CONTENTS

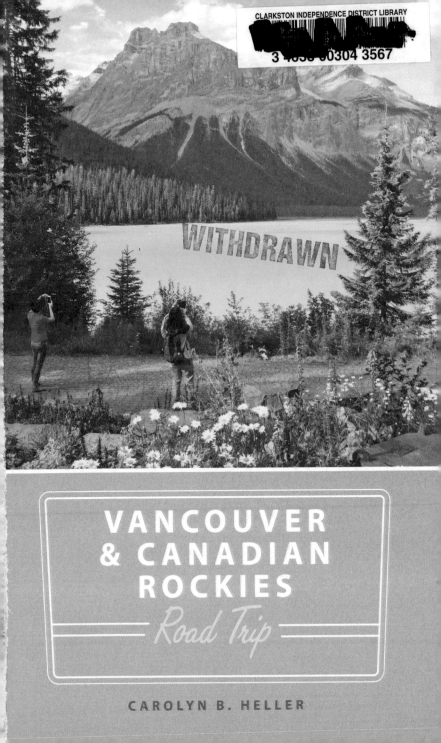

VANCOUVER & CANADIAN ROCKIES

Road Trip

CAROLYN B. HELLER

VANCOUVER AND CANADIAN ROCKIES ROAD TRIP

Quesnel

Mount Robson

Tête Jaune Cache

Valemount

97

5

Williams Lake

20

97

Kamloops to the B.C. Rockies

93 Mile

24

Little Fort

97

BRITISH COLUMBIA

Shuswamp Lake

99

Cache Creek

Sicamou

5

KAMLOOPS

Lillooet

97

Canoe

97

12

1

5

5A

Whistler and the Sea-to-Sky Highway

Mount Currie

Vernon

WHISTLER

Lytton

Merritt

The Okanagan

99

97C

KELOWNA

Saltery Bay

Egmont

Squamish

5

5A

Naramata

Penticton

33

Horseshoe Bay

Hope

Princeton

3

Okanagan Falls

Nanaimo

VANCOUVER

Vancouver

1

3A

Oliver

Rock Creek

Lake Cowichan

Manning Park

3

OSOYOOS

CANADA
UNITED STATES

Port Renfrew

Mill Bay

Sidney

Bellingham

97

Victoria and Vancouver Island

VICTORIA

20

WASHINGTON

Beecher Bay

DISCOVER
Vancouver & the Canadian Rockies

Snowy peaks, rushing rivers, and vineyard-lined valleys. Elaborate totem poles rising from the rainforest. Waterfront cities buzzing with outdoor cafés. Whales breaching and seals sunning just offshore. Clichés? Perhaps. But in Canada's most naturally spectacular region, these clichés are true. Stretching from Vancouver to the Rockies, western Canada is tailor-made for a road trip.

In Vancouver, an active city bordering the mountains and the sea, begin your trip by strolling or cycling through a 1,000-acre (400-hectare) rainforest park and exploring diverse cultures, from the original aboriginal inhabitants to modern-day communities that reflect the city's position on the Pacific Rim.

A 90-minute ferry ride across the Strait of Georgia, Victoria retains its British roots even as it has morphed into a contemporary city. It's now known as much for its locally produced wine, beer, and spirits as for its tradition of afternoon tea. Beyond Victoria, opportunities abound for exploring Vancouver Island's forests, waterways, and dramatic coastal regions.

Back on the mainland, the Sea-to-Sky Highway is one of Canada's most beautiful short drives, winding along the coast between Vancouver and Whistler. North America's largest winter sports mecca, Whistler is nearly as busy in spring, summer, and fall, with hikers, cyclists, and other adventurers exploring the peaks and lakes.

Travel east from Vancouver to the sunny Okanagan Valley, with its string of freshwater lakes, orchards, and Canada's only desert—and more than 200 wineries lining its back roads.

From the Okanagan, head to the Rocky Mountains. The Trans-Canada Highway passes through several of British Columbia's mountain national parks, including Mount Revelstoke, Glacier, Yoho, and Kootenay, each more dramatic than the last.

Just across the provincial border in Alberta are the marquee destinations of any western Canada road trip: Banff, Lake Louise, and Jasper. The region's best scenic drive takes you along the Icefields Parkway, with its incredibly blue lakes and the largest area of glacial ice in the Canadian Rockies.

Once you've had your fill of hiking, rafting, and savoring the mountain vistas, continue on to the gateway city of Calgary, which not only hosts Canada's biggest annual cowboy party but also offers distinctive museums and a pretty riverfront promenade. Or follow the southern route back toward Vancouver, exploring the Kootenays' funky mountain towns and detouring along B.C.'s Hot Springs Highway.

From the ocean to the mountains, there's plenty to experience, taste, and enjoy. Let's hit the road.

PLANNING YOUR TRIP

Where to Go

Vancouver

The rainforest meets the city in Vancouver, where massive **Stanley Park** and forests of glass-and-steel skyscrapers populate the downtown peninsula. The North Shore Mountains overlook the city skyline, while the sea hugs the city, with sandy beaches just steps from urban hotels. Yet this outdoor-oriented metropolis has plenty of culture as well, reflecting its First Nations heritage (the totem poles at the **Museum of Anthropology** are a must-see) and its contemporary Pacific Rim society. **Granville Island, Gastown,** and **Kitsilano** draw food-lovers to their locally focused restaurants, while the suburb of **Richmond** has some of the best Chinese food outside China. With its well-connected international airport and location just north of the U.S. border, 145 miles (230 kilometers) from Seattle, Vancouver is a convenient starting point for trips along the British Columbia coast and east to the Canadian Rockies.

Victoria and Vancouver Island

Across the Strait of Georgia at the southern tip of Vancouver Island, British Columbia's waterfront capital city of **Victoria** retains elements of its British heritage—visiting the world-class **Butchart Gardens** and taking afternoon tea at the grand **Fairmont Empress** are still beloved traditions for visitors—even as this increasingly cosmopolitan community booms with new restaurants and cocktail bars. Elsewhere on the island, you can **snorkel with seals,** take a **bear-watching tour,** or watch the waves crash along the Pacific coast.

Whistler and the Sea-to-Sky Highway

One of western Canada's most spectacular short drives, the **Sea-to-Sky Highway** connects Vancouver to the resort town of **Whistler.** Known for **winter sports,** Whistler has plenty to do in warmer weather, too, from riding the **gondolas** into the mountains, to **hiking, cycling,** and **canoeing,** to exploring the region's **aboriginal heritage.**

Kamloops to the B.C. Rockies

As you drive east from Vancouver and cross the Coast Mountains, you leave behind the green coastal rainforest and wind through the desert-like hills of British Columbia's interior. Here, the sunny city of **Kamloops** makes a convenient stopover point midway between Vancouver and the Rockies, with several small museums and an emerging wine industry. Continue east on the Trans-Canada Highway to a trio of national parks, **Mount Revelstoke, Glacier,** and **Yoho,** where you can hike, paddle the glacier-fed lakes, or enjoy the mountain scenery. Base yourself in towns like **Revelstoke** or **Golden** (only Yoho National Park has accommodations) and enjoy their cafés, restaurants, and comfortable lodgings.

Banff and Lake Louise

Banff National Park is a highlight of any Canadian Rockies road trip, with dramatic mountain peaks and natural hot springs, the sparkling blue **Lake Louise,** and more than 1,000 miles (1,600 kilometers) of hiking paths. Within the boundaries of Canada's first national park, the town of **Banff** bustles with restaurants, museums, and shops, and though its sidewalks can feel as jammed as New York City's during the busy summer season, there's always plenty of space out on the trails.

Jasper

The **Icefields Parkway** between Lake Louise and **Jasper** is one of Canada's great drives, where you can stop at the **Columbia Icefield** to walk on a glacier or hike among the glacier-capped peaks. Without Banff's crowds, **Jasper National Park** is equally beautiful, and as the largest park in the Canadian Rockies, there's ample room to explore its lakes, canyons, and mountains.

The Kootenays

The Kootenays region extends across

WHERE TO GO

paddling on Maligne Lake, Jasper National Park

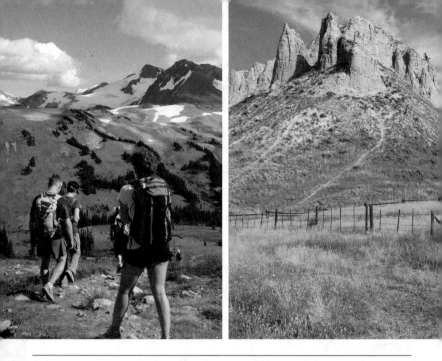

Clockwise from top left: hiking on Whistler Mountain; hoodoos near Kamloops; Vancouver's West End.

The Rockies by Train

This is a road-trip guide, of course, but western Canada, and particularly the Canadian Rockies region, is a fantastic destination to explore by train. So whether you combine road and rail travel, or simply head off on a rail-based holiday, here's where and how to explore the Rockies by train.

Two major rail carriers serve the Canadian Rockies region: **VIA Rail** (514/989-2626 or 888/842-7245, www.viarail.ca), which is Canada's national rail carrier, and the **Rocky Mountaineer** (604/606-7245 or 877/460-3200, www.rockymountaineer.com), a private rail tour company.

VIA Rail's flagship route, *The Canadian*, can take you 2,775 miles (4,466 kilometers) across the western two-thirds of the country, traveling between Toronto and Vancouver, with stops in Winnipeg (Manitoba), Saskatoon (Saskatchewan), Edmonton and Jasper (Alberta), and Kamloops (British Columbia) on its way to the coast.

Of course, you don't have to make this entire four-night, three-day journey; you can ride *The Canadian* between Vancouver and Jasper in the Canadian Rockies, which covers some of the rail route's most scenic terrain.

The Rocky Mountaineer offers several different Canadian Rockies rail trips, traveling between Vancouver, Banff, Lake Louise, Jasper, and Calgary. You can make a round-trip loop from the coast to the Rockies and back, or book a one-way journey through the Rockies between Vancouver and Calgary. Another route starts in Seattle and stops in Vancouver before continuing to the Rockies. You can book a Rocky Mountaineer holiday that covers rail fare and accommodations only or packages that include everything from gondola rides to helicopter tours, as well as all your transportation and accommodations. Check the website to review the tour options.

southeastern British Columbia, between the Rocky Mountains and the Okanagan Valley. Here, you can explore the diverse landscape of **Kootenay National Park,** follow the **Hot Springs Highway** to several natural mineral pools, hang out in funky mountain towns like **Fernie** and **Nelson,** or learn more about the First Nations who've lived in the area for more than 10,000 years. Delve into the history of other ethnic communities, too, including the Japanese Canadians who were sent to **internment camps** across B.C. during World War II, and the Russian pacifists known as the **Doukhobors** who settled here in the early 20th century.

The Okanagan

More than 200 **wineries** hug the lakeshores and rocky hills of the sunny Okanagan Valley in central B.C., often called the "Napa of the North." This agricultural region stretches from **Osoyoos,** in the desert-like lands near the U.S.

border, north to **Kelowna,** the area's largest city. If you love wine, or enjoy being outdoors along some of Canada's warmest **lakes,** plan to stop in the Okanagan as you drive between Vancouver and the Rocky Mountains.

Calgary

Canada's fourth-largest city has the closest airport to the Canadian Rockies, so you can start or end your Rocky Mountain travels here. Known for the annual **Calgary Stampede,** Calgary has the excellent **Glenbow Museum** of western Canadian history, art, and culture; **Heritage Park Historical Village,** the country's largest living history village; and a new **National Music Centre.** The city's restaurants regularly rank among the country's top dining spots. A short drive from Calgary, the **Canadian Badlands** has a completely different geological profile, with its unusual hoodoo rock formations and deep rocky canyons.

When to Go

High season in Vancouver and the Canadian Rockies runs from May through October, when most attractions and roads are open and the weather is generally warm and sunny. **July and August** are the region's peak travel months, with the sunny, temperate conditions balancing out the big crowds and high prices.

Ask the locals about the best time to visit the Canadian Rockies, though, and everyone will say **September.** The summer crowds begin to abate, the weather is still mild, and the trees take on their fall colors. Temperatures can remain pleasant into October, though the nights get colder, and snow frequently begins in late October or early November.

While the long days and fewer tourists make **May and June** a reasonable alternative for a Rockies trip, prepare for more rain than in the summer. You might have occasional damp days on the coast, but the Rockies can be hit with a "June monsoon" when the rain turns heavy. These showers bring spring flowers, so pack a raincoat and get outdoors anyway.

Winter is mild in Vancouver and Victoria; rain is common from November through March, but snow is unusual. As soon as you rise above coastal elevations, winter travelers should prepare for heavy snow. It snows *a lot* in the mountains of B.C. and in the Canadian Rockies, when severe weather can close highway mountain passes. Always check the forecast before you hit the road.

Before You Go

If you're traveling in the summer, particularly in July and August, consider booking your **hotel reservations** in advance. Many of the national park campgrounds fill up early, so **reserving a campsite** for summer or holiday travel is also a smart idea. Car reservations are recommended on **B.C. Ferries** in the summer as well.

Visitors to **Yoho National Park** should note that two park activities require advance reservations and careful attention to the reservations procedure and deadlines: visiting **Lake O'Hara** and touring the **Burgess Shale** fossil beds. Refer to the Yoho National Park section for specifics.

HIT THE ROAD

The Classic 15-Day Vancouver-Rockies Loop

On a **two-week drive,** you can road-trip from Vancouver to the Canadian Rockies and back, taking in many of western Canada's top attractions. See Vancouver's sights, then day-trip by ferry to Victoria, British Columbia's capital. Take another day to get outdoors in the mountains at Whistler. Get ready for the real mountains, though, as you head east, stopping in Mount Revelstoke, Glacier, and Yoho National Parks as you enter the Canadian Rockies. In Alberta, you'll visit Lake Louise, follow the scenic Icefields Parkway to Jasper, then return south for a couple of days outdoors in Banff National Park. From there, travel through B.C.'s Kootenays region, with stops in the fun towns of Fernie and Nelson, and go wine-tasting in the Okanagan Valley, on your way back to Vancouver and the coast.

You could also start and end the trip in Calgary, doing the loop in reverse.

Days 1-2
VANCOUVER

Start your tour in Vancouver, circling the scenic seawall in **Stanley Park,** snacking on **Granville Island,** and getting an introduction to aboriginal culture at the **Museum of Anthropology.** Explore **Chinatown** in the peaceful **Dr. Sun Yat-Sen Classical Chinese Garden** and in the neighborhood's growing number of hip restaurants, or head to the North Shore to hike and enjoy the views from **Grouse Mountain.** With several beaches right downtown, wrap up your day with a sunset stroll along the sand.

Day 3
VICTORIA
Vancouver to Victoria (round-trip)
95 mi (150 km)
6 hrs, including ferries
Make a day trip to Vancouver Island today for a quick visit to **Victoria.** From Vancouver, drive south on **Highway 99** to catch an early-morning **B.C. Ferry** from **Tsawwassen;** it's a 90-minute trip to **Swartz Bay.** When you leave the ferry terminal, follow Highway 17A to the **Butchart Gardens** to wander among the floral displays.

From the gardens, take Keating Cross Road east to **Highway 17** toward downtown Victoria. Park your car, then tour the **Inner Harbour,** have afternoon tea at the stately **Fairmont Empress,** and visit the **Royal British Columbia Museum.** Have a drink in one of the city's **craft breweries** and dinner in a contemporary bistro in or around **Chinatown,** before returning to Swartz Bay for the ferry back to Vancouver.

Day 4
WHISTLER
Vancouver to Whistler
75 mi (120 km)
2 hrs
Head north from Vancouver to pick up the **Sea-to-Sky Highway** (Hwy. 99), a scenic route between the mountains and the ocean that leads to the resort town of **Whistler.** Consider stopping in **Squamish** for a ride up the **Sea-to-Sky Gondola;** either have lunch with a view from the gondola summit or continue on to Whistler. Visit the **Squamish Lil'wat Cultural Centre** to learn more about the local First Nations community, then get outdoors, whether you choose to ride the **PEAK 2 PEAK Gondola,** climb the **Via Ferrata,** go **zip-lining,** or simply **take a hike.**

Best Scenic Drives

Peyto Lake, along the Icefields Parkway

Road-tripping in western Canada is one big scenic drive, so it's hard to pick just a few favorite routes. But here are some of the most spectacular sections of road in British Columbia and Alberta.

* **Sea-to-Sky Highway:** Highway 99 from Vancouver to Whistler winds between the mountains and the ocean, with views of offshore islands and snow-topped peaks around every bend. Stop at roadside kiosks to learn more about local First Nations communities (page 146).

* **Bow Valley Parkway, Banff National Park:** With numerous lookout points and stops for hikes, this 30-mile (48-kilometer) drive is an ever-so-scenic alternative to Highway 1 between Banff and Lake Louise (page 232).

* **Icefields Parkway:** Take your time on this 143-mile (230-kilometer) route between Lake Louise and Jasper, as you pass turquoise lakes, rushing waterfalls, and countless glacier-topped peaks. It's one of Canada's most spectacular drives (page 276).

* **Highway 3A along Kootenay Lake:** An alternate route between Nelson and the East Kootenays region, Highway 3A winds along the shores of Kootenay Lake and past one of B.C.'s quirkiest attractions: a house built from more than 500,000 empty bottles of embalming fluid (page 335).

Day 5
REVELSTOKE
Whistler to Revelstoke
315 mi (510 km)
6.5 hrs

Today is a long driving day as you set out for the mountains of eastern British Columbia. Leave Whistler on **Highway 99** north to **Highway 1** east; if you start early, you can reach **Kamloops** for lunch. Try to arrive at **Mount Revelstoke National Park** in time to zigzag up the **Meadows in the Sky Parkway** and take at least a short hike, before settling into the town of **Revelstoke** for dinner and a well-deserved rest.

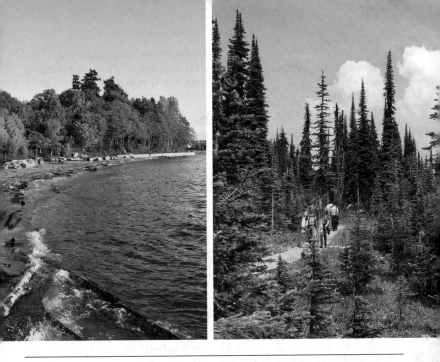

Clockwise from top left: Vancouver's Stanley Park; trails near the Meadows in the Sky Parkway summit in Mount Revelstoke National Park; Wapta Falls in Yoho National Park.

Day 6
GOLDEN AND YOHO NATIONAL PARK
Revelstoke to Field
125 mi (200 km)
2.5 hrs

After breakfast, make a brief stop at the **Revelstoke Railway Museum** to learn about the railroad's importance to this region before continuing east on Highway 1 toward **Glacier National Park.** Stretch your legs on the **Skunk Cabbage Boardwalk Trail** or the **Giant Cedars Boardwalk Trail** (in Mount Revelstoke National Park) or on Glacier's **Hemlock Grove Trail** before stopping at the **Rogers Pass Discovery Centre.** After checking out the exhibits, drive on to **Golden** for lunch; you could ride the gondola at **Kicking Horse Mountain Resort** to eat at the **Eagle's Eye Restaurant,** Canada's highest restaurant. Don't forget to move your clocks ahead; Golden is in the mountain time zone.

Keep going east on Highway 1 into **Yoho National Park.** Stop at the **Natural Bridge** and beautiful **Emerald Lake,** and if you have time, drive up to **Takakkaw Falls.** Have dinner and spend the night at one of the upscale lodges within the park.

Day 7
**LAKE LOUISE AND THE
ICEFIELDS PARKWAY**
Field to Jasper
160 mi (260 km)
4 hrs

Today will be another long one, but keep your camera handy. You'll pass through some of the most scenic terrain of the entire trip. It's just 20 minutes east on Highway 1 from Field in Yoho National Park to **Lake Louise,** where you can hike or paddle along its famous namesake lake.

From Lake Louise, turn north onto Highway 93, the **Icefields Parkway.** There are numerous places to ooh and aah along this route; highlights include **Peyto Lake, Wilcox Pass,** and the **Columbia Icefield,** where you can walk on the **Athabasca**

Glacier. Continuing toward Jasper, another pretty place to pause is **Athabasca Falls.** Arrive in Jasper for dinner and a microbrew in the local pub.

Day 8
JASPER
Start your morning with a ride up the **Jasper Sky Tram.** Return to town to pick up a picnic lunch and take a look through the **Jasper-Yellowhead Museum.** Bring your picnic to **Maligne Canyon** to hike through this deep limestone gorge.

In the afternoon, drive to **Maligne Lake** for a leisurely 90-minute cruise. Have an early supper in town, then head for **Miette Hot Springs** to wrap up your day with a relaxing visit to these natural mineral pools.

Days 9-10
BANFF
Jasper to Banff
180 mi (290 km)
4.5 hrs

If you didn't make all the stops you wanted along the **Icefields Parkway,** you have another chance today, since you'll retrace your steps southbound on this picturesque parkway. When you get back to Lake Louise, detour to glacier-fed **Moraine Lake** for a short hike or canoe paddle. Then follow the **Bow Valley Parkway** south toward Banff, stopping to walk along **Johnston Canyon.** In **Banff,** have a leisurely dinner and take a late-evening soak at **Banff Upper Hot Springs.**

Spend part of the next day at Banff's in-town attractions, including the **Cave and Basin National Historic Site, Banff Park Museum,** and **Whyte Museum of the Canadian Rockies,** and part of the day outdoors. Climb the **Mount Norquay Via Ferrata,** take a cruise on **Lake Minnewanka,** or ride the **Banff Gondola** and take a short hike at the top. In the evening, see a play, concert, or other event at the **Banff Centre.**

Best Hikes

- **High Note Trail, Whistler:** Accessed from the top of the Peak Express chair, this trail follows the alpine ridges, with great views of the Black Tusk peak (page 152).

- **Eva Lake Trail, Mount Revelstoke National Park:** Starting from the summit of the Meadows in the Sky Parkway, this 7.5-mile (12-kilometer) round-trip route takes you through wildflower meadows and boulder fields to a lovely alpine lake (page 187).

- **Iceline Trail, Yoho National Park:** If you're up for an all-day adventure, this challenging 13-mile (21-kilometer) round-trip trail begins near Takakkaw Falls and rewards hikers with spectacular glacier vistas (page 213).

- **Johnston Canyon, Banff National Park:** This easy trail along the cantilevered walkways through this rock canyon is among Banff's most dramatic; get an early start to beat the crowds (page 232).

- **Plain of Six Glaciers Trail, Lake Louise:** This 6.6-mile (10.6-kilometer) round-trip hike leads from the lakeshore up toward glacier-capped mountains en route to a historic teahouse, where you can stop for lunch or a sweet—or both (page 260).

- **Wilcox Pass, Jasper National Park:** What's the payoff for this moderate climb along the Icefields Parkway? Impressive views of the mountains and glaciers of the Columbia Icefield (page 278).

- **Maligne Canyon, Jasper National Park:** Hike the trails, over the bridges, and along the river through this deep limestone gorge, one of Jasper's most scenic spots (page 285).

Days 11-12
KOOTENAY NATIONAL PARK AND FERNIE
Banff to Fernie
220 mi (355 km)
4.5 hrs

Pick up coffee and pastries at Banff's best bakeshop, **Wild Flour Artisan Bakery.** Then, leaving Banff, take Highway 1 west and turn south on **Highway 93** into **Kootenay National Park.** Stop at **Marble Canyon** and the **Paint Pots,** and keep your bathing suit handy for a dip in the **Radium Hot Springs.** Continue south on Highway 93/95, where the town of **Invermere** has several options for lunch.

If you're interested in history, stop at **Fort Steele Heritage Town,** a living history village. Keep following Highway 93/95 south and turn east on **Highway 3** to **Fernie,** where you'll spend the night. In the morning, check out the **Fernie Museum,** browse the downtown shops, and have lunch in one of the cafés. After

you eat, head over to **Fernie Alpine Resort** to test your balance in the **Aerial Park** or go for a mountaintop **hike.**

Day 13
NELSON
Fernie to Nelson
200 mi (325 km)
4 hrs

Leave Fernie on Highway 3 west, stopping off at **St. Eugene Resort** in Cranbrook to visit the First Nations-run **Ktunaxa Interpretive Centre** in this former mission and residential school for aboriginal students; call first to be sure the center is open. Continue west on Highway 3, where you'll cross back into the Pacific time zone (set your watch back an hour), to the junction with **Highway 6,** where you go north to **Nelson.**

Visit **Touchstones Nelson: Museum of Art and History** and browse the shops along Baker Street. Stop at **Oso Negro Café** when you're ready for a coffee

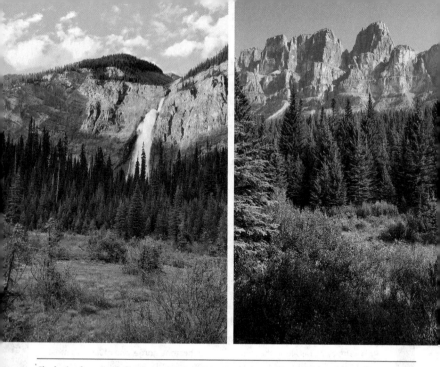

Clockwise from top left: Takakkaw Falls in Yoho National Park; cliffs along the Bow Valley Parkway in Banff National Park; Athabasca Glacier.

Aboriginal Culture

Aboriginal people have lived in western Canada for more than 10,000 years, and for many visitors, the opportunity to explore this traditional culture and its present-day manifestations is a highlight. Here are just a few of the numerous places across the region where indigenous culture remains strong.

+ **Bill Reid Gallery of Northwest Coast Art, Vancouver:** Dedicated to the work of Haida First Nations artist Bill Reid, this gallery showcases Reid's sculptures, carvings, and jewelry (page 38).

+ **Museum of Anthropology, Vancouver:** This excellent museum illuminates the culture of British Columbia's aboriginal peoples and traditional cultures from around the world (page 45).

+ **Skwachàys Lodge, Vancouver:** Stay at Canada's first aboriginal arts and culture hotel, where works by First Nations artists adorn the guest rooms (page 69).

+ **Meares Island:** Paddle by kayak or dugout canoe to this First Nations park across the harbor from Tofino, on Vancouver Island's Pacific coast (page 130).

+ **Wya Point Resort, Ucluelet:** The Ucluelet First Nation runs this remote Vancouver Island waterfront lodging, where works by aboriginal carvers decorate the upscale cabins (page 136).

+ **Squamish Lil'wat Cultural Centre, Whistler:** Learn about the history and present-day culture of the region's First Nations communities at this modern gallery (page 154).

+ **Kamloopa Powwow, Kamloops:** Most First Nations powwows welcome visitors, and this August celebration of First Nations culture, with dancers, drummers, and other performers, is one of western Canada's largest (page 179).

+ **Cross River Wilderness Centre, near Kootenay National Park:** Choose outdoor adventures or aboriginal experiences that reflect both the owner's Métis heritage and the local First Nations culture at this unique wilderness lodge (page 315).

+ **St. Eugene Resort, Cranbrook:** Set in a former mission that was once a residential school for aboriginal children, this First Nations-run hotel with an on-site interpretive center mixes its historic past with contemporary amenities (page 329).

+ **Nk'Mip Cellars, Osoyoos:** In the Okanagan Valley, the Osoyoos Indian Band runs Canada's first aboriginal-owned winery (page 375) and operates the adjacent Nk'Mip Desert Cultural Centre (page 379).

Most of western Canada's national parks, including Banff and Jasper in Alberta, and Mount Revelstoke, Glacier, Yoho, and Kootenay in B.C., offer interpretive programs focusing on First Nations culture. Another excellent source of information for visitors interested in aboriginal culture is the **Aboriginal Tourism Association of British Columbia** (604/921-1070 or 877/266-2822, www.aboriginalbc.com).

break. Another option is to tour the sobering **Nikkei Internment Memorial Centre** in New Denver, which is 60 miles (100 kilometers) north of Nelson on Highway 6. Nelson has lots of good restaurants, so take time to enjoy your evening meal.

Day 14
OKANAGAN VALLEY
Nelson to Osoyoos
165 mi (265 km)
3.5 hrs
From Nelson, follow Highway 6 west to Highway 3A south, and stop in **Castlegar**

at the **Doukhobor Discovery Centre** to learn about the pacifist Russian community that settled in B.C. in the early 1900s. Then take **Highway 3** west toward the Okanagan Valley.

You should arrive in the **Osoyoos-Oliver** area early enough to spend the afternoon sampling local **wineries.** Plan a special dinner at **The Sonora Room at Burrowing Owl** or **Miradoro Restaurant at Tinhorn Creek** to celebrate the end of your holiday.

Day 15
RETURN TO VANCOUVER
Osoyoos to Vancouver
250 mi (400 km)
5 hrs

If you're not in a rush to return to Vancouver, pick up freshly baked cinnamon buns at **The Lake Village Bakery** in Osoyoos, then stop at the **Nk'Mip Desert Cultural Centre** or take a morning stroll along Lake Osoyoos. When you're ready to hit the road, follow **Highway 3** west to Hope, where you pick up **Highway 1** toward Vancouver.

Options for Shorter Trips
FIVE DAYS ON THE B.C. COAST

If you have just five days, base yourself in **Vancouver** for three nights, which is enough time to see the sights and take a day trip along the **Sea-to-Sky Highway** to **Whistler.** On Day 4, catch the ferry to Vancouver Island to tour **Victoria;** you can stay the night there—the city has lots of good restaurants and lodgings—before returning to Vancouver.

Have a little more time? Extend your trip for two or three days by crossing Vancouver Island to **Tofino,** a laid-back beach town on the Pacific coast.

A WEEK IN THE ROCKIES

If you want to spend your time in the Canadian Rockies and you have just a week, start and end your trip in **Calgary.** Do a quick city tour, and then head for **Banff National Park,** just 90 minutes to the west. Spend two days in Banff to hike, canoe, or take a lake cruise, and check out the museums and shops in town. Drive west on Highway 1 to explore the highlights of **Yoho National Park,** then turn back east to **Lake Louise,** where you can stay near the famous lake.

From Lake Louise, allow at least half a day to drive the **Icefields Parkway** to **Jasper;** there are enough lakes, glaciers, and hiking trails to fill many hours. Give yourself two nights and at least one full day in **Jasper National Park.** Returning south, you'll backtrack along the Icefields Parkway, but it will give you a chance to see any sights you missed. Spend one more night in Banff or stop off east of the park in **Canmore,** before returning to Calgary and heading for home.

VANCOUVER TO BANFF AND CALGARY

If you don't have time to make a full loop from Vancouver to the Canadian Rockies and back, consider starting in Vancouver and doing a one-way weeklong road trip to Calgary. To begin in Calgary and drive to Vancouver, just reverse the order of this itinerary.

After spending a couple of days in **Vancouver,** head east on the Trans-Canada Highway; at Hope, follow Highway 5 east, then take Highway 97A to **Kelowna,** where you can visit several Okanagan Valley wineries and stay the night.

The next day, continue east on Highway 1 to **Mount Revelstoke** and **Glacier National Parks,** and overnight in **Golden.** Explore **Yoho National Park** and cross into Alberta to stay at **Lake Louise.** Take the **Bow Valley Parkway** south to **Banff,** where you can easily spend two days in **Banff National Park.** From Banff, it's only 90 minutes east on Highway 1 to **Calgary.**

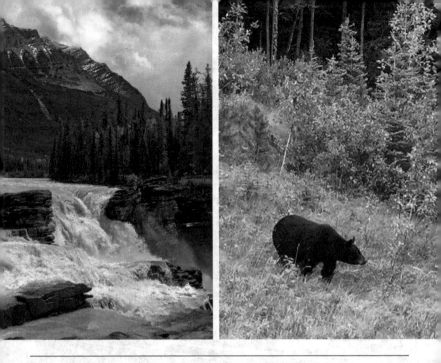

Clockwise from top left: Athabasca Falls in Jasper National Park; black bear; view from one of the hiking trails above Lake Louise.

Vancouver

Ringed with beaches and mountains, the glass-and-steel city of Vancouver mixes urban pleasures and outdoor adventures.

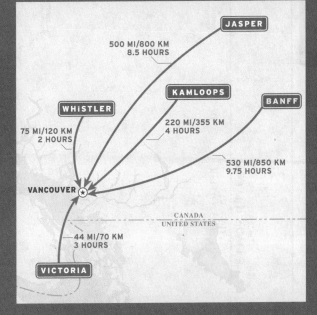

JASPER

500 MI/800 KM
8.5 HOURS

KAMLOOPS

BANFF

WHISTLER

220 MI/355 KM
4 HOURS

75 MI/120 KM
2 HOURS

530 MI/850 KM
9.75 HOURS

VANCOUVER ★

CANADA
UNITED STATES

44 MI/70 KM
3 HOURS

VICTORIA

Vancouver

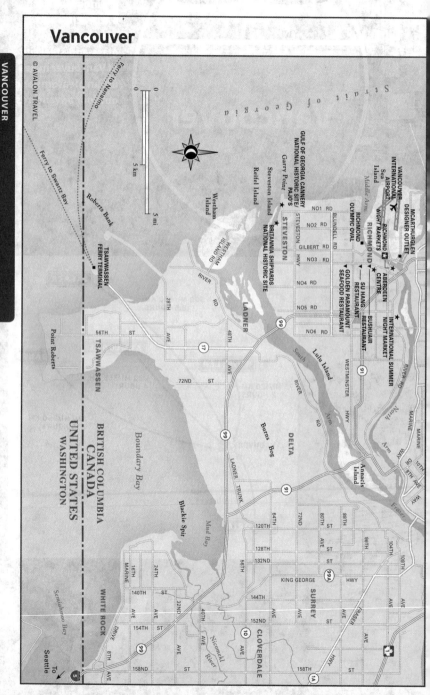

© AVALON TRAVEL

Ferry to Nanaimo

Ferry to Swartz Bay

Strait of Georgia

Roberts Bank

0   5 km
0   5 mi

Westham
Island

Reifel Island

Steveston Island

Garry Point

PAJO'S

GULF OF GEORGIA CANNERY
NATIONAL HISTORIC SITE

STEVESTON

BRITANNIA SHIPYARDS
NATIONAL HISTORIC SITE

Middle Arm

Sea
Island

VANCOUVER
INTERNATIONAL
AIRPORT

MCARTHURGLEN DESIGNER OUTLET

RICHMOND
NIGHT MARKETS

RICHMOND
OLYMPIC OVAL

NO1 RD

NO2 RD

STEVESTON
HWY

BLUNDELL RD

GILBERT RD

NO3 RD

NO4 RD

NO5 RD

NO6 RD

GOLDEN PARAMOUNT
SEAFOOD RESTAURANT

SU HANG
RESTAURANT

BUSHUAIR
RESTAURANT

ABERDEEN
CENTRE

INTERNATIONAL
SUMMER
NIGHT MARKET

Lulu Island

South

RIVER

Arm

WESTMINSTER HWY

91

NORTH ARM

MARINE WAY

10TH AVE

8TH AVE

RICHMOND

RIVER RD

WISHAM
ISLAND RD

RIVER
RD

LADNER

28TH

56TH ST

48TH

17

99

72ND ST

AVE

99

LADNER TRUNK

91

Burns Bog

DELTA

Annacis
Island

Fraser

River

TSAWWASSEN
FERRY TERMINAL

TSAWWASSEN

Point Roberts

BRITISH COLUMBIA
CANADA
UNITED STATES
WASHINGTON

Boundary Bay

Blackie Spit

Mud Bay

64TH

72ND

80TH
ST

88TH

96TH ST

104TH

108TH

AVE

AVE

16TH
MARINE

24TH

120TH

128TH

132ND

56TH

KING GEORGE HWY

99A

SURREY

AVE

ST

140TH ST

144TH

AVE

32ND

40TH

AVE

152ND

ST

AVE

CLOVERDALE

10

154TH

AVE

Nicomekl River

158ND ST

158TH ST

FRASER HWY

1A

WHITE ROCK

Semiahmoo Bay

DRIVE

8TH AVE

99

To
Seattle

5

Highlights

★ **Stanley Park:**
Crisscrossed with walking
trails and home to several
attractions, this 1,000-acre
(400-hectare) parkland on
the downtown peninsula
is Vancouver's urban jewel
(page 33).

★ **Bill Reid Gallery of
Northwest Coast Art:**
Dedicated to the life and
work of Haida First Nations
artist Bill Reid, this gallery
explores his vast output of
sculptures, carvings, and jewelry (page 38).

★ **Dr. Sun Yat-Sen
Classical Chinese Garden:**
Master craftsmen from
the Chinese city of Suzhou
constructed this peaceful
oasis, the first authentic Ming
Dynasty garden built outside
China (page 40).

★ **Granville Island:** This
former industrial district
underneath the Granville
Bridge bustles with galleries,
boutiques, breweries and
distilleries, theaters, and the
Public Market (page 43).

★ **Museum of
Anthropology:** This striking modern museum on the
University of British Columbia
campus illuminates the
culture of British Columbia's
aboriginal peoples and traditional cultures from around
the world (page 45).

★ **Grouse Mountain:** Ride
the tram up this North Shore
peak for a lumberjack show,
wildlife refuge, and mountaintop hiking trails, along
with spectacular views (page
50).

★ **Richmond Night
Markets:** From mid-May
through mid-October, the
suburb of Richmond hosts
two weekend night markets,
with Asian food stalls and a
festive carnival atmosphere
(page 53).

★ **English Bay Beach:** This
stretch of sand, right downtown, is a lively spot for strolling, swimming, or watching
the sunset (page 62).

★ **Pacific Spirit Regional
Park:** Stanley Park may get
all the glory, but this huge
rainforest park near the
University of British Columbia
has secluded walking trails
lined with massive trees
(page 63).

In a region of dramatic natural scenery, Vancouver cuts a dramatic urban figure.

Set on Pacific coastal inlets with forested mountains beyond, Vancouver is frequently named one of the world's most livable cities, even giving its name to a style of urban planning: "Vancouverism."

Thanks to Vancouverism, downtown Vancouver is a vibrant mix of residential and commercial development, dotted with parks and green spaces. Tall glass-and-steel towers sprout along the downtown peninsula, with "view corridors" providing peeks of the peaks and waterfront. The city's active population takes full advantage of the cycling lanes, walking paths, beaches, and parks, particularly its 1,000-acre (400-hectare) rainforest park right downtown.

Home to roughly two million people, the Vancouver region looks to the Pacific Rim. More than 40 percent of the metro area's population is of Asian descent, influencing the city in everything from urban design to art to food. Vancouver boasts, deservedly, of having the best Chinese cuisine outside China.

Another Vancouver influence to explore comes from its aboriginal people, who've lived on this part of the continent for thousands of years. Vancouver has several museums, galleries, and other attractions where you can get acquainted with First Nations culture. If you land at Vancouver's international airport, you'll see its extensive collection of native art welcoming visitors to the region.

Just 35 miles (57 kilometers) north of the U.S. border, Vancouver is a convenient starting point for trips along the British Columbia coast, east to the Okanagan Valley (a major wine-producing district), and on to the strikingly scenic Rocky Mountains. There's lots of gorgeous territory in this part of the world, and it all starts in the beautiful, livable city of Vancouver.

Getting to Vancouver

Driving from Seattle

It's a **145-mile (230-kilometer)** drive from Seattle, Washington, to downtown Vancouver. **I-5** takes you north from Seattle to the U.S.-Canada border. The **Peace Arch Crossing** on I-5 is open 24 hours daily. When you pass through the border checks, you'll be on **Highway 99** in British Columbia.

If traffic is backed up at the Peace Arch crossing, there's an **alternate border crossing** at the **Pacific Highway/Highway 543** (Exit 275 from I-5), which is also open 24 hours. Once you're through the border here, you'll be on B.C.'s **Highway 15.** Follow Highway 15 north for 1.9 miles (3 kilometers), and turn left (west) onto **8th Avenue.** In 1.2 miles (2 kilometers), merge onto **Highway 99** north.

Once you're on Highway 99, continue north through the **George Massey Tunnel** and then cross the **Oak Street Bridge** into Vancouver. To reach the downtown area, continue north on Oak Street until you reach West 41st Avenue. Turn left onto 41st Avenue, and then at the light, turn right onto Granville Street. Stay on Granville Street across the Granville Bridge into downtown. It's 35 miles (57 kilometers) from the border to downtown Vancouver.

The **Washington State Department of Transportation** (www.wsdot.com) and the **British Columbia Ministry of Transportation** (www.th.gov.bc.ca/ATIS) provide information about border delays on their websites. Illuminated signs along I-5 and Highway 99 in B.C. also show border wait times.

Driving from Victoria (via Ferry)

B.C. Ferries (888/223-3779, www.bcferries.com) provides frequent service between the Vancouver metropolitan area on the mainland and Vancouver Island. Ferries transport foot passengers,

Best Hotels

★ **Burrard Hotel:** Start your road trip at this old-time motor hotel that's been converted into a retro-chic lodging (page 66).

★ **Listel Hotel:** Original contemporary art distinguishes this low-rise lodging with a prime perch on Vancouver's main downtown shopping street (page 67).

★ **Fairmont Pacific Rim:** Vancouver's most elegant modern hotel is this luxurious Asian-influenced tower near the Coal Harbour waterfront (page 67).

★ **Rosewood Hotel Georgia:** Originally built in the 1920s, this classy restored hotel has upscale guest rooms, excellent eateries, and stylish lounges, all in a central downtown location (page 69).

★ **Skwachàys Lodge:** One-of-a-kind works by First Nations artists adorn the guest rooms at Canada's first aboriginal arts and culture hotel (page 69).

★ **Opus Hotel Vancouver:** At this cool Yaletown boutique lodging, the vibrantly hued rooms have windows into the baths. Don't be shy (page 70)!

★ **Corkscrew Inn:** Handcrafted art deco-style stained glass and an unusual collection of antique corkscrews give this Kitsilano B&B its wine-themed charm (page 70).

bicycles, cars, trucks, and recreational vehicles. Reservations ($15 at least 7 days in advance, $18.50 1-6 days in advance, $22 same-day travel) are recommended for vehicles, particularly if you're traveling on summer weekends or during holiday periods. Reservations are not available for walk-on passengers or bicycles.

Ferries from the Victoria area depart from the **Swartz Bay Terminal** (Hwy. 17), 20 miles (32 kilometers) north of Victoria via **Highway 17,** about a **30-minute** drive.

To travel between Victoria and Vancouver, take the **Swartz Bay-Tsawwassen Ferry** (one-way adults $16.90, ages 5-11 $8.45, cars $55.40, bikes $2). The ferry ride is **one hour and 35 minutes.**

On the mainland, the ferry docks at the **Tsawwassen Terminal** (1 Ferry Causeway, Delta), 24 miles (38 kilometers) south of Vancouver. Leaving the Tsawwassen terminal, follow **Highway 17/17A** to **Highway 99** north. Continue north on Highway 99 through the **George Massey Tunnel** and then cross the **Oak Street Bridge** into Vancouver. To reach the downtown area, continue north on **Oak Street** until you reach **West 41st Avenue.** Turn left onto 41st Avenue, and then at the light, turn right onto **Granville Street.** Stay on Granville Street across the **Granville Bridge** into downtown. Allow about **45 minutes** to drive from Tsawwassen to downtown Vancouver, with extra time during the morning and evening rush hours.

Driving from Whistler

Allow about **two hours** to make the **75-mile (120-kilometer)** drive between Whistler and Vancouver along the spectacular **Sea-to-Sky Highway.**

To get from Whistler to downtown Vancouver, follow **Highway 99** south to **Highway 1** east and take Exit 13, **Taylor Way,** toward Vancouver. At the foot of the hill, turn left onto **Marine Drive,** then bear right onto the **Lions Gate Bridge.** Many lanes merge onto the bridge here, so be prepared for delays. Once you've crossed the bridge, continue on **West Georgia Street** in downtown Vancouver.

Best Restaurants

★ **Yew Seafood & Bar:** This classy restaurant in the Four Seasons Hotel Vancouver promotes sustainable seafood, so you can enjoy modern fish fare while doing your part for the oceans (page 73).

★ **The Pie Shoppe:** When you need a pie break, head for this sliver of a bakery in Chinatown that turns out a changing array of sweet things in a crust (page 73).

★ **L'Abbatoir:** On the site of Vancouver's first jail, this chic Gastown dining spot now detains diners with creative cocktails and ever-evolving west coast plates (page 73).

★ **Farmer's Apprentice:** Imaginative multicourse tasting menus inspired by local products bring adventurous diners to this petite South Granville dining room (page 78).

★ **West:** A wall of wine, inventive cuisine, and gracious service make any meal feel like an occasion at this upscale South Granville restaurant (page 79).

★ **Dynasty Seafood:** Love dim sum? This Chinese dining spot serves some of Vancouver's finest. There are great views, too (page 79).

★ **The Acorn:** Vancouver's first upscale vegetarian bistro pleases vegetarians and omnivores alike with its creative plant-based cuisine (page 79).

Driving from Banff

The most direct route between Banff, in the Canadian Rockies, and Vancouver is to follow the **Trans-Canada Highway (Hwy. 1)** west. You'll pass through Yoho, Glacier, and Mt. Revelstoke National Parks and the city of Kamloops.

From **Kamloops**, take **Highway 5 (Coquihalla Hwy.)**, southbound, toward Merritt and Hope. Highway 5 meets **Highway 3**, which you take westbound to rejoin **Highway 1** at the town of Hope.

From **Hope**, continue west on Highway 1 toward Vancouver. After passing through the city of Burnaby, take Exit 25 for **McGill Street.** Follow McGill Street westbound, and turn left onto **Nanaimo Street.** At the intersection with **Dundas Street,** turn right onto Dundas. Dundas Street becomes **Powell Street,** which will take you into downtown Vancouver.

It's **530 miles (850 kilometers)** from Banff to Vancouver. The drive takes **9 to 9.5 hours.** From **Kamloops** to Vancouver, it's **220 miles (355 kilometers)** and takes **3.75 to 4 hours.**

Driving from Jasper

The **shortest route** between Jasper and Vancouver is to follow **Highway 16** west to **Highway 5 (Yellowhead Hwy.),** where you turn south toward Kamloops. At **Kamloops**, continue south on Highway 5, following the Banff-to-Vancouver directions above. This Jasper-to-Vancouver route is **500 miles (800 kilometers)** and takes about **8.5 hours.**

A **longer but scenic route** is to take the **Icefields Parkway (Hwy. 93)** south from Jasper to **Lake Louise,** where you turn west onto **Highway 1.** From there, follow the Banff-to-Vancouver directions above. From Jasper to Vancouver, this route is about **620 miles (1,000 kilometers)** and takes about **11.5 hours.**

Getting There by Air, Train, and Bus
By Air

The **Vancouver International Airport** (YVR, 3211 Grant McConachie Way, Richmond, 604/207-7077, www.yvr.ca) is a major international gateway with flights to Vancouver from across Canada,

Downtown Vancouver

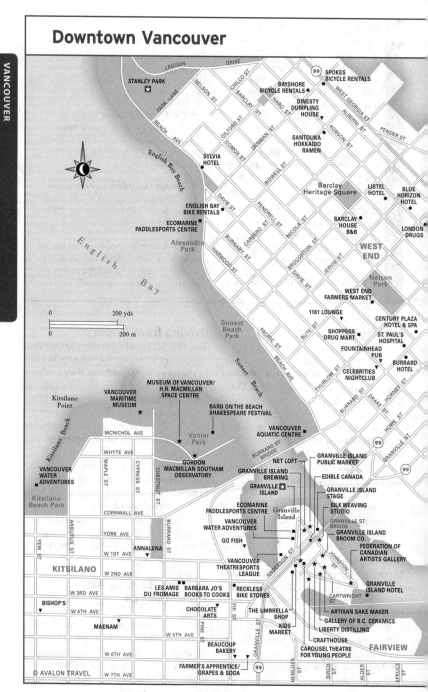

STANLEY PARK

SPOKES
BICYCLE RENTALS

BAYSHORE
BICYCLE RENTALS

DINESTY
DUMPLING
HOUSE

SYLVIA
HOTEL

SANTOUKA
HOKKAIDO
RAMEN

Barclay
Heritage Square

LISTEL
HOTEL

BLUE
HORIZON
HOTEL

ENGLISH BAY
BIKE RENTALS

BARCLAY
HOUSE
B&B

LONDON
DRUGS

ECOMARINE
PADDLESPORTS CENTRE

Alexandra
Park

WEST
END

English Bay Beach

English Bay

Nelson
Park

WEST END
FARMERS MARKET

1181 LOUNGE

CENTURY PLAZA
HOTEL & SPA

Sunset
Beach
Park

SHOPPERS
DRUG MART

ST. PAUL'S
HOSPITAL

FOUNTAINHEAD
PUB

BURRARD
HOTEL

CELEBRITIES
NIGHTCLUB

Kitsilano
Point

VANCOUVER
MARITIME
MUSEUM

MUSEUM OF VANCOUVER/
H.R. MACMILLAN
SPACE CENTRE

BARD ON THE BEACH
SHAKESPEARE FESTIVAL

VANCOUVER
AQUATIC CENTRE

Kitsilano Beach

VANCOUVER
WATER
ADVENTURES

Vanier
Park

GORDON
MACMILLAN SOUTHAM
OBSERVATORY

NET LOFT

GRANVILLE ISLAND
PUBLIC MARKET

GRANVILLE ISLAND
BREWING

EDIBLE CANADA

Kitsilano
Beach Park

GRANVILLE
ISLAND

GRANVILLE ISLAND
STAGE

ECOMARINE
PADDLESPORTS CENTRE

Granville
Island

SILK WEAVING
STUDIO

VANCOUVER
WATER ADVENTURES

GRANVILLE ISLAND
BROOM CO.

GO FISH

KITSILANO

ANNALENA

VANCOUVER
THEATRESPORTS
LEAGUE

FEDERATION OF
CANADIAN
ARTISTS GALLERY

GRANVILLE
ISLAND HOTEL

BISHOP'S

LES AMIS
DU FROMAGE

BARBARA JO'S
BOOKS TO COOKS

RECKLESS
BIKE STORES

CARTWRIGHT
ST

ARTISAN SAKE MAKER

MAENAM

CHOCOLATE
ARTS

THE UMBRELLA
SHOP

GALLERY OF B.C. CERAMICS

LIBERTY DISTILLING

KIDS
MARKET

CRAFTHOUSE

BEAUCOUP
BAKERY

CAROUSEL THEATRE
FOR YOUNG PEOPLE

FAIRVIEW

© AVALON TRAVEL

FARMER'S APPRENTICE/
GRAPES & SODA

0   200 yds
0   200 m

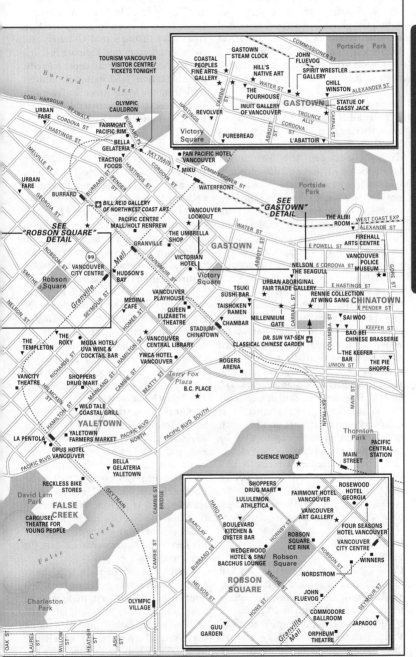

the United States, Mexico, Europe, Asia, and the Pacific, and connecting cities across the globe. The airport is located south of the city center in the suburb of Richmond; it's about 20-25 minutes from the airport to downtown by public transit or by car/taxi.

Ground Transportation

The **Canada Line** (604/953-3333, www.translink.ca), part of Vancouver's SkyTrain rapid transit system, runs directly between the Vancouver International Airport and downtown. If you don't have a lot of baggage, and you're not renting a car, it's the fastest and least expensive way to travel downtown from the airport. Trains run from about 5am to 1am daily. When you purchase a transit ticket at the YVR Airport station, you pay a $5 fee in addition to the regular transit fare.

Taxis wait outside the arrivals area of the domestic and international terminals. Fares between the airport and most Vancouver destinations are a **flat rate by zone.** To many destinations downtown or in Kitsilano, the flat-rate fare is $31. Other fares include Canada Place $35, Ballantyne Pier $36, Stanley Park $37, and the University of British Columbia $34. Gratuities are not included. Most cabs serving the airport accept credit cards. Note that returning to YVR by taxi, airport-bound cabs use their meters rather than the flat-rate system, so fares vary depending on your starting point and traffic conditions.

The major car rental companies all have offices at the Vancouver airport.

By Train
VIA Rail
Canada's national rail carrier, **VIA Rail** (514/989-2626 or 888/842-7245, www.viarail.ca), runs *The Canadian,* its flagship train, between Toronto and Vancouver. If you do the trip nonstop, Toronto to Vancouver takes four nights and three days. Major stops en route include Winnipeg, Saskatoon, Edmonton, Jasper, and Kamloops. *The Canadian* operates three times a week in each direction from May through mid-October, and twice a week from mid-October through April. The Vancouver rail depot is **Pacific Central Station** (1150 Station St.), a short walk from the Main Street SkyTrain station, where you can catch a train to other points downtown.

Amtrak
U.S. rail carrier **Amtrak** (800/872-7245, www.amtrak.com) operates two trains a day in each direction between Vancouver and Seattle; one of these trains continues to Portland, Oregon. In either Portland or Seattle, you can make connections to or from San Francisco, Los Angeles, and other California cities. Amtrak trains arrive and depart from Vancouver's **Pacific Central Station** (1150 Station St.).

Remember that when you arrive in Vancouver from the United States or travel from Vancouver to the United States, you're crossing an international border, and you need to allow time for customs and immigration procedures. Don't forget your passport!

The Rocky Mountaineer
The **Rocky Mountaineer** (1755 Cottrell St., at Terminal Ave., 604/606-7245 or 877/460-3200, www.rockymountaineer.com, mid-Apr.-mid-Oct.) is a privately run luxury train that offers rail trips between Vancouver, Banff, Lake Louise, Jasper, and Calgary. You can travel round-trip from Vancouver to the Canadian Rockies and back, or you can book a one-way journey through the Rockies from Vancouver to Calgary (or vice versa).

Unlike a standard train trip, many Rocky Mountaineer packages include a number of different activities, ranging from gondola rides to helicopter tours, with accommodations included along the way. It's also possible to book a Rocky Mountaineer holiday that includes rail fare and accommodations only; for example, they offer two-day train trips between Vancouver and Lake Louise, Banff, or Jasper. Rail packages start at $1,699 pp and go up depending on the destinations, the number of days of travel, and the level of service and accommodations.

All Rocky Mountaineer trains travel during the day and stop overnight in Kamloops en route to and from the Rockies. Note that in Vancouver, Rocky Mountaineer trains do not use Pacific Central Station, where VIA Rail and Amtrak trains depart; they have their own depot nearby.

By Bus
Pacific Central Station (1150 Station St.), the rail depot, is also the main Vancouver bus station. **Greyhound** (800/661-8747, www.greyhound.ca) runs buses to Vancouver from many Canadian and U.S. destinations.

Between Seattle and Vancouver, other bus services include **Bolt Bus** (877/265-8287, www.boltbus.com), which arrives and departs from Pacific Central Station, and **Quick Shuttle** (604/940-4428 or 800/665-2122, www.quickcoach.com), which stops at Canada Place and will also pick up or drop off passengers at a number of downtown hotels, with advance reservations. Bolt Bus takes four hours; Quick Shuttle takes four to five hours, depending on pick-up and drop-off locations.

Sights

★ Stanley Park
Like New York's Central Park or London's Hyde Park, Vancouver's **Stanley Park** is the city's beating green heart. Crisscrossed with walking trails, dense with trees, and home to several attractions, this 1,000-acre (400-hectare) parkland sits on the downtown peninsula, a short walk from the city's skyscraping towers. The waters of English Bay and

Burrard Inlet surround the park, making it even more scenic.

The Seawall, a 5.5-mile (9-kilometer) walking and cycling path, circles the perimeter of Stanley Park and passes many of the park's attractions. You can also follow the park's perimeter by car along Park Drive. TransLink's **bus 19** travels through downtown along West Pender and West Georgia Streets into the park.

Totem Poles at Brockton Point
When you enter the park from West Georgia Street, one of the first attractions you reach illustrates the region's First Nations heritage. Nine colorful **totem poles** stand at Brockton Point.

The park board purchased four of these hard-carved poles in the 1920s from the northern Vancouver Island community of Alert Bay. Several more came from Haida Gwaii (formerly known as the Queen Charlotte Islands) off the B.C. coast. Eventually, all of these poles were either returned to their original homes or sent to museums for preservation; the totems now standing in the park are replicas. A Squamish Nation artist, Robert Yelton, carved the newest pole, which was installed at Brockton Point in 2009.

Prospect Point
From **Prospect Point**, a lookout located at the highest spot in Stanley Park, you have great views of the Burrard Inlet, the North Shore mountains, and the Lions Gate Bridge. Built in 1938 and spanning 1,553 feet (473 meters), the **Lions Gate Bridge** is one of the world's longest suspension bridges.

You can stop for lunch or an ice cream cone at the **Prospect Point Restaurant** (5601 Stanley Park Dr., 604/669-2737, www.prospectpoint.com, 11am-5pm daily, mains $10-16), which serves salads, fish-and-chips, burgers, and beer overlooking the water. At the same location, the **Prospect Point Coffee Company** (9am-6pm Mon.-Fri., 9am-5pm Sat.-Sun.) sells java and pastries, and you can

Two Days in Vancouver

Start your day on **Granville Island** with coffee and a water view in the **Granville Island Public Market.** Browse the market food stalls early, before the crowds arrive, and pick up snacks or picnic fixings to enjoy when you're done shopping. Wander the island to explore the craft shops and galleries, too. If you're feeling energetic, rent a kayak or a stand-up paddleboard at **Ecomarine Paddlesports Centre** and spend an hour on the water paddling around the island.

After lunch, head west to the University of British Columbia campus to visit the **Museum of Anthropology,** which has a particularly strong collection of First Nations art, including an awe-inspiring gallery of totem poles. On your way back downtown, stop along West 4th Avenue in **Kitsilano** to browse some of the boutiques or refresh with a pastry from **Beaucoup Bakery** or a shot of rich drinking chocolate at **Chocolate Arts.**

Once you've returned to the city center, your next stop is **Stanley Park,** Vancouver's vast downtown green space. **Rent a bicycle** and circle the seawall, stopping to see the **totem poles at Brockton Point,** or if you're visiting with kids, tour the **Vancouver Aquarium Marine Science Centre,** Canada's largest aquarium. Either way, make time for a late-afternoon walk or a rest in the sand at **English Bay Beach,** which is also one of Vancouver's best spots to watch the sun set over the ocean.

Have dinner in Gastown or Chinatown at one of the deliciously fun contemporary restaurants, like **L'Abbatoir,** **Chambar,** or **Sai Woo.** Wrap up your evening with a nightcap nearby at **The Pourhouse** or the **Keefer Bar.**

The next morning, choose between an urban or outdoor experience. If it's a fine day, cross the Burrard Inlet to the North Shore and explore **Grouse Mountain,** where you can laugh at the lumberjack show, explore the wildlife refuge, go hiking, or simply take in the panoramic views.

Or stay in the city and tour the **Dr. Sun Yat-Sen Classical Chinese Garden,** which is the only authentic Ming Dynasty garden outside China; the **Bill Reid Gallery of Northwest Coast Art,** which showcases the work of a renowned First Nations artists; and the **Vancouver Art Gallery,** known for its collection of works by B.C. painter Emily Carr.

In the evening, if you're visiting between mid-May and mid-October, hop on the Canada Line and head for the **Richmond Night Market,** an Asian-style festival of street foods from China, Taiwan, Japan, and more. Or have supper in Richmond's **Golden Village,** where you'll find some of the best Chinese cuisine outside China.

If you'd rather stay closer to the downtown area, consider sampling the bounty of the seas at **Yew Seafood & Bar** or **Boulevard Kitchen & Oyster Bar,** get adventurous with dinner at **Farmer's Apprentice,** or indulge in a fine meal at **Hawksworth Restaurant** or **West** to wind up your two days in Vancouver with a delicious splurge.

---

get food to go at the **Signal Station Grill** (11am-6:30pm Mon.-Fri., 11am-7pm Sat.-Sun.).

Siwash Rock

Another landmark is **Siwash Rock,** a towering pillar just offshore that you can see from the Seawall on the park's west side. Topped with a wind-buffeted Douglas fir tree, the rock figures in a Squamish First Nations legend, which tells of a young father who the gods turned to stone to honor his commitment to his family.

Second and Third Beaches

Stanley Park has two sandy beaches along the Seawall on the park's western side. **Third Beach,** which is farther into the park, is quieter, while family-friendly

Second Beach is busier, with a seaside swimming pool and snack bar.

Vancouver Aquarium Marine Science Centre

Located in the center of Stanley Park and housing more than 50,000 marine creatures, the **Vancouver Aquarium** (845 Avison Way, 604/659-3474, www.vanaqua.org, 9:30am-6pm daily July-early Sept., 10am-5pm daily early Sept.-June, adults $29, seniors and students $20, ages 4-12 $15) is Canada's largest aquarium. Exhibits highlight Canadian environments, but also explore marine life from the Amazon to Africa to the Arctic. Besides perusing the exhibit halls, you can watch live shows throughout the day, including popular beluga whale, dolphin, shark, and penguin programs, and or immerse yourself in the films shown in the 4-D theater.

This popular attraction draws throngs of visitors, particularly in the busy summer months. Buy tickets online to avoid long waits at the door. In summer, visit before 11am or after 4pm when the crowds can be smaller; in winter, come in the mornings or after 2pm.

Stanley Park Nature House

An ecology center located on the park's Lost Lagoon, the **Stanley Park Nature House** (nature house 604/257-8544, program information 604/718-6522, www.stanleyparkecology.ca, 10am-5pm Tues.-Sun. July-Aug., 10am-4pm Sat.-Sun. Sept.-June, free) has exhibits about the plants and animals that live in the park.

Nature House staff lead periodic two-hour **discovery walks** (check the website for schedules; generally adults $10) highlighting the park's plants, birds, and wildlife. To find the nature house, enter the park near the intersection of Alberni and Chilco Streets, and walk toward the lagoon.

Downtown and the West End
Canada Place

Among Vancouver's most famous landmarks is **Canada Place** (999 Canada Pl., 604/665-9000, www.canadaplace.ca), its billowing white sails recalling a ship ready to set off to sea. Canada Place does have a seafaring function; the building, with its five 90-foot (27-meter) white sails made of Teflon-coated fiberglass, houses the city's cruise ship terminal. Also inside are the east wing of the Vancouver Convention Centre, the Pan Pacific Hotel Vancouver, and several attractions for visitors.

The coolest reason to visit Canada Place is **FlyOver Canada** (604/620-8455, www.flyovercanada.com, 10am-9pm daily, adults $19.95, seniors and students $17.95, ages 12 and under $14.95), a multimedia simulated flight that has you swoop and soar across the country, flying over Arctic peaks, past Toronto's CN Tower, and across the Canadian Rockies. You even feel the spray as you hover above Niagara Falls, and at one point, the Northern lights spread out around you. The FlyOver Canada experience lasts about 30 minutes; the flight itself is just eight minutes long.

While you're at Canada Place, you can follow the **Canadian Trail,** a walkway along the building's west promenade. Check out interpretive panels about Canada's ten provinces and three territories while enjoying the views of Stanley Park, Burrard Inlet, and the North Shore mountains. You'll frequently see massive cruise ships at the docks from spring through fall.

Olympic Cauldron

When Vancouver hosted the 2010 Winter Olympic Games, the candelabra-like **Olympic Cauldron** (Jack Poole Plaza, foot of Thurlow St.) burned brightly. Although it's now lit only for special events, the 33-foot-tall (10-meter) landmark still stands next to the Vancouver

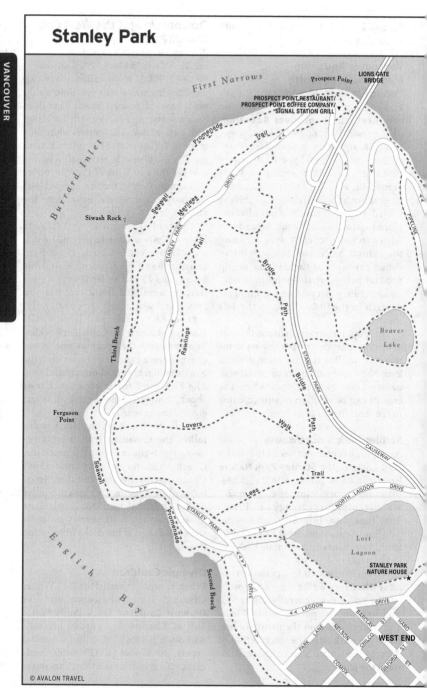

Stanley Park

First Narrows

Prospect Point

LIONS GATE BRIDGE

PROSPECT POINT RESTAURANT/
PROSPECT POINT COFFEE COMPANY/
SIGNAL STATION GRILL

Burrard Inlet

Promenade

Trail

Seawall

STANLEY PARK — Merilees

DRIVE

Siwash Rock

Trail

PIPELINE

Bridle

Path

Beaver Lake

Third Beach

Rawlings

STANLEY — PARK

Bridle

Path

Ferguson Point

Lovers

Walk

CAUSEWAY

Seawall

Lees

Trail

NORTH LAGOON

DRIVE

STANLEY PARK

Promenade

Lost Lagoon

STANLEY PARK NATURE HOUSE ★

English Bay

Second Beach

DRIVE

LAGOON

DRIVE

HARO

BARCLAY ST

NELSON

CHILCO ST

GILFORD ST

WEST END

PARK LANE

COMOX

© AVALON TRAVEL

First Narrows

NORTH VANCOUVER

Burrard Inlet

Seawall

STANLEY PARK

Promenade

Hummingbird Trail

AVISON WAY

DRIVE

ROAD

THEATRE UNDER THE STARS

VANCOUVER AQUARIUM MARINE SCIENCE CENTRE

TOTEM POLES AT BROCKTON POINT

Brockton Point

Hallelujah Point

STANLEY PARK DRIVE

THE SEAWALL

Deadman's Island (no public access)

Coal Harbour

WEST GEORGIA ST

SPOKES BICYCLE RENTALS

BAYSHORE BICYCLE RENTALS

DENMAN ST

ROBSON ST

ALBERNI ST

BIDWELL ST

| 0 | | 300 yds |
| 0 | | 300 m |

Convention Centre's west building, near the Coal Harbour waterfront.

Vancouver Lookout

Ride the glass elevator to the top of the **Vancouver Lookout** (555 W. Hastings St., 604/689-0421, www.vancouverlookout. com, 8:30am-10:30pm daily May-Sept., 9am-9pm daily Oct.-Apr., adults $16.25, seniors $13.25, students $11.25, ages 6-12 $8.25, families $41), for views across the city, Stanley Park, the waterfront, and the North Shore mountains. Although many downtown buildings now tower above this 30-story tower, which opened in 1977, it's a good place to get oriented. Your admission price includes a 20-minute tour highlighting local sights as you circle the observation platform. Even if you don't follow a tour, you can ask the guides to point out particular locations or tell you what you're seeing.

Lookout tickets are good all day, so you can check out the daytime views, then return to see the sunset or watch the evening lights twinkle.

★ Bill Reid Gallery of Northwest Coast Art

Born to a Haida First Nations mother and a European father, British Columbia artist Bill Reid (1920-1998) created more than 1,500 sculptures, carvings, and pieces of jewelry, most of which explore Haida traditions. The **Bill Reid Gallery of Northwest Coast Art** (639 Hornby St., 604/682-3455, www.billreidgallery.ca, 10am-5pm daily late May-early Sept., 11am-5pm Wed.-Sun. early Sept.-late May, adults $10, seniors and students $7, ages 5-17 $5, families $25) is dedicated to Reid's life and work.

Among the highlights of Reid's many works on display are *Mythic Messengers*, a 28-foot (8.5-meter) bronze frieze; more than 40 pieces of his gold and silver

Top to bottom: Canada Place; view from the Vancouver Lookout; Dr. Sun Yat-Sen Classical Chinese Garden.

jewelry; and several of Reid's pieces that the Canadian government featured on Canada's $20 bill. The gallery showcases other First Nations art, including a full-size totem pole carved by James Hart of Haida Gwaii, and hosts changing exhibits of aboriginal art of the northwest coastal region.

Vancouver Art Gallery

The permanent collection at the **Vancouver Art Gallery** (750 Hornby St., 604/662-4719, www.vanartgallery.bc.ca, 10am-5pm Wed.-Mon., 10am-9pm Tues., adults $20, seniors and students $15, children over age 5 $6, families $50, 5pm-9pm Tues. by donation) includes more than 10,000 artworks, emphasizing artists from western Canada. The gallery has a particularly strong collection of works by British Columbia-born artist Emily Carr (1871-1945), one of Canada's most important early-20th-century artists. Carr is known for her paintings of B.C.'s landscapes and its indigenous people.

Hosting changing exhibitions throughout the year, the gallery is currently housed in the former 1906 court building the architect Francis M. Rattenbury (1867-1935), who also designed Victoria's Parliament Building. Noted B.C. modern architect Arthur Erikson (1924-2009) incorporated the courthouse into the expanded gallery that was completed in 1983.

If you need a break while you're browsing, the **Gallery Café** (604/688-2233, www.thegallerycafe.ca, 9am-6pm Mon. and Wed.-Fri., 9am-9pm Tues., 10am-6pm Sat.-Sun., mains $8-11) is a peaceful spot for salads, *paninis*, quiche, or a glass of wine.

Vancouver Central Library

Why go to the library when you're on holiday? The **Vancouver Central Library** (350 W. Georgia St., 604/331-3603, www.vpl.ca, 10am-9pm Mon.-Thurs., 10am-6pm Fri.-Sat., 11am-6pm Sun., free) is both an architectural landmark and a hub of information, art, and events.

Designed by Israeli-Canadian architect Moshe Safdie and opened in 1995, the library building has a distinctive curved shape, modeled after Rome's Colosseum. Before you even get to the books, you can have coffee or a snack in one of several cafés in the library's light and airy interior atrium.

The library regularly hosts events from lectures to author talks to movies. Most are free; check the calendar on the library website to see what's going on.

Gastown and Chinatown

Vancouver's historic **Gastown** district got its name from a fast-talking British sailor and riverboat pilot turned saloon-keeper. In 1867, Captain John Deighton, nicknamed "Gassy Jack" for his habit of telling tall tales, promised local mill-workers that he'd serve them drinks if they'd build him a saloon on the shores of Burrard Inlet. The motivated mill-workers constructed the bar in just one day, and the fledging Gastown neighborhood took its title from Deighton's "Gassy" nickname.

Gastown, which centers along Water and Cordova Streets, between Richards and Main Streets, became part of the city of Vancouver in 1886. Many of its historic brick and stone buildings date to the early 1900s. There's a **statue of Gassy Jack** at Maple Tree Square, where Alexander, Carrall, Water, and Powell Streets converge.

Chinese immigrants began settling in Vancouver in the 1880s, and by the 1920s, Vancouver's **Chinatown** was thriving. However, in 1923, the Canadian government passed the Chinese Immigration Act, often called the Chinese Exclusion Act, which effectively stopped Chinese from immigrating to Canada. This lack of new residents, combined with the Great Depression of the 1930s, sent the neighborhood into decline. The Exclusion Act wasn't repealed until 1947.

Today, the ornate **Millennium Gate** (Pender St.), erected in 2002, marks the entrance to Chinatown. While the neighborhood still has Chinese markets, bakeries, and restaurants, hip new galleries, shops, and eateries are moving in. Chinatown's busiest streets are East Pender, Keefer, and Georgia between Carrall Street and Gore Avenue.

Waterfront Station (Cordova St., between Granville St. and Seymour St.), a transit hub for the SkyTrain, buses, and SeaBus, borders Gastown; the **Stadium/Chinatown** SkyTrain station (Beatty St. at Dunsmuir St.) is also nearby. Many TransLink buses, including buses 4, 7, 14, 16, 20, and 22, travel between downtown and Gastown or Chinatown.

Like many North American cities, Vancouver has a significant homeless population, many of whom congregate on Gastown's and Chinatown's streets. While that isn't a reason to avoid the area, use caution as you would in any urban neighborhood.

Gastown Steam Clock
Sure, it's touristy, but you'll still find yourself in front of this local icon, waiting for it to toot its steam whistle every 15 minutes. The historic-looking **Gastown Steam Clock** (Water St., at Cambie St.) actually dates back only to 1977, when area businesses commissioned clockmaker Ray Saunders to create the clock as part of the neighborhood's revitalization. Saunders based his clock on an 1875 design; it draws power from the city's underground steam heating system (and from three electric motors).

Gastown Art Galleries
Several Gastown art galleries show and sell works by traditional or contemporary aboriginal artists. Browsing is free at these commercial galleries.

On the main floor of Skwachàys Lodge, a boutique aboriginal art hotel, the **Urban Aboriginal Fair Trade Gallery** (29 W. Pender St., 604/558-3589, www.

urbanaboriginal.org, 10am-4pm Mon.-Fri., 11am-5pm Sat.-Sun.) showcases works by Canadian aboriginal artists. The nonprofit Vancouver Native Housing Society owns the gallery, and gallery proceeds help support the society's mission to provide affordable urban housing for aboriginal people.

Three-story **Hill's Native Art** (165 Water St., 604/685-4249, www.hills.ca, 9am-9pm daily) carries a large collection of First Nations arts and crafts, with more souvenir-style items on the lower level and high-quality artworks, carvings, and more on the upper floors.

Coastal Peoples Fine Arts Gallery (312 Water St., 604/684-9222, www.coastalpeoples.com, 10am-7pm daily mid-Apr.-mid-Oct., 10am-6pm daily mid-Oct.-mid-Apr.) specializes in Northwest Coast and Inuit artwork in their spacious, modern gallery.

At **Spirit Wrestler Gallery** (47 Water St., 604/669-8813, www.spiritwrestler.com, 10am-6pm Mon.-Sat., noon-5pm Sun.), you can view art from three cultures: western Canada's First Nations, the Inuit, and New Zealand's Maori.

Another specialist in Canadian aboriginal art, the **Inuit Gallery of Vancouver** (206 Cambie St., 604/688-7323, www.inuit.com, 10am-6pm Mon.-Fri., 11am-5pm Sat., noon-5pm Sun.) exhibits works by First Nations and Inuit people.

★ Dr. Sun Yat-Sen Classical Chinese Garden
From the building tiles to the pathway pebbles, all the components of the **Dr. Sun Yat-Sen Classical Chinese Garden** (578 Carrall St., 604/662-3207, www.vancouverchinesegarden.com, 10am-6pm daily May-mid-June and Sept., 9:30am-7pm daily mid-June-Aug., 10am-4:30pm daily Oct., 10am-4:30pm Tues.-Sun. Nov.-Apr., adults $12, seniors $10, students and children over age 5 $9, families $25) came from China, as did the 52 master craftsmen who arrived from Suzhou in 1985 to construct the

first authentic Ming Dynasty garden outside China.

Take one of the informative **garden tours** (included with admission), to learn more about the peaceful garden's design and construction. From mid-June through August, tours start on the hour 10am to 4pm with an additional tour at 5:30pm; check the garden website or phone for tour times during the rest of the year.

Adjacent to the garden is the free city-run **Dr. Sun Yat-Sen Park.** While built with Canadian materials and lacking the classical garden's Chinese pedigree, this smaller park is still a pretty spot to sit. Head for the shaded pagoda and watch the fish swim past.

Rennie Collection at Wing Sang

Vancouver real estate marketer Bob Rennie has assembled one of Canada's largest private collections of contemporary art. At the **Rennie Collection at Wing Sang** (51 E. Pender St., 604/682-2088, www.renniecollection.org, hours vary, free), a private museum in Chinatown's oldest structure, the 1889 Wing Sang Building, you can see changing exhibitions of these works by both established and emerging international artists. To visit an exhibit, you must reserve a spot on a free 50-minute guided tour, offered several times a week; book in advance on the gallery website.

Even if you don't go inside, walk far enough away from the gallery building to see British artist Martin Creed's 2008 neon sculpture, *Work No. 851: EVERYTHING IS GOING TO BE ALRIGHT,* installed on the upper facade.

Vancouver Police Museum

If you're creeped out by crime, give the **Vancouver Police Museum** (240 E. Cordova St., 604/665-3346, www.vancouverpolicemuseum.ca, 9am-5pm Tues.-Sat., adults $12, seniors and students $10, ages 6-18 $8, families $30), in the 1932 former city morgue and autopsy facility,

a pass. Yet if you're curious about some of shiny Vancouver's darker moments, plan a visit to this museum of policing, criminology, and various misdeeds.

In the museum's Sins gallery, you can check out their collection of counterfeit money, illegal drugs, and confiscated weapons. The True Crime gallery exhibits photos and evidence from notorious regional crimes, many of which remain unsolved. You can also visit the autopsy suite, last used in 1980, which has a collection of preserved human organs.

The museum runs two two-hour **Sins of the City Walking Tours** (May-Oct., adults $20, seniors, students, and ages 16-18 $16), where you can explore the underbelly of Gastown and Chinatown. The **Red Light Rendezvous Tour** (5pm Thurs., 3pm Sat.) tells you about the neighborhoods' brothels and the women who ran them, while on the **Vice, Dice, and Opium Pipes Tour** (3pm Fri.), you walk the beat of a 1920s cop, on the lookout for gambling dens, bootlegging joints, and other nefarious activity. While kids are allowed in the police museum, at their parents' discretion, the minimum age for these walking tours is 16.

The Police Museum is located east of Gastown, on the edge of Chinatown. **Buses 4 and 7** from downtown stop nearby.

Yaletown and False Creek

British naval officer and explorer George Henry Richards is credited with naming the waterway that separates downtown Vancouver from the rest of the city to the south. In 1859, Richards traveled up what he thought was a creek in search of coal deposits. However, Richards discovered that this waterway was actually an inlet of the Pacific Ocean. He named it **False Creek.**

Sawmills, rail yards, and other industrial developments once lined False Creek. On its northern shore, bounded by Nelson, Homer, Drake, and Pacific Streets, an eight-block warehouse district was built in 1900 in the neighborhood now known as **Yaletown.** Although the area grew derelict in the mid-1900s, its fortunes began to change when Vancouver hosted the Expo '86 World's Fair along False Creek's shores. These days, the renovated brick warehouses are home to a chic mix of condos, restaurants, boutiques, and drinking spots.

On the opposite side of False Creek, a new neighborhood developed, thanks to the 2010 Winter Olympic Games. The residential buildings where athletes lived during the Games have been transformed into the **Olympic Village,** also known as the Village at False Creek, comprising stylish condominiums, brewpubs, and cafés. Photographers: The Olympic Village provides a great vantage point for skyline photos.

To get to Yaletown's restaurants, shops, and pubs, you can take the Canada Line to **Yaletown/Roundhouse** station. From the Canada Line's **Olympic Village** station, across False Creek from downtown,

you can walk east along the Seawall to the village itself. The **Main Street/Science World** station on the SkyTrain's Expo and Millennium Lines is closest to the city's science museum and to the rail and bus depot.

Science World

What's that dome thing? The kids may want to check out the distinctive geodesic dome (constructed for Expo '86) that houses Vancouver's cool science museum, even before they venture inside.

Officially called **Science World at Telus World of Science** (1455 Quebec St., 604/443-7440, www.scienceworld.ca, 10am-5pm Mon.-Fri., 10am-6pm Sat.-Sun. Apr.-late June, 10am-6pm Fri.-Wed., 10am-8pm Thurs. late June-early Sept., 10am-5pm Tues.-Fri., 10am-6pm Sat.-Sun. early Sept.-Mar., extended hours during Dec. winter break and Mar. spring break, adults $23.25, seniors and students $18.50, ages 3-12 $15.25), the museum is full of hands-on exhibits about

Science World, on Vancouver's False Creek

the human body, natural world, light and sound, puzzles and illusions, and more. The littlest visitors have their own Kidspace, designed for children under age six. Live science shows and demonstrations take place throughout the day, and a rotating selection of films plays on the five-story-tall screen in the immersive OMNIMAX Theatre ($6 pp).

Outside in the **Ken Spencer Science Park,** you can explore more interactive exhibits about the local environment and issues of sustainability. The park even has its own chicken coop.

The easiest way to get to Science World from other downtown points is on the SkyTrain to the **Main Street/Science World Station.** The **Aquabus** (604/689-5858, www.theaquabus.com) and **False Creek Ferries** (604/684-7781, www.granvilleislandferries.bc.ca) also stop nearby.

B.C. Place

The odd-looking structure along False Creek that resembles a giant space ship

is **B.C. Place** (777 Pacific Blvd., 604/669-2300, www.bcplacestadium.com, subway: Stadium/Chinatown), a sports and concert arena. The Vancouver Whitecaps Major League Soccer team plays here, as does the B.C. Lions football team.

Outside the arena, near the intersection of Robson and Beatty Streets, is the **Terry Fox Memorial,** a series of four progressively larger sculptures by Vancouver artist Douglas Coupland. The memorial honors Fox, the B.C. man who embarked on a cross-Canada run in 1980 to raise money for cancer research after losing his own leg to the disease. Fox unfortunately had to stop his "Marathon of Hope," after running 5,342 kilometers (3,339 miles), when his cancer returned. Although Fox raised more than $24 million, he died of cancer at age 22 on June 28, 1981.

★ Granville Island

This former industrial district underneath the Granville Bridge, across False Creek from downtown, is now one of Vancouver's most popular attractions. **Granville Island** (604/666-6655, http://granvilleisland.com) entertains visitors with art galleries, boutiques, breweries and distilleries, and the lively Granville Island Public Market. Granville Island also draws theatergoers to its several stages.

The best time to visit Granville Island is on a weekday morning. The island, particularly the Public Market, gets packed with visitors in the afternoons and on weekends, especially in summer.

From downtown, most TransLink buses that follow Granville Street over the Granville Bridge take you within walking distance of Granville Island. **Bus 50,** which stops at West 2nd Avenue and Anderson Street, is most convenient. You can also take **buses 4, 7, 10, 14, or 16** to Granville Street at 5th Avenue; from there, it's a 10-15 minute walk to the island.

The **Aquabus** (604/689-5858, www.theaquabus.com) and **False Creek Ferries**

The Island the Olympics Built

Before hosting the 2010 Winter Olympic Games, Vancouver embarked on numerous building projects: the Canada Line subway connecting downtown and the airport, the Olympic Cauldron on the Coal Harbour waterfront, and the former Athletes Village on the shores of False Creek, which housed competitors during the Games and is now the fashionable Olympic Village district.

Yet one of the Olympics' most unusual legacies may be an artificial island. To build the Athletes Village, developers excavated a vast amount of rocks, sand, and gravel. More than 2 million cubic feet (60,000 cubic meters) of this excavated material was used to construct tiny **Habitat Island,** along Southeast False Creek.

Now city-owned parkland, Habitat Island has more than 200 native trees, shrubs, flowers, and grasses, and, as befits its name, it provides a habitat for birds, crabs, starfish, and other land and sea creatures.

Habitat Island is located on the False Creek waterfront, near the foot of Columbia Street, east of the Cambie Bridge. A rock pathway leads onto the island from the Seawall path. You can wander over to the island for a stroll or a picnic. Or simply explore the island that the Olympics built.

(604/684-7781, www.granvilleislandferries.bc.ca) can also take you across False Creek between downtown and Granville Island.

Granville Island Public Market

The island's main attraction is the year-round indoor **Granville Island Public Market** (1689 Johnston St., http://granvilleisland.com, 9am-7pm daily), where artistically arranged fruits garnish the produce stalls and you can nibble away the day on pastries, fudge, and other treats.

Start at **Blue Parrot Espresso Bar** (604/688-5127, www.blueparrotcoffee.com) for java with a water view. Sample the **salmon candy** (unexpectedly addictive cured, salty-sweet fish snacks) at any of the seafood counters, or line up with the locals for house-made charcuterie at **Oyama Sausage** (604/327-7407, www.oyamasausage.ca) or nut-studded grape loaves at **Terra Breads** (604/685-3102, www.terrabreads.com).

When you're looking for lunch, sample the soups at the **Stock Market** (604/687-2433, http://thestockmarket.ca) or the well-prepared salmon burgers at the **Market Grill** (604/689-1918). You might hope that the kids won't notice longtime favorite **Lee's Donuts** (604/685-4021), at least until it's time for dessert.

Net Loft

After you've explored the Public Market, browse the shops and galleries in the nearby **Net Loft** (1666 Johnston St., 10am-7pm daily).

Circle Craft Co-Operative (604/669-8021, www.circlecraft.net) sells ceramics, textiles, jewelry, and other work by B.C. craftspeople. The **Wickaninnish Gallery** (604/681-1057, http://wickaninnishgallery.com) shows First Nations art. Other fun shops are **Little Dream** (604/683-6930, http://dreamvancouver.com), which carries locally made fashions; **Paper-Ya** (604/684-2531, http://paper-ya.com), for fine papers, notebooks, origami, and other paper goods; and the **Granville Island Hat Shop** (604/683-4280, www.thehatshop.ca), where you can find almost anything to wear on your head.

Kids Market

On Granville Island, youngsters have their own marketplace, the **Kids Market** (1496 Cartwright St., 604/689-8447, www.kidsmarket.ca, 10am-6pm daily), where cute shops sell toys, games, and clothing. The kids can run around in the

Adventure Zone, an indoor playground, or outside in the **splash park** (late May-early Sept.).

Art Galleries

Along the island's lanes are many artist studios and galleries. Wander around to see what you discover, or look for some of these artisans.

Crafthouse (1386 Cartwright St., 604/687-6511, www.craftcouncilbc.ca, 10am-6pm daily May-Aug., 10:30am-5:30pm daily Sept.-Apr.) shows work by members of the Craft Council of B.C.

Federation of Canadian Artists Gallery (1241 Cartwright St., 604/681-2744, www.artists.ca, 10am-4pm Tues.-Fri., 10am-1pm and 1:30pm-4pm Sat.-Sun.) exhibits work by its member artists from across Canada.

Owned by the nonprofit Potters Guild of British Columbia, the **Gallery of B.C. Ceramics** (1359 Cartwright St., 604/669-3606, www.bcpotters.com, 10:30am-5:30pm daily Feb.-Dec., 10:30am-5:30pm Tues.-Sun. Jan.) displays pottery and ceramic work.

Harry Potter and his Quidditch team would covet the handmade sweepers from the **Granville Island Broom Co.** (1406 Old Bridge St., 604/629-1141, www.broomcompany.com, 10am-6pm daily).

At the **Silk Weaving Studio** (1531 Johnston St., 604/687-7455, www.silkweavingstudio.com, 10am-5pm daily), you'll find hand-woven scarves, shawls, and other garments.

Breweries and Distilleries

Thirsty? At Granville Island's breweries and distilleries, you can learn about the production process and sample the wares.

Granville Island Brewing (1441 Cartwright St., 604/687-2739, www.gib.ca, store 10am-8pm daily, taproom noon-8pm daily, tours noon, 2pm, and 4pm daily, adults $9.75) started producing craft beers back in 1984. Tour the brewery or try a sample in their Taproom.

Liberty Distilling (1494 Old Bridge St., 604/558-1998, www.thelibertydistillery.com, 11am-8pm daily, tours 11:30am and 1:30pm Sat.-Sun., $10) brews small batches of vodka, gin, and whiskey in their copper pot stills. Sample their hand-crafted products in the cocktail lounge, or take a weekend distillery tour.

At the **Artisan Sake Maker** (1339 Railspur Alley, 604/685-7253, www.artisansakemaker.com, 11:30am-6pm daily), Vancouver's only local producer of Japanese rice wine, learn how sake is brewed, and taste it, too.

Kitsilano and the West Side

West of Granville Island, the Kitsilano neighborhood has a great beach, lots of shops and restaurants (mostly along West 4th Ave.), and several museums in waterfront Vanier Park.

On the city's far west side, the University of British Columbia campus is worth visiting for its stellar Museum of Anthropology, and for several gardens and smaller museums.

Two more of Vancouver's notable parks and gardens—the VanDusen Botanical Garden and Queen Elizabeth Park—are located between Oak and Main Streets, near West 33rd Avenue.

★ Museum of Anthropology

If you're interested in exploring the culture of British Columbia's aboriginal peoples, and traditional cultures from around the world, don't miss the striking **Museum of Anthropology** (6393 NW Marine Dr., 604/822-5087, http://moa.ubc.ca, 10am-5pm Wed.-Mon., 10am-9pm Tues. mid-May-mid-Oct., 10am-5pm Tues.-Sun. mid-Oct.-mid-May, adults $16.75, seniors, students, and children over age 6 $14.50, families $44.75, 5pm-9pm Tues. $9 pp) on the University of British Columbia campus.

Canadian architect Arthur Erickson (1924-2009), whose other work includes Toronto's Roy Thompson Hall, the Museum of Glass in Tacoma, Washington, and many other cultural and governmental buildings around the world, designed the museum, which opened in 1976. The window-lined Great Hall provides a dramatic backdrop for the immense totem poles, traditional canoes, and elaborate carvings. The museum also houses the world's largest collection of works by noted Haida First Nations artist Bill Reid, including his massive cedar sculpture, *The Raven and the First Men*.

To reach the museum by public transit, take any **UBC-bound bus** (including buses 4 or 14 from downtown, bus 84 from the Olympic Village SkyTrain station, or bus 99 from the Broadway/City Hall SkyTrain station) to the last stop at the UBC bus loop. From there, you can walk to the museum in 10-15 minutes, or transfer to **shuttle bus C18,** which stops in front of the museum.

By car, it's about 25 minutes from downtown to the museum. Cross either the Granville or Burrard Bridges, and go west on West 4th Avenue. West of Blanca Street, 4th Avenue becomes Chancellor Boulevard, which circles the campus and meets NW Marine Drive. There's a parking lot at the museum.

Nitobe Japanese Garden

You could be in Japan as you stroll among the flowers, waterfalls, and koi ponds at the serene **Nitobe Japanese Garden** (1895 Lower Mall, UBC, 604/822-6038, www.botanicalgarden.ubc.ca, 9:30am-5pm daily Apr.-Oct., adults $7, seniors and students $5.50, ages 5-12 $4, families $16, 10am-2pm Mon.-Fri. Nov.-Mar. by donation), one of the most authentic traditional Japanese gardens in North America. The garden is particularly scenic in April and May, when the cherry blossoms bloom.

The garden is named for Dr. Inazo Nitobe (1862-1933), a professor, author, and advocate for East-West relations who served as Japan's representative to the League of Nations in the 1920s.

You can participate in a traditional **Japanese tea ceremony** (May-Sept., $10 pp in addition to garden admission) in the garden's teahouse on the last Saturday of the month. Ceremonies are held on the hour from 11am to 3pm, and reservations are recommended; call 604/939-7749 to reserve.

The garden is a short walk from the Museum of Anthropology. From the UBC bus loop, you can walk or take **shuttle bus C18.**

UBC Botanical Garden

A garden of native B.C. plants, a woodland garden, a traditional Asian garden: These are just a few groupings of the more than 10,000 trees and plants that thrive at the 70-acre (28-hectare) **UBC Botanical Garden** (6804 SW Marine Dr., UBC, 604/822-4208, www.botanicalgarden.ubc.ca, 9:30am-5pm daily, adults $9, seniors $7, ages 5-12 $5), where walking paths wend through the woods and grounds.

A more adventurous way to explore the garden is on the **Greenheart Canopy Walkway** (10am-4pm daily, adults $20, seniors $15, ages 5-12 $10, including garden admission), a 1,000-foot (308-meter) aerial trail system that takes you high into the rainforest canopy. You climb a series of swinging bridges to eight viewing platforms mounted in the trees.

Explore the walkway on your own or on a 45-minute **guided tour,** where your guide tells you about the surrounding second-growth forest. Though the area was once logged, many trees are more than a century old. You'll also learn how First Nations use various trees and plants, from carving canoes to traditional medicine.

The Botanical Garden is on the south side of the UBC campus. By public transit, take any **UBC-bound bus** (including buses 4 or 14 from downtown) to the last stop at the UBC bus loop; transfer to **shuttle bus C20,** which stops in front of the garden.

By car, it's about 25 minutes from downtown to the gardens. Cross the

Granville or Burrard Bridges, and go west on West 4th Avenue. West of Blanca Street, 4th Avenue becomes Chancellor Boulevard, which circles the campus and meets NW Marine Drive, which becomes SW Marine. There's a parking lot at the garden.

Beaty Biodiversity Museum

An 85-foot (26-meter) blue whale skeleton, the largest on display in Canada, greets visitors to the **Beaty Biodiversity Museum** (2212 Main Mall, UBC, 604/827-4955, www.beatymuseum.ubc.ca, 10am-5pm daily mid-May-mid-Oct., 10am-5pm Tues.-Sun. mid-Oct.-mid-May, adults $12, seniors, students, and ages 13-17 $10, ages 5-12 $8), a modern natural history gallery. The museum has more than two million specimens of bugs, fish, plants, fossils, and more, many of which come from B.C. and the surrounding regions.

The museum is near the center of the UBC campus, a short walk from the UBC bus loop.

Museum of Vancouver

Though its building resembles a flying saucer that might have landed in Kitsilano's Vanier Park, this city museum's unique structure, created by architect Gerald Hamilton, is actually designed to recall a traditional hat of the Haida First Nations people. Inside the **Museum of Vancouver** (1100 Chestnut St., 604/736-4431, www.museumofvancouver.ca, 10am-5pm Fri.-Wed., 10am-8pm Thurs., adults $15, seniors, students, and ages 12-18 $11, ages 5-11 $5), the exhibition spaces are no less distinctive.

The permanent galleries take you through Vancouver's past, from its aboriginal heritage to early settlement days to the hippie era of the 1960s, while the sometimes controversial temporary exhibitions explore social phenomena from happiness to sex. The museum hosts lectures, workshops, and social events that are as engaging as the exhibits themselves; check the calendar on their website for details.

The museum shares its building with the **H.R. MacMillan Space Centre** (1100 Chestnut St., 604/738-7827, www.spacecentre.ca; 10am-5pm daily late June-early Sept., 10am-3pm Mon.-Fri., 10am-5pm Sat., noon-5pm Sun. early Sept.-late June, adults $18, seniors and ages 12-18 $15, ages 5-11 $13, families $56), the city's planetarium, which has galleries of space exhibits to explore and astronomy shows throughout the day.

The Space Centre's **Gordon MacMillan Southam Observatory** (604/738-2855, Sat. year-round, Fri. early July-early Sept., evening show and stargazing adults $13, seniors and students $10, ages 5-11 $8, families $38) is also open for a planetarium show (7:30pm and 9pm) and guided stargazing (8pm-midnight) through the half-meter telescope. If you come only for the stargazing, admission is by donation.

The **Vanier Park Explore Pass** (adults $37, seniors, students, and ages 5-18 $30) includes admission to the Museum of Vancouver and the Space Centre, as well as the nearby Vancouver Maritime Museum.

Buses 2 and 22 travel from Burrard Street downtown into Kitsilano; get off at the corner of Cornwall Avenue and Chestnut Streets, where it's a short walk toward the water to the museum. Or take **False Creek Ferries** (604/684-7781, www.granvilleislandferries.bc.ca) to Vanier Park from Granville Island or downtown.

Vancouver Maritime Museum

Built in B.C. in the 1920s, the historic Arctic-exploring schooner *St. Roch* recorded several firsts. The ship was the first to sail the Northwest Passage from west to east (1940-1942) and the first to circumnavigate North America, when it traveled from Vancouver to Halifax via the Panama Canal in 1950.

When the ship was retired, the *St. Roch* came to rest at the **Vancouver Maritime Museum** (1905 Ogden St., 604/257-8300, www.vancouvermaritimemuseum.com, 10am-5pm Fri.-Wed., 10am-8pm Thurs. late May-early Sept., 10am-5pm Tues.-Wed. and Fri.-Sat., 10am-8pm Thurs., noon-5pm Sun. early Sept.-late May, adults $11, seniors, students, and ages 6-18 $8.50, families $30, 5pm-8pm Thurs. by donation), where it's now the centerpiece of the museum's exhibits about the high seas.

Climb aboard the *St. Roch* and learn more about its Arctic adventures. The museum has other hands-on exhibits designed for kids, as well as changing exhibitions about the Pacific Northwest and Arctic maritime history.

To reach the museum, on the waterfront in Vanier Park, take **buses 2 or 22** from Burrard Street downtown to the corner of Cornwall Avenue and Chestnut Street in Kitsilano. Or take **False Creek Ferries** (604/684-7781, www.granvilleislandferries.bc.ca) to Vanier Park from Granville Island or downtown.

South Granville Street

Granville Street, between West 5th and 15th Avenues, is worth browsing for its high-end boutiques and contemporary art galleries. Stop into **Douglas Reynolds Gallery** (2335 Granville St., 604/731-9292, www.douglasreynoldsgallery.com, 10am-6pm Mon.-Sat., noon-5pm Sun.) to explore exhibits of historic and contemporary Northwest Coast First Nations art, or see what's on view at **Bau-Xi Gallery** (3045 Granville St., 604/733-7011, www.bau-xi.com, 10am-5:30pm Mon.-Sat., 11am-5:30pm Sun.), which features contemporary fine art.

Buses 10, 14, and 16 travel along Granville Street over the Granville Bridge from downtown. Get off at Broadway, and you'll be in the heart of the South Granville neighborhood.

Top to bottom: totem pole at the Museum of Anthropology; Museum of Vancouver; Bloedel Conservatory at Queen Elizabeth Park.

VanDusen Botanical Garden

Wander the plant world without leaving Vancouver at the 55-acre (22-hectare) **VanDusen Botanical Garden** (5251 Oak St., 604/257-8335, www.vandusengarden. org; 9am-8:30pm daily June-Aug., 10am-6pm daily Sept., 10am-5pm daily Oct., 10am-4pm daily Nov., 10am-3pm daily Dec.-Jan., 10am-4pm daily Feb., 10am-5pm daily Mar., 9am-7pm daily Apr., 9am-8pm daily May, extended hours during Dec. Festival of Lights; Apr.-Sept. adults $11, seniors and ages 13-18 $8.25, ages 3-12 $5.75, families $25.75, Oct.-Mar. adults $8, seniors and ages 13-18 $5.75, ages 3-12 $4, families $17).

With more than 250,000 plants from around the globe, the garden contains varieties native to the Pacific Northwest, to other parts of Canada, and to ecosystems in the Himalayas, the Mediterranean, and South America. A one-hour **guided tour** (2pm daily and 10:30am Wed. Apr.-mid-Oct., 1pm Sun. mid-Oct.-Mar.) helps you explore what's growing.

From downtown, **bus 17** for Oak Street stops at West 37th Avenue at the garden entrance.

Queen Elizabeth Park

At **Queen Elizabeth Park** (4600 Cambie St., www.vancouver.ca, dawn-dusk daily), at the highest point in Vancouver, you can explore several gardens, have a picnic on its manicured grounds, or take photos of the city skyline and mountains. Also in the park are tennis courts, a pitch-and-putt golf course, and a lawn bowling field.

In a geodesic dome near the center of the park, the **Bloedel Conservatory** (604/873-7000, www.vancouver.ca, 9am-8pm Mon.-Fri., 10am-8pm Sat.-Sun. May-early Sept., 10am-5pm daily early Sept.-Apr., adults $6.50, seniors and students $4.50, ages 3-12 $3.25, families $15) houses three different ecosystems, including a tropical rainforest, subtropical rainforest, and desert environment, with native plants and more than 200

free-flying birds. It's a warm destination for a cold or rainy day.

To get to the park by public transit, take the Canada Line to **King Edward station**. Then either transfer to **bus 15** southbound on Cambie Street to West 33rd Avenue, or walk south on Cambie Street to the park entrance. Follow the trails through the trees or walk along the park road to reach the Conservatory; either way, it's a short but uphill climb.

Main Street and the East Side

Visit Vancouver's funky East Side for eclectic art galleries, craft breweries, cafés, and local boutiques.

Art Galleries

Several contemporary art galleries have moved into The Flats district, near the intersection of Main Street and East 2nd Avenue. All are free and welcome browsers interested in checking out the local art scene.

Stop into the **Equinox Gallery** (525 Great Northern Way, 604/736-2405, www.equinoxgallery.com, 10am-5pm Tues.-Sat.), **Monte Clark Gallery** (525 Great Northern Way, 604/730-5000, www.monteclarkgallery.com, 10am-5:30pm Tues.-Sat.), **Winsor Gallery** (258 E. 1st Ave., 604/681-4870, www.winsorgallery.com, 10am-6pm Tues.-Fri., 10am-5pm Sat.), and **Hot Art Wet City** (2206 Main St., 604/764-2266, www.hotartwetcity.com, noon-5pm Wed.-Sat.) to see what's happening.

It's a short walk to the galleries from the **Main Street/Science World** SkyTrain station. Or catch **buses 3 or 8,** which run along Main Street from downtown.

Breweries

The neighborhood around Main Street between 2nd and 8th Avenues has also become a center of local craft beer production. Perfect for a brewery crawl, several breweries with tasting rooms are within walking distance of each other:

- **33 Acres Brewing** (15 W. 8th Ave., 604/620-4589, www.33acresbrewing. com, 9am-11pm Mon.-Fri., 10am-11pm Sat.-Sun.)

- **Brassneck Brewery** (2148 Main St., 604/259-7686, www.brassneck.ca, 2pm-11pm Mon.-Fri., noon-11pm Sat.-Sun.)

- **Main Street Brewing Company** (261 E. 7th Ave., 604/336-7711, www.main-streetbeer.ca, 2pm-11pm Mon.-Thurs., noon-11pm Fri.-Sun.)

The North Shore

Across the Burrard Inlet from downtown Vancouver, the North Shore mountains provide the backdrop for the waterfront cities of North Vancouver and West Vancouver. For visitors, exploring these peaks—on the hiking trails, suspension bridges, or ski runs—is the best reason to cross the bridges from downtown.

Two bridges connect Vancouver to the North Shore. The Lions Gate Bridge is from Stanley Park across to West Vancouver, while the Ironworkers Memorial Second Narrows Bridge links Vancouver's east side to North Vancouver.

★ Grouse Mountain

Open for skiing and snowboarding in winter, and for hiking and lots of other activities from spring through fall, a half-day (or longer) trip to **Grouse Mountain** (6400 Nancy Greene Way, North Vancouver, 604/980-9311, www. grousemountain.com, 9am-10pm daily) lets you experience the mountains less than 40 minutes from downtown.

Take the **Skyride** (8:45am-10pm Mon.-Fri, 8:15am-10pm Sat.-Sun.), North America's largest tram system, to the **Peak Chalet,** where you can watch a film about the region's wildlife at the **Theatre in the Sky** or take in the entertaining 45-minute **Lumberjack Show** (noon, 2:30pm, and 4:30pm daily late

May-mid-Oct.), complete with log rolling, tree climbing, and ax throwing. The **Birds in Motion demonstration** (1:30pm, 3:30pm, and 5:30pm daily late May-late Sept.) shows off the skills of eagles, falcons, and other birds of prey, while at the **Grouse Mountain Refuge for Endangered Wildlife** you can learn more about bears, wolves, owls, and other creatures. Several self-guided **walking trails** start near the Peak Chalet, or you can take a 45-minute **guided eco-walk** (late May-Sept.) that departs several times a day.

The basic access tickets, called the **Alpine Experience** (adults $43.95, seniors $39.95, ages 13-18 $24.95, ages 5-12 $14.95, families $113.95), are available year-round and give you access to the Skyride, Theatre in the Sky, Lumberjack Show, Birds in Motion, wildlife refuge, and walking trails. To go higher up on the mountain, purchase a **Peak Experience ticket** (late May-Oct., adults $47.95, seniors $43.95, ages 13-18 $28.95, ages 5-12 $14.95, families $121.95), which adds a ride on the Peak Chairlift. The **Ultimate Experience** (late May-mid-Oct., adults $57.95, seniors $53.95, ages 13-18 $38.95, ages 5-12 $14.95, families $139.95) includes a visit to **The Eye of the Wind,** a mountaintop wind turbine.

For extra fees, you can add activities such as **zip-lining** ($109, including a Peak Experience ticket), **paragliding** (late June-Sept., $229, includes Peak Experience ticket if booked in advance), and **breakfast with the bears** (8:30am Sat.-Sun. late Mar.-late June and mid-Sept.-mid-Oct., 8:30am daily late June-mid-Sept., adults $64.95, seniors $59.95, ages 13-18 $44.95, ages 5-12 $34.95, families $184.95, includes Alpine Experience ticket) at the wildlife refuge.

Getting There

By car from downtown Vancouver, take West Georgia Street to the Lions Gate Bridge. Cross the bridge, turn right onto Marine Drive east, but move immediately into the left lane. Take the first left onto

Capilano Road and follow it up the hill to the Grouse Mountain parking lot (3 hours $6, full day $8).

You don't need a car to get to Grouse Mountain, though. The mountain runs a **free shuttle** (May-Sept., call or check the website for schedule) from Canada Place.

By public transportation, take the **SeaBus** from Waterfront Station to Lonsdale Quay and change to **bus 236** for Grouse Mountain, which will drop you at the mountain's base.

Capilano Suspension Bridge

The **Capilano Suspension Bridge** (3735 Capilano Rd., 604/985-7474, www.capbridge.com, 8:30am-8pm daily early May-early Sept., 9am-7pm daily early Sept.-late Sept., 9am-6pm daily late Sept.-mid-Oct., 9am-5pm daily mid-Oct.-Nov., 11am-9pm daily Dec.-early Jan., 9am-5pm daily early Jan.-mid-Mar., 9am-6pm daily mid-Mar.-late Apr., 9am-7pm daily late Apr.-late May, adults $37.95, seniors $34.95, students $30.95, ages 13-16 $24.95, ages 6-12 $12) draws daredevils who thrill to the swinging bridge, as well as others who want to explore this rainforest park.

Built in 1889, the 450-foot (137-meter) **Suspension Bridge** is a highlight, swaying 230 feet (70 meters) above the Capilano River. And yes, it does swing!

Before you cross the bridge, follow the **Cliffwalk,** a series of boardwalks and stairways cantilevered out over the river. If you're feeling brave, stand on the glass platform and look down (way down!) into the canyon where the river rushes below.

After you've made your way over the Suspension Bridge, explore the **Treetops Adventure,** a 700-foot (213-meter) network of gently swaying wooden bridges linking eight treehouse platforms. Many of the surrounding Douglas firs are up to 300 feet (90 meters) tall. Back on the ground, gentle **walking trails** lead through the rainforest.

Particularly in the summer high season, the least crowded times to visit the Capilano Suspension Bridge are before 11am or after 3pm.

Getting There

You can take a **free shuttle** to the suspension bridge from several locations downtown. One route stops at Canada Place, Hyatt Hotel (Melville St. at Burrard St.), Blue Horizon Hotel (1225 Robson St.), and the Westin Bayshore (1601 Bayshore Dr.); another picks up and drops off at the Century Plaza Hotel (1015 Burrard St.), Chateau Granville (Granville St. at Helmcken St.), Library Square (Homer St. at Robson St.), and Pacific Centre Mall (Georgia St. at Howe St.). Call or check the website for seasonal schedules.

By car from downtown, cross the Lions Gate Bridge onto Marine Drive east, then take the first left onto Capilano Road, following it up the hill to the Suspension Bridge. **Parking** is $5 for up to four hours. If you're also planning to visit Grouse Mountain, continue north on Capilano Road.

By public transportation, take the **SeaBus** from Waterfront Station to Lonsdale Quay and change to **bus 236** for Grouse Mountain. Get off at Ridgewood Avenue, a block from the suspension bridge.

Lynn Canyon Park

The 617-acre (250-hectare) **Lynn Canyon Park** (Park Rd., North Vancouver, www.lynncanyon.ca, 7am-9pm daily summer, 7am-7pm daily spring and fall, 7am-6pm daily winter, free) is a little farther from downtown than the Capilano bridge, but it has its own **suspension bridge** built back in 1912—and it's free.

Hiking trails wend through the park, including the **30 Foot Pool trail** and the **Twin Falls trail** that both lead to popular swimming areas (bring your bathing suit); both trails are easy and are 0.6 miles (1 kilometer) long, starting from the suspension bridge. The **Ecology Centre** (3663 Park Rd., North Vancouver,

The Best Chinese Food Outside China

Do you love Chinese food? Then you've come to the right city.

Closely linked to the Pacific Rim, Vancouver has more direct flights to China than any other North American city, and more than 40 percent of the population in metropolitan Vancouver is of Asian descent. These strong Asian influences permeate the city, from business culture to food. In particular, the Vancouver region has hundreds of Chinese restaurants, many serving high-end cuisine that rivals the fare in Hong Kong, Taipei, and Beijing.

Chinatown, near the city center, was once a vibrant immigrant community. While it still has Chinese markets, bakeries, and restaurants, new hip shops and eateries have moved in, making the neighborhood fun to explore but not necessarily the best place for traditional Asian meals.

For that, hop on the Canada Line to **Richmond,** the region's new Chinatown, where dozens of restaurants serve cuisines from across China. It's a 25-minute ride from downtown.

Whether you're looking for spicy Sichuan or Hunan fare, handmade noodles and dumplings like you'd see in Shanghai, delicately seasoned Cantonese seafood, or the hearty lamb dishes of China's western provinces, you'll find it in Richmond. Cafés serving bubble tea and Taiwanese shaved ice desserts draw a young crowd, while families pack the round tables of countless dim sum houses. Richmond's Alexandra Road, which runs for several blocks east from No. 3 Road, has so many restaurants that it's known locally as **"Food Street."**

The center of Richmond's Asian food scene is the **Golden Village,** along No. 3 Road from Cambie Road south toward Granville Avenue. From the Canada Line, get off at Aberdeen, Lansdowne, or Richmond/Brighouse stations, and you'll find plenty to eat.

604/990-3755, www.lynncanyonecologycentre.ca, 10am-5pm daily June-Sept., 10am-5pm Mon.-Fri., noon-4pm Sat. Sun. Oct.-May, donation $2) has kid-friendly exhibits about the region's plants and animals.

Getting There

To get to Lynn Canyon by car from downtown Vancouver, cross the Lions Gate Bridge, then turn right onto Marine Drive east. Take the first left onto Capilano Road, and go up the hill to the Highway 1 entrance. Follow Highway 1 east to Exit 19. Take Lynn Valley Road northeast to Peters Road. Turn right (east) onto Peters, which will take you into the park.

By public transit, take the **SeaBus** from Waterfront Station to Lonsdale Quay, then change to **bus 228** for Lynn Valley. The bus will take you to Lynn Valley Center, about a 15-minute walk from the park entrance.

Lonsdale Quay

A food and shopping complex overlooking the water adjacent to the SeaBus terminal, **Lonsdale Quay** (123 Carrie Cates Court, North Vancouver, 604/985-6261, www.lonsdalequay.com, 9am-7pm daily) is like a small-scale Granville Island Public Market. Vendors sell fruit, vegetables, seafood, sandwiches, and other prepared foods. **Green Leaf Brewing** (604/984-8409, www.greenleafbrew.com) makes craft beer; the **Artisan Wine Shop** (604/264-4008, www.artisanwineshop.ca) does complimentary wine-tastings.

The easiest way to get to Lonsdale Quay from downtown Vancouver is to take the **SeaBus** from Waterfront Station, a 12-minute ride.

Richmond

Vancouver is now considered the most Asian city outside Asia, and many of its Asian residents have settled in Richmond, a city of more than 200,000 on Vancouver's southern boundaries. More than half of Richmond's population is of Asian descent, with most from China, Taiwan, or Hong Kong.

Richmond has several multicultural attractions to explore and some of the best Chinese food in North America. The city's waterfront Steveston Village was important in the region's fishing history and still houses a bustling fish market and numerous seafood restaurants.

★ Richmond Night Markets

From mid-May through mid-October, Richmond's two weekend night markets are packed with visitors enjoying the Asian food stalls, quirky shopping opportunities, and general carnival atmosphere. Don't have dinner before you go, since there's plenty to sample: grilled kebabs, squid on a stick, bubble waffles, handmade tofu pudding, and many other Asian-style snacks; most dishes cost $5 or less. Vendors also sell cell phone cases, socks, electronic gadgets, and more.

The easiest way to get to either night market is to take the Canada Line from downtown to **Bridgeport Station.** From there, it's a 15-minute walk to the **Richmond Night Market** (8351 River Rd., 604/244-8448, www.richmondnightmarket.com, 7pm-midnight Fri.-Sat., 7pm-11pm Sun. mid-May-mid-Oct., adults $2.75, seniors and kids under 10 free). Just follow the crowds.

Alternatively, from Bridgeport Station, catch the free shuttle to the **International Summer Night Market** (12631 Vulcan Way, 604/278-8000, www.summernightmarket.org, 6pm-11pm Fri.-Sat., 6pm-10pm Sun. mid-May-mid-Oct., free), located behind the Home Depot store.

Golden Village

The Richmond branch of the Canada Line follows No. 3 Road through the

Top to bottom: Capilano Suspension Bridge; Richmond Night Market; fishing boats at Steveston Harbour.

district known as the **Golden Village,** the region's new Chinatown. You'll know you've arrived when the Chinese-language signs outnumber those in English, and Asian restaurants, markets, and shops line the strip malls and surrounding streets.

A good place to start exploring is **Aberdeen Centre** (4151 Hazelbridge Way, 604/270-1234, www.aberdeencentre. com, 11am-7pm Sun.-Wed., 11am-9pm Thurs.-Sat.), a glitzy Hong Kong-style shopping mall, with shops selling tea, electronics, clothing, Asian-language books, and more. On the third-floor, stop for excellent Cantonese, Sichuanese, Taiwanese, Japanese, and Korean fare in the busy food court. The mall has several good sit-down restaurants, too, including **Fisherman's Terrace Seafood Restaurant** (604/303-9739, dim sum 10am-3pm daily, dinner 5:30pm-10pm daily, dim sum $4-15, dinner mains $15-35) for dim sum, **Chef Hung Taiwanese Beef Noodle** (604/295-9357, www.chefhung-noodle.com, 11am-9pm Sun.-Thurs., 11am-9:30pm Fri.-Sat., mains $8-13) for Taiwanese noodle soup, and **Guu Richmond** (604/295-6612, www.guu-izakaya.com, 11:30am-2:30pm and 5pm-9pm Mon.-Thurs., 11:30am-3:30pm and 5pm-10pm Fri.-Sat., 11:30am-3:30pm and 5pm-9pm Sun., lunch mains $8-13, dinner small plates $5-13), a branch of Vancouver's popular Japanese *izakaya* mini chain.

Aberdeen Centre is one block from **Aberdeen Station,** at the corner of Cambie Road and Hazelbridge Way.

Steveston

Where the Fraser River meets the Pacific Ocean, the village of Steveston has long been a launching point for fishing boats, and it remains among Canada's largest commercial fishing ports. Fish vendors sell their catch along the docks, and numerous eateries serve local seafood. Steveston is also a departure point for whale-watching tours.

In the late 1800s, Steveston was not only a fishing hub; it also became a major center for salmon canning. The largest of the more than 15 canneries that lined the waterfront is now the **Gulf of Georgia Cannery National Historic Site** (12138 4th Ave., 604/664-9009, www.gulfofgeorgi-acannery.org, 10am-5pm daily, adults $7.80, seniors $6.55, ages 6-16 $3.90, families $19.60). Inside the 1894 cannery, you can see what it was like to work the canning line, alongside the Asian and European immigrant workers who were the main labor force. Other exhibits trace the history of the west coast fishing industry.

If you wonder how the multicultural community of fisherfolk, dockworkers, and cannery crews lived, visit the **Britannia Shipyards National Historic Site** (5180 Westwater Dr., 604/718-8050, http://britanniashipyard.ca, 10am-5pm daily May-Sept., noon-5pm Sat.-Sun. Oct.-Apr., free), a collection of restored homes and shops, many dating back to the 1880s, that housed Chinese, Japanese, European, and First Nations people. Stop into the 1885 Murakami House, where a Japanese family of 12 lived and worked between 1929 to 1942, or explore the west coast's last surviving Chinese bunkhouse, which once accommodated 75 to 100 Chinese cannery workers. To walk to the shipyards from the Steveston waterfront, follow the harborside path 0.6 miles (1 kilometer) east.

To reach Steveston by public transit, take the Canada Line to **Richmond-Brighouse Station,** then change to any Steveston-bound bus, including **buses 402, 407, or 410.**

By car from downtown, follow Granville Street south toward the Vancouver airport. After crossing the Arthur Laing Bridge, stay in the right lane and exit toward Richmond. Continue south on Russ Baker Way, which becomes No. 2 Road. At Westminster Highway, turn right (west). At No. 1 Road, turn left (south) and continue south to Steveston.

Entertainment and Events

For local event listings, see the **Georgia Straight** (www.straight.com), the **Vancouver Theatre Guide** (www.gvpta.ca) from the Greater Vancouver Professional Theatre Association, or **Inside Vancouver** (www.insidevancouver.ca). The blog **Miss 604** (www.miss604.com) also publishes monthly lists of upcoming events.

Nightlife
Downtown and the West End
First opened in 1930, **The Commodore Ballroom** (868 Granville St., 604/739-4550, www.commodoreballroom.com) hosts live concerts, featuring performers as diverse as the Tragically Hip, Lady Gaga, and Katy Perry.

Head to **The Roxy** (932 Granville St., 604/331-7999, www.roxyvan.com) when you want to dance. Their rockin' house bands play several nights a week. Sunday is country-western night.

Quiet enough for conversation, snug **Uva Wine & Cocktail Bar** (900 Seymour St., 604/632-9560, www.uvavancouver.com) serves creative cocktails, craft beer, and a long list of wines by the glass.

Secreted away on the fourth floor of the Rosewood Hotel Georgia, the outdoor **Reflections Lounge** (604/673-7043, www.rosewoodhotels.com, Apr.-Oct.), where you can sip your wine or classic cocktail on teak couches around a fire pit, brings Los Angeles glamour to Vancouver. The hotel's elegant **Prohibition Lounge** (604/673-7089, www.prohibitionrhg.com) has a roaring twenties theme, with music or DJs several nights a week.

Polished **Bacchus Lounge** (845 Hornby St., 604/608-5319, www.wedgewoodhotel.com) at the Wedgewood Hotel is appropriate for cocktails with a colleague or a consort. There's live piano music every evening.

Davie Street, in the West End, is the center of Vancouver's LGBT community, where nightspots include **Celebrities Nightclub** (1022 Davie St., 604/681-6180, www.celebritiesnightclub.com), a party-hardy dance club; the easygoing **Fountainhead Pub** (1025 Davie St., 604/687-2222, www.thefountainheadpub.com); and **1181 Lounge** (1181 Davie St., 604/787-7130, www.1181.ca), an upscale lounge and music spot.

Gastown and Chinatown
On a mild evening, join the crowds for drinks on the patio at **Chill Winston** (3 Alexander St., 604/288-9575, www.chillwinston.com), checking out Gastown's street life.

With a name like **The Pourhouse** (162 Water St., 604/568-7022, www.pourhousevancouver.com), you'd expect a joint that serves great cocktails—and you'd be right. The resident mixologists at this upscale Gastown saloon concoct drinks like the Alamo Flip (a blend of tequila, housemade root beer, chocolate bitters, egg, and cinnamon) and the Old Pal (rye, vermouth, and Campari).

Beer lovers need no excuse to visit **The Alibi Room** (157 Alexander St., 604/623-3383, www.alibi.ca), a low-key Gastown pub with 50 taps of local and imported craft beers.

The Keefer Bar (135 Keefer St., 604/688-1961, www.thekeeferbar.com), a hip Chinatown hideout, concocts aromatic cocktails using house-made bitters, teas, and syrups. Pair the Opium Sour (bourbon, grapefruit, tamarind, lemon, and poppy-seed tincture) or the Bloody Ming (vodka, guava, lemon, Worcestershire, and Tabasco) with the Asian-inspired small plates.

Granville Island
For brews with water views, **Dockside Lounge** (Granville Island Hotel, 1253 Johnston St., 604/685-7070, www.docksidevancouver.com) looks out across False Creek, with a patio perfectly positioned for drinks on a sunny afternoon.

The Arts

Tickets Tonight (Tourism Vancouver Visitor Centre, 210-200 Burrard St., 604/684-2787, www.ticketstonight.ca, 9am-5pm daily) sells same-day, half-price theater tickets. Check the current day's availability by phone, on the website, or via their Twitter feed, @TicketsTonight. You have to buy tickets in person, before noon for matinee performances and 4pm for evening shows. Tickets Tonight also sells full-price advance tickets to many local productions.

Theater

Vancouver's top repertory theater and the largest theater company in western Canada, the **Arts Club Theatre Company** (604/687-1644, http://artsclub.com) performs on three stages. Their main stage shows are held at the 650-seat **Stanley Industrial Alliance Stage** (2750 Granville St.) in the South Granville district. They also perform at the **Granville Island Stage** (1585 Johnston St.) next to the Public Market and at the **Goldcorp Stage at the BMO Theatre Centre** (162 W. 1st Ave.) in the Olympic Village.

The **Vancouver East Cultural Centre** (604/251-1363, http://thecultch.com), known locally as "The Cultch," hosts an eclectic season of theater, dance, and musical events. They have three performance spaces on the city's East Side: the 200-seat **Historic Theatre** (1895 Venables St.), the small black-box **Vancity Culture Lab** (also at 1895 Venables St.), and the nearby **York Theatre** (639 Commercial Dr.).

Another venue for diverse theatrical productions is the **Firehall Arts Centre** (280 E. Cordova St., 604/689-0926, http://firehallartscentre.ca), in a 1906 former city fire station on the edge of Chinatown.

From June through September, the **Bard on the Beach Shakespeare Festival** (604/739-0559, http://bardonthebeach.org) performs Shakespeare's plays under

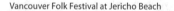

Vancouver Folk Festival at Jericho Beach

billowing white tents in Kitsilano's Vanier Park.

With a mix of professional and aspiring actors, **Theatre Under the Stars** (Malkin Bowl, 610 Pipeline Rd., information 604/734-1917, tickets 877/840-0457, http://tuts.ca) produces two summertime musicals outdoors in Stanley Park.

If you're traveling with kids, see what's on stage at Granville Island's **Carousel Theatre for Young People** (1411 Cartwright St., 604/669-3410, www.carouseltheatre.ca).

Comedy

The always-entertaining **Vancouver Theatre Sports League** (1502 Duranleau St., 604/738-7013, www.vtsl.com) performs regular improv shows at their waterside theater on Granville Island.

At **Yuk Yuk's Vancouver Comedy Club** (2837 Cambie St., 604/696-9857, www.yukyuks.com), you can see shows by local and visiting comedians.

Music

The **Vancouver Symphony Orchestra** (604/876-3434, www.vancouversymphony.ca) performs downtown in the historic **Orpheum Theatre** (601 Smithe St. at Granville St.).

Canada's second-largest opera company, the **Vancouver Opera** (604/683-0222, www.vancouveropera.ca) stages its productions in the 2,765-seat **Queen Elizabeth Theatre** (650 Hamilton St.).

On the University of British Columbia campus, the modern **Chan Centre for the Performing Arts** (6265 Crescent Rd., 604/822-2697, www.chancentre.com) hosts jazz, blues, and world music performers, as well as early music and chamber concerts.

Dance

Vancouver's professional contemporary ballet company, **Ballet BC** (855/985-2787, www.balletbc.com) presents several productions a year at the **Queen Elizabeth Theatre** (650 Hamilton St.).

DanceHouse (604/801-6225, www.dancehouse.ca) brings Canadian and international dance companies to the **Vancouver Playhouse** (630 Hamilton St.) downtown.

Cinema

Vancity Theatre (1181 Seymour St., 604/683-3456, www.viff.org), a modern repertory cinema downtown, shows independent and art films from around the world and hosts the Vancouver International Film Festival every autumn.

Summer Cinema in Stanley Park (www.freshaircinema.ca, July-Aug.) is a family-friendly series of free Tuesday-evening films shown outdoors at Ceperley Meadow off Stanley Park Drive, near Second Beach. Films begin at dusk. Bring a blanket or a lawn chair.

The Vancouver Police Museum (240 E. Cordova St., 604/665-3346, www.vancouverpolicemuseum.ca) presents a monthly film series, **Movies in the Morgue,** on the second Tuesday of the month September through May. They're not all horror films, but they do sell out, so book tickets in advance on the museum website.

Festivals and Events
Spring

Close to 50,000 runners and walkers take to the streets for the **Vancouver Sun Run** (www.vancouversun.com/sunrun, Apr.), a fun-for-all 10K that starts and ends downtown.

Dinners featuring chefs from across Canada, cooking workshops, a food expo, and lots of other delicious events draw foodies to the **EAT! Vancouver Food + Cooking Festival** (http://eat-vancouver.com, Apr.-May).

Bring the kids to Kitsilano's Vanier Park when the **Vancouver International Children's Festival** (www.childrensfestival.ca, May-June) offers family-friendly concerts, circus performers, crafts, and other activities.

Summer

Vancouver celebrates Canada's birthday, **Canada Day** (www.canadaplace.ca, July 1), with a parade, outdoor concerts, and celebratory fireworks over Burrard Inlet. Canada Place is the center of the festivities.

It's not just folk music at the long-established **Vancouver Folk Festival** (http://thefestival.bc.ca, July), which draws world beat, roots, blues, and yes, folk musicians from across Canada and around the world to Jericho Beach for three days of always eclectic music on multiple outdoor stages. It's great fun for all ages.

Fireworks displays over English Bay bring thousands of Vancouverites and visitors out for the **Celebration of Light** (http://hondacelebrationoflight.com, July-Aug.) that takes place over several summer evenings. The best viewing spots are at English Bay Beach, but you can see them from Kitsilano Beach and other beaches around False Creek.

The **Vancouver Pride Festival** (http://vancouverpride.ca, July-Aug.) features more than 20 events celebrating the city's large gay, lesbian, bisexual, and transgender community, culminating in a festive parade through the downtown streets.

Fall

For two weeks, the **Vancouver Fringe Fest** (www.vancouverfringe.com, Sept.) takes over Granville Island and other stages around town with innovative, quirky, and often surprising theater, comedy, puppetry, and storytelling performances.

Movie lovers line up at the **Vancouver International Film Festival** (www.viff.org, Sept.) to see the latest releases from Canadian, American, and international filmmakers.

The **Vancouver Writers Fest** (www.writersfest.bc.ca, Oct.), a week of readings, lectures, and other literary events, features more than 100 authors from across Canada and abroad.

East Vancouver artists open their studios to visitors during the popular **Eastside Culture Crawl** (www.culture-crawl.ca, Nov.). Whether you're in the market for artwork or just like to browse, most artists are interested in chatting with visitors.

Winter

The VanDusen Botanical Garden marks the holiday season with its annual **Festival of Lights** (http://vandusen-garden.org, Dec.), illuminating its garden paths with thousands of sparkling lights.

More than 2,000 intrepid people welcome the year at the **Polar Bear Swim** (www.vancouver.ca, Jan. 1), an annual New Year's Day dip in the sea at English Bay. It's fun to watch, even if you don't dive in. And in case you're wondering, it's cold.

Dozens of restaurants offer special menus, and you can join in food events, from chef dinners to wine-tastings to food tours, during **Dine Out Vancouver** (www.dineoutvancouver.com, Jan.), the city's annual celebration of dining that has grown into one of Canada's largest food and drink festivals.

Vancouver's Chinatown, and many venues in Richmond, mark the **Lunar New Year** (Jan.-Feb.) with parades, lion dances, music, fireworks, and other special events.

Shopping

If you're coming from a major city in the United States, you may be disappointed with the shopping options in Vancouver, since selections are typically smaller and prices higher than at similar stores south of the border. Of course, if the exchange rate is in your favor, shopping here may be a better value.

Regardless of your home base, products to look for in Vancouver include Canadian-designed clothing, local art, B.C. wines, and local food items. Vancouver has a number of well-stocked outdoor stores where you can find outdoor gear for your Canadian travels.

Shopping Districts
Downtown and the West End
Vancouver's main downtown shopping district is along **Robson Street,** between Jervis and Granville Streets. Department stores and boutiques line **Granville Street** as well. At **Pacific Centre Mall** (701 W. Georgia St., 604/688-7235, www.cfshops. com, 10am-7pm Mon.-Tues. and Sat., 10am-9pm Wed.-Fri., 11am-6pm Sun.), stores include Canadian and international brands such as Nordstrom, H&M, Banana Republic, Aritzia, and the Apple Store.

Gastown and Chinatown
Visit **Gastown** for smaller fashion boutiques and clothing by local designers. Several Gastown galleries carry high-quality First Nations art.

Chinatown still has its traditional herbalists, produce markets, and tea shops, but increasingly, the neighborhood is home to funky independent boutiques.

Kitsilano and the West Side
On Vancouver's West Side, the Kitsilano neighborhood mixes North American chains and local boutiques, centered along **West 4th Avenue** between Burrard and Vine Streets. There's a collection of ski and snowboard gear shops on 4th at Burrard.

Another street to browse is **South Granville** between West 5th and 15th Avenues, for high-end clothing and accessories and for contemporary art.

Main Street
Looking for clothes you won't find at the local mall? **Main Street,** between East 20th and 30th Avenues, is lined with independent boutiques, many carrying clothing by local and Canadian designers.

Richmond
The **McArthurGlen Designer Outlet-Vancouver Airport** (1000-7899 Templeton Station Rd., Richmond, 604/231-5525, www.mcarthurglen.com, 10am-9pm Mon.-Sat., 10am-7pm Sun.) has outlets and factory stores for brands that include Calvin Klein, Coach, Fossil, J.Crew, and Vans. Take the Canada Line (YVR branch) to Templeton Station.

Department Stores
The Vancouver flagship location of **Hudson's Bay** (674 Granville St., 604/681-6211, www.hbc.com, 9:30am-9pm Mon.-Sat., 11am-7pm Sun.), Canada's original department store, is in a 1914 building downtown.

For high-fashion designer clothing, with prices to match, visit **Holt Renfrew** (737 Dunsmuir St., 604/681-3121, www. holtrenfrew.com, 10am-7pm Mon.-Tues., 10am-9pm Wed.-Fri., 10am-8pm Sat., 11am-7pm Sun.) downtown.

Seattle-based **Nordstrom** (799 Robson St., 604/699-2100, www.nordstrom.com,

9:30am-9pm Mon.-Sat., 11am-7pm Sun.) has a large store at Vancouver's Pacific Centre Mall downtown.

You can often find deals on designer apparel and other clothing at **Winners** (http://winners.ca), a discount department store with branches downtown (798 Granville St., 604/683-1058, 9am-9pm Mon.-Sat., 10am-7pm Sun.) and near Broadway and Cambie (491 W. 8th Ave., 604/879-3701, 9am-9pm Mon.-Sat., 10am-7pm Sun.).

Clothing and Accessories

The now-ubiquitous yoga- and work-out-wear maker **Lululemon Athletica** (www.lululemon.com) got its start in Vancouver and still has its flagship stores downtown (970 Robson St., 604/681-3118, 10am-9pm Mon.-Sat., 10:30am-7:30pm Sun.) and in Kitsilano (2113 W. 4th Ave., 604/732-6111, 10am-7pm daily). A unique-to-Vancouver shop is **Lululemon Lab** (511 W. Broadway, at Cambie, 604/708-1126, www.lululemon-lab.com, 10am-6pm Mon.-Sat., 11am-6pm Sun.), a "concept store" offering prototypes and other clothing not carried at the other stores.

Shannon Wilson is married to Lululemon founder Chip Wilson, and J. J. Wilson is Chip's son. Together, they founded **Kit and Ace** (151 Water St., Gastown; 2235 W. 4th Ave., Kitsilano, 844/548-6223, www.kitandace.com, 10am-7pm Mon.-Sat., 11am-6pm Sun.), which designs and sells hip men's and women's clothing made from "technical cashmere" and other luxury fabrics.

For vintage, designer consignment, and smart new clothing, the fashion-conscious frequent **Front and Company** (3772 Main St., 604/879-8431, www.frontand-company.com, 11am-6:30pm daily).

The Vancouver designers who founded the boutique **Twigg & Hottie** (3671 Main St., 604/879-8595, www.we3.ca, 11am-6pm Mon.-Sat., noon-5pm Sun.) carry their own We3 label along with clothes and accessories by other local creators.

For clothing and accessories by emerging Canadian designers, check out **Two of Hearts** (www.twoofhearts.ca), in Kitsilano (1986 W. 4th Ave., 604/428-0998, 11am-6pm Mon. and Wed.-Sat., noon-5pm Sun.) and on the East Side (3728 Main St., 604/568-0998, 11am-6pm Mon.-Sat., noon-5pm Sun.).

Even if you're visiting in the sunny summertime, you may want as a souvenir Vancouverites' constant companion: an umbrella. With locations downtown (526 W. Pender St., 604/669-1707, 10am-6pm Mon.-Fri., 11am-5pm Sat.) and on Granville Island (1550 Anderson St., 604/697-0919, 10am-6pm daily), **The Umbrella Shop** (www.theumbrellashop.com) sells good-quality rain protectors in a broad range of colors and styles.

Canadian shoemaker **John Fleuvog** (837 Granville St., Downtown, 604/688-2828; 65 Water St., Gastown, 604/688-6228, www.fluevog.com, 10am-7pm Mon.-Wed. and Sat., 10am-8pm Thurs.-Fri., noon-6pm Sun.) launched his funky footwear line in Vancouver.

Kitsilano's **Gravity Pope** (2205 W. 4th Ave., 604/731-7673, www.gravitypope.com, 10am-9pm Mon.-Fri., 10am-7pm Sat., 11am-6pm Sun.) stocks style-conscious shoes for men and women.

Books

When you love to read about food as much as you love to eat it, visit **Barbara Jo's Books to Cooks** (1740 W. 2nd Ave., 604/688-6755, www.bookstocooks.com, 10:30am-6pm Tues.-Sat., noon-5pm Sun.-Mon.) for cookbooks, food magazines, food memoirs, and anything gourmet that you might want to peruse. The bookshop hosts chef talks, cooking demonstrations, and other food events, too.

Kidsbooks (2557 W. Broadway, 604/738-5335, www.kidsbooks.ca, 9:30am-6pm Mon.-Thurs. and Sat., 9:30am-9pm Fri., 11am-6pm Sun.) is Vancouver's best place to find reading matter for toddlers to teens. The Kitsilano shop stocks a large selection of titles by Canadian authors, plus games, crafts, and audio books.

Pulp Fiction Books (http://pulpfiction-booksvancouver.com) carries a large selection of new and used titles in Kitsilano (2754 W. Broadway, 604/873-4311, 11am-7pm daily) and in two East Side shops (2422 Main St., 604/876-4311, 10am-8pm Mon.-Wed., 10am-9pm Thurs.-Sat., 11am-7pm Sun.; 1830 Commercial Dr., 604/251-4311, 11am-7pm daily).

Wander into **Wanderlust** (1929 W. 4th Ave., 604/739-2182, www.wanderlustore. com, 10am-7pm Mon.-Fri., 10am-6pm Sat., noon-5pm Sun.), a well-stocked travel store in Kitsilano, for guidebooks, maps, luggage, and other travel gear. Also in Kitsilano, **The Travel Bug** (2865 W. Broadway, 604/737-1122, www.thetravel-bug.ca, 10am-6pm Mon.-Sat., noon-5pm Sun.) carries travel books and supplies.

Gourmet Goodies

Looking for a souvenir for a foodie friend or an edible memory from your Vancouver visit? **Edible Canada** (1596 Johnston St., 604/682-6675, www.edible-canada.com, 10am-6pm Mon.-Fri., 9am-6pm Sat., 9am-5pm Sun.), opposite the Granville Island Public Market, stocks locally produced salts, jams, vinegars, and more from around British Columbia and across Canada.

The friendly cheese mongers at **Les Amis du Fromage** (www.buycheese. com) will help you pick the perfect wedge, whether you're looking for locally made Brie or a pungent Époisses from France. Sampling is encouraged. The Kitsilano shop (1752 W. 2nd Ave., 604/732-4218, 9am-6pm Sat.-Wed., 9am-6:30pm Thurs.-Fri.) is a short walk from Granville Island; there's a second location in East Vancouver (843 E. Hastings St., 604/253-4218, 10am-6pm daily).

British Columbia's largest privately owned liquor store, **Legacy Liquor Store** (1633 Manitoba St., 604/331-7900, http://legacyliquorstore.com, 10am-11pm daily), in the Olympic Village, has an excellent selection of B.C. wines. They hold complimentary wine-tastings and other special events; check the website or phone for a schedule.

Another source of wines from B.C. and elsewhere is **Liberty Wine Merchants** (1660 Johnston St., 604/602-1120, www. libertywinemerchants.com, 9:30am-8pm Mon.-Thurs., 9:30am-9pm Fri., 9am-9pm Sat., 9am-8pm Sun.), near the Granville Island Public Market.

Outdoor Gear

If you need outdoor clothing and equipment, camping supplies, or cycling gear, head for Broadway between Yukon and Main Streets, where you'll find a cluster of outdoor shops. The largest, **MEC** (130 W. Broadway, 604/872-7858, www.mec. ca, 10am-7pm Mon.-Wed., 10am-9pm Thurs.-Fri., 9am-6pm Sat., 10am-5pm Sun.), as Mountain Equipment Co-op is known, is a Canadian chain stocking their own label and other brands of clothing, backpacks, and gear for hiking, bicycling, rock climbing, kayaking, and other sports.

Sports Junkies (102 W. Broadway, 604/879-6000, www.sportsjunkies. com, 10am-7pm Mon.-Wed., 10am-8pm Thurs.-Fri., 10am-6pm Sat., 10am-5pm Sun.) has good deals on new and used sports equipment and clothing for both kids and adults.

Visit **Three Vets** (2200 Yukon St., 604/872-5475, www.3vets.ca, 9:30am-6pm Mon.-Sat., 11am-5pm Sun.) for well-priced camping gear, clothing, and equipment that's functional rather than fashionable.

Near West 4th Avenue at Burrard in Kitsilano, several shops sell gear for skiing, snowboarding, surfing, and cycling, including **Comor** (1766 W. 4th Ave., 604/736-7547, www.comorsports. com, 10am-6pm Mon.-Wed. and Sat., 10am-8pm Thurs.-Fri., 11am-5pm Sun.), **West Coast Sports** (1675 W. 4th Ave., 604/732-4810, http://westcoastsports.ca, 10am-6pm Mon.-Sat., 11am-5pm Sun.),

Skiis & Biikes (1701 W. 3rd Ave., 604/738-3715, www.skiisandbiikes.com, 9am-7pm Mon.-Fri., 9am-5pm Sat., 10am-5pm Sun.), **Pacific Boarder** (1793 W. 4th Ave., 604/734-7245, www.pacificboarder.com, 10am-6pm Mon.-Wed. and Sat., 10am-8pm Thurs.-Fri., 11am-5pm Sun.), and **The Boardroom** (1749 W. 4th Ave., 604/734-7669, http://boardroomshop.com, 10am-6pm Mon.-Wed. and Sat., 10am-8pm Thurs.-Fri., 11am-5pm Sun.).

Sports and Recreation

Whale-Watching

Several whale-watch companies run trips from Vancouver or from Steveston Harbour in Richmond.

Wild Whales Vancouver (1806 Mast Tower Rd., 604/699-2011, www.whales-vancouver.com, mid-Apr.-Oct., adults $135, seniors and students $110, ages 3-12 $85) offers whale-watching trips leaving from Granville Island.

Steveston Seabreeze Adventures (12551 No. 1 Rd., Richmond, 604/272-7200, www.seabreezeadventures.ca, Apr.-Oct., adults $120, seniors and students $100, ages 3-12 $75) operates whale-watch trips from Steveston Village. They provide a **shuttle** (round-trip $7.50) from downtown Vancouver hotels. In the spring, they also offer 90-minute **sea lion tours** (Apr.-mid-May, adults $31.50, seniors and students $23.50, kids $18.50) to view migrating California sea lions.

Also departing from Steveston, **Vancouver Whale Watch** (210-12240 2nd Ave., Richmond, 604/274-9565, www.vancouverwhalewatch.com, Apr.-Oct., adults $130-140, seniors and students $100-140, ages 4-12 $75-140) offers whale-watching tours with a **shuttle** (round-trip $15) between Steveston and several downtown Vancouver hotels.

Beaches and Pools
Downtown and the West End

You don't have to leave downtown Vancouver to go to the beach. The city has several stretches of sand right downtown.

Along the Seawall on the west side of Stanley Park, you can swim or sun at quiet **Third Beach** or busier **Second Beach,** which has a seasonal snack bar as well as the kid-friendly seaside **Second Beach Pool** (Stanley Park Dr., 604/257-8371, www.vancouver.ca, May-Sept.).

As you'd expect from the name, **Sunset Beach** (Beach Ave. at Thurlow St.), along the Seawall near English Bay, is a west-facing beach with sunset views.

To swim year-round, head for the **Vancouver Aquatic Centre** (1050 Beach Ave., 604/665-3424, www.vancouver.ca, daily, adults $6.15, seniors and ages 13-18 $4.40, ages 3-12 $3.10, families $3.10 pp), a public 50-meter indoor pool near Sunset Beach downtown.

★ English Bay Beach

English Bay Beach (Beach Ave. at Denman St.), in the West End, is the busiest of the downtown beaches, fun for people-watching, swimming, or watching the sunset. You can follow the Seawall path from here into Stanley Park or around to Yaletown. In summer, you can rent kayaks and stand-up paddleboards.

Kitsilano and the West Side

Popular **Kitsilano Beach** (aka "Kits Beach," Cornwall Ave. at Arbutus St.) is a good swimming spot. In summer, serious beach volleyball players flock here, and you can rent kayaks or stand-up paddleboards. From the beach, you can follow the seawall path east around Vanier Park (popular with kite-flyers and home to the Museum of Vancouver and the Vancouver Marine Museum) to Granville Island. Next to the beach, **Kitsilano Pool** (2305 Cornwall St., 604/731-0011, www.vancouver.ca, daily May-Sept., adults $6.15, seniors and ages 13-18 $4.40, ages 3-12 $3.10, families $3.10 pp) is a 450-foot-long (135-meter) saltwater swimming pool with three water slides to entertain the kids.

West of Kitsilano, three connected beaches, **Jericho Beach** (Point Grey Rd. west of Alma St.), **Locarno Beach** (NW Marine Dr. at Trimble St.), and **Spanish Banks Beach** (NW Marine Dr. at Tolmie St.), draw families with sandy swimming areas and grassy stretches for picnicking and playing.

Water Sports

One of the best ways to explore Vancouver is from the water, since sheltered seas surround the city. You can head out on the water in a **kayak** or **stand-up paddleboard** from English Bay, False Creek, Kitsilano Beach, and Jericho Beach.

Ecomarine Paddlesports Centre (604/689-7575 or 888/425-2925, www. ecomarine.com) rents kayaks and stand-up paddleboards from several locations, and offers guided kayak and SUP tours. Find them on **Granville Island** (1668 Duranleau St., 9am-9pm daily late May-July, 9am-8pm daily Aug.-early Sept., 10am-6pm daily early Sept.-late May), **English Bay** (1700 Beach Ave., 10am-dusk Mon.-Fri., 9am-dusk Sat.-Sun. late May-early Sept.), and **Jericho Beach** (Jericho Sailing Centre, 1300 Discovery St., 10am-dusk Mon.-Fri., 9am-dusk Sat.-Sun. late May-early Sept.). Their last rentals go out two hours before sunset at English Bay and Jericho Beach, three hours before sunset on Granville Island; call them to confirm seasonal hours.

Vancouver Water Adventures (604/736-5155, www.vancouverwateradventures.com, May-Sept., call or check website for hours) rents kayaks and stand-up paddleboards, offers tours, rents Jet Skis, and teaches SUP yoga classes. They have branches on **Granville Island** (1812 Boatlift Lane) and on **Kitsilano Beach.**

Near the Olympic Village on False Creek, **Creekside Kayaks** (1 Athletes Way, 604/616-7453, www.creeksidekayaks.ca, 11am-dusk Mon.-Fri., 9am-5pm Sat.-Sun. mid-Apr.-mid-Oct.) rents kayaks and stand-up paddleboards.

Hiking
★ Pacific Spirit Regional Park

Although it's less well known than downtown's Stanley Park, **Pacific Spirit Regional Park** (604/224-5739, www. metrovancouver.org, dawn-dusk daily, free), on Vancouver's West Side near the University of British Columbia campus, is actually larger, measuring more than 1,800 acres (760 hectares). More than 40 miles (70 kilometers) of hiking trails wend through this dense rainforest. Most are gentle forest strolls, although some steeper routes lead from the park to Spanish Banks Beach.

You can access several park trails off West 16th Avenue between Discovery Street and Acadia Road; several others start from Chancellor Boulevard west of Blanca Street. Another park entrance is on West 29th Avenue at Camosun Street. Maps are posted at the start of most trails. For an online map, see the website of the **Pacific Spirit Park Society** (www.pacific-spiritparksociety.org).

Don't hike alone here. While you're close to the city, many trails quickly lead deep into the forest and feel quite remote.

The Grouse Grind

You can't call yourself a Vancouverite until you've hiked the Grind, or so say the many who've made the trek up Vancouver's best-known trail. Nicknamed "Mother Nature's Stairmaster," the **Grouse Grind** (6400 Nancy Greene Way, North Vancouver, 604/980-9311, www.grousemountain. com) is only 1.8 miles (2.9 kilometers) long, but it's essentially a mountain staircase that you climb straight up, gaining an elevation of 2,800 feet (850 meters). Along most of the trail, you're hiking in the forest. The reward comes at the top, with vistas across the city.

Average active hikers can generally complete the Grouse Grind, which has

2,830 steps, in about 90 minutes, but plenty of people need at least two hours. The very fit charge up the mountain in 30 to 60 minutes.

Hikers are allowed to walk uphill only. To return to the parking area, you ride down on the **Skyride** (one-way $10), the Grouse Mountain tram. Check the trail status if you're planning a spring or fall hike; there can be snow on the trail even when it's warm in the city.

To get to the Grouse Grind trailhead by car from downtown Vancouver, take West Georgia Street to the Lions Gate Bridge. Cross the bridge, turn right onto Marine Drive east, but move immediately into the left lane. Take the first left onto Capilano Road and follow it up the hill to the Grouse Mountain parking lot (3 hours $6, full day $8). The mountain runs a **free shuttle** (May-Sept., call or check the website for schedule) from Canada Place. By public transportation, take the **SeaBus** from Waterfront Station to Lonsdale Quay and change to **bus 236** for Grouse Mountain, which will drop you at the mountain's base.

Cycling

Vancouver prides itself on being bicycle-friendly, and the city has been adding off-street and dedicated cycling lanes throughout the area.

Vancouver's most popular cycling route runs along the **Seawall,** also signposted as the "Seaside Cycling Route." This paved path circles Stanley Park and follows False Creek through Yaletown and past Science World and the Olympic Village, Granville Island, and Kitsilano Beach. From Kits Beach, you can continue west on Point Grey Road, which becomes a bicycle-priority street west of MacDonald Street, then pedal the beachside paths along Jericho, Locarno, and Spanish Banks Beaches. You'll enjoy some of Vancouver's best views as you cycle this route.

English Bay Beach

Bike Rentals

Spokes Bicycle Rentals (1798 W. Georgia St., 604/688-5141, www.spokesbicycle-rentals.com, open daily, call or check the website for hours), **English Bay Bike Rentals** (1754 Davie St., 604/568-8490, www.englishbaybikerentals.com, 9am-6:30pm daily), and **Bayshore Bicycle Rentals** (745 Denman St., 604/688-2453, www.bayshorebikerentals.ca, 9am-dusk daily) are convenient to Stanley Park.

Reckless Bike Stores (www.reckless.ca) rents bicycles along the Seawall in **Yaletown** (110 Davie St., 604/648-2600, 9:30am-6:30pm Mon.-Fri., 9:30am-6pm Sat., 10am-6pm Sun.) and near **Granville Island** (1810 Fir St., 604/731-2420, 9:30am-6:30pm Mon.-Fri., 10am-5pm Sat., 11am-5pm Sun.).

Winter Sports
Skiing, Snowboarding, and Snowshoeing

Vancouver has three local mountains that offer downhill skiing and snowboarding, weather permitting, from December through March. It can often be snowing on the mountains when it's raining in the city, so check the mountain weather forecast if you're hoping for a snow day.

Grouse Mountain (6400 Nancy Greene Way, North Vancouver, 604/980-9311, www.grousemountain.com) is closest to downtown and the only mountain that's easily accessible by public transportation. There are 26 runs for downhill skiing and snowboarding, and snowshoeing is offered.

The largest of the North Shore mountains, **Cypress Mountain** (6000 Cypress Bowl Rd., West Vancouver, 604/926-5612, www.cypressmountain.com) hosted several events during the 2010 Winter Olympics. You can ski and snowboard on the mountain's 53 downhill trails. Cypress has a separate Nordic area with trails for cross-country skiing and snowshoeing.

Family-friendly **Mount Seymour** (1700 Mt. Seymour Rd., North Vancouver, 604/986-2261, www.mountseymour.com), the area's smallest ski area, has five lifts serving 40 downhill runs. It's a good spot for snowshoeing.

Ice Skating

You can ice skate right downtown at the **Robson Square Ice Rink** (800 Robson St., 604/209-8316, www.robsonsquare.com, 9am-9pm Sun.-Thurs., 9am-11pm Fri.-Sat. Dec.-Feb., free), underneath Robson Square, near the Vancouver Art Gallery. You can rent skates ($4) if you don't have your own.

During the 2010 Winter Olympic Games, the **Richmond Olympic Oval** (6111 River Rd., Richmond, 778/296-1400, www.richmondoval.ca) hosted the speed-skating events. You can practice your own skating moves during the Oval's public skating hours; rentals are available.

Spectator Sports

Vancouver is wild for hockey, particularly the city's National Hockey League team, the **Vancouver Canucks** (800/745-3000, http://canucks.nhl.com), whose regular season runs from October through April. The Canucks take to the ice at **Rogers Arena** (800 Griffiths Way, 604/899-7400, http://rogersarena.com, subway: Stadium/Chinatown).

Vancouver's professional Major League Soccer team, the **Vancouver Whitecaps** (604/669-9283, www.whitecapsfc.com), plays at **B.C. Place** (777 Pacific Blvd., 604/669-2300, www.bcplacestadium. com, subway: Stadium/Chinatown).

Curious as to how professional Canadian Football differs from its American cousin? Watch the **B.C. Lions** (604/589-7627, www.bclions.com) run the field at **B.C. Place** (777 Pacific Blvd., 604/669-2300, www.bcplacestadium. com, subway: Stadium/Chinatown).

The city's minor league baseball team, the **Vancouver Canadians** (604/872-5232, www.canadiansbaseball.com), play June through September at family-friendly **Nat Bailey Stadium** (4601 Ontario St., subway: King Edward), near Queen Elizabeth Park.

Accommodations

Most Vancouver accommodations are on the downtown peninsula, with a few B&Bs and smaller hotels in other parts of the city. Rates peak, and availability is limited, in July and August, so book early if you're planning a summer visit. At other times, especially during the slower winter season, hotel rates drop significantly from the high-season prices listed here.

Downtown and the West End
$150-250

Each of the six guest rooms at the **Barclay House B&B** (1351 Barclay St., 604/605-1351 or 800/971-1351, www.barclayhouse.

com, $150-250 d), in a yellow 1904 Victorian home in the midst of urban Vancouver, is decorated differently. The bay-windowed turquoise-accented Beach room has a queen bed and a cozy sitting area, while the Peak room, under the eaves on the top floor, has skylights and a claw-foot tub. Guests can mingle in the lounge or games room, both furnished with a mix of contemporary and antique pieces. Rates at this West End inn include parking, Wi-Fi, and a full breakfast.

Built in the 1960s, the **Blue Horizon Hotel** (1225 Robson St., 604/688-1411 or 800/663-1333, www.bluehorizon-hotel.com, $129-299 d, parking $17) was Vancouver's first high-rise. These days, all 214 rooms in this skinny 31-story tower are corner units, with private balconies and city views, as well as flat-screen TVs, mini fridges, Keurig coffeemakers, air-conditioning, and free Wi-Fi. The family suites on the 29th floor have a separate living room with a queen bed and double sofa bed, as well as a king bedroom. Other amenities include an indoor lap pool, a hot tub, and a sauna. Prices rise as you get higher in the building.

What better spot to start a road trip than at an old-time motor hotel gone glam? Built in 1956, the four-story ★ **Burrard Hotel** (1100 Burrard St., 604/681-2331 or 800/663-0366, www. theburrard.com, $179-239 d, parking $20) emerged from a makeover as a retro-chic mid-century-modern lodging. The best feature is the courtyard garden, with palm trees and a fire pit, hidden from the surrounding city hum. The 72 guest rooms are small (baths are particularly petite), but they're well designed with espresso makers, mini fridges, and flat-screen TVs. Rates include Wi-Fi, North American phone calls, a pass to a nearby health club, and use of the hotel's bicycles. Off the lobby, **Container Coffee** (604/568-3200, www.containercoffee.ca, 6am-8pm daily) serves pastries, coffee, beer, wine, and locally made ice cream.

The apartment-style **Century Plaza Hotel and Suites** (1015 Burrard St., 604/687-0575 or 800/663-1818, www.century-plaza.com, $129-299 d, parking $17) isn't fancy, but the studio and one-bedroom units have kitchen facilities and free Wi-Fi; outside the busy summer season, you can often find good deals here. The hotel has a fitness center, indoor pool, and a branch of the local Absolute Spa chain, and you're just a short stroll from most downtown attractions.

Original artworks adorn the lobby, corridors, and guest rooms at the low-rise 129-room ★ **Listel Hotel** (1300 Robson St., 604/684-8461 or 800/663-5491, www.thelistelhotel.com, $189-299, parking $37) on Vancouver's main downtown shopping street. The "museum" rooms feature works by First Nations artists, while staff from a local gallery decorated the eclectic "gallery" rooms. The standard units lack this artistic flare, but they're less expensive. Overall, the hotel is comfortable rather than deluxe. **Forage** restaurant (604/661-1400, www.foragevancouver.com, breakfast 6:30am-10am Mon.-Fri., 7am-10am Sat.-Sun., dinner from 5pm daily, brunch 10am-2pm Sat.-Sun., mains breakfast $8-15, brunch $9-18, dinner $15-38), which emphasizes B.C. ingredients, is a bonus. The Listel charges an additional 6 percent fee to cover Wi-Fi and North American phone calls.

In a restored 1908 building, the boutique **Moda Hotel** (900 Seymour St., 604/683-4251 or 877/683-5522, www.modahotel.ca, $127-260 d) has 67 cozy rooms. The smallest measure just 150 square feet (14 square meters), while standard doubles are 300-350 square feet (28-32 square meters), but they're smartly designed, with red accents, updated baths, air-conditioning, and free Wi-Fi and North American phone calls. You don't have to go far to eat and drink; **Uva Wine & Cocktail Bar** (604/632-9560, www.uvavancouver.com, 8am-1:45am Mon.-Sat., 8am-12:45am Sun.), **Red Card Sports Bar** (604/602-9570, www.redcardsportsbar.ca, from noon daily), and **Cibo Trattoria** (604/602-9570, www.cibotrattoria.com, breakfast 7am-11am Mon.-Fri., lunch 11:30am-2pm Mon.-Fri., brunch 7am-2pm Sat.-Sun., dinner from 5pm daily, mains breakfast $11-14, lunch $14-21, brunch $11-17, dinner $18-45) are all on the lobby level.

Sure, the ivy-covered **Sylvia Hotel** (1154 Gilford St., 604/681-9321 or 877/681-9321, www.sylviahotel.com, $160-259 d), constructed as an apartment building in 1912, is a little old-fashioned. But all units, from basic queens and kings to larger family suites, have free Wi-Fi and flat-screen TVs; some have kitchens, and the best rooms have million-dollar views of English Bay. Even if your room doesn't, you can walk out the front door to the beach, Stanley Park, and plenty of dining spots. Location, location, location.

Over $250

At the oldest of the Fairmont chain's downtown properties, the copper roof and stone gargoyles of the 1939 **Fairmont Hotel Vancouver** (900 W. Georgia St., 604/684-3131 or 866/540-4452, www.fairmont.com, $399-599 d, parking $39) make it a recognizable landmark amid the city's glass-and-steel towers. The least expensive of the 556 English manor-style guest rooms are small, but all come with modern amenities such as air-conditioning and flat-screen TVs, as well as the classic Fairmont service. For free Wi-Fi, sign up for Fairmont's complimentary frequent-stay program. The indoor pool is in a window-lined greenhouse space, and on the lower level, **Absolute Spa at the Fairmont** (604/684-2772, www.absolutespa.com) caters to men, although women are welcome.

High-tech, Asian-inspired ★ **Fairmont Pacific Rim** (1038 Canada Pl., 604/695-5300 or 877/900-5350, www.fairmont.com, $449-929 d, parking $43-48) is one of the city's most luxurious lodgings. Stearns & Foster beds topped with Italian linens, plush robes, and marble baths with soaker tubs make the 377 contemporary guest rooms feel like urban oases. And that's before you open the electronically controlled drapes to check out the city and harbor views, or head for the rooftop to lounge around the secluded swimming pool. When you're ready to venture out, the hotel's bicycle butler can outfit you with two-wheeled transportation, or you can book the complimentary car service for downtown outings. As at all Fairmont properties, Wi-Fi is free to Fairmont President Club members.

Though it fades into the urban cityscape, surrounded by newer and flashier towers, the **Four Seasons Hotel Vancouver** (791 W. Georgia St., 604/689-9333 or 866/223-9333, www.fourseasons.com, $450-970 d, parking $45) is a discretely deluxe property. Spread over 28 floors, its 372 traditionally decorated rooms and suites have down pillows and fluffy duvets, dark wood furnishings, flat-screen TVs, and free Wi-Fi; pick a room on the 20th floor or above for peekaboo mountain views. A hotel highlight is the private fourth-floor deck, with an indoor-outdoor pool and fitness facility facing the garden terrace. On the lobby level, **Yew Seafood & Bar** (604/692-4939, www.yewseafood.com, 7am-2:30pm and 5pm-10pm daily, mains breakfast $7-17, lunch $22-41, dinner $25-45) draws fish lovers with its emphasis on sustainable seafood.

Located above the cruise ship terminal at Canada Place, the 21-story **Pan Pacific Hotel Vancouver** (999 Canada Pl., 604/662-8111 or 800/663-1515, www.panpacific.com, $379-719 d, parking $39-43) is especially convenient if you're starting or ending your Vancouver stay on a boat, though even landlubbers appreciate the panoramic views of the harbor and North

Top to bottom: the Burrard Hotel, an old-time motor hotel gone glam; the Sylvia Hotel, opposite English Bay; Skwachàys Lodge, Canada's first aboriginal arts and culture hotel.

Shore mountains. Enjoy the vistas from the heated saltwater pool and from many of the 503 nautical-style guest rooms, outfitted with padded white-leather headboards, white duvets trimmed with navy piping, and maple furniture. Have a drink in the **Cascades Lounge** or on the **Patio Terrace** for more sea-to-sky views.

Originally built in the 1920s and still channeling that era's glamour, the ★ **Rosewood Hotel Georgia** (801 W. Georgia St., 604/682-5566 or 888/767-3966, www.rosewoodhotels.com, $499-989 d, parking $42) has 156 classy guest rooms and suites, done in blues, creams, and chocolate browns with Italian linens and luxe baths with heated floors. Make time to exercise in the indoor saltwater lap pool or the 24-hour fitness center, since the hotel's **Hawksworth Restaurant** (604/673-7000, www.hawksworthrestaurant.com, breakfast 6:30am-10:30am Mon.-Fri., 7am-10:30am Sat.-Sun., lunch 11:30am-2pm Mon.-Fri., brunch 10:30am-2pm Sat.-Sun., dinner from 5pm daily, mains breakfast $12-27, lunch $20-31, dinner $40-52) is among the city's top special-occasion dining spots and **Bel Café** (604/673-7000, http://belcafe.com, 6:30am-5:30pm Mon.-Fri., 7am-5:30pm Sat.-Sun.) is an upscale place for pastry. Room service is available around the clock, and when you need to venture out, the hotel's car service can chauffeur you around town.

You don't hear much buzz about the **Wedgewood Hotel & Spa** (845 Hornby St., 604/689-7777 or 800/663-0666, www.wedgewoodhotel.com, $328-628 d, parking $35), but guests at this fashionable hideaway seem to like it that way. The 83 traditional rooms and suites feature deluxe amenities like plush robes and slippers, twice-daily housekeeping, and homemade bedtime cookies. You can work out in the up-to-date fitness facility and relax in the eucalyptus steam room; there's also a full-service spa. Elegant **Bacchus Restaurant and Lounge** (604/608-5319, breakfast 6:30am-11am Mon.-Fri., 7am-11am Sat.-Sun., lunch 11:30am-2:30pm Mon.-Fri., brunch 11am-2pm Sat.-Sun., afternoon tea 2pm-4pm Sat.-Sun., dinner 5:30pm-10pm daily, mains breakfast $13-29, lunch $16-34, brunch $15-35, afternoon tea $35 pp, dinner $25-44) serves French-accented cuisine with west coast ingredients.

Gastown
$150-250

At ★ **Skwachàys Lodge** (31 W. Pender St., 604/687-3589 or 888/998-0797, http://skwachays.com, $189-229 d, parking $18), Canada's first aboriginal arts and culture hotel, aboriginal artists worked with hotel designers to craft 18 distinctive guest rooms in an early-20th-century brick Victorian. In the Poem Suite, poems and pencil drawings dance across walls; in the Moon Suite, artists painted a golden moon face on the ceiling watching over the bed below. An aboriginal-owned company created the hotel's bath products; Wi-Fi and both local and international calls are included in the rates. Guests can participate in sweat lodge or smudging ceremonies with an aboriginal elder, with advance reservations. An added benefit: Hotel profits help subsidize housing for First Nations artists.

The 47-room **Victorian Hotel** (514 Homer St., 604/681-6369, www.victorianhotel.ca, $145-225 d, parking $20) is a European-style boutique property in two brick buildings, dating to 1898 and 1908. While the least expensive rooms are tiny and share hallway baths, others are more spacious and have private baths. All tastefully mix period pieces and modern furnishings, with pillow-top mattresses, robes, flat-screen TVs, and iPod docks. Rates include Wi-Fi and continental breakfast.

Yaletown
Under $150

One of Vancouver's best options for travelers on a budget is the modern **YWCA Hotel Vancouver** (733 Beatty St.,

604/895-5830 or 800/663-1424, www. ywcavan.org, $75-90 s, $84-135 d, parking $15). The 155 rooms range from basic singles with either a hall bath or a semi-private bath (shared between two rooms) or doubles with hall, semi-private, or private facilities to larger units that accommodate three to five people. All have air-conditioning, flat-screen TVs, mini fridges, and free Wi-Fi. Guests can prep meals in one of the three common kitchens or grab a snack in the lobby café.

Over $250

A clear contender for the title of "Vancouver's coolest hotel," the boutique ★ **Opus Hotel Vancouver** (322 Davie St., 866/642-6787, http://vancouver.opushotel.com, $369-499 d, parking $39) outfitted its 96 guest rooms in eye-popping lime greens, magentas, purples, and vibrant oranges. Many of the spacious baths have a window into the bedroom, while in others, bath windows face outside (don't be shy!). Rooms aren't huge, though they come with high-tech toys like flat-screen TVs, Keurig coffeemakers, and iPads that you can use throughout your stay (with free Wi-Fi, of course). Staff greet guests with a complimentary glass of sparkling wine; to get around town, book the hotel's complimentary car service or borrow a gratis mountain bike.

Granville Island
Over $250

To stay right on Granville Island, book a room at the waterfront **Granville Island Hotel** (1253 Johnston St., 604/683-7373 or 800/663-1840, www.granvilleislandhotel.com, $209-389 d, parking $12). All the guest rooms are furnished differently; the nicest take advantage of the island location with balconies or water views. Wi-Fi is included, and the hotel has a small fitness room, though for a better workout, you can run along the Seawall or walk over to the well-equipped fitness facility at the nearby False Creek Community Center.

Kitsilano
$150-250

Glass artist Sal Robinson has outfitted ★ **Corkscrew Inn** (2735 W. 2nd Ave., 604/733-7276 or 877/737-7276, www. corkscrewinn.com, $165-300 d), the B&B that she co-owns with her husband, Wayne Meadows, in a 1912 Craftsman-style Kitsilano home, with her original art deco-inspired wine-themed stained glass. You'll see her work in the sitting areas, dining room, and the five guest rooms, which also have custom-designed baths; one features tiles that Robinson designed to depict the Empire State Building. The inn also takes its name from Meadows's collection of antique corkscrews, which he displays in a tiny "museum" on the lower level. Rates include a family-style hot breakfast, which might feature a wild salmon frittata or lemon ricotta pancakes.

The North Shore
$150-250

Convenient to mountain activities, eight-story **Pinnacle Hotel at the Pier** (138 Victory Ship Way, North Vancouver, 604/986-7437 or 877/986-7437, http:// pinnaclepierhotel.com, $209-329 d, parking $15) has panoramic views across the water to the Vancouver skyline. Of the 106 modern guest rooms, with Wi-Fi included, those on the harbor side have small step-out balconies, and if you open the bath blinds, you can take in the vistas while you soak in the tub. City-side rooms glimpse the mountains. In the health club, you can enjoy the seascape from the cardio and weight machines, waterside sundeck, or indoor Olympic-size pool. The hotel is a five-minute walk from Lonsdale Quay and a 15-minute ride on the SeaBus to downtown Vancouver.

Vancouver's Food Trucks

Vancouver's growing number of **food trucks** park downtown, purveying a global gamut of meals to go. A cluster of trucks sets up shop around the Vancouver Art Gallery along Howe and Hornby Streets, some park near the Queen Elizabeth Theatre on Cambie and Georgia Streets, while others locate closer to the waterfront along Burrard or Thurlow Streets. Most operate from 11am or 11:30am until 2:30pm or 3pm.

The best way to find what trucks are where is with the **Vancouver Street Food app** (http://streetfoodapp.com/vancouver), which also lists truck locations online. Some favorites include:

- **Mom's Grilled Cheese** (Howe St. at Robson St. and W. Cordova St. at Hornby St., http://momsgrilledcheese-truck.com) for, as you'd expect, grilled cheese sandwiches

- **Le Tigre Cuisine** (check the website for locations, www.letigrecuisine.ca) for Asian-fusion fare, including kick ass fried rice

- **The Kaboom Box** (Granville St. at W. Georgia St., www.thekaboombox.com) for hot smoked salmon sandwiches

- **Yolk's Breakfast Street Meet Truck** (Burrard St. at W. Pender St., http://yolks.ca) for free-range egg sandwiches and fresh beignets

- **Aussie Pie Guy** (check the website for locations, www.aussiepieguy.com) for hand-held Australian-style meat or vegetable pies

Food

What should you eat in Vancouver? Like any major North American city, Vancouver restaurants span the globe, serving meals that take cues from Italy, France, Spain, China, Japan, and more. But here's what Vancouver does best.

Vancouver is known for seafood, particularly salmon, halibut, oysters, and spot prawns, caught in regional waters. The city's restaurants have embraced the "eat local" movement, so look for seasonal produce and locally raised meats. With a large Asian population, Vancouver has some of the best Chinese food in North America, as well as good Japanese and Korean fare, and many non-Asian restaurants incorporate Pacific Rim influences in their dishes.

British Columbia wines, from the Okanagan Valley or Vancouver Island, are good accompaniments to most Vancouver meals, as are regionally brewed craft beers. Plenty of bartenders have adopted an "eat local" philosophy, too, incorporating locally grown herbs, house-made bitters, and other fresh ingredients into creative cocktails and alcohol-free drinks.

Downtown and the West End
Groceries and Markets
The **West End Farmers Market** (Comox St. at Thurlow St., www.eatlocal.org, 9am-2pm Sat. late May-late Oct.) purveys produce, baked goods, and prepared foods; several food trucks park here, too.

Upscale **Urban Fare** (305 Bute St., 604/669-5831; 1133 Alberni St., 604/648-2053; www.urbanfare.com, 7am-10pm daily) sells groceries and meals to go from two downtown locations.

Cafés, Bakeries, and Light Bites
When a gelato maker is obsessive about fresh ingredients and traditional Italian techniques, naturally he and his team make Vancouver's best gelato. Find it at tiny **Bella Gelateria** (1001 W. Cordova St., 604/569-1010, http://bellagelateria.com,

11am-10pm Sun.-Thurs., 11am-11pm Fri.-Sat.), near the Fairmont Pacific Rim Hotel.

Expect a queue at **Medina Café** (780 Richards St., 604/879-3114, www.medinacafe.com, 8am-3pm Mon.-Fri., 9am-3pm Sat.-Sun., mains $6-17), which is known for its sugar-studded Liège waffles and North African-influenced brunch fare. Try the tagine, a flavorful vegetable stew topped with poached eggs, merguez sausage, and preserved lemon.

For fresh salads, soups, and sandwiches near Canada Place, plow a path to cafeteria-style **Tractor Foods** (335 Burrard St., 604/979-0500, www.tractorfoods.com, 7am-10:30am Mon.-Fri. and 11am-9pm daily, mains $5-13). They have another location in Kitsilano (1903 W. 4th Ave., 604/222-2557, 11am-9pm daily).

Contemporary

In a chandelier-bedecked space at the Rosewood Hotel Georgia, sophisticated **Hawksworth Restaurant** (801 W. Georgia St., 604/673-7000, www.hawksworthrestaurant.com, breakfast 6:30am-10:30am Mon.-Fri., 7am-10:30am Sat.-Sun., lunch 11:30am-2pm Mon.-Fri., brunch 10:30am-2pm Sat.-Sun., dinner from 5pm daily, mains breakfast $12-27, lunch $20-31, dinner $40-52) attracts expense-account diners, couples celebrating occasions, and gourmets savoring a fine meal with solicitous service. From the foie gras torchon to *wagyu* flank steak to lobster with Korean rice cakes, it's all about the luxe ingredients in the regionally influenced contemporary fare. **TIP:** If the dinner prices are too rich, splurge on a leisurely lunch or a light bites at the bar.

Asian

Part of a local mini chain of *izakayas,* lively **Guu Garden** (888 Nelson St., 604/899-0855, www.guu-izakaya.com/garden, lunch 11:30am-2:30pm Mon.-Fri., noon-3pm Sat.-Sun., dinner 5:30pm-midnight Sun.-Thurs., 5:30pm-12:30am Fri.-Sat., small plates $4-16) serves Japanese

tapas designed to share, like grilled black cod cheeks, crispy cauliflower *karaage,* and sashimi-style tuna *tataki,* to pair with sake, *shochu,* or Japanese beer. Guu is on the top floor of a complex with a similarly named eatery on the main level, so be sure to go upstairs.

Watch the dumpling makers at work at **Dinesty Dumpling House** (1719 Robson St., 604/669-7769, www.dinesty.ca, 11am-3pm and 5pm-10pm Mon.-Fri., 11am-10pm Sat.-Sun., mains $7-23), and that's what you should order, too: Shanghai-style soup dumplings, pan-fried pork buns, and steamed vegetable and egg dumplings. Handmade noodles, fresh greens with garlic, and the unusual omelet with pickles are also tasty choices.

At **Santouka Hokkaido Ramen** (1690 Robson St., 604/681-8121, www.santouka.co.jp, 11am-11pm daily, mains $11-17), the local outpost of a Japan-based noodle shop chain, the signature dish is *tokusen toroniku ramen,* a rich, almost creamy soup made from pork cheek meat. This ramen revelation is worth the inevitable queue, but lingering is discouraged, so diners slurp and move on.

For sushi with a water view, visit **Miku** (200 Granville St., 604/568-3900, www.mikurestaurant.com, 11:30am-3pm and 5pm-10:30pm daily, mains $16-36), an upscale Japanese dining room opposite Canada Place. They're known for *aburi sushi,* fresh fish seared with a blowtorch.

A unique-to-Vancouver mash-up of hot dogs and Japanese flavors, **Japadog** concocts their signature sausages, like the *kurobuta* pork *terimayo,* sauced with teriyaki, mayonnaise, and seaweed, at a diminutive downtown restaurant (530 Robson St., 604/569-1158, www.japadog.com, 10am-10pm Mon.-Thurs., 10am-midnight Fri.-Sat., 10am-9pm Sun., mains $4-8) and at two downtown food trucks (899 Burrard St. at Smithe St.; Burrard St. at W. Pender St.).

Diners

Retro diner **The Templeton** (1087

Granville St., 604/685-4612, http://the-templeton.ca, 9am-11pm Mon.-Wed., 9am-1am Thurs.-Sun., mains $8-16), complete with tabletop jukeboxes and soda-fountain stools, has morphed into a cool purveyor of comfort foods. Dig into hearty plates of pancakes, creative omelets, or burgers, which you can pair with coffee or "big people drinks" (craft beer, local wines, and cocktails). Save room for an ice cream sundae or old-fashioned banana split.

Seafood

Sink into a cream-colored banquette at **Boulevard Kitchen & Oyster Bar** (845 Burrard St., 604/642-2900, www.boule-vardvancouver.ca, 6:30am-11pm daily, mains breakfast $9-29, lunch $17-27, dinner $27-47), where dishes like citrus-cured *hamachi,* roasted sablefish with *gailan* flan, or ling cod in a clam and ham hock ragout highlight local seafood in refined Asian-accented preparations. You could stop in for a glass of bubbly and fresh oysters at the bar, too.

The chefs at ★ **Yew Seafood & Bar** (791 W. Georgia St., 604/692-4939, www.yews-eafood.com, 7am-2:30pm and 5pm-10pm daily, mains breakfast $7-17, lunch $22-41, dinner $25-45), in the Four Seasons Hotel Vancouver, are passionate about sustainable seafood, so not only can you enjoy contemporary dishes like salmon with pickled shallots and bacon vinaigrette, lobster tacos, or a B.C. spot prawn salad, you're also doing your part for the oceans. It's a stylish setting for a business lunch, special dinner, or drinks with seafood small plates. Surprise: Yew also offers an upscale vegan menu.

Gastown and Chinatown

Many of Vancouver's most innovative restaurants have opened in Gastown and Chinatown, so visit these districts when you're hungry for what's new and cool.

Cafés, Bakeries, and Light Bites

Gastown is Vancouver's coffee central. Sip your java among the designers, techies, and laptop-toting cool kids at **Revolver** (325 Cambie St., 604/558-4444, www.revolvercoffee.ca, 7:30am-6pm Mon.-Fri., 9am-6pm Sat.) or **Nelson the Seagull** (315 Carrall St., 604/681-5776, www.nelsontheseagull.com, 8am-5pm Mon.-Fri. 9am-5pm Sat.-Sun.).

Vancouverites used to have to drive to Whistler for the decadent pastries and wholesome breads at **Purebread** (159 W. Hastings St., 604/563-8060, www.pure-bread.ca, 8:30am-5:30pm daily). But now Gastown has a Purebread of its own, with drool-inducing treats like fresh-baked scones, lemon chèvre brownies, and giant meringues.

A tiny sliver of a bakery in Chinatown, ★ **The Pie Shoppe** (721 Gore Ave., 604/338-6646, http://thepieshoppe.ca, 11am-6pm Tues.-Sun., slices $5-7, whole pies $20-30) turns out a seasonally changing array of sweet things in a crust. The delicious homemade options include blueberry, nectarine-cardamom, and chocolate pecan. Unless you're lucky enough to snag one of the few seats, ask for a fork and take your slice to go. Warning: The Pie Shoppe closes early if they run out of pie.

Contemporary

On the site of Vancouver's first jail, transformed into a multilevel space with exposed brick and polished woods, ★ **L'Abbatoir** (217 Carrall St., 604/568-1701, www.labattoir.ca, 5:30pm-10pm Sun.-Thurs., 5:30pm-10:30pm Fri.-Sat., brunch 10am-2pm Sat.-Sun., mains dinner $29-35, brunch $14-22) detains diners with creative cocktails (how about an avocado gimlet with herb-infused gin, schnapps, avocado, and lime?) and a changing menu of west coast plates. Meat eaters might bite into pan-fried sweetbreads or roast lamb with marinated eggplant, while fish fans might favor baked oysters or charcoal-grilled rockfish with peas, potatoes, and clams. At brunch, order the oversize scone mounded with house-made jam and clotted cream.

Combining tastes of North Africa and Belgium with local ingredients, **Chambar** (568 Beatty St., 604/879-7119, www.chambar.com, breakfast 8am-11:30am Mon.-Fri., lunch 11:30am-3pm Mon.-Fri., dinner from 5pm daily, brunch 8am-3pm Sat.-Sun., mains breakfast and brunch $9-20, lunch $15-29, dinner $24-33) pleases patrons all day in a window-lined rehabbed warehouse. Kick off your morning with a waffle studded with pearl sugar or breakfast paella topped with spicy sausage and a fried egg. Later, you might sup on Haida Gwaii halibut with sea asparagus or venison with fresh pasta and blue cheese. *Moules frites* (mussels with french fries) are a specialty.

In a sleekly renovated Chinatown space that once housed a chop suey joint, **Sai Woo** (158 E. Pender St., 604/568-1117, www.saiwoo.ca, 5pm-midnight Tues.-Sun., small plates $9-26) mixes up Asian, world-beat, and regional flavors. Look for eclectic dishes designed to share, like jerk chicken with radish cake and yams, Sichuan cured tuna with heirloom tomatoes, or pork belly braised in fermented red tofu and paired with taro puree. Creative cocktails like the frothy Sai Woo Sour (gin, Benedictine, lemon, ginger syrup, and an egg white) add to the entertainment.

Asian

At **Bao Bei Chinese Brasserie** (163 Keefer St., 604/688-0876, www.bao-bei.ca, 5:30pm-midnight Mon.-Sat., 5:30pm-11pm Sun., small plates $6-20), many menu items, from *mantou* (steamed buns) to fried rice, would be at home in a traditional Chinatown kitchen, but this modern lounge and eatery isn't your grandmother's Chinese restaurant. The buns are stuffed with pork belly and sweet peanuts, the fried rice is amped up with clams and salted halibut, and other dishes, like wok-charred octopus with mustard-root gnocchi, start in Asia

Sai Woo reflects Vancouver's Chinatown.

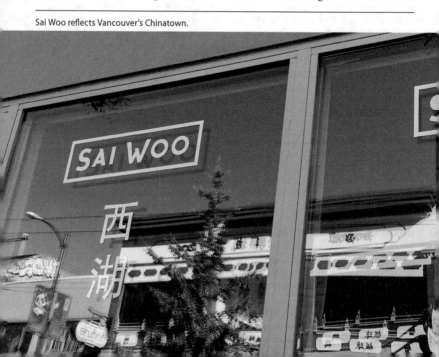

but wander the world. To drink? Clever cocktails, like Cheung Po the Kid, which blends rum, Dubonnet, pomegranate molasses, and house-made Chinese plum bitters.

Tsuki Sushi Bar (509 Abbott St., 604/558-3805, http://tsukisushibar.ca, 11:30am-2:30pm and 5pm-9:30pm Mon.-Fri., noon-3pm and 4:30pm-9pm Sat., mains $10-16) does one thing and does it well: preparing fresh sushi and sashimi. See what's on special, or try their *chirashi* bowl, an assortment of raw fish on rice. The same owners run a Japanese noodle shop next door, **Taishoken Ramen** (515 Abbott St., 778/737-3805, 11:30am-4pm and 5pm-9:30pm daily, mains $10-13), where the specialty is *tsukemen,* noodles served with a separate dipping broth.

Yaletown and False Creek
Groceries and Markets
The **Yaletown Farmers Market** (120 Mainland St., www.eatlocal.org, 2pm-6pm Thurs. early May-late Oct.) sells fresh produce, baked goods, and more outside the Yaletown/Roundhouse Canada Line station.

Italian and Pizza
The waterside branch of Vancouver's best gelato shop not only serves its fresh and delicious homemade frozen treats, **Bella Gelateria Yaletown** (1089 Marinaside Cres., 778/737-7890, http://bellagelateria.com, 9am-11pm daily, mains $9-20) is a full-fledged Neapolitan-style pizzeria, cooking up creative and traditional pies in their wood-burning oven.

The best way to dine at **La Pentola** (350 Davie St., 604/642-0557, www.lapentola.ca, 7am-10pm daily, mains lunch $14-24, dinner $18-35), the fashionable dining room at the Opus Hotel, is family-style ($60-75 pp), when the kitchen will send out a procession of contemporary Italian dishes. Even if you opt for a less opulent feast, you can still choose from antipasti like braised octopus with fried eggplant, house-made pastas (perhaps tagliatelle bolognese or agnolotti stuffed with duck confit and marsala currents), and mains that might include *branzano* with Swiss chard or veal osso buco. Save room for their sweet-tart lemon-cream dessert.

Seafood
Fresh seafood, simply prepared, is the lure at **Wild Tale Coastal Grill** (1079 Mainland St., 604/428-9211, www.wildtale.ca, 11:30am-late Mon.-Fri., 3pm-late Sat.-Sun., mains lunch $12-18, dinner $23-35). Start with something from the raw bar, maybe oysters or ceviche, then order the day's fresh catch. Easy, right?

Granville Island
Granville Island Public Market
The best place to eat on Granville Island, at least if you like to browse and graze, is inside the **Granville Island Public Market** (1689 Johnston St., http://granvilleisland.com, 9am-7pm daily), where vendors sell soups, sandwiches, sweets, and lots of goodies for a picnic.

⟡ Side Trip: The Fraser Valley

Southeast of Vancouver, this partly agricultural, partly suburban region along the Fraser River has several places to get outdoors as well as historic sites, wineries, and farms that welcome visitors. Explore this area as a day trip from Vancouver or as a stop when you're traveling between Vancouver and the Okanagan Valley.

A number of the region's producers have organized into a series of self-guided **Circle Farm Tours** (www.circlefarmtour.com), with loops through the communities of Langley, Abbottsford, Chilliwack, Agassiz, Harrison Mills, and Maple Ridge/Pitt Meadows. Pick up their brochure at local visitors centers or see details and maps on the website.

Fort Langley National Historic Site

At this former Hudson's Bay Company trading post, you can venture back to the 1800s, watching the blacksmith at work over his forge or trying your hand at panning for gold, aided by costumed interpreters.

The **Fort Langley National Historic Site** (23433 Mavis Ave., Fort Langley, 604/513-4777, www.pc.gc.ca, 10am-5pm daily, adults $7.80, seniors $6.55, ages 6-16 $3.90, families $19.60) not only illuminates the fur trade history and the traders' relationships with local First Nations, it also marks the site where British Columbia became a British Crown Colony in 1858. The fort is 28 miles (45 kilometers) east of Vancouver via Highway 1.

Fraser Valley Wineries

The fertile Fraser Valley grows much of Vancouver's fruits and vegetables, and it's also a small wine-producing area. You can get to the Fraser Valley wineries from Highway 99 near the U.S. border, or from Highway 1 east of Vancouver.

Vista D'Oro Farms & Winery (346 208th St., Langley, 604/514-3539, www.vistadoro.com, 11am-5pm Thurs.-Sun.) runs a tasting room in a little white farmhouse, where you can sample their most interesting product, a rich, port-like fortified walnut wine.

The Fraser Valley's oldest and largest winery is **Domaine De Chaberton Estate Winery** (1064 216 St., Langley, 604/530-1736, 10am-6pm Mon.-Wed., 10am-8pm Thurs.-Sat., 11am-6pm Sun., tours 2pm and 4pm daily Feb.-Nov., 3pm daily Dec.-Jan.), which makes red and white wines from less common estate-grown grapes such as bacchus and ortega. Their **Bacchus Bistro** (604/530-9694, lunch 11:30am-3pm Wed.-Sun., dinner 5:30pm-9pm Thurs.-Sat., mains lunch $13-24, dinner $19-28) serves French-inspired west coast fare.

Township 7 Winery (21152 16th Ave., Langley, 604/532-1766, www.township7.com, 11am-6pm daily), based in the Okanagan, doesn't make wine at its Langley location, but you can still sample the highly regarded chardonnay, merlot, sauvignon blanc, and other wines in the cave-like Langley tasting room.

Harrison Hot Springs

The main reason to detour to this scenic town along a glacier-fed lake, 80 miles (130 kilometers) east of Vancouver, is for the mineral pools that give the community its name.

Long considered a healing place, the area has two natural hot springs. The water is cooled before it's pumped into the **Harrison Hot Springs Public Pool** (101 Hot Springs Rd., 604/796-2244, 10am-8pm Mon.-Thurs., 10am-9pm Fri., 9am-9pm Sat., 9am-8pm Sun., adults $9, seniors and ages 5-14 $6.75, families $26.75), where you can soak and paddle in the still-warm 100°F (38°C) pool.

Another place to soak, and stay, is **Harrison Hot Springs Resort and Spa** (100 Esplanade Ave., 604/796-2244 or 866/638-5075, www.harrisonresort.com, $149-329 d), which has five mineral pools available to guests, plus an on-site spa. Accommodations range from basic rooms in the hotel's original 1926 section to more contemporary units in several newer wings.

Contemporary

Edible Canada Bistro (1596 Johnston St., 604/682-6681, www.ediblecanada.com, 11am-9pm Mon.-Thurs., 11am-10pm Fri., 9am-10pm Sat., 9am-9pm Sun., mains brunch $10-18, lunch $14-18, dinner $18-31), opposite the Public Market, creates contemporary dishes with ingredients from around British Columbia and across Canada. At midday, you might try a duck confit sandwich with cherry-onion relish or root vegetable hash with boar bacon and poached eggs; for supper, find plates like maple-glazed pork chops, wild salmon with braised lentils, or bison short ribs. They regularly partner with Canadian chefs to host special dinners; check the website for upcoming events.

Seafood

Like seafood? Then go fish—at **Go Fish** (1505 W. 1st Ave., 604/730-5040, 11:30am-6:30pm Tues.-Fri., noon-6:30pm Sat.-Sun., mains $8-20), an always busy take-out shack on the waterfront, a short walk from Granville Island. Choose fish-and-chips made from cod, salmon, or halibut, or go a little wild with a wild salmon sandwich, an oyster po' boy, or fish tacos. Expect lines on sunny days.

Kitsilano and the West Side

The West Side neighborhoods with the most interesting dining options include West 4th Avenue in Kitsilano, South Granville Street, and the Broadway-Cambie district, near the Broadway/City Hall Canada Line station.

Cafés, Bakeries, and Light Bites

With classic French pastries like croissants or buttery *kouign-amann*, and other baked treats like the kid-pleasing peanut butter sandwich cookies, petite **Beaucoup Bakery & Café** (2150 Fir St., 604/732-4222, www.beaucoupbakery.

Top to bottom: seafood at La Pentola; an artful plate at AnnaLena; pastries at Beaucoup Bakery & Café.

com, 7am-6pm Mon.-Fri., 8am-6pm Sat.-Sun.) makes a sweet stop for South Granville shoppers. It's a short walk from Granville Island, too.

If you like your chocolate rich, dark, and homemade, add **Chocolate Arts** (1620 W. 3rd Ave., 604/739-0475, www. chocolatearts.com, 10am-6pm Mon.-Sat., 10am-5pm Sun.), near Granville Island, to your itinerary. Try a shot of drinking chocolate (think espresso but with chocolate) or assemble a box of bonbons. For a treat, come for Haute Chocolat, a version of afternoon tea, with cocoa, house-made chocolates, petits fours, and other chocolaty pastries.

Overlooking the sea from the second floor of the Jericho Sailing Centre, **The Galley Patio and Grill** (1300 Discovery St., 604/222-1331, www.thegalley.ca, summer 10am-10pm Mon.-Fri., 9am-10pm Sat.-Sun., call for off-season hours, mains $10-19) cooks up simple, beach-friendly bites, including burgers, grilled salmon, and sweet potato fries, served on a deck with killer ocean views. Local beer is on tap. If you can't find a seat, take your food outside and picnic. Tip for morning beachcombers: The Galley also serves breakfast.

Contemporary

Though it's named for the chef's grandmothers, there's nothing old-fashioned about **AnnaLena** (1809 W. 1st Ave., 778/379-4052, www.annalena.ca, dinner from 5pm Tues.-Sun., brunch 10am-1:45pm Sat.-Sun., shared plates $13-33, brunch mains $8-10), a smart Kitsilano bistro with white walls, black banquettes, and west coast wood trimmings. The modern menu, designed to share, includes kale salad with fried cauliflower dressed with creamy tahini, seared trout with pickled cabbage puree, and lamb neck with chimichurri. To sip? Local microbrews, B.C. wines, and fun cocktails.

Chef-owner John Bishop helped pioneer Vancouver's farm-to-table movement long before the 100-mile diet was on the lips of every locavore. At his classy Kitsilano restaurant, **Bishop's** (2183 W. 4th Ave., 604/738-2025, www. bishopsonline.com, 5:30pm-11pm Tues.-Sun., mains $32-49), the polished staff can guide you to seasonal suppers that might start with asparagus served with giant kelp or a terrine of locally raised pork before continuing with Haida Gwaii halibut paired with fresh fennel or chicken roulade with Okanagan lentils and heirloom carrots. Finish with whipped goat Brie with oat biscuits or a brown-butter chocolate cake with cherries.

Though the name **Fable** (1944 W. 4th Ave., 604/732-1322, www.fablekitchen. ca, lunch 11:30am-2pm Mon.-Fri., dinner 5pm-10pm daily, brunch 10:30am-2pm Sat.-Sun., mains lunch $12-20, dinner $19-29)—"from farm to table"—may be a bit earnest, the kitchen has a sense of humor at this Kitsilano eatery, with starters like an oversize duck meatball that bursts open to sauce its tagliatelle, and sweets like "Oops, I dropped the dessert," a mash-up of rhubarb, vanilla custard, and ice cream. In between are hearty unpretentious plates featuring local seafood, meats, and fresh veggies.

Imaginative multicourse tasting menus inspired by local products bring adventurous diners to ★ **Farmer's Apprentice** (1535 W. 6th Ave., 604/620-2070, www.farmersapprentice.ca, brunch 11am-2pm Sat.-Sun., dinner 5:30pm-10pm daily, brunch mains $14-19, dinner tasting menus $50-55 pp), a petite South Granville dining room. Ling cod with epazote and radishes? Dry-aged duck with emmer and sea buckthorn? You won't find these creations on any other tables around town. The same team runs the more casual wine and tapas bar, **Grapes and Soda** (1541 W. 6th Ave., 604/336-2456, www.grapesandsoda.ca, 5pm-11pm Wed.-Sun., small plates $4-17) next door.

A wall of wine sets the sumptuous

scene at South Granville's ★ **West** (2881 Granville St., 604/738-8938, www.westrestaurant.com, lunch 11:30am-2:30pm Mon.-Fri., brunch 10:30am-2:30pm Sat.-Sun., dinner 5:30pm-10:30pm Sun.-Thurs., 5:30pm-11pm Fri.-Sat., mains lunch $17-27, dinner $30-40), where the gracious service and just-inventive-enough cuisine make any meal feel like an occasion. Wild salmon with zucchini noodles, a pork duo of braised cheek and crispy belly, or smoked duck with wilted kale are just some of the locally sourced plates you might encounter. Sweets are special, too, with choices like polenta coconut cake with yellow plum sauce and sweet corn ice cream, or a chocolate tasting plate.

Asian

★ **Dynasty Seafood** (777 W. Broadway, 604/876-8388, www.dynasty-restaurant.ca, 10am-3pm and 5pm-10:30pm daily, dim sum $3-8) serves some of Vancouver's best dim sum, a sophisticated mix of traditional and creative dumplings, buns, and other small bites. Highlights include lemony baked barbecue pork buns, steamed black truffle dumplings, and sweet sago pudding, a tapioca dessert. The busy second-floor dining room, with views of the downtown skyline and North Shore mountains, is a short walk west of the Broadway/City Hall Canada Line station.

Serving modern Thai cuisine in a minimalist Kitsilano space, **Maenam** (1938 W. 4th Ave., 604/730-5579, www.maenam.ca, lunch noon-2:30pm Tues.-Sat., dinner 5pm-10pm Mon.-Thurs., 5pm-11pm Fri.-Sat., mains lunch $14-19, dinner $15-21) brightens Vancouver's dark nights with banana blossom salad, grilled fermented sausage with crispy rice, and flavorful curries. If you can't decide, go for the six-course chef's menu ($40 pp).

Long considered Vancouver's top Japanese dining room, **Tojo's** (1133 W. Broadway, 604/872-8050, www.tojos.com, mains $18-55) is known for the high quality of its sushi and sashimi. For a special evening, sit at the sushi bar and order *omakase* (chef's choice, $80-120 pp), a parade of traditional and creative dishes. Sip rice wines and order small plates at **The Sake Bar** when you don't want a full meal.

First Nations

If you're keen to explore First Nations culture on your plate, visit **Salmon 'n' Bannock** (1128 W. Broadway, 604/568-8971, www.salmonandbannock.net, lunch 11:30am-3pm Mon.-Fri., dinner 5pm-9pm Mon.-Thurs., 5pm-10pm Fri.-Sat., mains lunch $10-18, dinner $12-45). This modern aboriginal bistro uses traditional ingredients in the elk burgers, game sausages, and bison tenderloin, and yes, there's plenty of salmon and bannock, a native bread, on the menu, too. Desserts include bannock bread pudding and homemade fruit pies.

Indian

Celebrated for its innovative riffs on Indian cuisine, **Vij's** (3106 Cambie St., 604/736-6664, www.vijsrestaurant.ca, dinner from 5:30pm daily, mains $19-29), which became equally famous for its no-reservations waiting lines, relocated in 2015 to a larger space, six blocks from the Broadway/City Hall Canada Line station. The no-bookings policy, and the modern Indian fare, from chickpeas in black cardamom curry to grilled venison atop tamarind-date puree to the signature lamb "Popsicles," remain unchanged; a cocktail or a cup of *chai* make the wait go more smoothly. **TIP:** The same owners' **Rangoli** (1488 W. 11th Ave., 604/736-5711, www.vijsrangoli.ca, 11am-10pm daily, mains $10-18) serves similarly interesting Indian dishes in a casual South Granville café.

Main Street and the East Side
Vegetarian

At ★ **The Acorn** (3995 Main St., 604/566-9001, www.theacornrestaurant.ca,

5:30pm-10:30pm Sun.-Wed., 5:30pm-11pm Thurs.-Sat., mains $17-20), Vancouver's most innovative vegetarian restaurant, plant food shakes off its crunchy-granola reputation with ambitious plates that would enhance any upscale table: kale salad with tempeh and smoked paprika croutons, beer-battered halloumi cheese with zucchini-potato pancakes, or eggplant, oyster mushroom, and macadamia cannelloni. The dining space isn't much larger than the restaurant's name, and they don't take reservations, so you might chill at the bar with a Pina Loca (rum, sherry, pandan coconut syrup, and pineapple juice) or an Olde Black (bourbon, blackberry and foraged chamomile syrup, and house-made blackberry-cacao bitters).

Richmond

Why come to Richmond to eat? For some of the best Chinese food outside China. You might also find yourself in Richmond to explore the waterfront in Steveston or on your way to the Vancouver International Airport.

Asian

In an ordinary strip mall, **Golden Paramount Seafood Restaurant** (8071 Park Rd., 604/278-0873, 10:30am-3pm and 5pm-10pm Wed.-Mon., dim sum $4-16, subway: Richmond/Brighouse) is a first-rate spot for Hong Kong-style dim sum. Try the pan-fried oysters, *congee* (rice porridge), and steamed dumplings filled with pork and crab, or survey what other tables are eating and politely point. Reservations are recommended, particularly on weekends.

Su Hang Restaurant (100-8291 Ackroyd Rd., 604/278-7787, www.su-hang.ca, 11am-3pm and 5pm-10pm daily, mains $12-44, subway: Lansdowne) specializes in Shanghai dishes, from delicate *xiao long bao* (pork-filled soup dumplings) to fresh fish or crab to meaty pork ribs. To sample their signature dish, Hangzhou beggar chicken, order a

Pajo's

day in advance. At lunchtime, they serve Shanghai-style dim sum. Make a reservation; the restaurant is small.

Like spice? **Bushuair Restaurant** (Empire Centre, 121-4540 No. 3 Rd., 604/285-3668, 11am-midnight daily, mains $12-22, subway: Aberdeen) prepares the blistering hot cuisine of China's Hunan province. Choose any preparation with smoked bacon or pickled chilies, which give dishes their distinctive Hunan flavors. The whole fish buried in chili peppers is a showstopper.

Seafood
A favorite among the seafood restaurants lining Steveston's waterfront, **Pajo's** (12351 3 Ave., 604/272-1588, www.pajos. com, 11am-7pm daily Feb.-Oct., mains $8-21) is a simple picnic-on-the-pier spot known for its fish and chips, which you can order with cod, salmon, or halibut. Prepare to wait when the sun shines; they close in foul weather.

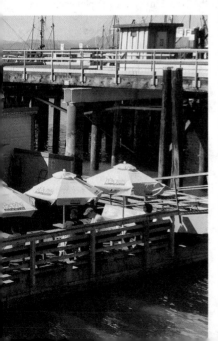

Information and Services

Visitor Information
Near Canada Place, the **Tourism Vancouver Visitor Centre** (200 Burrard St., plaza level, 604/683-2000, www.tourismvancouver.com, 9am-5pm daily) provides helpful information about the city. Inside the visitors center, **Tickets Tonight** (604/684-2787, www.ticketstonight.ca, 9am-5pm daily) sells half-price same-day theater and event tickets.

Tourism Vancouver's **Inside Vancouver blog** (www.insidevancouver.com) details goings-on around town and provides event listings. **Destination BC** (www.hellobc.com), the provincial tourism agency, has a useful website with information about Vancouver and destinations across the province. The **City of Vancouver** website (http://vancouver.ca) provides details about city-run parks, theaters, and transportation. **TransLink** (www.translink.ca), the city's public transit system, has an online trip-planning function that can help you get around town.

Media and Communications
The city's local daily newspapers include the *Vancouver Sun* (www.vancouversun. com) and *Vancouver Province* (www. theprovince.com). The daily Toronto-based *Globe and Mail* (www.theglobeandmail.com) covers news across Canada, including Vancouver, as does the **CBC** (www.cbc.ca), Canada's public television and radio outlet.

The *Georgia Straight* (www.straight. com) provides arts and entertainment listings, restaurant reviews, and area news. Other community news outlets include the *Vancouver Courier* (www.vancourier.com) and the *WestEnder* (www. westender.com). *Vancouver Magazine* (http://vanmag.com), a glossy monthly also available online, covers city news, restaurants, and events.

The online **Scout Magazine** (http://scoutmagazine.ca) features Vancouver restaurant and food stories. **Miss 604** (www.miss604.com) and **Vancouver is Awesome** (http://vancouverisawesome.com) are established local blogs.

Medical Services

Call 911 for assistance in an emergency.

Vancouver General Hospital (920 W. 10th Ave., 604/875-4111) has a 24-hour emergency room, which will assist patients ages 17 and older. If children under 17 need emergency medical attention, take them to **B.C. Children's Hospital** (4480 Oak St., 604/875-2345 or 888/300-3088, www.bcchildrens.ca).

Downtown, you can get 24-hour emergency care at **St. Paul's Hospital** (1081 Burrard St., 604/682-2344, www.providencehealthcare.org). On the University of British Columbia campus, the **UBC Urgent Care Clinic** (UBC Hospital, Koerner Pavilion, 2211 Wesbrook Mall, 604/822-7121, www.vch.ca, 8am-10pm daily) is a good choice for X-rays and nonemergency medical issues.

Several locations of **Shoppers Drug Mart** (www.shoppersdrugmart.ca) have 24-hour pharmacies, including branches in the **West End** (1125 Davie St., 604/669-2424), on **Broadway** near Vancouver General Hospital (885 W. Broadway, 604/708-1135), and **Kitsilano** (2302 W. 4th Ave., 604/738-3138). Other centrally located branches have extended hours, including **Robson and Burrard** downtown (748 Burrard St., 778/330-4711, 8am-midnight daily) and **Yaletown** (1006 Homer St., 604/669-0330, 8am-midnight Mon.-Sat., 9am-midnight Sun.).

London Drugs (www.londondrugs.com), another Canadian pharmacy chain, has several downtown locations that are open late, including 710 Granville Street (604/448-4802, 8am-10pm Mon.-Fri., 9am-10pm Sat., 10am-8pm Sun.) and 1187 Robson Street (604/448-4819, 9am-10pm Mon.-Sat., 10am-10pm Sun.).

Getting Around

You don't need a car to get around downtown Vancouver. The downtown peninsula is easy to navigate on foot, cabs are readily available, and the city has a good public transportation system with its SkyTrain subway and comprehensive bus network. It can be faster to go by car to some places outside downtown, like the University of British Columbia or the North Shore, but these destinations are not difficult to reach by transit.

TIP: If you're planning to rent a car in Vancouver for your Canadian road trip, you can save money by picking up that car when you're ready to leave the city, instead of when you arrive. And you won't have to pay for parking during your Vancouver stay.

By Subway and Bus

TransLink (604/953-3333, www.translink.ca) runs the city's public transportation system. Use the **Trip Planner** feature on the TransLink website to plot your route.

Transit Fares and Passes

Vancouver transit fares (one-zone/two-zone/three-zone adults $2.75/$4/$5.50, seniors, students, and ages 5-13 $1.75/$2.75/$3.75) are divided into **three zones,** based on the distance you travel. **Pay a basic one-zone fare** if:

- your trip is entirely within the Vancouver city limits.

- you're traveling only by bus. All bus trips are one zone, regardless of distance.

- you're traveling anywhere after 6:30pm on weekdays or all day Saturday, Sunday, and holidays.

If you're taking the SkyTrain between downtown Vancouver and the airport Monday through Friday before 6:30pm, you need to pay a two-zone fare; during those hours, the SeaBus between Vancouver and North Vancouver is also a two-zone trip.

When you board the SkyTrain at the YVR Airport station, you pay a $5 surcharge in addition to the regular transit fare.

If you're going to be riding transit extensively, buy a **day pass** (adults $9.75, seniors, students, and ages 5-13 $7.50), which covers one day of unlimited travel on the SkyTrain, buses, and SeaBus across all zones.

How to Buy Tickets and Passes

At SkyTrain or SeaBus stations, buy a ticket or day pass from the vending machine, which accepts cash, credit cards, and debit cards.

On the bus, you can pay your fare in cash; you need exact change. If you've bought a ticket on the SkyTrain or SeaBus within the previous 90 minutes, you can use that same ticket on the bus.

For any mode of travel, you can also buy a **Compass Card,** an electronic stored-value card, which gives you a **discounted fare** (one-zone/two-zone/three-zone adults $2.10/$3.15/$4.20). Buy Compass Cards at station vending machines, online (www.compasscard.ca), or at London Drugs stores around the city.

When you purchase a Compass Card, you're charged a $6 card deposit. You can get your deposit back when you no longer need the card, either by returning your card in person to the **Compass Customer Service Centre** (Stadium-Chinatown Station) or to the **West Coast Express Office** (Waterfront Station), or by mailing in a refund request. See the TransLink website for mail-in refund instructions.

How to Use a Compass Card

Before boarding the SkyTrain or SeaBus, tap your Compass Card at the fare gates. After your trip, tap out your card as you exit the station, so the system can calculate the correct fare and debit it from your card balance. **Remember to tap out,** or you'll be charged the maximum fare.

When you board a bus, tap your card on the card reader. You don't have to tap out when you get off the bus, since all bus trips are a one-zone fare.

By SkyTrain

Vancouver's **SkyTrain** subway has three lines that converge downtown at Waterfront Station.

The **Canada Line** (5am-1am daily) has several downtown stops, and its two branches can take you between downtown and the airport (take the YVR branch) or other destinations in Richmond (the Richmond-Brighouse branch).

The **Expo Line** (5am-1:30am Mon.-Fri., 6am-1:30am Sat., 7am-12:30pm Sun.) and **Millennium Line** (5:30am-1:30am Mon.-Fri., 6:30am-1:30am Sat., 7:30am-12:30pm Sun.) both travel between downtown and Vancouver's eastern suburbs; take either of these lines to Chinatown, Main Street (near Science World), or points farther east.

By Bus

The main bus routes in downtown Vancouver run along Granville, Burrard, Robson, Georgia, Pender, Hastings, and Davie Streets. Useful routes outside downtown travel along West 4th Avenue, Broadway, Oak, Cambie, and Main Streets.

At any bus stop, text the posted stop number to 33333 and you'll receive a reply listing the next buses scheduled to arrive at that stop.

Bus schedules vary by route, but regular service begins between 5am and 6pm and runs until 1am or 2am. Vancouver also has 12 **Night Bus** routes that provide limited service into the wee hours; get schedules on the TransLink website (www.translink.ca).

By Ferry
Aquabus and False Creek Ferries

Two privately run ferry services shuttle passengers across False Creek between downtown, Granville Island, Science World, and several other points. Schedules vary seasonally, but in summer, service starts around 6:45am-7am and continues until after 10pm. These ferries aren't part of the TransLink system and require separate tickets.

The colorful **Aquabus Ferries** (604/689-5858, www.theaquabus.com; adults $3.25-5.50, day pass $15, seniors and ages 4-12 $1.75-3.75, day pass $13) stop at the foot of Hornby Street, Granville Island, Yaletown's David Lam Park, Stamps Landing, Spyglass Place near the Cambie Bridge, the foot of Davie Street in Yaletown, Plaza of Nations, and Olympic Village. They operate 12-passenger mini-ferries, as well as 30-passenger boats that accommodate bicycles.

False Creek Ferries (604/684-7781, www.granvilleislandferries.bc.ca; adults $3.25-5.50, day pass $15, seniors and ages 4-12 $1.75-3.75, day pass $11) follow a similar route, stopping at the Vancouver Aquatic Centre in the West End, Granville Island, Vanier Park (near the Maritime Museum and Museum of Vancouver), David Lam Park, Stamps Landing, Spyglass Place, the foot of Davie Street, Plaza of Nations, and Olympic Village.

SeaBus

The **SeaBus** (604/953-3333, www.translink.ca) ferry is the fastest route between downtown and North Vancouver's Lonsdale Quay, taking just 12 minutes to cross the Burrard Inlet. TransLink bus and SkyTrain tickets are also valid on the SeaBus.

By Taxi

In downtown Vancouver, you can usually hail taxis on the street or find cabs waiting at hotels, restaurants, bars, and transit stations.

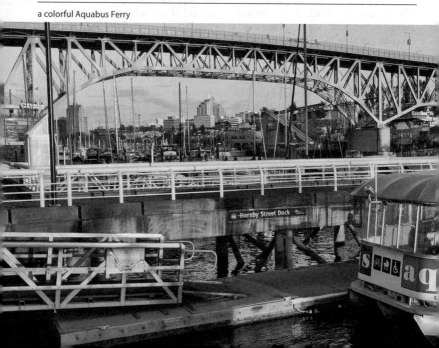

a colorful Aquabus Ferry

You can also phone for a cab or book one online. Local taxi companies include **Blacktop & Checker Cabs** (604/731-1111, www.btccabs.ca), **MacLure's Cabs** (604/831-1111, www.maclurescabs.ca), **Vancouver Taxi** (604/871-1111, www.avancouvertaxi.com), and **Yellow Cab** (604/681-1111, www.yellowcabonline.com).

Vancouver taxis are metered, with a base fare of $3.20 plus $1.84 per kilometer, except for trips starting at Vancouver International Airport; from the airport, you'll pay a **flat rate by zone** ($31-37) to most Vancouver destinations. Cabs accept cash and credit cards.

By Car
Parking
Vancouver's on-street **parking meters** ($1-6 per hour) operate from 9am to 10pm daily, including holidays. Rates vary by location. You can park at most metered spaces for up to two hours. Pay for parking using coins, credit cards, or the **Pay by Phone app** (604/909-7275, www.paybyphone.com).

You can also park at city-run parking garages and lots. Find these **EasyPark** (www.easypark.ca) locations and rates online, or look for their bright orange signs. EasyPark garages are usually less expensive than privately owned parking facilities.

Many residential neighborhoods, including the West End, Kitsilano, and Main Street, reserve some street parking for residents. Don't park in spaces marked "Parking by permit only," or you can be ticketed.

Car Rental
The major car rental companies have offices at Vancouver International Airport, including **Alamo** (604/231-1400 or 888/826-6893, www.alamo.ca), **Avis** (604/606-2847 or 800/230-4898, www.avis.ca), **Budget** (604/668-7000 or 800/268-8900, www.budget.ca), **Discount** (604/207-8140 or 800/263-2355, www.discountcar.com), **Dollar** (604/606-1656 or 800/800-6000, www.dollar.com), **Enterprise** (604/303-1117 or 800/261-7331, www.enterprise.com), **Hertz** (604/606-3700 or 800/654-3001, www.hertz.ca), **National** (604/273-6572 or 888/826-6890, www.nationalcar.ca), and **Thrifty** (604/207-7077 or 800/847-4389, www.thrifty.com). Most also have downtown locations.

Victoria and Vancouver Island

British Columbia's capital city mixes historic and hip, while the island's Pacific coast lures ocean-lovers with surf, sand, and rainforest trails.

WHISTLER

60 MI/100 KM
3.25 HOURS

14 MI/23 KM
2.25 HOURS

130 MI/210 KM
3 HOURS

NANAIMO

VANCOUVER

TOFINO

CANADA
UNITED STATES

75 MI/115 KM
1.75 HOURS

44 MI/70 KM
3 HOURS

VICTORIA

Vancouver Island

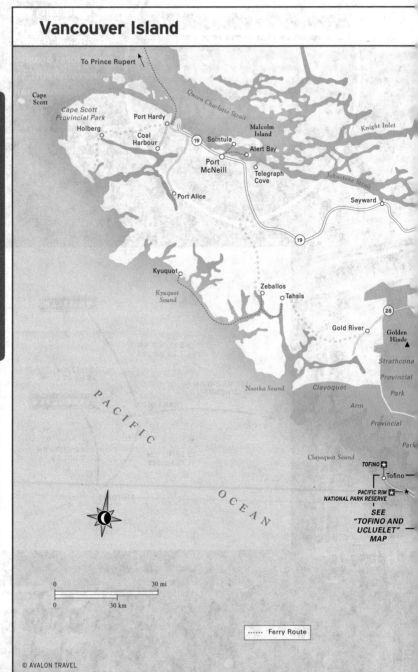

To Prince Rupert

Cape Scott

Cape Scott Provincial Park

Queen Charlotte Strait

Knight Inlet

Holberg

Port Hardy

Coal Harbour

19

Sointula

Malcolm Island

Alert Bay

Port McNeill

Telegraph Cove

Johnstone Strait

Port Alice

Sayward

19

Kyuquot

Kyuquot Sound

Zeballos

Tahsis

28

Gold River

Golden Hinde ▲

Strathcona Provincial Park

Nootka Sound

Clayoquot Arm

Provincial

Park

Clayoquot Sound

TOFINO ✚

Tofino

PACIFIC RIM NATIONAL PARK RESERVE ✚

★

SEE "TOFINO AND UCLUELET" MAP

PACIFIC

OCEAN

0 ___ 30 mi

0 ___ 30 km

······ Ferry Route

© AVALON TRAVEL

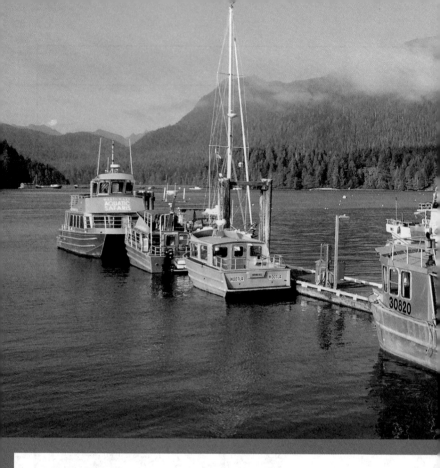

Highlights

★ **Victoria's Inner Harbour:** Buskers, ferries, floatplanes, and travelers all converge on Victoria's waterfront, where the city's major sights are located (page 97).

★ **Royal British Columbia Museum:** Trace British Columbia's roots at this museum of cultural and natural history (page 97).

★ **Butchart Gardens:** Elaborate floral displays and holiday lights make these gardens one of Vancouver Island's most popular year-round attractions (page 109).

★ **Whale-Watching:** You may spot orcas, humpbacks, or gray whales from the whale-watching boats that depart from Victoria (page 112).

★ **Snorkeling with Seals:** Suit up and snorkel up close with harbor seals on this unique half-day adventure from Nanaimo (page 121).

★ **Pacific Rim National Park Reserve:** Explore the rainforest and beaches in this lush oceanfront national park (page 124).

★ **Tofino:** This funky town on Vancouver Island's far west coast has beautiful beaches, great restaurants, and a chill surfer vibe, plus lots of on-the-water excursions (page 126).

Vancouver Island offers lots of ways to relax, from enjoying a cup of tea or a glass of wine to snorkeling with seals, watching whales, and catching waves.

British Columbia's capital city, Victoria, is located at the southern tip of Vancouver Island, across the Strait of Georgia from the city of Vancouver. You can easily spend a day or more taking in the sights along the Inner Harbour, venturing offshore for a whale watch, or enjoying traditional afternoon tea. A boom in contemporary restaurants, craft breweries, and cool cocktail bars means that you'll eat and drink well, too. Just outside of Victoria, the Cowichan Valley is a growing wine region, where you can sip and sample what's new at the winery tasting rooms.

North of Victoria, Nanaimo is an alternate ferry port between Vancouver and the island; it's the most convenient route between Vancouver and Tofino on the island's west coast. Besides an attractive waterfront and historic attractions, Nanaimo is worth a stop for a unique adventure: snorkeling with a colony of seals who live near the city's harbor. Be sure to sample a sweet Nanaimo bar, too.

Vancouver Island's striking west coast is the region's ocean playground. You can explore the beaches and rainforest trails in the Pacific Rim National Park Reserve, and unwind in the sand-and-surf communities of Tofino and Ucluelet. Day-trip to a remote hot springs, kayak to a First Nations island, or go on a whale- or bear-watching excursion. Oceanfront resorts and fine casual restaurants (seafood is a specialty) keep you comfortable when you come in from the sea.

Getting to Victoria and Vancouver Island

Driving from Vancouver (via Ferry)

B.C. Ferries (888/223-3779, www.bcferries.com) provides frequent service between the Vancouver metropolitan area on the mainland and Vancouver Island. Ferries transport foot passengers, bicycles, cars, trucks, and recreational vehicles. Reservations ($15 at least 7 days in advance, $18.50 1-6 days in advance, $22 same-day travel) are recommended for vehicles, particularly if you're traveling on summer weekends or during holiday periods. Reservations are not available for walk-on passengers or bicycles.

The two ferry docks of metropolitan Vancouver are both outside the city center. The **Tsawwassen Terminal** (1 Ferry Causeway, Delta), the departure point for ferries to Victoria, is 24 miles (38 kilometers) south of Vancouver. The **Horseshoe Bay Terminal** (6750 Keith Rd., West Vancouver), where ferries leave for Nanaimo, is on the North Shore, 12 miles (20 kilometers) northwest of downtown; if you're heading for Tofino or Ucluelet on the island's west coast, the most direct route is to take the ferry from Horseshoe Bay to Nanaimo and continue west from there.

Watch your speed approaching the ferry terminals on both the mainland and the island. Speed limits drop suddenly, and police frequently ticket unwary motorists.

To Victoria

Take the **Tsawwassen-Swartz Bay Ferry** (one-way adults $16.90, ages 5-11 $8.45, cars $55.40, bikes $2) to travel between Vancouver and Victoria. The ferry ride is **one hour and 35 minutes.**

To drive from **Vancouver to Tsawwassen,** head south on **Oak Street,** following the signs for **Highway 99**

Best Hotels

★ **Abbeymore Manor B&B:** This 1912 Victorian home houses the city's friendliest B&B (page 113).

★ **Fairmont Empress:** Victoria's grand hotel overlooking the Inner Harbour has been welcoming guests, and serving traditional afternoon tea, since the early 1900s (page 114).

★ **Magnolia Hotel & Spa:** Catering to both business and leisure travelers, this well-run boutique property is convenient to Victoria's harbor and downtown sights (page 114).

★ **Oak Bay Beach Hotel:** The lovely seaside swimming pool is reason enough to stay at this Victoria resort. The contemporary ocean-view rooms are a bonus (page 114).

★ **BriMar Bed & Breakfast:** Recipe for a west coast holiday: Mix three spacious guest rooms on Tofino's Chesterman Beach with a helpful host and hearty breakfasts (page 132).

★ **Wickaninnish Inn:** Overlooking the surf in Tofino, this rustic yet elegant, art-filled inn is Vancouver Island's most deluxe beach getaway spot (page 133).

★ **Wya Point Resort:** The Ucluelet First Nation runs this unique west coast property where the wood-frame cottages, decorated with works by native carvers, sit on a remote ocean cove (page 136).

---

south, and cross the **Oak Street Bridge** into Richmond. Stay on Highway 99 through the **George Massey Tunnel.** Exit onto **Highway 17** south toward the Tsawwassen ferry terminal. Allow about **45 minutes** to drive from downtown Vancouver to Tsawwassen, with extra time during the morning and evening rush hours.

From late June through early September, ferries between Tsawwassen and Swartz Bay generally run every hour between 7am and 9pm daily, and every two hours the rest of the year; however, there are frequent variations, so check the B.C. Ferries website (www. bcferries.com) for the schedule before you travel.

The **Swartz Bay Terminal** (Highway 17) is 20 miles (32 kilometers) north of Victoria at the end of **Highway 17,** about a **30-minute** drive. After you exit the ferry at Swartz Bay, follow Highway 17 south, which goes directly into downtown Victoria, where it becomes Blanshard Street.

To Nanaimo
Via Horseshoe Bay

The most direct route between Vancouver and Nanaimo is to take the **Horseshoe Bay-Departure Bay Ferry** (one-way adults $16.90, ages 5-11 $8.45, cars $55.40, bikes $2). The ferry ride is **one hour and 40 minutes.**

From downtown **Vancouver to Horseshoe Bay,** take **West Georgia Street** to the **Lions Gate Bridge.** Watch the signs carefully as you approach Stanley Park en route to the bridge to stay in the proper lane. The center lane on the three-lane bridge reverses its travel direction at different times of the day, typically creating two travel lanes into the city in the morning and two travel lanes toward the North Shore during the afternoon rush hour.

After you cross the Lions Gate Bridge, bear left toward Marine Drive west/ Highway 1/Highway 99. Enter **Marine Drive** and stay in the far right lane to take the first right onto **Taylor Way** (the sign says "Whistler"). Follow Taylor Way up the hill, and exit left onto **Highway 1**

Best Restaurants

★ **OLO:** Local ingredients star on the always-changing menu at this stylish yet casual Chinatown restaurant, one of Victoria's most inventive eateries (page 117).

★ **Little Jumbo:** Victoria's cocktail connoisseurs find their way to this speakeasy-style joint hidden at the end of a hallway, where the kitchen is as creative as the bar (page 117).

★ **Brasserie L'Ecole:** A warm welcome and updated French bistro fare have made this edge-of-Chinatown eatery a long-standing Victoria favorite (page 118).

★ **Zambri's:** This sleek dining room serves modern Italian cuisine in Victoria's equally modern Atrium Building (page 118).

★ **Bistro at Westwood Lake:** Why dine at a Nanaimo tennis club? For fine contemporary dishes, gracious service, and serene lake views (page 122).

★ **The Wolf in the Fog:** Oysters in a potato web? The west coast's most imaginative dishes come from the open kitchen at this relaxed Tofino dining spot (page 134).

★ **The Pointe at the Wickaninnish Inn:** The crashing Pacific waves provide the backdrop for fresh seafood and an extensive wine list at Tofino's most romantic dining room (page 134).

west. Continue on Highway 1 to the ferry terminal. The drive from downtown to Horseshoe Bay generally takes about **30 minutes,** but allow extra time during the morning and afternoon commute times.

From late June through early September, ferries between Horseshoe Bay and Departure Bay generally make eight or nine trips daily, with six or seven daily runs the rest of the year; check the B.C. Ferries website (www.bcferries.com) for the seasonal schedule.

The **Departure Bay Terminal** (680 Trans-Canada Hwy., Nanaimo) is two miles (3 kilometers) north of downtown Nanaimo.

Via Tsawwassen

Another route between the mainland and Nanaimo is the **Tsawwassen-Duke Point Ferry** (one-way adults $16.90, ages 5-11 $8.45, cars $55.40, bikes $2). The ferry ride is **two hours.** Ferries run 6 to 8 times per day. Consider this route if you are traveling to the Nanaimo area from points south of Vancouver.

The **Duke Point Terminal** (400 Duke Point Hwy., Nanaimo) is off Highway 1, nine miles (16 kilometers) south of downtown Nanaimo.

To Tofino and Ucluelet

A road trip from **Vancouver to Tofino** involves taking a ferry from the mainland to Nanaimo, and then driving west across the island; allow **six hours** to make the journey.

From Vancouver, drive northwest to the Horseshoe Bay Ferry Terminal and take the **Horseshoe Bay-Departure Bay Ferry** to Nanaimo.

Although the drive from **Nanaimo to Tofino** is just **130 miles (210 kilometers),** it takes at least **three hours,** longer if you stop to sightsee en route. When you exit the Departure Bay ferry terminal, follow the signs to **Highway 19/Parksville.** Just past Parksville, exit onto **Highway 4** westbound toward Port Alberni. **Check your gas;** there are no gas stations between Port Alberni and the Pacific coast.

Highway 4 winds its way across the island, over and around the mountains that form the island's spine. At several points, the road becomes quite narrow and curvy; don't be in a rush to make this trip. If you find that a line of impatient drivers is forming behind you, use one of the pullouts to move over and allow them to pass.

Highway 4 comes to a T at the **Tofino-Ucluelet junction.** Turn right (north) onto the Pacific Rim Highway toward Tofino; it's 20 miles (32 kilometers) from the junction into town. Make a left if you're going to Ucluelet, which is five miles (9 kilometers) south of the junction.

Driving from Whistler (via Ferry)
Via Horseshoe Bay

If you're traveling between Whistler and Vancouver Island, you don't have to go through the city of Vancouver. You can take the **B.C. Ferries** (888/223-3779, www.bcferries.com) service from Horseshoe Bay to Nanaimo's Departure Bay terminal.

To get from **Whistler to Horseshoe Bay,** follow **Highway 99** south **60 miles (100 kilometers).** Allow about **75 to 90 minutes** for the drive.

The **ferry to Departure Bay is one hour and 40 minutes.** The **Departure Bay Terminal** (680 Trans-Canada Hwy., Nanaimo) is two miles (3 kilometers) north of downtown Nanaimo.

From Departure Bay, it's **75 miles (115 kilometers)** south to **Victoria** via **Highway 1,** which takes **1.75 hours,** and **130 miles (210 kilometers)** west to **Tofino,** via **Highways 19 and 4,** a **three-hour** drive.

Via Tsawwassen

If you want to go directly from Whistler to Victoria, another option is to drive through Vancouver to the Tsawwassen Terminal. You have to allow time to navigate Vancouver's traffic, but the overall travel time is similar to traveling from Horseshoe Bay.

From **Whistler to Tsawwassen,** follow **Highway 99** south to **Highway 1** east and take Exit 13, **Taylor Way,** toward Vancouver. At the foot of the hill, turn left onto **Marine Drive,** then bear right onto the **Lions Gate Bridge.** Many lanes merge onto the bridge here, so be prepared for delays. Once you've crossed the bridge, continue on **West Georgia Street** in downtown Vancouver, and turn right onto **Howe Street,** following the signs for Highway 99. Howe Street will take you over the **Granville Bridge** and onto **Granville Street.** At West 59th Avenue, turn left onto **Park Drive** and then right onto **Oak Street.** Continue across the **Oak Street Bridge** into Richmond and onto **Highway 99.** After you pass through the **George Massey Tunnel,** exit onto **Highway 17** toward Tsawwassen. This route between Whistler and Tsawwassen is **105 miles (165 kilometers)** and should take you **2.5 hours,** but allow extra time for traffic or for a stop downtown.

Getting There by Air

The fastest way to travel between Vancouver and Victoria or Nanaimo is by floatplane or helicopter. Both take off and land from the city centers, making this option convenient for a car-free day trip. It's more expensive than taking the ferry, but the scenery over the Gulf Islands and Strait of Georgia is impressive. Check the carriers' websites for schedules and occasional fare discounts. It's also possible to fly from Vancouver or Victoria to Tofino.

If you're coming from farther away, you can fly to Victoria's international airport from a number of U.S. and Canadian cities.

By Air to Victoria

Harbour Air (604/274-1277 or 800/665-0212, www.harbourair.com, 35 minutes, one-way adults $210) flies frequently throughout the day between the **Vancouver Harbour Flight Centre** (1055 Canada Pl., behind the Vancouver Convention Centre, 604/274-1277) and the **Victoria Inner Harbour Centre** (1000 Wharf St., 250/384-2215).

Helijet (800/665-4354, www.helijet. com, 35 minutes, one-way adults $199, seniors $157) departs frequently throughout the day between **Vancouver Harbour Heliport** (455 Waterfront Rd., near Waterfront Station, 604/688-4646) and **Victoria Harbour Heliport** (79 Dallas Rd., 250/386-7676), between the Ogden Point Cruise Ship Terminal and Fisherman's Wharf. One child (ages 2-11) flies free with each adult; additional one-way children's fares are $79.

A number of airlines serve **Victoria International Airport** (YYJ, 1640 Electra Blvd., Sidney, 250/953-7533, www.victoriaairport.com), which is north of downtown. **Air Canada** (www.aircanada.com) flies between Victoria and Vancouver, Calgary, Toronto, or San Francisco. **WestJet** (www.westjet.com) has flights between Victoria and Calgary, Edmonton, Kelowna (B.C.), Las Vegas, and Phoenix. **Alaska Air** (www.alaskaair.com) makes the quick hop between Victoria and Seattle.

By Air to Nanaimo
Harbour Air (604/274-1277 or 800/665-0212, www.harbourair.com, 20 minutes, one-way adults $105) flies regularly between the **Vancouver Harbour Flight Centre** (1055 Canada Pl., 604/274-1277) and Nanaimo's **Pioneer Waterfront Plaza** (90 Front St., 250/714-0900).

Helijet (800/665-4354, www.helijet.com, 20 minutes, one-way adults $109, seniors $97) buzzes across the water Monday through Friday between **Vancouver Harbour Heliport** (455 Waterfront Rd., near Waterfront Station, 604/688-4646) and **Nanaimo Harbour Heliport** (Port of Nanaimo Welcome Centre, 100 Port Dr.). One child (ages 2-11) flies free with each adult; additional one-way children's fares are $79.

By Air to Tofino
The **Tofino-Long Beach Airport** (YAZ, Pacific Rim Highway, www.tofinoairport.com) is seven miles (11 kilometers) southeast of the town of Tofino and 18 miles (30 kilometers) northeast of Ucluelet.

Orca Airways (888/359-6722, www.flyorcaair.com) has regular flights to Tofino from the **South Terminal at Vancouver International Airport** (5220 Airport Rd. S., Richmond, www.yvr.ca, year-round, one hour, one-way adults $175-220) and from the **Victoria International Airport** (1640 Electra Blvd., Sidney, 250/953-7533, www.victoriaairport.com, mid-May-mid-Oct., one hour, one-way adults $225-270).

KD Air (800/665-4244, www.kdair. com, one-way adults $175-190) also flies between Vancouver's South Terminal and Tofino.

Getting There by Bus and Ferry
To travel between Vancouver to Victoria without your own car (and without splurging on a flight), the easiest option is to take a direct bus service that picks up passengers at several points downtown, takes you onto the ferry, and continues into downtown Victoria.

It's also possible to reach the island ferries by public transportation in Vancouver, Victoria, and Nanaimo. Although you'll need to allow more time, you'll also save some cash.

There's a bus-ferry-bus combination that will get you to Tofino from Vancouver, but it's not a very fast route. Buses also run to Tofino from Nanaimo's Departure Bay Ferry Terminal, where the ferries from Vancouver arrive, and from downtown Victoria.

By Direct Bus to Victoria
BC Ferries Connector (604/428-9474 or 888/788-8840, www.bcfconnector.com, one-way bus adults $44.95, seniors or B.C. resident adults $31.20, students $25.25, ages 5-11 $22.48), operated by Wilson's Transportation, transports passengers between downtown Vancouver and downtown Victoria. The bus takes you to the Tsawwassen Ferry Terminal and drives onto the ferry. At Swartz Bay,

you reboard the bus and travel to downtown Victoria. Trips depart several times daily in each direction, and reservations are required; the entire trip takes about four hours.

In Vancouver, the BC Ferries Connector bus originates at **Pacific Central Station** (1150 Station St.). For a slightly higher fare (one-way bus adults $49.95, seniors or B.C. resident adults $38.20, students $30.25, ages 5-11 $24.98), you can schedule a pickup from many downtown Vancouver hotels. In Victoria, the coach takes you to the **Victoria Bus Station** (700 Douglas St.), behind the Fairmont Empress Hotel, one block from the Inner Harbour.

The BC Ferries Connector fare does not include a ferry ticket (one-way adults $16.90, ages 5-11 $8.45), which you must purchase in addition to your bus ticket.

By Public Transit to Victoria

If you don't have a lot of luggage, it's possible to take public transit between downtown Vancouver and the Tsawwassen Ferry Terminal and from the Swartz Bay Ferry Terminal to downtown Victoria. It's much cheaper than the BC Ferries Connector option, but it takes a little longer.

In Vancouver, take the **Canada Line** to Bridgeport Station, where you change to **bus 620 for Tsawwassen Ferry** (www.translink.ca, one-way adults $5.50, seniors, students, and ages 5-13 $3.75). The total trip takes about an hour.

After taking the **Tsawwassen-Swartz Bay Ferry** (www.bcferries.com, 1 hour and 35 minutes, one-way adults $16.90, ages 5-11 $8.45), catch **B.C. Transit bus 70 for Swartz Bay/Downtown Express** (www.bctransit.com/victoria, 50 minutes, one-way $2.50 pp) to downtown Victoria.

By Public Transit to Nanaimo

From downtown Vancouver, **bus 257 for Horseshoe Bay Express** (www.translink.ca, 45 minutes, one-way adults $4, seniors, students, and ages 5-13 $2.75) runs to the Horseshoe Bay Ferry Terminal from several stops along West Georgia Street. The slightly slower **bus 250 for Horseshoe Bay** (www.translink.ca, 55 minutes, one-way adults $4, seniors, students, and ages 5-13 $2.75) follows a similar route. Alternatively, **Greyhound** (www.greyhound.ca) operates several buses daily to the Horseshoe Bay Ferry Terminal from **Pacific Central Station** (1150 Station St., 45 minutes, adults $5.05-15.20).

After taking the **Horseshoe Bay-Departure Bay Ferry** (www.bcferries.com, 1 hour and 40 minutes, one-way adults $16.90, ages 5-11 $8.45), catch **B.C. Transit bus 2** (www.bctransit.com/nanaimo, 20 minutes, one-way adults $2.50, seniors, students, and ages 5-11 $2.25) from the Departure Bay Ferry Terminal to downtown Nanaimo.

By Bus to Tofino

Tofino Bus (250/725-2871 or 866/986-3466, www.tofinobus.com) can take you to Tofino starting from Vancouver's **Pacific Central Station** (1150 Station St., 7.5 hours, adults $62, seniors and students $56, ages 2-11 $46). This route runs in partnership with Greyhound, which provides bus service from Vancouver to Horseshoe Bay, where you board the Horseshoe Bay-Departure Bay Ferry to Nanaimo. After arriving at the Nanaimo ferry terminal, you transfer to the Tofino Bus to the west coast. You must purchase a ferry ticket in addition to the bus fare.

Tofino Bus can also take you to Tofino from **Nanaimo's Departure Bay Ferry Terminal** (4 hours, adults $46, seniors and students $42, ages 2-11 $23) and from downtown **Victoria** (6.5 hours, adults $69, seniors and students $62, ages 2-11 $36).

Victoria

The British Empire lived long and prospered in British Columbia's capital city,

Victoria. British explorer James Cook became the first non-aboriginal person to set foot in what is now British Columbia, when he landed on Vancouver Island's west coast in 1778. Sixty-five years later, the Hudson's Bay Company established a trading post on the island's southeastern corner, naming it Fort Victoria, after the British queen.

Victoria is still known for its British traditions, particularly elegant afternoon tea, and as Canada's warmest region, Victoria has been a popular destination for retirees. These days, though, Victoria has shed its reputation as a destination for "the newly wed and the nearly dead." It's an increasingly modern, multicultural community that's drawing entrepreneurs, passionate foodies, and other independent types, with cultural attractions, vibrant restaurants, and plenty to do in the mild outdoors.

Sights
Downtown
★ Victoria's Inner Harbour
Victoria's harbor is the center of activity downtown, with ferries and floatplanes coming and going, buskers busking, and plenty of tourists soaking up the scene and the sun. Many companies offering whale-watching tours and other water-based excursions have their offices along the waterside promenade, and **Tourism Victoria** (812 Wharf St., 250/953-2033, www.tourismvictoria.com, 9am-5pm daily) runs a visitor information center here, with public restrooms.

Victoria Harbour Ferry (250/708-0201, www.victoriaharbourferry.com) operates a **water taxi** (11am-5pm daily Mar. and Oct., 11am-7pm daily Apr.-mid-May, 10am-9pm daily mid-May-mid-Sept.) around the Inner Harbour in cute colorful boats, with stops at Fisherman's Wharf, the Delta Victoria Ocean Pointe Resort, and many other waterside points. Fares vary by distance; a basic one-zone trip, which includes many Inner Harbour points, is $5 pp. They also offer 45-minute

harbor tours (11am-5pm daily Mar. and Oct., 11am-7pm daily Apr.-mid-May, 10am-9pm daily mid-May-mid-Sept., adults $25, seniors and students $23, under age 13 $13, families $60), departing every 20 minutes from the Causeway Marina in front of the Fairmont Empress Hotel.

Fairmont Empress Hotel
A landmark on the Inner Harbour, the **Fairmont Empress** (721 Government St., 250/384-8111, www.fairmont.com) has cast its grand ivy-covered visage across Victoria's waterfront since 1908. Architect Francis M. Rattenbury designed and built the hotel as one of the Canadian Pacific Railway's majestic château-style lodgings. British royals have slept here, including Prince Charles and Camilla in 2009, as have U.S. presidents and numerous celebrities, including Katharine Hepburn, Bob Hope, John Travolta, Harrison Ford, and Barbra Streisand.

Even if you're not staying at the Empress, you can walk through its public spaces, dine in its restaurants and lounges, or take afternoon tea (a Victoria tradition). On the front lawn, check out the beehives where Fairmont staff harvest honey to use in the property's kitchen.

Walkabouts Historical Tours (www.walkabouts.ca) offers 90-minute historic tours of the Empress (10am daily mid-May-mid-Oct., adults $13, ages 6-12 $6.50). The entertaining costumed guides tell you about the building's heritage and the colorful characters who resided in the hotel over the years. Reserve your tour in person or by phone at the Fairmont Empress Dining Reservations Desk (250/995-4688).

★ Royal British Columbia Museum
Tracing British Columbia's cultural and natural history, the **Royal British Columbia Museum** (675 Belleville St., 250/356-7226, http://royalbcmuseum.bc.ca, 10am-5pm daily late Sept.-late

Victoria

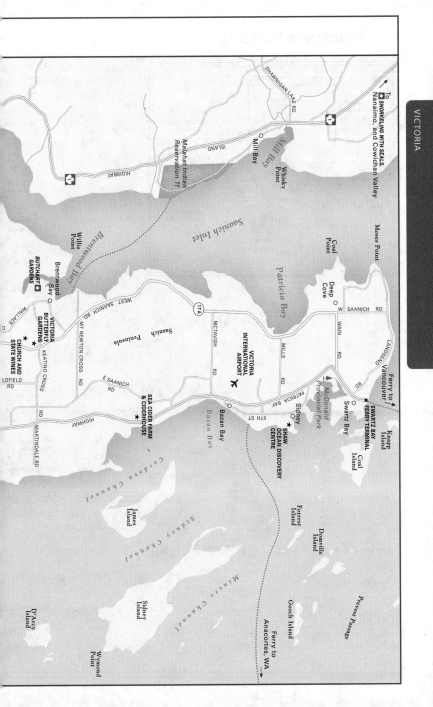

To **SNORKELING WITH SEALS,** Nanaimo, and Cowichan Valley

SHAWNIGAN LAKE RD

Malahat Indian Reservation 11

ISLAND

HIGHWAY

Mill Bay

Whisky Point

Willis Point

Brentwood Bay

Saanich Inlet

Moses Point

Coal Point

Deep Cove

Patricia Bay

BUTCHART GARDENS

Brentwood Bay

WALLACE

VICTORIA BUTTERFLY GARDENS

WEST SAANICH RD

MT NEWTON CROSS RD

Saanich Peninsula

MCTAVISH RD

17A

MILLS RD

W SAANICH RD

WAIN RD

LANGSDON RD

Ferry to Vancouver

Knapp Island

CHURCH AND STATE WINES

KEATING CROSS RD

VICTORIA INTERNATIONAL AIRPORT

Coal Island

OLDFIELD RD

E SAANICH RD

MARTINDALE RD

HIGHWAY

SEA CIDER FARM & CIDERHOUSE

Bazan Bay

5TH ST

McDonald Provincial Park

Sidney

PATRICIA BAY

SHAW OCEAN DISCOVERY CENTRE

Swartz Bay

SWARTZ BAY FERRY TERMINAL

Cordova Channel

James Island

Sidney Channel

Bazan Bay

Forrest Island

Domville Island

Prevost Passage

D'Arcy Island

Sidney Island

Miners Channel

Gooch Island

Ferry to Anacortes, WA

Wymond Point

Downtown Victoria

ESQUIMALT RD

MAP AREA

★ PHILLIPS BEER

★ SPINNAKERS GASTRO BREWPUB

Victoria Harbour

GOVERNMENT ST
DOUGLAS ST
BLANSHARD ST

JOHNSON ST
YATES ST

★ CRAIGDARROCH CASTLE

SUPERIOR ST
SIMCOE ST
OSWEGO ST

ART GALLERY OF GREATER VICTORIA ★

VICTORIA HARBOUR HELIPORT

ST

DALLAS RD

● BEACONSFIELD INN

★ EMILY CARR HOUSE

Beacon Hill Park

FAIRFIELD RD
COOK ST
MOSS ST

ABBEYMOORE MANOR B&B

VILLA MARCO POLO INN

Ogden Point Breakwall

Holland Point

★ BEACON HILL CHILDREN'S FARM

ROSS BAY CEMETERY ★

Juan de Fuca Strait

Finlayson Point

Clover Point

JOHNSON ST BRIDGE

STORE ST

CHINATOWN

SWIFT ST

OLO ▼

SWANS BREWPUB ★

Market Square

STORE ST
WHARF ST
WADDINGTON

0 ———————— 200 yds
0 ———————— 200 m

KIMTA RD

SONGHEES RD

Victoria   Harbour

Laurel Point

Centennial Park

Inner Harbour

RED FISH BLUE FISH ▼

VICTORIA INNER HARBOUR CENTRE

ORCA SPIRIT ADVENTURES ■

WHALE-WATCHING ★

FISHERMAN'S WHARF/ BARB'S FISH 'N' CHIPS ★

■ EAGLE WING TOURS

■ ORCA SPIRIT ADVENTURES

KINGSTON ST

SUPERIOR ST

INN AT LAUREL POINT

QUEBEC ST

MONTREAL ST
KINGSTON ST
PENDRAY ST

BELLEVILLE ST

Quadra Park

ROBERT BATEMAN CENTRE ★

OSWEGO ST

QUEBEC ST

OSWEGO HOTEL ●

© AVALON TRAVEL

JAM CAFÉ ▼

HERALD ST

BRASSERIE
L'ECOLE ▼

VICTORIA
PUBLIC MARKET ▼

BALMORAL ST

DOUGLAS ST

BLANSHARD ST

QUADRA ST

VENUS SOPHIA
TEA ROOM &
VEGETARIAN EATERY ▼

FISGARD ST

★ GATE OF
HARMONIOUS INTEREST

SILK ROAD
TEA ■

FAN TAN ALLEY

FAN TAN ★
ALLEY

PANDORA ST

Centennial
Square

CORMORANT ST

MASON ST

PANDORA ST

STILL LIFE
FOR HIM ■

BAGGINS
SHOES

STILL LIFE
FOR HER ■

MEC ■

SUASION ■

LULULEMON ■

JOHNSON ST

JOHNSON ST

SMOKING
LILY ■

GOVERNMENT ST

LEGACY
ART GALLERY
DOWNTOWN ★

BROAD ST

DOUGLAS ST

BLANSHARD ST

PIG BBQ ▼
JOINT

HEAD OVER HEELS ■

ZAMBRI'S ▼

YATES ST

YATES ST

ALLEY

LANGLEY ST

REBAR ▼

TROUNCE ALLEY

VIEW ST

FOO ▼
ASIAN STREET
FOOD

VIEW ST

THE MARKET
ON YATES ▼

To
Café Brio
→

SPRINGTIDE
WHALE WATCHING ■

LITTLE
JUMBO ▼

MUNRO'S
BOOKS ■

FORT ST

NORTH 48 ▼

BROAD ST

CHOUX CHOUX
CHARCUTERIE ▼

FORT ST

CHORIZO & CO. ▼

QUADRA ST

CHOCOLAT, CHOCOLATIERE
DE VICTORIA ▼

FISHHOOK ▼

BE LOVE ▼

BROUGHTON ST

GORDON ST

BROUGHTON ST

Pioneer
Square

COURTNEY ST

MAGNOLIA ●
HOTEL & SPA ★

VICTORIA
BUG ZOO ★

COURTNEY ST

TOURISM VICTORIA
INFORMATION CENTRE ■

HUMBOLDT ST

BURDETT AVE

PRINCE OF
WHALES ■

GOVERNMENT ST

FAIRMONT
EMPRESS
HOTEL ★

FAIRFIELD RD

RUPERT TERR

VICTORIA'S
INNER HARBOUR ✚

HUMBOLDT ST

THE PEDALER ■

TRE ▼
FANTASTICO

LE PETIT ▼
DAKAR

VICTORIA
BUS STATION ■

BELLEVILLE ST

DOUGLAS ST

BLANSHARD ST

QUADRA ST

To
Beaconsfield
Inn

BRITISH COLUMBIA
PARLIAMENT BUILDING ★

ROYAL BRITISH ✚
COLUMBIA MUSEUM

Thunderbird
Park

Beacon Hill Park

HELMCKEN ★
HOUSE

May, 10am-5pm Sun.-Thurs., 10am-10pm Fri.-Sat. late May-late Sept., adults $23, seniors, students, and ages 6-18 $17, families $72) was founded in 1886. A highlight is the First Peoples Gallery, with totem poles, masks, regalia, and other indigenous objects, along with exhibits that illuminate the lives of Canada's first inhabitants.

You can take a one-hour **guided tour** (included with museum admission); check the calendar on the museum's website or in the lobby for tour times and topics. To spread out your museum meanderings over two consecutive days, buy a discounted **two-day ticket** (adults $34.50, seniors, students, and ages 6-18 $25.50, families $108).

The museum has an **IMAX Theatre** (IMAX only adults $11.95, seniors and ages 6-18 $9.75, students $10.75, with museum admission adults $32.95, seniors and ages 6-18 $26.75, students $27.75), showing a changing selection of movies on the big screen.

Adjacent to the museum, several totem poles stand in **Thunderbird Park.** Also outside is the 1852 **Helmcken House,** the oldest public building in B.C. still on its original site; the Hudson's Bay Company built the cabin for Dr. John Sebastian Helmcken and his wife, Cecilia Douglas. A physician and politician, Helmcken helped bring B.C. into the Canadian Confederation, though he allegedly once said that Canada would eventually be absorbed into the United States.

B.C. Parliament Building

Although Vancouver, on the mainland, is a much larger city, Victoria has been the provincial capital since British Columbia joined the Canadian Confederation in 1871. The seat of the provincial government is the B.C. Legislative Assembly, which convenes

Top to bottom: Victoria's Inner Harbour; totem pole at the Royal British Columbia Museum; marching band at the B.C. Parliament Building.

One Day in Victoria

Catch an early-morning ferry from Vancouver to Swartz Bay and head straight for the **Butchart Gardens** to wander the blossom-lined paths. When you've had your fill of flowers, drive to downtown Victoria and get oriented with a quick stroll around the **Inner Harbour.** Continue up Government Street to the narrow lanes of **Chinatown,** then browse the boutiques along Lower Johnson Street.

Wander into the grand **Fairmont Empress** for a glimpse of the city's Victorian past; for the full Empress experience, book **afternoon tea** in the hotel's elegant tea room. Or if you'd rather a more contemporary lunch, **Zambri's** serves fine Italian fare.

After lunch, visit the **Royal British** Columbia Museum to learn more about the region's cultural and natural history, take a short tour of the **Parliament Building,** or stop into the **Robert Bateman Centre** to explore the work of this noted B.C. artist. If you'd prefer an outdoor adventure, go **whale-watching;** plenty of tour boats depart from the Inner Harbour.

Unwind over drinks in one of Victoria's lounges, or do a beer crawl to sample the city's **craft breweries.** Then enjoy dinner at **Brasserie L'Ecole** if you're in the mood for a French bistro experience or **OLO** if you prefer more adventurous cuisine paired with creative cocktails.

After dinner, settle into your hotel or take the late ferry back to Vancouver, after your very full Victoria day.

---

in the stately 1897 **Parliament Building** (501 Belleville St., 250/387-8669, tour information 250/387-3046, www.leg.bc.ca, tours 9am-5pm daily mid-May-early Sept., 9am-5pm Mon.-Fri. early-Sept.-mid-May, free), overlooking the Inner Harbour.

Thousands of twinkling white lights illuminate the Parliament Building, making the copper-roofed stone structure even more photogenic at night than it is during the day. British-born architect Francis M. Rattenbury (1867-1935) designed the building, winning a design competition and his first major commission less than a year after he arrived in B.C. from England at age 25.

On 30- to 45-minute tours of the grand building, you'll learn more about the province's history and governmental operations. In the legislative chambers, for example, desks are set two sword-lengths apart so that no one would get injured during the years when members of parliament carried swords.

Other notable features include a cedar canoe in the rotunda that Steven L. Point, the first aboriginal Lieutenant Governor

of British Columbia, carved in 2010, and stained glass work commemorating Queen Victoria's diamond jubilee.

Tours are free, but **reservations are required.** Book your tour at the tour information kiosk, which is outside the building during the summer season and inside the main entrance fall through spring. On weekdays, visitors can also explore the building on their own (9am-5pm Mon.-Fri.).

Robert Bateman Centre

Artist and naturalist Robert Bateman is a notable Canadian wildlife painter. Born in Ontario in 1930, he made an epic round-the-world journey in a Land Rover before returning to Canada to teach and paint, eventually relocating to B.C.'s Salt Spring Island. View his paintings and learn more about his interesting life at the **Robert Bateman Centre** (470 Belleville St., 250/940-3630, http://batemancentre.org, 10am-9pm daily June-Sept., 10am-5pm daily Oct.-May, adult $12.50, seniors and students $8.50, ages 6-18 $6, families $25), in the 1924 beaux arts Steamship Terminal on the Inner Harbour.

Two Scandals and a Murder

Architect Francis Mawson Rattenbury became one of British Columbia's most notable architects at the turn of the 20th century, designing Victoria's Parliament Building, the Empress Hotel, and the Vancouver Court House, which now houses the Vancouver Art Gallery. Yet Rattenbury became enmeshed in two marital scandals that tarnished his reputation and eventually led to his grisly murder.

In 1898, not long after he completed work on the Parliament Building, Rattenbury married Florence Nunn, and they had two children. However, as his professional stature grew, his personal life deteriorated, and by the early 1920s, he and Florence were living in different sections of their Oak Bay home, communicating only through their daughter.

At a reception at the Empress Hotel in 1923, Rattenbury met a young musician, Alma Pakenham, nearly 30 years his junior, and they began a very public affair. Florence initially refused Rattenbury's request for a divorce, agreeing only after he moved Alma into their home, where Florence still lived.

Rattenbury's indiscrete behavior scandalized Victoria society. Even after he and Alma married in 1925, they were never accepted in the community.

In 1929, they moved to England to start fresh. Instead, they became embroiled in another scandal. Rattenbury had begun drinking, and when they settled in England, his alcoholism worsened, triggering depression and, reportedly, impotence. After they hired 18-year-old George Stoner as a chauffeur, Alma began an affair with the teenager.

Apparently jealous that Alma had any relationship at all with her husband, Stoner attacked Rattenbury in their home, hitting him repeatedly on the head with a mallet. When Rattenbury died not long after the attack, both Alma and Stoner were charged with murder.

After a public trial at London's Old Bailey that mesmerized the city, Alma was found innocent and Stoner guilty, sentenced to die by hanging. Four days later, apparently distraught by the scandal and by her lover's sentence, Alma committed suicide by stabbing herself to death.

Despite the trail's verdict, Alma became the villain in the court of public opinion, accused of corrupting an innocent boy. Stoner's death sentence was commuted to life in prison.

For the murder of the eminent B.C. architect whose life deteriorated into scandal, George Stoner served only seven years in jail.

Victoria Bug Zoo

If you're not afraid of ants, tarantulas, and other crawling, flying, or wriggling insects, visit this fascinating little museum devoted to the world of bugs. The **Victoria Bug Zoo** (631 Courtney St., 250/384-2847, www.victoriabugzoo.ca, 10am-5pm Mon.-Thurs., 10am-6pm Fri.-Sun., adults $10, seniors $9, ages 11-18 $8, ages 3-10 $7) houses more than 40 insect species, as well as Canada's largest ant colony, which you can view through a clear wall. Guides are on hand to share fun bug facts.

Fisherman's Wharf

Can you imagine yourself living on the water? With your house *in* the water? The residents of the 30 compact floating houses in the Float Home Village at **Fisherman's Wharf** (1 Dallas Rd., www.fishermanswharfvictoria.com) do just that. Wander the docks and envision life in this colorful waterfront community; these are private homes, though, so do respect residents' privacy.

Fisherman's Wharf has several outdoor eateries, including ever-popular Barb's Fish 'n' Chips, touristy shops, and kayak rentals. From the Inner Harbour, it's a lovely walk along the waterfront on the **David Foster Harbour Pathway**, or you can catch the **Victoria Harbour Ferries** (www.victoriaharbourferry.com).

Emily Carr House

Known for her paintings of British Columbia's landscape and its native people, artist Emily Carr (1871-1945) is considered one of Canada's most important early-20th-century painters. Unusual for a woman of her era, she made several solo trips to remote First Nations communities, where she wanted to document what she believed was the disappearing indigenous culture. She didn't begin seeing commercial success until late in her life, after a 1927 National Gallery of Canada exhibit featured some of her work; the now-famous artist managed a Victoria apartment building for 15 years to support herself.

Set in a Victorian home in Victoria's James Bay neighborhood where she was born and spent her childhood, **Emily Carr House** (207 Government St., 250/383-5843, www.emilycarr.com, 11am-4pm Tues.-Sat. May-Sept., adults $6.75, seniors and students $5.75, ages 6-18 $4.50, families $17) is a museum about her life and work and about B.C. society during her era.

Beacon Hill Park

Established in 1882, the 200-acre (81-hectare) **Beacon Hill Park** (bounded by Douglas, Southgate, and Cook Streets and the Dallas Road waterfront, www.beaconhillpark.ca, free) is Victoria's urban green space, with flower gardens, walking paths, and several attractions, including one of the **world's tallest totem poles,** measuring nearly 128 feet (39 meters) tall, and the **Mile 0 marker,** in the park's southwest corner, which denotes the start of the 5,000-mile (8,000-kilometer) Trans-Canada Highway.

Near the center of the park, **Beacon Hill Children's Farm** (Circle Dr., 250/381-2532, www.beaconhillchildrensfarm.ca, 10am-4pm daily Mar.-Apr. and early Sept.-mid-Oct., 10am-5pm daily May-early Sept., free) has wandering peacocks, furry alpacas, and a petting zoo. A highlight is the daily **goat stampede** (10:10am and 5:10pm daily summer, 10:10am and 4:10pm daily spring and fall), when the farm's goats race between their sleeping barn and the petting area. It's one of those things you just have to see!

The **Cameron Bandshell,** near Arbutus and Bridge Ways, hosts summertime **Concerts in the Park** (250/361-0500, www.victoria.ca, 1:30pm Fri.-Sun. mid-June-mid-Sept., free), with performances ranging from classical to swing to jazz and blues.

Legacy Art Gallery

The **Legacy Art Gallery Downtown** (630 Yates St., 250/721-6562, http://uvac.uvic.ca, 10am-4pm Wed.-Sat., free), a small satellite of the University of Victoria's art collections, has changing shows that typically feature contemporary artists with British Columbia connections.

Chinatown

Settled in the 1850s, Victoria's **Chinatown** (Fisgard St. at Government St.) is the oldest in Canada. Although it has now shrunk to a couple of blocks around Fisgard Street, where the neighborhood's gateway, the **Gate of Harmonious Interest,** stands, the district was once Canada's largest Chinese settlement.

After B.C.'s gold rush drew the first Chinese immigrants, the community really began to grow as Chinese workers arrived in Victoria on their way to jobs on the Canadian Pacific Railway. More than 17,000 Chinese immigrants came to Canada between 1881 and 1884.

Today, you'll find a few Chinese-run shops and restaurants and many non-Asian boutiques and eateries. One remaining landmark is narrow **Fan Tan Alley** (between Fisgard St. and Pandora Ave.), a lane just three to six feet (1 to 2 meters) wide, where, somehow, several shops have managed to squeeze in.

Breweries

Victoria's craft beer scene has bubbled up in recent years, with a cluster of breweries in an industrial district north of the downtown core, and other microbreweries and brewpubs scattered around the city. Here's where to find the suds:

- **Swans Brewpub** (506 Pandora Ave., 250/361-3310, http://swanshotel.com, 11:30am-1am Mon.-Wed., 11:30am-2am Thurs.-Fri., 9am-2am Sat., 9am-midnight Sun.)

- **Phillips Beer** (2010 Government St., 250/380-1912, www.phillipsbeer.com, store 10am-5pm Mon., 10am-6pm Tues.-Thurs., 10am-7pm Fri., 11am-6pm Sat., tours 4pm Tues.-Thurs., 2pm Fri.-Sat., $6, reservations recommended)

- **Vancouver Island Brewing Co.** (2330 Government St., 250/361-0005, http://vanislandbrewery.com, store 10am-6pm Mon.-Sat., tours 1pm and 3pm Fri.-Sat., $7)

- **Moon Under Water Brewery and Pub** (350 Bay St., 250/380-0706, www.moonunderwater.ca, 11:30am-11pm Mon.-Thurs. and Sat., 11:30am-midnight Fri., 11:30am-8pm Sun.)

- **Hoyne Brewing Co.** (2740 Bridge St., 250/590-5758, http://hoynebrewing.ca, noon-6pm Mon.-Fri., 11am-6pm Sat.)

- **Spinnakers Gastro Brewpub** (308 Catherine St., 250/386-2739, www.spinnakers.com, 11:30am-11pm daily)

East of Downtown
Abkhazi Garden
The story of this manicured garden is a love story between a British woman born in Shanghai and an erstwhile prince from the Republic of Georgia. Marjorie Pemberton-Carter, known as Peggy, first

---

Top to bottom: Chinatown's Gate of Harmonious Interest; Fan Tan Alley; Swans Brewpub.

met Prince Nicholas Abkhazi in Paris in the 1920s. Although they wrote to each other over the years, circumstances kept them apart; during World War II, each spent time in prisoner of war camps—Nicholas in Germany and Peggy in Shanghai.

En route from China to Britain in 1945, Peggy stopped to see friends in Victoria. Her visit turned more permanent when she purchased an overgrown lot and decided to build a summer home. Peggy had lost contact with Nicholas, but he wrote to her in early 1946; they met later that year in New York, and by November, they had returned to Victoria and married.

The home and garden that the newly-weds built on Peggy's property, and where they lived for more than 40 years, became the **Abkhazi Garden** (1964 Fairfield Rd., 778/265-6466, http://blog.conservancy. bc.ca, 11am-5pm daily Apr.-Sept., 11am-5pm Wed.-Sun. Oct.-Mar., last admission 1 hour before closing, $10 donation). The compact garden, just over one acre (0.4 hectares), features a rhododendron woodland with large Garry Oak trees, a winding path known as the Yangtze River, and a variety of other plantings around the site's natural rock formations.

Peggy's 1947 summer home is now **The Teahouse at Abkhazi Garden** (778/265-6466, www.abkhaziteahouse. com, 11am-5pm daily May-Sept., 11am-5pm Wed.-Sun. Oct.-Apr., mains $11-18), which serves soups, salads, and light meals as well as traditional afternoon tea ($28).

From downtown Victoria, take B.C. Transit **bus 7** for UVIC (one-way $2.50) from Douglas and View Streets and get off on Fairfield Road at Foul Bay Road, opposite the garden.

Craigdarroch Castle

Like any good British-inspired city, Victoria has a castle, a grand stone Romanesque revival structure, complete with turrets, stained glass, and Victorian-era artifacts.

Robert Dunsmuir, a Scottish immigrant who made his fortune mining coal on Vancouver Island, built the 39-room mansion, known as **Craigdarroch Castle** (1050 Joan Cres., 250/592-5323, www.the-castle.ca, 9am-7pm daily mid-June-early Sept., 10am-4:30pm daily early Sept.-mid-June, adults $13.95, seniors $12.95, students $8.95, ages 6-12 $5), in the late 1880s. Sadly, Dunsmuir died before the castle was finished. His wife Joan lived here with three of her unmarried daughters (the Dunsmuirs had 10 children) from the castle's completion in 1890 until she died in 1908.

With more than 20,000 square feet (1,880 square meters) of floor space, the castle, now a National Historic Site, is decorated as it would have been in the Dunsmuirs' time, with lavish Victorian appointments, including sculptures, paintings, books, and period furnishings.

From downtown Victoria, any of the Fort Street buses (one-way $2.50), including B.C. Transit **bus 14** for UVIC, **bus 15** for UVIC, or **bus 22** for Hillside Mall, will drop you near the castle. On foot, allow 30 to 35 minutes from the Inner Harbour.

Art Gallery of Greater Victoria

Built around an 1899 Victorian mansion that now houses the museum shop, the **Art Gallery of Greater Victoria** (1040 Moss St., 250/384-4171, www.aggv.ca, 10am-5pm Mon.-Sat., noon-5pm Sun. mid-May-mid-Sept., 10am-5pm Tues.-Sun. mid-Sept.-mid-May, adults $13, seniors and students $11, ages 6-17 $2.50, families $28) has a significant collection of work by Victoria-born painter Emily Carr and one of Canada's most extensive Asian art holdings. The gallery's changing exhibitions typically showcase Canadian or Asian works.

The Art Gallery is 1.5 miles (2.3 kilometers) east of the Inner Harbour. B.C. Transit **bus 15** for UVIC (one-way $2.50), which runs along Fort Street, will drop you at the corner of Fort Street and Fernwood Road, around the corner from the gallery. You can easily combine visits to the Art Gallery and nearby Craigdarroch Castle.

Ross Bay Cemetery

Many notable Victorians are buried in the historic **Ross Bay Cemetery** (Fairfield Rd. at Stannard Ave., dawn-dusk daily, free) that stretches between Fairfield Road and the Dallas Road waterfront. The Victorian-era cemetery's most visited grave is that of artist Emily Carr (1871-1945), near the intersection of Fairfield Road and Arnold Avenue. The cemetery is also the final resting place of Sir James Douglas, who served as British Columbia's first governor from 1858 to 1864, and Robert Dunsmuir, who built Craigdarroch Castle. The cemetery includes sections for different Christian denominations, with separate areas for First Nations and Chinese people, and a potter's field, where the poor were buried.

Cemetery maps are available online from the **Old Cemeteries Society of Victoria** (250/598-8870, www.oldcem. bc.ca). The society offers **tours** ($5) focusing on different aspects of the cemetery's history. In July and August, tours are offered every Sunday at 2pm, while September through June, tours generally run on the first and third Sundays; check their website for a schedule.

From Douglas Street in downtown Victoria, B.C. Transit **buses 3 or 7** (one-way $2.50) will take you along Fairfield Road to the cemetery. It's a 35- to 40-minute walk from the Inner Harbour.

The Saanich Peninsula

The Saanich Peninsula extends north of downtown Victoria to the communities of Saanich, North Saanich, Sidney, and Brentwood Bay. Partly suburban and partly a rural landscape of farms, forests,

Top to bottom: Victoria Spirits craft distillery; Hatley Castle; one of the whale-watching outfitters at Victoria's Inner Harbour.

and fields, the peninsula is worth exploring for one major attraction—the popular Butchart Gardens—and for several smaller sights; it's also home to several wineries and distilleries. The Swartz Bay Ferry Terminal, with boats to Vancouver and several of the Gulf Islands, is at the northern tip of the Saanich Peninsula.

★ Butchart Gardens

How did a cement factory and limestone quarry become one of Vancouver Island's most popular garden attractions? Jennie Butchart and her husband, Robert, moved to the island from Ontario in the early 1900s, where Robert established a quarry and cement business, and Jennie became the company's chemist. The Butcharts built a large manor nearby and began planting flowers around it.

The Butcharts named their estate Benvenuto, Italian for "welcome," and by the 1920s, more than 50,000 people were visiting their gardens every year. Now, nearly one million visitors annually come to ogle the floral displays at the 55-acre (22-hectare) **Butchart Gardens** (800 Benvenuto Ave., Brentwood Bay, 250/652-5256, www.butchartgardens.com, 9am-10pm daily mid-June-early Sept., 9am-5pm daily early-late Sept., 9am-4pm daily Oct., 9am-3:30pm daily Nov., 9am-9pm daily Dec.-early Jan., 9am-3:30pm daily early Jan.-Feb., 9am-4pm daily Mar., 9am-5pm daily Apr.-mid.-June; mid-June-Sept. adults $32.10, students 13-17 $16.05, ages 5-12 $3, reduced rates in other seasons).

When the company limestone quarry was exhausted, Jennie had the former pit transformed into what is now known as the Sunken Garden. Other highlights include the Rose Garden, the Italian Garden, and the serene Japanese Garden. On summer Saturday nights (July-early Sept.), **fireworks shows** are choreographed to music. During the winter holidays, the pathways twinkle with thousands of lights.

The Butchart Gardens are located 14 miles (23 kilometers) north of Victoria and 12.5 miles (20 kilometers) south of the Swartz Bay Ferry Terminal. From downtown Victoria, **B.C. Transit bus 75** (one-way $2.50) can take you to the gardens in about 45 minutes.

Victoria Butterfly Gardens

Don't be surprised if a common Mormon or a blue morpho lands on your head inside this tropical greenhouse. More than 3,000 butterflies dart and flutter around the palm trees and exotic plants at the family-friendly **Victoria Butterfly Gardens** (1461 Benvenuto Ave., Brentwood Bay, 250/652-3822 or 877/722-0272, www.butterflygardens.com, 10am-5pm daily early Mar.-Oct., 10am-4pm daily Nov.-early Mar., extended hours Dec., last admission 1 hour before closing, adults $16, seniors and student $11, ages 5-12 $5), which houses about 75 different species from around the world.

The Butterfly Gardens are 12 miles (20 kilometers) north of Victoria and 11 miles (18 kilometers) south of the Swartz Bay Ferry Terminal, near the Butchart Gardens. **B.C. Transit bus 75** (one-way $2.50) can take you from downtown Victoria in about 40 minutes.

Shaw Ocean Discovery Centre

A small modern aquarium on the waterfront in the town of Sidney, the **Shaw Ocean Discovery Centre** (9811 Seaport Pl., Sidney, 250/665-7511, www.ocean-discovery.ca, 10am-5pm daily July-early Sept., 10am-4:30pm daily early Sept.-June, last admission 30 minutes before closing, adults $15, ages 7-17 $8, ages 3-6 $5) focuses on the marine life of the Salish Sea, the waters surrounding southern Vancouver Island. More than 3,500 creatures, representing 150 different species, are typically on view. On Saturday and Sunday, marine-themed games, crafts, and other special activities add to the fun for kids.

Along Highway 17, the aquarium is 17

miles (28 kilometers) north of downtown Victoria and four miles (6.5 kilometers) south of the Swartz Bay Ferry Terminal. **B.C. Transit buses 70 and 72** (one-way $2.50) stop in Sidney en route between Victoria and the ferry terminal. Get off at 5th Street and Beacon Avenue, and walk down Beacon to the aquarium.

Wineries and Distilleries

You don't have to go far from Victoria to go wine-tasting, with several wineries and distilleries across the Saanich Peninsula.

One of the region's more established wineries, **Church and State Wines** (1445 Benvenuto Ave., Central Saanich, 250/652-2671, www.churchandstatewines.com, 11am-6pm Fri.-Sun. mid-late Apr., 11am-6pm daily May-Oct.) launched with just 10 acres (4 hectares) on the island and now has a winery and vineyards in the Okanagan Valley as well. Try their wines at the tasting bar or with lunch in the **Bistro** (11am-3pm Wed.-Sun. June-Oct., mains $17-21).

On a 10-acre (4-hectare) farm with more than 1,300 apple trees, **Sea Cider Farm & Ciderhouse** (2487 Mt. St. Michael Rd., Saanichton, 250/544-4824, www.seacider.ca, 11am-4pm daily May-Sept., 11am-4pm Wed.-Sun. Oct.-Apr.) produces traditional fermented artisanal ciders.

The master distillers at craft distillery, **Victoria Spirits** (6170 Old W. Saanich Rd., Victoria, 250/544-8217, www.victoriaspirits.com, tastings and tours 11am-5pm Fri.-Sun. May-Sept.), infuse their signature Victoria Gin with a custom blend of botanicals. They make an aged Oaken Gin and an unusual hemp vodka, too.

West of Downtown

Wend your way through the suburbs west of the city center to reach another of Victoria's famous castles.

Butchart Gardens

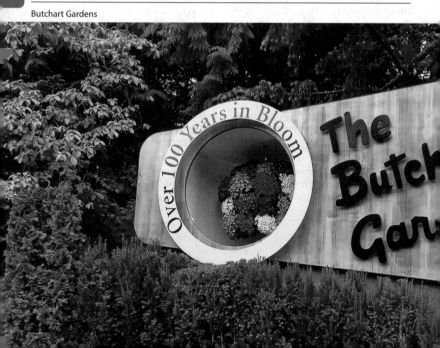

Hatley Park National Historic Site

Given that his father, Robert, built Craigdarroch Castle, perhaps it's no surprise that James Dunsmuir (1851-1920) and his wife, Laura, wanted a castle of their own, particularly as the parents of 12 children. The 1908 Edwardian stone manor that they constructed, now known as **Hatley Castle** at the **Hatley Park National Historic Site** (2005 Sooke Rd., 250/391-2511, www.royalroads.ca, 10:15am-3pm daily, adults $18.50, seniors $15.75, ages 6-17 $10.75, families $51), has 40 rooms, including 22 bedrooms and eight baths.

You can visit the castle, on the campus of Royal Roads University, on a one-hour **guided castle tour** (11:45am and 2:45pm Sat.-Sun. May-early Sept.) that takes you through the main-floor rooms and offers up details about the Dunsmuir family's history. The castle's upper floors, used as university offices, aren't part of the tour. Another option is the one-hour **guided estate tour** (10:30am, 11:45am,

1:30pm, and 2:45pm Mon.-Fri., 10:30am and 1:30pm Sat.-Sun. May-early Sept.), which focuses on the castle's exterior and gardens, along with the family's story.

If you don't have time for a tour, or if you're visiting outside the summer season, visit just the manicured **gardens** (adults $5, seniors $4, ages 6-17 $3.50, families $15) or the small **museum** (free) about the Dunsmuir family.

Hatley Park is 7.5 miles (12 kilometers) west of the Inner Harbour. While it's possible to get here by public transit, it's much faster to come by car.

Festivals and Events

Honoring Victoria's namesake queen, the city's **Victoria Day** festivities (www.tourismvictoria.com, May) include a parade downtown.

Aboriginal dancers, singers, and musicians perform at Victoria's three-day **Aboriginal Cultural Festival** (www.aboriginalbc.com, June), which also showcases works by First Nations artists.

It's not just mimes aping visitors at the annual **Victoria International Buskers Festival** (http://victoriabuskers.com, July). Professional street performers from around the world, including magicians, jugglers, flame throwers, acrobats, and more, show their stuff on stages around the city.

Food and wine lovers celebrate Vancouver Island's bounty at **Taste: Victoria's Festival of Food and Wine** (www.victoriataste.com, July), a weekend of wine-tastings, seminars, and dinners.

The annual **Victoria Symphony Splash** (www.victoriasymphony.ca, Aug.) includes a live performance by the Victoria Symphony from a floating stage moored in the Inner Harbour.

The **Victoria Fringe Fest** (http://victoriafringe.com, Aug.) is an 11-day festival of weird and often wonderful theater, comedy, and storytelling performances.

The **Victoria Classic Boat Festival** (www.classicboatfestival.ca, Sept.)

celebrates the island's maritime heritage with boat parades, races, and other events.

Shopping

Shops line Government Street, stretching north from the Inner Harbour, many selling T-shirts, Canadian flag patches, and other souvenirs. Lower Johnson Street in Chinatown has more distinctive local clothing, jewelry, and shoes.

Clothing and Accessories

In Chinatown, **Lower Johnson Street** between Government and Wharf is a mix of trend-conscious chains like yoga-wear maker **Lululemon** (584 Johnson St., 250/383-1313, www.lululemon. com, 10am-8pm Mon.-Sat., 10am-7pm Sun.) and locally run boutiques, including **Still Life for Her** (550 Johnson St., 250/386-5658, http://stilllifeboutique. com, 10:30am-6pm Mon.-Thurs. and Sat., 10:30am-8pm Fri., 11am-5pm Sun.) and its companion store **Still Life for Him** (560 Johnson St., 250/386-5655, http:// stilllifeboutique.com, 10:30am-6pm Mon.-Thurs. and Sat., 10:30am-8pm Fri., 11am-5pm Sun.), **Suasion** (552 Johnson St., 250/995-0133, http://shopsuasion. com, 10:30am-6pm Mon.-Sat., 11am-5pm Sun.), and **Smoking Lily** (569A Johnson St., 250/382-5459, www.smokinglily.com, noon-5pm Tues.-Sun.).

Sneaker fans run into **Baggins Shoes** (580 Johnson St., 250/388-7022, http:// bagginsshoes.com, 10am-6pm Mon.-Wed. and Sat., 10am-7pm Thurs.-Fri., 11am-6pm Sun.), which has one of the world's largest selections of Converse styles. In the Atrium Building, **Head Over Heels** (1323 Blanshard St., 250/590-5154, www.headoverheelsvictoria.ca, 10:30am-5:30pm Mon.-Sat., noon-4pm Sun.) sells fashion-forward shoes.

Books

Nobel prize-winning author Alice Munro and her former husband Jim opened **Munro's Books** (1108 Government St., 250/382-2464, www.munrobooks.com, 9am-6pm Mon.-Wed. and Sat., 9am-9pm Thurs.-Fri., 9:30am-6pm Sun.) in 1963. Although the writer is no longer involved in its management, this well-stocked old-school bookstore in a grand 1909 former bank carries titles by Canadian authors and other books of local interest.

Gourmet Goodies

Stocking a mind-boggling variety of teas, with helpful labels about their ingredients, flavors, and caffeine content, **Silk Road Tea** (1624 Government St., 250/704-2688, www.silkroadteastore.com, 10am-6pm Mon.-Sat., 11am-5pm Sun.) also carries tea-related products and cosmetics. Take a seat at their tea bar to rest your shopping-weary feet over a fresh-brewed cup, or book a massage in their on-site spa. They have a second location in the Victoria Public Market (1701 Douglas St., 778/433-9838, 10am-5:30pm Mon.-Sat., 11am-5pm Sun.).

Outdoor Gear

If you need clothing or supplies for outdoor adventures, head for the Victoria location of **MEC** (Mountain Equipment Co-op, 1450 Government St., 250/386-2667, www.mec.ca, 10am-7pm Mon.-Wed., 10am-9pm Thurs.-Fri., 9am-6pm Sat., 11am-5pm Sun.), Canada's largest retailer of outdoor wear and sports gear.

Sports and Recreation
★ Whale-Watching

The waters off Vancouver Island, the Gulf Islands, and Washington's San Juan Islands are home to several pods of resident orcas (also known as killer whales), particularly during the summer. Pods of transient orcas, as well as Pacific gray whales, humpback whales, and minke whales, migrate through the region.

Numerous Victoria-based companies offer three- to five-hour whale-watching tours from April through October, though summer (July and August) is peak season for both whales and travelers. Some operators use inflatable zodiac boats, which give you a rougher but more exhilarating ride. Others use larger boats for a calmer trip and more shelter from the weather, a better choice on rainy days or choppy seas. Victoria's whale-watching tour companies include:

- **Orca Spirit Adventures** (250/383-8411 or 888/672-6722, www.orcaspirit. com, adults $105, ages 13-17 $85, ages 3-12 $75), with departures from two Inner Harbour locations: 950 Wharf Street, at the Harbour Air Terminal, or 146 Kingston Street, at the Coast Harbourside Hotel

- **Prince of Whales** (812 Wharf St., 250/383-4884 or 888/383-4884, www. princeofwhales.com, adults $115, ages 13-17 $95, ages 5-12 $85)

- **Eagle Wing Tours** (Fisherman's Wharf, 12 Erie St., 250/384-8008 or 800/708-9488, www.eaglewingtours.com, adults $125, ages 9-15 $95, ages 2-8 $75)

- **SpringTide Whale Watching** (1119 Wharf St., 250/384-4444 or 800/470-3474, www.victoriawhalewatching. com, adults $105, seniors $95, ages 13-18 $85, ages 2-12 $75)

Accommodations

Victoria's hotels are clustered around the Inner Harbour. In some surrounding neighborhoods, you'll find B&Bs and other good-value lodgings.

Under $150

An old motel given new life as a funky retro lodging, **Hotel Zed** (3110 Douglas St., 250/388-4345 or 800/997-6797, www. hotelzed.com, $99-209 d), decorated in vibrant oranges, turquoises, fuchsias, and purples, is Victoria's most fun place to stay. The 63 rooms have rotary phones (with free local calls), comic books in the baths, and complimentary Wi-Fi. The indoor-outdoor pool has a bubblegum-pink water slide. A hip diner-style restaurant, **The Ruby** (250/507-1325, http://therubyvictoria.com, 8am-9pm daily, mains $9-18), cooks big breakfasts and roasts free-range chicken; downstairs, there's a Ping-Pong lounge. It's two miles (3 kilometers) north of the Inner Harbour, but the hotel runs a free shuttle downtown in their vintage VW bus.

$150-250

In a 1912 Victorian home in the residential Rockland neighborhood, ★ **Abbeymore Manor B&B** (1470 Rockland Ave., 250/370-1470 or 888/801-1811, www.abbeymoore.com, $159-299 d) looks formal, with polished woodwork, oriental rugs, and period furnishings, but the longtime owners keep things comfortable with help-yourself coffee, tea, soft drinks, and snacks, a book- and game-filled guest library, and hearty morning meals. The five guest rooms are all traditionally appointed, while the three suites (two on the garden level and one on the top floor) are more modern. Wi-Fi and local calls are included; no kids under 14.

To capture Victoria's traditional ambiance, stay at the **Beaconsfield Inn** (998 Humboldt St., 250/384-4044 or 888/884-4044, www.beaconsfieldinn. com, $159-249 d), a nine-room B&B in a 1905 Edwardian manor furnished with antiques, stained-glass windows, and chandeliers. Most guest rooms have fireplaces and whirlpool tubs; all have down comforters and Wi-Fi. Rates include full breakfast, afternoon tea and cookies, and evening sherry. No kids under 12.

Noted Canadian architect Arthur Erickson designed one wing of the **Inn at Laurel Point** (680 Montreal St., 250/386-8721 or 800/663-7667, $149-323, parking $17), where most of the contemporary suites are angled to take advantage of the property's waterfront views. The Laurel Wing units are more conventional, but the harbor vistas from these rooms aren't bad either. With a quiet setting a short walk from the busy Inner Harbour, the Pacific Rim-style lodging has an indoor pool and a sundeck facing a Japanese garden. The well-regarded **Aura Restaurant** is open for breakfast, lunch, and dinner. Wi-Fi is included.

Over $250

A bit removed from the Inner Harbour's fray, but still an easy stroll from the sights, the condo-style **Oswego Hotel** (500 Oswego St., 250/294-7500 or 877/767-9346, www.oswegovictoria. com, $190-310 d, 2-bedroom unit $350-595, parking $15-20) has 80 stylish, urban studio, one-bedroom, and two-bedroom units. All have kitchen facilities with granite counters, stainless-steel appliances, and French-press coffeemakers, as well as large baths with soaker tubs. The upper-floor suites have expansive city views. Wi-Fi is included.

A landmark on the Inner Harbour, the ★ **Fairmont Empress** (721 Government St., 250/384-8111 or 800/441-1414, www. fairmont.com, $449-749, parking $30) charms with its polished staff and stately public spaces. The classically furnished guest rooms vary from petite to grand, but you're here for the heritage and gracious service as much as the physical space. An indoor pool and well-equipped health club keep you busy, while the Willow Stream Spa keeps you pampered. The hotel's restaurant serves contemporary fare with produce from the rooftop garden and around the island, paired with B.C. wines and local craft beers; the Empress is famous for its traditional **afternoon tea.** Join Fairmont's complimentary President's Club to get Wi-Fi access; otherwise, it's $14 per day.

★ **Magnolia Hotel & Spa** (623 Courtney St., 250/381-0999 or 877/624-6654, www.magnoliahotel.com, $239-419 d, parking $24), a well-managed boutique lodging two blocks from the Inner Harbour, caters to both business and leisure travelers. The 64 rooms are decorated in soothing greys and creams, with mini fridges, single-cup coffeemakers, complimentary Wi-Fi, and flat-screen TVs. The best rooms are on the sixth and seventh floors above the surrounding buildings; from the corner units, you can see the Parliament Building, illuminated at night. Work out in the compact gym or borrow a complimentary bike to go touring. The staff is quick with a greeting or to offer assistance, from directions to restaurant recommendations.

A stay at the ★ **Oak Bay Beach Hotel** (1175 Beach Dr., 250/598-4556 or 800/668-7758, www.oakbaybeachhotel. com, $188-568 d) feels like an escape to a seaside resort, particularly when you swim or soak in the heated mineral pools that front the ocean. The 100 generously sized suites have electric fireplaces, flat-screen TVs, kitchen facilities, and deluxe baths. The panoramic vistas from the water-facing rooms are spectacular. Rates include Wi-Fi, local calls, and parking. **The Snug,** a British-style pub, serves classics like fish-and-chips and bangers and mash with a cold pint; **Kate's Café** keeps guests and locals supplied with coffee and pastries. The hotel is in the residential Oak Bay district, east of downtown.

To stay in an upscale Italian Renaissance manor, the deluxe **Villa Marco Polo Inn** (1524 Shasta Pl., 250/370-1524, www.villamarcopolo.com, $239-339 d), built in 1923, is in the Rockland district. The four romantic guest suites entice with European linens, Persian carpets, fireplaces, and a plush Silk Road style. Breakfasts feature homemade muffins, organic produce, and locally made charcuterie, with a sweet or savory entrée. Lounge in the garden or the wood-paneled library, checking your email if you must (Wi-Fi and local calls are included), but if you laze with your beloved in your double soaker tub instead, your messages can surely wait.

Food
Afternoon Tea
The **Fairmont Empress** (721 Government

St., 250/384-8111, www.fairmont.com, 11:30am-4:45pm daily, reservations recommended, May-Sept. adults $63, ages 12 and under $31.50, Oct.-Apr. adults $53, ages 12 and under $26.50) has been offering afternoon tea since the hotel opened in 1908. Upholding that tradition, the regal tea room still serves an estimated 500,000 cups of tea every year, along with tiered trays of finger sandwiches, scones with jam and clotted cream, and assorted pastries.

The Dining Room at Butchart Gardens (800 Benvenuto Ave., Brentwood Bay, 250/652-8222, www.butchartgardens.com, noon-3pm daily Apr.-Sept., adults $33.75, ages 11 and under $18.95) serves traditional afternoon tea in spring and summer, with a mix of sweet and savory items. From October through March, the Gardens offer High Tea (adults $32.50, ages 11 and under 18.95), adding warm dishes like quiche and Cornish pasty to the menu of sandwiches and desserts. Vegetarian versions of both afternoon tea and high tea are available.

In the traditionally British neighborhood of Oak Bay, the **White Heather Tea Room** (1885 Oak Bay Ave., 250/595-8020, www.whiteheather-tearoom.com, 11:15am-5pm Tues.-Sat., last seating 3:45pm) offers a traditionally British afternoon tea in several sizes, from the Wee Tea ($20 pp) to the Not-So-Wee Tea ($25.50) to the Big Muckle Giant Tea For Two ($58 for 2, each additional person $29).

For a less formal (and meat-free) tea, visit **Venus Sophia Tea Room & Vegetarian Eatery** (540 Fisgard St., 250/590-3953, www.venussophia.com, afternoon tea 11am-4:30pm daily, adults $28, kids $18), a pretty-in-pink Chinatown storefront. Choose among their signature teas to pair with a

Top to bottom: Oak Bay Beach Hotel; afternoon tea at the Fairmont Empress; Victoria Public Market.

Victoria's Chocolate Project

David Mincey is passionate about chocolate. The owner and resident chocolate obsessive at the **Chocolate Project** (Victoria Public Market, 1701 Douglas St.) is on a mission to improve the chocolate that is produced around the world and that we eat closer to home.

In his stall in Victoria's Public Market, Mincey carries single origin, sustainably produced chocolate from many different countries. If you stop to chat, he'll tell you about the horrors of conventional chocolate production; he says that most commercial chocolate comes from West African plantations where enslaved people provide the labor, which is how companies can produce chocolate bars selling for $3 or less. He can tell you about the small businesses and individual growers across the globe who produce the chocolate he sells, many of whom he has visited personally.

The Chocolate Project has no website or even official hours, but you can find Mincey at his stand most Fridays, Satur-

the focus of the Chocolate Project

days, and Sundays during Public Market hours (10am-5:30pm Mon.-Sat., 11am-5pm Sun.), offering tastings, running impromptu workshops, and generally preaching the chocolate gospel. His chocolate bars start around $10 each, and he'll convince you that they're worth it.

seasonally changing assortment of sandwiches, baked goods, and sweets.

Groceries and Markets

In a historic building that once housed the Hudson's Bay department store, the **Victoria Public Market** (1701 Douglas St., 778/433-2787, http://victoriapublicmarket.com, 10am-5:30pm Mon.-Sat., 11am-5pm Sun.) draws foodies with stalls selling cheeses, chocolate, tea, olive oil, pie, and other goodies, plus a seasonal **farmers market** (11am-3pm Wed. and Sat. Mar.-Nov.).

Another snacking destination is Fort Street, where upscale food shops include **Chorizo & Co** (807 Fort St., 250/590-6393, 8:30am-5pm Mon.-Tues., 8:30am-10pm Wed.-Fri., 11am-10pm Sat.), a Spanish deli and tapas bar; **Choux Choux Charcuterie** (830 Fort St., 205/382-7572, www.chouxchouxcharc.com,

10am-5:30pm Tues.-Fri., 10am-5pm Sat.) for cured meats and artisanal cheese; and **Chocolat, Chocolatiere de Victoria** (703 Fort St., 250/381-0131, www.chocolat-victoria.ca, 9:30am-6pm Mon.-Sat.) for handmade chocolates.

To buy groceries close to downtown, head for **The Market on Yates** (903 Yates St., 250/381-6000, www.themarketstores.com, 7am-11pm daily), a well-stocked local food store.

Cafés, Bakeries, and Light Bites

Well-prepared coffee, baked goods, and light meals such as salads, charcuterie, and pastas draw locals and visitors to the sunny patio or cozy interior at **Tre Fantastico** (810 Humboldt St., 250/590-8014, www.caffefantastico.com, 7am-10pm daily), a café set a short stroll from the Inner Harbour.

For a quick exotic meal, stop into **Le**

Petit Dakar (711 Douglas St., 250/380-3705, www.lepetitdakarbc.ca, 11am-5pm Mon.-Wed., 11am-7pm Thurs.-Fri., mains $7-11), a tiny Senegalese takeaway. The personable chef-owner will guide you through the small menu where you might dig into *mafe* (a meat stew enriched with peanut butter), black-eyed bean ragout, or chicken curry.

Canada isn't known as a barbecue nation, but **Pig BBQ Joint** (1325 Blanshard St., 250/590-5193, www.pigbbqjoint.com, 11am-10pm daily, mains $8-18) does a fine job with its pulled pork, smoked chicken, and beef brisket. In this casual downtown joint, expect big flavors, but don't expect niceties like utensils or plates.

Contemporary

Taking its name from a Chinook word meaning "hungry," ★ **OLO** (509 Fisgard St., 250/590-8795, www.olorestaurant. com, 5pm-midnight Sun.-Thurs., 5pm-1am Fri.-Sat., mains $18-46) doesn't just satisfy your hunger. This fashionably relaxed Chinatown restaurant, decorated with woven wooden light fixtures that dangle from the ceiling like outsized birds' nests, delights guests with its innovative seasonal fare, from delicate spot prawn bisque or poached halibut under a blanket of herbs to the popular burger garnished with tomato jam and garlic mayo. If you're feeling adventurous, order the "family meal" for your table and let the kitchen prepare a multicourse chef's-choice feast.

★ **Little Jumbo** (506 Fort St., 778/433-5535, www.littlejumbo.ca, 4pm-midnight Tues.-Thurs. and Sun., 4pm-1am Fri.-Sat., mains $21-32) feels like a secret speakeasy, set at the end of a narrow hallway. In the cozy narrow room with exposed brick walls and green lights illuminating the banquettes, the well-stocked bar and hard-working bartenders draw cocktail connoisseurs (they'll make you delicious "mocktails," too, if you're keeping with the Prohibition theme), but the kitchen is serious as well. Even simple dishes, like fresh green salads or platters of house-made charcuterie, are thoughtfully prepared, and you might find innovations like albacore tuna *poke* (chopped raw fish) topped with creamy avocado sorbet.

You'll want to eat your vegetables when they're as delicious as the fried Brussels sprouts salad at **North 48** (1005 Langley St., 250/381-2428, www.northfortyeight. com, 11:30am-10pm Tues.-Thurs., 11:30am-11pm Fri.-Sat., mains $12-26), a downtown restaurant and lounge, where the menu mixes comfort foods such as mussels and clams in a broth of bacon and local beer with cool creations like octopus tacos. Tiki cocktails and even nonalcoholic drinks like the house-made ginger beer add to the fun.

Café Brio (944 Fort St., 250/383-0009 or 866/270-5461, www.cafe-brio. com, from 5:30pm daily, mains $15-33) is an old-favorite with a modern Mediterranean menu. Look for dishes like grilled local octopus with cherry tomato and fennel risotto, pan-roasted halibut with cauliflower, or hand-cut tagliatelle with potatoes, green beans, and pesto. Note to grazers, or those with small appetites: you can order most dishes in full or half portions. The wine list is strong on B.C. labels.

An unassuming order-at-the-counter eatery, **Part and Parcel** (2656 Quadra St., 778/406-0888, www.partandparcel.ca, 11:30am-9pm Tues.-Sat., mains $7-13) surprises with the first-rate quality of its straightforward but innovative dishes. On the changing menu that leans heavily on salads and sandwiches, super-fresh greens might be topped with spring rhubarb, fresh tuna might come sandwiched with pickled green beans, and pillowy gnocchi might sport a creamy sesame sauce. In the Quadra Village neighborhood, not quite two miles (3 kilometers) north of the Inner Harbour, this local joint is an easy pit stop on the way to or from the Swartz Bay ferry.

Asian

For a quick bite with flavors from across Asia, pop into **Foo Asian Street Food** (769 Yates St., 250/383-3111, www.foofood.ca, 11:30am-10pm Mon.-Sat., 11:30am-9pm Sun., mains $8-13) for a short rib *bánh mì,* pork fried rice, butter chicken, and other crowd-pleasing dishes that take cues from Vietnam, China, India, Japan, and Thailand. They don't have many seats, but they do have local beer on tap.

Diners

A favorite joint for breakfast or brunch is funky **Jam Café** (542 Herald St., 778/440-4489, www.jamcafevictoria. com, 8am-3pm daily, mains $8-15), where the hip takes on diner classics include fried oatmeal, red velvet pancakes, and chicken and waffles. Come hungry, and be prepared to line up; they don't take reservations.

French

A long-standing French bistro on the edge of Chinatown, ★ **Brasserie L'Ecole** (1715 Government St., 250/475-6260, www.lecole.ca, 5:30pm-11pm Tues.-Sat., mains $18-34) continues to charm with its warm welcome and its just-classic-enough menu. You might find local trout paired with lentil fritters and squash puree, braised sausage with spaetzle, or *steak frites.* They stock a long list of Belgian beers and French wines. No reservations.

Italian

The modern Italian fare at ★ **Zambri's** (820 Yates St., 250/360-1171, www.zambris.ca, lunch 11:30am-3pm Mon.-Sat., dinner 5pm-9pm Sun.-Thurs., 5pm-10pm Fri.-Sat., brunch 10:30pm-2pm Sun., mains lunch $9-16, dinner $17-32), in the equally modern Atrium Building, makes one of Victoria's best meals, Italian or otherwise. The pastas, like penne with gorgonzola and peas or orecchiette with house-made sausages and rapini, are always good choices, as are the pizzas, or you can try more elaborate mains like tuna *alla livornese* (sauced with onions, tomatoes, olives, and wine) or beef tenderloin paired with polenta. Save room for desserts like panna cotta or chocolate *pot de crème.*

Seafood

It's a little hard to find, but that hasn't stopped the hordes from lining up at the wharf-side shipping container housing **Red Fish Blue Fish** (1006 Wharf St., 250/298-6877, www.redfish-bluefish. com, 11am-9pm daily, mains $6-22), a busy seafood takeaway at the foot of Broughton Street. Choose tempura-battered Pacific cod, wild salmon, B.C. halibut, or oysters for your fish-and-chips. The hand-rolled fish tacos and salmon sandwich with pickled cucumbers are other popular picks.

Reel in a quick bite at **Fishhook** (805 Fort St., 250/477-0470, www.fishhookvic. com, 11:30am-7pm Mon.-Sat., noon-7pm Sun., mains $6-13), which specializes in seafood *tartines,* open-faced sandwiches topped with cured, broiled, or smoked fish. Try the sablefish with kale and house-made pickles or the tuna melt with cheddar and caramelized broccoli. This casual café also makes an array of fish curries.

A Victoria institution on Fisherman's Wharf, **Barb's Fish 'n' Chips** (1 Dallas Rd., 250/384-6515, 11am-dark daily mid-Mar.-Oct., mains $6-19) has been serving up seafood since 1984. It's one mile (1.6 kilometers) west of downtown; you can also get here on the Victoria Harbour Ferry (250/708-0201, www.victoriaharbourferry.com).

Vegetarian

You can order a local craft beer or a "superfood" cocktail (perhaps the Coastal Gin & Tonic made with spirulina and bull kelp) at cool, laid-back **Be Love** (1019 Blanshard St., 778/433-7181, http://beloverestaurant.ca, 11am-9:30pm Sun.-Thurs., 11am-10pm Fri.-Sat., mains lunch $13-15, dinner $14-21), a bright vegetarian café where veggie-friendly doesn't mean ascetic. Try a salad like arugula and melon with shaved fennel and pumpkin seeds or the Vitality Bowl, a mix of greens, quinoa, avocado, sauerkraut, and poached eggs topped with miso-ginger dressing. Want a booze-free beverage? Note the big vats of *kombucha* above the bar.

An old favorite among plant-eaters and their omnivorous dining companions, **Rebar** (50 Bastion Square, 250/361-9223, www.rebarmodernfood.com, 11:30am-9pm Mon.-Fri., 8:30am-9pm Sat.-Sun., mains $10-18) serves vegetarian comfort food like curries, enchiladas, and stir-fries, along with a few seafood dishes. Their almond burger is a classic. Save room for a sweet, like a homey ginger molasses cookie or gooey carrot cake.

Information and Services
Visitor Information

Tourism Victoria (812 Wharf St., 250/953-2033, www.tourismvictoria.com, 9am-5pm daily) runs a year-round information center on the Inner Harbour, with helpful staff who can assist you in booking tours and accommodations. The building has public restrooms, too.

Tourism Vancouver Island (www.vancouverisland.travel) publishes a guide to things to do across the island, available online and in print from area visitors centers.

Media and Communications

The **Victoria *Times Colonist*** (www.timescolonist.com) is the city's daily newspaper. Based in Victoria, *Eat Magazine* (www.eatmagazine.ca) covers the Vancouver Island food scene. *Monday Magazine* (www.mondaymag.com) reports on arts, entertainment, food, and recreation. Tourism Victoria's **Going Local blog** (www.tourismvictoria.com/blog) features local happenings and area travel.

Medical Services

Victoria General Hospital (1 Hospital Way, 250/727-4212 or 877/370-8699, www.viha.ca) and **Royal Jubilee Hospital** (1952 Bay St., 250/370-8000 or 877/370-8699, www.viha.ca) provide emergency medical services. The pharmacy at **Shoppers Drug Mart** (3511 Blanshard St., 250/475-7572, www.shoppersdrugmart.ca) is open 24 hours daily.

Getting Around

Victoria's Inner Harbour is compact and walkable, easy to navigate without a car. It's possible to reach sights outside the city center on the region's public buses, although to explore farther afield on Vancouver Island, having your own vehicle is more convenient.

By Bus

B.C. Transit (250/382-6161, http://bctransit.com/victoria, one-way $2.50) runs buses around Victoria, to Butchart Gardens, and to the Swartz Bay ferry terminal. Hours vary by bus route, but major routes typically begin service between 6am and 7am and stop service between 11pm and midnight. Service to the Swartz Bay ferry begins at 5:30am Monday through Saturday and 6:30am on Sunday.

By Ferry

Victoria Harbour Ferry (250/708-0201, www.victoriaharbourferry.com, 11am-5pm daily Mar. and Oct., 11am-7pm daily Apr.-mid-May, 10am-9pm daily mid-May-mid-Sept.) can take you around the Inner Harbour in their cute colorful boats, stopping at Fisherman's Wharf, the Delta Victoria Ocean Pointe Resort, and many other waterside points. Fares vary by distance; a basic one-zone trip is $5 pp.

By Taxi

You can usually find taxis near the Inner Harbour and the Fairmont Empress Hotel. Victoria taxi rates start at $3.25, plus $1.88 per kilometer. Local cab companies include **Bluebird Cabs** (250/382-2222, www.taxicab.com) and **Yellow Cab of Victoria** (250/381-2222, www.yellowcabvictoria.com).

By Car

Victoria's downtown sights are all clustered around the Inner Harbour, so if you've driven downtown, park your car and do your exploring on foot. Having a car is handy to visit attractions outside downtown or on the Saanich Peninsula.

Parking

Pay for downtown **on-street parking** (Mon.-Sat. 9am-6pm $1.50-3 per hour) at the nearby pay stations with coins or credit cards. Parking is free in the evenings and on Sunday.

The city has five centrally located public parking garages ($2 per hour, $12 per day) open 24 hours daily: **Bastion Square Parkade** (575 Yates St.), **Broughton Street Parkade** (745 Broughton St., below the Central Library), **Centennial Square Parkade** (645 Fisgard St.), **Johnson Street Parkade** (750 Johnson St.), and **View Street Parkade** (743 View St.). Rates are in effect 8am-6pm Monday-Saturday; parking is free in the evenings and on Sunday.

You can also park in these city-run surface lots ($2.25 per hour, $13.50 per day): **900 Wharf Street** (near the Harbour Air terminal) and **820 Courtney Street.** There's no free parking in these lots; pay rates are in effect 24 hours daily.

Car Rentals

Avis (800/879-2847, www.avis.ca), **Budget** (250/953-5300 or 800/668-9833, www.budget.ca), **Hertz** (800/263-0600, www.hertz.ca), and **National** (250/656-2541 or 800/227-7368, www.nationalcar.ca) have rental desks at Victoria International Airport. **Enterprise** (250/655-7368, www.enterprise.com) has a nearby off-airport location. Both Budget and National also have rental offices downtown, near the Inner Harbour.

By Bicycle

Victoria is a bike-friendly city. Among the scenic routes for visitors on bikes are **Dallas Road,** which skirts the seashore on the city's southern edge, and **Fairfield Road,** which passes Ross Bay Cemetery.

Running along a former rail line, the 35-mile (55-kilometer) **Galloping Goose Trail** takes you from Victoria west to the town of Sooke. You can follow the 18-mile (29-kilometer) **Lochside Regional Trail,** another rail trail, between Swartz Bay and Victoria.

Located behind the Empress Hotel, **The Pedaler** (719 Douglas St., 778/265-7433, http://thepedaler.ca, 9am-6pm daily May-Sept., call for off-season hours) has a fleet of modern bikes for rent (1 hour $10, 2 hours $14, full-day $28). They also run fun **guided cycling tours**, including the two-hour **Castles, Hoods & Legends** (adults $49, youth $45), a short tour of Victoria's major sights; the three-hour **Beans & Bites** ($89), which takes you through several Victoria neighborhoods with stops for coffee, pastries, and other snacks; and the three-hour **Hoppy Hour Ride** ($89), sampling Victoria's craft breweries.

Nanaimo

This city of 85,000 on Vancouver Island's east coast, 70 miles (110 kilometers) north of Victoria, is an alternate ferry port between the city of Vancouver and the island, convenient if you're traveling to Tofino on the island's west coast. British Columbia's third-oldest city, Nanaimo is worth a stop for its pretty waterfront, historic sites, and a unique adventure: snorkeling with a colony of seals who live near the harbor. Be sure to sample a Nanaimo bar, the local signature sweet.

Sights and Recreation
Nanaimo Museum

The modern **Nanaimo Museum** (100

Side Trip: Sipping Through the Cowichan Valley

The **Cowichan Valley,** located along Highway 1 between Victoria and Nanaimo, is a growing west coast wine-producing district, an easy day-trip from Victoria.

The **British Columbia Wine Institute** (www.winebc.com) has details about all the Cowichan Valley wineries, but you can start planning your Cowichan trip with these well-regarded stops:

• **Unsworth Vineyards** (2915 Cameron Taggart Rd., Mill Bay, 250/929-2292, www.unsworthvineyards.com, 11am-5pm Mon.-Tues., 11am-6pm Wed.-Sun. mid-May-mid-Oct., 11am-4pm Mon.-Tues., 11am-5pm Wed.-Sun. mid-Oct.-mid-May), a family-owned winery, has an upscale **Restaurant** (lunch and dinner from 11am Wed.-Sun., mains $15-27) in a restored 1907 farmhouse overlooking the vineyards.

• **Merridale Ciderworks** (230 Merridale Rd., Cobble Hill, 250/743-4293, www.merridalecider.com, 11am-5pm daily) makes sparkling cider, brandies, and fortified wines. Their **Bistro** (noon-3pm Mon.-Fri., 11am-3pm Sat.-Sun.) serves casual comfort food.

• **Venturi-Schulze Vineyards** (4235 Vineyard Rd., Cobble Hill, 250/743-5630, www.venturischulze.com, 10am-4:30pm Wed.-Sun.), another family-owned winemaker, produces organic wines from estate-grown grapes.

• **Zanetta Winery** (5039 Marshall Rd., Duncan, 250/748-2338, http://zanatta.ca, noon-4:30pm Wed.-Sun. May-Oct., call for off-phone hours) was the region's first estate winery, launched in 1992.

• **Averill Creek Vineyard** (6552 North Rd., Duncan, 250/709-9986, www.averillcreek.ca, 11am-5pm daily) has a patio where you can bring a picnic to enjoy with your wine.

Museum Way, 250/753-1821, www.nanaimomuseum.ca, 10am-5pm daily mid-May-early Sept., 10am-5pm Mon.-Sat. early Sept.-mid-May, adults $2, seniors and students $1.75, ages 5-12 $0.75) tells the stories of the city's development, from its First Nations communities to its days as a mining hub, when the Hudson's Bay Company established a coal mine nearby. Other exhibits focus on the city's quirkier traditions, like its annual summer bathtub race.

The Bastion

Built in 1853 by the Hudson's Bay Company, **The Bastion** (95 Front St.), on the Nanaimo waterfront, is the city's oldest structure and North America's only original wooden bastion (fortified tower). The first-floor exhibit area talks about the Hudson's Bay Company and its trading activities; the upper floors illustrate the building's military uses.

Outside the Bastion, stop to watch the midday **cannon firing ceremony** (noon daily mid-May-early Sept.), with a local bagpiper and a really big bang.

★ Snorkeling with Seals

Looking for a unique adventure? A colony of harbor seals lives around Snake Island, a rock outcropping located 15 minutes by boat from Nanaimo harbor. **Sundown Diving** (22 Esplanade Rd., 250/753-1880, www.sundowndiving.com) runs half-day tours ($100 pp) to the island, where you can **snorkel with the seals.**

The tour starts at the company's downtown shop, where you're outfitted with a wetsuit, hood, booties, gloves, and snorkeling gear. Your guide will take you to the harbor, where you board the motorboat to Snake Island. Scoot into the water to swim alongside these marine creatures, which are surprisingly graceful as they glide through the sea.

Bring a bathing suit, towel, and water bottle. You don't need snorkeling experience, but you should be comfortable swimming in deep water.

Accommodations

If you're going to stay over in Nanaimo, the friendly **Buccaneer Inn** (1577 Stewart Ave., 250/753-1246 or 877/282-6337, www.buccaneerinn.com, $75-200 d) is the closest place to sleep near the Departure Bay ferry terminal. In this basic but well-maintained family-run motel, many of the nautical-themed rooms and suites have kitchens. Parking, Wi-Fi, and free local phone calls. The inn is on a busy road, although traffic typically quiets at night.

The modern 15-story **Coast Bastion Hotel** (11 Bastion St., 250/753-6601 or 800/716-6199, www.coasthotels. com, $145-290 d) overlooks the harbor downtown, with water vistas from its upper floors; request a corner unit for prime views. The 179 rooms have all the expected amenities, including white linens with colorful accents, air-conditioning, coffeemakers, flat-screen TVs, safes, and included Wi-Fi and local calls. The hotel has a fitness room and spa. Park in the nearby city parkade ($8.50 for 24 hours) or let the hotel valet deal with your car for an additional $8.

Oh, the views! At **MGM Seashore B&B** (4950 Fillinger Cres., 250/729-7249, www.mgmbandb.com, $199-275 d), with three guest rooms in a residential neighborhood north of town, the panoramas stretch across the water, particularly out on the mammoth deck, where you can soak in the hot tub. Owners Marilyn and Glenn McKnight start guests' stays with a welcome Nanaimo bar, serve a full breakfast, and stock a guest lounge with espresso, tea, books, and movies. The Honeymoon Suite has a whirlpool tub positioned toward the ocean vistas, while the Sunset Room, with a round king bed, opens to the deck. The more basic King Room could accommodate a family, with a king bed and two singles.

Food

Start your day with pastries and coffee from **Mon Petit Choux** (120 Commercial St., 250/753-6002, www.monpetitchoux. ca, 8am-5pm Mon.-Sat., 9am-5pm Sun., mains $6-11), a sunny French-style café downtown. Beyond the sweets, they serve breakfasts (including scrambled eggs with smoked salmon or a *croque madame* on house-made brioche) and light lunches, from quiche to sandwiches on their own baguettes.

Despite its name, the **Modern Café** (221 Commercial St., 250/754-5022, www.themoderncafe.ca, 11am-11pm Mon.-Wed., 11am-midnight Thurs.-Sat., 10am-11pm Sun., mains lunch $12-18, dinner $14-28) is one of Nanaimo's oldest restaurants, serving food and drinks in its pub-style space downtown since 1946. Burgers, sandwiches, salads, and several types of macaroni and cheese are the lunchtime draws, while the dinner menu adds heartier plates like maple-glazed ribs or grilled steak. To drink? A Nanaimo bar martini!

The wood-burning oven takes center stage at **La Stella Trattoria** (321 Wesley St., 778/441-4668, www.lastellatrattoria. com, 5pm-9:30pm Wed.-Sun., mains $14-18) in Nanaimo's Old City Quarter, 0.5 miles (800 meters) up the hill from the harbor, turning out crisp-crusted pizzas topped with fresh ingredients like arugula, prosciutto, and locally produced *bocconcini*. Handmade pastas and Italian salads give you options beyond the pies.

When you pull up to the Westwood Tennis Club, a 15-minute drive west of downtown, you'd never guess that behind the courts is a fine lakeside bistro. The ★ **Bistro at Westwood Lake** (2367

On the Nanaimo Bar Trail

The city of Nanaimo has its own namesake dessert: the **Nanaimo bar.** This sweet treat, which became popular in the 1950s, has three layers: a nutty base of coconut, cocoa, and graham cracker crumbs, with a custard filling and a thick dark chocolate coating on top. You can find Nanaimo bars at bakeries all around town.

You can get more adventurous with your Nanaimo bars, too, if you follow the city's **Nanaimo bar trail.** At more than 30 stops, you can sample numerous variations on the Nanaimo bar theme. There's a rich, creamy vegan version at **Powerhouse Living Foods** (200 Commercial St., 250/571-7873, www. powerhouseliving.ca) and a whipped cream-slathered deep-fried wonder at **Pirate Chips** (1-75 Front St., 250/753-2447, www.pirate-chips.com). Several watering holes, including the **Modern Cafe** (221 Commercial St., 250/754-5022, www. themoderncafe.ca) and **Acme Food Co.** (14 Commercial St., 250/753-0042, http://

deep-fried Nanaimo bars at Pirate Chips

acmefoodnanaimo.com), even serve a Nanaimo bar martini.

Get a guide to the Nanaimo bar trail on the website of **Tourism Nanaimo** (www. tourismnanaimo.com) or pick up a copy at the **Nanaimo Visitor Centre.**

Arbot Rd., 250/753-2866, www.westwoodlake.com, lunch 11:30am-2:30pm Tues.-Fri., dinner 5pm-10pm Tues.-Sat., mains lunch $11-17, dinner $23-29) serves comfortably creative dishes, like B.C. halibut with lemon-caper aioli or steak in a soy-ginger marinade, in a lovely dining room and patio overlooking peaceful Westwood Lake. The three-course evening prix-fixe menu ($35) is a good value. Before or after your meal, loop the lake on the 3.5-mile (5.5-kilometer) walking trail.

Information and Services

Tourism Nanaimo (www.tourismnanaimo.com) runs the year-round **Nanaimo Visitor Centre** (2450 Northfield Rd., 250/751-1556 or 800/663-7337, 9am-5pm Mon.-Sat., 10am-3pm Sun.), off Highway 19 northwest of the city center, and provides information about the area.

The West Coast

Vancouver Island's west coast can feel like the edge of the world. After you climb the winding road up and over the spines of mountains in the center of the island, you finally reach the west shore, where the Pacific waves crash along the beach. Here are the ocean sands and peaceful coastal rainforests of the island's first national park, along with two easygoing west coast towns, larger Tofino to the north and Ucluelet to the south. These peninsula communities have whale-watching tours, First Nations canoe trips, and plenty of other outdoor adventures, as well as good restaurants and beachfront lodges.

The weather on the west coast can be cooler, damper, and more changeable than elsewhere on the island. Bring

The Island's Biggest Trees

Heading west from Nanaimo toward Vancouver Island's west coast, you'll pass through a section of old-growth rainforest, with massive trees that began their lives more than 800 years ago.

In **Cathedral Grove,** which is part of **MacMillan Provincial Park** (Hwy. 4, 250/474-1336, www.env.gov.bc.ca, dawn-dusk daily, free), you can follow two short trails through these forests of giants.

The biggest trees—colossal Douglas firs—are on the south side of the highway. The largest measures more than 30 feet (9 meters) around. On the north side of the road, the trail passes through groves of ancient western red cedars and along the shore of Cameron Lake.

Cathedral Grove is 40 miles (65 kilometers) west of Nanaimo and 10 miles (16 kilometers) east of Port Alberni. Highway 4 runs directly through the park; there's a parking lot near the big trees.

Cathedral Grove

layers, rain gear, and shoes or boots that can get wet.

Whatever the weather, the west coast is a laid-back region where local surfers carry their boards on their bikes, and cocktail hour can seem like a sacred ritual. And it's hugely popular with travelers: Tofino's population of 2,000 can swell to more than 20,000 on weekends in July and August.

Don't worry, though. Even in midsummer, there's plenty of room here at the edge of the world.

★ Pacific Rim National Park Reserve

With 14 miles (22 kilometers) of sandy beaches and dunes backed by coastal rainforest, the reserve protects a wide swath of Vancouver Island's west coast. Established in 1970, it was the island's first national park.

Visiting the Park

The **Pacific Rim National Park Reserve** has three geographically separate components. Most visitors head directly to the park's **Long Beach Unit** (Pacific Rim Hwy., 250/726-3500, www.pc.gc.ca), north of the Tofino-Ucluelet junction. The park visitors center is here, as is the longest beach on the island's west coast. You can camp, too, although you can easily day-trip to the park from Tofino or Ucluelet.

You can reach the park's **Broken Islands Group,** offshore in Barkley Sound, only by boat. Check the park website for recommended tour operators who organize guided kayaking or sailing tours to the islands.

Also part of the park is the 47-mile (75-kilometer) **West Coast Trail** (May-Sept.), a rugged backpacking route.

Park Passes and Fees

Purchase a **day pass** (adults $7.80, seniors $6.80, ages 6-16 $3.90, families $19.60) for the Pacific Rim National Park Reserve at the **Pacific Rim Visitor Centre** (2791 Pacific Rim Hwy., Ucluelet), at the park's **Kwisitis Visitor Centre** (Wick Beach, off

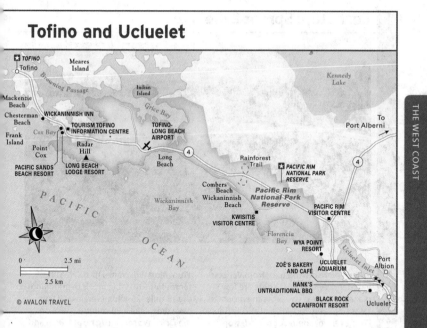

Tofino and Ucluelet

Pacific Rim Hwy.), or from vending machines at parking lots within the park.

Buying a Parks Canada **annual discovery pass** (adults $67.70, seniors $57.90, ages 6-16 $33.30, families $136.40), valid for a year, is a good deal if you're spending at least a week in one or more parks. It's good at more than 100 national parks and national historic sites across Canada. Buy annual passes online from Parks Canada or at any park visitors center.

For both day and annual passes, family passes cover up to seven people in a single vehicle.

Visitors Center
Start your park visit at the **Kwisitis Visitor Centre** (485 Wick Rd., off Pacific Rim Hwy., 250/726-3524, www.pc.gc.ca, 10am-4:30pm Wed.-Sun. Apr.-May, 8am-7pm daily June-early Sept., 10am-5pm Thurs.-Sun. early Sept.-mid-Nov., call for winter hours). The park encompasses the traditional territory of the Nuu-chah-nulth First Nation, and you can get an introduction to their culture though the center's exhibits.

Sports and Recreation
Beaches
Confusingly, **Wickaninnish Beach** is not the beach where the deluxe Wickaninnish Inn is located; that hotel is on Chesterman Beach. Rather, the wide dune-backed Wick Beach is adjacent to the park visitors center.

North of Wick Beach and adjacent to old-growth forest, **Long Beach** creates the longest sand dune on Vancouver Island; it's more than nine miles (16 kilometers) long.

Hiking
Several gentle hiking trails start from the park's Kwisitis Visitor Centre. The three-mile (5-kilometer) **Nuu-chah-nulth Trail** is an easy loop with interpretive panels about First Nations culture. You can branch from this trail onto the 0.5-mile (800-meter) **South Beach Trail** that leads to a pebble beach with often spectacular

Rest Stop: Sproat Lake

Sproat Lake

When you're driving to or from Vancouver Island's west coast, there are few places to stop as you cross the mountains between Port Alberni and Tofino. For a break or some good food, stop at **Sproat Lake Landing** (10695 Lakeshore Rd., Port Alberni, 250/723-2722, www.sproatlakelanding.com), where **Drinkwaters Social House** (11am-11pm Mon.-Fri., 9am-11pm Sat.-Sun.) serves farm-to-table meals overlooking the 15-mile (25-kilometer) lake. If you have time, take a 90-minute cruise on the *Drinkwater IV* **tugboat** (10am and 2pm daily spring-fall, $45). Book one of the seven modern guest rooms ($140-250) if you want a longer rest; the best have lake views.

waves; don't swim here, though, due to the strong currents. The gentle **Shorepine Bog Trail,** a 0.5-mile (800-meter) loop, takes you through an old-growth temperate rainforest.

Camping

Above the beach, 7.5 miles (12 kilometers) north of the Tofino-Ucluelet junction, **Green Point Campground** (www.pc.gc.ca, late June-early Nov., $17.60-23.50) has 94 drive-in sites and 20 forested walk-in sites with flush toilets and running water but no showers.

The walk-in sites include five **equipped camping sites** ($55), which are handy if you're not traveling with your own camping gear. The equipped sites come with a tent that sleeps 4 to 6 people, sleeping pads, a tarp shelter, stove, and lantern. You need to bring sleeping bags or bedding, cooking supplies, food, and other personal items. Remember your flashlights.

Make campsite **reservations** (877/737-3783, www.reservation.parkscanada. gc.ca) online or by phone, beginning in March for the upcoming season. Reservations are especially recommended for stays between mid-June and August.

★ Tofino

Like all of the west coast, the Tofino area was First Nations territory where generations of fishers and hunters lived and foraged, both on the mainland and on the islands offshore. Spanish explorers first ventured to the region in the late 1700s, followed quickly by British

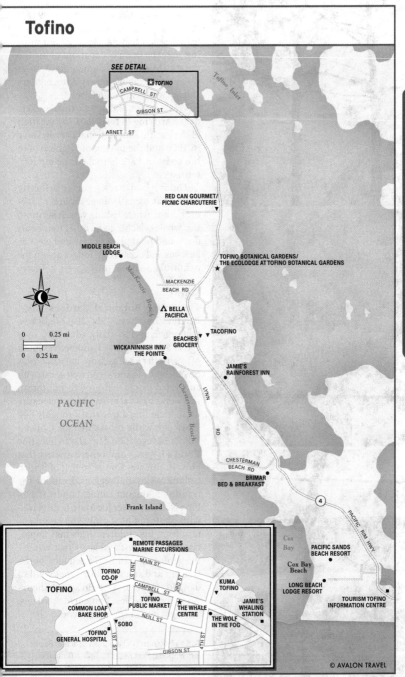

Tofino

SEE DETAIL

★ TOFINO

CAMPBELL ST

GIBSON ST

Tofino Inlet

ARNET ST

RED CAN GOURMET/
PICNIC CHARCUTERIE

MIDDLE BEACH
LODGE

TOFINO BOTANICAL GARDENS/
THE ECOLODGE AT TOFINO BOTANICAL GARDENS

★

MacKenzie Beach

MACKENZIE
BEACH RD

▲ BELLA
PACIFICA

▼ TACOFINO

BEACHES
GROCERY

WICKANINNISH INN/
THE POINTE

JAMIE'S
RAINFOREST INN

PACIFIC

OCEAN

0   0.25 mi

0   0.25 km

Chesterman Beach

LYNN
RD

CHESTERMAN
BEACH RD

BRIMAR
BED & BREAKFAST

④

PACIFIC RIM HWY

Frank Island

Cox
Bay

Cox Bay
Beach

PACIFIC SANDS
BEACH RESORT

LONG BEACH
LODGE RESORT

TOURISM TOFINO
INFORMATION CENTRE

REMOTE PASSAGES
MARINE EXCURSIONS

MAIN ST

2ND ST

3RD ST

TOFINO
CO-OP

CAMPBELL ST

KUMA
TOFINO

TOFINO

TOFINO
PUBLIC MARKET

★ THE WHALE
CENTRE

JAMIE'S
WHALING
STATION

COMMON LOAF
BAKE SHOP

NEILL ST

THE WOLF
IN THE FOG

▼ SOBO

1ST ST

TOFINO
GENERAL HOSPITAL

4TH ST

GIBSON ST

© AVALON TRAVEL

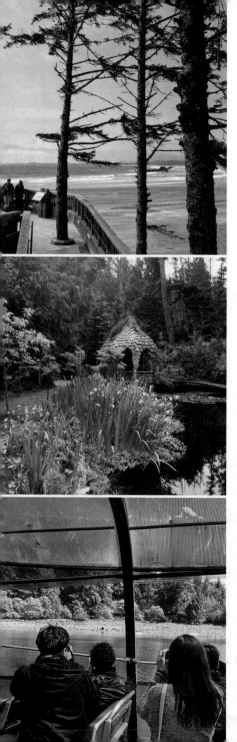

expeditions, but it wasn't until 1909 that the town of Tofino was officially established, when fishing, logging, and mining were the main occupations along the coast. Tofino's nickname comes from these hardscrabble jobs and the region's stormy winters: Tough City.

While surfers and other nature-seekers began arriving in the 1960s, the creation of the Pacific Rim National Park Reserve in 1970 and the paving of Highway 4 to the coast in 1972 launched the modern tourist era.

Today, laid-back, surfer-friendly Tofino has a small village around its scenic harbor, where fishing vessels set off to sea, whale-watching and other tour boats dock, and float planes come and go. The beaches and oceanfront lodges are on the peninsula, south of town.

Sights

The **Tofino Botanical Gardens** (1084 Pacific Rim Hwy., 250/725-1220, www. tbgf.org, 9am-dusk daily, adults $10, over age 11 $6), two miles (3 kilometers) south of town, offer a refuge from the wilderness of Vancouver Island's wild west coast, with cultivated plants, old-growth rainforest, and works by local artists. Many plants are local, including a tree that's roughly 800 years old, while others include Chilean rainforest vegetation, Himalayan lilies (the world's largest), and other varieties that grow in climates similar to that of British Columbia's coastal regions. Examine the traditional dugout canoe, handmade by First Nations carver Joe Martin, displayed with photos of his family and commentary from his children. Kids may appreciate the chickens and goats that wander the garden's grounds. Named for Charles Darwin and stocked with "books full of dangerous ideas," **Darwin's Café** (hours vary) serves coffee, homemade pastries, and light breakfasts and lunches.

Top to bottom: Wickaninnish Beach in Pacific Rim National Park Reserve; Tofino Botanical Gardens; bear-watching near Tofino.

Two Days on Vancouver Island's West Coast

Start your day with a morning stroll along the beach; **Chesterman Beach** is one of the area's most beautiful. Then wander through the **Tofino Botanical Gardens** to explore the old-growth rainforest, stopping at the garden's **Darwin's Café** when it's time for a coffee break.

Have lunch at the orange food truck, **Tacofino.** Then head for **Pacific Rim National Park Reserve** to check out the displays in the **Kwisitis Visitor Centre** and hike near the shore. Later, take a **surfing lesson,** go swimming, or book a **First Nations Dugout Canoe Tour** with the excellent guides at T'ashii Paddle School. Have dinner at **The Wolf in the Fog,** where the don't-miss appetizer is the potato-crusted oyster, and any local seafood is bound to be stellar.

The next morning, pick up coffee and a ginger scone at **Common Loaf Bakery,** before heading for the waterfront for an offshore excursion. Take a full-day trip to **Hot Springs Cove,** a kayak excursion to **Meares Island,** or a shorter **whale-watching** or **bear-watching tour.**

After your tour, clean up and drive to the **Wickanninish Inn** for a cocktail in their window-lined lounge facing the sea. If your budget allows, stay for a special dinner at **The Pointe,** or if you'd rather have a more casual meal, head into town for a restorative bowl of ramen at **Kuma Tofino** or the wild salmon chowder at **SoBo.** Either way, stop to take a few sunset photos over the harbor to remember your west coast adventures.

The Whale Centre (411 Campbell St., 250/725-2132, www.tofinowhalecentre.com, 9am-5pm daily May-June and Sept.-Oct., 8am-8pm daily July-Aug., hours vary Nov.-Apr., free) has a little museum with a grey whale skeleton and information about local marine life.

Tours and Excursions

To really experience the west coast, get off-shore to explore the coastline and nearby islands, and look for the wildlife that populates the region. Most tours operate from March or April through October or November, although trips can be postponed or cancelled if the seas get too rough.

The following companies are among those offering tours in the Tofino area:

- **Remote Passages Marine Excursions** (51 Wharf St., 250/725-3330 or 800/666-9833, www.remotepassages.com)

- **Ocean Outfitters** (368 Main St., 250/725-2866 or 877/906-2326, www.oceanoutfitters.bc.ca)

- **T'ashii Paddle School** (250/266-3787 or 855/883-3787, www.tofinopaddle.com)

- **The Whale Centre** (411 Campbell St., 250/725-2132 or 888/474-2288, www.tofinowhalecentre.com)

Hot Springs Cove/Maquinna Marine Provincial Park

A full-day trip to these remote hot springs is a highlight for many Tofino visitors. Located 27 nautical miles (50 kilometers) northwest of Tofino, **Hot Springs Cove,** in Maquinna Marine Provincial Park at the north end of Clayoquot Sound, is accessible only by boat (adults $125-130, under age 13 $79-105) or float plane (adults $199, under age 13 $179).

Traveling by boat (1.5 to 2 hours each way), you may spot whales, sea lions, and even bears or other wildlife, so you might consider this trip an alternative to a separate whale-watching tour. With the float plane option, you save a little time, traveling one way by boat, the other on a scenic 20-minute flight.

Once you arrive at the dock, it's a one-mile (1.6-kilometer) walk on a boardwalk through the rainforest to the natural hot springs. Climb down the rocks and take a natural hot shower in the gushing sulfur springs, then soak in the rock pools. The water temperature averages a soothing 110°F (43°C).

There's a rustic shelter with change rooms and a pit toilet above the springs and a restroom near the docks. Don't forget your bathing suit, towel, and water bottle. Sports sandals or water shoes will protect your feet from the rocks. Bring snacks or a picnic to enjoy before or after you soak.

Meares Island

Declared a park by the Tla-o-qui-aht and Ahousaht First Nations, **Meares Island**—its traditional name is *Wanachis-Hilthhoois*—is across the harbor from the village of Tofino.

A popular way to get to the island is on a half-day **kayak excursion** ($79). Some companies also run **water shuttles** (adults $25-30, under age 12 $20) to the island. Tour companies also collect a $3-5 park pass fee.

Once you arrive on Meares Island, you can hike through the rainforest on the moderate 1.9-mile (3 kilometer) round-trip **Big Tree Trail,** which takes you into an old-growth forest, where some trees are more than 1,000 years old.

For experienced hikers, the island's steep, challenging **Lone Cone Trail** leads up to a 2,395-foot (730-meter) peak with panoramic views across the island and the sound. It's only 0.6 miles (1 kilometer) in each direction, but it's essentially a vertical trail.

Whale-Watching

On **whale-watching excursions** (adults $89-109, under age 13 $69-79) from Tofino, you'll likely spot Pacific gray whales. You might also see humpback whales, bald eagles, sea lions, harbor seals, and occasionally orcas or porpoises.

As on the trips that depart from Victoria, you can choose from a tour in an inflatable zodiac, which gives you a choppier but more thrilling ride, or on a larger, more sheltered boat, which would be more comfortable in inclement weather. On either type of craft, whale-watching tours typically last two to three hours.

Bear-Watching

From Tofino, you can take a boat through Clayoquot Sound to several spots where it's possible to observe the area's resident population of black bears. On these **bear-watching excursions** (adults $89-99, under age 13 $69-79), the tour boats dock offshore, where, if you're lucky, you'll spot bears foraging along the rocky beaches or in the tidal pools.

You stay on the boat throughout these two- to three-hour tours. Bring a camera with a telephoto lens for the best photos, since the boats must remain a safe distance away from the animals.

First Nations Dugout Canoe Tours

First Nations-owned **T'ashii Paddle School** (250/266-3787 or 855/883-3787, www.tofinopaddle.com) offers several excellent paddling tours in hand-carved dugout canoes, where you'll learn about local indigenous communities and their traditional culture.

Departing from Jamie's Whaling Station (606 Campbell St.), excursions include a two-hour **Harbour Canoe Tour** (late May-mid-Oct., $65 pp), which is especially lovely at sunset; a **Meares Island Canoe Tour** (Mar.-Oct., $80 pp), a four-hour paddling and hiking excursion; and a full-day **Lemmens Inlet Canoe Tour** (Mar.-Oct., by request only, $130 pp). Check the website for specific departure times.

Sports and Recreation
Beaches

Sandy beaches line the peninsula that stretches south from Tofino to Ucluelet. All are along the Pacific Rim Highway, listed here from north to south.

Sheltered **MacKenzie Beach** is closest to Tofino, with several resorts and campgrounds.

Beginning surfers hone their skills on the south end of 1.7-mile (2.7-kilometer) **Chesterman Beach,** one of Tofino's most scenic and popular stretches of sand. Toward the beach's north side, you can explore the tide pools at low tide.

Home to several resorts, including Pacific Sands and Long Beach Lodge, **Cox Bay Beach** has a popular surf break. At the bay's northern tip, you can explore several tidal caves, accessible only at low tide. The Wickaninnish Inn is on North Chesterman Beach.

Continuing south, you'll reach the beaches in Pacific Rim National Park Reserve, including **Long Beach** and **Wickaninnish Beach.**

Surfing

Tofino is western Canada's **surfing** capital (yes, Canada really has a surfing capital), with plenty of places to take lessons or catch the waves. While you can surf year-round, hardcore surfers come in winter when the waves are biggest; if you're just getting started, summertime is warmest, with the gentlest surf.

With a crew of women as instructors, **Surf Sister Surf School** (250/725-4456, www.surfsister.com) specializes in teaching women to surf, although they offer lessons for both men and women.

The **Surf Club Adventure Centre** (250/725-2442, www.longbeachlodgeresort.com) at the Long Beach Lodge Resort is another highly regarded surf school, teaching group and private lessons.

Hiking

The **Rainforest Education Society** (250/725-2560, www.raincoasteducation.org) offers free one-hour interpretive walks in July and August that explore the tide pools and rainforest along Cox Bay. Check the website for the schedule and other details.

Guides from the First Nations-owned **T'ashii Paddle School** (250/266-3787 or 855/883-3787, www.tofinopaddle.com) lead winter **Cultural Walks on the Schooner Cove Trail** (mid-Dec.-Mar. 11am daily, $80 pp) in Pacific Rim National Park Reserve that combine a gentle hike through the old-growth rainforest with information about local First Nations culture. Book in advance on their website.

Festivals and Events

In early spring, gray whales begin returning to the waters off Vancouver Island's west coast. During the weeklong **Pacific Rim Whale Festival** (www.pacificrimwhalefestival.com, Mar.), you can learn more about these creatures with presentations, documentary films, guided walks, whale-watching tours, and other events.

The **Tofino Food and Wine Festival** (www.tofinofoodandwinefestival.com, June) is a weekend of dining, sipping, and toe-tapping to live music, on the grounds of the Tofino Botanical Gardens.

Celebrating local bivalves, the **Clayoquot Oyster Festival** (www.oyster-gala.com, Nov.) brings seafood lovers to town for oyster farm tours, restaurant events, a gala party, and plenty of oyster eating.

Accommodations

Tofino's nicest accommodations are south of town, along the peninsula beaches. Book in advance for summer high season (mid-June-mid-Sept.). In winter, many lodgings offer **storm watching** packages, when the big winter surf and rain rolls in.

$150-250

Once a field station for research groups, **The Ecolodge at Tofino Botanical Gardens** (1084 Pacific Rim Hwy., 250/725-1220, www.tbgf.org, $149-199 d) is a simple comfortable lodge in the midst of the botanical gardens. Guests gather in the great room for continental breakfast or just to relax; you can use the kitchen to prep meals or browse the lodge's nature library. Eight basic, colorfully decorated rooms share two large baths. Two additional suites, with private baths, have family-friendly nooks with bunk beds. There are no TVs, but Wi-Fi is included, as is garden admission.

At **Jamie's Rainforest Inn** (1258 Pacific Rim Hwy., 250/725-2323 or 855/433-2323, www.tofinorainforestinn.com, $209-249 d), a well-kept motel facing the woods on the inlet side of the highway, the 38 rooms have microwaves, mini fridges, coffeemakers, and included Wi-Fi. The king-bed rooms have gas fireplaces, and the larger units include kitchenettes with cooktops. Ask about discounts on whale-watching and other tours from their affiliated adventure company, **Jamie's Whaling Station** (www.jamies.com).

Overlooking two beaches and the offshore islands, **Middle Beach Lodge** (400 MacKenzie Beach Rd., 250/725-2900 or 866/725-2900, www.middlebeach.com, $155-465 d) offers a variety of accommodations. The original lodge has tiny, no-frills rooms with no TVs or closets, but the nicest of these economical units have ocean views. In the main lodge, rooms are slightly larger with wooden floors and flat-screen TVs; choose an end unit upstairs for the best water vistas. Also on the forested property are roomy cabins with kitchen facilities; some have sleeping lofts, fireplaces, or hot tubs. Your room almost doesn't matter when you take in the panoramic views from the overstuffed chairs in the wood-beamed great room, where a deluxe continental breakfast buffet (included in the rates) is served.

Over $250

The three gold-and-burgundy guest rooms at the cedar-shingled ★ **BriMar Bed & Breakfast** (1375 Chesterman Beach Rd., 250/725-3410, www.brimarbb.com, $259-319 d) look right onto Chesterman Beach, close enough to hear the surf. On

dugout canoe tour with T'ashii Paddle School

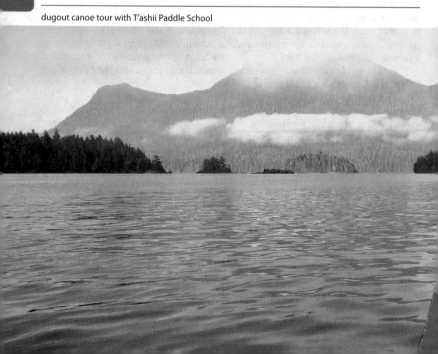

the second floor, the spacious Moonrise Room has an equally spacious private bath, while the slightly smaller Sunset Room has a private bath across the hall. The secluded Loft Unit, under the eaves, runs the whole length of the top floor. Rates include Wi-Fi and an ample breakfast, with fruit, granola, yogurt, baked goods, and a hot dish like eggs benedict or baked french toast. Guests can help themselves to coffee and tea at all hours and store snacks in the hallway fridge.

Even if you're not staying at the **Long Beach Lodge Resort** (1441 Pacific Rim Hwy., 250/725-2442, www.longbeachlodgeresort.com, $199-439 d, cottages $449-589), have a drink or a meal in the resort's inviting **Great Room,** with walls of windows facing the ocean. The lodge has a highly regarded surf club, where both kids and adults can learn to ride the waves. When it's time to sleep, choose from 41 studio units in the main lodge, with sturdy Douglas fir furnishings, or from 20 two-bedroom cottages

in the forest, set back from the beach. Solo travelers: in the off-season, the resort regularly offers excellent discounts for individual guests.

Opened in 1972 on the beach at Cox Bay, **Pacific Sands Beach Resort** (1421 Pacific Rim Hwy, 250/725-3322, www.pacificsands.com, $235-365 d, 2-bedroom unit $490-850) has grown to encompass a variety of units in several buildings. Most of the modern condo-style beach houses have two bedrooms and views across the lawn to the waterfront. In other buildings, the studio to two-bedroom units are smaller but still feel airy and beachy. All suites have full kitchens, handy since there's no restaurant on-site, though the lobby coffee bar sells drinks, snacks, and quick meals. Rent beach cruiser bikes to go cycling or gather the gang in the gazebo to roast marshmallows.

The most deluxe lodging on Vancouver Island's west coast is the ★ **Wickaninnish Inn** (500 Osprey Lane, 250/725-3100 or 800/333-4604, www.wickinn.com, $310-900 d), which nestles into 100 acres (40 hectares) of old-growth rainforest on Chesterman Beach. Behind the unassuming gray exteriors, the inn is filled with aboriginal art and 75 rustic yet elegant accommodations with earth-tone furnishings, gas fireplaces, flat-screen TVs hidden in cabinets that open by remote control, soaker tubs, and heated bath floors. Wi-Fi and bicycles are complimentary. The **Ancient Cedars Spa** has seven treatment rooms, including one set dramatically above the rocks; guests can join daily yoga classes. Local musicians perform at the **Driftwood Café** (named for its bar made of driftwood), which serves coffee, pastries, and light meals. **The Pointe,** the inn's premier restaurant, is among the region's finest.

Food

For a small community, Tofino has a significant food culture, emphasizing innovative uses of local seafood and produce. Outside the summer months, many restaurants have reduced hours, so call to confirm before you set out. Except for The Pointe at the Wickaninnish Inn, Tofino's eating places are casual; patrons often look like they've wandered directly off a boat because, most likely, they have.

Groceries and Markets

The area's largest grocery store is **Tofino Co-op** (140 First St., 250/725-3226, www. tofinocoop.com, 8:30am-9pm daily summer, call for off-season hours). South of town, tiny but well-stocked **Beaches Grocery** (1184 Pacific Rim Hwy., 250/725-2237) carries fruits and vegetables, baked goods, and other food items, from chips to Asian chili sauce.

Find local produce, prepared foods, and crafts at the **Tofino Public Market** (Tofino Village Green, 3rd St. and Campbell St., www.tofinomarket.com, 10am-2pm Sat. late May-Sept.).

Cafés, Bakeries, and Light Bites

From local hippies to texting teens to travelers, everyone stops into the red house that's home to long-standing **Common Loaf Bake Shop** (180 1st St., 250/725-3915, 8am-6pm daily) for delectable cinnamon buns, ginger scones, breads, and muffins. They make soup, sandwiches, and pizza, too.

In an industrial building on the town's south side, **Red Can Gourmet** (700 Industrial Way, 250/725-2525, www.redcangourmet.com, 9am-8pm Wed., 9am-9pm Thurs.-Sat., 9am-8pm Sun., mains lunch $8-15, dinner $17-25) cooks gourmet take-out fare, from sandwiches and salads midday to more substantial dinner plates, such as seafood curry with smoked tofu or beef tenderloin, as well as pizza.

Tiny **Picnic Charcuterie** (Industrial Way, behind Red Can Gourmet, 250/889-5738, www.picniccharcuterie.com, 10am-5pm Tues.-Sat., 11am-4pm Sun.) sells their own cured and smoked meats, with a selection of local and imported cheeses.

Contemporary

Oysters in a potato web? Rare tuna with confit pork and wasabi? Some of the west coast's most imaginative dishes come out of the open kitchen at ★ **The Wolf in the Fog** (150 4th St., 250/725-9653, www. wolfinthefog.com, 5pm-midnight daily, mains $15-32), where the second-floor dining room sparkles with polished wood and the big windows look out toward the harbor. While there's some serious technique and respect for local ingredients here, the chefs don't take themselves too seriously, with plates like the Block Party, a for-the-table feast of fried chicken, barbecued ribs, pulled pork, cornbread, and greens, or the Spanish Bombshell, scallops and other shellfish served with potatoes, focaccia, and saffron aioli. To drink, try a cocktail like The Angler, with smoked salmon-infused vodka, maple, ginger, and fresh orange, or a Cedar Sour, with cedar-infused rye. The bottom line? Good food, good drinks, good fun.

Though the name is short for "sophisticated bohemian," airy **SoBo** (311 Neil St., 250/725-2341, www.sobo.ca, 11:30am-9pm daily, mains lunch $10, dinner $16-35), with sunny yellow walls and floor-to-ceiling windows, is more refined than hippie, serving modern worldbeat fare at lunch and dinner. Noon-hour dishes roam from Asian salad to huevos rancheros to pizza, while in the evening, you might try cedar-planked salmon, whiskey-braised beef brisket, or seafood stew. SoBo is justifiably famous for its smoked wild fish chowder.

Tofino's special-occasion restaurant, ★ **The Pointe at the Wickaninnish Inn** (500 Osprey Lane, 250/725-3106, www. wickinn.com, 8am-2pm and 5pm-9pm daily, mains dinner $30-46, brunch $12-24) emphasizes local seafood, foraged ingredients, and regional products. The polished staff and walls of curved windows wrapping the ocean panoramas around you don't hurt either. You might start with ginger-cured foie gras or with a Pacific Harvest of mussel custard, kelp, clams, and pickled sea asparagus, as a prelude to snapper and shrimp paired with prawn dumplings and grilled cucumber or roast duck in a hemlock jus. There are sweets, of course, from a platter of petit fours to fancy s'mores. Can't decide (or ready to splurge)? Choose a four- to six-course tasting menu ($85-100 pp) with optional wine pairings.

Asian
When you crave a restorative bowl of ramen, head for **Kuma Tofino** (101-120 4th St., 250/725-2215, www.kumatofino. com, 4pm-11pm Wed.-Sun., mains $10-14), a modern Japanese eatery. Sake and local craft beer stand up to sharing plates like crispy chicken *karaage,* fresh tuna *tataki,* and bright house-made pickles.

Mexican
Before it became a Mexican mini chain with branches in Vancouver and Victoria, **Tacofino** (1184 Pacific Rim Hwy., 250/726-8288, www.tacofino.com, 11am-8pm daily, mains $4-12) was a taco truck in Tofino ("Taco-fino," get it?). This orange truck parked behind a surf shop south of town channels a surfer vibe with tacos (try the tuna with seaweed and ginger), burritos, and slushie drinks like tangy lime-mint "freshies." Park at one of the long outdoor tables, or take yours to the beach.

Information and Services
The **Pacific Rim Visitor Centre** (2791 Pacific Rim Hwy., Ucluelet, 250/726-4600, www.pacificrimvisitor.ca, 10am-4:30pm daily, longer hours in summer), at the Tofino-Ucluelet junction, where Highway 4 meets the Pacific Rim Highway, provides information about the region. **Parks Canada** staff are on hand to offer visitor services (10am-4:30pm Wed.-Sun. Apr.-May, 8am-7pm daily June-early Sept., 9:30am-5pm daily early Sept.-mid-Oct.) for Pacific Rim National Park Reserve spring through fall.

Tofino Tourism (www.tourismtofino. com) has a detailed website with useful trip-planning tips. They run the **Tofino Information Centre** (1426 Pacific Rim Hwy., Tofino, 250/725-3414 or 888/720-3414, www.tourismtofino.com, 9am-7pm daily mid-June-early Sept., 10am-5pm daily early-Sept.-mid-June), 4.5 miles (7 kilometers) south of downtown Tofino and 15.5 miles (25 kilometers) north of the Tofino-Ucluelet junction.

Small **Tofino General Hospital** (261 Neill St., 250/725-4010, www.viha.ca) offers 24-hour emergency services.

Getting Around
Easy to explore on foot, the town of Tofino is just a few blocks square, with most shops and restaurants along Campbell or Main Streets, between 1st and 4th Streets. To travel between town and the beaches, it's easiest to have your own car, although it's possible to cycle or take a bus.

By Car
From its junction with Highway 4, the Pacific Rim Highway runs 20 miles (32 kilometers) up the peninsula to the town of Tofino, passing Pacific Rim National Park Reserve and beaches along the way. In town, the highway becomes Campbell Street.

If you arrive in Tofino without a car, you can rent one from **Budget** (188 Airport Rd., 250/725-2060, www.bcbudget.com) at the Tofino airport.

By Bus
The free **Tofino Transit shuttle bus** (www. tofinobus.com, 11am-8pm daily late June-early Sept.) runs during the summer between town and Cox Bay, with stops near several beaches. Buses leave about once an hour in each direction, so check the schedule online before setting out.

By Bike
Cycling is a good way to travel between the village of Tofino and the beaches. Ride along the 3.75-mile (6-kilometer)

Multi-Use Path, locally known as the MUP, a fairly flat, paved trail that parallels Highway 4 from town to Cox Bay. **TOF Cycles** (660 Sharp Rd., 250/725-2453, www.tofcycles.com) or **Tofino Bikes** (1180 Pacific Rim Hwy., 250/725-2722, http://tofinobike.com), both located between Mackenzie and Chesterman Beaches, rent bikes.

Ucluelet

Once considered the workaday counterpart to more upscale Tofino, 25 miles (40 kilometers) to the north, Ucluelet (population 1,600) is coming into its own as a holiday destination. While it's close enough to Pacific Rim National Park Reserve to explore the trails and beaches, you can also enjoy the sand and hiking routes in and around town.

Sights and Recreation

Ucluelet Aquarium (180 Main St., 250/726-2782, www.uclueletaquarium. org, 10am-5pm daily mid-Mar.-Nov., adults $14, seniors and students $10, ages 4-17 $7) has a rare "catch and release" philosophy. In the spring, staff bring in sealife from the local waters of Clayoquot and Barkley Sounds to populate the kids'-eye-level tanks, releasing them in the autumn back to the wild. The "please touch" displays are fun for youngsters and not-so-youngsters alike.

For hikers, the **Wild Pacific Trail** (www. wildpacifictrail.com) has several moderate options at the foot of the Ucluelet peninsula. The 1.6-mile (2.6-kilometer) **Lighthouse Loop** starts and ends on Coast Guard Road south of Terrace Beach. The hillier **Artist Loop** takes you 1.7 miles (2.8 kilometers) along the cliffs starting from either Brown's Beach or Big Beach Park near Black Rock Oceanfront Resort. Get a map on the trail website or from the Pacific Rim Visitor Centre.

Accommodations and Camping

The Ucluelet First Nation runs the unique ★ **Wya Point Resort** (2695 Tofino-Ucluelet Hwy., 250/726-2625 or 844/352-6188, www.wyapoint.com), which has several lodging options on a remote section of coast. Nine wood-frame **lodges** ($349 one-bedroom, $559 two-bedroom), decorated with works by First Nations carvers, are upscale cabins, each sleeping four to six, with solid hand-built bed frames, living rooms with sleep sofas, full kitchens, and spacious decks above Ucluth Beach. Fifteen heated **yurts** ($150-175) made of thick canvas offer more rustic accommodations. You can cook outside on the barbecue and sleep inside on the sofa bed; some yurts also have bunk beds for the kids. Shared washrooms are nearby. The third option is the **campground** (early-Mar.-mid-Oct., $35-65), where some sites overlook the ocean and others sit in the forest near the beach.

Family-friendly 133-room **Black Rock Oceanfront Resort** (596 Marine Dr., 250/726-4800 or 877/762-5011, www. blackrockresort.com, $169-379 d) has everything you need for a beach getaway. Modern studios and one-bedroom suites in the main lodge, decorated in earthy greens and blacks, have kitchen facilities, spacious baths with heated floors and soaker tubs, and free Wi-Fi. Choose a fourth-floor room for the best views. Surrounded by trees in separate buildings, the Trail Suites range from studios to two-bedroom units. On the sea-facing deck is a plunge pool and two hot tubs; inside is a small fitness room and spa. Borrow a complimentary bicycle to go exploring. When you get hungry, **Fetch Restaurant,** specializing in seafood, cooks up breakfast, lunch, and dinner; **Float Lounge** serves drinks and light meals.

Food

Stop into **Zoë's Bakery and Café** (250 Main St., 250/726-2253, 7:30am-4pm Tues.-Fri., 8am-4pm Sat.-Sun., mains $5-10) for pastries, soups, quiche, sandwiches, and other baked goods. Try the

Savory Breakfast Egg Bake Thingy, a delicious mash-up of sourdough bread cubes and bacon, topped with an egg. Zoë's is also known for its carrot cake.

Curing their own meats and sourcing ingredients locally may not make this barbecue joint nontraditional, but at **Hank's Untraditional BBQ** (1576 Imperial Lane, 250/726-2225, www. hanksbbq.ca, 5pm-10pm daily, mains $15-18), it does make things good. Lead off with spicy hoisin duck wings, mustardy turkey wings, or crispy smelts before muscling into the main event, whether it's juniper-rubbed pork cheeks, coffee- and cocoa-rubbed beef brisket, or pulled chicken with maple barbecue sauce.

Information and Services

Get local information at the **Pacific Rim Visitor Centre** (2791 Pacific Rim Hwy., Ucluelet, 250/726-4600, www.pacificrim-visitor.ca, 10am-4:30pm daily, longer hours in summer) at the Tofino-Ucluelet junction.

Whistler and the Sea-to-Sky Highway

To explore the outdoors in any season, follow this scenic drive to western Canada's year-round playground.

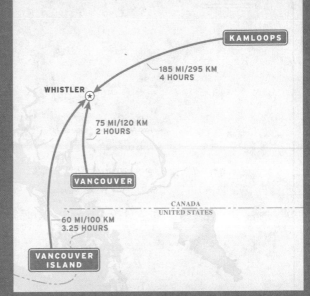

KAMLOOPS

185 MI/295 KM
4 HOURS

WHISTLER

75 MI/120 KM
2 HOURS

VANCOUVER

CANADA
UNITED STATES

60 MI/100 KM
3.25 HOURS

VANCOUVER
ISLAND

Sea-to-Sky Highway

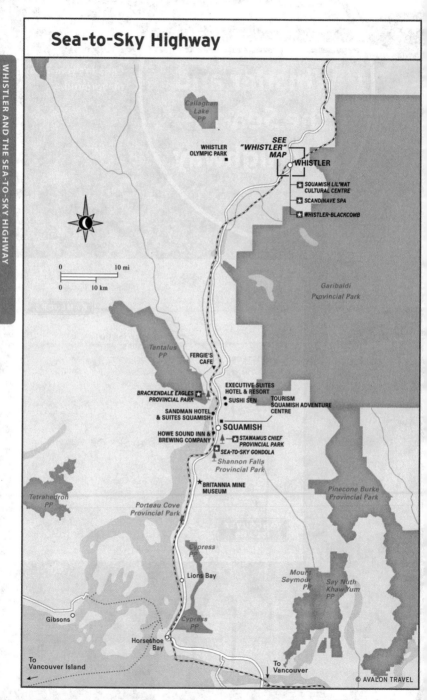

© AVALON TRAVEL

Whistler

The Sea-to-Sky Highway, one of western Canada's most stunning roadways, connects Vancouver to the year-round outdoor mecca of Whistler.

Just a two-hour drive, it's perfect for a day trip or as part of a longer exploration. Whistler offers not just North America's largest snow sports resort but also plenty of opportunities for hiking, biking, paddling the glacier-fed lakes, and exploring the region's First Nations heritage.

Between Whistler and Vancouver, the town of Squamish is a hot spot for outdoor activities, including excellent hiking and the region's best white-water rafting. For those looking for gentler adventures,

Highlights

★ **Sea-to-Sky Gondola:**
A 10-minute ride up this
2,790-foot (850-meter)
Squamish peak gives you
expansive views of Howe
Sound and the surrounding
mountains. There's a sus-
pension bridge, lots of hiking trails, and a great patio
at the top (page 146).

★ **Brackendale Eagles
Provincial Park:** One of
North America's largest
populations of bald eagles
spends the winter months

in this park near Squamish
(page 148).

★ **Stawamus Chief
Provincial Park:** For strong
hikers, a day hike up the
rocky summit known as the
Chief is a popular adventure
(page 149).

★ **Whistler-Blackcomb:**
From skiing and snowboarding to hiking, canoeing, rock
climbing, and zip-lining, if it's
an outdoor adventure, you

can do it at this mountain
resort (page 151).

★ **Squamish Lil'wat
Cultural Centre:** Learn
about the Whistler region's
First Nations communities
at this modern museum and
cultural facility (page 154).

★ **Scandinave Spa:** After
your Whistler adventures,
ease your sore muscles into
the hot and cold pools at this
Scandinavian-style soaking
spa (page 155).

Squamish's Sea-to-Sky Gondola delivers stellar mountain views and access to mountaintop hiking trails.

Getting to Whistler

Driving from Vancouver

Allow about **two hours** to make the **75-mile (120-kilometer)** drive between Vancouver and Whistler along the spectacular **Sea-to-Sky Highway.**

From downtown Vancouver, take **West Georgia Street** to the **Lions Gate Bridge.** Watch the signs carefully as you approach Stanley Park en route to the bridge to stay in the proper lane. The center lane on the three-lane bridge reverses its travel direction at different times of day, typically creating two travel lanes into the city in the morning and two travel lanes toward the North Shore during the afternoon rush hour.

After you cross the Lions Gate Bridge, bear left toward Marine Drive west/ Highway 1/Highway 99. Enter **Marine Drive** and stay in the far right lane to take the first right onto **Taylor Way** (the sign says "Whistler"). Follow Taylor Way up the hill, and exit left onto **Highway 1** west. Continue on Highway 1 until it merges with **Highway 99 (Sea-to-Sky Hwy.).** Stay on Highway 99 through Squamish and into Whistler.

Driving from Kamloops

If you're driving to Whistler from Kamloops or from points farther east in the Canadian Rockies, follow **Highway 1** west. At Kamloops, continue west on Highway 1 to **Cache Creek,** where you make a sharp right turn onto **Highway 97** north, following the signs for "BC-99/Prince George/Lillooet." When Highways 97 and 99 meet, take **Highway 99** west, which will take you through Lillooet, Pemberton, and on into Whistler. Kamloops to Whistler is **185 miles (295 kilometers),** a **four-hour** drive.

Driving from Vancouver Island (via Ferry)

If you're traveling between Vancouver Island and Whistler, you don't have to go through the city of Vancouver. Take the **B.C. Ferries** (888/223-3779, www.bcferries.com) service from Nanaimo's Departure Bay Terminal to Horseshoe Bay, which is on the mainland northwest of Vancouver. The **Horseshoe Bay-Departure Bay Ferry** (one-way adults $16.90, ages 5-11 $8.45, cars $55.40, bikes $2) takes **one hour and 40 minutes.**

The **Departure Bay Terminal** (680 Trans-Canada Hwy., Nanaimo) is two miles (3 kilometers) north of downtown Nanaimo.

From **Horseshoe Bay,** drive north on **Highway 99 (Sea-to-Sky Hwy.).** It's **60 miles (100 kilometers)** from Horseshoe Bay to Whistler; allow about **75-90 minutes** for the drive.

From late June through early September, ferries between Horseshoe Bay and Departure Bay generally make eight or nine trips daily, with six or seven daily runs the rest of the year; check the B.C. Ferries website (www.bcferries.com) for the seasonal schedule.

Getting There by Air or Bus
By Air

A dramatic way to travel between Vancouver and Whistler, if your budget allows, is by floatplane, which takes you above Howe Sound, the Gulf Islands, and the surrounding peaks.

Harbour Air (604/274-1277 or 800/665-0212, www.harbourair.com, 45 minutes, one-way adults $200) flies twice daily in each direction between the **Vancouver Harbour Flight Centre** (1055 Canada Pl., behind the Vancouver Convention Centre, 604/274-1277) and **Green Lake** (8069 Nicklaus North Blvd.), two miles (3 kilometers) north of Whistler Village. There's a free shuttle between the Green Lake terminal and the village. The shuttles operate in conjunction with the flight schedules.

Best Hotels

★ **AAVA Whistler Hotel:** This modern, sociable hotel catering to active travelers is a good-value option, close to all the activities in Whistler Village (page 161).

★ **Four Seasons Whistler Hotel:** Solicitous staff and all sorts of amenities help make this grand lodging one of Whistler's top resort hotels (page 163).

★ **Fairmont Chateau Whistler:** Designed like an upscale mountain lodge, this classic Canadian hotel is convenient for hiking, skiing, or just cocooning in the comfortable rooms (page 163).

★ **Nita Lake Lodge:** Whistler's only lakeside accommodation, this contemporary hotel has large suites, rooftop hot tubs, a full-service spa, and kayaks, canoes, and stand-up paddleboards for guests (page 164).

By Bus

To visit Whistler without a car, **Greyhound** (800/661-8747, www.greyhound.ca, about 2.5 hours, one-way adults $17-38) operates several buses a day between Vancouver and Whistler and is the least expensive option. In Vancouver, the bus depot is at **Pacific Central Station** (1150 Station St.). In Whistler, the bus stops in **Creekside** (2029 London Lane) and **Whistler Village** (4230 Gateway Dr.).

Pacific Coach Lines (604/662-7575 or 800/661-1725, www.pacificcoach.com, one-way adults $55, ages 5-11 $27.50) runs buses several times daily between downtown Vancouver and Whistler Village. The trip takes 2.5 hours. The downtown stops are on Burrard Street at Alberni Street outside the Fairmont Hotel Vancouver, and at Melville Street adjacent to the Hyatt Vancouver. You can also take their **YVR Whistler SkyLynx bus** (one-way adults $65, ages 5-11 $32.50) directly between Vancouver International Airport and Whistler, which takes three hours.

Squamish

Located midway between Vancouver and Whistler along the Sea-to-Sky Highway (Hwy. 99), the town of Squamish is perched between the Coast Mountains and Howe Sound. Cafés, local eateries, and a few shops populate the town's sleepy downtown, while along Highway 99, strip malls and fast-food joints give Squamish a mountain-suburban feel. The real action in Squamish, though, is outdoors.

It's a popular destination for all manner of outdoor adventures, including hiking, rock climbing, and white-water rafting. You can see the area's most famous peak, the Stawamus Chief, from the highway, or tackle the Chief on a day hike.

Squamish takes its name from the Squamish First Nation, the people whose traditional territory encompasses the modern-day town. In more recent times, mining was an important contributor to the local economy; a historic mine is now a visitor attraction. Another Squamish attraction, if you're passing through between December and February, are bald eagles; one of North America's largest populations of eagles spends the winter months near Squamish.

Squamish makes an easy day trip from Vancouver or a stopover between Vancouver and Whistler. It's 40 miles (65 kilometers) from Vancouver to Squamish, a one-hour drive, and 37 miles (60 kilometers) between Squamish and Whistler, which takes 45 minutes.

Best Restaurants

★ **Purebread:** Whistler's best bakery offers an irresistible array of sweet treats, homemade breads, and savory pastries (page 165).

★ **Araxi:** Long considered one of Whistler's top dining spots, Araxi features regional ingredients, from fresh oysters to produce grown on area farms (page 165).

★ **Bearfoot Bistro:** Serving imaginative multicourse prix-fixe dinners, this stylish dining destination houses one of western Canada's largest wine cellars and features live jazz (page 165).

★ **Aura Restaurant:** Overlooking the lake at Nita Lake Lodge, this casual yet sophisticated dining room has both a lovely waterside location and fine contemporary cuisine (page 166).

Sights and Activities
Britannia Mine Museum

Beginning in 1904 and continuing through much of the 20th century, the Britannia Beach area south of Squamish was copper mining territory. During its heyday, the Britannia Mine produced more copper than any other mine in the British Empire. Workers from more than 50 countries settled here, living in barracks by the water or in a company town high in the surrounding hills.

While the Britannia Mine provided valuable resources and jobs for decades, it also created environmental havoc, particularly on the local water supply. After the mine closed in 1974, its environmental impacts took years to remediate.

The mine site is now the **Britannia Mine Museum** (1 Forbes Way, Britannia Beach, 604/896-2233 or 800/896-4044, www.britanniaminemuseum.ca, 9:30am-5:30pm daily, last tour 4pm, adults $27, seniors and ages 13-18 $23, ages 5-12 $18.50, families $99), where you can explore the mine's complicated history and get a glimpse of what it was like to work in the 130-mile (210-kilometer) network of tunnels underground. Begin the 45-minute tour by donning a hard hat and riding a train into the mine. Guides demonstrate explosives, drilling tools, and how the "muck" (rocks sparkling with copper) was hauled out of the tunnels.

Above ground, tours continue in the 1923 mill building that rises nearly 20 stories into the hill; inside, workers had to climb 375 steps to reach the building's highest level. You can also explore a museum building and watch an interesting 15-minute film about the mine's history. Tours are offered throughout the day, but schedules vary seasonally; check the website or phone for tour times. The temperature in the mine (54°F/12°C) can feel chilly, so bring a sweater.

The Britannia Mine Museum is located 32 miles (52 kilometers) north of Vancouver and 7.5 miles (12 kilometers) south of Squamish, along Highway 99.

Shannon Falls Provincial Park

Pull off the highway between Britannia Beach and Squamish for a short stroll to B.C.'s third highest waterfall. At **Shannon Falls Provincial Park** (Hwy. 99, 604/986-9371, www.env.gov.bc.ca, dawn-dusk daily, free), the falls descend 1,100 feet (335 meters) in a narrow, rushing gush. An easy 0.25-mile (400-meter) walking trail leads through the forest to the falls.

Beyond the falls, up a short steep trail (there are stairs), you can hike to another viewpoint for a closer look at the cascading waters.

Shannon Falls is 36 miles (58 kilometers) north of Vancouver and 1.25 miles (2 kilometers) south of Squamish. The park has a snack bar and restrooms with

Scenic Drive: The Sea-to-Sky Highway

Horseshoe Bay

Highway 99, the Sea-to-Sky Highway, is one of western Canada's most beautiful drives. And in a region full of beautiful drives, that's high praise.

At its southern end, the winding road that leads from West Vancouver to Whistler hugs the shores of Howe Sound, where the Gulf Islands rise from the water. You can stop at **Horseshoe Bay** (http://horseshoebayvillage.com), where the ferries depart for Vancouver Island and B.C.'s Sunshine Coast, to stroll the harbor and admire the vistas.

Another stopping point is **Porteau Cove Provincial Park** (www.env.gov.bc.ca), which has a small pebbly beach along a scenic stretch of coastline.

In **Squamish** (www.exploresquamish.com), you have views both of the waterfront and the mountains, particularly the iconic Stawamus Chief that looms above the highway. As you continue toward **Whistler** (www.whistler.com), the road begins to climb, and both forests and peaks surround you.

Keep your camera handy, but pull off at one of the many turnouts to take in the views. At several viewpoints, informational kiosks explore the region's First Nations heritage, a "Cultural Journey" designed in partnership with Whistler's **Squamish Lil'Wat Cultural Centre** (www.slcc.ca).

With rock faces plunging down to the roadway and forested islands just offshore, you can easily become distracted by the scenery, so drive carefully. Watch your speed, too, as the speed limit changes frequently, as do the number of travel lanes.

From October through March, drivers are required to have winter tires or carry (and know how to use) chains, since sections of Highway 99 can become snow-covered and slippery.

Yet, whatever the season, this drive is a striking one, so pack up the car, and hit the road from sea to sky.

---

flush toilets (snack bar and restrooms open mid-May to mid-Oct.).

★ Sea-to-Sky Gondola

For spectacular views of Howe Sound, the Chief, and the surrounding mountains, take a ride up the **Sea-to-Sky Gondola** (36800 Hwy. 99, 604/892-2550, www.seatoskygondola.com, 10am-5pm daily, longer hours on summer weekends, adults $37.95, seniors $35.95, ages 13-18 $23.95, ages 6-12 $13.95, families $95.95).

A 10-minute trip in the eight-passenger gondola whisks you up to the 2,790-foot (850-meter) summit, where you can enjoy the vistas, have lunch on the deck at the Summit Lodge, and access a network of hiking trails.

TIP: Purchase your gondola tickets online at least 24 hours before your visit to save a few dollars.

Once you've taken the gondola to the summit, a highlight is the **Sky Pilot Suspension Bridge,** a 330-foot (100-meter) span that crosses from the Summit Lodge to a viewing platform with expansive views. If you're afraid of heights, don't worry; you don't have to cross the bridge to reach most of the hiking trails.

Another adventure that begins from the gondola summit is the **Via Ferrata** (604/892-2550, www.seatoskygondola.com, daily May-Oct., call for tour times, over age 7 $109, families $425). This "iron way" gives you the experience of rock climbing without needing any special climbing skills or experience. With a guide, you take a short hike down from the Summit Lodge. From there, you clip into a safety cable, cross bridges and a catwalk, and climb a series of steel rungs up the rock face. You'll have beautiful views as you climb, but skip this activity if you're acrophobic. The tour is 1.5 hours. You have to purchase a gondola ticket in addition to the Via Ferrata tour fee. Kids under 8 are not allowed on the Via Ferrata.

Hiking

A number of hiking trails start at the gondola summit. Two are easy walking paths: the 0.25-mile (400-meter) **Spirit Trail,** a flat loop trail with interpretive panels about the region's First Nations, and the **Panorama Trail,** a one-mile (1.6-kilometer) loop that takes you to a lookout with excellent views of the Stawamus Chief.

Also starting from the summit is the

Top to bottom: Britannia Mine Museum; Sea-to-Sky Gondola; Sky Pilot Suspension Bridge.

moderate **Wonderland Trail.** This forested one-mile (1.6-kilometer) loop has a couple of slightly steeper segments, before flattening out as it circles small Wonderland Lake.

Experienced hikers can pick from several challenging trails that begin at the gondola summit, including the intermediate **Shannon Basin Loop Trail** (6 miles/9.7 kilometers), and the more difficult **Al's Habrich Ridge Trail** (7.5 miles/12 kilometers) and **Skyline Ridge Trail** (15 miles/24 kilometers). Check with gondola staff for trail conditions before attempting these longer hikes, and be sure you have water, snacks, warm clothing, and a rain-resistant jacket, even if it's sunny and warm when you set out; the mountain weather here can change quickly.

Want a workout? You can hike *up* to the gondola summit on the **Sea-to-Summit Trail** and then ride the gondola (one-way $10) back down. It's a 4.5-mile (7.5-kilometer) steady climb; average hikers should allow three to five hours.

Winter Activities

The Sea-to-Sky Gondola is open year-round. From December through April, weather-permitting, trails are open for winter walking and snowshoeing, and there's also a tube park where kids can slide down a hill on inner tubes. Before planning a winter visit, phone for trail conditions and current operating hours.

Food

The small **Basecamp Café** (9am-3pm daily) at the gondola base sells coffee, drinks, trail mix, pastries, and a few sandwiches, but it's worth waiting till you get to the **Summit Restaurant and Edge Bar** (10am-5:30pm daily, mains $9-14), in the lodge at the top of the gondola, for a meal with a view. The kitchen cooks up burgers, sandwiches, salads, and baked goods, and serves beer from Squamish's own Howe Sound Brewing Company. If you prefer to picnic, you can bring your own food.

Parking

Although you can park for free in the lot at the gondola base, stays in this lot are limited to three hours. If you're planning to do a longer hike or linger at the top (or if this parking area is full), park in the free lot at Darrell Bay, on Highway 99 opposite Shannon Falls Provincial Park, 0.3 miles (500 meters) south of the gondola.

To walk from the Darrell Bay parking area to the gondola base, carefully cross Highway 99 toward Shannon Falls, and follow the Shannon Falls Connector Trail, which has signs directing you toward to the Sea-to-Sky Gondola.

★ Brackendale Eagles Provincial Park

From late November through mid-February, hundreds of bald eagles come to winter north of Squamish in the now-protected 1,865-acre (755-hectare) environs of **Brackendale Eagles Provincial Park** (www.env.gov.bc.ca, dawn-dusk daily Apr.-Sept.). It's one of the most significant winter eagle populations in North America. In a recent peak year, volunteers counted more than 3,700 eagles in the vicinity.

You can't actually enter the park during the eagle season; it's closed to visitors between October and March to provide a protected habitat for the birds. However, you can watch the eagles from across the river. **Eagle Run Park** (Government Rd., dawn-dusk daily), along the municipal dyke, has several viewing points where you can spot the birds. Bring binoculars if you have them. In December and January on the weekends, volunteer interpreters staff the Eagle Run viewing area (9:30am-3:30pm Sat.-Sun.) and can tell you more about the eagles and their migration patterns.

Coming from Vancouver or points south, follow Highway 99 past downtown Squamish, turn left (west) onto Mamquam Road, and then go right (north) on Government Road toward Brackendale.

Festivals and Events

Wondering how lumberjacks get their jollies? At the **Squamish Days Loggers Sports Festival** (www.squamishdays.ca, July-Aug.), a weekend of family fun, you can watch competitions in ax-throwing, tree-climbing, birling (also known as log rolling), and other events, and enjoy pancake breakfasts, bed races, barbecues, and more.

Sports and Recreation

Hiking

★ Stawamus Chief Provincial Park

Looming above Highway 99 just north of the Sea-to-Sky Gondola, the rocky cliff known as the Chief has long been a must-do climb for experienced hikers and rock-climbers. A challenging, but popular, day hike takes you from the Chief's base to the top of the cliffs in the **Stawamus Chief Provincial Park** (Hwy. 99, 604/986-9371, www.env.gov.bc.ca or http://seatoskyparks.com, dawn-dusk daily).

The Chief actually has three summits, and you can choose to hike one or all. **First Peak,** at 2,000 feet (610 meters), draws the most hikers; from the summit, you have great views of Howe Sound. From the parking lot to the First Peak summit is just 2.5 miles (4 kilometers) round-trip. However, because the trail is quite steep, most hikers allow two to three hours.

Second Peak, at 2,150 feet (655 meters), has lots of viewpoints from its summit, looking across Howe Sound, the town of Squamish, and the mountains in nearby Garibaldi Provincial Park. From the parking lots, it's three miles (5 kilometers) round-trip to the Second Peak. Allow four to five hours.

Third Peak is the tallest of the three summits, rising 2,300 feet (702 meters). You can hike to Third Peak directly from the base or continue from the Second Peak trail. Either route is 4.5 miles (7 kilometers) round-trip; allow five to seven hours.

The hikes up The Chief are considered intermediate-level adventures. Note, though, that on the routes to First and Second Peaks, there are sections where you need to climb ladders or grab onto chains to help you reach the top. For all these hikes, bring water, snacks, a rain jacket, and warm layers. Get an early start, and especially in the summer, hike on a weekday if you want to avoid congestion on these often-busy trails.

Garibaldi Provincial Park

The region's largest provincial park, the 750-square-mile (1,942-square-kilometer) **Garibaldi Provincial Park** (www.env.gov.bc.ca), extends from Squamish north to Whistler and beyond. Hikers have a lot of territory to explore in this vast park, with more than 55 miles (90 kilometers) of hiking trails.

The southernmost section of the park, **Diamond Head,** is closest to Squamish and includes the park's namesake, the 8,786-foot (2,678-meter) Mount Garibaldi. For experienced day-hikers, a scenic trail in the Diamond Head area leads up to **Elfin Lakes** (7 miles/11 kilometers, each way); allow three to five hours one-way. To find the trailhead, turn east off Highway 99 onto Mamquam Road, 2.5 miles (4 kilometers) north of Squamish. Follow the paved road past the Squamish Golf and Country Club, and take the gravel road just after the Mashiter Creek Bridge. In 3.7 miles (6 kilometers), turn left onto the Garibaldi Park road, which will take you to the parking lot. It's 10 miles (16 kilometers) from the highway to the parking area.

Farther north, you can do several day hikes in the park's **Black Tusk/Garibaldi Lake** sector. It's a six-mile (9-kilometer) climb to **Garibaldi Lake.** Allow three to four hours each way; the trail has an elevation change of nearly 2,800 feet (850 meters). From the same starting point, you can hike to **Taylor Meadows.** This 4.75-mile (7.5 kilometer) route follows the Garibaldi Lake trail for the first 3.75 miles (6 kilometers) before heading up into the alpine meadows. Allow three to four hours each way; the trail also has an elevation change of about 2,800 feet (850 meters). The Garibaldi Lake parking lot is 23 miles (37 kilometers) north of Squamish or 12 miles (19 kilometers) south of Whistler, along Highway 99.

At the park's higher elevations, snow is usually on the ground from October until June or July. Check the trail conditions report on the park website before you set out.

Rafting

Two rivers in the Squamish area offer white-water rafting adventures. Trips on the **Cheakamus River** are gentler, with class I and II rapids, good for family excursions. The faster **Elaho-Squamish River,** with class III and IV rapids, will give you more of a thrill. For the Elaho trips, kids generally need to be at least 12 years old and weigh at least 90 pounds (40 kilograms).

SunWolf Rafting (70002 Squamish Valley Rd., 604/898-1537 or 877/806-8046, www.sunwolf.net) offers full-day Elaho River trips (June-Sept., adults $169, ages 12-16 $155) that include a barbecue lunch. They also run half-day Cheakamus River Family trips (June-Sept., adults $99, ages 5-12 $69). In winter, when hundreds of eagles nest at Brackendale Eagles Provincial Park, SunWolf operates guided **Eagle Float Tours** (Dec.-mid-Feb., adults $110, ages 5-12 $75) that enable you to view the eagles from the river, closer than you can see them from the shore.

Canadian Outback Rafting (40900 Tantalus Rd., 866/565-8735, www.canadianoutbackrafting.com) runs Elaho River trips (May-Sept., adults $145, ages 13-16 $135) and Cheakamus River float trips (May-Sept., adults $95, ages 5-16 $66). Whistler-based **Wedge Rafting** (211-4293 Mountain Square, Whistler, 604/932-7171 or 888/932-5899, http://wedgerafting.com) operates Elaho (May-Sept., adults $169, ages 12-16 $155) and

Cheakamus (May-Sept., adults $99, ages 6-16 $69) trips as well.

Accommodations and Food

If you want to stay overnight in Squamish, the town has several mid-range chain hotels off Highway 99, including the **Executive Suites Hotel and Resort** (40900 Tantalus Rd., Garibaldi Highlands, 604/815-0048 or 877/815-0048, www.executivesuitessquamish.com, $125-229 d) and the **Sandman Hotel & Suites Squamish** (39400 Discovery Way, 604/848-6000 or 800/726-3626, www.sandmanhotels.ca, $149-199).

Howe Sound Inn & Brewing Company (37801 Cleveland Ave., 604/892-2603, www.howesound.com) is a brewery, a restaurant, and a place to stay. Rates at the 20-room **inn** (www.howesound-inn.com, $89-129 d) include Wi-Fi and a brewery tour. The **brewpub** (11am-midnight Mon.-Thurs., 11am-1am Fri., 8am-1am Sat., 8am-midnight Sun., mains $11-18) serves pizzas, salads, burgers, and other pub fare to pair with the craft beer.

A popular spot for breakfast, **Fergie's Café** (70002 Squamish Valley Rd., Brackendale, 604/898-1537 or 877/806-8046, www.sunwolf.net, 8am-3pm daily, mains $12-15) serves home-style classics with local ingredients, like eggs benedict, pulled pork hash, Nutella french toast, and burgers.

Locals recommend **Sushi Sen** (40382 Tantalus Way, Garibaldi Highlands, 604/898-8235, www.sushisensquamish.com, lunch 11:30am-2pm Tues.-Fri., dinner 5pm-9pm Tues.-Thurs., 5pm-9:30pm Fri., 4pm-9:30pm Sat., 4pm-9pm Sun., mains $8-21) when they need a *maki* or *nigiri* fix. While the menu emphasizes sushi, you can choose a few other Japanese standards, including chicken teriyaki or tempura.

Information and Services

At the Squamish Adventure Centre, just off Highway 99, **Tourism Squamish**

One Day in Whistler

If you've come to North America's largest winter sports resort during the ski season, you'll likely spend your day out on the snow. But if you're at Whistler before the snow falls, here's how to organize a great one-day trip.

Whistler is located on the traditional territory of two First Nations, so start your day with a visit to the modern **Squamish Lil'wat Cultural Centre,** where you can learn about the history and present-day culture of these two communities. If you want to know more about how Whistler became the outdoor resort it is today, wander over to the informative **Whistler Museum** that tells the stories of many area entrepreneurs.

Then you want to get outdoors, whether you head up the mountain for a ride on the **PEAK 2 PEAK Gondola**

that wings you between Whistler and Blackcomb Mountains, challenge yourself with a climb on the **Via Ferrata,** go **zip-lining, mountain biking,** or simply **take a hike.** The biggest challenge might be seeing how many activities you can fit into your single day.

When you've had your fill of outdoor adventure, unwind at the forested **Scandinave Spa Whistler,** a Scandinavian-style bath experience where you alternate between hot soaks and cold plunges.

Then choose one of Whistler's top dining rooms, perhaps **Araxi** or the **Bearfoot Bistro,** for a leisurely evening meal. At Bearfoot Bistro, you can even have a nightcap in their **Ketel One Ice Room,** the coldest vodka tasting room in the world—a unique way to cap off your active Whistler day.

(38551 Loggers Lane, 604/815-4994 or 877/815-5084, www.tourismsquamish. com, 8am-5pm daily) provides lots of information about the region, including details about hiking trails. The building has a café and restrooms, handy for a Sea-to-Sky pit stop.

Whistler

More than two million visitors every year make their way to this mountain town that has a permanent population of only 10,000. The core of the village is an Alpine-style pedestrian plaza, where restaurants, pubs, and shops line the walkways, and all paths lead, sooner or later, to the ski lifts. Most come to get outdoors—to ski or snowboard in winter, and to hike, cycle, canoe, kayak, rock-climb, or zip-line in the warmer months. Others simply want to stroll through the pedestrian village and perhaps ride the gondola to gaze across the mountains.

Just a two-hour drive from Vancouver, Whistler is close enough for a day trip. If you enjoy outdoor adventures, though, you might want to spend two days or more. There's plenty to do!

Whistler has several neighborhoods stretching along Highway 99, with the main **Whistler Village** about midway through the area. **Creekside,** where there's a separate base village with its own lifts, and **Function Junction,** a more industrial area with some of the town's services, are south of Whistler Village. The **Upper Village** and the **Blackcomb** base areas are just north of Whistler Village.

Sights and Activities
★ Whistler-Blackcomb

From more than 200 trails for skiing and snowboarding, to mountain biking, gondola rides, hiking, zip-lining, and much more, the two-mountain **Whistler-Blackcomb Resort** (604/967-8950 or 800/766-0449, www.whistlerblackcomb. com) has scads of outdoor things to do all year long.

PEAK 2 PEAK Gondola

Whistler's **PEAK 2 PEAK Gondola** (10:15am-5pm daily late May-late Sept., 10:15am-5pm Sat.-Sun. late Sept.-mid-Oct., adults $49.95-54.95, seniors and ages 13-18 $42.95-47.95, ages 7-12 $24.95-27.95) runs 2.73 miles (4.4 kilometers) between Whistler and Blackcomb Mountains. It holds the world's record for the longest unsupported span (that is, the straight-line distance between two towers) at 1.88 miles (3,024 meters) and for the highest lift of its kind, rising 1,427 feet (436 meters) above the valley floor. It transports skiers and snowboarders between the two mountains in winter, and from spring through fall, it's open to sightseers to enjoy the peaks' panoramas.

Allow about two hours for a sightseeing trip on the PEAK 2 PEAK Gondola. The PEAK 2 PEAK ride itself takes about 20 minutes, but to reach the gondola station, you need to take either the Whistler Village Gondola or chair lifts on Blackcomb mountain, which add another 25 minutes each way. If you plan to go hiking, allow additional time.

Gondola tickets are typically cheaper if you buy them online in advance, but check the weather forecast first. The views are obviously best on a sunny, clear day.

Via Ferrata

Do you want to try rock climbing but don't have any training or experience? Consider Whistler's **Via Ferrata** (604/938-9242, www.mountainskillsacademy.com, 4 hours, adults $129, ages 14-18 $119, families $449), a guided climbing route that's open to anyone who's reasonably fit, even if you've never done any climbing. The name comes from the Italian for "iron way," and the Via Ferrata route includes a series of iron rungs built into the mountain, which provide hand grips and footholds as you ascend the rock face. You clip onto to a series of safety cables during your climb, which you do in small groups with a guide. Your guide will give you tips as you ascend and talk you through some of the more challenging sections.

The Via Ferrata route starts with a short hike up from the Whistler Roundhouse (at the top of the Whistler gondola) across a boulder field or a snowy slope or both, depending on the season, to the start of the climbing route. After your climb, you hike or take the chairlift back to your starting point. Wear sturdy hiking shoes, and bring a rainproof jacket and a small backpack with water and snacks.

You need to purchase a PEAK 2 PEAK Gondola ticket in addition to the Via Ferrata tour ticket. Via Ferrata tours are seasonal, generally beginning in late June or early July and continuing until early October; tours typically start at 9am or 1pm, but call or check the website to confirm.

Lift-Accessed Hiking

Whistler-Blackcomb has lots of hiking trails, from short easy strolls to all-day adventures, that you can access from the lifts or gondolas.

From the top of the Whistler gondola or the Whistler side of the PEAK 2 PEAK Gondola near the Roundhouse Lodge, you can access the moderate **Harmony Lake Trail and Loop,** a 1.6-mile (2.5-kilometer) round-trip circuit through the forest to pretty Harmony Lake. You can extend this hike on the steeper 0.7-mile (1.1-kilometer) **Harmony Meadows Trail,** which connects to the Harmony Lake route.

For a more challenging hike with panoramic views, take the Peak Express chair (a short walk from the Roundhouse Lodge) to the start of the 5.8-mile (9.4-kilometer) **High Note Trail.** This trail follows the mountain ridges, with great views of the Black Tusk peak in Garibaldi Provincial Park and Cheakamus Lake far below. You can circle back on the trail and ride the lift down, or for an all-day

Whistler Village

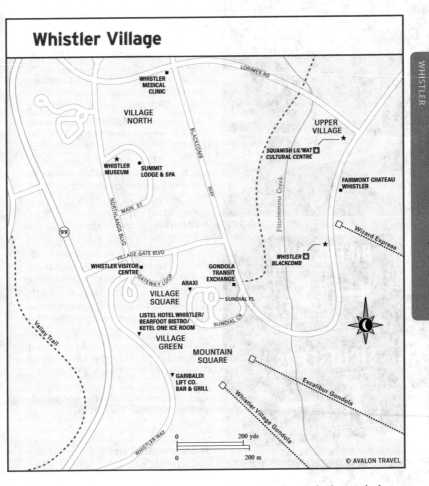

adventure, hike back down to the village; the latter route is about 14 miles (22 kilometers).

Pick up a trail map showing these and other hiking routes at the **Whistler Visitor Centre** (4230 Gateway Dr.) or get one online at the website of **Whistler-Blackcomb** (www.whistlerblackcomb.com).

Lift-Accessed Mountain Biking

Have you seen those cyclists, suited up in knee pads, elbow pads, helmets, and other protective gear, flying down the mountain trails? At Whistler-Blackcomb,

you can join them, whether you're learning to mountain bike or whizzing down those trails yourself at North America's largest mountain bike park.

From mid-May through mid-October, 70 trails across three different areas are open to mountain bikers, who take their bikes up the lifts.

You can choose a package including lift tickets and lessons (one-day $129-149) or, if you know what you're doing, buy a lift ticket (one-day adults $65) and hit the trails on your own. Bike rentals are available at shops around the village.

Winter Sports

In winter, Whistler-Blackcomb has 37 lifts providing access to more than 200 trails across 8,171 acres (3,300 hectares), so you can ski or snowboard here for days and still discover new terrain.

Whistler Village is at an elevation of 2,214 feet (675 meters), while the highest lift takes you up to nearly 7,500 feet (2,284 meters), so the weather can be very different at the base than it is in the alpine regions. Even when there's no snow in the village, the mountains are typically covered in the white stuff from late November into April.

Lift tickets (one-day adults $125) are most expensive when you walk up to the ticket window and purchase a single-day, same-day ticket. Discounts are available when you buy tickets online in advance, purchase multiday tickets or passes, or sometimes when you buy your tickets as part of a package with your lodging. The **Edge Card** program offers discounts to residents of British Columbia, Washington State, and Oregon, with larger savings for advance purchases. Explore all the pricing options and details at **Whistler-Blackcomb** (604/967-8950 or 800/766-0449, www. whistlerblackcomb.com).

★ Squamish Lil'wat Cultural Centre

For centuries before Whistler was an outdoor holiday destination, aboriginal communities called the region home. Discover this heritage at the **Squamish Lil'wat Cultural Centre** (4584 Blackcomb Way, 604/964-0999 or 866/441-7522, www.slcc.ca, 9:30am-5pm daily, adults $18, seniors and students $13.50, ages 6-12 $8, families $49), a fascinating multimedia exploration of the two First Nations whose traditional territory encompasses the Whistler region.

Top to bottom: rest stop on Whistler's Via Ferrata; lift-accessed hiking and biking; Squamish Lil'wat Cultural Centre.

After rhythmic beats of a drum and a traditional First Nations welcome song greet you, watch a short film about the history and present-day culture of these two communities. Then check out the exhibits, from hand-carved canoes to woven baskets to information about aboriginal languages. You can often try out a native craft or chat with "cultural ambassadors," museum staff who come from the Squamish or Lil'wat communities. The center's **Thunderbird Café** uses local ingredients in dishes like Squamish salmon chowder, Lil'wat venison chili, and bannock (a biscuit-like bread), and the gift shop sells locally made crafts.

In summer, admission on Tuesday is by donation. Ask about discounts for B.C. residents, too.

Whistler Museum

Like many ski "villages" with their alpine facades and purpose-built pedestrian strolls, Whistler can seem like a manufactured community. The **Whistler Museum** (4333 Main St., 604/932-2019, www.whistlermuseum.org, 11am-5pm Fri.-Wed., 11am-9pm Thurs., suggested donation $5) tells the history of how the present-day Whistler-Blackcomb resort came to be and the stories of the entrepreneurs and innovators who made it happen.

Another way to learn more about the town and its heritage is to take the museum's one-hour **Valley of Dreams Walking Tour** (1pm daily June-Aug., donation), starting at the Whistler Visitor Centre (4230 Gateway Dr.). You'll hear tales of the community's entrepreneurial women, the year of the naked skiers, and much more.

Whistler Olympic Plaza

Whistler joined Vancouver in hosting the 2010 Winter Olympic Games. One legacy of the Games is now a popular photo stop: in front of the colorful Olympic rings that adorn **Whistler Olympic Plaza** in the village. Also in the plaza is an outdoor amphitheater, where concerts, festivals, and other special events take place.

Audain Art Museum

Whistler scored an art-world coup when Vancouver businessman and philanthropist Michael Audain decided to build a 56,000-square-foot (5,200-square-meter) gallery in this mountain town to house much of his extensive art collection. Focusing on British Columbia artists from the region's earliest eras to the present, the **Audain Art Museum** (4350 Blackcomb Way, www.audainartmuseum.com, 10am-5pm Sat.-Mon. and Wed., 10am-9pm Thurs.-Fri., adults $18, ages 16 and under free), new in 2016, has one of Canada's largest collections of work by early-20th-century artist Emily Carr; other highlights include 19th-century Northwest Coast masks and Vancouver photography.

★ Scandinave Spa

To unwind after a day on the mountains, head for **Scandinave Spa Whistler** (8010 Mons Rd., 604/935-2424 or 888/935-2423, www.scandinave.com, 10am-9pm daily, adults $60, minimum age 19), a Scandinavian-style bath experience set among the trees. You alternate between heat—in a series of hot pools, saunas, and steam baths—and brief cold plunges in a chilled pool or shower, following each sequence with a period of relaxation in the lounges or in a hammock in the forest. To make the experience even more tranquil, the spa has a "silence" policy; you can't talk in the bath area.

Bring your own bathing suit. The spa provides towels and lockers. Several types of massage treatments are available for an additional fee.

Scandinave Spa is located two miles (3.5 kilometers) north of Whistler Village, along Highway 99.

Entertainment and Events
Nightlife

One of Whistler's most popular pastimes

Whistler on a Budget

Whistler is one of those destinations where there are more things to do than you could pack into a summer-long stay, but many of those activities can be budget-blowing adventures. If you're watching your loonies but still want to enjoy the best of what Whistler has to offer, follow these tips for organizing your Whistler stay.

♦ **Come off-season.** If you can schedule your Whistler visit for the spring (May-early June) or fall (Sept.-Oct.), you'll often find lower rates for accommodations and occasional deals for tours and activities.

♦ **Look for free or low-cost activities.** You can hike or cycle many trails around Whistler without purchasing a lift ticket to go up on the mountain. Go for a swim in area lakes or visit the Whistler Museum (by donation). Window-shopping in the village

and walking the Valley Trail are both free, too.

♦ **Maximize your spending.** If you do buy a lift ticket for sightseeing or hiking, get an early start and spend as much time as you'd like up on the mountain. You can stay on the mountain all day on your single ticket.

♦ **Pack a lunch.** Look for accommodations with kitchen facilities, so you can prepare some of your own meals, even if it's just fruit and yogurt for breakfast or a sandwich for the trail. Another option is to have your big meal out at lunch when restaurant prices are a little lower than in the evenings.

♦ **Go easy on the booze.** Many of Whistler's bars and après-ski hangouts have free live music for the price of a drink. But you don't have to spend the money for *several* drinks to enjoy the tunes.

is après (aka après-ski, literally "after skiing"), and what do you do after a day in the mountains but hit the pub? Here are several places where the party starts when the lifts close.

Merlin's Bar and Grill (4553 Blackcomb Way, 604/938-7700, 11am-1am daily), located at the Blackcomb Mountain base, often has live music, as does the **Garibaldi Lift Company** (4165 Springs Lane, 604/905-2220, 11am-1am daily), at the base of the Whistler gondola. In the Creekside area, **Dusty's Bar & BBQ** (2040 London Lane, 604/905-2171, 11am-1am daily) has been pouring pints since the 1960s.

The laid-back **Dubh Linn Gate Irish Pub** (Pan Pacific Whistler Mountainside, 4320 Sundial Cres., 604/905-4047, www. dubhlinngate.com, 8am-1am daily June-Oct., 7am-1am daily Nov.-May), steps from the Whistler Village lifts, keeps 25 varieties of beer on tap and offers a long list of single-malt scotch. They serve an

authentic Irish breakfast and varied pub fare throughout the day.

Bearfoot Bistro (4121 Village Green, 604/932-3433, http://bearfootbistro. com, dinner from 6pm daily) is among Whistler's best restaurants, but it's also a destination for drinkers: Their **Ketel One Ice Room** is the coldest vodka tasting room in the world. Don a heavy parka (which the restaurant provides) and venture into the frosty tasting room, with its carved ice walls and year-round temperature of -25°F (-32°C). Choose a tasting flight ($48) from their selection of 50 different vodkas, made in destinations as diverse as Poland, the Ukraine, or Pemberton, B.C.

Several Whistler hotels have more sedate drinking scenes, more upscale lounge than rowdy party, including the **Mallard Lounge at the Fairmont Chateau Whistler** (4599 Chateau Blvd., 604/938-8000, www. fairmont.com, 11am-midnight Sun.-Thurs., 11am-1am Fri.-Sat.), known for its martinis and creative seasonal cocktails, and the **Sidecut Bar at the Four Seasons Whistler** (4591 Blackcomb Way, 604/935-3400, www.fourseasons.com, from 11am daily). **Cure Lounge at Nita Lake Lodge** (2131 Lake Placid Rd., 604/966-5700, www.nitalakelodge.com, from 11:30am daily), in the Creekside area, has a great patio overlooking the lake.

What about a private wine-tasting at your hotel or condo? **Taste Whistler** (604/902-9463 or 844/470-9463, www.tastewhistler.com, from $79-99 pp) creates customized wine-tastings for groups of friends, families, or corporate events, from a Wine 101 sampler to a B.C. wine or champagne tasting, and they'll come to you.

The Arts

The **Whistler Arts Council** (604/935-8410, www.artswhistler.com) hosts concerts, films, and other productions as part of their Performance Series at Maury Young Arts Centre (4335 Blackcomb Way).

For something a little different, see what's happening at **The Point Artist-Run Centre** (5678 Alta Lake Rd., www.thepointartists.com), which presents live music during July and August in the Saturdays at the Point events, as well as occasional music, film, theater, and dance performances throughout the year. The facility is south of the village on the west side of Alta Lake.

Festivals
Spring and Summer Events

Plenty of special events bring visitors to Whistler in the spring and summer. There's something on the calendar most weekends from late May through Canadian Thanksgiving in mid-October.

Bring the kids to the annual **Whistler Children's Festival** (www.whistlerchildrensfestival.com, July), a weekend of family-friendly arts, crafts, and entertainment ranging from African dancing to First Nations drumming.

A "celebration of mindful living,"

Wanderlust Whistler (www.wanderlust.com, July-Aug.) includes several days of yoga classes, meditation workshops, concerts, lectures, guided hikes, and local food.

Crankworx Freeride Mountain Bike Festival (www.crankworx.com, Aug.) draws wild and crazy mountain bikers to town for a week of downhill and cross-country cycling, stunt riding, and plenty more two-wheeled fun.

One of Whistler's top restaurants hosts the **Araxi Longtable Series** (www.araxi.com, Aug.-Sept.), lavish alfresco dinners highlighting the region's late-summer bounty.

Fall and Winter Events

Whistler isn't only about sports. The town shows its artistic side during the annual **Whistler Writers Festival** (www.whistlerwritersfest.com, Oct.), when Canadian and international authors conduct readings, teach seminars, participate on panels, and mingle with guests to discuss their work.

Why come to Whistler in November, when it's chilly for hiking and cycling but too early to ski? Because that's when Whistler hosts a bang-up food and wine festival. The annual **Cornucopia Festival** (www.whistlercornucopia.com, Nov.) draws food and wine lovers from far and wide for two weeks of wine-tastings and seminars, guest chef events, special dinners, and lots of parties.

Whistler Film Festival (www.whistlerfilmfestival.com, Dec.) screens up to 90 movies, including world premieres, features, documentaries, and shorts during this five-day international competition. At least 50 percent of the films are Canadian. You might even spot a celebrity or two.

Whistler hosts one of North America's largest gay and lesbian ski weeks, the **Whistler Pride and Ski Festival** (www.gaywhistler.com, Jan.). It's eight days of LGBTQ-friendly snow sports, après-ski events, parties, concerts, and more.

Sports and Recreation
Hiking and Biking

Winding 25 miles (40 kilometers) through the Whistler area, the paved **Valley Trail** (www.whistler.ca) is open to both walkers and cyclists. You can follow short stretches of the trail, for example, between the Blackcomb base area and Whistler Village, or head north to Green Lake or south to the Creekside area and beyond.

Close to Whistler Village (you can follow the Valley Trail), **Lost Lake Park** has several easy hiking and cycling trails. Walkers can circle the lake on the Lost Lake Loop trail, while mountain bikers can follow several single-track routes through the park.

Whistler has several areas of old-growth forest with massive trees. A moderate five-mile (8-kilometer) loop hike takes you through one of these forests along the **Ancient Cedars Trail,** where the trees are up to 1,000 years old. The trailhead is north of the village; take Highway 99 north past Green Lake and turn left onto 16-Mile Forest Service Road. It's three miles (5 kilometers) from the highway to the parking area. Bring mosquito repellent, since this area can be buggy.

Get trail maps showing these and other trails from the **Whistler Visitor Centre** (4230 Gateway Dr.) or online from the Whistler municipality website (www.whistler.ca) or from Whistler.com.

Zip-Lining

Fancy a ride on the longest zip line in Canada or the United States? **Ziptrek Ecotours** (604/935-0001 or 866/935-0001, www.ziptrek.com) offers several different zip-line options, including **The Sasquatch** (daily May-mid-Oct., 1.5 hours, adults $119, seniors and ages 10-14 $99), which runs more than 7,000 feet (2 kilometers), starting on Blackcomb Mountain and zipping down to the Whistler side.

Ziptrek also offers **The Eagle** (daily year-round, 2.5-3 hours, adults $139, seniors and ages 6-14 $119), which takes

Ketel One Ice Room at Bearfoot Bistro

you down five zip lines and across four treetop bridges. If zip-lining is your passion, you can combine the Sasquatch and Eagle tours (4.5 hours, adults $199, seniors and ages 10-14 $179). Newcomers to zip-lining, or younger kids, may prefer **The Bear** (year-round, 2.5-3 hours, adults $119, seniors and ages 6-14 $99), a slightly gentler combination of zip lines and bridges. Hours vary seasonally, so call or check the website for details.

Superfly Ziplines (211-4293 Mountain Square, 604/932-0647, www.superfly-ziplines.com, 9am-5pm daily, 3 hours, adults $129-149, ages 7-13 $99) has a zip-line tour that includes a 0.6-mile (1 kilometer) line that's more than 500 feet (150 meters) high.

Treetop Adventures

If you're looking for an activity that's gentler than zip-lining but still gets you high in the trees, consider a two-hour **TreeTrek Canopy Walk** (604/935-0001 or 866/935-0001, www.ziptrek.com, daily

year-round, call or check the website for tour times, adults $39, seniors and ages 6-14 $29), which follows a series of bridges suspended among the old-growth forest on Blackcomb Mountain. The highest of the eight viewing platforms rises nearly 200 feet (60 meters) above the forest floor; the oldest trees in the area are about 800 years old. On this excursion offered by Ziptrek Ecotours, your guide will introduce you to the local ecology as you explore the woods.

Want more of a challenge? Superfly's **Treetop Adventure Course** (211-4293 Mountain Square, 604/932-0647, www.superflyziplines.com, 9am-5pm daily, $59) takes you through the treetops on a ropes course, where you navigate swaying bridges, rope swings, tightropes, and zip lines. Kids not tall enough to reach 71 inches (180 centimeters) can try the **Kids Treetop Adventure Course** ($29), designed for youngsters ages 7-14 who can reach to 55 inches (140 centimeters).

Bobsled and Skeleton

During the 2010 Winter Olympic Games, the **Whistler Sliding Centre** (4910 Glacier Lane, 604/964-0040, www.whistlersportlegacies.com) hosted the bobsled, skeleton, and luge competitions. You can live out your almost-Olympic dreams with rides down the same slippery track that the Olympic athletes used.

In summer, whiz down the track in the **Rolling Thunder** (Thurs.-Mon. late June-early Sept., advance reservations required, $89 pp), a bobsled on wheels. A pilot steers your sled, which holds up to four passengers, and can reach speeds of 50 mph (80 km/h). Kids must be at least 12 to ride (12- and 13-year-olds must have an adult accompany them; those ages 14 to 18 need a parent or guardian present to sign a waiver). Participants must also be between 4 foot 6 and 6 foot 5 (137 to 196 centimeters) and weigh between 85 and 285 pounds (39 to 129 kilograms).

In winter, the **Thunder on Ice** (daily early Dec.-late Mar., advance reservations required, $169 pp) bobsled experience sends you down the ice at even faster speeds: up to 75 mph (120 km/h). The sled holds a pilot and one or two guests. For this experience, you must be between ages 14 and 75; youth ages 14 to 16 must ride with a parent or guardian, and those ages 17 and 18 must have a responsible adult sign a waiver. All participants must be between 4 foot 6 and 6 foot 8 (137 to 203 centimeters) and weigh between 90 and 270 pounds (41 to 122 kilograms) with your winter clothing on.

If you're really adventurous, ride head-first on the skeleton down the icy track. **Lightening on Ice** (daily early Dec.-late Mar., advance reservations required, $169 pp) gives you two solo runs, where you may find yourself hurtling down the track at close to 60 mph (100 km/h). Minimum age for the skeleton is 16, and the maximum is 75. Parents or guardians must sign a waiver for youth under age 19, and all participants must be between 4 foot 6 and 6 foot 5 (137 to 198 centimeters) and weigh between 90 and 220 pounds (41 to 120 kilograms) with your winter clothing on.

To reach the Whistler Sliding Centre from Whistler Village, follow Blackcomb Way to Glacier Lane.

Water Sports

One of Whistler's most peaceful outdoor experiences is a kayak or canoe tour along the **River of Golden Dreams.** **Whistler Eco Tours** (604/935-4900 or 877/988-4900, www.whistlerecotours. com) offers three-hour guided (adults $120, under age 13 $84) or self-guided (adults $80, under age 13 $56) paddles that start on Alta Lake, travel through a scenic wetlands area, and wrap up at beautiful Green Lake. On the guided tour, your guide will tell you about the area's ecology and give you paddling tips. Both the self-guided and guided options are family-friendly and include transportation back to the village.

Whistler Eco Tours also rents single kayaks ($25 per hour) and canoes, double kayaks, stand-up paddleboards, and pedal boats (all $30 per hour) from their base in Wayside Park on Alta Lake, between the village and Creekside.

You can **swim** in several Whistler-area lakes, although the water can be chilly. You'll find beaches at **Alpha Lake** near Creekside, **Alta Lake** between Creekside and the village, **Lost Lake** near the village, and **Green Lake,** a large glacier-fed lake north of the village.

Prefer to do your swimming indoors? Then visit the **Meadow Park Sports Centre** (8625 Hwy. 99, 604/935-7529, www.whistler.ca, adults $8.25, ages 13-18 $5, ages 4-12 $4.25), a public recreational facility with a 25-meter lap pool as well as a kids pool with a lazy river. Located two miles (three kilometers) north of the village, the center and pool are generally open 6am-10pm daily, but call or check the website for seasonal variations.

Winter Sports

As an alternative to skiing and snowboarding on Whistler-Blackcomb, go to the **Whistler Olympic Park** (5 Callaghan Valley Rd., 604/964-0060, www.whistlersportlegacies.com, late Nov.-early Apr., weather permitting) for **cross-country skiing** (weekday/weekend adults $19/$25, seniors $10/$25, ages 7-18 $10/$15), **snowshoeing** (weekday/weekend adults $10/$15, ages 7-18 $5/$8), and **tobogganing** (weekday/weekend $10/$15 per vehicle). Gear rentals are available. The park is 15 miles (23 kilometers) from the village; follow Highway 99 south to Callaghan Valley Road.

Accommodations and Camping

Whistler accommodations include a range of hotels and condominium buildings. Hotels provide more services, such as on-site restaurants, ski valets, and concierge staff; some, but not all, have kitchenettes or in-room fridges and microwaves. Renting a condo is often less expensive, particularly for a family, and you'll have a kitchen where you can prepare some meals. Many Whistler hotels charge for overnight parking, so factor that fee into your lodging budget.

Whistler has two "peak" seasons. The main high season is during the winter for skiing and snowboarding, which typically begins in late November and continues until April. There's also a "mini peak" during July and August, when visitors come for hiking, biking, and other summer activities. The most expensive time to stay at Whistler is during the Christmas-New Year holiday, when rates soar. The February-March school holiday weeks are also pricy. During the rest of the year, lodging rates are usually lowest midweek.

Check the **Tourism Whistler website** (www.whistler.com) for lodging deals, particularly if you're making last-minute plans. The **Whistler-Blackcomb website** (www.whistlerblackcomb.com) sometimes posts discounts on accommodations as well.

Under $150

Built as part of the Athletes Village for the 2010 Winter Olympics, the **HI-Whistler Hostel** (1035 Legacy Way, 604/962-0025 or 866/762-4122, www.hi-hostels.ca, $33-38 dorm, $82-134 d) still feels new, offering dorm beds as well as good-value, basic, but modern private rooms with flat-screen TVs and en-suite baths—worth considering even if you don't normally stay in a hostel. Dorms sleep eight in four bunk beds, each with reading lights, electrical outlets, lockers, and shared washrooms. Parking and Wi-Fi are free, and common areas include a café, a TV room, a lounge with a pool table, a big shared kitchen, and an outdoor terrace. Rates are highest December through February, when the hostel can have more of a ski-party atmosphere. Summer is typically quieter, when staff organize guided hikes, local brewery tours, and other activities. The hostel is five miles (8 kilometers) south

of Whistler Village; at the Function Junction crossroads, turn east onto Cheakamus Lake Road. B.C. Transit buses to the village stop out front.

$150-250

Catering to skiers and snowboarders in winter, and to cyclists and other active guests in summer, the ★ **AAVA Whistler Hotel** (4005 Whistler Way, 604/932-2522 or 800/663-5644, www.aavawhistlerhotel.com, $135-330 d, parking $19) will loan you a complimentary Go-Pro camera to record your day's adventures (neat, right?). While it's not upscale (hotel staff say, "We don't valet your car, but we do valet your bike"), this 192-room lodging feels sociable, with several lobby seating areas and a communal worktable with a charging station. There's space to lounge on the outdoor deck, too, around the compact pool and hot tub. Outfitted with one king, two queens, or a queen plus a sofa bed, the guest rooms are crisp and modern, with mini fridges, safes, and Keurig coffeemakers; the prime top-floor units have vaulted ceilings. Wi-Fi and local calls are free. You can walk to the Whistler base in about 10 minutes.

Feeling funky? The boutique 41-room **Adara Hotel** (4122 Village Green, 604/905-4009 or 866/502-3272, www.adarahotel.com, $119-319 d, parking $20) goes beyond typical ski-lodge style, starting from its lobby, furnished with curvaceous orange banquettes, a massive stone fireplace, and stylized antler sculptures; you can grab coffee and a breakfast bar here in the morning, or give the resident dog a pat. Out on the sun-deck is a small hot tub and summer-only pool. Standard rooms have electric fireplaces, French-press coffeemakers, mini fridges, microwaves, and modern baths with rain showers, but the coolest units are the lofts, with a bedroom upstairs and a living area below. Wi-Fi is included.

The three-story **Listel Hotel Whistler** (4121 Village Green, 604/932-1133 or 800/663-5472, www.listelhotel.com,

$139-369 d, parking $20) is simple but comfortable, with a quiet location off the Village Stroll yet close to the lifts at the Whistler base. Most of the 98 rooms are standard units with two queen beds, free Wi-Fi, coffeemakers, and mini fridges. There's a hot tub (but no pool) on the outdoor patio. Rates include continental breakfast. The excellent **Bearfoot Bistro** (604/932-3433, http://bearfootbistro.com, dinner from 6pm daily, prix fixe $78-108 pp) is on the property.

At the serene boutique **Summit Lodge and Spa** (4359 Main St., 604/932-2778 or 888/913-8811, www.summitlodge.com, $130-479 d, parking $20), the 81 studio and one-bedrooms suites, with cherry furnishings, all have kitchenettes. Wi-Fi and local calls are included, and you can borrow a complimentary bike to cycle around town. The Asian-style **Taman Sari Royal Heritage Spa** (604/938-5982, www.tamansarispa.com) uses traditional Javanese herbs in many of its treatments. Other hotel amenities include a sauna, a hot tub, and a year-round outdoor pool. You're surrounded by lots of good restaurants, and it's a 10- to 15-minute walk to the lifts.

Most of the studio units at the 84-room **Whistler Pinnacle Hotel** (4319 Main St., 604/938-3218 or 888/999-8986, www. whistlerpinnacle.com, $129-280 d, parking $19), a quieter older property off the Village Stroll, have full kitchens (handy if you don't want to eat out for every meal), gas fireplaces, included Wi-Fi and local calls, and modern baths with whirlpool tubs to soak away any adventure-induced aches and pains. The units on the fourth floor feel larger, with vaulted ceilings. There's a guest laundry, as well as a small outdoor lap pool. Guests get a discount at the on-site **Quattro Italian Restaurant** (604/905-4844, http://quattrorestaurants. com, 5:30pm-10pm daily, mains $24-48); the modern French **Alta Bistro** (604/932-2582, www.altabistro.com, from 5:30pm daily, mains $29-39) is the other on-property dining option.

Four Seasons Whistler Hotel

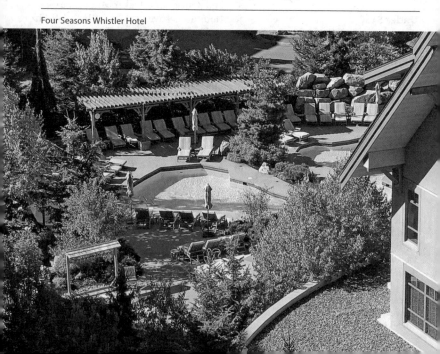

Over $250

With a solicitous staff and all sorts of amenities, ★ **Four Seasons Whistler Hotel** (4591 Blackcomb Way, 604/935-3400, www.fourseasons.com, $399-539 d, $675-1,399 suite, parking $39) is among Whistler's top resort hotels. Decorated in ski-lodge earth tones, the 273 rooms and suites have gas fireplaces, big closets, mini fridges, and flat-screen TVs; ask for an upper-floor unit for slope-side views. If you haven't gotten enough exercise on the mountain, you can work out in the 24-hour fitness room or swim in the heated outdoor pool. The three hot tubs and eucalyptus steam room are popular après-ski, as is the library-style **Sidecut Bar**. Located in Whistler's Upper Village, the Four Seasons isn't a ski-in, ski-out property, but the hotel offers a free ski concierge, so you can leave your gear slope-side. A complimentary car service can take you around town.

Like a grand mountain lodge, the ★ **Fairmont Chateau Whistler** (4599 Chateau Blvd., off Blackcomb Way, 604/938-8000 or 800/606-8244, www.fairmont.com, $299-619 d, parking $35-39) keeps you comfortable, whether you're in your room, exploring the property, or out in the village. The 550 rooms and suites, some with views of the slopes, have down duvets, fluffy bathrobes, flat-screen TVs, and Keurig coffeemakers. The Fairmont charges a daily resort fee ($12 per room), which covers most of the things you'd want to do, including Internet access, use of the indoor and outdoor pools and the well-equipped health club, yoga classes, tennis, a shuttle to take you to various village destinations, and valet service for your skis, bikes, or golf clubs. The **Mallard Lounge** is popular for après-ski cocktails, and the hotel has several other dining outlets, including **The Grill Room** (6pm-9pm daily, mains $33-59) for steak and seafood and the more casual **Wildflower Restaurant** (7am-10:30am and 6pm-9pm Mon.-Fri., 7am-11am and 6pm-9pm Sat.-Sun., mains breakfast $10-30, dinner $22-49).

You can't stay much closer to the lifts than at the 121-unit all-suite **Pan Pacific Whistler Mountainside** (4320 Sundial Cres., 604/905-2999 or 888/905-9995, www.panpacific.com, $279-689 d, parking $28-32), steps from Blackcomb's Excalibur gondola. Decorated with cherry-hued Craftsman-style furnishings, the studio, one-bedroom, and two-bedroom units all have full kitchens, gas fireplaces, flat-screen TVs, and DVD players. The studios nominally sleep four, with a queen-size Murphy bed and a sleep sofa, but the larger suites are more comfortable for families. Other amenities include a heated outdoor saltwater pool, two hot tubs, complimentary Wi-Fi, and free local phone calls. The **Dubh Linn Gate Irish Pub** (604/905-4047, www.dubhlinngate.com, 8am-1am daily June-Oct., 7am-1am daily Nov.-May, mains $14-25) is popular for drinks and pub fare, with more than 25 beers on tap and live music most nights.

Slightly farther from the gondolas than its sister property, the **Pan Pacific Whistler Village Centre** (4299 Blackcomb Way, 604/966-5500 or 888/966-5575, www.panpacific.com, $169-539 d, parking $28-32) has a more modern boutique feel, but similar amenities: suites ranging from studios to three bedrooms with full kitchens, a saltwater lap pool, two hot tubs, a sauna, and a fitness facility. Rates include breakfast, Wi-Fi, local calls, and a complimentary shuttle to get around the village. You can store your ski or snowboard gear at the Pan Pacific Mountainside.

Set on a lake in the Creekside area, ★ **Nita Lake Lodge** (2131 Lake Placid Rd., 604/966-5700, www.nitalakelodge. com, $289-559 d, 2-bedroom suites $409-849, parking $20-30) is a beautiful setting for a stay in any season. The 77 spacious contemporary suites—studio, one-, and two-bedroom units on four floors—have fireplaces, compact kitchenettes hidden in an armoire, and modern baths with rain showers and soaker tubs; the best units have lake views. You can choose all kinds of activities, from lounging in the rooftop hot tubs to kayaking, canoeing, or stand-up paddle boarding on the lake, or riding up the Valley Trail on the complimentary bicycles. There's a full-service spa, as well as a yoga studio that offers discounts for hotel guests. Three restaurants, the more formal **Aura Restaurant** (7am-11:30am and 5:30pm-9pm Mon.-Sat., 7am-2pm and 5:30pm-9pm Sun., call for off-season hours, mains breakfast $10-15, dinner $20-30) overlooking the lake, **Cure Lounge** (11:30am-11pm Mon.-Sat., 10am-11pm Sun., mains $13-25), and casual **Fix Café** (6:30am-3:30pm daily, mains $5-13), which serves pastries, coffee, and sandwiches, give you plenty of dining options. The hotel offers a free shuttle to the village or the Creekside gondola.

Camping and Cabins

The **Riverside Resort** (8018 Mons Rd., 604/905-5533, www.whistlercamping. com) has several lodgings options, including campsites for tents and RVs, yurts, and sturdy log cabins. It's located two miles (3.5 kilometers) north of the village.

The 14 family-friendly **cabins** ($199-239), with solid wood furnishings, have a living room, small kitchen, bedroom with a queen bed, and bath on the main level, plus a sleeping loft with two twin beds. They're equipped with electricity and even a flat-screen TV. The **yurts** ($99-139) are more rustic, but they still have electricity and heat. Sleeping up to five, most have a bunk bed with a single over a double bed, and either a futon couch or a separate single with a trundle bed. Washrooms with showers are a short walk away. **Campsites for RVs** ($48-60) include both fully and partially serviced sites. There's a quiet wooded walk-in **tent campground** ($20-35) with sites along the river.

The campground's main building has a small market and café; bicycle rentals are available. Other amenities include a guest laundry, a kids playground, a volleyball court, and a putting course. The Valley Trail crosses the campground property, so you can follow it into town.

Condo Rentals

You can book many condo accommodations through the **Tourism Whistler** (www.whistler.com) and **Whistler-Blackcomb** (www.whistlerblackcomb. com) websites and through many of the standard online booking services for hotels. You can also find condos through **Airbnb** (www.airbnb.com).

TIP: Check locally based rental agencies, including **alluraDirect** (604/707-6700 or 866/425-5872, www.alluradirect. com), which sometimes offer deals that the larger booking services don't have.

Food

Like many resort towns, Whistler offers several splurge-worthy dining rooms. If you're watching your budget, you'll need to pick your dining spots carefully, but burgers, pizza, and diner-style meals can fuel you up at moderate prices. Another money-saving option, when you're staying in a condo or lodging with kitchen facilities, is to have one or more meals "at home" or pack a lunch for your outdoor adventures.

Groceries and Markets

The **Whistler Farmers Market** (Upper Village Stroll, Blackcomb Village Base, 11am-4pm Sun. June-mid-Oct., 3pm-7pm Wed. July-Aug.) brings locally grown produce and other goodies to the village every weekend from late spring through fall, with an additional weekday market in midsummer.

Whistler Marketplace IGA (4330 Northlands Blvd., 604/938-2850, www.marketplaceiga.com, 9am-9pm daily) is the largest and most centrally located grocery store in the village.

Handy to pick up a snack or the toothpaste you forgot, the **Whistler Grocery Store** (4211 Village Square, 604/932-3628, www.whistlergrocery.com, 8am-11pm daily) keeps long hours and is the closest market to the slopes. If you're staying in the Creekside area, your go-to grocery is **Whistler's Creekside Market** (305-2071 Lake Placid Rd., 604/938-9301, www.creeksidemarket.com, 8am-10pm daily).

Cafés, Bakeries, and Light Bites

★ **Purebread** (www.purebread.ca), Whistler's best bakery, offers an irresistible array of treats, from scones and croissants to lemon crumble bars, salted caramel bars, and oversized brownies. For a savory snack, opt for a Pudgie Pie, a portable pastry that might be stuffed with goat cheese, potatoes, or other veggies. If you're packing for a picnic, try the Dysfunction Ale bread, a hearty loaf made with spent grains from the Whistler Brewing Company. Purebread has two Whistler branches: a convenient **Village location** (Main St., Olympic Plaza, 604/962-1182, 8:30am-5:30pm daily) and their original **Function Junction shop** (1-1040 Millar Creek Rd., 604/938-3013, 8:30am-5pm daily) on the south side of town.

Contemporary

Long considered one of Whistler's top restaurants, ★ **Araxi** (4222 Village Square, 604/932-4540, www.araxi.com, dinner from 5pm daily, brunch 10am-2pm Sat.-Sun., mains $30-53) emphasizes regional ingredients, whether it's fresh oysters (there is an oyster bar, with oyster happy hour 3pm-5pm daily) or produce grown on local farms. The menu might include chorizo-crusted B.C. halibut with roasted tomato fondue or pan-roasted duck breast with parmesan-mushroom polenta and caramelized pears. Sate your sweet tooth with the warm Valrhona chocolate fondant or the refreshing lemon tart.

With more than 20,000 bottles, ★ **Bearfoot Bistro** (4121 Village Green, 604/932-3433, http://bearfootbistro.com, dinner from 6pm daily, prix fixe $78-108 pp) has one of the largest wine cellars in western Canada, the better to pair with their modern Canadian cuisine. Accompanied by live jazz, dinners are multicourse prix-fixe affairs that might start with an heirloom tomato salad with ricotta *salata* or scallop ceviche with pickled watermelon rind, and continue with arctic char paired with artichoke *agnolotti*, beef striploin with roasted bone marrow and oyster mushrooms, or za'atar-rubbed grilled quail. Of course, there are sweets, including ice cream that they whip up tableside, mixing cream with liquid nitrogen. If you prefer a lighter meal, perhaps oysters and champagne, a game burger, or duck confit with a chili-honey glaze, take a seat in their less formal **champagne lounge** (from 4pm Mon.-Fri., from 3pm Sat.-Sun., small plates $12-22), which is open from après-ski until late evening.

Overlooking the village and up 21

steps from the street, **21 Steps Kitchen + Bar** (4433 Sundial Place, 604/966-2121, www.21steps.ca, 5:30pm-midnight daily, mains $15-36) serves crowd-pleasing comfort food, from roast chicken, pork schnitzel, and bison steak to pasta. You can also stop in for cocktails and small plates, like orange-soy braised pork ribs or cheesy baked mushroom caps.

Popular for breakfast, casual **Elements Urban Tapas Parlour** (102B-4359 Main St., 604/932-5569, www.elementswhistler.com, 8am-2pm and 5pm-10pm Sun.-Thurs., 8am-2pm and 5pm-11pm Fri.-Sat., mains breakfast and lunch $9-18, dinner small plates $9-26) serves plates to share later in the day, from a wild salmon combo plate (offering the fish cured, maple-smoked, and raw), or mini venison burgers topped with gruyère, to bison short ribs paired with pineapple salsa. The restaurant is located in the Summit Hotel building.

★ **Aura Restaurant** (2131 Lake Placid Rd., 604/966-5715, www.nitalakelodge.com, 7am-11:30am and 5:30pm-9pm Mon.-Sat., 7am-2pm and 5:30pm-9pm Sun., call for off-season hours, mains breakfast $10-15, dinner $20-30) at Creekside's Nita Lake Lodge is worth a visit even if you're not staying at this lakefront hotel, both for its fine contemporary fare and for the lovely lakeside setting. You might begin with a seasonal salad or tuna *crudo* dressed with citrus vinaigrette, accompanied by a watermelon martini or a Violaceus Fizz (a blend of lavender-infused gin and lemon soda). For your main course, you could try seared scallops with sweet pea puree, fresh B.C. salmon, or cider-brined pork chops with a side of grilled asparagus, cauliflower gratin, or a shareable platter of garden veggies.

Asian

A longtime favorite for Japanese fare, upscale **Sushi Village** (11-4340 Sundial Cres., 604/932-3330, http://sushivillage.com, lunch noon-2pm Fri.-Sun., dinner from 5:30pm daily, mains $16-38) has been keeping Whistler in *nigiri, maki,* teriyaki, and tempura since the 1980s. Another popular spot for Japanese meals is **Sushi Sachi** (106-4359 Main St., 604/935-5649, www.sachisushi.com, lunch noon-2pm Tues.-Fri., dinner from 5:30pm daily, mains $13-30) at the Summit Lodge.

Part grocery store and part quick-serve Japanese eatery, **Fuji Market** (205-4000 Whistler Way, 604/962-6251, www.fuji-market.ca, 10am-9pm daily, mains $5-12) stocks ready-made sushi and cooks up ramen, tempura, and other inexpensive Japanese bites. You can pick up wasabi peas, jars of kimchi, and other Asian ingredients. It's in a strip mall on the edge of the village, near the Whistler Conference Centre.

Burgers

Like burgers? **Splitz Grill** (4369 Main St., 604/938-9300, www.splitzgrill.com, 11am-9pm daily, mains $5-13) has 'em, and they're not just traditional beef patties. You can get lamb, bison, lentil, even salmon. Line up at the counter, order your burger, and choose from a large selection of toppings. *Poutine,* fries, and beer are the favored accompaniments.

Diners

For fuel-me-up breakfasts and hearty meals served with friendly sass, head for the **Southside Diner** (2102 Lake Placid Rd., Creekside, 604/966-0668, www.southsidediner.ca, 7am-9pm Sun.-Thurs., 7am-10pm Fri.-Sat., mains breakfast $7-15, lunch and dinner $10-16), off Highway 99 in the Creekside area. Morning menus get you going with breakfast *poutine* (home fries topped with poached eggs, sausage, cheese curds, and gravy), "big-ass pancakes" (yes, they're big), and the usual egg suspects. Later in the day, you can stuff yourself with burgers, sandwiches, meatloaf, or macaroni and cheese.

Italian and Pizza

A life raft of good value in a sea of expensive eateries, family-friendly **Pasta Lupino** (121-4368 Main St., 604/905-0400, www.pastalupino.com, 11am-9pm daily, mains lunch $7-12, dinner $14-18) serves a small menu of Italian classics, including spaghetti and meatballs, lasagna, and chicken parmigiana. In the evenings, pasta dinners come with soup or salad, plus homemade focaccia.

The wood-fired oven turns out traditional Neapolitan-style pizzas at **Pizzeria Antico** (101-4369 Main St., 604/962-9226, www.pizzeriaantico.ca, noon-10pm Sun.-Wed., noon-11pm Thurs.-Sat., mains lunch $9-20, dinner $13-20), like the Prosciutto con Ruccola, topped with arugula, prosciutto, tomato, and mozzarella, or the Funghi, sauced with porcini cream and layered with roasted mushrooms and onions. Several fresh salads, grilled *paninis* (at lunch), and pastas (at dinner) round out the menu.

Vegetarian

You might walk away with a green mustache after slurping down a fresh juice or smoothie at **The Green Moustache** (122-4340 Lorimer Rd., 604/962-3727, http://greenmoustachejuice.com, 8am-6pm daily, mains $7-10), a tiny juice bar and vegetarian eatery. In the morning, they serve Breakfast Bowls, like muesli or chia pudding topped with nuts, berries, and house-made almond or cashew milk. Later in the day, order a big salad or the Buddha Bowl, a blend of rice and quinoa piled high with fresh veggies.

Information and Services
Visitor Information

Tourism Whistler (www.whistler.com) should be your starting point for information about the Whistler region. The website has lots of details about the area,

Top to bottom: tuna crudo at Aura Restaurant; "big-ass pancakes" at the Southside Diner; Pizzeria Antico.

both on and off the mountain, and they run the year-round **Whistler Visitor Centre** (4230 Gateway Dr., 604/935-3357 or 877/991-9988, www.whistler.com/whistler-visitor-centre) in the village, which supplies maps, answers questions, and books accommodations and activities. Hours vary seasonally, but the visitors center is open at least 8am-6pm daily; it stays open until 8pm or 10pm on busy weekends and holiday periods.

Whistler-Blackcomb (604/967-8950 or 800/766-0449, www.whistlerblackcomb.com) books lift tickets, equipment rentals, ski and snowboard lessons, and accommodations (reservations 604/296-5316 or 888/403-4727), and can provide information about other mountain activities in every season. Check the website for toll-free reservations numbers from many different countries.

Media and Communications

Pique Newsmagazine (www.piquenewsmagazine.com) covers the Whistler area and provides events listings. The *Whistler Question* (www.whistlerquestion.com) is another local news source.

Medical Services

The **Whistler Health Care Centre** (4380 Lorimer Rd., 604/932-4911, www.vch.ca, 8am-10pm daily) provides emergency medical services to both locals and visitors. Doctors are on-call after hours.

The Whistler area has several medical clinics that will see visitors for minor issues, including the **Whistler Medical Clinic** (4380 Lorimer Rd., 604/932-3977, www.whistlermedicalclinic.com), **Northlands Medical Clinic** (101-4359 Main St., in the Summit Lodge complex, 604/932-8362, www.northlandsclinic.com), and **Town Plaza Medical Clinic** (40-4314 Main St., 604/905-7089, www.medicalclinicwhistler.com).

Rexall (103-4360 Lorimer Rd., 604/932-2303; 4212 Village Square, 604/932-4251, www.rexall.ca, 9am-9pm daily, 9am-7pm daily) has two Whistler

pharmacies. **Shoppers Drug Mart** (121-4295 Blackcomb Way, 604/905-5666, www.shoppersdrugmart.ca, 9am-9pm daily) also provides pharmacy services.

Getting Around
By Car

Whistler Village is a pedestrian zone, so you have to leave your car outside the village proper. Whistler has several public **parking lots** where you can park all day.

Day lots 1 to 5, on Blackcomb Way near Lorimer Road, are closest to Whistler Village. Lots 4 and 5 are always free. Lots 1, 2, and 3, which are closer to the lifts, are paid lots ($2 per hour, $8 per day) until 5pm; they're free from 5pm to 3am. Closer to the Blackcomb Base, off Glacier Lane, day lots 6, 7, and 8 are also free. From November through March, you can't park overnight in any of the day lots; between April and October, you can park for up to 72 hours.

In the Creekside area, you can park free in the Creekside base underground garage. Follow London Lane off Highway 99.

Public paid parking is available at Whistler Conference Centre (4010 Whistler Way, per hour/day $1 per hour, $10 per day, 24-hour maximum), Whistler Public Library (4329 Main St., per hour/day $1 per hour, $10 per day, 24-hour maximum), and Whistler Municipal Hall (4325 Blackcomb Way, $1 per hour, 4-hour maximum).

By Bus

B.C. Transit (604/932-4020, http://bctransit.com/whistler, $2.50 pp) runs several bus routes through the Whistler area that are useful if you're staying outside of the central Whistler Village. The **Whistler Creek** route travels between the village and Creekside, and the **Valley Connector** links many of Whistler's residential neighborhoods with the Whistler Gondola Exchange, where you can board the mountain gondola.

Two bus routes are free during the

winter season, including the **Upper Village/Benchlands** route that can take you to the village from condos in those neighborhoods, and the **Marketplace Shuttle** between the Whistler Gondola Exchange and the Marketplace shopping center.

The Valley Connector route operates 5:15am-3:30am daily. The other routes vary seasonally; call or check the website for hours.

By Taxi

Whistler has two local taxi companies: **Whistler Resort Cabs** (604/938-1515, www.resortcabs.com) and **Whistler Taxi** (604/932-3333, www.whistlertaxi.com). Both operate 24 hours daily. Taxi fares average $5 within Whistler Village, $10 between the village and Creekside, and $15 between the village and other Whistler neighborhoods.

Kamloops to the B.C. Rockies

Deserts. Forests. Alpine peaks. The region from British Columbia's interior to the Rocky Mountains is among western Canada's most beautiful and diverse.

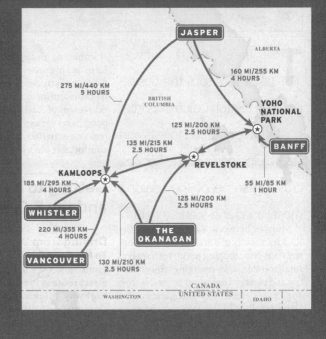

JASPER

ALBERTA

160 MI/255 KM
4 HOURS

275 MI/440 KM
5 HOURS

BRITISH
COLUMBIA

YOHO
NATIONAL
PARK

125 MI/200 KM
2.5 HOURS

★

BANFF

135 MI/215 KM
2.5 HOURS

★

REVELSTOKE

KAMLOOPS

185 MI/295 KM
4 HOURS

★

55 MI/85 KM
1 HOUR

WHISTLER

125 MI/200 KM
2.5 HOURS

220 MI/355 KM
4 HOURS

THE
OKANAGAN

VANCOUVER

130 MI/210 KM
2.5 HOURS

CANADA
UNITED STATES

WASHINGTON

IDAHO

Kamloops to the B.C. Rockies

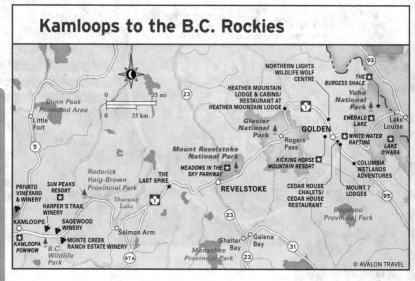

© AVALON TRAVEL

The Trans-Canada Highway takes you from the desertlike hills of British Columbia's interior to the evergreen forests and stark alpine peaks of the Rockies, crossing some of the region's most varied and scenic terrain.

Midway between Vancouver and the Rockies, the city of Kamloops makes a logical road-trip stopping point, with several small museums, an emerging wine industry, and plenty of desert sunshine. Nearby, Sun Peaks Resort offers hiking and cycling along its rolling hills in summer and more than 130 trails for skiing and snowboarding once the snow starts to fall.

As you continue east, Highway 1 climbs through the Purcell and Selkirk mountain ranges en route to the Rockies, passing directly through three striking national parks: Mount Revelstoke, Glacier, and Yoho have plenty of scenic drives, numerous hiking trails, shimmering glacier-fed lakes, and one of Canada's highest waterfalls. Important in Canada's early development, particularly its transcontinental railroad, the mountain towns of Revelstoke and Golden are good bases for exploring the parks, with outdoor activities, cool restaurants, and comfortable places to spend the night.

Getting to Kamloops and the B.C. Rockies

Driving from Vancouver
To Kamloops

From Vancouver to Kamloops, the **most direct route** is to take the **Trans-Canada Highway (Highway 1)** east to Hope. Continue east at Hope onto **Highway 3**, then exit onto **Highway 5 (Coquihalla Hwy.)** north. Follow the Coquihalla over the mountains to Kamloops. It's **220 miles (355 kilometers)** from Vancouver to Kamloops via this route, which takes **3.75 to 4 hours.**

An alternate route from Vancouver to Kamloops takes you through the **scenic Fraser Canyon.** Take **Highway**

Highlights

★ **Kamloopa Powwow:** One of western Canada's largest celebrations of First Nations' culture brings dancers, drummers, and other performers to Kamloops every August (page 179).

★ **Sun Peaks Resort:** This ski resort near Kamloops has lots to do outdoors in the warmer months, especially mountain hiking and biking (page 182).

★ **Meadows in the Sky Parkway:** In Mount Revelstoke National Park, this winding 16-mile (26-kilometer) road climbs to over 6,500 feet (2,000 meters) above sea level, with great hiking at the top (page 186).

★ **White-Water Rafting:** The Kicking Horse River east of Golden is one of the region's top spots for white-water rafting, with long stretches of Class 3 and Class 4 rapids (page 198).

★ **Kicking Horse Mountain Resort:** From getting up close with a grizzly bear to whizzing downhill in North America's highest bike park, this mountain getaway near Golden offers lots of warm-weather experiences—plus serious powder skiing in winter (page 203).

★ **Lake O'Hara:** Make your reservation early if you'd like to catch the shuttle bus to this Yoho National Park lake,

so picturesque—and popular—that Parks Canada limits visitor access (page 208).

★ **Emerald Lake:** As scenic as its name suggests, this green beauty in Yoho National Park is a lovely spot for canoeing, hiking, or enjoying the surrounding mountain landscape (page 210).

★ **The Burgess Shale:** Geologists have discovered some of the world's oldest fossils in these layers of rocks in Yoho National Park. Reserve in advance for a challenging guided hike to the fossil beds (page 211).

Best Hotels

★ **The Cube Hotel:** For travelers on a budget, this Revelstoke lodging mixes the relaxed vibe of a guesthouse with the style of a boutique hotel (page 191).

★ **Sutton Place Hotel Revelstoke Mountain Resort:** This condo-style property at the base of the ski lifts accommodates couples, friends, and families in its contemporary suites, ranging from studios to three-bedroom units (page 191).

★ **Cedar House Chalets:** These modern wood-framed chalets near Golden are stocked with everything you need for a mountain getaway (page 201).

★ **Emerald Lake Lodge:** You can't ask for a prettier setting than that of these comfortable guest rooms, overlooking one of Yoho National Park's most spectacular bodies of water (page 214).

★ **Cathedral Mountain Lodge:** In these upscale cabins in Yoho National Park, you don't have to rough it to live out your log-cabin dreams (page 214).

1 to Hope and continue north on Highway 1 through Boston Bar and Cache Creek, where the highway turns east to Kamloops. This Fraser Canyon route is **270 miles (430 kilometers)** from Vancouver to Kamloops and it takes **five hours.**

To the B.C. Rockies

If you're heading on to the Rockies from Kamloops, pick up **Highway 1** in Kamloops, which continues east to Revelstoke, Golden, and Yoho National Park. The drive from Kamloops to **Revelstoke** is **135 miles (215 kilometers)** and takes **2.5 hours;** from Kamloops to **Golden,** it's **225 miles (360 kilometers)** and takes **four hours;** from Kamloops to **Yoho,** it's **260 miles (415 kilometers)** and takes **4.75 to 5 hours.**

Driving from Whistler

If you want to stop off in Whistler between Vancouver and Kamloops, take the following route. After following Highway 99 (Sea-to-Sky Hwy.) from Vancouver to Whistler, continue north on **Highway 99.** It will join **Highway 97,** and at **Cache Creek,** you'll meet up with the **Trans-Canada Highway (Highway 1)** east to Kamloops. This

Vancouver-Whistler-Kamloops route is **260 miles (420 kilometers)** and takes **5.75 to 6 hours;** the **Whistler-Kamloops** leg is **185 miles (295 kilometers)** and takes **four hours.**

Driving from Kelowna (Okanagan)
To Kamloops

Driving from Kelowna, in the Okanagan wine region, to Kamloops, you have two options: Follow **Highway 97C** west to **Merritt,** where you pick up **Highway 5** to Kamloops; this route is **130 miles (210 kilometers)** and takes you through some beautifully remote ranchlands. Or take **Highway 97** north, which forks to the northwest and continues to Kamloops; this second option is **105 miles (165 kilometers)** and follows some scenic stretches of lakeshore. The Merritt route is longer, but the roads are faster. Either option will take about **2.5 hours.**

To the B.C. Rockies

From Kelowna to Revelstoke, Golden, or Yoho, take **Highway 97** north, then continue north on **Highway 97A.** At **Sicamous,** turn east onto the **Trans-Canada Highway (Hwy. 1),** which leads east to these mountain destinations. The

Best Restaurants

★ **Painted Pony Café:** Sample traditional aboriginal dishes at this homey Kamloops diner, run by a First Nations family (page 180).

★ **La Baguette:** This sociable café is the place for coffee and pastries in Revelstoke (page 192).

★ **Woolsey Creek Bistro:** Revelstoke's most accomplished restaurant cooks up a world-rambling menu in a sunny yellow house (page 193).

★ **Restaurant at Heather Mountain Lodge:** Near the east entrance to Glacier National Park, this lodge serves inventive meals using lots of wild ingredients. The mountain setting is gorgeous, too (page 197).

★ **Eagle's Eye Restaurant:** With wraparound mountain views and an elevation of 7,700 feet (2,350 meters), this contemporary eatery at Kicking Horse Mountain Resort is Canada's highest restaurant (page 206).

trip from Kelowna to **Revelstoke** is **125 miles (200 kilometers)** and takes **2.5 hours.**

Driving from Banff

The **Trans-Canada Highway (Hwy. 1)** is the direct route from Banff to British Columbia. The road will take you west into B.C. to Yoho, Golden, Revelstoke, and Kamloops. The drive from Banff to **Yoho** is **55 miles (85 kilometers)** and takes **one hour.** From Banff to **Kamloops,** it's **310 miles (495 kilometers)** and takes **5.5 to 5.75 hours.**

Driving from Jasper

The **shortest route** between Jasper and Kamloops is to follow **Highway 16** west to **Highway 5 (Yellowhead Hwy.),** where you turn south toward Kamloops. The trip from Jasper to **Kamloops** via this route is **275 miles (440 kilometers)** and takes **five hours.**

A **longer but scenic route** is to take the **Icefields Parkway (Hwy. 93)** south from Jasper to **Lake Louise,** where you turn west onto **Highway 1.** You'll pass through Yoho, Glacier, and Mount Revelstoke National Parks and into the city of Kamloops. The drive from Jasper to **Yoho National Park** via this route is **160 miles (255 kilometers)** and it takes **3.5 to 4 hours.** Driving this scenic route from Jasper to **Kamloops,** the trip is **415 miles (665 kilometers)** and takes **8.25 to 8.75 hours.**

Getting There by Air, Train, or Bus

The most convenient way to get to Kamloops from most B.C. or Alberta destinations is with your own vehicle, although there are options to fly, take the train, or travel by bus. To reach any of the B.C. national parks easily, you need a car.

By Air

Air Canada (888/247-2262, www.aircanada.ca) flies to the regional **Kamloops Airport** (YKA, 3035 Airport Rd., 250/376-3613, www.kamloopsairport.com) from Vancouver and Calgary. **WestJet** (888/937-8538, www.westjet.com) serves Kamloops from Calgary and Edmonton. **Central Mountain Air** (888/865-8585, www.flycma.com) flies to Kamloops from Kelowna and from several northern B.C. communities, including Fort St. John, Prince George, Smithers, and Terrace. The airport is seven miles (11 kilometers) west of downtown Kamloops.

Budget Car Rental (250/374-7368 or 888/368-7368, www.budget.ca), **Enterprise Rent-a-Car** (250/376-2883 or 888/305-8051, www.enterprise.com), and **National Car Rental** (250/376-4911, www.nationalcar.ca) have offices at the Kamloops Airport.

By Train

The Canadian, the **VIA Rail** (514/989-2626 or 888/842-7245, www.viarail.ca) Vancouver-Toronto train, stops in Kamloops. You can travel westbound to Vancouver or eastbound to Jasper and points farther east, including Edmonton, Saskatoon, Winnipeg, and Toronto. However, between Vancouver and Kamloops (10 hours) or between Kamloops and Jasper (8.25 hours), the train is significantly slower than driving. *The Canadian* operates three times a week in each direction from May through mid-October, and twice a week from mid-October through April.

By Bus

Greyhound (800/661-8747, www.greyhound.ca) can take you to Kamloops (725 Notre Dame Dr., 250/374-1212) from Vancouver (4.5-5.25 hours, one-way adults $30-81), Kelowna (2.5-3.5 hours, one-way adults $18-47), Revelstoke (2.5-3.5 hours, one-way adults $23-62), Golden (4.75-5.5 hours, one-way adults $36-92), Banff (7-8 hours, one-way adults $45-115), and many other destinations across western Canada.

Kamloops

Its name comes from *T'kemlups,* a Secwepemc First Nations' word meaning "the meeting of the rivers." Kamloops, a city of 85,000 at the confluence of the South Thompson and North Thompson Rivers and at the intersection of Highways 1, 5, and 97, is a convenient stopping point when you're traveling across the province. This dry region has a hot, almost desertlike climate in summer; it gets an average of 8.6 inches (218 millimeters) of rain every year, compared with more than 43 inches (1,100 millimeters) in coastal Vancouver. The city has several small museums, an emerging wine industry, and lots of sunshine.

Sights and Recreation

Secwepemc Museum and Heritage Park

A residential school for aboriginal children operated from the 1890s to 1978 on the grounds of what is now the **Secwepemc Museum and Heritage Park** (200-330 Chief Alex Thomas Way, 250/828-9749, www.secwepemcmuseum.com, 8:30am-4:30pm daily June-early Sept., 8am-4pm Mon.-Fri. early Sept.-May, adults $10, seniors and students $7, ages 7-17 $6, families $20), first in a wooden schoolhouse and later in the 1920s red brick building that still stands on the site.

The museum details the history of the Shuswap First Nation (Shuswap is the English name for the Secwepemc people), whose traditional lands cover 56,000 square miles (145,000 square kilometers) between the Fraser River and the Rocky Mountains. Exhibits include regalia and other clothing, dugout canoes, profiles of chiefs and other band members, information about the Shuswap language and culture, and details about the residential schools, both here and elsewhere in B.C.

Museums and Galleries

Stop into the contemporary building in downtown Kamloops that houses the **Kamloops Art Gallery** (465 Victoria St., 250/377-2400, www.kag.bc.ca, 10am-5pm Mon.-Wed. and Fri.-Sat., 10am-9pm Thurs., adults $5, seniors, students, and ages 7-13 $3, families $10) for exhibits of works by regional artists, including aboriginal artists. Admission is free on Thursday.

Kamloops Courthouse Gallery (7 W. Seymour St., 250/314-6600, http://kamloopscourthousegallery.ca, 10am-5pm Tues.-Fri., 10am-4pm Sat.), a local artists cooperative, shows and sells work by its members in the stately former provincial court building that dates to the early 1900s.

Kamloops Museum (207 Seymour St., 250/828-3576, www.kamloops.ca/

Kamloops

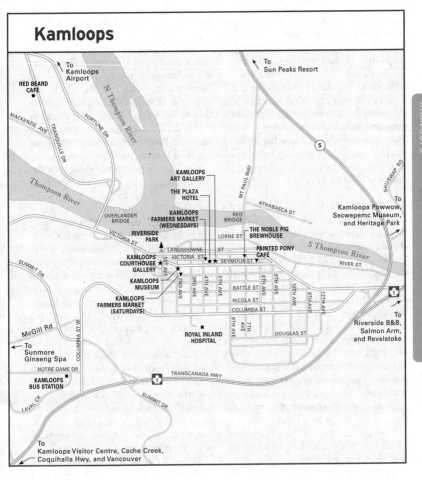

museum, 9:30am-4:30pm Tues.-Wed. and Fri.-Sat., 9:30am-7:30pm Thurs. May-Oct., donation adults $3, ages 17 and under $1) has both permanent and changing exhibits about the history of the Kamloops region.

Riverside Park

On the South Thompson River in downtown Kamloops, **Riverside Park** (Lorne St.) has a sandy riverside swimming beach with a splash park for the kids, as well as changing rooms and restrooms. The park also has a rose garden and a riverfront walking trail. Every evening in July and August, at the park's Rotary Bandshell, there's **Music in the Park** (250/828-3611, www.tourismkamloops. com, 7pm daily July-Aug., free), a series of free 90-minute concerts.

Sunmore Ginseng Spa

A unique East-meets-West spa in Kamloops incorporates locally grown ginseng, which has long been used in traditional Chinese medicine, into massage oils, facial treatments, steam baths, and soaks.

Furnished with Buddha sculptures, traditional Japanese wooden bathtubs, and other art and accessories from Asia, the **Sunmore Ginseng Spa** (925 McGill Place, 250/372-2814, www.sunmoreginseng.com, 10am-5pm Tues.-Sat., treatments $130-300) is a full-service spa. In addition to standard massage and facial treatments, you can select services like a ginseng body wrap, which includes a ginseng-honey body mask to smooth and hydrate your skin, or enjoy the ginseng steam room, where ginseng helps open your pores and detoxify your body. It's a one-of-a-kind way to relax.

B.C. Wildlife Park

If you're hoping to see Canadian wildlife as you journey across the region, start at the nonprofit **B.C. Wildlife Park** (9077 Dallas Dr., 250/573-3242, www.bcwildlife.org, 9:30am-5pm daily May-early Sept., 9:30am-4pm daily Mar.-Apr. and early-Sept.-Oct., 9:30am-4pm Sat.-Sun. Nov.-Feb., Apr.-early Sept. adults $14.95, seniors $12.95, ages 3-17 $10.95, families $49, early-Sept.-Mar. adults $13, seniors $10, ages 3-17 $8, families $40), where wolves, coyotes, moose, elk, eagles, owls, and other animals live in large outdoor enclosures. You may even get a glimpse of the rare white Kermode or "spirit" bear that's native to the B.C. coast.

The best time to visit the wildlife park, which has little shade along its pathways, is in the morning or on a cool or overcast day. On summer afternoons, the animals take shelter from the strong desert sun, and so should you. The park is 12 miles (20 kilometers) east of Kamloops, off Highway 1.

Wineries

While the wine-making industry in the Kamloops area is a drop in the wine cask compared to the well-developed wineries in B.C.'s Okanagan Valley, you can stop and sip at several local vineyards.

The first winery in the Kamloops region, **Harper's Trail Winery** (2761 Shuswap Rd., 250/573-5855, http://harperstrail.com, call for hours) released their initial vintage in 2011 and now produces riesling, pinot gris, cabernet franc, and other varieties that you can sample in the wood-paneled tasting room. Picnickers are welcome on the wraparound patio, facing the vineyards and desert hills. The winery is 12 miles (19 kilometers) east of downtown Kamloops. Taking Highway 1 is a little faster, but the drive along Shuswap Road past the desert cliffs and hoodoos is more scenic.

Credited with coining the phrase, "Hands up!," notorious train robber Billy Miner held up his last Canadian train in 1906 on the ranchlands that now house **Monte Creek Ranch Estate Winery** (2420 Miner's Bluff Rd., Monte Creek, 250/573-5399 or 855/633-9463, www.montecreekranchwinery.com, 10am-6pm daily). This Wild West history inspired the winery's Hands Up varieties, including a white blend of frontenac blanc, viognier, and la crescent grapes, and a red made primarily from merlot and cabernet sauvignon. The tasting room, 20 miles (33 kilometers) east of Kamloops along Highway 1, is in a striking modern barn-inspired structure with a landmark bell tower, opened in 2015 with views of the Lions Head rock face, desert headlands, and surrounding vines. On the Terrace, the winery's wine bar, you can sip wine while nibbling cheese or charcuterie.

Other Kamloops-area wineries include **Privato Vineyard & Winery** (5505 Westsyde Rd., 250/579-8739, http://privato.ca, 10am-5pm daily May-Oct., by appointment Nov.-Apr.), an 80-acre family-run farm that produces chardonnay, pinot noir, and rosé wines, and **Sagewood Winery** (589 Meadow Lark Rd., 250/573-1921, http://sagewoodwinery.ca, 1pm-5pm Wed.-Sun. mid-June-Oct., call for off-season hours), where you can sample their riesling, gewürztraminer, pinot noir, and other varieties.

Festivals and Events
Kamloops Cowboy Festival

Considered the largest cowboy fest in

Canada, the **Kamloops Cowboy Festival** (www.bcchs.com, Mar.) is four days of cowboy music, cowboy poetry, cowboy dinner theater, and other things cowboy.

★ Kamloopa Powwow

One of western Canada's largest celebrations of First Nations culture, the annual **Kamloopa Powwow** (Secwepemc Powwow Grounds, Chief Alex Thomas Way, 250/828-9700, http://tkemlups.ca, August, $10 per day, $20 for the weekend) draws aboriginal families and visitors from near and far for three days of traditional music, drumming, and dancing. Try to arrive for one of the Grand Entry processions, where all the participating dancers assemble in the powwow arena. Vendors sell First Nations crafts, souvenirs, and snacks ranging from hot dogs to bannock to Indian tacos. You can bring your own food and drinks, but no alcohol is allowed on the powwow grounds.

Accommodations
Under $150

From several decks, an outdoor hot tub, and a swimming dock, you can enjoy views of the Thompson River and the desert cliffs beyond, when you stay at the **Riverside Bed & Breakfast** (2664 Thompson Dr., 250/374-1043 or 888/400-1043, www.riversidebnb.ca, $129-159 d), five miles (7.5 kilometers) east of the city center. The four comfortable, air-conditioned guest rooms have private baths, mini fridges, microwaves, and coffeemakers; Wi-Fi, local phone calls, and parking are included. Owners Cynthia and Gordon James dress in spiffy chef's coats to serve a full family-style breakfast in the dining room, which has more river views.

The orange stucco building doesn't look too stylish from the outside, but inside **The Plaza Hotel** (405 Victoria St.,

Top to bottom: moose at the B.C. Wildlife Park; Harper's Trail Winery; Monte Creek Ranch Estate Winery.

250/377-8075 or 877/977-5292, www.theplazahotel.ca, $119-169 d, parking $8), built in 1928 on downtown Kamloops's main street, are 67 updated guest rooms, with flat-screen TVs, mini fridges, and air-conditioning. Rates include Wi-Fi, local and long-distance calls, a hot breakfast, and access to the indoor pool and fitness facilities at the nearby YMCA; also complimentary are drop-in yoga classes at a local studio.

$150-250

Like an estate in Kentucky's horse-racing country, the **South Thompson Inn and Conference Centre** (3438 Shuswap Rd. E., 250/573-3777 or 800/797-7713, www.souththompsonhotelkamloops.com, $159-249), east of downtown, has an equestrian theme, with a dark-paneled bourbon lounge and 56 guest rooms named for thoroughbreds. Rooms are traditionally furnished, with included Wi-Fi and balconies overlooking either the river or across the lawns to the desert hills. Also facing the river is an outdoor pool and hot tub. Guests can help themselves to complimentary morning coffee and tea in the lobby; continental breakfast ($9.95) is also available. The inn's restaurant, **Madisens** (dinner from 5:30pm daily, mains $15-36), serves traditional dishes like New York steak with blue cheese butter, pistachio-crusted rack of lamb, and local trout with lemon-caper sauce.

Food

The **Kamloops Farmers Market** (250/682-7975, www.kamloopsfarmersmarket.com) has two downtown locations. On Saturday (8am-12:30pm Sat. late Apr.-Oct.) it's in the 200 block of St. Paul Street between 2nd and 3rd Avenues; on Wednesday (8am-2pm Wed. May-Oct.) it's in the 400 block of Victoria Street between 4th and 5th Avenues.

Launched by a First Nations family, the homey ★ **Painted Pony Café** (705 Victoria St., 250/828-1131, www.

hikers at Sun Peaks Resort

paintedponycafe.com, 9am-9pm Mon.-Sat., 10am-2pm Sun., mains breakfast $8-14, lunch and dinner $8-24) uses aboriginal ingredients and traditional recipes for breakfast, lunch, and dinner. Morning meals might include an egg sandwich on bannock, fried quail, salmon cakes topped with poached eggs, or a deer steak, while later in the day, you can dig into buffalo burgers, elk stew, or cedar-planked salmon.

Try a tasting flight of house-brewed beers at **The Noble Pig Brewhouse** (650 Victoria St., 778/471-5999, http://thenoblepig.ca, 11:30am-11pm Mon.-Wed., 11:30am-midnight Thurs.-Sat., 3pm-10pm Sun., mains $13-21), a downtown brewpub and eatery where you might sample Honey Badger pale ale, Prodigal Swine dark amber, or Imperialist Pig IPA. To go with your drinks, crispy breaded pickles are an addictive starter, while beer enlivens main dishes from *coq au bier* (beer-braised chicken) to beer-and-bacon macaroni and cheese

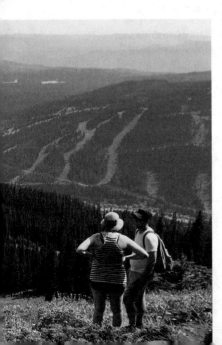

to burgers topped with porter-flavored barbecue sauce.

When you can't decide between coffee or a beer, head to the north side of the Thompson River to the **Red Beard Café** (449 Tranquille Rd., 250/376-0083, www.redbeardcafe.com, 7am-10pm Mon.-Thurs., 7am-11pm Fri.-Sat., 8am-10pm Sun., mains $4-15), which is part coffee shop and part beer garden. They're serious about both brews, roasting their own coffee and pouring B.C. craft beers from more than a dozen taps. The munchies range from breakfast toasts (try the bacon-avocado or the Nutella-pear) to small plates like hummus and crostini or pulled pork tacos.

Information and Services

Tourism Kamloops (www.tourismkamloops.com) has a helpful website with detailed information about the region and things to do. They also run the **Kamloops Visitor Centre** (1290 W. Trans-Canada Hwy., 250/374-3377 or 800/662-1994, 9am-5pm Mon.-Fri. Jan.-mid-May, 8:30am-6pm Mon.-Fri., 9am-6pm Sat.-Sun. mid-May-late Sept., 8:30am-6pm Mon.-Fri., 9am-6pm Sat., 10am-3pm Sun. late Sept.-Oct., 8:30am-5pm Mon.-Fri. Nov.-Dec.); take Exit 368 from Highway 1.

The main hospital facility for the Kamloops region, **Royal Inland Hospital** (311 Columbia St., 250/374-5111, www.interiorhealth.ca) has a 24-hour emergency room.

Getting Around

Downtown Kamloops is compact and walkable, although many accommodations and activities are outside the downtown core, most easily explored by car.

The **Kamloops Transit System** (250/376-1216, http://bctransit.com/Kamloops, one-way $2) runs buses across the city. Use the Trip Planner function on their website to figure out if you can get where you're going by bus.

Service hours vary by bus route and

day of the week, so check the schedule online before you set out. Major routes begin service between 6am and 7am Monday through Friday (between 7am and 8:30am Saturday and Sunday) and run until between 11pm and midnight.

★ Sun Peaks Resort

When you turn off Highway 5 north of Kamloops, you quickly leave behind the desert-dry hills and begin to climb through the pines to Sun Peaks Resort.

Sun Peaks is 35 miles (56 kilometers) from the city, less than an hour's drive, and offers summertime relief from Kamloops's heat with plenty of outdoor activities. In winter, it's B.C.'s second-largest ski and snowboard resort after Whistler-Blackcomb.

At the base of the mountain, Sun Peaks has a compact village with several hotels, restaurants, and shops. Compared to a large resort like Whistler, the village here is tiny, although it has everything you need for a mountain getaway.

Sports and Recreation

Hiking

In summer, you can take the **Sunburst Express Chair** (www.sunpeaksresort. com, 10am-5pm daily late June-early Sept., adults $19, seniors and ages 13-18 $16, ages 6-12 $13) up to an elevation of 6,000 feet (1,850 meters) to access a 22-mile (35-kilometer) network of easy and intermediate hiking trails. Colorful wildflowers carpet the slopes, usually peaking in late July or early August.

If you'd rather not hike alone, or if you'd like to learn more about the area flora and fauna while you walk, book a two-hour guided **alpine nature hiking tour** (10am and 1pm daily late June-early Sept., $25 pp, $12 per additional person).

Mountain Biking

Mountain bikers can explore more than 35 lift-accessed trails in the **Sun Peaks Bike Park** (www.sunpeaksresort.com, 10am-5pm daily late June-early Sept.,

half-day adults $34, seniors and ages 13-18 $29, ages 6-12 $20, full-day adults $42, seniors and ages 13-18 $36, ages 6-12 $25).

Sun Peaks also has a network of **cross-country bicycle trails,** ranging from beginner to advanced, many of which you can access without purchasing a lift ticket. Get a trail map online (www.sunpeaksresort.com) to plan your routes. If you're new to mountain or cross-country biking, consider an **introduction to cross-country mountain biking** package (www.sunpeaksresort.com, 10am and 1pm daily late June-early Sept., $89) that includes a bike rental, lift ticket, and two-hour lesson. Or book a **guided cross-country alpine tour** (www.sunpeaksresort.com, 10am and 1pm daily late June-early Sept., $39 pp, $12 per additional person) for an introduction to the mountain's trail network.

Elevation Bike Ski Board (Sun Peaks Grand Hotel, 250/578-5555, www.sunpeaksresort.com/elevation) rents bikes and related gear for downhill and cross-country cycling.

Mountain Cross Carts

Imagine whizzing down the mountain in a grown-up go-kart. If that sounds like your thing, try out Sun Peaks' **mountain cross carts** (www.sunpeaksresort.com, 11am-8pm daily late June-early Sept., 11am-6pm Fri.-Sun. early-Sept.-late Sept., $25). After you and your cart ride up a platter lift, you drive your vehicle back down a winding 1,680-foot (512-meter) course, at speeds up to 35 mph (55 km/h). If that doesn't sound fast, remember you're in a go-kart. Your ticket lets you do four laps of the course; the minimum age is 14.

Stand-Up Paddleboarding

On Heffley Lake, off Tod Mountain Road on the way to Sun Peaks Resort, **Paddle Surfit** (2388 Heffley Lake Rd., Heffley Creek, 250/318-0722, www.paddlesurfit.com, 2 hours $50) rents stand-up paddleboards. The two-hour rentals include a lesson as well as all the paddling gear. Call or check the website for hours.

Winter Sports

With a skiable area of 4,270 acres (1,728 hectares) spread across three mountains, Sun Peaks Resort is the second-largest **winter sports resort** in Canada (www.sunpeaksresort.com, lift tickets adults $86, seniors and ages 13-18 $69, university students $77, ages 6-12 $43). The ski and snowboard season runs from late November to early April. Eleven lifts serve 133 trails, rated 10 percent novice, 58 percent intermediate, and 32 percent expert.

Accommodations

Most Sun Peaks accommodations are "ski-in, ski-out," or within walking distance of mountain activities. **Sun Peaks Resort Central Reservations** (250/578-5399, http://sunpeaksresort.com) assists with lodging bookings at the several slope-side hotels or nearby condo buildings. Summer rates are much lower than the winter season prices.

Close to the lifts, the large **Sun Peaks Grand Hotel and Conference Centre** (3240 Village Way, 250/578-6080 or 844/774-7263, www.sunpeaksgrand.com, $139-434, parking $13-18) has an upscale dark-wood lobby and comfortable traditional guest rooms. An outdoor heated pool and three outdoor hot tubs can soak away any adventure-induced aches and pains.

Another handy-to-the-lifts option with an outdoor hot tub, the **Coast Sundance Lodge** (3160 Creekside Way, 250/578-0200 or 800/716-6199, www.coasthotels.com, $135-305, parking $10) has 84 updated rooms with kitchenettes or full kitchens.

Food

Bluebird Market (3250 Village Way, 250/578-2414, 11:30am-6:30pm Mon.-Thurs., 11:30am-9pm Fri., 10am-9pm Sat., 10am-6:30pm Sun.) sells basic groceries, snacks, and essentials. Otherwise, the nearest full-service supermarket is in Kamloops, so stock up in advance if you want to prepare your own meals.

Tiny **Bolacco Café** (Coast Sundance Lodge, 3160 Creekside Way, 250/578-7588, 8am-5pm daily, mains $4-7) squeezes a lot of good cheer, as well as espresso and fresh-baked pastries, into its pint-size space. Try the berry scones.

Specializing in both savory and sweet crepes, like spinach and feta or strawberries with Nutella, **Tod Mountain Café** (3170 Creekside Way, 250/571-0545, http://todmountaincafe.ca, call for hours, mains $4-10) also serves breakfast all day, sandwiches, and smoothies.

The **Voyageur Bistro** (Kookaburra Lodge, 3270 Village Way, 250/578-5268, http://voyageurbistro.ca, 4pm-9pm daily, mains $18-34) injects some Canadiana into its pub-fare-and-more menu. The soup of the day comes with bannock (a traditional aboriginal fried bread), the burger is made with bison, and the mains include cider-braised rabbit and *tourtière*, French-Canadian meat pie. There's *poutine*, too, of course. Frequent live music adds Canadian beats.

Information and Services

Contact **Sun Peaks Resort** (1280 Alpine Rd., Sun Peaks, 250/578-5474, http://sunpeaksresort.com) for information about the mountain and various activities. For winter conditions, call the **Snow Report** (250/578-7232).

During the winter ski season, **Sun Star Shuttle** (250/554-8005, http://sunstarshuttle.com, late Nov.-early Apr., one-way adults $45, ages 6-12 $26) runs between the Kamloops Airport and Sun Peaks Resort several times a day. Reservations are required. They also provide transportation from early April through late November with three days' advance notice. Summer rates are $99 pp, or $68.75 pp for two or more passengers.

To get to Sun Peaks for a day of

Rest Stop: Salmon Arm

If you need a break along Highway 1 as you're driving toward B.C.'s national parks, stop in Salmon Arm, a pleasant town on Shuswap Lake, 68 miles (110 kilometers) east of Kamloops and 65 miles (105 kilometers) west of Revelstoke.

Sights and Activities

Cheese-lovers should detour to **Gord's Gouda at Grass Fed Dairy** (1470 50 St. SW, 250/832-4274, www.gortsgoudacheese.bc.ca, 8:30am-5pm Mon.-Sat.), a family-run dairy just west of Salmon Arm that produces delicious gouda and several other varieties of cheese. You can watch the cheesemakers at work while the kids check out the cows in the barn or run around with the chickens. The dairy is about five minutes' drive from Highway 1. From the highway, bear right onto Salmon River Road. Take the first right onto 10th Avenue SW, which will turn left and become 50th Street SW.

Stretch your legs with a walk in **Marine Peace Park at Salmon Arm Wharf** (750 Marine Park Dr. NE, 250/832-4044, www.salmonarm.ca), which has trails along the lake and a boardwalk on the pier, where you might spot ospreys or blue herons. It's a nice spot for a picnic. If you're passing through on a summer evening, you might take in **WOW! Wednesday on the Wharf** (www.salmonarmartscentre.ca, 6:45pm Wed. mid-June-Aug.), a series of free concerts outdoors in the park.

For a more artistic break, see what's happening at the **Salmon Arm Arts Centre** (70 Hudson Ave. NE, 250/832-1170, www.salmonarmartscentre.ca, 11am-4pm Tues.-Sat., donation), which operates a small art gallery.

Food

What's a rest stop without pie? **Shuswap Pie Company** (331A Alexander St. NE, 250/832-7992, www.shuswappiecompany.ca, 7:30am-5:30pm Mon.-Fri., 9am-3pm Sat.), a café and bakery in downtown Salmon Arm, sates your baked goods cravings with a variety of savory and sweet pies. The coffee is good, too.

weekend skiing, you can take the **Kamloops Ski & Ride Shuttle Bus** (www.sunpeaksresort.com, Sat.-Sun. early Dec.-late Mar., one-way $15, round-trip $25). The shuttle picks up passengers from several locations throughout Kamloops and takes you to the mountain in the morning, then returns you to town in the afternoon.

Mount Revelstoke National Park

Mount Revelstoke National Park's main attraction is a great drive: the zigzagging Meadows in the Sky Parkway that climbs steeply to an elevation of more than 6,500 feet (2,000 meters). From the top of the parkway, you can walk up the only mountain in Canada's national park system that you can summit by hiking just a short distance from your car. And lest you think that this snaking road to the summit is a modern innovation, the parkway was constructed between 1911 and 1927. Work on the road actually began before the region became a national park in 1914.

Located in the Selkirk range of B.C.'s Columbia Mountains, Mount Revelstoke National Park has longer hikes, too, including a number of great day hikes from the Meadows in the Sky summit. Another highlight at the summit area are the summer wildflowers that carpet the slopes with color, peaking in early to mid-August.

The visitor season is short here, however; the parkway summit is typically open only from July through September. The rest of the year, it's too snow-covered to travel.

Driving from the west along the

The Last Spike

The idea of a railroad crossing the entire continent became an obsession in 19th-century Canada. After Canadian Confederation in 1867, when the country was established with its four founding provinces of Ontario, Quebec, New Brunswick, and Nova Scotia, the railroad was seen as key to the new nation's expansion. In fact, the promise of a transcontinental railroad was a major factor in convincing British Columbia to join the Confederation in 1871.

In 1880 the Canadian government signed a contract with the Canadian Pacific Railway (CPR) Company to construct this national rail line, and construction immediately began pushing west. Because the CPR couldn't recruit enough workers in B.C., they looked overseas, particularly to China. Roughly 15,000 Chinese laborers eventually helped build Canada's transcontinental railroad.

In 1885, Craigellachie, B.C., in the mountains west of Revelstoke, was the site of a historic milestone. It's where the last spike was driven along the Canadian Pacific Railway, marking the completion of the country's 3,100-mile (5,000-kilometer) transcontinental railroad.

At **The Last Spike Visitor Centre,** 103 miles (165 kilometers) east of Kamloops and 28 miles (45 kilometers) west of Revelstoke along Highway 1, there's a historic marker commemorating the event, as well as restrooms and a gift shop.

Trans-Canada Highway (Hwy. 1), the turnoff for Revelstoke, the town closest to the park, is just before you get to the exit for the Meadows in the Sky Parkway. From the east, Highway 1 skirts, and in some cases crosses, the park's southern boundary after passing through Glacier National Park.

The park doesn't have accommodations, road-accessible campgrounds, food, or other services, so plan to stay in Revelstoke. The nearest Parks Canada campgrounds are at Glacier National Park.

Visiting the Park
Entrances

The main entrance to Mount Revelstoke National Park is at the base of the Meadows in the Sky Parkway, off Highway 1 near Revelstoke. Highway 1 runs through parts of the park, and some hiking trails begin just off the highway.

Park Passes and Fees

A **day pass** (adults $7.80, seniors $6.80, ages 6-16 $3.90, families $19.60) for Mount Revelstoke National Park is valid until 4pm on the day after you purchase it. You can buy a park pass at the entrance to the Meadows in the Sky Parkway.

Purchasing a Parks Canada **annual discovery pass** (adults $67.70, seniors $57.90, ages 6-16 $33.30, families $136.40), which is valid for a year, is a good deal if you're spending at least a week in one or more parks. It's accepted at more than 100 national parks and national historic sites across Canada. You can buy an annual pass online from Parks Canada or at any park visitors center.

For both day and annual passes, family passes cover up to seven people arriving together in a single vehicle, whether or not they're actually related.

Visitors Centers

Park information is available in the town of Revelstoke at the **Revelstoke Visitor Information Centre** (301 Victoria Rd. W., 250/837-5345 or 800/487-1493, www.revelstokechamber.com, 8:30am-7pm Mon.-Fri., 9am-7pm Sat.-Sun. June-Sept., 8:30am-4:30pm Mon.-Fri. Oct.-May) or at the **Parks Canada information office** (301B 3rd St. W., 250/837-7500, www.pc.gc.ca, 8am-noon and 1pm-4:30pm Mon.-Fri.).

Revelstoke

To Revelstoke Dam

To Mount Revelstoke National Park

BEST WESTERN PLUS REVELSTOKE

THE NOMAD FOOD COMPANY

MONASHEE LODGE

To Kamloops

To Shelter Bay and Nakusp

REVELSTOKE RAILWAY MUSEUM

PHARMASAVE REVELSTOKE

LE MARCHE

PEOPLES DRUG MART

LA BAGUETTE

WOOLSEY CREEK BISTRO

REVELSTOKE MUSEUM

PARKS CANADA

THE CUBE HOTEL

VALHALLA PURE OUTFITTERS

THE MODERN BAKESHOP & CAFE

REVELSTOKE VISITOR INFORMATION CENTRE

FREE SPIRIT SPORTS

GRIZZLY PLAZA

REVY OUTDOORS

GRIZZLY BOOK & SERENDIPITY SHOP

To Rogers Pass, Glacier National Park, and Golden

TRANSCANADA HWY

EASTERN ACCESS RD

Queen Elizabeth Park

Columbia River

Illecillewaet River

SCALE NOT AVAILABLE

QUEEN VICTORIA HOSPITAL

To Sutton Place Hotel, Revelstoke Mountain Resort

© AVALON TRAVEL

Getting Around

While Mount Revelstoke National Park is located just outside the town of Revelstoke, there are no public transportation options or shuttle services that operate to or within the park. You need a car to get around.

★ Meadows in the Sky Parkway

The park's 16-mile (26-kilometer) **Meadows in the Sky Parkway** climbs steeply from an elevation of 1,315 feet (400 meters) to over 6,500 feet (2,000 meters). As the road rises and twists around the 16 switchbacks, snaking its way up the mountain, you can stop at several viewpoints; the Revelstoke Viewpoint looks down on the town in the valley below, while other lookouts offer vistas across the mountains.

It's not just about the drive, though. Once you reach the end of the parkway, you can access a number of hiking trails, ranging from easy to challenging.

You'll need to leave your car at the Balsam Lake parking lot, since the road is not open to private cars all the way to the mountain summit. From the parking area, it's a 0.6-mile (1-kilometer) walk to the summit, either on the **Upper Summit Trail,** a gently climbing, wooded, dirt and gravel path, or along the road. Alternatively, take the free **summit shuttle bus** (10am-5:30pm daily July-Sept., weather permitting), which runs every 15 to 20 minutes, up to the Heather Lake summit area. If you're heading up late in the day, confirm the time that the last shuttle returns. Before or after your time at the summit, take a few minutes to walk around tiny **Balsam Lake.**

Allow about three hours for your Meadows in the Sky excursion. It takes 35 to 45 minutes to drive each way, plus time to get from the parking lot to the summit area. Plan at least an hour to hike and enjoy the views at the summit; you could easily spend an entire day if you'd like to do one of the longer hikes.

The parkway is generally open from May to October, but snow can remain at higher elevations until July or August, which means that the summit area is typically accessible only between mid-late July and late September. Confirm road conditions and open hours with the park staff before you set out.

The **Meadows in the Sky Parkway Entrance Station** (8am-5pm daily mid-June-mid-Sept., 9am-5pm daily mid-May-mid-June and mid-Sept.-early Oct.) is 0.5 miles (800 meters) northeast of Revelstoke off Highway 1.

The parkway closes to uphill drivers at 5:30pm, but you can return downhill until 8:30pm May to August, until 6:30pm in September, and until 5:30pm in October.

Bring water and whatever food you might need; there are restrooms but no other services along the Meadows in the Sky Parkway and at the summit area. Bring extra layers of clothing, too, since it's always cooler up on the mountain than it is in town.

Hiking

Mount Revelstoke National Park has several trails from the summit area of the Meadows in the Sky Parkway. Other trails are to the east, off Highway 1.

From the Meadows in the Sky Summit

You get panoramic views across the mountains and down to the Columbia River from the **Firetower Trail,** a gentle 0.3-mile (480-meter) climb to the 1927 Summit Firetower, a cabin with a cupola-style lookout on top. Park firefighters used the tower as a lookout until 1987, when satellite fire monitoring and aerial fire patrols replaced the human guards.

Another easy trail is the **First Footsteps Trail,** a 0.6-mile (1-kilometer) loop, which has First Nations art, interpretive panels, and viewpoints along the way. You can also follow the 10-minute **Heather Lake Trail** around the subalpine lake of the same name.

If you have more time, an excellent intermediate-level hike follows the **Eva Lake Trail** through wildflower meadows and boulder fields to a beautiful alpine lake, which is named for Eva Hobbs, a Revelstoke teacher and avid hiker who discovered the lake on a 1909 outing with the Revelstoke Mountaineering Club. The trail is 7.5 miles (12 kilometers) round-trip. Along the way, you have the option to make a short detour to **Miller Lake.**

A more difficult hike climbs the **Jade Lakes Trail** (11 miles/18 kilometers round-trip), crossing the Jade Lake Pass into the alpine regions above the tree line. The Eva Lake, Miller Lake, and Jade Lakes trails all start from the same point but divide along the way.

From Highway 1

As you travel Highway 1 between Revelstoke and Glacier National Park, you can stop off for several easy walks that illustrate different ecosystems within Mount Revelstoke National Park.

Have you ever seen a giant skunk cabbage? They look like, well, gigantic cabbages, and you can see them as you wander across the marshes and wetlands along the **Skunk Cabbage Boardwalk Trail,** an easy 0.75-mile (1.2-kilometer) loop. If you visit in May when their yellow flowers bloom, you'll understand the "skunk" component of their name. The trail is 17 miles (28 kilometers) east of Revelstoke, off Highway 1.

You typically find temperate rainforest climates along the British Columbia coast and in other coastal regions. B.C.'s Columbia Mountains, including sections of Mount Revelstoke National Park, house the world's only *inland* temperate rainforest, including plentiful old-growth forests where western red cedar and western hemlock predominate. Explore this old-growth forest on the **Giant Cedars Boardwalk Trail,** a 0.3-mile (480-meter) boardwalk that loops past massive cedars, some of which are more than 500 years old. The trail starts 19 miles (30 kilometers) east of Revelstoke.

Revelstoke

Transportation, forestry, and increasingly tourism drive the economy of Revelstoke, a community of 7,200 in B.C.'s Selkirk and Monashee mountains. Located on the Columbia River outside Mount Revelstoke National Park, the town is an outdoor-oriented place, drawing hikers and cyclists in summer, and skiers and snowboarders during the colder months. The Revelstoke Mountain Resort is famous for its powder skiing; the area gets 40 to 60 feet (12 to 18 meters) of snow in a typical winter season.

Sights and Recreation

Located in the town's former post office, the **Revelstoke Museum** (315 1st St. W., 250/837-3067, www.revelstokemuseum.ca, 10am-5pm Mon.-Sat., 11am-5pm Sun., adults $5, seniors $4 and over age 12 $2, families $12) helps answer the

---

Top to bottom: First Footsteps Trail; Skunk Cabbage Boardwalk Trail; Giant Cedars Boardwalk Trail.

question, "Why is Revelstoke here?" It's because of the railroad that the modern-day town developed, beginning in the 1880s as a construction base for workers building the transcontinental railroad. When the trains began to run—10 passenger trains every day once passed through town—the Canadian Pacific Railway was the region's major employer, drawing workers from across Canada and from China, Italy, and Scandinavia. Those Scandinavian settlers helped introduce Revelstoke to the sport that dominates today's tourism economy: skiing.

To learn more about Revelstoke's railroad history, including how the railroad was built and the people who built it, visit the **Revelstoke Railway Museum** (719 Track St. W., 250/837-6060, www.railwaymuseum.com, 9am-5pm daily May-mid-Oct., adults $10, seniors $8, ages 8-16 $5, ages 4-7 $2, families $22). Inside you can climb aboard a steam locomotive or imagine traveling in high style in the 1929 "Business Car No. 4," where the white tablecloths are set for dinner. Practice your skills as an engineer on the diesel locomotive simulator, or explore the stories of the Chinese railroad workers. Outside are more historic rail cars, including a coal car, a snowplow, and a caboose. You don't have to be a train buff to enjoy this well-designed museum.

North America's fourth-largest river, the Columbia, starts in British Columbia and flows through Washington and Oregon to the Pacific Ocean. The massive Revelstoke Dam, completed in 1984 after eight years of construction, harnesses the Columbia to produce electricity, generating 25 percent of B.C.'s power. At the **Revelstoke Dam Visitor Centre** (Hwy. 23, 250/814-6697 or 800/224-9376, http://bchydro.com/revelstoke, 10am-4pm daily mid-May-early Sept., adults $6, seniors and ages 6-18 $5, families $15), three miles (5 kilometers) north of Revelstoke via Highway 23, you can learn about the dam's construction and operation; take the elevator up to a viewing area at the top of the dam 30 stories above the river. B.C. Hydro, the provincial electric company, runs the visitors center, so the exhibits have an industry perspective, but they're still interesting if you're curious about rivers, dams, and power generation.

For a short hike in town, follow the paved **Revelstoke Greenbelt Trails.** One route starts in Centennial Park, behind the Revelstoke Community Centre (600 Campbell Ave.), and meanders east along the Columbia and Illecillewaet Rivers. Another option is the Revelstoke Dyke Walk; cross the Big Eddy Bridge from Wilson Avenue at the west end of town and turn left onto the dyke.

Revelstoke Mountain Resort

Unlike many ski mountains with a large purpose-built village at the base, **Revelstoke Mountain Resort** (2950 Camozzi Rd., 250/814-0087 or 866/373-4754, www.revelstokemountainresort. com), a 10-minute drive from the center of Revelstoke, has only a hotel, a few food outlets, and a couple of shops. Many of the visitors who come to ski or snowboard in winter or to hike and bike in summer come to the mountain to get outdoors and return to town to eat and sleep. Yet there's plenty to do at this 3,121-acre (1,263-hectare) mountain resort.

Summer Activities

Although Revelstoke's peak season is winter, the resort is developing summer activities. You can take the gondola up the mountain for a buffet **breakfast at the Revelation Lodge** (7am-noon Mon.-Fri., breakfast till 11am, 7am-2pm Sat.-Sun., breakfast till 1pm, late June-early Sept., gondola only adults $15, seniors and under age 13 $10, gondola plus buffet breakfast adults $32, seniors and under age 13 $16) where your bacon and eggs come with views across the valley. The vistas are even better from the patio tables. If you're feeling energetic, hike back down to the base after your meal.

Revelstoke Mountain also has several lift-accessed **mountain biking trails** (late June-early Sept.).

Selkirk Tangiers Heli Skiing (250/837-5378 or 800/663-7080, www.selkirk-tangiers.com, July-early Sept.) offers summertime helicopter tours that depart from Revelstoke Mountain Resort. They run **helicopter sightseeing tours** (12-30 minutes, $119-299 pp) exploring the nearby mountains; **helicopter picnics** (2.5-3.5 hours, $329 pp), combining a sightseeing tour with a mountain picnic lunch; half-day and full-day **heli-hiking tours** ($399-479 pp); and even a **heli-biking adventure** ($345 pp), for advanced riders only, where the helicopter drops you at the summit of Mount Cartier and you ride the challenging 7,000-foot (2,135-meter) descent back down to the Columbia River valley.

Winter Sports

Revelstoke Mountain is open for **skiing and snowboarding** (www.revelstokemountainresort.com, adults $61-86, seniors and over age 12 $42-64, ages 6-12 $20-32) from late November to mid-April. The mountain's ski and snowboard terrain leans heavily toward the expert and intermediate categories. Only 7 percent of the runs are classified as "beginner." Lift ticket prices vary with the season and the number of days purchased; you can usually save money buying your tickets online in advance.

Other winter activities include **snowshoe tours** (www.revelstokemountainresort.com, 1.5-2.5 hours, adults $40-60, ages 11-16 $25-50, ages 8-10 free) and **dog-sled tours** (www.revelstokemountainresort.com, 3 hours, $199 single, $279 double). Book online or through the resort's activity center.

Events

Every evening from late June through the end of August, head downtown for **free live music** (6:30pm-9:30pm)

historic rail cars at the Revelstoke Railway Museum

outdoors at Grizzly Plaza (Mackenzie St. at Victoria St.).

Shopping

If you need clothing or gear for your outdoor adventures, look in Revelstoke. The downtown area has several sport shops, including **Free Spirit Sports** (203 1st St. W., 250/837-9453, www.freespiritsports.com, 9:30am-6pm Mon.-Fri., 9:30am-5pm Sat., 11am-4pm Sun.), **Revy Outdoors** (201 Mackenzie Ave., 250/814-2575, 10am-6pm Mon.-Fri., 9am-6pm Sat., 11am-4pm Sun.), and **Valhalla Pure Revelstoke** (213 Mackenzie Ave., 250/837-5517, http://vpo.ca, 9:30am-6pm Mon.-Sat., noon-5pm Sun.).

You don't know what treasures you might find at the **Grizzly Book and Serendipity Shop** (208 Mackenzie Ave., 250/837-6185, www.grizzlybook.com, 9:30am-5:30pm Mon.-Sat.), part independent bookstore and part jewelry and gift shop. They've been supplying Revelstoke with things to read since 1989.

Accommodations

Revelstoke has several chain motels along Highway 1, but it's much nicer to get off the highway and into town.

Under $150

Located downtown, ★ **The Cube Hotel** (311 Campbell Ave., 250/837-4086, www.cubehotel.ca, $88-128 d) pairs the relaxed vibe of a simple guesthouse with the style of a modern boutique hotel. Guests can hang out in the cool communal lounge space with lime green walls and overstuffed couches, where a complimentary continental breakfast is served. You can prep meals in the shared kitchen. The 21 no-frills guest rooms provide a space to sleep, plus essentials like free Wi-Fi, flat-screen TVs, sinks, and toilets; seven individual shower rooms are down the hall.

The 18 utilitarian rooms at **Monashee Lodge** (1601 3rd St. W., 250/814-2553, www.monasheelodgerevelstoke.com, $124-155 d), a basic two-story motel west the town center, come with comfortable beds, mini fridges, and Keurig coffeemakers; some have microwaves. The helpful owners can tell you about the area; in winter, they serve a continental breakfast.

$150-250

The newest of Revelstoke's chain motels, the **Best Western Plus Revelstoke** (1925 Laforme Blvd., 250/837-2043 or 855/837-2043, http://revelstokebestwestern.com, $166-207 d) is off Highway 1 on the west end of town. The parking-lot surroundings are uninspiring, but the 87 rooms have pillow-top mattresses, mini fridges, microwaves, safes, and coffeemakers. There's an outdoor pool and two hot tubs. Wi-Fi and breakfast are included in the rates.

Over $250

The nicest hotel in town isn't actually in town; it's the contemporary condo-style ★ **Sutton Place Hotel Revelstoke Mountain Resort** (2950 Camozzi Rd.,

250/814-5000 or 866/378-8866, www.suttonplace.com/revelstoke, $205-450 d, 2-bedroom suite $305-590, 3-bedroom suite $385-700) at the base of Revelstoke Mountain Resort. The 205 suites, ranging from studios to three-bedroom units, all have fireplaces, fully equipped kitchens, and washer-dryers. Other amenities include an outdoor heated pool and hot tub, a spacious fitness room, a spa, and underground parking. In winter, you're steps from the lifts; in summer, you can go exploring with one of the complimentary mountain bikes.

Food

You'd expect that an eatery named ★ **La Baguette** (607 Victoria Rd., Unit 103, 250/837-3755, 6:30am-7pm daily, mains $5-15) would make excellent breads and pastries, and you'd be right; they even bake their own bagels. But this popular café doesn't stop there. First-rate coffee plus a changing assortment of sandwiches, pizzas, and pastas round out the menu. The same owners run **Le Marché** (607 Victoria Rd., Unit 101, 9am-7pm daily), a gourmet grocery around the corner, where you can pick up charcuterie, well-priced cheeses, organic produce, and some prepared foods—perfect for picnicking in the national parks.

A busy breakfast and lunch spot, **The Modern Bakeshop & Café** (212 Mackenzie Ave., 250/837-6886, http://themodernbakeshopandcafe.com, 7am-5pm Mon.-Fri., 7am-4pm Sat., mains $2.50-8) serves coffee and pastries in the morning (try the pumpkin muffins), plus sandwiches and soups at midday. Their veggie rolls are a good grab-and-go snack for the trail.

Nomads and locals alike stop into **The Nomad Food Company** (1601 Victoria St. W., 250/837-4211, 11am-9pm daily summer, 11am-8pm daily winter, mains $7-15) for cooked-to-order burgers, *paninis*, *poutine*, and other diner-style fare. With a few tables inside and picnic tables out in the parking lot, it's nothing fancy, but

Woolsey Creek Bistro

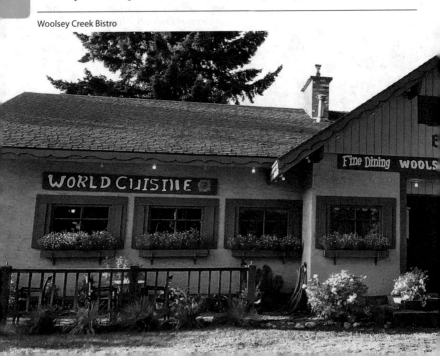

everything is hearty, fresh, and moderately priced.

A sunny yellow house is home to the ★ **Woolsey Creek Bistro** (604 2nd St. W., 250/837-5500, www.woolseycreekbistro.ca, 5pm-9pm daily, mains $18-40), Revelstoke's most accomplished restaurant, where you can enjoy the world-rambling creations in the spacious casual dining room or on the outdoor patio. The simple house salad of greens topped with grilled pineapple, goat cheese, and dates is first-rate, or for a more original starter, try the Petit Baluchon, a phyllo pouch filled with braised rabbit and served atop poached pears. Mains include butternut squash ravioli with a fennel-orange-caper sauce, Thai-style coconut-tamarind sablefish, and bison short ribs. Save room for a dessert like the dark-chocolate truffle cake or a fresh fruit sorbet.

Information and Services

Staff at the **Revelstoke Visitor Information Centre** (301 Victoria Rd. W., 250/837-5345 or 800/487-1493, www.revelstokechamber.com, 8:30am-7pm Mon.-Fri., 9am-7pm Sat.-Sun. June-Sept., 8:30am-4:30pm Mon.-Fri. Oct.-May) can assist with information about the Revelstoke region and other destinations across the province. If you're interested in hiking, they can advise you about area trails and provide a hiking map.

Tourism Revelstoke (www.seerevelstoke.com) publishes a free guide to the area that's available online and in print at the Visitor Information Centre.

Parks Canada maintains a year-round information office (301B 3rd St. W., 250/837-7500, www.pc.gc.ca, 8am-noon and 1pm-4:30pm Mon.-Fri.) in the city's post office building.

The emergency room at Revelstoke's **Queen Victoria Hospital** (1200 Newlands Rd., 250/837-2131, www.interiorhealth.ca) is open 24 hours daily, seven days a week. Local pharmacies include **Pharmasave Revelstoke** (307 W. Victoria Rd., 250/837-2028, www.pharmasaverevelstoke.com, 9am-6pm Mon.-Thurs. and Sat., 9am-9pm Fri., 11am-5pm Sun.) and **Peoples Drug Mart** (555 Victoria Rd., 250/837-5191, www.peoplesdrugmart.com, 9am-6pm Mon.-Sat., 11am-4pm Sun.).

Getting Around

Revelstoke's downtown area is compact and walkable. The city has limited bus service around town, run by **B.C. Transit** (250/837-3888, http://bctransit.com/revelstoke, 8am-5pm Mon.-Sat., adults $2, seniors and children over age 5 $1.75). To explore the national parks outside town, you need a car.

When Revelstoke Mountain Resort is open for skiing and riding in winter, **Revelstoke Resort Shuttle** (250/837-2268, www.revelstokeresortshuttle.ca, one-way $3, round-trip $5) has frequent service between downtown and the mountain.

Two Days in B.C.'s National Parks

You really need more than two days to take in even the highlights of B.C.'s national parks, but here's how to make the most of a short trip through the mountains, stopping in Mount Revelstoke, Glacier, and Yoho National Parks.

Get an early start with a drive up Mount Revelstoke's **Meadows in the Sky Parkway.** The winding road that climbs to an elevation of more than 6,500 feet (2,000 meters) opens at 8am daily in summer. From the parking area, catch the free shuttle to the summit, where you can hike one of the loop trails to capture the views across the mountains.

Head down the Parkway and stop in **Revelstoke** at the **Revelstoke Railway Museum** to learn about the railroad's importance in the development of this mountain region. After a quick lunch at **La Baguette,** start heading east along Highway 1.

Stretch your legs with a walk on the **Skunk Cabbage Boardwalk Trail** or the **Giant Cedars Boardwalk Trail,** short walkways that highlight different local ecosystems.

Continue east into **Glacier National Park,** enjoying the vistas of the mountains. Stop into the **Rogers Pass Discovery Centre** to explore the exhibits and watch one of the informative films about avalanche control, bear safety, or other eco-topics.

Your destination for dinner is the **Restaurant at Heather Mountain Lodge,** where the chef uses lots of wild ingredients in the creative mountain fare. Remember if you're booking a dinner reservation that you've crossed into a new time zone—it's an hour later here than the B.C. coast. Spend the night at the lodge or continue into **Golden** for more lodging options.

In the morning, if you're up for an adventure, go **rafting on the Kicking Horse River** or take a more gentle canoe or kayak excursion at **Columbia Wetlands Adventures.**

Back in the car, drive east into **Yoho National Park.** If you have time, hike to **Wapta Falls** near the park's western entrance; it's the largest waterfall along the Kicking Horse River. Closer to the center of the park, stop to see the unusual **Natural Bridge** en route to gorgeous **Emerald Lake.** Hike the trail that loops around the lake, rent a canoe for a leisurely paddle, and take lots of photos.

Have dinner and stay in Yoho at one of the lodges: **Emerald Lake Lodge, Cathedral Mountain Lodge,** or in the tiny town of Field, **Truffle Pigs.**

In the morning, try to take at least one more hike, perhaps to **Takakkaw Falls** or, if you've booked ahead, to **Lake O'Hara.** Then relax, knowing that you've seen the highlights of three of British Columbia's spectacular mountain national parks.

Glacier National Park

As you might guess from its name, Glacier National Park is known for the broad glaciers and jagged mountains that populate its 333,000-acre (135,000-hectare) expanse. Established in 1886 along with Yoho National Park, not long after the completion of Canada's transcontinental railroad, it was British Columbia's first national park and the second national park in Canada, after Banff. It is not connected to the U.S. national park of the same name.

Most early visitors to Glacier National Park came by rail, after the transcontinental railroad opened the region to tourism. It wasn't until 1962 when the Rogers Pass section of the Trans-Canada Highway, which runs east-west across the park, was completed and visitors began road-tripping in and around the park.

A number of sights and short hiking trails are just off the Trans-Canada (Hwy. 1). If you're short on time, go directly to the **Rogers Pass Discovery Centre,** which has well-designed exhibits about the park and the surrounding areas.

Visiting the Park

The best months to visit Glacier National Park are July through early September. Much of the park's terrain is at high mountain elevations, and the region gets heavy snow during the winter months. While the park is technically open year-round, the weather makes many areas inaccessible between October and May. Park staff advise contacting them before visiting in spring (Apr.-June) or fall (Sept.-Oct.) for an update on road conditions and to confirm what's open.

TIP: Fill your gas tank in Revelstoke or Golden. There are no gas stations or other services between these two towns or anywhere in Glacier National Park.

Entrances

The Trans-Canada Highway (Hwy. 1) runs through Glacier National Park. Glacier's western boundary is 10 miles (16 kilometers) east of Mount Revelstoke National Park. The east entrance is 35 miles (57 kilometers) west of Golden.

Park Passes and Fees

There is no entrance gate when you approach Glacier National Park from the west, so purchase your park pass at the **Revelstoke Visitor Information Centre** in Revelstoke. Similarly, if you're coming from the east, you can buy your park pass at the **British Columbia Visitor Centre** in Golden. If your first stop in Glacier National Park will be the visitors center at Rogers Pass, purchase your pass there.

A **day pass** (adults $7.80, seniors $6.80, ages 6-16 $3.90, families $19.60) for Glacier National Park is valid until 4pm on the day after you purchase it.

Buying a Parks Canada **annual discovery pass** (adults $67.70, seniors $57.90, ages 6-16 $33.30, families $136.40), which is valid for a year, is a good deal if you're spending at least a week in one or more parks. It's valid at more than 100 national parks and national historic sites across Canada. Buy your annual pass online from Parks Canada or at any park visitors center.

For both day and annual passes, the family passes cover up to seven people in a single vehicle, whether or not they're actually related.

If you're driving through the park along Highway 1 without stopping, a park pass isn't required. However, you need a pass if you get out of your car anywhere within the park boundaries.

Visitors Centers

The **Rogers Pass Discovery Centre,** which houses the **Glacier National Park Visitor Centre** (Hwy. 1, 250/837-7500, www.pc.gc.ca, 9am-5pm daily mid-May-mid-June, 8am-7pm daily mid-June-late Sept., 9am-5pm daily late Sept.-late Nov., 7am-4pm Sat.-Mon., 7am-12:30pm and 1:30pm-4pm Tues.-Fri. late Nov.-Apr.), is at the Rogers Pass summit, 45 miles (72 kilometers) east of Revelstoke and 50 miles (80 kilometers) west of Golden.

Reservations

Glacier National Park's campgrounds are first-come, first-served; reservations are not possible.

Getting Around

There are no public transportation options or shuttle services that operate in Glacier National Park, so you need to have a car to get around.

Sights and Activities

Canada's coast-to-coast Trans-Canada Highway is the longest highway in the world, running 4,849 miles (7,821 kilometers) from Victoria, on British Columbia's Vancouver Island, to St. John's, Newfoundland. It was officially completed at **Rogers Pass,** in Glacier National Park, which helped open the region for tourism. Canadian prime minister John Diefenbaker led the opening ceremony at the pass in 1962.

You can learn more about the highway's history and construction, as well as the area's wildlife and weather, with the informative exhibits at the **Rogers Pass Discovery Centre** (Hwy. 1, 250/837-7500, www.pc.gc.ca, 9am-5pm daily mid-May-mid-June, 8am-7pm daily mid-June-late Sept., 9am-5pm daily late Sept.-late Nov., 7am-4pm Sat.-Mon., 7am-12:30pm and 1:30pm-4pm Tues.-Fri. late Nov.-Apr.), which is also the park's visitors center.

At an elevation of 4,364 feet (1,330 meters), Rogers Pass is the third-highest point on the Trans-Canada Highway, and the pass is all too frequently closed in winter due to heavy snow or avalanche danger. If you have time, watch the film *The Snow Wars,* about managing avalanche risks. Although the film was made in the late 1970s, and communications technology (and hairstyles) have advanced, technicians still use the same processes for testing the snow quality to predict avalanche risk and use blasts of the same military howitzers to trigger controlled avalanches around the region. You can see those howitzers on display in front of the Discovery Centre as well.

Also at the Rogers Pass summit is the **Memory Garden,** where interpretive plaques document milestones in the construction of the Trans-Canada Highway and offer memorials to those who lost their lives in area avalanches.

The Rogers Pass Discovery Centre is at the Rogers Pass summit, 45 miles (72 kilometers) east of Revelstoke and 50 miles (80 kilometers) west of Golden.

Hiking

Glacier National Park has 87 miles (140 kilometers) of hiking trails. Some park trails are just off Highway 1, but they're not always well-marked. Watch carefully for signs as you approach your stopping point.

Check the **Parks Canada Trail Conditions Report** (www.pc.gc.ca) online or ask about trail status at the **Glacier National Park Visitor Centre** before setting out on any long hikes.

Hemlock Grove

The **Hemlock Grove Trail** is a short 0.2-mile (350-meter) boardwalk trail that loops through old-growth cedars and hemlocks. These trees are big! The trail is on the west side of the park, on the north side of Highway 1.

Rock Garden

For mountain views, follow the **Rock Garden Trail** up a series of rock staircases and stepping stones. A quarter-mile (400-meter) loop, it's not long, but a few sections can be steep and slippery in wet weather. Like the Hemlock Grove trail, the trailhead is on the west side of the park, on the north side of Highway 1.

Bear Creek Falls

The 0.6-mile (1-kilometer) **Bear Creek Falls Trail** leads down a short, somewhat steep trail to a pretty waterfall. The turnoff from Highway 1 is sharp and not well-marked, so watch carefully for the trailhead sign, 5.5 miles (9 kilometers) east of the park visitors center.

Avalanche Crest

For a longer day hike, the **Avalanche Crest Trail,** five miles (8.2 kilometers) round-trip, climbs from the trailhead in the Illecillewaet Campground (1.9 miles/3 kilometers west of the Rogers Pass summit) up into an alpine basin, where you have panoramic views over Rogers Pass. This steep trail has an elevation gain of 2,600 feet (800 meters). Allow at least five hours for this hike.

Asulkan Valley

The **Asulkan Valley Trail** takes you to the tongue of the Illecillewaet Glacier. Another steep route, this trail starts gently as it leaves the trailhead in the Illecillewaet Campground, but after the 2.5-mile (4-kilometer) mark, the pitch goes up much more sharply. The trail is

8.6 miles (13.8 kilometers) round-trip, with an elevation gain of 2,850 feet (869 meters). Plan six to seven hours for this hike.

Accommodations and Food

Glacier National Park has three rustic drive-in campgrounds, but no other accommodations or food concessions. The park is close enough to the towns of Revelstoke and Golden that staying in either of these communities is an option.

If you don't want to camp, the best accommodations near the park are the **Heather Mountain Lodge & Cabins** (5400 Hwy. 1 W., Golden, 250/344-7490 or 866/344-7490, http://heathermountainlodge.com, late June-mid-Sept., $154-185 d, $300 cabin), located 1.2 miles (2 kilometers) outside the park's east gate. The 22 mountain-style guest rooms in a two-story motel block have been updated with light wood furnishings, modern baths, flat-screen TVs, free Wi-Fi, and Nespresso machines. Even nicer, and far more romantic, are the two private log cabins, with king beds, woodstoves, in-floor heating, rain showers, and deep soaker tubs. The lodge is 53 miles (89 kilometers) east of Revelstoke and 33 miles (55 kilometers) west of Golden. From December through mid-April, the lodge is reserved for clients booked on heli-skiing trips with their sister company, **Great Canadian Heli-Skiing** (250/344-2326 or 866/424-4354, http://canadianheli-skiing.com).

Serving creative mountain fare with lots of wild ingredients, the ★ **Restaurant at Heather Mountain Lodge** (7:30am-10pm daily late June-mid-Sept., mains $13-37) is well worth a stop, even if you're not staying at the lodge. To share, or to start, try the charcuterie plate, with smoked duck breast "ham," snowshoe hare galantine, pork rillettes, and bannock, or the Railman's Picnic, which includes house-canned sockeye and chicken thighs, homemade cheese, pickled egg, wild spruce tips, and an assortment of pickles and relishes. Among the hearty mains, look for the game cheeseburger topped with brie, barbecue sauce, and horseradish beet relish, or the free-range Alberta beef steak. Veggie lovers, your dish is the Vegetable Patch, with maple-smoked beans, jicama slaw, blueberry-quinoa pilaf, roasted potatoes, kale, grilled leeks, and a slab of buttery corn bread. The dining room, with a high wood-beamed ceiling and a stone fireplace, looks out to the nearby mountains. If you're making a reservation, note that the lodge is in the mountain time zone, the same as Alberta but one hour later than Glacier National Park and the B.C. coast.

Camping

Glacier National Park's three campgrounds, all along Highway 1 near the center of the park, are open only during the summer months. Since reservations aren't accepted, plan to arrive before noon to make sure you get the site you want.

None of the campgrounds have showers, RV hookups, or laundry facilities. Most sites are designed to accommodate tents or small RVs, so if you're driving a big rig, you might need to look elsewhere.

The largest camping area, 60-site **Illecillewaet Campground** (late June-late Sept., $21.50), is 1.9 miles (3 kilometers) west of the Rogers Pass summit. The **Loop Brook Campground** (July-Aug., $21.50), three miles (5 kilometers) west of the summit, has 20 campsites. Both of these campgrounds have restrooms with flush toilets and drinking water.

The park also has a 15-site primitive campground, **Mount Sir Donald Campground** (July-Aug., $15.70), with no facilities. It's 0.6 miles (1 kilometer) west of the Loop Brook Campground.

Time Zones

While most of British Columbia is in the Pacific time zone and Alberta is in the mountain time zone, some B.C. national parks and communities close to the Alberta border are on mountain time. Here's how to set your clocks:

* **Revelstoke:** Pacific time

* **Mount Revelstoke National Park:** Pacific time

* **Glacier National Park:** Pacific time

* **Golden:** mountain time

* **Yoho National Park:** mountain time

* **Kootenay National Park:** mountain time

* **Fernie:** mountain time

* **Cranbrook:** mountain time

Golden and Vicinity

One of the most centrally located towns in the B.C. Rockies, Golden makes a good base for visiting the region's national parks. It's set between Glacier to the west and Yoho to the east; Mount Revelstoke, Kootenay, Lake Louise, and Banff are all within a short drive.

Located at the confluence of the Columbia and Kicking Horse Rivers, the Golden region was an important travel route for aboriginal people who lived in the area for millennia. Now its river location makes Golden a center for white-water rafting and river float trips. Just west of town is Kicking Horse Mountain Resort, which offers serious powder skiing in winter and a variety of outdoor experiences during the summer season.

When you're wandering through this town of 3,750, stop to see the **Kicking Horse Pedestrian Bridge** (8th Ave. N.), over the Kicking Horse River. You wouldn't think it's a record-breaker, but at 151 feet (46 meters) across, it's the longest freestanding pedestrian bridge in North America.

Note that Golden is in the mountain time zone, the same as Alberta and one hour later than Vancouver and the B.C. coast.

Sights and Recreation
★ White-Water Rafting

Golden is a center for white-water rafting, with Class 3 and 4 rapids on the Kicking Horse River east of town. Several local outfitters offer half- and full-day **white-water rafting trips** ($90-165), as well as gentler family-oriented rafting tours ($35-70). Many trips have minimum age requirements, so check ahead if you're traveling with kids or teens.

Golden's rafting season typically runs from May through September, with the highest river levels and fastest water in June and early July.

Glacier Raft Company (612 7th St. N., 250/344-6521 or 877/344-7238, www.glacierraft.com) runs a variety of on-the-water adventures, from an introductory white-water experience to several wet-and-wild rafting trips. They also offer a laid-back two-hour guided inflatable **kayak tour** (ages 10 and up $70) that begins on a gentle section of the Kicking Horse River and continues to the point where the Kicking Horse meets the Columbia.

Alpine Rafting (101 Golden Donald Upper Rd., 250/344-6778 or 888/599-5299, www.alpinerafting.com) runs a similar range of white-water tours, as well as a **catrafting** option, where you run the river on an inflatable boat with two pontoons.

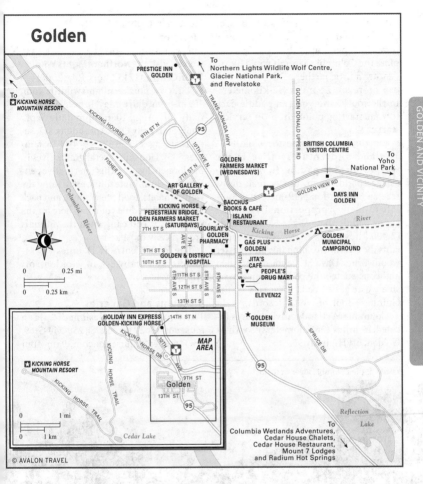

Golden

Other Kicking Horse rafting outfitters include **Hydra River Guides** (2936 Kicking Horse Rd., 403/762-4554 or 800/644-8888, www.raftbanff.com), **Wet N' Wild Adventures** (1509 Lafontaine Rd., 250/344-6546 or 800/668-9119, www.wetnwild.bc.ca), and **Wild Water Adventures** (Beaverfoot Rd., 403/522-2211 or 888/647-6444, http://wildwater.com).

Columbia Wetlands Adventures

Explore the gentle Columbia River and its wetlands ecosystems on an excursion with **Columbia Wetlands Adventures** (2629 Hwy. 95, Parson, 250/348-2235 or 888/244-7117, www.wetlandsadventures.com, 9:30am-6pm daily May-Sept.). You can take a self-guided **dock walk** ($7 pp) on the boardwalk through the marshes, peruse their wetlands library, stocked with bird and animal books, or bring a picnic to enjoy on the riverside dock.

To get out on the water, take a 2.5-hour **guided float tour** (10am and 2pm daily May-Sept., adults $69, ages 4-15 $25), where you might spot deer, elk, or even a bear. You can also rent **canoes** (2 hours $49, full-day $60), **kayaks** (single 2 hours $40, full-day $60, double 2 hours $50, full-day $90), **stand-up paddleboards** ($25 per hour, full-day $90), and **pedal boats** ($30 per hour, full-day $90) to explore the Columbia River. If you'd like to venture a little farther afield, their staff can drop you 7.5 miles (12 kilometers) to the south, and you can paddle back to your starting point; drop-off services start at $25.

On the lawn outside the Columbia Wetlands Adventures office is the **world's largest paddle** (www.worldslargestpaddle.com, dawn-dusk daily, free), a 60-foot-long (19-meter), 9-foot-tall (3-meter) proportionally correct canoe paddle that weighs 5,300 pounds (2,400 kilograms). Mark Teasdale, who runs the adventure company, and master woodworker Dave Stonehouse designed and constructed the paddle from a massive western red cedar. Yes, it's in the Guinness Book of World Records.

Columbia Wetlands Adventures is located 16 miles (26 kilometers) south of Golden, off Highway 95.

Northern Lights Wildlife Wolf Centre

For a close-up look at Canada's gray wolves, visit the **Northern Lights Wildlife Wolf Centre** (1745 Short Rd., 250/344-6798, www.northernlightswildlife.com, 10am-6pm daily May-June, 9am-7pm daily July-Aug., 10am-6pm daily Sept., noon-5pm daily Oct.-Apr., adults $12, seniors and ages 12-16 $9, ages 4-11 $6, families $35). Housing several gray wolves in outdoor enclosures, this interpretive center offers 30-minute tours, explaining the wolves' habits, food preferences, and pack structure. Schedule your stop here for the morning, if you can, when the animals are typically most active.

The Wolf Centre is 11 miles (18 kilometers) northwest of Golden, off Highway 1.

Museums and Galleries

The small but well-designed **Golden Museum** (1302 11th Ave. S., 250/344-5169, www.goldenbcmuseum.com, 9am-4pm

kayaks at the Columbia River wetlands

Mon.-Fri., adults $5, seniors and students $3, children $2, families $10) tells the stories of the region's history, from its First Nations and Métis communities to its early explorers, to the importance of the railroad to the region. British explorer David Thompson was the first non-aboriginal person to settle in Golden, when he arrived in 1807 with his Métis wife, Charlotte Small, and their four children as part of a mapping expedition for the Northwest Company. Thompson and Small were married for 55 years and eventually had 14 children, although they remained in the Golden area for just a few years. Later, Golden had one of the earliest Sikh temples in Canada, when many Sikhs moved from the Vancouver region to work in the logging industry.

The **Art Gallery of Golden** (516 9th Ave. N., 250/344-6186, www.kickinghorseculture.ca, 10:30am-5:30pm Mon.-Sat., 11am-4pm Sun. July-Aug., 10:30am-5:30pm Mon.-Sat. Sept.-June) is part gallery and part craft boutique,

showing and selling works by regional artists.

Events

In June, July, and August, **Kicking Horse Culture** (250/344-6186, http://kickinghorseculture.ca) organizes the Summer Kicks series of concerts and other arts events. Check the website or call for the schedule and details.

Accommodations and Camping

Most of Golden's chain motels are along or just off Highway 1, including the **Holiday Inn Express Golden-Kicking Horse** (1120 14th St. N., 250/344-4664 or 877/660-8550, www.ihg.com/holidayinnexpress), the **Prestige Inn Golden** (1049 Trans-Canada Hwy., 250/344-7990 or 877/737-8443, www.prestigehotelsandresorts.com), and the **Days Inn Golden** (1416 Golden View Rd., 250/344-2216 or 877/311-2216, www.daysinngolden.ca).

More accommodations are available at the Kicking Horse Mountain Resort, a 15-minute drive from the town center.

High on a hill off Highway 95 south of town, the ★ **Cedar House Chalets** (735 Hefti Rd., 250/290-0001, www.cedarhousechalets.com, $240-330 d) are seven contemporary wood-frame cottages, ranging from one to three bedrooms, on 10 acres of forested land. All units have wood stoves, private hot tubs, and decks with barbecues, and they're stocked with board games, flat-screen TVs, and DVD players. The smallest unit, the romantic Adventure Chalet, has a loft bed; the high-ceilinged three-bedroom Mountain View Chalet has the best mountain vistas. Wi-Fi and phone calls (local, national, and even international) are included in the rates. You can have dinner on-site at the **Cedar House Restaurant** (250/344-4679, 5pm-10pm daily mid-June-mid-Sept., 5pm-10pm Wed.-Sun. mid-May-mid-June, mid-Sept.-Oct., and Dec.-mid-Apr., mains $26-39).

Jo-Anne and Dave Best came from the UK to ski western Canada's mountains.

Their ski holiday turned permanent when they settled on a 68-acre (28-hectare) property south of Golden, where they keep horses and rent out three up-scale self-catering cottages. The secluded **Mount 7 Lodges** (891 Crandall Rd., 250/344-8973 or 888/344-8973, www.mount7lodges.com, $260-440 for 2-8 people), all built using local wood, include the two-bedroom Deer Lodge, the three-bedroom, two-bath Bear Lodge, and the four-bedroom, four-bath Eagle Lodge. All have open-plan living rooms, full kitchens, private hot tubs, and Wi-Fi included.

Camping

Located along the Kicking Horse River at the east end of town, the popular **Golden Municipal Campground** (1411 9th St. S., 250/344-5412 or 866/538-6625, www.goldenmunicipalcampground.com, June-Oct., $28 tent sites, $31-35 electrical sites) has 72 campsites, including 32 with power. There are showers, laundry facilities, and included Wi-Fi. A limited number of sites are available for winter camping ($30) November through May.

Food
Groceries and Markets

Tiny **Golden Farmers Market** (www.goldenfarmersmarket.com, noon-5pm Wed., 10am-3pm Sat. mid-June-Sept.) has two downtown locations selling fresh fruits and vegetables, baked goods, and craft items. The Saturday market is in Spirit Square, next to the Kicking Horse Pedestrian Bridge; on Wednesday, the market sets up in the parking lot next to the Kicking Horse Chamber of Commerce building on Highway 95.

Cafés, Bakeries, and Light Bites

Locals sip coffee on the couches at **Jita's Café** (1007 11th Ave. N., 250/344-3660, call for hours, mains $8-11), a colorful hangout with Indian flavors and lots of veggie-friendly options. In addition to coffee drinks and baked goods, the café, which is open for breakfast and lunch, serves several breakfast dishes (eggs, burritos, bagels), curries, and sandwiches. The house-made veggie burger is excellent.

Stocking new and used books, **Bacchus Books & Café** (409 9th Ave. N., 250/344-5600, www.bacchusbooks.ca, 9am-5:30pm Mon.-Sat., 10am-4pm Sun., mains $5-13) also has a second-floor eatery. Stop in for coffee and pastries or soup and a sandwich; there's a rack of magazines to peruse while you munch.

Contemporary

In a log house on the river, **Island Restaurant** (101 10th Ave., 250/344-2400, www.islandrestaurant.ca, 9am-9pm daily, mains breakfast $7-15, lunch and dinner $12-26) serves a crowd-pleasing "Canadian mountain fusion" menu that includes sandwiches and salads, house-made pastas, and hearty plates like buffalo in mushroom-brandy sauce. Island is open for breakfast as well. On a warm day, ask for a patio table.

In a wood-beamed house with a patio facing the mountains, the **Cedar House Restaurant** (735 Hefti Rd., 250/344-4679, 5pm-10pm daily mid-June-mid-Sept., 5pm-10pm Wed.-Sun. mid-May-mid-June, mid-Sept.-Oct., and Dec.-mid-Apr., mains $26-39) serves contemporary Canadian fare using lots of local organic ingredients. After sipping a glass of B.C. wine or local craft beer, you might sup on steelhead trout paired with charred tomato and fennel relish, merlot-braised bison short ribs, or an asparagus-spring pea risotto. Cedar House is located off Highway 95 south of town.

Ask Golden residents where to eat, and nearly everyone recommends **Eleven22** (1122 10th Ave. S., 250/344-2443, www.eleven22.ca, 5pm-10pm daily, mains $12-25), a comfortably upscale bistro in a renovated house. Start with a shared plate like stilton fondue with marinated vegetables, lamb meatballs with tomato-bacon jam, or a mountain salad piled with greens, feta cheese, sunflower and pumpkin seeds, and cranberries. The menu crosses the globe with mains like sausage and cabbage, *nasi goreng* (Malaysian rice with chicken, chorizo, and prawns), and duck breast paired with a Moroccan squash tart, but the drink list leans local with plenty of B.C. beers and wines.

Asian

Sometimes you find interesting food in surprising places. A local gas station, **Gas Plus Golden** (818 10th Ave. S., 250/344-2222, mains $7-13), cooks up Korean dishes, including *bi-bim-bap* and *bulgogi*, as well as fried chicken with potato wedges.

Information and Services

Tourism Golden (www.tourismgolden. com) provides regional information on its website, which also has an online trip-planning tool.

In a modern building above town, the provincially operated **British Columbia Visitor Centre** (111 Donald Upper Rd., 250/344-7711, www.hellobc.com, 9am-5pm daily mid-May-late June and Sept., 9am-8pm daily late June-early Sept., 9am-4pm daily Oct.-mid-May) can help with area details.

The **Golden & District Hospital** (835 9th Ave. S., 250/344-5271) has a 24-hour emergency room. **Gourlay's Golden Pharmacy** (826 9th St., 250/344-8600, www.gourlayspharmacygolden.ca, 9am-5pm Mon.-Fri.) and **People's Drug Mart** (1104 10th Ave. S., 250/344-6821, www. peoplesdrugmart.com, 9am-6pm Mon.-Sat., 10am-4pm Sun.) fill prescriptions and sell medical supplies.

★ Kicking Horse Mountain Resort

At **Kicking Horse Mountain Resort** (1500 Kicking Horse Trail, Golden, 250/439-5425 or 866/754-5425, www.kickinghorseresort.com), a mountain playground just outside Golden, there's plenty to do in both summer and winter. The resort is

set in the Purcell Mountains, surrounded by the peaks of the Rocky and Selkirk Ranges.

To reach Kicking Horse Mountain, from Highway 95 (10th Ave. N.) in Golden, take 7th Street North toward the river, where it turns right and joins Kicking Horse Drive. Kicking Horse Drive crosses the river, becomes Kicking Horse Trail, and leads up the mountain to the resort, nine miles (14 kilometers) from Golden.

Summer Activities

For information about all the summer activities at the resort, contact the **Kicking Horse Mountain Activity Centre** (250/439-5425 or 866/754-5425, www. kickinghorseresort.com), located at the base of the mountain.

In summer, you can take the **Golden Eagle Express Gondola** (10am-2:30pm daily late May-late June, 10am-4:30pm daily late June-Aug., 10am-3pm Mon.-Thurs., 10am-4pm Fri.-Sun. Sept., adults $33.95, seniors and students $19.95, ages 6-12 $15.95, families $83.95) to the mountain summit for sightseeing, hiking, or a meal at the Eagle's Eye Restaurant.

Grizzly Bear Interpretive Centre

You may not see a bear in the wild as you travel across western Canada, but you can get close to a grizzly at Kicking Horse Mountain. At the **Grizzly Bear Interpretive Centre** (9:45am-2:15pm daily late May-late June, 9:45am-4pm daily late June-Aug., 9:45am-3pm Mon.-Thurs., 9:45am-4pm Fri.-Sun. Sept., adults $24.95, seniors and students $18.95, ages 6-12 $13.95, families $70.95), a mountainside bear sanctuary, Boo, an orphaned grizzly bear born in 2002 in B.C.'s northern Cariboo region, roams a 20-acre (8-hectare) habitat. You can watch the omnivorous Boo digging, foraging, and munching on seeds, fruits, meat, or sometimes field mice that he hunts. He needs to chow down throughout the summer to reach his average hibernation weight of 750 pounds (340 kilograms).

Learn more about bears and their habits on one-hour interpretive tours, which run on the hour, beginning at 10am (there's no 1pm tour). The best time to visit is in the morning, when Boo is likely to be most active.

To reach the bear reserve, take the Catamount Chairlift from the mountain base. You can purchase tickets for the bear reserve alone, or buy an **Adventure Pass** (adults $38.95, seniors and students $29.95, ages 6-12 $19.95, families $114.95), a combined ticket for the reserve and the sightseeing gondola.

Hiking

From the top of the Golden Eagle Express Gondola, you can access several **hiking trails,** from the relatively easy 20- to 30-minute CPR Ridge Walk, which has several lookout points across the mountains, to the challenging Terminator Ridge Hike up to the T2 Summit. Get hiking information and trail maps online or from the resort Activity Centre.

Via Ferrata

The Kicking Horse **Via Ferrata** (late June-Sept.) is a great adventure, an "iron way" route that enables nonclimbers to experience alpine climbing. The two-hour **Discovery Route** (adults $129, ages 12-17 $119, families $399) is a good starting point if you've never experienced a Via Ferrata. For more of a challenge, try the longer **Ascension Route** (adults $169, ages 12-17 $159, families $549), which typically takes three to four hours.

Advance reservations are required for both tours; call or check the website for specific tour times. No rock-climbing experience is necessary for either route,

Top to bottom: cottage at the Cedar House Chalets; Grizzly Bear Interpretive Centre at Kicking Horse Mountain Resort; Eagle's Eye Restaurant, Canada's highest restaurant.

although you should be generally fit and be comfortable with heights.

Mountain Biking

Kicking Horse Mountain's 31 **mountain biking trails** (full-day adults $46.95, seniors and students $37.95, ages 6-12 $23.95, families $117.95), accessed from the **Golden Eagle Express Gondola** (10am-4:30pm daily late June-Aug., 10am-4:30pm Fri.-Sun. Sept.) or the **Catamount Chair Lift** (10am-4pm daily late June-Aug., 10am-4pm Fri.-Sun. Sept.), make up the highest bike park in North America. The trails range from beginner to expert, and both equipment rentals and lessons are available.

Winter Sports

Kicking Horse Mountain Resort is known for the powder conditions on its 120-plus **skiing** and **snowboarding** runs (one-day adults $89.95, seniors $71.95, ages 13-17 $67.95, ages 6-12 $35.95). The mountain covers more than 2,800 acres (1,130 hectares), with the fourth-highest vertical drop in North America (4,133 feet/1,260 meters). Over 60 percent of the terrain is rated "advanced" or "expert." The winter season typically runs from mid-December to mid-April.

Kicking Horse has introduced **fat-tire biking** as a winter sports option. You can ride these specially designed bicycles, with their low gears and fat tires, on snow-covered trails. The resort offers rentals, lessons, and guided tours. Contact the resort Activity Centre for details.

Accommodations

Rates at the resort's lodgings are highest during the winter months (Dec.-Mar.), so they can be a good value for a summer stay.

Kicking Horse Lodging (250/439-1160 or 877/754-5486, www.kickinghorselodging.com) manages several accommodations at the resort, including **Glacier Mountaineer Lodge** (1549 Kicking Horse Trail, $159-379 d, 2-bedroom suite $269-379), homey condos steps from the gondola. In addition to standard hotel rooms, the building has one- and two-bedroom suites with full kitchens, washer-dryers, gas fireplaces, included Wi-Fi, and comfortable lodge-style furnishings. While you might prefer to overlook the ski runs, even the units facing away from the slopes have views to the more distant surrounding mountains. The outdoor hot tub, sauna, and steam room are popular après-ski.

Owned by former ski racer Felix Belczyk, who competed on the Canadian team in the 1988 and 1992 Winter Olympic Games, the 10-room **Copper Horse Lodge** (Cache Close, 250/344-7644 or 877/544-7644, www.copperhorselodge.com, Dec.-Apr. and late May-early Oct., $205-340 d), 0.25 miles (400 meters) from the lifts, has 10 sizeable guest rooms with windows looking out to the mountains, all with mini fridges and coffee-tea stations. You can check out a wall of photos of Belczyk and other Olympians or soak in the outdoor hot tub. In winter, the lodge allows kids 12 and older only, but summer accommodations are open to families. Rates include breakfast (continental in summer, a hot meal in winter) served in **Corks Restaurant** (250/344-6201) on the lodge's lower level; Corks is also open to nonguests daily for dinner (mains $18-34).

The most surprising place to stay in the Golden area might be at the top of the Kicking Horse Mountain gondola station, where two private suites at the **Eagle's Eye** (250/439-5425 or 866/754-5425, www.kickinghorseresort.com, $900-1,500 d), above the restaurant of the same name, let you lodge in romantic seclusion at 7,700 feet (2,347 meters) elevation. Yes, it's wildly expensive, but rates include a personal butler to pamper you and a private chef to prepare your meals. In winter, you have a private ski guide to show you the best runs, and since you're already at the top of the gondola when the lifts open, you can get into the powder before anyone else. The suites themselves are homey, rather than over-the-top upscale, with pine walls and modern baths, but their views of the mountain peaks are priceless.

Food

It's Canada's highest restaurant: At the top of the gondola station on Kicking Horse Mountain, the ★ **Eagle's Eye Restaurant** (250/439-5425 or 866/754-5425, www.kickinghorseresort.com, mains lunch $16-21) perches at 7,700 feet (2,347 meters). Whether you ride up in summer to take in the sweeping mountain views (they're great from the picture windows inside and even better from the outdoor patio), or stop off to refuel between ski runs in the winter, the creative plates aren't typical ski-café fare. Dig into dishes like wild mushroom tagliatelle, a kale and smoked salmon caesar salad, or grilled Alberta beef strip loin with mashed yams. The restaurant is open for lunch during both the summer and winter seasons and for dinner on Friday and Saturday evenings from December to March; call or check the website for hours. Note that you need to purchase a lift ticket to get to the restaurant, although gondola and meal packages are available.

At the gondola base, the **Double Black Café** (www.kickinghorseresort.com, mains $5-15) sustains you for your mountain adventures with breakfast sandwiches, hot soup, muffins, gelato, and coffee. Sit on the patio outside or at the window-facing counters indoors, which both look out to the slopes.

Yoho National Park

As you drive through British Columbia's mountain regions, it's hard to imagine that each place you visit could be more stunning than the next. But when you reach Yoho National Park, hugging the provincial boundary between B.C. and Alberta, you have to conclude that the scenery is spectacular. How fitting that the park's name comes from a Cree expression for "wonder" and "awe."

Yoho National Park covers 507 square miles (1,310 square kilometers) on the western slopes of the Canadian Rockies, between Golden and Lake Louise. More than 30 mountains within the park rise to nearly 10,000 feet (3,000 meters). Established in 1886, Yoho now protects stunning glacial lakes, some of Canada's highest waterfalls, and fossil beds that are among the world's oldest. A popular destination for hikers, Yoho also played an important role in Canada's railroad history.

Visiting the Park

Yoho National Park is open year-round, although many park services, including the visitors center and the park's campgrounds, are available only from May through mid-October, and several destinations can remain snow-covered even into June. Due to the risk of avalanches, Yoho Valley Road, which leads to Takakkaw Falls, is usually open only from late June until mid-October.

The tiny town of **Field** is near the center of the park. The park visitors center is here, as are a couple of restaurants, a small grocery, a gas station, and an inn. Beyond Field, the park has limited services.

Entrances

Yoho's western entrance is along Highway 1, east of Golden. There's no park entrance gate, so if you're coming from the west, buy your park pass in Golden at the **British Columbia Visitor Centre** (111 Donald Upper Rd., 250/344-7711, www.hellobc.com).

Yoho's eastern entrance is also along Highway 1, west of Lake Louise. If you're coming from the east, you can purchase a park pass at the **Lake Louise Visitor Information Centre** (Samson Mall, Lake

Yoho National Park and Vicinity

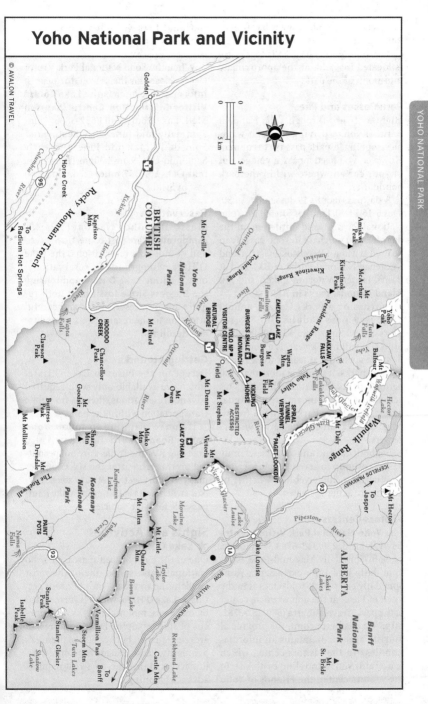

© AVALON TRAVEL

Louise, 403/522-3833, www.bannflake-louise.com).

The **Yoho National Park Visitor Centre** is located in Field, at the approximate mid-point of the park.

Park Passes and Fees

Highway 1 runs through Yoho National Park. If you're driving through without stopping, a park pass isn't required. However, you need a pass if you get out of your car anywhere within the park boundaries.

A **day pass** (adults $9.80, seniors $8.30, ages 6-16 $4.90, families $19.60) for Yoho National Park is valid until 4pm on the day after you purchase it. Yoho passes can be used at Mount Revelstoke, Glacier, and Kootenay National Parks in B.C. and at Banff, Jasper, Waterton Lakes, and Elk Island National Parks in Alberta.

Purchasing a Parks Canada **annual discovery pass** (adults $67.70, seniors $57.90, ages 6-16 $33.30, families $136.40), valid for a year, is a good deal if you're spending at least a week in one or more parks. It's good at more than 100 national parks and national historic sites across Canada. You can buy an annual pass online from Parks Canada (www.pc.gc.ca) or at any of the parks' visitors centers.

For both day and annual passes, family passes cover up to seven people arriving together in a single vehicle, whether or not they're actually related.

Visitors Centers

The **Yoho National Park Visitor Centre** (Hwy. 1, Field, 250/343-6783, www.pc.gc.ca, 9am-5pm daily May-mid-June, 9am-7pm daily mid-June-early Sept., 9am-5pm daily early Sept.-mid-Oct.) is in the town of Field, at the approximate center of the park. **Travel Alberta** (800/252-3782, http://travelalberta.com), the provincial tourism agency, maintains an information desk in the visitors center, which is useful if you're traveling east. Also in the visitors center, the **Friends of Yoho**

National Park (250/343-6393, www.friendsofyoho.ca) run a gift shop and organize special events.

When the Yoho National Park Visitor Centre closes for the season, the nearest information center is the **Lake Louise Visitor Information Centre** (Samson Mall, Lake Louise, 403/522-3833, 9am-7pm daily mid-June-early Sept., 9am-5pm daily May-mid-June and early Sept.-mid-Oct., 9am-4:30pm Thurs.-Sun. mid-Oct.-Apr.), 17 miles (27 kilometers) east of Field.

Reservations

Most of Yoho National Park's **campgrounds** are first-come, first-served and do not take reservations; the Lake O'Hara campground is reservations-only. Visiting **Lake O'Hara** and touring the **Burgess Shale** fossil beds both require advance reservations and careful attention to the reservations procedure and deadlines.

Getting Around

Except for the buses to Lake O'Hara, which are available only with required advance reservations, there is no public transportation within the park.

If you're planning to follow **Yoho Valley Road** toward Takakkaw Falls, note that RVs and trailers are not permitted on this road after the six-kilometer mark. A short section of very steep, narrow switchbacks at this point make it impassable for large vehicles.

Sights and Activities
★ Lake O'Hara

One of the most beautiful areas of Yoho National Park is also one of the most challenging to reach—not because getting to **Lake O'Hara,** which is surrounded by meadows, mountain peaks, and dozens of smaller alpine lakes, requires an arduous journey, but because of the area's popularity, Parks Canada has limited visitor access to the lake, so a visit requires advance planning.

Getting There

Private cars are not allowed on the Lake O'Hara road, so for day visitors, the only way to visit is on the Parks Canada shuttle bus or by hiking in seven miles (11 kilometers) from the Lake O'Hara parking lot, which is eight miles (13 kilometers) east of Field and 7.5 miles (12 kilometers) west of Lake Louise.

To take the **Parks Canada shuttle bus** (mid-June-early Oct., round-trip adults $14.70, ages 6-16 $7.30), you must make **advance reservations** (519/826-5391 or 877/737-3783, www.reservations.parks-canada.gc.ca) online or by phone in early spring for the coming season. Typically, reservations for the entire season **sell out on the first day** they become available. Check the Parks Canada website (www.pc.gc.ca) for reservation instructions, and be ready to make your booking as early as possible. In addition to the ticket price, there's a reservation fee of $4.50 per ticket online and $6.25 per ticket by phone for one or two people; for three or more people, it's a flat rate of $11 online or $13.50 by phone.

While reservations aren't required to return from the lake, pay attention to the bus schedule, as there are typically just a few departures per day, and you don't want to miss the last bus.

If you aren't able to make a reservation for the shuttle, you can hike to the lake on the access road. You might be able to buy a one-way ticket (adults $9.75, ages 6-16 $4.75) to return from the lake on the bus, but only if space is available. If you choose to hike, be prepared to hike both ways.

Hiking

Once you've managed to get to the lake, it's a great destination for day hikes, from easy strolls to more adventurous mountain treks.

One of the most popular easier routes is the **Lake O'Hara Shoreline Trail,** a 1.7-mile (2.8-kilometer) loop. The **Lake Oesa Trail,** which is two miles (3.2 kilometers)

each way, starts on the Lake O'Hara Shoreline Trail, before climbing up to a cliff overlooking the lake; the elevation gain is 787 feet (240 meters). The 3.7-mile (5.9-kilometer) **Opabin Plateau Circuit** takes you to a hanging valley on top of a cliff above Lake O'Hara, with an elevation gain of 820 feet (250 meters).

Get a more detailed description of these and all the Lake O'Hara trails on the Yoho National Park website (www.pc.gc.ca) or from the Yoho National Park Visitor Centre.

Lake O'Hara Campground

Unlike the rest of the Yoho campgrounds, where you can't make a reservation, you can stay overnight at the 30-site **Lake O'Hara Campground** (mid-June-Sept., $9.80) only by reservation. You'll have to be on the ball to book a campsite; all sites are usually reserved on the first morning that they become available, three months in advance.

To reserve a Lake O'Hara site, you must phone the **Yoho National Park reservation line** (250/343-6433, 8am-noon and 1pm-4pm mountain time Mon.-Fri. Apr.-May, 8am-noon and 1pm-4pm daily June-Sept., reservation fee $11.70) exactly three months before your desired stay. You can book a site for up to three nights.

When you make your camping reservation, you also reserve a spot on the **Parks Canada shuttle bus** (adults $14.70, ages 6-16 $7.30). The amount of luggage you can bring is restricted, so check the details on the Yoho National Park website (www.pc.gc.ca).

Lake O'Hara Lodge

A stay at the remote **Lake O'Hara Lodge** (250/343-6418 or 403/678-4110, www.lakeohara.com, mid-June-early Oct. and late Jan.-early Apr., $650-730 d, cabins $920-930), built in 1926, takes you off the grid near the scenic lake. The eight rooms in the rustic main lodge each have two twin beds and share two large baths.

In the summer or fall, you can stay in a log cabin with a private bath; some are on the lakeshore, while others (with a sofa bed and a Murphy bed to accommodate up to four) are on a knoll above the lake.

Rates include three meals a day, afternoon tea, and transportation to the property on the lodge's private shuttle. Since no private cars are allowed on the Lake O'Hara road, guests catch the shuttle at the Lake O'Hara parking lot off Highway 1; it departs twice a day in each direction.

★ Emerald Lake

Emerald Lake is as beautiful as its name suggests, its waters shimmering light green, turquoise, and deep emerald as the sunlight bounces off the mountains and moves across the sky and behind the clouds. It's one of the park's most visited spots, with tour buses disgorging hordes of visitors who snap photos and hop back on their buses. But stay awhile. You can follow an easy trail around the lake and leave many of the other visitors behind, or rent a canoe to go for a paddle and admire the surrounding cliffs.

The 3.25-mile (5.2-kilometer) mostly flat Emerald Lake trail leads through the forest around the lake. Allow about two hours for a leisurely lake circuit.

From a lakeside boathouse, Emerald Sports (250/343-6000, www.khsc.ca/emerald-sports) rents canoes and rowboats (10am-5pm daily May-June and Sept.-Oct., 9am-7pm daily July-Aug., $40 per hour, 2 hours $65) from spring through fall. In winter it rents snowshoes (noon-4pm Mon.-Fri., 10am-4pm Sat.-Sun. Dec.-Mar., $10 per hour, $5 per additional hour, $20 per day) and cross-country skis ($15 per hour, $5 per additional hour, $25 per day).

Overlooking the lake, Emerald Lake Lodge (250/343-6321, www.crmr.com) has several restaurants that are open to nonguests. You can also picnic near the lake.

To reach Emerald Lake, follow Emerald Lake Road off Highway 1, west of Field. Try to visit early in the morning or late in the afternoon, when the crush of visitors may have lessened slightly.

Natural Bridge

On your way to Emerald Lake, stop to see the Natural Bridge (Emerald Lake Rd.), an unusual rock formation on the Kicking Horse River with a swirl of water rushing through it. Surrounded by mountain peaks and pines, the natural bridge is a scenic spot for photos. Several hiking and cycling trails start nearby, including the 2.3-mile (3.6-kilometer) Kicking Horse-Amiskwi trail and the 7.8-mile (12.6-kilometer) Kicking Horse-Otterhead trail, which both follow old fire roads.

Takakkaw Falls

One of the highest waterfalls in Canada, Takakkaw Falls (Yoho Valley Rd.) is 833 feet (254 meters) tall. The falls, which cascade down a rock face in the Yoho Valley, are especially lovely late in the day when the afternoon or early evening sun illuminates the water. A short walking trail leads from the parking area to the base of the falls.

To reach the falls, follow Yoho Valley Road off Highway 1; the falls are 11 miles (17 kilometers) northeast of Field. Because Yoho Valley Road has a short section of steep, narrow switchbacks, RVs and other large vehicles are not permitted to continue on this road beyond the switchbacks.

Spiral Tunnels

To complete the transcontinental railroad that would link Canada's Pacific coast with its eastern regions, Canadian Pacific Railway engineers needed to find a route across the Rocky Mountains. The route they chose, through the Kicking Horse Pass, required a precipitous descent—four times steeper than the average rail grade at the time—on what became known as the "Big Hill."

Unfortunately, climbing and

descending the Big Hill, which is in present-day Yoho National Park, turned out to be complicated and dangerous. The first train that tried to travel through the pass derailed, killing three workers. Engineer J. E. Schwitzer eventually came up with a solution: the **Spiral Tunnels,** two looping tracks that allowed trains to make a more gradual descent. Completed in 1909, these tunnels are still in use.

You can watch trains enter and leave these unusual tunnels from two viewpoints. From the **Lower Spiral Tunnel Viewpoint** (Hwy. 1, 4.7 miles/7.5 kilometers east of Field), you can see trains pass through the tunnel on Mount Ogden. From the **Upper Spiral Tunnel Viewpoint** (Yoho Valley Rd., 1.5 miles/2.3 kilometers from Hwy. 1), you can watch the tunnel through Cathedral Mountain.

While an average of 25 trains pass through the tunnels every day, the schedule is irregular, but if you're lucky, you'll get to see a train make its looping way through this engineering innovation.

★ The Burgess Shale

In 1909, American geologist Charles Walcott made a surprising discovery in the mountains near the town of Field. The well-preserved fossils that he unearthed were the remains of soft-bodied marine organisms that once lived in the Cambrian Sea in what is now Yoho National Park. Among the world's oldest fossils, they're estimated to be 505 million years old.

The area where Walcott discovered the fossils, known as **the Burgess Shale,** encompasses layers of fossil-filled rocks on Fossil Ridge between Wapta Mountain and Mount Field. To recognize the importance of its geological legacy, the Burgess Shale has been designated a UNESCO World Heritage Site.

The **Yoho National Park Visitor Centre** (Hwy. 1, Field) has an exhibit where you

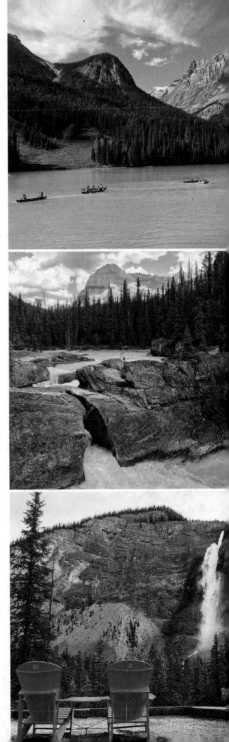

Top to bottom: Emerald Lake; Natural Bridge; Takakkaw Falls.

can learn more about the Burgess Shale fossils.

Burgess Shale Guided Hikes

Park visitors can tour the Burgess Shale fossil beds on a **full-day guided hike,** which you must reserve in advance. Make reservations with **Parks Canada** (877/737-3783, www.reservations.parkscanada. gc.ca, reservations fee $11 online, $13.50 by phone), beginning in early January for the coming season. Check the website to confirm when reservations will become available; you'll want to book them as early as possible. You can choose from two different guided Burgess Shale hikes in Yoho National Park. There's also a guided Burgess Shale hike in Kootenay National Park.

One of the guided hikes is to **Walcott Quarry** (Fri.-Mon. and Wed. mid-July-early Sept., Fri.-Sun. Sept., adults $70, seniors $59.50, ages 8-16 $35). You need to hike a challenging trail, a 13-mile (21-kilometer) round-trip route with an elevation gain of 2,710 feet (825 meters). Parks Canada staff caution that this elevation change is the equivalent of climbing up and down the stairs in a 234-story building. Along the way, as you traverse the striking mountain scenery, your guide will explain more about the Burgess Shale, the fossils and their importance, and local wildlife. Hikes depart from the Takakkaw Falls parking lot on Yoho Valley Road at 7am; expect to be on the trail for 10.5 hours.

An alternate guided hike takes you to the **Mount Stephen Fossil Bed** (Sat.-Mon. mid-June-mid-Sept., adults $55, seniors $46.75, ages 8-16 $27.50), where railroad workers found fossils even before Walcott made his groundbreaking discovery. This seven-hour hike is shorter but steeper than the Walcott Quarry hike, with an elevation gain of 2,610 feet (795 meters) on a five-mile (8-kilometer) round-trip hike. This hike departs from the **Yoho National Park Visitor Centre,** off Highway 1 in Field, at 7am.

Field

The small town of **Field,** in the center of Yoho National Park, was settled in the 1880s when the Canadian Pacific Railway was built through Kicking Horse Pass. Originally a service center for the trains that were climbing the Big Hill, the town began developing tourist infrastructure when the Mt. Stephen House hotel opened in 1886. In the early 1900s, up to 12 passenger trains passed through Field each day.

Though the Mt. Stephen House is no longer standing, another town landmark is: the **CPR Water Tower,** which was built in 1930 to supply the steam trains with water. The 70-foot (21-meter) tower was retired in 1952 when diesel engines replaced their steam counterparts.

In summer, the Friends of Yoho National Park offer one-hour **historic walking tours of Field** (250/343-6393, www.friendsofyoho.ca, 8pm Tues. and Thurs. July-Aug., free) that depart from the Field Community Centre (315 Stephen Ave.), near the water tower. If you prefer to wander on your own, you can get a copy of the Friends' historic map of Field online or at the park visitors center.

Hiking

With more than 250 miles (400 kilometers) of hiking trails, Yoho has plenty of options for hikers of all levels.

Wapta Falls

Near the park's western boundary, 16 miles (26 kilometers) west of Field, the **Wapta Falls Trail** (mid-June-mid-Oct.) is a moderate hike with a big payoff: up-close views of the largest waterfall on the Kicking Horse River.

Most of the 2.9-mile (4.6-kilometer) round-trip trail is fairly easy, with gentle ups and downs. Just above the first point where the falls come into view, the trail switchbacks down more sharply, but your reward from the next viewpoints is a full-on view of the falls with rocky peaks

How the Kicking Horse River Got Its Name

Beginning near the Alberta border, the Kicking Horse River runs through Yoho National Park before descending through a series of rapids as it approaches the town of Golden and joins the Columbia River. But who'd name a river Kicking Horse?

In 1858, the British exploring party known as the Palliser Expedition became the first non-aboriginal people to venture into the Yoho area. One day, while trying to recover a runaway horse near the

river that fed Wapta Falls, James Hector, a member of the expedition, was kicked in the chest and presumed dead. The other members of his party began digging his grave. Fortunately, before they lowered Hector into the ground, one of his companions noticed Hector's eye blink.

Hector recovered enough to continue on the expedition. His fellow explorers named the river where he had nearly met his demise for the animal that would have sent him to the grave: the Kicking Horse.

beyond. Then you can descend another short segment to the riverbank, where you'll be close enough to the falls, which are 98 feet (30 meters) high and 490 feet (150 meters) wide, to feel their spray.

Hoodoos

To see a series of hoodoos, pillar-like rock formations created from glacial debris, follow the steep **Hoodoos Trail,** which begins in the Hoodoo Creek Campground, 14 miles (23 kilometers) west of Field off Highway 1. This 3.2-mile (5.2-kilometer) round-trip trail climbs steeply, with an elevation gain of 1,066 feet (325 meters), so take it slow and allow at least 2.5 hours for the hike.

Twin Falls

The mostly forested **Twin Falls Trail** (mid-June-mid-Oct.), leading to the 260-foot (80-meter) waterfall of the same name, begins at the Takakkaw Falls parking lot on Yoho Valley Road, 10.5 miles (17 kilometers) northeast of Field. This hike is 10.2 miles (16.4 kilometers) round-trip, with an elevation gain of 985 feet (300 meters); allow approximately six hours.

Iceline

One of the most popular all-day hikes in Yoho National Park, the challenging 13-mile (21-kilometer) round-trip **Iceline Trail** rewards hikers with spectacular glacier views before climbing down through

meadows in the Little Yoho Valley and past Laughing Falls. With a 2,329-foot (710-meter) elevation gain, this trail takes most hikers about eight hours.

For a slightly shorter hike, you can follow an alternate Iceline route to **Celeste Lake,** a 10.9-mile (17.5-kilometer) round-trip route with a 2,280-foot (695-meter) elevation gain. This variation still takes about seven hours.

The trailhead for the Iceline Trail is near the Whiskey Jack Hostel. Park nearby at the Takakkaw Falls parking lot, on Yoho Valley Road, 10.5 miles (17 kilometers) northeast of Field.

Accommodations and Food

Yoho National Park has two upscale lodges, both of which have dining rooms that are open to nonguests. The park also has a rustic hostel near Takakkaw Falls. In the town of Field, within the park boundaries, there's a small inn with a restaurant, and many homeowners rent rooms to guests. If you can't find accommodations in the park, or if you want other lodging options, consider staying in Golden or Lake Louise and making day trips to Yoho.

Around the Park

Why stay at the remote **HI-Yoho National Park Whiskey Jack Hostel** (Yoho Valley Rd., 778/328-2220 or 866/762-4122, www. hihostels.ca, late June-Sept., $28 dorm), a rustic cabin with no electricity? Because you can step onto the porch for views of nearby Takakkaw Falls or easily access several excellent hiking routes, including the Iceline Trail, which begins right at the hostel. Guests share three bunk rooms, each outfitted with nine beds and a small private bath with a flush toilet and hot shower. Propane powers the lamps and the appliances in the shared kitchen. Bring food and a flashlight, and charge your batteries before you arrive. The hostel has no phone, cell service, or Wi-Fi.

You can't ask for a lovelier setting than that of ★ **Emerald Lake Lodge** (Emerald Lake Rd., 800/663-6336, www.crmr.com, $275-475 d), on the shores of the gorgeous green lake. The property has 85 comfortable, though not luxurious, guest rooms in 37 cabins; many cabins have two units on the main level and two upstairs. With standard rooms, studios, and one-bedroom suites, the accommodations all have fireplaces and balconies, with natural wood furnishings and fans but no air-conditioning. The Club House has a hot tub, a sauna, and a small gym, while the main lodge, constructed from hand-hewn wood, has a restaurant, a lounge, and a second-floor games room with the second-oldest snooker table in Canada. Expect to disconnect while you're here: Wi-Fi is available in the main lodge only, and there's no cell phone service.

Emerald Lake Lodge has several dining options, open to both guests and nonguests. The more formal **Mount Burgess Dining Room** (250/343-6321, 7am-11am and 5:30pm-9:30pm daily, reservations required, mains breakfast $12-16, dinner $28-40) overlooks the lake; it's known for game meats like caribou medallions or buffalo steak. In the casual **Kicking Horse Lounge** (11am-11pm daily, mains $15-20), you can order from the dining room menu or from a lighter lounge selection, including a signature charcuterie plate for two. In summer, you can have drinks or lunch (salads, burgers, pizza, and sandwiches) at **Cilantro on the Lake** (11am-5pm daily June-Sept., mains $15-20), on the water near the bridge to the property. Cilantro's **take-out window** (10am-5pm daily June-Sept.) sells ice cream, coffee, and cold drinks.

What's more Canadian than a stay in a log cabin? At ★ **Cathedral Mountain Lodge** (Yoho Valley Rd., 250/343-6442 or 866/619-6442, www.cathedralmountain-lodge.com, late May-early Oct., $280-495 d), which has 31 upscale cabins near the Kicking Horse River, you don't have to rough it to live out your log-cabin dreams. They're furnished with custom log beds, down duvets, soaker tubs, and porches with Adirondack chairs; the premier units have stone fireplaces and mini fridges. Five of the units can sleep up to four people; family cabins have a king bed on the main floor and a loft with two twins. Originally built in the 1930s to accommodate railroad workers and miners, the high-ceilinged, wood-framed main lodge building now houses the **Riverside Dining Room** that serves a buffet breakfast (7am-10:30am daily, included in the room rates) and dinner (5:30pm-9:30pm daily, mains $21-40) to guests and nonguests. Guests can order a packed lunch ($36 for 2 people) to take on your park adventures. The lodge is located 0.6 miles (1 kilometer) from Highway 1. The only minor quibble with the otherwise serene setting is that you can sometimes hear the distant traffic hum.

In Field

A list of **rooms to rent** (www.field.ca, $140-270 d) in private homes in the town of Field is available online. Book early, especially if you're visiting in July and August, as availability is limited.

Truffle Pigs Bistro and Lodge (100 Center St., Field, 250/343-6303, www.trufflepigs.com, Dec.-Oct.) runs a well-loved restaurant (breakfast 7am-10:30pm daily, lunch 11am-3pm daily, dinner 5pm-9pm daily May-Sept., call for off-season hours, mains lunch $13-18, dinner $26-36) in a post-and-beam mountain lodge, where you can lunch on smoked brisket, *bulgogi* pork-belly nachos, or salads like the Roasted, Toasted, Fried, with millet, walnuts, pumpkin seeds, chickpeas, kale, and goat cheese. In the evening, the inventive mains include the 48-Hour Bender short ribs (marinated for two days in beer) and the Frolicking Foie Gras Lily Pad (flatbread topped with pear coulis, *bocconcini,* and seared foie gras). If you want to crawl under the covers after your meal, the lodge ($120-220 d) has 13 guest rooms with queen beds, mini fridges, microwaves, private baths, and included Wi-Fi.

In a cozy yellow house, funky **Siding Café** (318 Stephen Ave., Field, 250/343-6002, www.thesidingcafe.ca, 10am-5pm daily, longer hours in summer, mains $8-15) serves breakfast, burgers, sandwiches, and a tasty rice bowl with tofu, spinach, beets, and carrots sauced with a garlicky tahini dressing. It's also the town's liquor store.

Camping

At Yoho's four main campgrounds, sites are first-come, first-served, so arrive early in the day, especially in July and August. It's possible to camp from mid-May to mid-October, although not all campgrounds remain open during the entire period.

The centrally located 88-site **Kicking Horse Campground** (Yoho Valley Rd., late May-mid-Oct., $27.40) is the park's largest camping area and the only one with flush toilets and showers. Nearby, the **Monarch Campground** (mid-May-late May and late June-early Sept., $17.60) has 44 sites.

Near the waterfalls of the same name, **Takakkaw Falls Campground** (Yoho Valley Rd., late June-mid-Oct., $17.60) has 35 walk-in sites.

The 30-site **Hoodoo Creek Campground** (late June-early Sept., $15.70) is off Highway 1 near the park's west entrance.

Information and Services

The **Yoho National Park Visitor Centre** (Hwy. 1, Field, 250/343-6783, www.pc.gc.ca, 9am-5pm daily May-mid-June, 9am-7pm daily mid-June-early Sept., 9am-5pm daily early Sept.-mid-Oct.), a basic grocery, and a gas station are located in the town of Field.

Yoho National Park currently has no cell phone coverage; you might get a signal in Field but not elsewhere in the park. The park has no Wi-Fi, although the lodges offer Internet access for guests.

Outside the park, the nearest town is Lake Louise, which has a small food market, gas stations, park information, and a medical clinic. Lake Louise is 17 miles (27 kilometers) east of Field via Highway 1. For more services, go to Golden, 35 miles (57 kilometers) to the west, or Banff, 55 miles (85 kilometers) to the east.

Banff and Lake Louise

A highlight of any Canadian Rockies road trip, Banff National Park is one of Canada's most-visited destinations, for good reason.

JASPER — 145 MI/230 KM 3.75 HOURS

LAKE LOUISE

35 MI/57 KM 0.75 HOUR

BANFF

CALGARY

490 MI/790 KM 9 HOURS

80 MI/130 KM 1.5 HOURS

265 MI/425 KM 5.25 HOURS

80 MI/130 KM 2 HOURS

85 MI/140 KM 2 HOURS

BRITISH COLUMBIA

ALBERTA

THE OKANAGAN

THE KOOTENAYS

VANCOUVER

Banff and Lake Louise

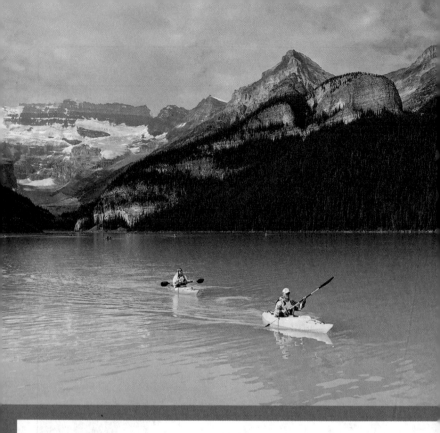

Highlights

★ **Mount Norquay Via Ferrata:** An exciting way to explore the rock faces and mountains above Banff, this "iron way" is a guided climbing route that doesn't require rock-climbing expertise (page 230).

★ **Bow Valley Parkway:** A scenic alternative to Highway 1 between Banff and Lake Louise, this route through the mountains includes numerous hikes and lookout points along the way. The trail along the cantilevered walkways through Johnston Canyon is one of the park's most dramatic (page 232).

★ **Cave and Basin National Historic Site:** Learn the story of Canada's first national park and its underground hot springs at this Banff historic attraction. And yes, there's really a cave (page 234).

★ **Banff Upper Hot Springs:** At 5,200 feet (1,585 meters), these outdoor mineral pools high on Sulphur Mountain are the highest hot springs in Canada (page 236).

★ **The Banff Centre:** Banff's artistic life centers

on this modern campus of theaters, concert halls, and galleries just above town (page 240).

★ **Lake Louise:** A highlight of any Canadian Rockies trip is a photo stop at this strikingly blue lake, framed by the surrounding mountains and glaciers (page 256).

★ **Moraine Lake:** Near Lake Louise, this glacier-fed lake is popular for leisurely canoe paddles, woodland strolls, and lakeside photographs (page 261).

With dramatic mountain peaks, hot springs, and sparkling lakes, Banff National Park is one of western Canada's most spectacular destinations.

An underground hot spring led to the creation of Canada's first national park. Now, more than three million visitors every year come to soak in the mineral-rich waters, hike the more than 1,000 miles (1,600 kilometers) of hiking trails, drive the scenic byways lined with craggy mountain peaks, or simply enjoy the glacier-fed lakes.

Start your Rocky Mountain adventures in the town of Banff, within the national park boundaries. This town of just under 8,500 people has museums, gardens, historic sites, and easy access to many of the park's hiking trails. It's home to the Banff Centre, where plays, concerts, lectures, and other artistic events draw world-class performers and add vibrancy to this small town's cultural life. You can eat a bison burger, fresh trout, or renowned Alberta beef, whether you dine in a classic mountain lodge, high in an alpine meadow, or around an evening campfire. Banff is even home to its own "castle in the Rockies"— the iconic Fairmont Banff Springs Hotel.

Another Canadian Rockies icon is 35 miles (57 kilometers) northwest of the town of Banff: the impossibly beautiful Lake Louise. With sparkling blue water and glacier-capped peaks beyond, Lake Louise makes a stunning backdrop for photos. It's a starting point for several great hikes, too, including two trails to historic mountain teahouses. You can tour Lake Louise on a day trip from Banff, ideally including a drive up the scenic Bow Valley Parkway, or escape to one of its rustic yet elegant mountain lodges or the classic lakeside hotel.

With a famous trio of peaks called the Three Sisters, the town of Canmore, just

20 minutes' drive southeast of Banff, is a quieter alternative to staying within Banff National Park. You're close enough to make day trips to all the park sights, and the town has good restaurants and several attractions of its own, particularly for outdoor enthusiasts.

Banff National Park can be your base for exploring elsewhere in the Canadian Rockies. Both Banff and Lake Louise are close enough to Yoho National Park and Kootenay National Park that you can stay in the Banff area and make day trips to these other mountain parks. The Icefields Parkway, one of the Rockies' best scenic drives, begins in Lake Louise and takes you north to Jasper.

Getting to Banff and Lake Louise

Driving from Vancouver

The most direct route from Vancouver to the Banff area is to take the **Trans-Canada Highway (Highway 1)** east to **Hope.** Continue east at Hope onto **Highway 3,** then exit onto **Highway 5 (Coquihalla Hwy.)** north. Follow the Coquihalla over the mountains to **Kamloops,** where you rejoin **Highway 1.** Stay on Highway 1 past Revelstoke, Golden, and Yoho National Park into Alberta, where you'll reach Lake Louise first and then Banff.

The drive from Vancouver to **Lake Louise** is **490 miles (790 kilometers)** and takes **8.5 to 9 hours.**

To **Banff,** continue east from Lake Louise on **Highway 1.** The trip from Vancouver to Banff is **530 miles (850 kilometers)** and takes **9 to 9.5 hours.**

Driving from Jasper

From Jasper to **Lake Louise,** follow the scenic **Icefields Parkway (Hwy. 93)** south; it's **145 miles (230 kilometers)** and takes **3.25 to 3.75 hours** (but allow additional time for stops at the many scenic points along the way).

Best Hotels

★ **Juniper Hotel:** Staying at this fun mid-century-modern Banff lodging adds some style to your Rocky Mountain holiday (page 242).

★ **Fairmont Banff Springs Hotel:** Arguably the grandest hotel in the Canadian Rockies, this castle-like property blends history with mineral pools, mountain-view lounges, and other resort amenities (page 243).

★ **Grande Rockies Resort:** This comfortable condo-style lodging in Canmore is an alternative to the bustle of Banff—still just a short drive from the national park (page 253).

★ **Moraine Lake Lodge:** There's plenty to do at this rustic yet elegant, off-the-grid escape on the shores of Moraine Lake near Lake Louise, from canoeing to guided hikes to upscale dining (page 265).

★ **Fairmont Chateau Lake Louise:** You can't sleep closer to the famous lake than at this luxury lodging (page 266).

To **Banff,** continue east from Lake Louise on **Highway 1.**

Driving from the Kootenays
From Kootenay National Park

Follow **Highway 93** north through Kootenay National Park and into Alberta to the junction with Highway 1. Turn west on **Highway 1** to Lake Louise; turn east for Banff. It's **80 miles (130 kilometers)** from the town of Radium Hot Springs at the park's southern boundary to **Lake Louise,** a **1.75- to 2-hour** drive. From Radium to **Banff,** it's **85 miles (140 kilometers),** also a **1.75- to 2-hour** drive.

From Fernie

Follow **Highway 3** west from Fernie to **Highway 93** north and continue through **Kootenay National Park.** At **Highway 1,** turn west for Lake Louise or east for Banff. It's **215 miles (350 kilometers),** a **four-hour** drive, between Fernie and either Banff or Lake Louise.

From Nelson

If you're driving from Nelson to Banff or Lake Louise, you can choose from several different routes.

The most direct routing is to leave Nelson heading south on **Highway 6.** At **Highway 3,** turn east. When you reach **Cranbrook,** go north on **Highway 93,** and continue through **Kootenay National Park.** Once you cross into Alberta and reach **Highway 1,** turn west to Lake Louise or east to Banff. Allow about **six hours** for this **310-mile (500-kilometer)** drive to either Lake Louise or Banff.

For a scenic drive along the shore of **Kootenay Lake,** leave Nelson on **Highway 3A** towards **Balfour,** where you catch the free, 35-minute **Kootenay Lake Ferry** (250/229-4215, www.th.gov.bc.ca, 6:30am-9:40pm daily) across the lake to **Kootenay Bay.** Take **Highway 3A** south, which winds along the lakeshore to **Creston,** where you can pick up **Highway 3** east. Follow the directions (above) to Cranbrook, Kootenay National Park, and Lake Louise or Banff. This Kootenay Lake alternative is also **310 miles (500 kilometers)** between Nelson and either Lake Louise or Banff, but budget an extra hour (about **seven hours** total) for the ferry and for the slower drive along Highway 3A.

Yet another scenic option takes you from Nelson through the **B.C. national parks** along Highway 1 en route to Lake Louise and Banff. Leave Nelson traveling north on **Highway 6** toward New Denver and Nakusp. At **Nakusp,** continue north on **Highway 23.** When you

Best Restaurants

★ **Wild Flour Artisan Bakery:** Sweet and savory pastries, sandwiches, and fresh salads make this Banff bakery an excellent breakfast or lunch stop (page 244).

★ **Park Distillery:** From house-made spirits to hearty campfire fare (they really set things on fire!), this lively Banff distillery-lounge is deliciously fun (page 244).

★ **The Sleeping Buffalo:** Yes, you can sample buffalo at this upscale dining room at Banff's Buffalo Mountain Lodge, where game meats, west coast seafood, and local produce are specialties (page 244).

★ **PD3 by Blake:** Fasten your seat belts, diners! Canmore's coolest dining spot serves eclectic Asian-inspired plates in a silver double-decker bus (page 254).

★ **Crazyweed Kitchen:** Long considered Canmore's best restaurant, this modern kitchen still charms with its inventive world-beat menu and relaxed vibe (page 254).

★ **Plain of Six Glaciers Teahouse:** The only way to reach this historic Lake Louise teahouse is by hiking up from the lakeshore, but you'll appreciate your lunch (or rich chocolate cake) all the more (page 260).

★ **Mount Fairview Dining Room at Deer Lodge:** A short stroll from Lake Louise but miles from the tourist frenzy, this serene log-walled restaurant serves modern mountain meals (page 267).

reach **Galena Bay,** take the free, 20-minute **Upper Arrow Lake Ferry** (250/265-2105, www.th.gov.bc.ca, 5:30am-12:30am daily) across the lake to **Shelter Bay.** Continue on **Highway 23** north until you meet Highway 1 at **Revelstoke.** Turn east onto **Highway 1,** which takes you through Mount Revelstoke, Glacier, and Yoho National Parks and into Alberta. This route is **295 miles (475 kilometers),** or about **6.5 hours,** between Nelson and **Lake Louise,** and **335 miles (535 kilometers),** or **seven hours,** from Nelson to **Banff,** although you may need to allow extra time for the ferry crossing.

Driving from Kelowna (Okanagan)

To travel from Kelowna, in the Okanagan Valley, to Banff, take **Highway 97** north, then continue north on **Highway 97A.** At **Sicamous,** turn east onto the **Trans-Canada Highway (Hwy. 1)** that will take you into Alberta. It's **300 miles (480 kilometers)** from Kelowna to Banff, which takes **5.75 to 6 hours.**

Driving from Calgary

The **Trans-Canada Highway (Hwy. 1)** heads west from Calgary to **Banff.** The **80-mile (130-kilometer)** drive takes about **90 minutes,** weather and traffic permitting.

To **Lake Louise,** continue west from Banff on **Highway 1;** Calgary to Lake Louise is **115 miles (185 kilometers),** a **2.25-hour** drive.

Getting There by Air, Train, and Bus
By Air

Calgary International Airport (YYC, 2000 Airport Rd. NE, 403/735-1200, http://yyc.com) is the closest airport to Banff. The airport is on Calgary's northeast side, 90 miles (145 kilometers) from Banff.

From the Calgary airport, you can take a scheduled shuttle directly to Banff. Both the **Banff Airporter** (403/762-3330 or 888/449-2901, www.banffairporter. com, one-way adults $58.95, seniors $50.11, ages 2-12 $29.48) and **Brewster**

Banff Airport Express (403/762-6700 or 866/606-6700, www.brewster.ca, one-way adults $57, ages 6-15 $28.50) make the trip in about two hours and stop at most Banff hotels.

Brewster Banff Airport Express also runs buses from the Calgary airport to Lake Louise (3.25-3.5 hours, one-way adults $78, ages 6-15 $39).

By Train

VIA Rail, Canada's national rail carrier, does not provide service to Banff. However, the **Rocky Mountaineer** (877/460-3200, www.rockymountaineer.com, mid-Apr.-mid-Oct.), a privately run luxury train, does, offering rail packages between Vancouver, Lake Louise, and Banff. You can travel round-trip from Vancouver to the Canadian Rockies and back, or book a one-way journey through the Rockies starting in either Vancouver or Calgary.

You can purchase a Rocky Mountaineer holiday with rail fare and accommodations only; the company offers a two-day train trip between Vancouver and Banff. Other packages add in a variety of activities and tours. All Rocky Mountaineer trains travel during the day and stop overnight in Kamloops en route to and from the Rockies.

Rail packages start at $1,699 pp and vary by the destination, number of days of travel, and level of service and accommodations.

By Bus

Brewster Banff Airport Express (403/762-6700 or 866/606-6700, www.brewster.ca), which provides bus service between the Calgary airport and both Banff and Lake Louise, can also pick you up or drop you off in downtown Calgary (2.5 hours, one-way adults $57, ages 6-15 $28.50). Brewster buses can take you between Banff and Lake Louise (1 hour, one-way adults $26, ages 6-15 $13) year-round. The buses stop at several downtown Calgary hotels, most Banff hotels, and several locations in Lake Louise.

Greyhound (800/661-8747, www.greyhound.ca) operates several buses a day between the **Banff bus depot** (327 Railway Ave., Banff, 403/762-1091) and Calgary (1.75 hours, one-way adults $16.50-36.50), Canmore (30 minutes, one-way adults $5.20-9.70), and Lake Louise (45 minutes, one-way adults $15-23). From Calgary, Canmore, or Banff, the buses continue to the **Lake Louise bus depot** (Samson Mall, Lake Louise, 403/522-3870).

Greyhound runs buses to Banff from several points in B.C., including Vancouver (13-16 hours, one-way adults $65-128), Kelowna (8 hours, one-way adults $80-115), Revelstoke (4-4.5 hours, one-way adults $45-64), and Golden (2 hours, one-way adults $25-38). These buses stop at Lake Louise en route to Banff.

Banff National Park

Established in 1885, Canada's first national park is also one of its most popular, welcoming more than three million visitors in an average year. Banff National Park covers an area of 2,564 square miles (6,641 square kilometers) and has more than 1,000 miles (1,600 kilometers) of hiking trails. You could hike in the park for years and never repeat the same route.

The towns of Banff and Lake Louise are both within the national park boundaries. Banff is larger, with a full complement of accommodations, restaurants, and in-town attractions, while Lake Louise is essentially a village with two famous lakes. Based in either community, though, you can easily reach most national park sites.

Visiting the Park
Entrances

The **Banff East Gate** is on Highway 1,

west of Canmore. Coming from Calgary, Canmore, or anywhere east of Banff, you must stop here and purchase a park pass, if you haven't bought your pass in advance.

Traveling east on Highway 1 from British Columbia, you enter Banff National Park at the Alberta-B.C. provincial boundary.

If you're driving south on the Icefields Parkway (Hwy. 93) between Jasper and Lake Louise, you enter Banff National Park along the way. The northern section of the parkway is within Jasper National Park, while the southern sector is within Banff's boundary. You must have a valid park pass to travel anywhere on the Icefields Parkway.

Park Passes and Fees

A **day pass** (adults $9.80, seniors $8.30, ages 6-16 $4.90, families $19.60) for Banff National Park is valid at both Banff and Jasper and for travel along the Icefields Parkway; it's also good at Kootenay, Yoho, Mount Revelstoke, Glacier, Waterton Lakes, and Elk Island National Parks. Lake Louise is within the Banff National Park boundaries, so you must have a park pass to visit the lake area as well. A day pass is good until 4pm on the day after you purchase it. You can purchase your park pass online from **Banff Lake Louise Tourism** (www. banfflakelouise.com) or at any park visitors center or entrance gate.

Purchasing a Parks Canada **annual discovery pass** (www.pc.gc.ca, adults $67.70, seniors $57.90, ages 6-16 $33.30, families $136.40), valid for a year, is a good deal if you're spending at least a week in one or more parks. It's good at more than 100 national parks and national historic sites across Canada. Buy an annual pass online from Parks Canada or at any of the parks' visitors centers.

For both day and annual passes, the family passes cover up to seven people in a single vehicle, whether or not they're actually related.

Visitors Centers

In the town of Banff, both **Parks Canada** (www.pc.gc.ca) and **Banff-Lake Louise Tourism** (www.banfflakelouise.com) staff the **Banff Visitor Information Centre** (224 Banff Ave., 403/762-8421, 9am-7pm daily late June-early Sept., 9am-5pm daily early Sept.-late June), providing information about the national park and surrounding area. You can purchase park passes, pick up park maps, and get hiking tips here.

There's a seasonal **Banff Visitor Information Desk** (327 Railway Ave., 9am-5pm daily May-Dec.) in the Banff Heritage Train Station, which is the Greyhound bus depot.

Another park visitors center is at Lake Louise. **Parks Canada** (www. pc.gc.ca) provides park information, sells park passes, and handles camping inquiries at the **Lake Louise Visitor Information Centre** (Samson Mall, 403/522-3833, 9am-7pm daily mid-June-early Sept., 9am-5pm daily May-mid-June and early Sept.-mid-Oct., 9am-4:30pm Thurs.-Sun. mid-Oct.-Apr.), where staff from **Banff-Lake Louise Tourism** (www.banfflakelouise. com) assist visitors as well.

Reservations

The campgrounds in Banff National Park that accept reservations include all the Tunnel Mountain Campground sites; the Lakeside-area sites at Two Jack Lake Campground, including the oTENTiks (platform tents); the Johnston Canyon Campground on the Bow Valley Parkway; and the two Lake Louise Campgrounds. Make **campsite reservations** (877/737-3783, www.reservation.parkscanada. gc.ca) online or by phone.

Sights and Recreation

These sights and things to do within the park are near the town of Banff.

Lake Minnewanka

For a relaxing activity where you can

Banff National Park

© AVALON TRAVEL

Two Days in Banff

Have two days to spend in Banff National Park? Here's how to make the most of your time.

Get oriented with a walk around the town of Banff, with stops at some of its historic sites and museums: the **Cave and Basin National Historic Site,** which tells the story behind Canada's first national park; the **Banff Park Museum,** in a historic log building; or the **Whyte Museum of the Canadian Rockies,** which traces the area's cultural and artistic roots.

When you're done at the museums, take a lunch break. Have soup, salad, or a sandwich at the **Wild Flour Artisan Bakery,** but don't leave without a fresh-baked sweet.

If you're feeling adventurous in your quest for the best mountain views, book a tour on the **Mount Norquay Via Ferrata,** an exciting guided climbing experience that requires no previous rock-climbing expertise; the vistas from the top of the ridge are spectacular. Or go for a hike: The three-mile (4.8-kilometer) **Tunnel Mountain Trail** is close to town and climbs up to a lookout point with views across the Bow Valley.

Catch your breath at glacier-fed **Lake Minnewanka,** the largest lake in Banff National Park, where you can take a leisurely one-hour narrated cruise.

Have an early dinner at the **Park Distillery,** perhaps a vodka cocktail (they brew their own) and the flaming raclette, then see a concert, play, or other event at the **Banff Centre.** For a post-performance nightcap, stop into the Wine Bar at the Banff Centre's **Three Ravens Restaurant.**

The next day, get up early and fortify yourself with breakfast at the **Juniper Bistro,** where the views from the terrace help get your morning off to a good start. Then pack a picnic lunch and drive along the scenic **Bow Valley Parkway.** You want to get to **Johnston Canyon,** a dramatic rock canyon with cantilevered walkways through the gorge, to hike to the **Lower Falls** before the crowds descend on this extremely popular trail. Continue your hike to the **Upper Falls** and if you have the time, keep going toward the **Ink Pots,** a series of colorful pools. Have your picnic along the trail or at another quiet spot along the parkway.

Back in town, drive up Sulphur Mountain for an afternoon ride in the **Banff Gondola.** Walk the boardwalk trail and make plenty of stops to take in the mountain panoramas.

Just down the road from the gondola base, have a relaxing soak in the mineral pools at **Banff Upper Hot Springs.** Then, to wrap up your two days in Banff, sit down for a leisurely evening meal at **The Sleeping Buffalo,** which specializes in game meats, or try one of the dining spots like the Austrian-themed **Waldhaus** at the grand **Fairmont Banff Springs Hotel.**

rest your hiking feet, take a leisurely one-hour **cruise on Lake Minnewanka** (403/762-3473, www.brewster.ca, adults $54.95, ages 6-15 $27.50, 11am, 1pm, 3pm, and 5pm daily early-mid-May; departures on the hour 10am-6pm daily mid-May-mid-Sept.; departures on the hour noon-5pm daily mid-Sept.-mid-Oct.), an azure glacial lake surrounded by mountain peaks. From late July through early September, there are additional cruise departures on the half hour between noon and 4pm. The boats are covered, so you're protected from the sun or other inclement weather.

The largest lake in Banff National Park, Minnewanka is 12.5 miles (20 kilometers) long and nearly one mile (1.6 kilometers) across at its widest point. Its name comes from the Stoney First Nation, who called the lake Minn-waki, or "Lake of the Spirits." During your cruise, a guide provides commentary about the lake, the wildlife in the vicinity, and how the remains of a town lie underneath the lake's waters.

Town of Banff and Vicinity

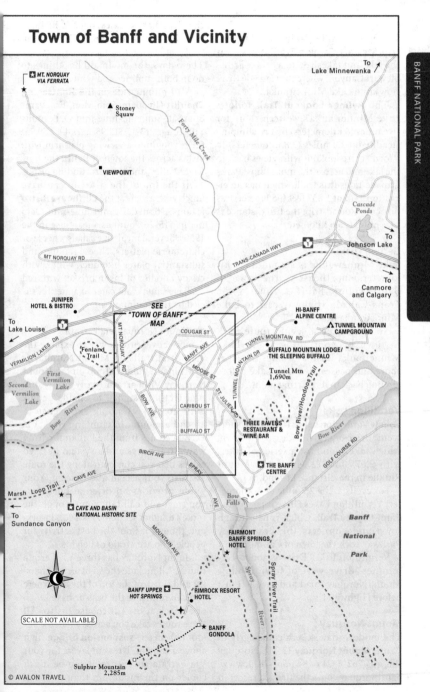

To Lake Minnewanka

★ MT. NORQUAY VIA FERRATA

▲ Stoney Squaw

Forty Mile Creek

■ VIEWPOINT

Cascade Ponds

To Johnson Lake

MT NORQUAY RD

TRANS-CANADA HWY

To Canmore and Calgary

JUNIPER HOTEL & BISTRO

SEE "TOWN OF BANFF" MAP

HI-BANFF ALPINE CENTRE

▲ TUNNEL MOUNTAIN CAMPGROUND

To Lake Louise

COUGAR ST

TUNNEL MOUNTAIN RD

BUFFALO MOUNTAIN LODGE/ THE SLEEPING BUFFALO

VERMILION LAKES DR

Fenland Trail

BANFF AVE

MOOSE ST

TUNNEL MOUNTAIN DR

Tunnel Mtn 1,690m ▲

First Vermilion Lake

Second Vermilion Lake

MT NORQUAY RD

BOW AVE

ST JULIEN RD

Bow River/Hoodoos Trail

Bow River

Bow River

CARIBOU ST

GOLF COURSE RD

BUFFALO ST

THREE RAVENS RESTAURANT & WINE BAR

BIRCH AVE

★ THE BANFF CENTRE

SPRAY AVE

CAVE AVE

Marsh Loop Trail ★

Bow Falls

■ CAVE AND BASIN NATIONAL HISTORIC SITE

To Sundance Canyon

Banff

MOUNTAIN AVE

FAIRMONT BANFF SPRINGS HOTEL

National

Spray River

Spray River Trail

Park

SCALE NOT AVAILABLE

BANFF UPPER HOT SPRINGS ■

RIMROCK RESORT HOTEL

★ BANFF GONDOLA

Sulphur Mountain 2,285m ▲

© AVALON TRAVEL

Hiking

The easy 1.9-mile (3-kilometer) round-trip **Stewart Canyon Trail** starts near the lake and takes you to a bridge across Stewart Canyon, where the Cascade River flows into Lake Minnewanka.

The **Aylmer Lookout Trail** follows Lake Minnewanka's western shore for five miles (8 kilometers) before climbing steadily up 2.4 miles (3.8 kilometers) to a former fire lookout with views back to the lake and across the mountains. Parks Canada rates this trail, which has an elevation gain of 1,837 feet (560 meters), as difficult. Round-trip, the full distance is 14.7 miles (23.6 kilometers).

Getting There

Lake Minnewanka is six miles (10 kilometers) northeast of the town of Banff. Follow Banff Avenue or the Trans-Canada Highway east to Lake Minnewanka Road.

You can take a scenic route back to town by continuing along Lake Minnewanka Road as it hugs the lakeshore and passes Two Jack Lake before circling back to its starting point.

Vermilion Lakes

Follow **Vermillion Lakes Drive** for a short scenic drive or bicycle ride close to town, which takes you past a series of lakes, with 9,675-foot (2,949-meter) Mount Rundle in the distance beyond.

For cyclists, the 2.7-mile (4.3-kilometer) Vermillion Lakes Drive is part of the **Banff Legacy Trail,** which runs through town and connects the Bow Valley Parkway with the town of Canmore.

Vermillion Lakes Drive is about five-minutes' drive west of town. Follow Mount Norquay Road and turn left just before Highway 1.

Mount Norquay

The modern-day ski era came early to Banff. **Mount Norquay** (2 Mt. Norquay Rd., 403/762-4421 or 844/667-7829, www.banffnorquay.com), the first ski resort in the Canadian Rockies, opened in 1926, installed its first mechanized rope tow in 1938, and by 1948, it had a chairlift, too. These days, the mountain has things to do in both summer and winter.

A 10-minute ride on the **Sightseeing Chairlift** (10:30am-6pm Mon.-Fri., 9am-6pm Sat.-Sun. mid-June-mid-Oct., adults $19.95, ages 13-17 $14.95, ages 4-12 $9.95) takes you up to a viewing platform with vistas across the town of Banff, the Bow River Valley, and the surrounding peaks.

At the top of the lift, you can have lunch with a view at the **Cliffhouse Bistro** (11am-5:30pm daily mid-June-mid-Oct., mains $15-26), built as a teahouse in the 1950s. Several meal-size salads, cheese or charcuterie platters, cheese fondue, and substantial plates like duck wings with crispy noodles or bison brisket with red cabbage sauerkraut cater to appetites fueled by the mountain air.

★ Mount Norquay Via Ferrata

A more adventurous way to explore the views and trails on Mount Norquay is to arrange a guided climb on the **Mount Norquay Via Ferrata** (daily mid-June-mid-Oct.). Designed to enable people with no rock climbing experience to ascend a mountain climbing trail, Via Ferrata comes from the Italian for "iron way." Iron rungs and a system of fixed cables that you clip onto along the route assist in your ascent and descent. Your guide provides an orientation before you start and can talk you through the route's tougher sections. It's a good workout, though it's not the best activity for people who are afraid of heights.

Mount Norquay has three Via Ferrata routes. All include the sightseeing chairlift and finish at the top of the lift, where you can return to the base or have lunch or a snack at the Cliffhouse Bistro. All three routes take you across a narrow 98-foot (30-meter) **suspension bridge** high above a canyon. Dress in layers for your Via Ferrata adventure; it can be much cooler on the mountain than in town, but you'll get warm as you climb. Bring water, too.

For an introduction to the Via Ferrata, take the **2.5-hour Explorer Route** (9am, noon, and 3pm Mon.-Thurs., 9am and 3pm Fri.-Sun. mid-June-mid-Oct., $139), which has plenty of challenge, but this shorter route doesn't take you all the way to the top of the ridge.

The **4-hour Ridgewalker Route** (8:30am, 10:30am, 12:30pm, and 2:30pm daily mid-June-mid-Oct., $179) climbs up to spectacular views at the top of the Norquay ridge. This half-day excursion has a longer and steeper downhill section than the Explorer Route.

On the **6-hour Mountaineer Route** (8:30am Fri.-Sun. mid-June-mid-Oct., additional 11:30am departure when the 8:30am tour is full, $299), you follow the same route as the Ridgewalker with an additional traverse along the alpine ridge to Mount Norquay's 8,038-foot (2,450-meter) East Summit. You also cross a **three-wire suspension bridge** (imagine a tight rope with two guide wires) over a deep chasm. This tour includes lunch and après-climb refreshments at the Cliffhouse Bistro.

Skiing and Snowboarding

In winter, compact, family-friendly **Mount Norquay** (9am-4pm daily mid-Nov.-Dec. and Apr., 9am-4pm Sun.-Thurs., 9am-4pm and 5pm-10pm Fri.-Sat. Jan.-Mar., adults $65, seniors and ages 13-17 $50, ages 6-12 $25, under age 6 free) has 60 runs spread over 190 acres (77 hectares) for skiing and snowboarding, including night skiing. The terrain is rated 20 percent beginner, 36 percent intermediate, 28 percent advanced, and 16 percent expert. There's also a **tube park** (10:30am-4pm daily mid-Nov.-Dec. and Apr., 10:30am-4pm Sun.-Thurs., 10:30am-4pm and

The Bow Valley Parkway

La promenade de la Vallée-de-la-Bow

Top to bottom: in the clouds on Mount Norquay; climbing the Mount Norquay Via Ferrata; entering the Bow Valley Parkway.

5pm-9pm Fri.-Sat. Jan.-Mar., adults $30, seniors and ages 13-17 $25, ages 4-12 $20). In addition to the standard full-day lift tickets and multiday passes, you can purchase tickets for two-, three-, or four-hour increments.

Getting There

From town, take Lynx Street to Mount Norquay Road, which will cross over Highway 1 and climb up the mountain to the ski area. It's a 15-minute drive.

The **Banff-Mount Norquay shuttle** (9:30am-6:40pm Mon.-Fri., 7:40am-6:40pm Sat.-Sun.) can take you between downtown Banff hotels and the mountain. In the summer season (mid-June-mid-Oct.) the shuttle is free and runs several times daily.

During the winter ski season, the **Ski Bus** shuttle (daily late Dec.-late Apr., adults $10, ages 6-12 $5) has three morning pickups in town and returns several times throughout the afternoon. For night skiing, the **Night Ski Bus** (Fri.-Sat. Jan.-Mar., adults $5, ages 6-12 $5) picks up three times in town during the late afternoon and returns three times in the evening.

★ Bow Valley Parkway

The most direct route between Banff and Lake Louise is the Trans-Canada Highway (Hwy. 1), but a prettier alternative is the more scenic **Bow Valley Parkway** (Hwy. 1A), a 30-mile (48-kilometer) secondary route. If you drove straight through, the Bow Valley route would add about 15 minutes of travel time. In fact, because you'll likely make numerous stops for hiking, picnicking, or simply enjoying the mountain views, plan on far more than 15 minutes extra for this scenic drive.

You must have a valid national park pass to travel on the Bow Valley Parkway, whether or not you plan to stop en route.

To protect wildlife in the area, Parks Canada restricts travel on the parkway in the spring (Mar.-late June). Check the

Parks Canada website (www.pc.gc.ca) for details on road closures.

Johnston Canyon

Thirteen miles (22 kilometers) west of Banff, **Johnston Canyon** is the most popular stop on the Bow Valley Parkway. Though it can be packed with walkers, the trail through the woods and along the cantilevered walkways through this rock canyon rates among the park's most dramatic scenic stops. Come early in the morning for fewer crowds.

The busiest path is the **Johnston Canyon Lower Falls Trail**, a 1.5-mile (2.4-kilometer) round-trip walk along a gentle path and several catwalks to the first set of waterfalls.

Continue past the Lower Falls on the **Johnston Canyon Upper Falls Trail**, which is slightly steeper, with an elevation gain of 394 feet (120 meters). It's three miles (4.8 kilometers) round-trip from the parking lot to the Upper Falls, which are nearly 100 feet (30 meters) high.

If you have more time, you can keep hiking beyond the Upper Falls on the **Ink Pots Trail**, which leads to a series of brightly colored pools. This moderate trail, with an elevation gain of 705 feet (215 meters), is 6.7 miles (10.8 kilometers) round-trip from the parking area.

Castle Junction

Highway 93, which travels south into Kootenay National Park, meets Highway 1 and the Bow Valley Parkway at **Castle Junction**, 19 miles (31 kilometers) west of Banff. Nearby, you can spot the spiky limestone and granite cliffs of 9,076-foot (2,766-meter) Castle Mountain.

A challenging full-day hike with a long steady climb takes you behind Castle Mountain to **Rockbound Lake**. With an elevation gain of 2,493 feet (760 meters), this trail is 10.4 miles (16.8 kilometers) round-trip. The trailhead is on the east side of Castle Junction.

The **Castle Lookout** was once a fire tower where fire spotters watched for blazes in the national park. Though the tower is gone, this 4.6-mile (7.4-kilometer) round-trip hike with an elevation gain of 1,706 feet (520 meters), leads up to a lookout point with views across the Bow Valley. The trailhead is three miles (5 kilometers) west of Castle Junction.

Storm Mountain Viewpoint

Storm Mountain, 10,310 feet (3,155 meters) tall, gets its name from its dramatic rain and snowstorms. You can see the mountain, along with several nearby peaks, from a pullout along the Bow Valley Parkway, west of Castle Junction. It's a pretty spot for a picnic.

Castle Mountain Internment Camp

From 1915 to 1917, during World War I, the **Castle Mountain Internment Camp** housed immigrants of Ukrainian, Austrian, Hungarian and German descent who were considered enemy aliens. Though the camp is gone, you can pull off the parkway at a memorial plaque, with information about this and other wartime camps in Canada.

Camping

Campsite **reservations** (877/737-3783, www.reservation.parkscanada.gc.ca) are accepted online or by phone for all the Tunnel Mountain Campground sites and for Lakeside-area sites at Two Jack Lake, and they're highly recommended if you'll be traveling from June through September. The other areas are first come, first served. Only Tunnel Mountain has electrical service and RV hookups.

Tunnel Mountain

Close to town, the **Tunnel Mountain Campground** (Tunnel Mountain Rd., tent sites $27.40, electrical sites $32.30-38.20) is the largest camping area in Banff National Park. It's divided into three sections: **Tunnel Mountain Village I** (mid-May-early Oct.) with 618 sites, **Tunnel Mountain Village II** (year-round) with 188 sites, and **Tunnel Mountain Trailer**

Court (mid-May-early Oct.), which has 321 sites exclusively for trailers and large RVs up to 50 feet (15 meters). All the Tunnel Mountain areas have washrooms with flush toilets and showers.

Two Jack Lake

Near Lake Minnewanka, 7.5 miles (12 kilometers) northeast of the town of Banff, the **Two Jack Lake Campground** (Lake Minnewanka Loop Rd.) accommodates tents and small RVs in two different areas: Main and Lakeside.

Located a five-minute drive from Two Jack Lake, **Two Jack Lake Main** (late June-early Sept., $21.50) has 380 sites. The restrooms have flush toilets but no showers. If you don't have your own camping gear, consider one of the 22 **equipped camping sites** ($55) at Two Jack Lake Main, which come with a six-person tent, sleeping pads, a stove, and a lantern. You still need to bring sleeping bags or bedding, cooking supplies, food, flashlights, and other personal items.

Many camping spots are right on the lake at the 64-site **Two Jack Lake Lakeside** (mid-May-early Oct., $27.40), which includes 23 walk-in tent sites. This area has both flush toilets and showers, as well as 10 **oTENTiks** ($120), canvas-walled platform tents that sleep up to six. The oTEN-Tiks have one double and two queen beds, heat, and electricity, as well as an outdoor barbecue and fire pit. You need to bring your own sleeping bags or bedding, as well as food, dishes, and cooking supplies.

Bactrax (225 Bear St., Banff, 403/762-8177, www.campingbanff.com, 8am-8pm daily) rents camping gear and cooking supplies if you don't have your own.

Bow Valley Parkway

Three of the national park campgrounds are along the Bow Valley Parkway (Hwy. 1A) between Banff and Lake Louise.

Opposite the Johnston Canyon trailhead, 14 miles (22 kilometers) from the town of Banff, **Johnston Canyon**

Campground (Bow Valley Parkway, late May-late Sept., $27.40) has 132 sites for tents and small RVs. The campground has restrooms with flush toilets and hot showers.

The 43-site Castle Mountain Campground (Bow Valley Parkway, late May-mid-Sept., $21.50) accommodates tents and small RVs; there are flush toilets but no shower facilities. It's 21 miles (34 kilometers) from Banff and 17 miles (28 kilometers) from Lake Louise.

Small Protection Mountain Campground (Bow Valley Parkway, late May-early Sept., $21.50) has just 14 sites. The restrooms have flush toilets but no showers. The campground is 11 miles (17 kilometers) from Lake Louise.

Town of Banff

On an August afternoon in the town of Banff, which has a population of just under 8,500, pedestrians stroll the sidewalks shoulder-to-shoulder, stopping for snacks or browsing the shops. Located entirely within the boundaries of Banff National Park, the town of Banff is the park's bustling heart.

Most of the park's accommodations, restaurants, and services are in town, as are some national park sights, along with numerous other privately run museums, gardens, and attractions. There's plenty to see and do.

The Bow River bisects the town. The town center, many of its restaurants and shops, the Banff Centre, and Tunnel Mountain are located between Highway 1 and the river. The Cave and Basin National Historic Site, Banff Upper Hot Springs, Banff Gondola, and the famous Fairmont Banff Springs Hotel are all south of the river.

Sights and Activities
★ Cave and Basin National Historic Site
How did Banff become Canada's first

national park? The story begins with a bubbling mineral spring in an underground cave.

The Cave and Basin National Historic Site (Cave St., 403/762-1566, www.pc.gc. ca, 10am-5pm Tues.-Sun. mid-May-June and early-Sept.-mid-Oct., 10am-5pm daily July-early Sept., 11am-5pm Wed.-Sun. mid-Oct.-mid-May, adults $3.90, seniors $3.40, ages 6-16 $1.90, families $9.80) tells the park's story, beginning in 1883 when three railroad workers stumbled on a sulfurous spring in a grotto—the Cave that you can still walk into today, through a dimly lit rock-lined tunnel. Through exhibits at this historic site, you can learn more about the development of Canada's national park system and about the hot springs in the area. You can also check out the Basin hot springs pool (although you can no longer take a soak here).

The Cave and Basin area also played a role during World War I, when the site housed a wartime internment camp, one of 24 camps in Canada for prisoners of war, most of whom were civilians of German or Eastern European heritage. Overall, Canada interned 8,579 people between 1914 and 1920. An on-site exhibit tells you more about this sobering history.

Getting There
The Cave and Basin National Historic Site is across the Bow River from the town center. Cross the Banff Avenue bridge, turn right onto Cave Avenue, and continue for 0.8 miles (1.3 kilometers) to the museum.

On weekends in spring through fall, you can get to the site on Roam Transit Route 4: Cave and Basin bus (www.roam-transit.com, 9am-6:50pm Fri.-Sun. late May-Sept., one-way adults $2, seniors and ages 6-12 $1, day pass $5) from town.

Buffalo Nations Luxton Museum
Journalist, adventurer, and entrepreneur Norman Luxton (1876-1962), along with

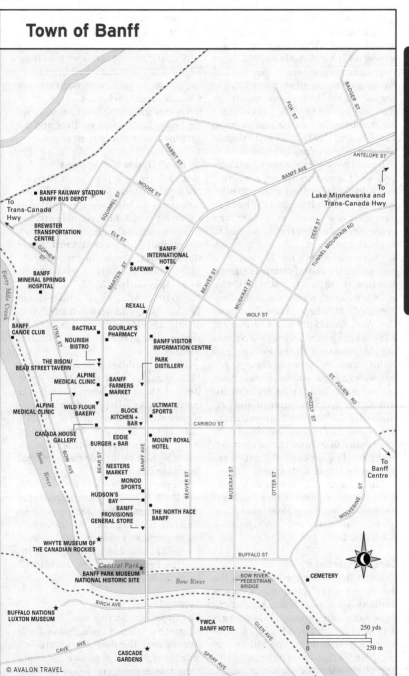

Town of Banff

sea captain John Voss, attempted to sail around the world in a 100-year-old, 30-foot (9-meter) red cedar dugout canoe, setting off from Victoria in 1901. After stops in Tahiti and Samoa, they reached Fiji, where Luxton, ill with fever, had to abandon the endeavor; Voss eventually reached England in 1904. Luxton made his way back to Canada and came to Banff, hoping that the mountain climate would help him return to health.

Luxton took over the then-bankrupt *Crag and Canyon* newspaper, remaining as publisher from 1902 until 1951. He invested in real estate, had his hand in numerous other ventures in town, and in the 1950s, decided that he wanted to establish a museum.

That museum, in a fort-like structure now called the **Buffalo Nations Luxton Museum** (1 Birch Ave., 403/762-2388, www.buffalonationsmuseum.com, 10am-7pm daily May-Sept., 11am-5pm daily Oct.-Apr., adults $10, seniors $9, over age 5 $5), has exhibits about the First Nations people, primarily of the Rockies and plains regions. It's a quirky, old-style gallery, showcasing beadwork, drums, moccasins, pipes, and taxidermy animals. Among the museum's more unusual artifacts are a bison skull, unearthed in downtown Banff and carbon dated to be more than 6,000 years old, and dioramas of the Sun Dance ritual, which involved piercing and other self-torture.

The museum is across the Bow River from the town center. Cross the Banff Avenue bridge, turn right onto Cave Avenue, and make the first right onto Birch Avenue.

Cascade Gardens

You can (sometimes) escape from the downtown Banff crowds at **Cascade Gardens** (Cave St. at Banff Ave., dawn-dusk daily, free), peaceful flower gardens with fanciful burl log bridges and benches, terraced into the hill behind the 1936 park administration building. The gardens are open year-round,

weather permitting, although the flowers are most vibrant between June and September.

A classic Banff photo spot is in front of the administration building, looking across the gardens through town to Cascade Mountain beyond.

From town, follow Banff Avenue over the bridge across the Bow River, and the gardens are directly in front of you.

★ Banff Upper Hot Springs

You can't bathe at the Cave and Basin National Historic Site, where the discovery of an underground spring led to the creation of Banff National Park, but you can soak in the mineral pools high on Sulphur Mountain at **Banff Upper Hot Springs** (1 Mountain Ave., 403/762-1515 or 800/767-1611, www.pc.gc.ca, 9am-11pm daily mid-May-mid-Oct., 10am-10pm Sun.-Thurs., 10am-11pm Fri.-Sat. Nov.-mid-May, last admission 30 minutes before closing, adults $7.30, seniors and ages 3-17 $6.30, families $22.50).

The first bathhouse here was built in 1886, though the current Queen Anne Revival stone bathhouse, which was constructed as a Depression-era unemployment relief project, dates to 1932. At 5,200 feet (1,585 meters), surrounded by mountains, the Upper Hot Springs are at the highest elevation of any mineral springs in Canada.

The pool waters are kept between 98°F and 104°F (37-40°C). The minerals that give the waters their unique composition are a mix of sulfate, calcium, bicarbonate, magnesium, and sodium. You can rent towels ($1.90) and swimsuits ($1.90), including historic "bathing costumes." Lockers are available for $1.

Getting There

The Upper Hot Springs are 2.5 miles (4 kilometers) south of town. Follow Banff Avenue over the Bow River, turn left onto Spray Avenue, then turn right onto Mountain Avenue, and follow the signs for 2.2 miles (3.6 kilometers) to the hot springs parking lot.

You can also take the **Roam Transit Route 1: Sulphur Mountain bus** (www.roamtransit.com, 6:15am-11:30pm daily, one-way adults $2, seniors and ages 6-12 $1, day pass $5) between town and the springs.

Banff Gondola

The **Banff Gondola** (Mountain Ave., Sulphur Mountain, 403/762-2523, www.brewster.ca, 8am-7pm daily mid-Apr.-mid-May, 8am-9pm daily mid-May-early Sept., 8am-7pm daily early Sept.-mid-Oct., 10am-5pm daily mid-Oct.-mid-Apr., adults $39.95, ages 6-15 $19.95) whisks you to the top of Sulphur Mountain, an eight-minute ride to an elevation of 7,486 feet (2,281 meters), where views of six surrounding mountain ranges spread out in all directions. The original gondola, which opened on this site in 1959, was the first in Canada.

At the top of the gondola, you can follow the **Banff SummitWalk**, a 0.6-mile (1-kilometer) boardwalk that leads to several observation platforms and to the **Sanson Peak Weather Observatory,** a historic observatory station that opened in 1903. It's named for Norman Bethune Sanson (1862-1949), who hiked up to this station more than 1,000 times over a 30-year period to monitor the area weather. Sanson also served as the curator of the Banff Park Museum from 1896 to 1932.

If you'd like to follow in Sanson's footsteps and hike Sulphur Mountain yourself instead of riding up in the gondola, follow the 3.5-mile (5.5-kilometer) **Sulphur Mountain Trail.** It starts from the Upper Hot Springs parking lot on Mountain Avenue and switchbacks up the mountain slopes, with an elevation gain of 2,149 feet (655 meters). You can purchase a **one-way gondola ticket** (mid-May-Sept. $19.95, Oct.-mid-May free) to save your knees from the hike back down.

In summer, when the gondola gets busy midday, visit before 11am or after 5pm to avoid long lines. From mid-May to early September, if you ride the gondola between 6 and 9pm, rates are $5 off.

As this book went to press, Brewster Travel, the company that runs the gondola, had launched a redevelopment project, including a new upper terminal building with revamped food outlets and a cinema, slated to open in late 2016.

Getting There

The Banff Gondola is located 2.6 miles (4.2 kilometers) south of town, beyond the Banff Upper Hot Springs. Follow Banff Avenue over the Bow River, turn left onto Spray Avenue, then turn right onto Mountain Avenue, which leads up to the gondola parking area.

The **Roam Transit Route 1: Sulphur Mountain bus** (www.roamtransit.com, 6:15am-11:30pm daily, one-way adults $2, seniors and ages 6-12 $1, day pass $5) can take you between town and the gondola.

Fairmont Banff Springs Hotel

Built in 1888 as one of the original Canadian Pacific Railway hotels, the **Fairmont Banff Springs Hotel** (405 Spray Ave., 403/762-2211 or 866/540-4406, www.fairmont.com) is as much a landmark as it is a lodging. While fire destroyed the original wooden hotel building, the stately stone château that now stands on the site, with more than 700 guest rooms, was constructed in 1928, and is designated a National Historic Site of Canada. Even if you're not staying at "The Castle in the Rockies," you might want to explore its grand public spaces, have a drink on its mountain-view terrace, or book **afternoon tea** in the Rundle Lounge (noon-3:30pm daily, $42).

The hotel is on the south side of the Bow River. From town, cross the Banff Avenue Bridge, turn left onto Spray Avenue, and follow it one mile (1.6 kilometers) to the hotel.

Taking the Waters

In 1883, three railroad workers stumbled on a sulfurous spring in an underground cave in what is now the town of Banff. Although aboriginal people had known about the region's hot springs for centuries, Frank McCabe and brothers William and Tom McCardell recognized that the springs they had "found" were a new tourism opportunity, and potentially, a chance to make a lot of money. They wrote to the Canadian government, staking a claim to the springs.

However, after legal battles ensued, Canada's federal government, led by the country's first prime minister, John A. Macdonald, stepped in, creating the Hot Springs Reserve in 1885. That protected area was eventually expanded into Banff National Park, the first in Canada's national park system.

As McCabe and the McCardell brothers predicted, the Canadian Rockies' hot springs became a draw for tourists, particularly after Canada's transcontinental railroad was completed. The general manager of the Canadian Pacific Railway, William Cornelius Van Horne, was keen to build traffic on the new railroad. He launched the construction of several mountain lodges to accommodate these rail travelers, including the Mount Stephen House in Field, B.C., now in Yoho National Park; the Glacier House at B.C.'s Rogers Pass; and a property that he hoped would create a new standard of Rocky Mountain luxury: the Banff Springs Hotel.

When the grand Banff Springs Hotel, now part of the Fairmont chain, opened in 1888, it helped put Banff on the tourist map. Trainloads of visitors came to "take the waters," soaking in the region's mineral pools.

Today, visitors to the Canadian Rockies still come for the mineral-rich waters at **Banff Upper Hot Springs** and in the mineral pools at the **Fairmont Banff Springs Hotel.** In Jasper National Park, you can soak in **Miette Hot Springs,** and in Kootenay National Park at **Radium Hot Springs.** Several more hot springs along B.C.'s Highway 93/95 have given that road the nickname "The Hot Springs Highway."

Even if more people travel to the Canadian Rockies these days by road than by rail, those 19th-century rail workers were right about one thing: Tourists will come from far and wide to "take the waters."

TIP: To take those iconic photos of the Fairmont Banff Springs Hotel surrounded by forests and backed by the mountains, you need to get some distance away from the hotel. From town, follow Buffalo Street toward the Banff Centre. The point where the road turns sharply uphill is known as **Surprise Corner.** Pull off here, walk up to the lookout platform above the Bow River, and you'll see the hotel standing regally amid the trees.

Banff Park Museum National Historic Site

Wandering into the **Banff Park Museum National Historic Site** (91 Banff Ave., 403/762-1558, www.pc.gc.ca, 10am-5pm Wed.-Sun. mid-May-June and early-Sept.-mid-Oct., 10am-5pm daily July-early Sept., adults $3.90, seniors $3.40, ages 6-16 $1.90, families $9.80) is like stumbling into the home of a 19th-century mountain explorer.

Opened in 1903, the log building itself is a historic attraction; it still has its original honey-hued wood paneling. Most of the collection inside, which includes taxidermy animals native to the Banff area, including bears, bison, and big-horned sheep as well as all kinds of birds, was acquired between 1900 and the 1930s. The museum's oldest specimen is a red-breasted merganser, which was mounted in 1860—before Canada had even become Canada.

There's a library where you can browse wildlife books and magazines, and a "discovery room" with please-touch activities for the kids. Head upstairs to find the "cabinet of curiosities," housing various oddities that people donated to the museum.

Whyte Museum of the Canadian Rockies

Founded by local artists and philanthropists Peter Whyte and Catharine Robb Whyte, the **Whyte Museum of the Canadian Rockies** (111 Bear St., 403/762-2291, www.whyte.org, 10am-5pm daily, adults $8, students over age 11 $4) explores mountain history, art, and culture.

Exhibits showcase the Rocky Mountains' First Nations communities, early explorers, and mountain guides and skiers who helped develop the area for winter tourism. The museum also has an art gallery with a changing roster of exhibitions.

In summer, the museum offers 90-minute **Historic Banff Walks** (10:30am Sat.-Sun. July-Aug.), with stories about the people who helped build the town.

Sports and Recreation
Hiking

Starting right in town, a popular intermediate-level hike goes up the **Tunnel Mountain Trail** to a lookout point with views across the Bow Valley. The trail is three miles (4.8 kilometers) round-trip, with a series of switchbacks to moderate the climb; the elevation gain is 850 feet (260 meters). The trailhead is near the Banff Centre on St. Julien Road.

Another hike to take for its panoramic views is the **Sulphur Mountain Trail.** The trailhead starts from the Upper Hot Springs parking lot on Mountain Avenue and switchbacks up the mountain slopes, with an elevation gain of 2,149 feet (655 meters). The trail is 3.5 miles (5.5

Top to bottom: Banff Upper Hot Springs; Banff Gondola; Fairmont Banff Springs Hotel.

kilometers) each way. If you don't want to walk back down, you can purchase a one-way ticket on the **Banff Gondola** (403/762-2523, www.brewster.ca, mid-May-Sept. $19.95, Oct.-mid-May free).

The **Surprise Corner to Hoodoos Trail** (3 miles/4.8 kilometers each way) is an easy hike along the Bow River to a group of hoodoos, unusual limestone rock formations. The trail begins at Surprise Corner (Buffalo St.), which also has an overlook with views to the Fairmont Banff Springs Hotel. For a one-way walk, catch the **Roam Transit Route 2: Tunnel Mountain bus** (www.roamtransit.com, 6:15am-11:30pm daily, one-way adults $2, seniors and ages 6-12 $1, day pass $5) back to town from the Tunnel Mountain Campground.

Canoeing and Kayaking

Take a laid-back paddle down the Bow River with a canoe or kayak rental from the **Banff Canoe Club** (403/762-5005, www.banffcanoeclub.com, 10am-6pm daily mid-May-mid-Oct., $36 per hour, $20 each additional hour). Their docks are on the river bank at the corner of Wolf Street and Bow Avenue. They also offer 1.5-hour guided **Voyageur Canoe Tours** (11am and 1pm daily mid-May-mid-Oct., adults $45, ages 6-12 $20).

Cycling

The **Rocky Mountain Legacy Trail** (403/762-1556, www.pc.gc.ca) is a paved 17-mile (27-kilometer) multiuse path that begins at the Bow Valley Parkway and travels through the town of Banff before running parallel to Highway 1 east to the town of Canmore. Nearly 14 miles (22 kilometers) of the route are within the boundaries of Banff National Park, where it's known as the Banff Legacy Trail. Pick up a trail map at area visitors centers or online from the Banff National Park website.

Rent bikes from **Bactrax** (225 Bear St., 403/762-8177, www.snowtips-bactrax.com), **Banff Cycle** (100 Owl St.,

403/985-4848, www.banffcycle.com), or **Ultimate Sports** (206 Banff Ave., 403/762-0547, www.ultimatebanff.com).

Entertainment and Events
★ The Banff Centre

The Banff Centre (107 Tunnel Mountain Dr., box office 403/762-6301 or 800/413-8368, www.banffcentre.ca) describes itself as "the largest arts and creativity incubator on the planet." Established in the 1930s as the Banff School of Drama, and quickly renamed the Banff School of Fine Arts, the Banff Centre provides professional development and training programs in a variety of artistic fields, including music, theater, dance, literature, painting, photography, sculpture, film, and new media. This campus-like complex of buildings on a hill overlooking the town presents a full calendar of performances, events, and exhibitions that are open to the public.

Festivals and Events

SpringstART (www.banfflakelouise.com, Apr.) is a week of art exhibitions and workshops, concerts, films, and other events celebrating mountain culture.

All summer long, the **Banff Summer Arts Festival** (www.banffcentre.ca, June-Aug.) presents more than 100 events, including concerts, dance, lectures, readings, and films on the Banff Centre campus.

The Banff Centre also hosts the **Banff Mountain Film and Book Festival** (www.banffcentre.ca, Nov.), nine days of movies, book talks, lectures, and other events that incorporate a mountain theme.

The **Winterstart Festival** (www.banfflakelouise.com, Nov.-Dec.) kicks off the winter season with **Bon Appétit Banff** (mid-Nov.), when local restaurants offer special fixed-price menus. Get started on your holiday shopping at the **Banff Christmas Market** (www.banffchristmasmarket.com, late Nov.), then bring the family to the annual **Santa Claus Parade of Lights** (Dec.).

Shopping

Canada House Gallery (201 Bear St., 800/419-1298, www.canadahouse.com, 9:30am-6pm Sun.-Thurs., 9:30am-7pm Fri.-Sat.) shows work by Canadian artists, including Inuit art from Canada's Arctic regions.

Banff has several outdoor gear shops, including **Monod Sports** (129 Banff Ave., 403/762-4571 or 866/956-6663, www.monodsports.com, 10am-8pm daily) and **The North Face Banff** (124 Banff Ave., 403/762-0775, www.thenorthfacebanff.com, 9am-9pm Sun.-Thurs., 9am-10pm Fri.-Sat.).

Ultimate Sports (206 Banff Ave., 403/762-0547, www.ultimatebanff.com, call for hours) sells and rents gear for skiing, snowboarding, and cycling. **Bactrax** (225 Bear St., Banff, 403/762-8177, www.campingbanff.com, 8am-8pm daily) rents camping gear, including tents, sleeping bags, and cooking supplies.

There's a branch of the **Hudson's Bay** (125 Banff Ave., 403/762-5525, www.hbc.com, 9:30am-10pm Mon.-Sat., 9:30am-9pm Sun.) department store in the center of town.

Accommodations

Book early if you're visiting in July and August, as accommodations generally fill up well in advance. Staying south of Banff in the town of Canmore is a reasonable alternative if Banff is overly busy.

Under $150

Banff's best budget lodging is the **YWCA Banff Hotel** (102 Spray Ave., 403/762-3560, www.ywcabanff.ca), in a former hospital building overlooking the Bow River, opposite Cascade Gardens. Not only does it offer simple, moderately priced rooms, but revenue from the hotel funds a local domestic violence prevention program. Single ($99-109) and double ($129-149) rooms have a bed, desk, and fan; the more expensive ones have private baths. Two family rooms ($189-199) accommodate up to six people. On the lower level, bunk-bedded dorms ($38-40 pp) sleep 6 to 10; most have their own washrooms with showers. None of the rooms has a TV, but you can catch your favorite show in the lounge, which also has a take-one, leave-one book library. There's a shared kitchen and guest laundry; Wi-Fi and parking are free. A small café serves light meals at breakfast, lunch, and dinner; in winter, room rates include continental breakfast.

Banff has a busy year-round hostel, the **HI-Banff Alpine Centre** (801 Hidden Ridge Way, 778/328-2220 or 866/762-4122, www.hihostels.ca, $34-46 dorm, $91.52-140 d), off Tunnel Mountain Road. Sleeping options include four- to six-bed female, male, or mixed dorms, private doubles with a queen bed (with or without en suite baths), and private stand-alone log cabins with two double beds, a sitting area with a sofa and TV, and a bath. All rates include Wi-Fi and a town bus pass (ask at the front desk). The hostel has a restaurant, a pub, and a shared kitchen; staff organize group hikes and nightlife excursions.

$150-250

While it's best known for its arts programs, the **Banff Centre** (107 Tunnel Mountain Dr., 403/762-6308 or 800/884-7574, www.banffcentre.ca, $189-339 d) also offers hotel accommodations on its wooded campus above town. These aren't student dorms; rather, they're comfortable mid-range hotel rooms. The most modern units are in the Professional Development Centre, where standard rooms have dark woodsy furnishings and either one king or two queen beds; one-bedroom suites have a separate living room. A $15 facility fee covers Wi-Fi, parking, and access to the nearby Sally Borden Building, which houses a fitness center, a swimming pool, a climbing wall, and a running track, as well as several dining outlets.

Despite its traditional exterior, the **Banff International Hotel** (333 Banff

Ave., 403/762-5666 or 877/442-2623, www.brewster.ca, $150-319 d) has 160 contemporary guest rooms, updated with grey faux-wood wallpaper, red desk chairs, and modern baths. Wi-Fi is included in the rates, as is underground parking. Other amenities include a whirlpool tub, a sauna, a steam room, and a fitness facility as well as a guest laundry. Tour operator Brewster Travel runs the hotel, so its on-site activities office books excursions; ask about package rates for lodging and tours.

Also part of the Brewster Travel family, the simply appointed **Mount Royal Hotel** (138 Banff Ave., 403/762-3331 or 877/442-2623, www.brewster.ca, $140-329 d), in the center of town, has small standard rooms, larger premium rooms, and junior suites with separate sitting areas. Rates include Wi-Fi and parking, although the limited spaces are first-come, first-served. The guest laundry is handy for long-term travelers and outdoor adventurers, who also appreciate the hot tub and sauna.

At the 50-room ★ **Juniper Hotel** (1 Juniper Way, 403/762-2281 or 866/551-2281, http://thejuniper.com, $129-269 d), a redone 1950s lodge, there's plenty to see, inside and out, from the locally themed artwork and First Nations artifacts throughout the hallways, to the scenic vistas from the mountainside guest rooms. Rooms are mid-century-modern, with clean-lined cherry furnishings, earth-toned upholstery, and updated baths with stone counters and floors. There's no pool, but there is a small outdoor hot tub. Open for breakfast and dinner, the **Juniper Bistro** has an expansive mountain-view terrace. The hotel is 1.2 miles (2 kilometers) outside the town center, at the base of the road to the Mount Norquay Ski Area. Parking and

Top to bottom: kayaks for rent at the Banff Canoe Club; Banff Centre; pool with a view at the Fairmont Banff Springs Hotel.

Wi-Fi are included, and you can catch a shuttle into town or to the ski hill.

Over $250

Up the hill from the town center, the **Buffalo Mountain Lodge** (700 Tunnel Mountain Rd., 403/762-2400 or 800/661-1367, www.crmr.com, $209-329 d) has 108 lodge-style rooms, all with wood-burning fireplaces, TVs, DVD players, included Wi-Fi, and patios or balconies, in several different buildings. The top units are the "premier" rooms in log cabin-like lodges on the property's upper level, with pine ceilings and in-floor heating in the baths. Other accommodations are in townhouse units or standard hotel rooms. Parking is complimentary, as is ski and bike storage. You can soak in the large outdoor hot tub. The excellent **Sleeping Buffalo Restaurant** serves breakfast to guests and is open to the public for lunch and dinner.

On Sulphur Mountain, below the Banff Upper Hot Springs and Banff Gondola, the **Rimrock Resort Hotel** (300 Mountain Ave., 403/762-3356 or 888/746-7625, www.rimrockresort.com, $258-748 d) is a classic luxury hotel. Among its 343 guest rooms, the premier mountain-view units come with either traditional furnishings and rose-print duvets or, in the Elegance rooms, with mid-century-modern style. Facilities include an indoor pool, a sauna, a hot tub, a 24-hour fitness center, and a spa. Two lounges (martinis are a specialty), a casual café, and two restaurants, including the upscale French-inspired **Eden** (403/762-1848, www.banffeden. com, 6pm-9pm daily, reservations required, prix fixe $79-197), ensure that you won't want for food or drink.

Known as "The Castle in the Rockies," the ★ **Fairmont Banff Springs Hotel** (405 Spray Ave., 403/762-2211 or 866/540-4406, www.fairmont.com, $479-779 d, resort fee $12 per day, parking $25-39) remains both a regional landmark and the town's most distinctive accommodations. Once you've settled into this stately stone manor, you might wish you had an appointment secretary to schedule all your activities, with its mountain-view indoor and outdoor pools, tennis courts, golf course, croquet lawn, bowling alley, large fitness center offering yoga and other exercise classes, and deluxe spa. Hotel guests can take a free one-hour **heritage tour** (1pm daily) of the property. The hotel's 764 guest rooms range from cozy 200-square-foot (19-square-meter) nooks to expansive suites fit for a queen (yes, more than one monarch has stayed here). Join the complimentary Fairmont President's Club to avoid the $14.95-per-day charge for Wi-Fi; members also get discounted entry to the hotel's **mineral pools.** Otherwise, a day pass to these lovely indoor hot baths is $69 ($49 after 4pm); admission to the baths is complimentary with a massage, facial, or other spa treatment.

The Fairmont's numerous dining outlets include the **1888 Chop House** (403/762-6860, www.1888chophouse. com, 6pm-9pm Tues.-Sat., mains $35-68), which focuses on wild game and Alberta beef; Austrian-themed **Waldhaus** (6pm-9pm Wed.-Sat., mains $36-51); **Rundle Lounge** (noon-3:30pm daily, $42), which offers daily afternoon tea; wood-paneled **Grapes Wine Bar,** serving cheeses, charcuterie, and vino; and **Samurai Sushi Bar,** where the fish is flown in from Vancouver.

Food
Groceries and Markets

At the **Banff Farmers Market** (Bear St. at Caribou St., www.thebanfffarmersmarket.com, 10am-6pm Wed. early June-late Sept.), you can find fresh produce, bison jerky, baked goods, prepared foods, and crafts.

Banff has several grocery stores, including **Nesters Market** (122 Bear St., 403/762-3663, www.nestersmarket. com, 8am-11pm daily) and **Safeway** (318 Marten St., 403/762-5378, www.safeway. ca, 8am-11pm daily). **Banff Provisions**

General Store (115 Banff Ave., 403/985-0983, www.banffprovisions.com, 9am-10pm daily) sells snacks and gourmet goodies.

Cafés, Bakeries, and Light Bites

Cheerful ★ **Wild Flour Artisan Bakery** (101-211 Bear St., 403/760-5074, www.wildflourbakery.ca, 7am-4pm Mon.-Thurs., 7am-5pm Fri.-Sun., mains breakfast $3.50-7, lunch $6-10) is always busy, and with good reason. From morning pastries, house-made granola, and frittata sandwiches to good-value lunchtime combos of soup, focaccia, sandwiches, or fresh salads, like kale with apples, cranberries, and pumpkin seeds, there's lots of deliciousness on your overflowing plate. Come at off-hours to snag a table or counter seat, or take your fresh-baked brownie, unusual fig-anise cookie, or other goodies for the trail.

Contemporary

Brewing their own vodka and serving fun "campfire food," ★ **Park Distillery** (219 Banff Ave., 403/762-5114, www.parkdistillery.com, lunch 11am-5pm daily, dinner 5pm-late daily, mains lunch $14-29, dinner $14-44) literally sets things ablaze in this lively ski lodge-style pub; when you order the oka raclette, a delectably gooey mix of melted cheese and potatoes accompanied by pickled vegetables and pretzel bread, your server sets it on fire at your table. Other plates come from the kitchen's wood-fired grill, from wild trout to rotisserie chicken to charred rib eye, and there's a long list of spirits and brews beyond their own. To get the scoop on the spirited scene, take a 30-minute **distillery tour** (3:30pm Wed.-Sun.).

Where's the wildlife at **The Bison** (211 Bear St., 403/762-5550, www.thebison.ca, 5pm-10pm Mon.-Sat., 10am-10pm Sun., mains $19-49)? The chefs can get wild in the open kitchen at this bustling bistro, where the second-floor dining room overlooks town and the mountains. And there's wildlife on the plates, too, when you graze on starters like elk-topped gnocchi *poutine* or buffalo-style lamb ribs, before going where the signature bison roam: carpaccio with pickled mushrooms, braised short ribs with baby potatoes, ravioli with a squash puree, or a burger with cheese curds and smoked bacon.

When you're on the lookout for light bites and cocktails, there's **Block Kitchen + Bar** (5-201 Banff Ave., 403/985-2887, www.banffblock.com, 11am-2am daily, mains lunch $14-16, all-day small plates $5-26). From midday to late night, the MediterrAsian sharing plates include tandoori prawns, Silk Road chicken, skewers, and smoked buffalo flatbread. At lunch, you can choose from a menu of world-roaming sandwiches, like Thai beef with pickled vegetables or hummus with green olive and sun-dried tomato tapenade.

Yes, you can sample buffalo at ★ **The Sleeping Buffalo** (700 Tunnel Mountain Rd., 403/760-4484, www.crmr.com, lunch noon-3pm daily, dinner 5:30pm-9pm Sun.-Thurs., 5:30pm-10pm Fri.-Sat., mains lunch $14-20, dinner $26-40), from a buffalo pastrami sandwich at lunch to a buffalo duo of grilled strip loin and braised short ribs in the evening. The house-made charcuterie platter, a sharing plate for two, includes cured game as well, but there are fresh salads, free-range chicken, and west coast seafood options if meat isn't your thing. There's nothing sleepy about this upscale wood-beamed dining room at Buffalo Mountain Lodge, although you may need a nap after the warm flourless chocolate quinoa cake, served with caramelized bananas and brandy ice cream.

Juniper Bistro (Juniper Hotel, 1 Juniper Way, 403/763-6219, www.thejuniper.com, breakfast 7am-11am Mon.-Sat., 7am-1pm Sun., dinner 5pm-9pm Sun.-Thurs., 5pm-10pm Fri.-Sat., mains breakfast $10-15, dinner $17-35) starts with a lovely setting, with a wall of windows facing the mountains and a spacious outdoor terrace with even better views. It's an excellent choice for a leisurely breakfast, with creative plates like avocado eggs Benedict on a biscuit with peach-poblano chutney, huevos rancheros topped with smoked pork, or savory bacon- and gruyère-stuffed french toast with sweet-and-sour tomato relish. In the evening, try the caesar salad with *sous vide* egg and seared tuna, rabbit rillettes with fig crackers, or Moroccan-spiced lamb with Israeli couscous. They don't serve dinner on Monday or Tuesday in the off-seasons; call ahead to confirm.

To dine before or after a show, or to enjoy fine modern fare with a valley view, head to the Banff Centre and its **Three Ravens Restaurant** (Sally Borden Bldg., 4th Fl., 107 Tunnel Mountain Dr., 403/762-6300, www.banffcentre.ca, 5pm-9pm daily, mains $30-41), where there's plenty to applaud on the imaginative menu. You might open with house-cured sturgeon with bacon sand or elk tartare with smoked mascarpone, before a second act of ancient grain *aranchini* with red pepper jam, bison with spiced popcorn, or a pork sampler of roasted tenderloin, braised belly, and candied ham. For a nightcap or a snack, take a seat at the **Wine Bar** (4pm-midnight daily, shared plates $9-45), which offers plates to share such as an antipasto platter and a three-cheese fondue.

Burgers

Deep-fried pickles, saucy chicken wings, hipster hot dogs, and classic *poutine* may grab your attention, but at **Eddie Burger + Bar** (6-137 Banff Ave., 403/762-2230, www.eddieburgerbar.ca, 11:30am-2am daily, mains $11-17), the name says it all. You want something on a bun, whether it's Alberta beef, bison, chicken, veggies, or even elk, and something from the bar. The milk shake bar has classics

Top to bottom: lunch at the Wild Flour Artisan Bakery; raclette at Park Distillery; on the terrace at Juniper Bistro.

like vanilla or chocolate, newcomers like Nutella or chocolate raspberry, and "high-octane" concoctions like the Monkey's Lunch (vanilla ice cream, Kahlúa, and crème de banana) or the Burt Reynolds, with vanilla ice cream, spiced rum, and butter ripple schnapps.

Diners

Although it started life as a steakhouse and still serves traditional Alberta beef, family-friendly **Melissa's Missteak** (218 Lynx St., 403/762-5511, www.melissasmissteak.com, 7am-9:30pm daily, mains breakfast $5-19, lunch $9-20, dinner $23-45) is at least as beloved for its hearty breakfasts: eggs benedict, Swiss apple pancakes, french toast, and the expected variations on the bacon-and-eggs theme. At lunchtime you can still order breakfast, or choose burgers, deep-dish pizza, or sandwiches like old-fashioned hot turkey.

Pizza

The choices are simple at the **Bear Street Tavern** (211 Bear St., 403/762-2021, www.bearstreettavern.ca, 11:30am-midnight Tues.-Sun., mains $15-18): pizza and craft beer. The pies build on the basics with options like the Bison (smoked bison, edamame, and caramelized onions) or the Wheeler Hut (wild mushrooms, pine nuts, truffle oil, and pesto). For the suds, they typically have eight local brews on tap and more microbrews in the bottle. If you're not into pizza, there's pork belly mac-and-cheese or smoked chicken wings with *piri piri* sauce. It's on the lower level of the same space that houses The Bison restaurant.

Vegetarian

Vegetarians, and anyone who's eaten their fill of Alberta beef, will appreciate the interesting plant-based fare at **Nourish Bistro** (110-211 Bear St., 403/760-3933, www.nourishbistro.com, 11:30am-10pm daily, mains lunch $13-18, dinner $13-26). At lunch, you can choose from veggie burgers, a grain and plant "nourishment bowl," or a vegan "mac and squeeze" made with quinoa noodles and coconut sauce. In the evening, when plates are designed to share, you can start with their popular nachos and order stuffed peppers, mushroom ravioli, and other dishes in either full- or half-portions.

Information and Services
Visitor Information

The **Banff Visitor Information Centre** (224 Banff Ave., 403/762-8421, www.banfflakelouise.com, 9am-7pm daily late June-early Sept., 9am-5pm daily early Sept.-late June) provides information about things to do in the area and keeps an updated list of available accommodations. **Parks Canada** (www.pc.gc.ca) staff are also on hand with park maps, brochures, and tips.

To learn more about Banff's historic buildings, or to plan your own walking tour, check out the town of Banff's online guide, **Walking Through Banff's History** (www.banff.ca).

Media and Communications

Banff's local newspapers include *The Crag and Canyon* (www.thecragandcanyon.ca) and the *Rocky Mountain Outlook* (www.rmoutlook.com).

The Canadian Rockies edition of *Where* magazine (www.where.ca) lists events and other things to do in Banff, Lake Louise, and surrounding mountain areas.

Medical Services

Banff Mineral Springs Hospital (305 Lynx St., 403/762-2222, www.albertahealthservices.ca) provides 24-hour emergency services. **Alpine Medical Clinic** (Unit 201A, Bison Courtyard, 211 Bear St., 403/762-3155, www.banffmedical.com, 8:30am-7pm Mon.-Thurs., 8:30am-5pm Fri., 9am-5pm Sat.-Sun.) accepts visitors for minor health issues.

Banff-area pharmacies include **Gourlay's Pharmacy** (220 Bear St.,

403/762-2516, www.gourlayspharmacy.ca, 9am-7pm Mon.-Fri., 9am-6pm Sat., 10am-5pm Sun.) or **Rexall** (317 Banff Ave., 403/762-2245, www.rexall.ca, 9am-8pm Mon.-Thurs., 9am-9pm Fri.-Sat., 10am-6pm Sun.).

Getting Around

Highway 1, the Trans-Canada Highway, connects Banff with Lake Louise to the west and Canmore and Calgary to the east. The center of town is south of the highway and north of the Bow River. The town is compact and easy to get around on foot.

Several attractions and accommodations, including the Cave and Basin National Historic Site, Banff Upper Hot Springs, the Banff Gondola, and the Fairmont Banff Springs Hotel are on the south side of the Bow River. A bridge on Banff Avenue crosses the river.

If you're on foot, you can cross on the **Bow River Pedestrian Bridge.** Built in 2013, this graceful timber footbridge across the river is east of the Banff Avenue bridge. On the town side, you can access the footbridge along the river or via the Bow River Trail, near the corner of Buffalo and Muskrat Streets. On the south side, the footbridge takes you to Glen Avenue, behind the YWCA Banff Hotel.

By Car

Banff town streets get very congested during the summer season, so you may find it less frustrating to get around on foot or by public transit, when you can.

Parking

You can park for free on the street and in a number of lots and parkades around the town of Banff. The time limits vary from 15 minutes to 12 hours, so check the signs before you leave your car. On residential streets without a posted time limit, you can park for up to 72 hours.

The easiest way to find parking is using the **Banff Parking app** (www.banffparking.ca), which indicates where you can park for how long and how busy each location typically is. You can search for spots for cars, RVs, and bicycles. The **Town of Banff** (www.banff.ca) also has parking map on its website.

There's a large open parking lot on Buffalo Street near the Bow River. Along the river, Bow Street is lined with street parking spaces.

Car Rentals

Car rental companies with Banff locations include **Avis** (Cascade Plaza, Wolf St. at Banff Ave., 403/762-3222, www.avis.ca), **Budget** (202 Bear St., 403/226-1550, www.budgetcalgary.ca), **Enterprise** (Lynx St. and Caribou St., 403/762-2688, www.enterprise.ca), and **Hertz** (Fairmont Banff Springs Hotel, 405 Spray Ave., 403/762-2027, www.hertz.ca).

By Bus

Roam Transit (403/762-0606, www.roam-transit.com) operates several bus routes throughout the Banff area. If you can match your travel times with the bus schedule, taking the bus can be a viable way to get around town. Banff was the first municipality in Canada to run an all-hybrid electric transit fleet.

Route 1: Sulphur Mountain (6:15am-11:30pm daily) travels through town along Banff Avenue, then crosses the river and follows Mountain Avenue to Banff Upper Hot Springs and the Banff Gondola.

Route 2: Tunnel Mountain (6:15am-11:30pm daily) runs from the Tunnel Mountain Campground through town along Banff Avenue, across the river, and along Spray Avenue to the Fairmont Banff Springs Hotel.

Route 4: Cave and Basin (late May-Sept., 9am-6:50pm Fri.-Sun.) is a seasonal weekend-only route that can take you between town, the Cave and Basin National Historic Site, Banff Upper Hot Springs, and the Banff Gondola.

To travel between Banff and Canmore,

you can take **Route 3: Banff-Canmore Regional** (6am-9:50pm Mon.-Wed., 6am-10:50pm Thurs.-Fri., 9am-9:50pm Sat., 9am-7:50pm Sun.).

Use the **trip planner function** on the Roam Transit website (www.roamtransit.com) to figure out what bus to take. The system also has a real-time bus-tracking feature that lets you know when the next bus is arriving.

Transit Fares and Passes

Purchase **local fares** (one-way adults $2, seniors and ages 6-12 $1) or day passes ($5), good for multiple rides throughout the day, on the bus. You can also buy **regional fares** (one-way adults $6, seniors and ages 6-12 $3) or day passes (adults $15, seniors and ages 6-12 $7.50) on the Canmore buses.

Pay for your bus fares with exact change if you can. The electronic fare boxes on the buses don't give change; if you don't have exact change, they issue you a **change voucher** that you can redeem at the **Bow Valley Regional Transit Customer Service Centre** (221 Beaver St.), **Banff Town Hall** (110 Bear St.), **Fairmont Banff Springs Hotel** (405 Spray Ave.), **Brewster Transportation Centre** (100 Gopher St.), **Explore Rockies Activity Centre** (Banff International Hotel, 333 Banff Ave.), and other locations around town.

Transfers are free between local routes (1, 2, and 4) and are valid for up to 30 minutes. You can also transfer from the Route 3 regional route to one of the local routes. If you're starting your trip on a local route but plan to transfer to the Canmore bus, buy your regional ticket when you first board the local bus so you can transfer to the regional bus without paying an extra fare.

By Taxi

Banff Taxi and **Taxi Taxi,** both part of the **Banff Transportation Group** (403/762-0000, www.banfftransportation.com), provide 24-hour cab service. Taxis wait

Bow River Pedestrian Bridge

at stands around town; you can also hail them on the street or phone for a cab.

Tours

Brewster Travel Canada (403/762-6700 or 866/606-6700, www.brewster.ca) offers several Banff sightseeing tours (4.5-6 hours, adults $96-131, ages 6-15 $50-68), with options that include the Banff Gondola, a Lake Minnewanka cruise, or both. They also run day tours of Banff starting in Calgary or Canmore. From Banff, they operate tours to Lake Louise, the Columbia Icefield, and Jasper as well. You can buy tickets online or at their **Explore Rockies Activity Centres** at the **Brewster Transportation Centre** (100 Gopher St., 800/760-6934, 7am-9pm daily), **Banff International Hotel** (333 Banff Ave., 403/760-3291, 10am-8pm Mon.-Thurs., 8:30am-8pm Fri.-Sun.), or **Cave and Basin** (311 Cave Ave., 403/760-3353, noon-4pm Wed.-Sun.).

Discover Banff Tours (Sundance Mall, 215 Banff Ave., 403/760-5007 or 877/565-9372, www.banfftours.com, 7:30am-8pm daily) offers a **Discover Banff & Its Wildlife Tour** (mid-Apr.-mid-Oct., 3 hours, adults $56, ages 6-12 $30), with stops at Bow Falls, the Fairmont Banff Springs Hotel, Surprise Corner, Hoodoos Lookout, Lake Minnewanka, and Two Jack Lake. From Banff, they also run half-day and full-day tours to **Lake Louise, guided hiking tours, helicopter tours,** and **horseback riding tours.**

To learn more about Banff history, public art, and local characters, take a free one-hour **Off the Beaten Path Walking Tour** (403/762-8421, www.banfflakelouise.com, noon and 3pm Tues.-Wed. and Fri.-Sun. early July-Aug.), departing from Banff Avenue Square (200 block of Banff Ave.).

Canmore

Just 16 miles (25 kilometers) southeast of the town of Banff and 65 miles (105 kilometers) due west of Calgary, Canmore is a quieter alternative to staying within Banff National Park. You're close enough to make day trips to all the park sights, and the town, with a population of 13,000, has attractions of its own, particularly for outdoor enthusiasts. With several good restaurants, it's worth a stop for a meal, even if you're only passing through.

Surrounded by mountains, Canmore is known for the Three Sisters, a triad of peaks named Faith, Charity, and Hope, also called the Big, Middle, and Little Sisters, that you can see from around the town. The Three Sisters Mountain is the highest in the Canmore area, with Big Sister rising to 9,632 feet (2,936 meters).

Sights and Activities

Downtown Canmore has several art galleries to browse, including **Carter-Ryan Gallery and Live Art Venue** (705 Main St., 403/621-1000, www.carter-ryan.com, 11am-6pm Sun.-Fri., 10am-6pm Sat.), which shows the colorful paintings and the soapstone carvings of aboriginal

Winter Fun in the Canadian Rockies

Most road-trippers travel through the Canadian Rockies from spring through fall, when the roads are usually snow-free and the weather is temperate. But for adventurous travelers and snow-lovers, a winter holiday in the Canadian Rockies can be wondrous.

Downhill Skiing and Snowboarding

Banff has one of the longest ski seasons in North America, typically beginning in mid-November and extending until late May. Three ski areas are within the boundaries of Banff National Park: Mount Norquay, Sunshine Village, and Lake Louise. Farther north, you can ski at Marmot Basin in Jasper National Park.

The first ski area in the Canadian Rockies, family-friendly **Mount Norquay** (844/667-7829, www.banffnorquay.com) is closest to the town of Banff, just 15-minutes' drive up the winding Mount Norquay Road.

Much larger **Sunshine Village** (877/542-2633, www.skibanff.com), with 145 runs across more than 3,300 acres (1,335 hectares) of skiable terrain, has one of Canada's longest ski seasons, lasting from early November through late May. The ski area also has Canada's first heated chairlift. Sunshine Village is 11 miles (18 kilometers) from town.

The **Lake Louise Ski Resort** (877/956-8473, www.skilouise.com), just two miles (3.3 kilometers) from the Samson Mall, is the biggest of the Canadian Rockies winter sports resorts, with 145 runs and plenty of off-piste skiing across its 4,200 skiable acres (1,700 hectares). The season generally runs from early November to early May.

Jasper's **Marmot Basin** (866/952-3816, www.skimarmot.com) has the highest base elevation of all Canada's winter sports resorts, so you can usually ski or snowboard from early November until early May. The 86 runs take you across 1,675 acres (678 hectares) of terrain.

Other Winter Activities

Cross-country skiers have lots of terrain to explore in Banff and Lake Louise. The **Castle Junction** area along the Bow Valley Parkway has 5.4 miles (8.7 kilometers) of easy groomed trails, while closer to town, the popular **Spray River Trail West** starts at the Fairmont Banff Springs Hotel and follows the rolling river valley. Beginning at the Lake Minnewanka parking lot, the **Cascade Valley Trail** is another local favorite. At **Lake Louise,** you can ski along the lakeshore and, when the lake itself has frozen solid, directly onto the lake.

You can usually go **snowshoeing** in the Canadian Rockies between late December and early April. When **Tunnel Mountain Drive** in the town of Banff closes to vehicles in the winter, it becomes a snowshoeing route, with views of Cascade Mountain. This trail also connects with the **Surprise Corner to Hoodoos Viewpoint Trail.**

Want to try **dogsledding?** Based in Canmore, both **Snowy Owl Sled Dog Tours** (403/678-4369, www.snowyowltours.com) and **Howling Dog Tours** (403/678-9588, www.howlingdogtours.com) offer several different dogsledding tours, including transportation from most Banff hotels. **Kingmik Dog Sled Tours** (403/763-7789, www.kingmikdogsledtours.com) runs excursions from Lake Louise.

artist Jason Carter. Also on view is artwork from the children's book series, *Who Is Boo: The Terrific Tales of One Trickster Rabbit,* which Carter illustrated and author Bridget Ryan wrote.

Learn about the brewing process, and sample the suds, at Canmore's microbrewery, the **Grizzly Paw Brewing Company** (310 Old Canmore Rd., 403/678-2487, www.thegrizzlypaw.com, tasting room 11am-5pm Sun.-Thurs., 11am-7pm Fri.-Sat., tours 3pm Thurs., 1pm, 2:30pm, and 4pm Fri.-Sun.). You can also taste the brews, along with burgers, salads, and other pub fare, at their downtown **restaurant** (622 8th St., 403/678-9983, 11am-10pm Sun.-Thurs., 11am-11pm Fri.-Sat., mains $14-18).

An unusual, if commercial, attraction is the **Ammonite Factory** (106 Bow Meadows Cres., 403/678-1786, www.ammonite-factory.com, 10am-5pm Mon.-Sat., noon-5pm Sun., tours 10am, 11am, and noon daily). Alberta's official gemstone, ammonite is a multicolored stone that comes from a fossilized snail-like sea creature. Located 2.5 miles (4 kilometers) southeast of the town center, the storefront has exhibits about the stone's origin, mining, and processing, and sells jewelry and other products made from the stone.

Sweep over the Canmore region and get a close-up view of the Three Sisters peaks on an excursion with **Alpine Heli Tours** (91 Bow Valley Trail, 403/678-4802, www.alpinehelicopter.com). Tour options include the 12-minute Three Sisters Peaks Tour ($124); the 25-minute Royal Canadian Tour ($249), which starts with the Three Sisters tour route, before flying through the Goat Range Pass and along the Sundance Range in Banff National Park; and the 30-minute Mount Assiniboine Glacier Tour ($289), which adds views of the 11,870-foot (3,611-meter) peak dubbed the "Matterhorn of the Canadian Rockies."

Sports and Recreation

Among Canmore's numerous hiking routes, a favorite is the **Grassi Lakes Trail,** which climbs up to two turquoise ponds. This 2.4-mile (3.8-kilometer) round-trip trail, with an elevation gain of 820 feet (250 meters), has two forks. The easier branch ascends gently along a gravel road, but the more difficult route, a forest trail with a short steep section near the top, has far better views. The trailhead is off Highway 742, west of town.

When you're ready to play indoors, head for **Elevation Place** (700 Railway Ave., 403/678-8920, www.elevationplace.ca, pool only adults $8, seniors and

students $6, ages 12-17 $5, ages 3-11 $4, full facility adults $15, seniors and students $12, ages 12-17 $8, ages 3-11 $5), Canmore's modern public recreation center, which has a swimming pool, fitness equipment, and a climbing gym.

Festivals and Events

Alberta's longest-running folk fest, the **Canmore Folk Music Festival** (403/678-2524, www.canmorefolkfestival.com, Aug.) is a weekend-long showcase of folk, world, blues, and roots music that began back in 1978.

Accommodations

Most of Canmore's hotels and motels are on or near the Bow Valley Trail (Hwy. 1A), which parallels Highway 1 east of the city's downtown.

Under $150

From the exterior, the **Rocky Mountain Ski Lodge** (1711 Bow Valley Trail, 403/678-5445 or 800/665-6111, www.rockyski.ca, $99-169 d) says "basic motel," but the five buildings that make up this well-maintained older lodging have a range of comfortable, updated rooms. Of the 83 units, 41 are standard guest rooms with mini fridges and included Wi-Fi, while 42 are apartment-style, such as lofts ($169-219) with a bedroom upstairs and living room below, and two-bedroom units ($179-229). Some rooms have microwaves; others have full kitchens. The owner, a former Swiss Guide and mountaineer, has outfitted the lobby with ski team memorabilia and free coffee. The family-friendly property has a hot tub, a sauna, and guest laundry; outside are barbecues, picnic tables, and a kids play area.

$150-250

The motto at **Silver Creek Lodge** (1818 Mountain Ave., 403/678-4242 or 877/598-4242, www.silvercreekcanmore.ca, $150-260 d, 2-bedroom suite $219-325), which is far more upscale that the chain motels

Canmore

To Banff

MOUNTAIN AVE

1A

SILVER CREEK
LODGE

PALLISER TRAIL

BOW VALLEY

LARCH AVE

SILVER TIP RD

ROCKY MOUNTAIN
SKI LODGE

17TH ST

SILVER TIP DR

CRAZYWEED
KITCHEN

FAIRHOLME DR

TRANS-CANADA HWY

TRAIL

COMMUNITEA
CAFÉ

RAILWAY AVE

CANMORE
GENERAL HOSPITAL

PD3 BY BLAKE

CPR TRESTLE
BRIDGE

CANMORE MOUNTAIN
FARMERS MARKET

GOURLAY'S
PHARMACY

TOURISM
CANMORE

SHOPPERS
DRUG MART

BENCHLANDS TR

THE IRON GOAT
PUB & GRILL

CAFÉ BOOKS

GRANDE ROCKIES
RESORT

REXALL

6TH AVE

ELEVATION
PLACE

MAIN ST

GRIZZLY PAW
BREWING COMPANY

COUGAR CREEK DR

CARTER-RYAN
GALLERY

GRIZZLY PAW
BREWING COMPANY

To
Grassi Lakes Trail

Bow River

Centennial
Park

5TH ST

TRANS-CANADA HWY

THREE SISTERS DR

RUNDLE DR

8TH AVE

7TH AVE

6TH AVE

5TH AVE

4TH AVE

1A

SOLARA
RESORT & SPA

SPRAY LAKES RD

2ND

1ST ST

Millennium
Park

Spring Creek

Policeman's Creek

BOW VALLEY TRAIL

Cougar Creek

ALPINE
HELI TOURS

Quarry
Lake

Canmore
Creek

To
Ammonite Factory and
Grotto Canyon

THREE SISTERS DR

LAWRENCE GRASSI RIDGE

To
Calgary

WILSON WAY

Bow River

THREE SISTERS PKWY

0   0.25 mi

0   0.25 km

© AVALON TRAVEL

that surround it, is "Mountain Zen," and it feels like a quiet oasis with vaguely Asian decor. Most of the 70 condo units are one- or two-bedroom suites with dark wood furnishings, electric fireplaces, sleep sofas in the living rooms, full kitchens with stone floors, soaker tubs, and washer-dryers; a few are smaller studios with kitchenettes. Each suite has its own Wi-Fi unit. A small interior fitness room has weights and two cardio machines; three outdoor hot tubs, a steam room, and a day spa give you more pampering options. The **Wild Orchid Asian Bistro** (403/679-2029, www.wildorchidbistro. com, 5pm-10pm Mon.-Tues. and Thurs., 4pm-10pm Fri.-Sun., mains $15-29) serves sushi and other Asian-influenced small plates.

The kids might dive right down the water slide at the ★ **Grande Rockies Resort** (901 Mountain St., 403/678-8880 or 877/223-3398, www.granderockies. com, $189-389 d, 2-bedroom suite $269-449), where the two indoor pools help make this urban-style property fun for families. Mom and Dad may head for the hot tub, compact third-floor fitness room, or small day spa, which offers couples massage. In the all-suite main building, the contemporary one- and two-bedroom units have full kitchens with granite countertops, stainless steel appliances, and washer-dryers. On the lobby level, **Habitat Restaurant and Bar** (403/679-5228, breakfast 7am-11pm daily, dinner 5pm-9:30pm Wed.-Sun., mains $26-36) serves a breakfast buffet ($14.95) with salads, seafood, and Alberta meats in the evening. If you don't need as much space, the adjacent annex has economical studios, more like standard hotel rooms, furnished in the same modern style but without kitchen facilities. Rates include Wi-Fi and parking.

Over $250

At swank **Solara Resort & Spa** (187 Kananaskis Way, 403/609-3600 or 877/778-5617, www.solararesort.ca,

$229-509 d, 2-bedroom suite $279-599, 3-bedroom suite $439-749), the one- to three-bedroom suites sprawl across three stone and wood buildings, with an outdoor courtyard in the center of the complex. The rustic-luxe suites have full modern kitchens with a wine fridge to chill your vino, fireplaces, and washer-dryers; the premium units on the top floor have vaulted ceilings. For your workout, visit the spacious and airy fitness center, with a sauna, steam room, and hot tub, as well as a full-service spa. You can go adventuring on the complimentary bikes, while younger guests can play in the indoor splash park or wading pool (there's no regular swimming pool). An on-site movie theater shows films on the weekends.

Food
Groceries and Markets
The **Canmore Mountain Farmer's Market** (7th Ave., www.tourismcanmore.com, 10am-6pm Thurs. mid-June-mid-Oct.) sells fresh produce, baked goods, prepared foods, and crafts.

Cafés, Bakeries, and Light Bites
With a long lists of teas and a vegetarian-friendly menu, bright and airy **Communitea Café** (117-1001 6th Ave., 403/688-2233, www.thecommunitea. com, 9am-6pm daily, mains $6-14) can refresh you from morning till late afternoon. For breakfast, you might try the apple berry crumble (fruit compote topped with homemade granola); a *panini,* like the Chinook (wild smoked salmon, scrambled eggs, avocado, spinach, and red pepper spread) or the Elvis (peanut butter, banana, honey, and bacon); or the Big Breakfast Bowl (eggs, avocado, quinoa, tomato, and yams on a bed of greens topped with hummus and salsa). Lunchtime brings salads, sandwiches, wraps, and rice bowls.

Café Books (100-826 Main St., 403/678-0908, www.cafebooks.ca, 9:30am-7pm Sun.-Thurs., 9:30am-9pm

Fri.-Sat.) sells new and used titles and also has a **tearoom** across the hall from the main shop.

Contemporary .

Fasten your seat belts, diners. Canmore's coolest dining spot is ★ **PD3 by Blake** (806 Main St., 403/675-3663, www.blake-canmore.com, May-Oct.), in a silver 1960s double-decker bus parked in a courtyard off Main Street. It's actually two different restaurants. **PD3 Street** (noon-late Thurs.-Sun., 5pm-late Mon., mains $11-17), a take-out window with adjacent picnic tables, serves eclectic Asian-inspired street food, like the Backpacker, a tempura shrimp taco piled with Vietnamese slaw and dressed with peanut sauce, or the Ichi-bun, a pork and prawn patty slathered with turmeric mayo and Sriracha. A sit-down dining room upstairs inside the bus, **PD3 Upper Saloon** (lunch noon-5pm daily, dinner 5pm-late daily, lunch prix-fixe $30-35, dinner mains $17-43, prix-fixe $99) is even more adventurous; you

might find pork belly "candy," scallops with chorizo and hominy grits, or garlic-poached cauliflower steak with Korean chili paste and carrot puree.

Long considered Canmore's best restaurant, ★ **Crazyweed Kitchen** (1600 Railway Ave., 403/609-2530, www.crazyweed.ca, lunch 11:30am-3pm Thurs.-Sun., dinner 5pm-9:30pm Sun.-Thurs., 5pm-10pm Fri.-Sat., mains lunch $14-20, dinner $18-38) still charms with its inventive world-beat menu and relaxed "food is fun" vibe. You can make a meal of small plates, like the house-made *lab-neh* with shaved fennel and kalamata olives or crispy kung pao chicken wings, or a pizza from the wood-fired oven, though then you'd miss out on mains, like the miso-crusted sablefish with wilted spinach or the pan-fried pork chop served with a parmesan potato cake. Either way, save room for sweets, like the warm chocolate and *medjool* date cake or the Passionfruit Ice Box, a frozen tropical fruit treat topped with brûlée meringue.

Canmore's coolest restaurant is PD3 by Blake, set up in this vintage double-decker bus.

Pub Fare

Perched on a hill east of the city center, **The Iron Goat Pub & Grill** (703 Benchlands Trail, 403/609-0222, www.irongoat.ca, 11am-11pm daily, mains $14-36) has a vast but perpetually packed patio with panoramic views of the Three Sisters and other nearby mountains. The menu has updated pub fare, including the always-requested chipotle-mango duck wings, meatloaf, pizza, and plenty of craft beer on tap.

Information and Services

Tourism Canmore (907A 7th Ave., 855/678-1295, www.tourismcanmore.com, 8:30am-5pm daily) runs the helpful downtown Visitor Information Centre that provides details about the region.

Medical Services

You can get 24-hour emergency medical attention at **Canmore General Hospital** (1100 Hospital Pl., 403/678-5536, www.albertahealthservices.ca).

If you need pharmacy services in Canmore, try **Gourlay's Pharmacy** (120-1151 Sidney St., 403/678-5288, www.gourlayspharmacy.ca, 9am-6pm Mon.-Fri., 10am-5pm Sat.), **Rexall** (901 8th St., 403/678-4301, www.rexall.ca, 9am-6pm Mon.-Sat.), or **Shoppers Drug Mart** (933 Railway Ave., 403/678-8750, www.shoppersdrugmart.ca, 9am-10pm daily).

Getting Around

Highway 1 runs through Canmore on its way between Calgary and Banff. In Canmore's compact and walkable downtown, numbered streets run east-west; 8th Street is the main street. Numbered avenues run north-south.

By Bus

Roam Transit (403/762-0606, www.roam-transit.com) runs regular buses between Canmore and Banff (6am-9:50pm Mon.-Wed., 6am-10:50pm Thurs.-Fri., 9am-9:50pm Sat., 9am-7:50pm Sun., one-way adults and ages 13-18 $6, seniors and ages 6-12 $3, day pass adults and ages 13-18 $15, seniors and ages 6-12 $7.50).

By Bicycle

You can ride your bike between Canmore and Banff along the paved **Rocky Mountain Legacy Trail** (403/762-1556, www.pc.gc.ca). It's 14 miles (22 kilometers) each way. If you don't want to ride both ways, you can put your bike on the Roam Transit bus for your return trip.

Lake Louise

Lake Louise is both a famous body of water and the name of the nearby village, located less than 45 minutes' drive from the town of Banff.

Like Banff, the village of Lake Louise, which has fewer than 1,200 residents, is within Banff National Park. However, the village isn't a quaint community that you can stroll and explore. The area's commercial center is the decidedly not

One Day in Lake Louise

Start your Lake Louise day not at the famous lake that gives the village its name but at another strikingly beautiful body of water: **Moraine Lake.** Located 8.7 miles (14 kilometers) from Lake Louise Village, Moraine Lake can get so busy during the day that Parks Canada closes the Moraine Lake Road, so you'll want to get there early, ahead of the crowds. Take a leisurely stroll along the lakeshore, then **rent a canoe** to go for a paddle.

When you leave Moraine Lake, **Lake Louise** should be your next stop. Take your lakeside photos, then if you're up to a long hike, follow the 6.6-mile (10.6-kilometer) round-trip **Plain of Six Glaciers Trail** that takes you to the far side of

Lake Louise and between several glacier-topped peaks. Have lunch and a pot of tea at the remote **Plain of Six Glaciers Teahouse.** Alternatively, it's a shorter hike up to the **Lake Agnes Teahouse,** another scenic setting for a sandwich or a snack.

After your hike, change clothes and have a cocktail in the Lakeside Lounge at the **Fairmont Chateau Lake Louise,** because you can't have enough opportunities to admire the lake. Then enjoy a leisurely dinner nearby at the **Mount Fairview Dining Room at Deer Lodge** for modern mountain fare, from house-made charcuterie to the triple chocolate mousse. You've earned it.

quaint Samson Mall, a cluster of shops off Highway 1, including the visitors center, a grocery, a liquor store, and several cafés. Nearby, along Village Road, are a number of hotels.

Across the Bow River is where Lake Louise gets interesting. From here, Lake Louise Drive takes you to the famous lake, with a few lodgings and restaurants. Moraine Lake Road (open spring-fall only) leads to the area's other notable body of water: Moraine Lake.

★ Lake Louise

The main sight at **Lake Louise** is, of course, the lake, the brilliant blue glacier-fed body of water surrounded by mountain peaks. The ice-topped mountain that you see on the opposite side of the lake is the 11,365-foot (3,464-meter) Mount Victoria, which sits on the Continental Divide between B.C. and Alberta, with the Victoria Glacier on its Lake Louise-facing side. Lake Louise is just 1.5 miles (2.5 kilometers) long and 295 feet (90 meters) deep.

The first non-aboriginal person to see the lake, Thomas Wilson, a Canadian Pacific Railway employee whose Stoney First Nation guides brought him to the

lakeshore in 1882, named it Emerald Lake for the color of its water. It was later renamed to honor Queen Victoria's fourth daughter, Princess Louise Caroline Alberta. The blue-green lake in nearby Yoho National Park, which Wilson also named, kept the Emerald Lake title.

The castle-like structure on the lakeshore is the stately **Fairmont Chateau Lake Louise** (www.fairmont.com). Built by the Canadian Pacific Railway as a log chalet in the 1890s (a fire destroyed the original building), the hotel has been rebuilt and expanded, with several wings dating from 1912 to 2004. It now has more than 500 guest rooms.

In summer, Parks Canada staff offer free two-hour **Lake Louise Lakeshore Guided Walks** (10am Thurs. July-Aug.), introducing you to the history and ecology of the area. They post a Parks Canada banner on the lakeshore to mark the meeting point.

The best times to visit Lake Louise are early in the morning (many people swear by the sunrise here) or late in the day. In July and August, try to avoid arriving between 10am and 4pm, when the parking lots can be a congested

Lake Louise and Vicinity

To Jasper National Park

To Skoki Lodge

ICEFIELDS PARKWAY

Pipestone

Herbert Lake

93

Whitehorn Mountain

Bow

River

Corral Creek

To Field and Golden

Kicking Horse Pass

(CLOSED TO VEHICLES)

1

1A

Ross Lake

LAKE LOUISE SKI RESORT

SEE "LAKE LOUISE" MAP

WHITEHORN RD

Lipalian Mtn

ALBERTA
BRITISH COLUMBIA

Mt Niblock

LAKE LOUISE

LITTLE BEEHIVE

Lake Agnes
LAKE AGNES TEA HOUSE

BIG BEEHIVE

Mt Whyte

Lake Louise

Louise Creek

LAKE LOUISE

93

Banff

National

Park

BOW VALLEY PARKWAY

PLAIN OF SIX GLACIERS TEA HOUSE

Fairview Mtn

Saddleback

MORAINE LAKE RD

Bow River

BOW VALLEY

Mt Victoria 3,459m

Victoria Glacier

Mt Aberdeen

Creek

1

TRANS-CANADA HIGHWAY

Abbot Pass

The Mitre

Giant Steps

Paradise Creek

Paradise Valley

Lake Annette

To Lake O'Hara

Mt Lefroy

Lake Oesa

Bow Range

Mt Temple

Valley of the Ten Peaks

Creek

To Banff

0   1 mi
0   1 km

Hungabee Mountain

Pinnacle Mtn

Sentinel Pass

Larch Valley

MORAINE LAKE LODGE

Moraine Creek

Panorama Ridge

Wenkchemna Peak

Eiffel Peak

Eiffel Lake

Moraine Lake

Mt Biddle

Yoho National Park

Neptuak Mtn

Wenkchemna Glacier

MORAINE LAKE

Mt Babel

Consolation Lakes

Deltaform Mtn

Mt Tuzo

Mt Allen

Mt Bowlen

Mt Little

Mt Fay

Taylor Lake

Kootenay National Park

Quadra Mountain

© AVALON TRAVEL

Lake Louise

© AVALON TRAVEL

nightmare, and sightseers jockey for position to take their photos in front of the famous lake. In most years, the lake is at least partly frozen from October or November into May.

Despite the crowds, Lake Louise remains a must-see on any Canadian Rockies trip. Whether you go hiking or canoeing, or simply sit by the lake, it's one of the region's most stunning spots.

Hiking

Walk even a short distance along the **Lake Louise Lakeshore Trail** and you'll get away from the hordes who cluster in front of the Fairmont hotel. The flat trail follows the lakeshore for 1.25 miles (2 kilometers). You can't circle the lake on foot, so return the way you came.

The short but steep **Fairview Lookout Trail** starts behind the Lake Louise boathouse and climbs up to viewpoints over the lake. This trail is 1.25 miles (2 kilometers) round trip, with an elevation gain of 328 feet (100 meters).

Several other hiking trails start from the lakeshore, and they can also take you away from the crowds and offer different views of the lake and surrounding mountains. If you live close to sea level, you may notice the elevation when you're hiking near Lake Louise. The village is located at 5,033 feet (1,530 meters), and many trails climb from the lakeshore into the mountains. Take it slow until you're acclimated.

Hike to the Lake Agnes Teahouse

One of the most popular hikes at Lake Louise is the **Lake Agnes Trail,** which takes you through the forests above the lakeshore and past small Mirror Lake. Your destination is the **Lake Agnes Teahouse** (www.lakeagnesteahouse. com, 9am-6pm daily early June-early Sept., 10am-5:30pm daily early Sept.- mid-Oct., mains $9-15, tea $6-7.50, pastries $3-7, cash only), a rustic log cabin overlooking Lake Agnes, where you can have soup and a sandwich (the homemade bread is excellent), or a pastry with a pot of tea (the teahouse carries more than 100 varieties).

This moderate 4.2-mile (6.8-kilometer) round-trip trail does climb steadily, gaining 1,263 feet (385 meters) of elevation between the lakeshore and the teahouse.

Once you arrive at the teahouse, expect to wait a while for your lunch, even after you get a table; the kitchen is small and the crowds can be large.

Beyond Lake Agnes, you can climb the switchback trail to **Big Beehive,** a beehive-shaped crag. The trail gains 443 feet (135 meters) of elevation in one mile (1.6 kilometers) from Lake Agnes. Your reward for the climb is a panorama across Lake Louise.

Another side trip takes you to **Little Beehive,** once the site of a fire lookout, with views of the Bow Valley. This trail is 0.6 miles (1 kilometer) each way, with a 355-foot (105-meter) elevation gain from Lake Agnes.

From Lake Agnes, you can continue to the Plain of Six Glaciers Teahouse, following the **Highline Trail** between them. This route is nine miles (14.6 kilometers)

Top to bottom: Big Beehive near Lake Agnes; Lake Agnes Teahouse, a popular hiking destination; on the Plain of Six Glaciers Trail.

in total, starting and ending on the Lake Louise shore.

Hike to the Plain of Six Glaciers

The **Plain of Six Glaciers Trail** is an intermediate-level 6.6-mile (10.6-kilometer) round-trip route that takes you to the far side of Lake Louise, then up and between mountain peaks that are topped with glaciers year-round. This trail has an elevation gain of 1,198 feet (365 meters).

The trail goes to the ★ **Plain of Six Glaciers Teahouse** (9am-6pm daily July-Aug., 9am-5pm daily late June and Sept.-mid-Oct., mains $9-13, tea $3-4, pastries $5-7.50), where you can enjoy tea, snacks, or a light lunch; the teahouse is known for its substantial slabs of rich chocolate cake. Swiss guides working for the Canadian Pacific Railway built the stone-and-wood teahouse in 1926.

If you want to go farther, take the two-mile (3-kilometer) round-trip trail, with an elevation gain of 165 feet (50 meters), to the **Abbot Pass Viewpoint,** where you can look down onto the Lower Victoria Glacier and look up to Abbot Hut, one of the highest buildings in Canada.

For an excellent full-day hike, you can walk to both the Lake Agnes and Plain of Six Glaciers Teahouses, following the **Highline Trail** between them. This route is nine miles (14.6 kilometers) in total.

Canoeing

A serene way to explore the lake is by canoe. You can rent a canoe at the **Fairmont Chateau Lake Louise Boathouse** (8:30am-8pm daily July-Aug., 11am-7pm daily June and Sept., 30 minutes $55, 1 hour $65) on the lakeshore.

Horseback Riding

With **Brewster Adventures** (403/762-5454, www.brewsteradventures.com), you can visit Lake Louise's historic teahouses on horseback on either the three-hour **Lake Agnes Teahouse Half-Day Ride** (9am and 1pm daily late May-mid-Oct., $150) or the four-hour **Plain of**

Moraine Lake

Six Glaciers Teahouse Ride (9am and 1pm daily late May-mid-Oct., $150).

Getting There

From Highway 1 or Lake Louise Village, follow Lake Louise Drive 2.6 miles (4.2 kilometers) to the lake. Parking is available is several lots that are tiered above the lake. At busy times, these lots fill, and you may need to park along the road and walk back to the lake.

In the summer, and on other busy days, **Mountain Park Transportation** (403/522-2525, one-way adults $5, ages 3-12 $3) runs a shuttle that can take you between the Samson Mall, Lake Louise Campground, and the Fairmont Chateau Lake Louise. Call or check at the **Lake Louise Visitor Information Centre** for the shuttle schedule.

★ Moraine Lake

Glacier-fed **Moraine Lake,** in the Valley of the Ten Peaks, is another impossibly blue body of water surrounded by sharp mountain peaks and glaciers. It's a beautiful setting for a hike or a leisurely canoe paddle.

As at Lake Louise, the best times to visit Moraine Lake are in the early morning or early evening. Come at sunrise if you can, or at least before 11am; otherwise, you might consider waiting until after 5pm when the crowds thin, especially if you're visiting in the peak months of July and August. The road to the lake is typically open only mid-May to mid-October.

The **Snowshoe Café** (8am-7pm daily June-Sept.) at the Moraine Lake Lodge is a quick-service café selling sandwiches, pastries, drinks, and ice cream. In the evenings, the lodge's lake-view **Walter Wilcox Dining Room** (5:30pm-9pm daily June-Sept., mains $30-49) accommodates hotel guests first, but nonguests can dine here if space is available.

Hiking

Several hiking trails begin in the Moraine Lake area. Follow the easy **Lakeshore Trail** for up to one mile (1.5 kilometers) along the lake.

The **Consolation Lakes Trail,** 3.6 miles (5.8 kilometers) round-trip with an elevation gain of 213 feet (65 meters), takes you into alpine meadows with views of the Quadra Glacier.

On the **Larch Valley/Minnestimma Lakes Trail,** you hike into a larch forest above Moraine Lake, with great views of the Ten Peaks. It's a 5.3-mile (8.6 kilometer) round-trip hike with a 1,755-foot (535-meter) elevation gain.

Branching off from the Larch Valley Trail, the moderate **Eiffel Lake Trail,** which is seven miles (11.2 kilometers) round-trip with an elevation gain of 1,213 feet (370 meters), leads up to an alpine lake with panoramas across the Valley of the Ten Peaks.

Note that Parks Canada issues seasonal **bear restrictions** for many of the Moraine Lake trails. During months when bears can be in the area, hikers must walk in groups of at least four and carry bear spray. Talk with park staff at the **Lake Louise Visitor Information Centre** (Samson Mall, 403/522-3833) or check the trail status on the website of **Parks Canada** (www.pc.gc.ca).

Canoeing

One of the most peaceful ways to explore this scenic lake is by canoe. Moraine Lake Lodge rents **canoes** (10am-4:30pm daily June-Sept., $55 per hour) from a lakeside dock.

Getting There

From Highway 1 or Lake Louise Village, follow Lake Louise Drive to the Moraine Lake turnoff and continue onto Moraine Lake Road. It's 8.7 miles (14 kilometers) from Lake Louise Village to Moraine Lake.

On busy summer days, the crowds at the lake can grow overwhelming. At that point, which can happen regularly in late morning and early afternoon, Parks Canada restricts traffic on Moraine Lake Road, preventing cars from entering the road until other cars leave the area.

Mountain Park Transportation (403/522-2525, round-trip adults $25, ages 3-12 $12) runs a seasonal shuttle that can take you to Moraine Lake from the Samson Mall, Lake Louise Campground, or the Fairmont Chateau Lake Louise. Call or check at the **Lake Louise Visitor Information Centre** for the shuttle schedule.

Lake Louise Gondola

From spring through fall, you can ride the **Lake Louise Gondola** (Whitehorn Dr., 403/522-3555 or 877/956-8473, www. lakelouisegondola.com, 9am-4pm daily mid-May-mid-June, 8:30am-5:30pm daily mid-June-July, 8:30am-6pm daily Aug.-early Sept., 10am-4pm daily early Sept.-mid-Oct., adults $31.95, ages 6-15 $15.95) at the Lake Louise ski resort to take in the views over the mountains, go hiking, visit a wildlife center, or have a

wildflowers near the Lake Louise Gondola

drink or a meal overlooking the peaks. You might even spot a grizzly bear.

Scan the meadows and woods for wildlife as you take the 14-minute ride up to an elevation of 6,850 feet (2,088 meters). In summer, grizzly and black bears come to forage for dandelions, berries, and other edibles along the slopes near the lift. You might also spot cougars, mountain goats, deer, wolves, or bighorn sheep. Check the calendar in the gondola ticket office to find out what animals the staff or other guests have recently seen.

Wildlife Interpretive Centre

A short walk from the top of the gondola, the **Wildlife Interpretive Centre** (free with gondola ticket) has exhibits about bears and other creatures, including elk, moose, bighorn sheep, deer, gray wolves, and mountain goats, that live in the region. Staff offer **interpretive programs** (10am, noon, and 2pm daily) about the animals and also lead **guided walks,** including a daily 45-minute "Trail of the

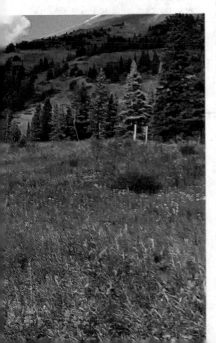

Great Bear" walk (on the hour 9am-5pm daily, adults and children over age 4 $6), about bear behavior and safety, plus tips on what to do if you see a bear.

In the same building, with a lovely mountain-view patio, the **Whitehorn Bistro** (10am-3pm daily early June-late June, 10am-4:30pm daily late June-July, 10am-5pm daily Aug.-early Sept., 10:30am-3pm daily early Sept.-mid-Oct., mains $21-27) serves upscale plates from salads and burgers to pheasant or rabbit fricassee with tagliatelle, along with craft beer and creative cocktails.

Hiking

Several hiking trails begin at the top of the gondola. A 1.1-mile (1.7-kilometer) round-trip loop takes you to the **Kicking Horse Viewpoint,** at an elevation of 7,497 feet (2,285 meters). A 2.1-mile (3.4-kilometer) round-trip trail leads to the **Ptarmigan Valley Viewpoint,** at 7,930 feet (2,417 meters).

Since bears and other wildlife frequent the mountain's lower slopes, you aren't allowed to hike in this area, so you have to begin your hike at the upper gondola station. Even on the upper trails, gondola staff recommend that you don't hike alone and suggest traveling in groups of four.

Skiing and Snowboarding

In winter, **Lake Louise Ski Resort** (877/956-8473, www.skilouise.com, 9am-4pm daily early Nov.-early May, full-day adults $92, seniors and ages 13-17 $72, ages 6-12 $35, under age 6 free) is the largest in the Canadian Rockies, with 145 runs and additional off-piste skiing across its 4,200 skiable acres (1,700 hectares).

Getting There

The gondola base is two miles (3.3 kilometers) from Lake Louise Village, about a five-minute drive. Take Lake Louise Drive across Highway 1 toward the entrance to the Bow Valley Parkway. Follow

Bears!

A highlight of a Canadian Rockies road trip is spotting local wildlife. Banff National Park is home to 53 species of mammals, and you'll likely see deer, bighorn sheep, and plenty of inquisitive squirrels as you explore the Banff and Lake Louise areas. If you're lucky, you might also catch a glimpse of larger mammals, like elk, cougars, or bears.

Two different bear species live in the Canadian Rockies: grizzlies and black bears. It's not the color that determines the bear type, though. While grizzlies are typically brown, their fur can range from almost blond to black, and black bears can be black, brown, blond, even nearly white.

One of the most noticeable differences between the two species is that grizzly bears have a prominent hump on their backs. It's a mass of muscle that looks like a large bump between their shoulders.

Approximately 20,000 grizzly bears currently live in western Canada, with roughly three-quarters in British Columbia and the remainder in western Alberta, Yukon, and the Northwest Territories. Parks Canada estimates that just 65 grizzlies reside within Banff National Park. Jasper National Park has a grizzly population of about 109, Yoho has 11 to 15, and Kootenay National Park has 9 to 16.

Black bears are much more common across North America, with an estimated Canadian population of more than 380,000, although they're somewhat less frequently seen in Banff National Park, where Parks Canada calculates that 20 to 40 black bears live. Among the other Rocky Mountain national parks, Jasper's black bear population is about 90, Yoho's is 20 to 50, and Kootenay's is 30 to 50.

Where to Learn More

At Lake Louise, ride the **Lake Louise Gondola** (403/522-3555 or 877/956-8473, www.lakelouisegondola.com) up to the mountainside **Wildlife Interpretive Centre** for exhibits, presentations, and guided hikes about bears and other wildlife.

Near Golden, B.C., the **Grizzly Bear Interpretive Centre at Kicking Horse Mountain Resort** (250/439-5425 or 866/754-5425, http://kickinghorseresort.com) houses an orphaned grizzly bear and offers regular interpretive tours where you can learn more about bears and their habits.

In Vancouver, bears live at the **Grouse Mountain Refuge for Endangered Wildlife** (604/980-9311, www.grouse-mountain.com), which offers wildlife education programs.

In central B.C., you can check out wolves, coyotes, moose, elk, eagles, owls, and even the rare white Kermode or "Spirit" bear, at the **B.C. Wildlife Park** (9077 Dallas Dr., Kamloops, 250/573-3242, www.bcwildlife.org).

---

the signs for the Lake Louise Ski Resort onto Whitehorn Drive.

You can catch a **free shuttle** to the gondola base from the Lake Louise hotels or the Samson Mall. Call or check the gondola website for the shuttle pick-up schedule.

Accommodations and Camping
Under $150

Lake Louise doesn't have any really cheap beds, but the least expensive accommodations are at the **HI-Lake Louise Alpine Centre** (203 Village Rd., 403/522-2201 or 866/762-4122, www.hihostels.ca, $30-42 dorm, $92-140 d) in a post-and-beam lodge on a wooded lot. The dorms sleep four to six, in either female, male, or mixed rooms. The private rooms with shared baths come with either one double, two singles, or a bunk bed with a double and a single. You can also choose a private room with an en suite bath. Both Wi-Fi and parking are included. Common areas include two shared kitchens, a TV and games room, and a playroom for the kids. The hostel's **Bill Peyto's Café** (7:30am-9:30pm daily, mains breakfast $6-13, lunch and dinner $12-22) serves breakfast, lunch, and dinner.

$150-250

A simple, comfortable motel, the **Mountaineer Lodge** (101 Village Rd., 403/522-3844 or 855/556-8473, www.mountaineerlodge.com, $144-339 d) has 78 rooms and suites in two buildings. In the main lodge, guests can soak in the indoor hot tub or have complimentary coffee in the sitting room; the second structure is a two-story drive-up motel block, where a complimentary breakfast buffet is served. Handy for road trippers: Rooms in both buildings include mini fridges, microwaves, coffeemakers, and free Wi-Fi, and there's a guest laundry.

Spread over five buildings, the **Lake Louise Inn** (210 Village Rd., 403/522-3791 or 800/661-9237, www.lakelouiseinn.com, $139-375 d) has 247 guest rooms, ranging from basic doubles to more upscale hotel rooms to condo-style units with full kitchens, all with flat-screen TVs and Wi-Fi included. The main building, where the lobby, two restaurants, and a sports bar are located, has an indoor pool, a hot tub, and a small gym with several cardio machines. Three buildings have guest laundries. Because the rooms are all so different, ask for details or photos when you book.

The wood and stone **Deer Lodge** (109 Lake Louise Dr., 403/522-3991 or 800/661-1595, www.crmr.com, $159-369 d) was built in the 1920s, complete with a turret, a massive stone fireplace, and heavy wood beams. The compact guest rooms in the original building still have that rustic style, with no TVs; if you don't need frills, they're a good value. The newer wing's units are much larger and more contemporary, with cherry furnishings and modern baths. The lodge has Wi-Fi included in the rates and a guest laundry. Common spaces include a games room with a pool table, and best of all, a rooftop hot tub with glacier views. The 71-room lodge is just few minutes' walk from Lake Louise, so while you don't have lake vistas, you don't need your car to explore the lakeshore.

Over $250

Noted Canadian modernist architect Arthur Erikson (1924-2009) designed ★ **Moraine Lake Lodge** (Moraine Lake Rd., 403/522-3733 or 877/522-2777, www.morainelake.com, June-Sept., $425-755 d), which opened in 1991, with 33 guest rooms spread out between the main lodge and several townhouse-style blocks of wood-frame cabins along the shore of the Lake Louise area's other notable lake. Rooms have handmade log beds with down duvets, rustic furnishings, and wood floors; some units have wood-burning fireplaces. At this adult-oriented property, room rates include breakfast, canoe rentals, guided hikes with a staff naturalist, and evening interpretive programs. Dinners in the lake-view **Walter Wilcox Dining Room** (5:30pm-9pm daily, mains $30-49) might feature steelhead trout with smoked tomato chutney, Alberta beef tenderloin, or rack of venison with braised cabbage. The lodge operates off the grid, generating its own electricity; there's no air-conditioning, TVs, or phones, although Wi-Fi is included in the rates.

Originally built in 1942 and significantly expanded over the years, **The Post Hotel** (200 Pipestone Rd., 403/522-3989 or 800/661-1586, www.posthotel.com, $280-775 d) recalls an elegant ski lodge in the Alps, with an indoor saltwater pool, a hot tub, a fitness room, a guest library, and a full-service spa. Guests stay in 60 rooms, 29 suites, or 5 cabins, outfitted with simple traditional furnishings and complimentary Wi-Fi. Dining options include the deluxe **main dining room** (7am-11am, 11:30am-2pm, and 5pm-9pm daily, mains lunch $17-40, dinner $42-88), a fondue restaurant called **Fondue Stübli** (5pm-9pm daily, mains $85-130 for 2), and the more casual **Outpost Pub**

(4:30pm-midnight Mon.-Fri., noon-midnight Sat.-Sun., mains $17-20).

You can't stay closer to the famous lake than at the ★ **Fairmont Chateau Lake Louise** (111 Lake Louise Dr., 403/522-3511 or 866/540-4413, www.fairmont.com, $442-1,429 d, parking $25-30), a grand lakeside lodging. It's hard to imagine that this lavish lodge started life as a log chalet in the 1890s (the original building was destroyed in a fire). With several wings dating from 1912 to 2004, the 550 traditional rooms vary from petite doubles overlooking the grounds or surrounding mountains to expansive suites with views across the lake. The hotel has an indoor heated pool, a fitness center, and a spa, and staff can arrange guided hikes (half-day adults $49, ages 8-12 $24, full-day adults $69, ages 8-12 $34), voyageur canoe tours (adults $45, ages 8-12 $22), and a variety of other activities. You can even take the hotel dog for a stroll along the lakeshore (free). Dining outlets range from a 24-hour deli to a Swiss fondue restaurant to a contemporary lake-view dining room. It's a splurge, yes, but it's the only lodging directly on Lake Louise. If you're traveling outside the peak summer months, check their website for off-season specials.

Camping

Parks Canada runs two campgrounds in the Lake Louise area, 0.6 miles (1 kilometer) from the village and 2.5 miles (4 kilometers) from the lake. Both have washrooms with flush toilets and hot showers.

The seasonal **Lake Louise Tent Campground** (late May-late Sept., $27.40) has 206 sites for tent campers. At the **Lake Louise Trailer Campground** ($32.30), the 187 fully serviced sites are open to campers year-round.

You can make campsite **reservations** (877/737-3783, www.reservation.parks-canada.gc.ca) online or by phone for both Lake Louise campgrounds; reservations are strongly recommended for summer stays.

Fairmont Chateau Lake Louise

Food

Lake Louise does not have a tremendous range of food options, and nothing is inexpensive.

TIP: The major hotels all have high-end restaurants, but most also have pubs or casual dining spots that are more moderately priced.

Groceries and Markets

The **Village Market** (Samson Mall, 403/522-3894, 8:30am-9pm daily) sells basic groceries and picnic supplies.

Cafés, Bakeries, and Light Bites

Pick up coffee and breakfast-to-go or sandwiches for a lunchtime picnic at the tiny **Trailhead Café** (Samson Mall, 403/522-2006, 7am-6pm daily, mains $6-10).

Contemporary

Known for game meats, like bison and elk, the wood-beamed ★ **Mount Fairview Dining Room at Deer Lodge** (109 Lake

Louise Dr., 403/522-4202, www.crmr. com, 7am-11am and 6pm-9pm daily, mains breakfast $13-16, dinner $27-40) pleases patrons with contemporary dishes using mountain-region ingredients. Lunch is served in the log-walled **Caribou Lounge** (11am-10pm daily, mains $15-19) or out on the patio (June-Sept.). An excellent plate to share, at lunch or dinner, is the Rocky Mountain charcuterie platter, with air-dried buffalo, elk salami, smoked duck, game pâté, along with a cranberry relish and a unique pickled "mustard melon." Other options include a salad of duck confit, butternut squash, quinoa, and wild rice; roasted salmon with salsa verde; or caribou medallions with a yam and leek gratin.

If you want to eat by the lakeshore, the **Fairmont Chateau Lake Louise** (111 Lake Louise Dr., dining reservations 403/522-1601, www.fairmont.com) has several dining options. For a quick bite, the cafeteria-style **Chateau Deli** (open 24 hours) sells sandwiches, salads, and pastries. You can try Swiss fondue, wiener schnitzel, bratwurst, and other European classics at **The Walliser Stube** (6pm-9pm daily, mains $39-52). The hotel's main dining room, **The Fairview** (generally 6pm-9pm daily, call for seasonal hours, mains $36-48, 3-course prix fixe $85), prepares contemporary dishes like charred peach and kale salad with pickled radish, black garlic gnocchi, or beef tenderloin with king mushrooms. Like many Fairmont properties, Chateau Lake Louise also offers traditional **afternoon tea** (noon-3pm daily, $43).

Pub Fare

You don't have to be a hostel guest to eat at **Bill Peyto's Café** (203 Village Rd., 403/522-2200, www.hihostels.ca, 7:30am-9:30pm daily, mains breakfast $6-13, lunch and dinner $12-22), the easygoing family-friendly eatery at the HI-Lake Louise hostel. You just have to appreciate hearty pub grub, including burgers, wraps, chili, and pasta, at moderate (at least for a resort town) prices. Try the bison burger. In the morning, the café serves breakfast basics: eggs, pancakes, hot cereal.

Information and Services
Visitor Information

Both **Parks Canada** (www.pc.gc.ca) and **Banff-Lake Louise Tourism** (www.banfflakelouise.com) staff the **Lake Louise Visitor Information Centre** (Samson Mall, 403/522-3833, 9am-7pm daily mid-June-early Sept., 9am-5pm daily May-mid-June and early Sept.-mid-Oct., 9am-4:30pm Thurs.-Sun. mid-Oct.-Apr.). The visitors center also has free Wi-Fi as well as exhibits about the geology of the region, illustrating how its lakes and mountains came to be, and short films about the national park.

Even when the office is closed, you can check out maps and other area details posted on the information boards outside.

Medical Services

Lake Louise Medical Clinic (200 Hector Rd., 403/522-2184, www.llmc.ca, 9am-noon and 1:30pm-4:30pm Mon., Wed., and Fri.-Sat., 1pm-6pm Tues. and Thurs.), opposite the visitors center, can take care of minor medical issues. It offers urgent care services, if necessary, outside regular office hours. The closest hospital is in Banff.

Getting Around
By Car

Lake Louise is 35 miles (57 kilometers) northwest of the town of Banff, a 45-minute drive, and 17 miles (27 kilometers) east of Field, B.C., in the center of Yoho National Park, a one-hour drive. Highway 1 runs west from Lake Louise into B.C. or east toward Banff. The scenic Bow Valley Parkway is an alternate route between Banff and Lake Louise; it's a 30-mile (48-kilometer) drive. From Lake Louise, you can go north on the Icefields Parkway (Hwy. 93) to Jasper.

Once you arrive in Lake Louise Village, it's 2.6 miles (4.2 kilometers) along Lake Louise Drive to the lake itself. To Moraine Lake, follow Lake Louise drive to the Moraine Lake turn-off and continue on Moraine Lake Road. Moraine Lake Road is open only from mid-May to mid-October.

Car Rentals

National (Samson Mall, 403/522-3870, www.nationalcar.ca) rents cars in Lake Louise. You'll have more car rental options in Banff or Calgary.

By Shuttle Bus

Mountain Park Transportation (403/522-2525) runs a seasonal shuttle among the Samson Mall, Lake Louise Campground, Fairmont Chateau Lake Louise, and Moraine Lake. Call or check at the **Lake Louise Visitor Information Centre** for the shuttle schedule.

From the Village to Chateau Lake Louise, round-trip fares are adults $10, ages 3-12 $6. Between the Village and Moraine Lake, round-trip fares are adults $25, ages 3-12 $12. The shuttles accept cash only.

By Bike

If you're a fit cyclist, you can pedal from Lake Louise Village to Lake Louise (2.6 miles/4.2 kilometers) or to Moraine Lake (8.7 miles/14 kilometers). Use caution on these hilly, heavily traveled roads. **Wilson Mountain Sports** (Samson Mall, 201 Village Rd., 403/522-3636 or 866/929-3636, www.wmsll.com) rents bikes.

Sightseeing Tours

Brewster Travel Canada (403/762-6700 or 866/606-6700, www.brewster.ca) offers Lake Louise sightseeing tours (daily May-mid-Oct.) that include stops along the Bow Valley Parkway, lunch at the Fairmont Chateau Lake Louise, and free time to explore the lake. Tours run from Banff (9.5 hours, adults $83, ages 6-15 $42), Canmore (12 hours, adults $93, ages 6-15 $47), or Calgary (14 hours, adults $103, ages 6-15 $52). You can buy tickets online or in Banff at the **Explore Rockies Activity Centres** at the **Brewster Transportation Centre** (100 Gopher St., 800/760-6934, 7am-9pm daily), **Banff International Hotel** (333 Banff Ave., 403/760-3291, 10am-8pm Mon.-Thurs., 8:30am-8pm Fri.-Sun.), or **Cave and Basin** (311 Cave Ave., 403/760-3353, noon-4pm Wed.-Sun.).

Another Brewster Travel tour, **Mountain Lakes and Waterfalls** (daily May-mid-Oct.), includes time at Lake Louise, Moraine Lake, and Takakkaw Falls in Yoho National Park. You can start this tour in Lake Louise (5-6 hours, adults $83-93, ages 6-15 $42-47), Banff (8.5-9.5 hours, adults $123, ages 6-15 $62), Canmore (12 hours, adults $133, ages 6-15 $67), or Calgary (10.5-14 hours, adults $143, ages 6-15 $72). Except for the Lake Louise departures, the tour includes a picnic lunch at the Fairmont Chateau Lake Louise. Brewster Travel has an office, **Explore Rockies Lake Louise** (Fairmont Chateau Lake Louise, 403/522-1695, 7:30am-5:30pm daily May-mid-Oct.), if you want to get information or tickets locally.

Discover Banff Tours (Sundance Mall, 215 Banff Ave., Banff, 403/760-5007 or 877/565-9372, www.banfftours.com, 7:30am-8pm daily) offers a **Full Day Explore Lake Louise Tour** (mid-Apr.-mid-Oct., 10 hours, adults $72, ages 6-12 $40) that includes transportation to and from Banff to Lake Louise, a picnic lunch, and time to explore the lake on your own. Their half-day **Lake Louise & Moraine Lake Tour** (mid-Apr.-mid-Oct., 4.5 hours, adults $69, ages 6-12 $35) begins and ends in Banff and takes you along the Bow Valley Parkway to both Lake Louise and Moraine Lake.

Lake Louise Historical Walking Tours (403/762-8421, www.banfflakelouise. com, 10am, 11:30am, 2pm, and 3:30pm Mon., Wed., and Sat. July-Aug., free) tell you about the Lake Louise area and look inside the Fairmont Chateau Lake Louise and Deer Lodge. These one-hour tours meet on the shore of Lake Louise near the canoe docks.

Jasper

From the spectacular Icefields Parkway to the Canadian Rockies' largest national park, the Jasper region wows with dramatic glaciers, mountain peaks, and strikingly blue lakes.

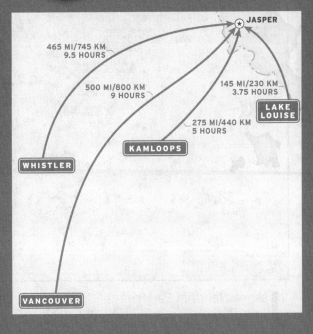

JASPER

465 MI/745 KM
9.5 HOURS

500 MI/800 KM
9 HOURS

145 MI/230 KM
3.75 HOURS

LAKE LOUISE

275 MI/440 KM
5 HOURS

KAMLOOPS

WHISTLER

VANCOUVER

JASPER

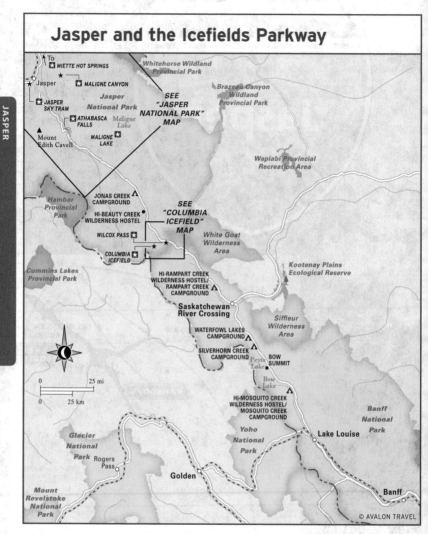

Jasper and the Icefields Parkway

To Miette Hot Springs

Whitehorse Wildland Provincial Park

Jasper

JASPER SKY TRAM

MALIGNE CANYON

Jasper National Park

ATHABASCA FALLS

Maligne Lake

Mount Edith Cavell

MALIGNE LAKE

SEE "JASPER NATIONAL PARK" MAP

Brazeau Canyon Wildland Provincial Park

Wapiabi Provincial Recreation Area

JONAS CREEK CAMPGROUND

Hamber Provincial Park

HI-BEAUTY CREEK WILDERNESS HOSTEL

WILCOX PASS

COLUMBIA ICEFIELD

SEE "COLUMBIA ICEFIELD" MAP

White Goat Wilderness Area

Kootenay Plains Ecological Reserve

Cummins Lakes Provincial Park

HI-RAMPART CREEK WILDERNESS HOSTEL/ RAMPART CREEK CAMPGROUND

Saskatchewan River Crossing

Siffleur Wilderness Area

WATERFOWL LAKES CAMPGROUND

SILVERHORN CREEK CAMPGROUND

Peyto Lake

BOW SUMMIT

Bow Lake

0   25 mi

0   25 km

HI-MOSQUITO CREEK WILDERNESS HOSTEL/ MOSQUITO CREEK CAMPGROUND

Yoho National Park

Lake Louise

Banff National Park

Glacier National Park

Rogers Pass

Golden

Banff

Mount Revelstoke National Park

© AVALON TRAVEL

Jasper National Park offers glacial peaks, turquoise lakes, cascading waterfalls, and dramatic canyons that you can explore on trails, by boat, or simply from the highway.

Many people arrive in Jasper via the scenic Icefields Parkway (Hwy. 93), which runs between Lake Louise and Jasper. Along the way, you'll travel through the Columbia Icefield, the largest area of glacial ice in the Canadian Rockies, where you can walk on a section of the Athabasca Glacier, get a thrill on the Glacier Skywalk (a glass-floored bridge that arcs over a canyon), or hike up to a dramatic

Highlights

★ **Wilcox Pass:** If you do one hike along the Icefields Parkway, make it this moderate climb that rewards you with impressive views of the surrounding glaciers (page 278).

★ **Columbia Icefield:** At the largest area of glacial ice in the Canadian Rockies, you can walk on a section of the Athabasca Glacier (page 278).

★ **Athabasca Falls:** Backed by mountain peaks, this powerful waterfall along the Icefields Parkway is an appealing photo opportunity (page 281).

★ **Maligne Canyon:** Hike on the trails and over the bridges through this deep limestone gorge that shows off how mountain rivers can carve through rocks (page 285).

★ **Maligne Lake:** Explore the turquoise waters of the largest natural lake in the Canadian Rockies and cruise to scenic Spirit Island (page 285).

★ **Miette Hot Springs:** Soak in Jasper's natural mineral-rich hot springs, the warmest in the Canadian Rockies (page 289).

★ **Jasper Sky Tram:** Ride this gondola for great views of the national park and the town of Jasper; then hike to the top of Whistlers Mountain for even better vistas (page 292).

Best Hotels

★ **Glacier View Inn:** The name says it all: The best of the simply furnished rooms at the Columbia Icefield Glacier Discovery Centre have views of the Athabasca Glacier (page 281).

★ **Patricia Lake Bungalows:** This family-run and family-friendly lakeside property offers a range of well-kept accommodations from standard hotel rooms to deluxe cabins (page 296).

★ **The Crimson:** For urban style in small-town Jasper, book a room in this 1950s lodge that has been converted into a boutique motel (page 298).

★ **Fairmont Jasper Park Lodge:** Jasper's most luxurious lodging is a full-service lakeside resort with a heated pool, an 18-hole golf course, a lake-view spa, and plenty of other amenities (page 298).

viewpoint looking across to the ice-topped mountains.

As the largest park in the Canadian Rockies, Jasper National Park has plenty to see, but even in the peak of summer, it doesn't normally have the crowds that clog the sidewalks in Banff. Oh, plenty of people come to Jasper; the park averages more than two million visitors every year. Yet, with more than 4,335 square miles (11,228 square kilometers) of protected land, Jasper has much more space.

The compact town of Jasper is located entirely within the boundaries of the national park. Most accommodations, restaurants, and other services are in or around town, although many park attractions are an hour's drive or more from the town site.

So take time to explore. It takes a little more effort to discover Jasper's attractions, but this incredible region is totally worth it.

Getting to Jasper

Driving from Banff

From Banff, go north on **Highway 1** to **Lake Louise,** where you take the scenic **Icefields Parkway (Hwy. 93)** to Jasper. The Icefields Parkway runs **145 miles (230 kilometers)** from Lake Louise to Jasper, which takes **3.25 to 3.75 hours.**

The total trip from **Banff** to Jasper is **180 miles (290 kilometers)** and takes **4 to 4.5 hours.**

Driving from Vancouver
Via Highway 5

The **shortest route** from Vancouver directly to Jasper is via **Highway 5 (Yellowhead Hwy.).**

Leave Vancouver, heading east on the **Trans-Canada Highway (Hwy. 1)** to **Hope.** Continue east at Hope onto **Highway 3,** then exit onto **Highway 5** north toward Kamloops. At **Kamloops,** continue north on Highway 5 until it intersects with **Highway 16** north of Valemount. Follow Highway 16 east to Jasper.

This Vancouver-to-Jasper route is **500 miles (800 kilometers)** and takes **8.5 to 9 hours.** From **Kamloops** to Jasper, the trip is **275 miles (440 kilometers)** and takes **five hours.**

Via Highway 1

A **longer but scenic route** through the mountains of eastern B.C. is to take **Highway 1** east from Kamloops.

From Vancouver, head east on the **Trans-Canada Highway (Hwy. 1)** to **Hope.** Continue east at Hope onto **Highway 3,** then exit onto **Highway 5** north toward Kamloops. From **Kamloops,** drive east on Highway 1. You'll travel through Mount Revelstoke, Glacier, and Yoho National Parks en route to Lake Louise. At **Lake**

Best Restaurants

★ **Bear's Paw Bakery:** At Jasper's favorite baked-goods purveyor, you can start your day with excellent scones or sticky buns (page 298).

★ **Patricia Street Deli:** It's nothing fancy, but this Jasper take-out spot makes excellent sandwiches,

convenient for taking out on the trails (page 298).

★ **Orso Trattoria:** The lake views alone are worth a visit to this modern Italian restaurant at the Fairmont Jasper Park Lodge; it also serves traditional afternoon tea (page 299).

Louise, turn north on the **Icefields Parkway (Hwy. 93)** to Jasper.

From Vancouver, this route is about **620 miles (1,000 kilometers)** and takes **11.5 to 12 hours.** From **Kamloops** to Jasper, the trip is **415 miles (665 kilometers)** and takes **8.25 to 8.75 hours.**

Driving from Whistler

If you're traveling to Jasper from Whistler, follow **Highway 99** north, until it joins **Highway 97,** and then meets up with the **Trans-Canada Highway (Hwy. 1).** Take Highway 1 east to Kamloops.

From **Kamloops,** either pick up **Highway 5** north to **Highway 16** east to Jasper, or continue east on **Highway 1** to **Lake Louise,** and then take the **Icefields Parkway (Hwy. 93)** to Jasper.

The trip from Whistler to Jasper via **Highways 5 and 16** is **465 miles (745 kilometers)** and takes **9 to 9.5 hours.** The route via **Highways 1 and 93** is **600 miles (965 kilometers)** and takes **12 to 12.5 hours.**

Driving from Edmonton

Edmonton to Jasper is **225 miles (365 kilometers),** a straight **four-hour** drive west on **Highway 16.**

Getting There by Air, Train, and Bus

By Air

Edmonton International Airport (YEG, 1000 Airport Rd., 780/890-8900 or 800/268-7134, http://flyeia.com) is the closest major airport to Jasper. You can

fly directly to Edmonton from many Canadian and U.S. cities, and from Amsterdam, London, and Reykjavik.

Car rental companies with offices at the Edmonton Airport include **Alamo** (780/890-7345 or 877/222-9075, www.alamo.ca), **Avis** (780/890-7596 or 800/879-2847, www.avis.ca), **Budget** (780/890-4801 or 800/268-8900, www.budget.ca), **Enterprise** (780/980-2338 or 800/261-7331, www.enterprise.com), **Hertz** (780/890-4435 or 800/263-0600, www.hertz.ca), and **National** (780/890-7345 or 800/227-7368, www.nationalcar.ca).

SunDog Tours (780/852-4056 or 888/786-3641, www.sundogtours.com, one-way adults $99, kids $59) runs a shuttle between the Edmonton Airport and Jasper. It operates once daily in each direction, offering pickups and drop-offs at several Jasper hotels. The trip takes approximately 5.5 hours.

By Train

Both VIA Rail, Canada's national passenger rail carrier, and the privately run Rocky Mountaineer train have service to the **Jasper Train Station** (607 Connaught Dr.), which is conveniently located in the center of town opposite Parks Canada's **Jasper Information Centre** (500 Connaught Dr.).

VIA Rail

On its flagship route, *The Canadian,* **VIA Rail** (514/989-2626 or 888/842-7245, www.viarail.ca) trains arrive in

Jasper from the west via Vancouver and Kamloops, and from the east from Edmonton, Saskatoon, Winnipeg, and Toronto. *The Canadian* operates three times a week in each direction from May through mid-October, and twice a week from mid-October through April.

Another VIA Rail route runs to Jasper three times a week from Prince Rupert and Prince George in northern British Columbia. The full Jasper-Prince Rupert trip is 720 miles (1,160 kilometers) and takes two days. This train travels only during the daylight hours, so you stop overnight in Prince George. Prince Rupert is a starting point for trips to the Queen Charlotte Islands. From Prince Rupert, you can also travel aboard B.C. Ferries south to Vancouver Island.

The Rocky Mountaineer

The deluxe **Rocky Mountaineer** (877/460-3200, www.rockymountaineer.com, mid-Apr.-mid-Oct.) can take you to Jasper from Vancouver or Seattle. The classic Journey Through the Clouds runs from Vancouver to Jasper, with an overnight stop in Kamloops; they also offer a version of this trip that starts in Seattle. Another option is the three-day Rainforest to Gold Rush route, which takes you to Jasper from Vancouver with overnight stops in Whistler and in the northern B.C. city of Quesnel.

Unlike a standard train trip, many Rocky Mountaineer packages include a number of different activities, ranging from gondola rides to helicopter tours, with accommodations included along the way. It's also possible to book a Rocky Mountaineer holiday that includes rail fare and accommodations only, such as a two-day train trip between Vancouver and Jasper. Rail packages start at $1,699 pp and depend on destinations, number of days of travel, and the level of service and accommodations.

By Bus

Between May and late October, **Brewster**

Banff Airport Express (403/762-6700 or 866/606-6700, www.brewster.ca) runs a daily bus in each direction between Jasper and Lake Louise (3.75 hours, one-way adults $77, ages 6-15 $38.50), Banff (5.5 hours, one-way adults $87, ages 6-15 $43.50), the Calgary International Airport (7.25 hours, one-way adults $128, ages 6-15 $64), and downtown Calgary (8 hours, one-way adults $128, ages 6-15 $64). The bus also stops at the Columbia Icefield Centre.

Greyhound (800/661-8747, www.greyhound.ca) provides regular service to the **Jasper Bus Depot** (607 Connaught Dr., 780/852-3926) from Edmonton (5 hours, one-way adults $36-85) and Kamloops (5.5 hours, one-way adults $41-87). From Vancouver (10.5 hours, one-way adults $76-162), you have to transfer at Kamloops.

The Icefields Parkway

The 143-mile (230-kilometer) route between Lake Louise and Jasper is one of Canada's most spectacular drives. Highway 93, known as the Icefields Parkway, takes you past rushing waterfalls, turquoise lakes, and countless glacier-topped peaks. This scenic road helped open the Jasper region to tourism when the highway was completed in 1940.

Most people make the drive in anywhere from four hours to one day, with lots of stops en route. If you want to stay longer, the parkway has a couple of lodgings, several campgrounds, and a network of rustic wilderness hostels.

The southern section of the Icefields Parkway is within the boundaries of Banff National Park, while the northern sector is part of Jasper National Park. You must have a valid **national park pass** (www.pc.gc.ca, adults $9.80, seniors $8.30, ages 6-16 $4.90, families $19.60) to drive anywhere on the parkway. If you don't already have a pass or need to purchase a pass for additional days, you can buy it at the **Lake Louise Visitor Information Centre** (Samson Mall, Lake Louise, 403/522-3833) before driving north or at the Parks Canada **Jasper Information Centre** (500 Connaught Dr., Jasper, 780/852-6176) if you're traveling south.

The Icefields Parkway is open year-round, although the road's limited services don't operate in winter, and heavy snows, primarily between December and March, can close the road for a day or more. Don't make this trip in winter, unless you have winter tires and you're comfortable in winter driving conditions.

At any time of year, be prepared for changeable weather. Since the parkway climbs through the mountains and crosses several mountain passes, the weather can vary significantly as you change elevation.

Note that there's currently no cell phone service along most of the Icefields Parkway.

Sights and Recreation

These highlights along the Icefields Parkway are listed from south to north, that is, from Lake Louise to Jasper. Parks Canada publishes **The Icefields Parkway Driving Guide,** available online (www.pc.gc.ca) and at park visitors centers, with more details about stopping points and hiking trails along this scenic route.

Bow Lake

At **Bow Lake,** a scenic stretch-your-legs and take-a-photo spot just 23 miles (37 kilometers) north of Lake Louise, the Wapta Icefield rises above the opposite lakeshore.

If you're ready for a picnic, follow the short road from the parking area (to your left as you face the lake) that leads to a quiet grove of lakeside picnic tables.

Top to bottom: landscape along the Icefields Parkway; rest stop on the Wilcox Pass Trail; Athabasca Glacier.

Bow Summit and Peyto Lake

Take time to stop at **Peyto Lake,** where a paved trail climbs steeply up from the parking lot to a viewpoint overlooking this brilliant-turquoise glacier-fed lake. It's worth the 10-minute hike for this photogenic panorama.

For a longer hike, continue past the Peyto Lake lookout on the **Bow Summit Trail,** which follows an old fire road up to another scenic viewpoint. This route is 3.6 miles (5.8 kilometers) round-trip, with an elevation gain of 804 feet (245 meters).

The turnoff for these trails is 25 miles (40 kilometers) north of Lake Louise.

★ Wilcox Pass

Have time for only one hike along the Icefields Parkway? Hike the **Wilcox Pass Trail,** a five-mile (8-kilometer) round-trip route that climbs up to a ridge and alpine meadows with spectacular views across the glaciers of the Columbia Icefield. This trail is an intermediate-level hike with an elevation gain of 1,100 feet (335 meters).

Even if you don't hike the entire route, walk up 1.5 miles (2.4 kilometers) to the first viewpoint, where the vistas spread out across glacier-topped peaks.

To reach the trailhead, turn off the Icefields Parkway at the Wilcox Campground, 79 miles (127 kilometers) north of Lake Louise or 67 miles (108 kilometers) south of the town of Jasper.

★ Columbia Icefield

If you want to explore glaciers, you'll want to visit the **Columbia Icefield,** the largest area of glacial ice in the Canadian Rockies. Measuring 77 square miles (200 square kilometers), the Icefield comprises several individual glaciers: the Saskatchewan, Columbia, Stutfield, Dome, and Athabasca. The Icefield region is unique in North America for being a triple watershed, the only point on the continent where water flows to three oceans: the Pacific, the Atlantic, and the Arctic.

Columbia Icefield Glacier Discovery Centre

The starting point for exploring the Icefield is the **Columbia Icefield Glacier Discovery Centre** (Hwy. 93, www.brewster.ca, daily mid-Apr.-mid-Oct.), 81 miles (130 kilometers) north of Lake Louise and 64 miles (103 kilometers) south of Jasper, which has a small Parks Canada exhibit area and a theater. It's also the departure point for several Icefield tours. The center has a cafeteria, which operates from 8:30am until the last tours depart daily, and a more upscale dining room (6pm-9pm daily).

A tourist mecca, the Icefield Centre gets jammed, particularly on summer afternoons, when waiting times for tours can be lengthy. Get here before 11am if you can.

Athabasca Glacier

Resembling a frozen river extending almost down to Highway 93, the **Athabasca Glacier** is visible from the road and from the Icefield Centre. It's not only the most accessible of the Columbia Icefield glaciers; it's the most visited glacier in North America.

Currently measuring 2.5 square miles (6 square kilometers), the Athabasca Glacier has been receding as the region's climate has warmed. It has lost close to one mile (1.5 kilometers) of its length and nearly half its volume during the last century. Some experts think that the glacier may disappear completely in 50 years.

The most popular way to explore the glacier is on the **Columbia Icefield Glacier Adventure** (10am-4pm daily mid-late Apr., 10am-5pm daily May, 9am-6pm daily June-early Sept., 10am-5pm daily Sept., 10am-4pm daily early-mid-Oct., adults $54.95, ages 6-15 $27.50), where you drive onto a section of the ice in Ice Explorer buses, fat-tire snowcat coaches. When you get off the bus, you have about 15 minutes to walk directly on the glacier.

The Glacier Adventure tours depart from the Icefield Centre every 15 to 30

Columbia Icefield

minutes. Allow about 90 minutes for this tour; you board a bus that takes you across the road to a transfer point, where you climb onto the Ice Explorer vehicles. From there, you drive up through a rocky chasm of glacial moraine and into the alpine region above the tree line. As part of the short ride to the ice, the snowcats descend a nail-biting 32 percent grade down toward the glacier.

Without taking the Glacier Adventure tour, it's possible to walk the 1.1-mile (1.8-kilometer) round-trip **Toe of the Athabasca Glacier Trail,** which starts across the road from the Icefield Centre and takes you to the glacier's base. However, since the Athabasca Glacier has more than 2,000 crevasses, Parks

Canada staff caution that you shouldn't wander on your own onto the glacier. The **Forefield Trail** (2.2 miles/3.6 kilometers round-trip) also begins opposite the Icefield Centre and traverses the glacier's moraines and left-behind debris.

Glacier Skywalk

For a different perspective on the Columbia Icefield, and to give yourself a thrill, take the **Glacier Skywalk Tour** (866/606-6700, www.brewster.ca, 10am-5pm daily May, 9am-6pm daily June-early Aug., 9am-7pm daily Aug., 10am-5pm daily Sept., 10am-6pm daily early-mid-Oct., adults $29.95, ages 6-15 $14.95).

The Skywalk is a steel bridge arcing

115 feet (35 meters) out over the Sunwapta Valley. The most exciting (or terrifying, depending on your perspective) part of the Skywalk is a section with a glass floor, where you can look directly down into the canyon, 918 feet (280 meters) below.

The Skywalk isn't just about thrills, though. A self-guided **audio tour** (included with the tour price) explores a series of interpretive panels with details about the icefield glaciers, geologic changes, and local wildlife and plants. Another interesting section of the exhibit details how the Skywalk was designed and built. Guides are on hand to answer your questions.

You can't drive yourself to the Skywalk. The tour includes a five-minute shuttle, which departs every 15 minutes from the Columbia Icefield Glacier Discovery Centre and brings you to the start of the Skywalk. You can stay at the Skywalk as long as you'd like during the operating hours; most visitors spend 40 to 60 minutes.

Tangle Falls

Four miles (7 kilometers) north of the Icefield Centre, 114-foot (35-meter) **Tangle Falls** stream down the rock face in several tiers, making the cascade especially photogenic. In winter, when the falls freeze, experienced ice climbers attempt to scale their frozen flow.

Tangle Falls are on the east side of the parkway, 85 miles (140 kilometers) north of Lake Louise and 60 miles (100 kilometers) south of Jasper.

Sunwapta Falls

Another waterfall viewpoint is at **Sunwapta Falls,** 111 miles (179 kilometers) north of Lake Louise and 34 miles (54 kilometers) south of Jasper. The main (upper) falls are closest to the parking area. You can also walk 0.6 miles (1 kilometer) along the river to Lower Sunwapta Falls.

Thousands of years ago, receding glacial ice left behind U-shaped valleys. When larger valleys were carved more

Athabasca Falls

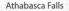

deeply into the rock than smaller valleys, these smaller valleys appeared to hang at a higher elevation where the valleys converged, leaving a path for waterfalls to form and flow. These hanging valleys created Sunwapta Falls and many of the other waterfalls in the Jasper region.

★ Athabasca Falls

At 955 miles (1,538 kilometers), the Athabasca River is Alberta's longest. Along the river, near where Highway 93 meets Highway 93A, south of Jasper, a set of waterfalls along the river crash into the canyon below.

What makes **Athabasca Falls** worth a stop on your Icefields Parkway tour isn't their height; they're only 75 feet (23 meters) high. But the strong rushing river causes the falls to cascade dramatically through the canyon. With a row of mountain peaks behind the falls, it's a photo-worthy spot.

A short paved path leads from the parking area to a viewpoint over the falls.

Cross the bridge and walk around to the overlooks on the other side of the river for even better falls views.

Athabasca Falls are close enough to Jasper, 19 miles (30 kilometers) to the south, that you can visit them either from town or as you're traveling the Icefields Parkway. The falls are 126 miles (203 kilometers) north of Lake Louise.

Accommodations and Camping

Many people travel the Icefields Parkway as a day trip from Banff, Lake Louise, or Jasper, but it's possible to stay overnight along the way.

Located on the third floor of the Columbia Icefield Glacier Discovery Centre and run by tour operator Brewster Travel Canada, the ★ **Glacier View Inn** (877/442-2623, www.brewster.ca, May-Oct., $199-269 d) has 32 large, simply furnished rooms, many with views across to the Athabasca Glacier. Some units have lofts with either one queen or two twin beds, plus either a queen or twins on the main level, sleeping up to four. All have flat-screen TVs with satellite service, landline phones, and free Wi-Fi, but the area has no cell coverage. Rooms also have coffee pots and teakettles; guests can have breakfast and dinner (not included in the room rates) in the dining room downstairs. Book several months in advance for stays in July and August.

Wilderness Hostels

Hostelling International-Canada (778/328-2220 or 866/762-4122, www.hihostels.ca) runs several rustic wilderness hostels along Highway 93 between Lake Louise and Jasper. "Rustic" means no indoor plumbing, showers, electricity, or Wi-Fi, but they'll give you a bunk in a cabin in the woods. From south to north:

- **HI-Mosquito Creek Wilderness Hostel** (May-mid-Oct. and mid-Nov.-early Apr., $25.14-27.24 dorm, $66-68 d) has both dorms and private rooms. It's located 18 miles (29 kilometers) north of Lake Louise.

- **HI-Rampart Creek Wilderness Hostel** (May-mid-Oct. and mid-Nov.-early Apr., $25.14-27.24 dorm), 56 miles (90 kilometers) north of Lake Louise and 88 miles (142 kilometers) south of the town of Jasper, has dorm rooms only.

- **HI-Hilda Creek Wilderness Hostel** ($25.14-27.24 dorm) has just six dorm beds and no staff. It's 4.5 miles (7 kilometers) south of the Icefields Centre, 75 miles (121 kilometers) north of Lake Louise.

- **HI-Beauty Creek Wilderness Hostel** ($25.14-27.24 dorm) is open year-round but staffed only mid-May to mid-October. The hostel is 11 miles (17 kilometers) north of the Icefields Centre, 55 miles (87 kilometers) south of Jasper.

- **HI-Athabasca Falls Wilderness Hostel** ($24.22-26.24 dorm, $63.58-65.60 d) has both dorm beds and private rooms in five rustic cabins. It's 20 miles (32 kilometers) south of Jasper.

Camping

Parks Canada operates a number of primitive campgrounds along the Icefields Parkway. Most have outhouses and no water or electricity, and none accept reservations. Mosquito Creek, Silverhorn Creek, Waterfowl Lakes, and Rampart Creek are in Banff National Park; Wilcox, Columbia Icefield, Jonas Creek, Honeymoon Lake, and Kerkeslin are within Jasper National Park's boundaries.

From south to north:

- **Mosquito Creek Campground** (June-mid-Oct., $17.60) is 15 miles (24 kilometers) north of Lake Louise, with 32 unserviced sites for tents or RVs.

- **Silverhorn Creek Campground** (late June-early Sept., $15.70), with 67 sites, is 32 miles (52 kilometers) north of Lake Louise. Silverhorn Creek has no running water; the nearest water is three miles (5 kilometers) north at Waterfowl Lakes Campground.

- **Waterfowl Lakes Campground** (late June-early Sept., $21.50) has a washroom with flush toilets and hot and cold water (but no showers) for its 116 sites. This campground is 35 miles (57 kilometers) north of Lake Louise.

- **Rampart Creek Campground** (June-mid-Oct., $17.60) has 50 sites, 55 miles (88 kilometers) north of Lake Louise.

- **Wilcox Campground** (early June-Sept., $15.70) has 46 sites that Parks Canada recommends for small motorhomes or trailers. It's just south of the Icefields Centre, near the trailhead for the Wilcox Pass Trail; it's 67 miles (108 kilometers) south of the town of Jasper.

- **Columbia Icefield Campground** (mid-May-mid-Oct., $15.70) is the place to camp if you want to be close to the Athabasca Glacier. The 33 tent-only sites are convenient to the Icefields Centre, 66 miles (106 kilometers) south of Jasper.

- **Jonas Creek Campground** (mid-May-early Sept., $15.70), 48 miles (78 kilometers) south of Jasper, is a quiet area with 25 sites for tents or small RVs.

- **Honeymoon Lake Campground** (mid-June-early Sept., sites $15.70), 33 miles (53 kilometers) south of Jasper, is a lakeside area not far from Sunwapta Falls. Its 35 sites accommodate tents and small motorhomes.

- **Kerkeslin Campground** (mid-June-early Sept., $15.70) has 42 sites for tents or small RVs, 22 miles (36 kilometers) south of Jasper.

Food

Services are limited along the Icefields Parkway, and the food choices are generally uninspiring, so consider packing a picnic or at least bringing water and snacks.

Off Highway 93 at Saskatchewan Crossing, 50 miles (80 kilometers) north of Lake Louise, **The Crossing Resort** (403/761-7000, www.thecrossingresort. com, mid-Mar.-mid-Nov.) has several food outlets, including **The Crossing Café,** a cafeteria serving breakfast, lunch, and dinner; **Mt. Wilson Restaurant,** open for lunch and dinner; and **The Parkway Pub,** a sports bar offering lunch, dinner, and drinks (if you're not the designated driver).

At the **Columbia Icefield Glacier Discovery Centre** (Hwy. 93, www.brewster.ca, mid-Apr.-mid-Oct. daily), you can have breakfast, lunch, or snacks in the cafeteria, which operates from 8:30am until the last tours depart daily. If the burgers, sandwiches, and other plates aren't special, the views across the road to the Athabasca Glacier are. Also in the Icefield Centre is a more upscale dining room (6pm-9pm daily), open for dinner.

Sunwapta Falls Resort (Hwy. 93, 780/852-4852 or 888/828-5777, www. sunwapta.com, mid-May-mid-Oct.), 111 miles (179 kilometers) north of Lake Louise and 34 miles (54 kilometers) south of Jasper, has a **deli** (7:30am-6pm daily, mains breakfast $7-13, lunch $10-17), serving eggs, french toast, and oatmeal in the morning, and soups, stews, and burgers midday, as well as premade sandwiches, muffins, yogurt, and fruit to go. In the evening, the window-lined white-tablecloth **Endless Chain Ridge Dining Room** (mains $19-35) is worth a stop for its candlelit setting and hearty mountain dishes: pan-seared rainbow trout, game meat pot pie, and Alberta beef steaks. Reservations are recommended.

Information and Services

Parks Canada (780/852-6288, www.pc.gc. ca, 10am-5pm daily early May-late Sept.) has a seasonal information desk in the Icefields Centre.

Check your fuel before you set out. **Gas** is available only at Lake Louise, Saskatchewan Crossing (50 miles/80 kilometers, north of Lake Louise), and Jasper.

There is currently **no cell phone service** for most of the length of the Icefields Parkway, between Lake Louise and the Athabasca Falls area, 20 miles (32 kilometers) south of Jasper.

Tours

Several companies offer day trips along the Icefields Parkway from Banff, Lake Louise, or Jasper.

Brewster Travel Canada (403/760-6934 or 800/760-6934, www.brewster.ca, May-mid.-Oct.) runs a one-day, one-way **Rockies Discovery and Glacier Adventure Tour** of the Icefields Parkway. You can start in Calgary (12 hours, adults $226, ages 6-15 $114), Canmore (10.5 hours, adults $216, ages 6-15 $109), Banff (9.5 hours, adults $206, ages 6-15 $104), or Lake Louise (8.5 hours, adults $196, ages 6-15 $99) and travel north to the Columbia Icefields, where your tour ticket includes a buffet lunch, the Columbia Icefield Glacier Adventure, and the Glacier Skywalk. The tour concludes in Jasper. You can also do the tour southbound, starting in Jasper and ending in Lake Louise, Banff, Canmore, or Calgary.

Another Brewster Travel option is the **Columbia Icefield Discovery Tour,** which provides round-trip transportation to the Columbia Icefield from Banff (9.5 hours, adults $206, ages 6-15 $104), Lake Louise (7 hours, adults $196, ages 6-15 $99), Jasper (5.5 hours, adults $176, ages 6-15 $88), Canmore (12 hours, adults $216, ages 6-15 $109), or Calgary (14 hours, adults $226, ages 6-15 $114). These tours also include lunch, the Glacier Adventure, and the Glacier Skywalk, and return to your starting point.

SunDog Tours (780/852-4056 or 888/786-3641, www.sundogtours.com, May-mid-Oct.) runs a **Columbia Icefields**

THE ICEFIELDS PARKWAY

Tour (5-6 hours, adults $79, under age 12 $45) that starts and ends in Jasper. It stops at Athabasca Falls and at the Columbia Icefields Centre, where you have the option to do the Glacier Tour or Glacier Skywalk (not included). You can also do these SunDog tours one-way from Jasper to Lake Louise (9 hours, adults $99, under age 12 $75) or from Jasper to Banff (10 hours, adults $119, under age 12 $85), or vice versa, starting in Lake Louise or Banff and ending in Jasper.

Alternatively, SunDog runs round-trip tours that start and end in either Lake Louise (8 hours, adults $174, ages 6-15 $93) or Banff (9 hours, adults $174, ages 6-15 $93) and travel to the Columbia Icefield. These tours include a box lunch and the Glacier Explorer adventure.

Jasper National Park

Jasper National Park is the largest park in the Canadian Rockies, stretching across 11,228 square kilometers (4,335 square miles) in western Alberta. Initially created as a forest reserve in 1907, Jasper became a full-fledged national park in 1930.

Visiting the Park
Entrances

Coming from Lake Louise, Banff, or points south, you enter Jasper National Park along Highway 93, the Icefields Parkway.

Highway 16, the Yellowhead Highway, runs through the park. The park's west gate is on Highway 16 near the Continental Divide, at the B.C.-Alberta provincial border. The east gate is 19 miles (30 kilometers) southwest of the town of Hinton, also along Highway 16.

Park Passes and Fees

A day pass (adults $9.80, seniors $8.30, ages 6-16 $4.90, families $19.60) for Jasper National Park is valid until 4pm on the day after you purchase it. Jasper day passes are also valid at Banff National Park. You need a park pass to travel the Icefields Parkway.

Purchasing a Parks Canada annual discovery pass (adults $67.70, seniors $57.90, ages 6-16 $33.30, families $136.40), valid for a year, is a good deal if you're spending at least a week in one or more parks. It's good at more than 100 national parks and national historic sites across Canada. Buy an annual pass online from Parks Canada or at any of the parks' visitors centers.

For both day and annual passes, the family passes cover up to seven people in a single vehicle, whether or not they're actually related.

Visitors Centers

Parks Canada runs the Jasper Information Centre (500 Connaught Dr., 780/852-6176, www.pc.gc.ca, 9am-5pm daily mid-Mar.-mid-May, 9am-7pm daily mid-May-mid-Sept., 9am-5pm daily mid-Sept.-Oct., 10am-5pm Wed.-Sun. mid-Dec.-mid-Mar.) in the town of Jasper, one block from the VIA Rail train station. The Friends of Jasper National Park (780/852-4767, www.friendsofjasper. com) operate a shop that sells books and souvenirs in the same location.

The Information Centre's rustic stone building is itself a National Historic Site. British Colonel Maynard Rogers, the park's first superintendent, built the stone structure as his home in 1913, using rocks excavated from the building site and from the nearby river. It was the first major building to be constructed at the Jasper town site after the government designated the surrounding region as Jasper Forest Park, a 5,000-square-mile (13,000-square-kilometer) protected area.

Reservations

You can make campsite reservations (877/737-3783, www.reservation.parks-canada.gc.ca) online or by phone for four of the campgrounds in Jasper National Park: Whistlers, Wapiti, Wabasso, and

One Day in Jasper

If you have just one day, get an early start. Jasper National Park is a big area to explore.

Start with a ride up the **Jasper Sky Tram** to get oriented with views across a wide swath of the park. Or if you'd rather begin the day with a hike, follow the 2.4-mile (3.8-kilometer) **Old Fort Point Trail,** which climbs to a viewpoint high above town.

Stop at the **Jasper-Yellowhead Museum** to learn more about the history of the Jasper region, then walk over to **Bear's Paw Bakery** or **Patricia Street Deli** to pick up a picnic lunch. Take your picnic to **Maligne Canyon,** where you can hike along the deep limestone gorge,

past rushing springs and striking rock formations.

In the afternoon, drive to **Maligne Lake** for a 90-minute cruise on this impossibly scenic glacier-fed lake to tiny Spirit Island, one of the park's most photographed spots. Or rent a canoe or kayak from the historic boathouse and go for a leisurely lake paddle.

Have an early supper back in town, then head for **Miette Hot Springs** to wrap up your day with a relaxing soak in these natural mineral pools. If you're not ready to call it a night, stop for a microbrew at the **Jasper Brewing Company,** the local brewpub, where, over a pint, you can recap the highlights of your Jasper day.

Pocahontas. Reservations are advised especially for July and August stays.

Sights and Recreation
★ Maligne Canyon
According to local legend, a 19th-century Belgian explorer tried to cross a river in the Jasper area. When the rough waters swept away all his belongings, he dubbed the river *maligne* (ma-LEEN), French for "evil" or "wicked." The name stuck to the river, the canyon, and the nearby lake that still bear the moniker. Fortunately, there's nothing especially wicked about scenic **Maligne Canyon,** a deep limestone gorge that showcases nature's carving power.

Several bridges cross the canyon, from First Bridge near the main canyon parking lot to Sixth Bridge, which is off Maligne Road to the west.

The **Maligne Canyon Trail** takes you through the gorge, past rushing springs and striking rock formations. An especially nice way to explore the canyon is to follow the trail from **Fifth Bridge;** from there, it's 1.4 miles (2.2 kilometers) to First Bridge at the top of the canyon. The trail gains 325 feet (100 meters) in elevation en route, with the steepest

sections around the Second and Third Bridges. For a slightly longer hike, start at Sixth Bridge, which adds one mile (1.6 kilometers) of gentle forest trail each way.

You can hike through the canyon in either direction, but the views are most dramatic when you go into the canyon from the Sixth or Fifth Bridges toward the First.

Near First Bridge is **Maligne Canyon Restaurant** (780/852-3583, www.malignecanyon.com, 9am-6pm daily Apr.-June and Sept.-Oct., 8am-7pm daily July-Aug.) with a coffee bar, cafeteria, art gallery, and gift shop.

To the canyon, follow Highway 16 east from the town of Jasper to Maligne Road. It's about a 15-minute drive from town. Watch for the turn-offs for Sixth Bridge and Fifth Bridge, both clearly marked, if you plan to start your hike from these points; both have small parking areas at the trailheads.

★ Maligne Lake
One of Jasper's loveliest lakes is glacier-fed **Maligne Lake,** where mountains and glaciers surround the turquoise waters. At 13.6 miles (22 kilometers) long, it's

Jasper National Park

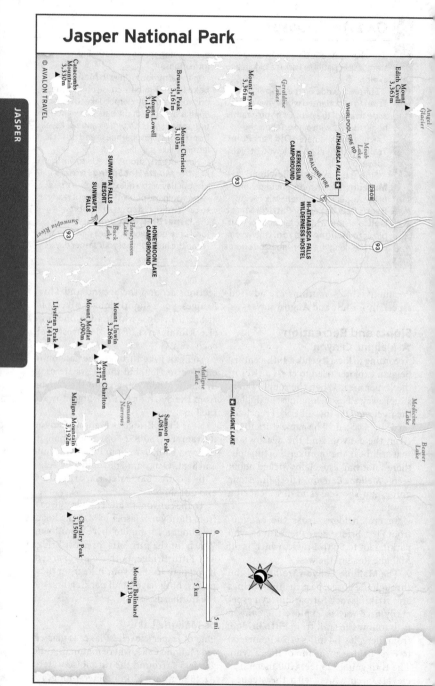

© AVALON TRAVEL

Catacombs Mountain
3,330m

Mount Edith Cavell
3,363m

Angel Glacier

Brussels Peak
3,161m

Mount Lowell
3,150m

Mount Fryatt
3,361m

Geraldine Lakes

WHIRLPOOL FIRE RD

ATHABASCA FALLS

Moab Lake

Mount Christie
3,103m

GERALDINE FIRE RD

KERKESLIN CAMPGROUND

HI-ATHABASCA FALLS WILDERNESS HOSTEL

280B

93

SUNWAPTA FALLS RESORT

SUNWAPTA FALLS

Sunwapta River

93

Buck Lake

Honeymoon Lake

HONEYMOON LAKE CAMPGROUND

93

Llysfran Peak
3,141m

Mount Moffat
3,090m

Mount Unwin
3,268m

Mount Charlton
3,217m

Maligne Lake

Medicine Lake

Samson Narrows

MALIGNE LAKE

Maligne Mountain
3,192m

Samson Peak
3,081m

Beaver Lake

Chivalry Peak
3,150m

Mount Balinhard
3,130m

0   5 km
0   5 mi

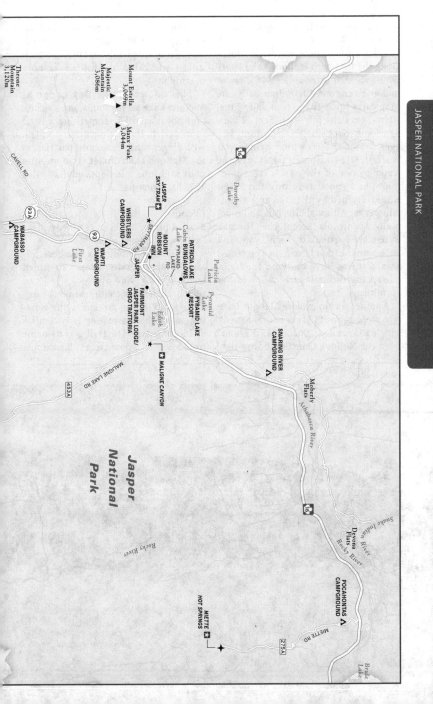

Throne Mountain 3,120m

Majestic Mountain 3,086m

Mount Estella 3,069m

Manx Peak 3,044m

CAVELL RD

93A

WABASSO CAMPGROUND

93

First Lake

WAPITI CAMPGROUND

WHISTLERS CAMPGROUND

JASPER SKY TRAM

JASPER

MOUNT ROBSON INN

SKYTRAM RD

Cabin Bungalows

PATRICIA LAKE

Patricia Lake

PYRAMID LAKE

Pyramid Lake

PYRAMID LAKE RESORT

Dorothy Lake

16

FAIRMONT JASPER PARK LODGE/ ORSO TRATTORIA

Edith Lake

MALIGNE LAKE RD

453A

MALIGNE CANYON

SNARING RIVER CAMPGROUND

Moberly Flats

Athabasca River

Jasper National Park

Rocky River

16

Devona Flats

Snake Indian River

Rocky River

Snake River

POCAHONTAS CAMPGROUND

MIETTE RD

275A

MIETTE HOT SPRINGS

Brule Lake

the largest natural lake in the Canadian Rockies.

Take a 90-minute narrated **cruise** along the lake with **Maligne Lake Tours** (780/852-3370 or 866/625-4463, www.malignelake.com, 10am-3pm daily late May-early June, 10am-4pm daily June, 10am-5pm daily July-early Sept., 10am-4pm daily Sept.-early Oct., adults $67, ages 5-14 $33.50), which brings you 9.5 miles (14 kilometers) across the water to one of the park's most photographed spots: tiny forested Spirit Island, framed by the lake and mountain peaks. Although Spirit Island is actually a peninsula (except when the lake waters are particularly high), you can't walk onto the island itself; it's a protected area. Cruises leave daily on the hour, late spring through early fall, weather permitting.

Another way to explore Maligne Lake is to rent a **canoe** ($30 per hour) or **kayak** (single $35 per hour, double $45 per hour) from the **Maligne Lake Boathouse** (late May-early Oct.), a historic wooden structure built in 1928. Note that you can't get all the way to Spirit Island in these craft unless you camp along the lakeshore overnight.

The cafeteria-style **Day Lodge at Maligne Lake** serves soups, sandwiches, and hot meals. For something a little more lavish, linger over afternoon tea, with finger sandwiches and pastries, at the **Maligne Lake Chalet** (1:30pm-4pm daily mid-June-mid-Sept., adults $34), a 1927 log structure.

Hiking

Several hiking trails start near the Day Lodge at Maligne Lake.

To hike along Maligne's lakeshore, follow the **Mary Schaffer Loop** trail, which leads to a lakeside overlook. You can turn back here, or continue into the forest before circling around to the starting point; the entire loop is two miles (3.2 kilometers). The trail gets its name from a Quaker woman from Philadelphia

Maligne Lake

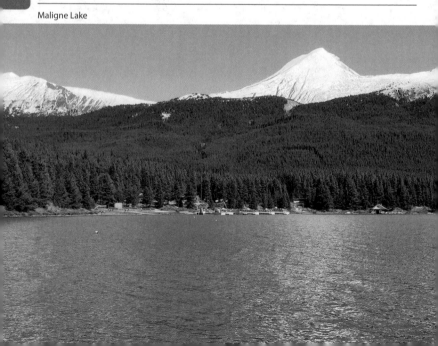

who explored and wrote about the lake in 1907.

Leading through the woods, the 1.7-mile (2.7-kilometer) **Moose Lake Loop** takes you through the site of a centuries-old landslide.

One of the steepest trails in the Maligne area, the **Opal Hills Loop,** a five-mile (8.2-kilometer) loop with an elevation gain of 1,510 feet (460 meters), has great mountain vistas. Check with Parks Canada staff at the **Jasper Information Centre** before hiking here in July and early August, when bears often frequent the area.

Another steep route, the 6.5-mile (10.4-kilometer) round-trip **Bald Hills Trail** rewards hikers with views of the lake and surrounding peaks. It has an elevation gain of 1,640 feet (500 meters).

Getting There

Maligne Lake is 29 miles (47 kilometers) east of town, about an hour's drive. From Highway 16, go east on Maligne Lake Road. Make sure you have enough fuel to get to the lake and back; there are no services en route.

To get to Maligne Lake without a car, take the **Maligne Lake Shuttle** (780/852-3370 or 866/625-4463, www.malignelake.com, late May-early Oct., one-way adults $30, ages 5-14 $15), which departs every morning from several stops in Jasper. The shuttle goes back to town three times later in the day.

Medicine Lake

En route to Maligne Lake, you'll pass **Medicine Lake** (Maligne Lake Rd.), an unusual "disappearing" lake.

The Maligne River feeds Medicine Lake, and in summer, waters from nearby melting glaciers cause the lake to fill. In fall and winter, when the snow melt stops, the lake begins to disappear, draining out through sinkholes at the lake bottom. The water then flows through an underground cave system, before surfacing 10 miles (16 kilometers) downstream in Maligne Canyon. The Maligne River is considered among the largest "sinking rivers" in the western hemisphere.

In 2015, triggered by a lightning strike, the Excelsior Wildfire decimated more than 2,300 acres (966 hectares) of forest along Medicine Lake. You'll see the charred remains of this severe fire all along the lakeshore.

★ Miette Hot Springs

Underground streams fuel hot springs throughout the Canadian Rockies, but the hottest of these mineral-rich waters flows into Jasper's **Miette Hot Springs** (Miette Rd., 780/866-3939, www.pc.gc.ca, early 10:30am-9pm daily May-mid-June, 9am-11pm daily mid-June-early Sept., 10:30am-9pm daily early Sept.-mid-Oct., adults $6.05, seniors and ages 3-17 $5.15, families $18.35). Its source is a steamy 129°F (54°C), though the waters are cooled to around 104°F (40°C) before they reach the large public soaking pools. The minerals concentrated in the Miette springs include sulfate, calcium, bicarbonate, magnesium, and sodium.

You can rent towels ($1.90) and swimsuits ($1.90), including early-20th-century bathing costumes (fun for those holiday photos!). Lockers are $1. You can't wear street shoes into the pool area, so bring water sandals or flip-flops if you'd rather not walk barefoot.

Before or after your soak in the pool, you can hike the **Source of the Springs** trail, a moderate 1.9-mile (3-kilometer) loop from the pool area, to see where the sulfurous waters come from. Along the way, you pass the ruins of the original pool building, built in the 1930s.

The hot springs are an hour's drive from the town of Jasper. Take Highway 16 east for 27 miles (44 kilometers) and turn right (south) onto Miette Road. From the Highway 16/Miette Road junction, it's 11 miles (17 kilometers) to the springs.

Mount Edith Cavell

Edith Cavell was a British nurse who worked in German-occupied Belgium during World War I. In 1915, a German firing squad executed Cavell after she was caught helping Allied soldiers escape across the border from Belgium to the Netherlands. Jasper's 11,046-foot (3,367 meter) Mount Edith Cavell bears her name.

You can drive up toward the mountain's north face on the snaking 8.7-mile (14-kilometer) Cavell Road, which is located off Highway 93A south of town.

At the top of the road, follow the **Path of the Glacier** trail, a short one-mile (1.6-kilometer) walk to a lookout opposite the Angel Glacier, which perches on the mountain above Cavell Pond. Expect snow on the surrounding mountains (and sometimes on the trail) at any time of year.

Camping

You can make **reservations** (877/737-3783, www.reservation.parkscanada.gc.ca) online or by phone for four Jasper

Medicine Lake

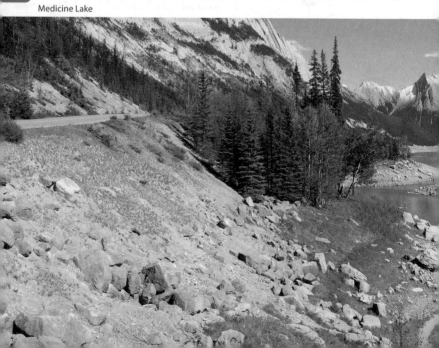

National Park campgrounds: Whistlers, Wapiti, Wabasso, and Pocahontas. Reservations are advised, particularly in July and August. You can make reservations starting in January for the upcoming year.

Whistlers Campground (Hwy. 93, 2.2 miles/3.5 kilometers south of Jasper, May-mid-Oct., $22.50-27.40 tent sites, $32.30-38.20 electrical sites) is Jasper's largest, with 781 sites that can accommodate everything from tents to big motor homes. The campground has washrooms with hot showers. The Whistlers area also has **oTENTiks** ($90), canvas-walled platform tents that sleep up to four adults and two children, with one queen bed, two bunk beds, and two lounge chairs that convert to single beds. Although the oTENTiks have electric lights and baseboard heaters, there are no outlets for charging phones or other electronics.

Like Whistlers, **Wapiti Campground** (Hwy. 93, 3.5 miles/5.4 kilometers south of Jasper, $27.40 tent sites, $32.30 electrical sites) accommodates both tents and RVs and has washrooms with hot showers. It has 362 sites available from May through mid-October; 93 sites are open for winter camping (mid-Oct.-Apr.).

Wabasso Campground (Hwy. 93A, 10 miles/16.5 kilometers south of Jasper, mid-June-early-Sept., $21.50), located off Highway 93A, which is quieter than the main Highway 93, has 231 sites for tents and small RVs. The washrooms have hot water but no showers.

Pocahontas Campground (Hwy. 16, mid-May-mid-Sept., $21.50) is off Highway 16, near the Miette Hot Springs, 28 miles (45 kilometers) east of the town of Jasper. Its 140 sites accommodate tents and small RVs. There is running water and flush toilets but no showers or electricity.

Snaring River Campground (Hwy. 16, mid-May-mid-Sept., $15.70) is also off Highway 16, but it's closer to town, eight miles (13 kilometers) to the east. It has 66 sites, some along the river, for tents and small RVs; some tent sites are in a more private, walk-in-only area. It's a rustic campground without showers, electricity, or flush toilets—just outhouses.

Town of Jasper

Set along the Athabasca River entirely within the national park, the compact town of Jasper has a year-round population of about 5,000. In summer, that number can swell to over 20,000 as seasonal workers arrive to cater to the influx of high-season visitors.

A good way to get oriented, while learning something about Jasper's heritage, is on a 90-minute historical walking tour of the town, **Jasper: A Walk in the Past** (www.friendsofjasper.com, 7:30pm daily late May-early Sept., free). Offered by the Friends of Jasper National Park, the tour is complimentary, but advance tickets are required; pick them up from the Friends store in the **Jasper**

Marilyn Monroe's Adventures in Jasper

The Canadian Rockies are glamorous enough without celebrity visitors, but Jasper had its moment in the Hollywood sun when an American movie icon came to town.

In 1953, director Otto Preminger, who subsequently became recognized for films like *Anatomy of a Murder* and *Exodus*, arrived in Jasper to make a new movie. *River of No Return* would star Robert Mitchum and Rory Calhoun along with the actress formerly known as Norma Jeane Mortenson: **Marilyn Monroe.**

The blond bombshell had all sorts of now-legendary escapades in Jasper while making this Wild West epic. Most famously, staff at the Jasper Park Lodge (now the Fairmont) refused to allow her to enter the dining room because she was wearing inappropriate attire for a woman: blue jeans. (Decades later, designer Tommy Hilfiger bought a pair of jeans that Monroe wore in the film at auction for US$37,000.)

Monroe injured her leg while filming a rafting scene in Jasper, and according to rumors, she was also escorted out of the Athabasca Hotel—on the arms of two dashing Mounties—for causing some sort of drunken commotion.

Monroe and director Preminger had a stormy relationship during the film, too. The director reportedly sniped that "Directing Marilyn Monroe was like directing Lassie. You needed 14 takes to get each one of them right."

What remains of Monroe's Jasper visit, beyond these (perhaps apocryphal) stories and the film itself, are photos of the star in this mountain setting. Local photographer Ray O'Neill, who came to town in 1942 and lived in Jasper for the next 45 years, had his 15 minutes of fame when he photographed Monroe during the filming. Some of his images are online at **Jasper Photography** (www.jasperphotography.com), and you may be able to view others at the **Jasper-Yellowhead Museum.** *Look* magazine staff photographer John Vachon also photographed the star during her time in Jasper; his photos are collected in the book *Marilyn, August 1953: The Lost Look Photos*.

While *River of No Return*, released in 1954, may be fading into history, it was still Jasper's Hollywood moment. After all, no matter how gorgeous your mountains are, it's not every day that Marilyn Monroe comes to town.

Information Centre (500 Connaught Dr.), which is also where the tour departs.

Sights and Activities
Jasper-Yellowhead Museum

How did Jasper get its name? Who are the Métis and what role did they play in Jasper's settlement? What's the story behind Jasper National Park?

If you're curious about these and other questions about the Jasper area, visit the **Jasper-Yellowhead Museum & Archives** (400 Bonhomme St., 780/852-3013, www.jaspermuseum.org, 10am-5pm daily June-Sept., 10am-5pm Thurs.-Sun. Oct.-May, adults $6, seniors, students, and over age 5 $5). The well-designed displays and artifacts trace the region's history from its aboriginal people to the early explorers and traders, the development of the railroad, the establishment of the national park, and the first days of tourism. The museum also sells used books (by donation) if you need to top up your vacation library.

★ Jasper Sky Tram

For great views, ride the **Jasper Sky Tram** (Whistlers Rd., 780/852-3093 or 866/850-8726, www.jasperskytram.com, 10am-5pm daily Apr.-mid-May, 9am-6pm daily mid-May-late June, 9am-8pm daily late-June-early Sept., 10am-5pm daily early-Sept.-Oct., adults $37, ages 6-15 $18.50, families $92.50), a seven-minute gondola trip that takes you 7,500 feet (2,300

Town of Jasper

To Pyramid Lake

To Hwy 16

To MALIGNE CANYON, MALIGNE LAKE, and MIETTE HOT SPRINGS

JUNIPER ST

16

PYRAMID LAKE RD

YELLOWHEAD HWY

Pyramid Benchland Trail

BONHOMME ST

COLIN CRESCENT

GEIKIE ST

ASPEN AVE

THE CRIMSON

ROBINSONS FOODS

CONNAUGHT DR

PATRICIA ST

CEDAR AVE

JASPER-YELLOWHEAD MUSEUM & ARCHIVES ★

To Mina Lakes

BEAR'S PAW BAKERY

JASPER HERITAGE FIREHALL

ELM AVE

JASPER INFORMATION CENTRE

WILDLIFE MUSEUM/ WHISTLER'S INN

SETON-JASPER HEALTHCARE CENTRE

MALIGNE AVE

REXALL

FAMOSO PIZZERIA

JASPER TRAIN STATION

PATRICIA STREET DELI

THE OTHER PAW

THE DOWNSTREAM

PHARMASAVE

JASPER BREWING COMPANY

PARK PLACE INN

MIETTE AVE

JASPER FARMERS MARKET

EVIL DAVE'S GRILL

PINE AVE

To Icefields Parkway, Banff (Banff National Park) and Prince George, BC

To Old Fort Point

0   200 yds
0   200 m

© AVALON TRAVEL

meters) above the national park and the town of Jasper. Book your tram ticket online to avoid the lines, especially in midsummer.

Want even better vistas of the surrounding snow-topped mountains? Then hike above the gondola station along the 0.75-mile (1.2-kilometer) dirt and shale path to the summit of Whistlers Mountain, elevation 8,100 feet (2,500 meters). On a clear day, you can see Mount Robson; at 12,972 feet (3,954 meters), it's the highest peak in the Canadian Rockies. The hike to the summit is a moderate climb that should take 45 to 60 minutes round-trip, although in spring and fall, parts of the path can be snow-covered.

The Sky Tram is five miles (8 kilometers) south of town; take Highway 93 south to Whistlers Road. **SunDog Tours** (780/852-4056 or 888/786-3641, www.sundogtours.com, adults $42, ages 5-12 $28) runs shuttles to the Sky Tram from town with pickups at several hotels; check the website or call for schedules. Prices include your tram ticket and transportation.

Sports and Recreation
Hiking
You don't have to go far from town to find scenic hiking trails. The **Jasper Discovery Trail** is a 5.2-mile (8.3 kilometer) loop that circles the town. It's marked with a bear symbol and has informational signs and kiosks along the way.

Old Fort Point is a rocky hill that rises above the Athabasca River. From the top, you have panoramic views of the town and the entire Jasper valley. You can climb straight up to the top, starting with 80 wooden steps and continuing on a steep dirt-and-rock path, but the easier route is to follow the **Old Fort Point Trail** (2.4 miles/3.8 kilometers), which begins as a gentle trail through the woods, then climbs steadily up to the lookout point; the elevation gain is 425 feet (130 meters). From the top, you can either circle

back the way you came, or go down the front face to the steps. To reach the trailhead, follow Highway 93A to the Old Fort Point/Lac Beauvert access road; there's a parking lot at the base of the trail.

The **Valley of the Five Lakes Trail,** a moderate 2.8-mile (4.5-kilometer) loop, takes you past five different bodies of water, which are all a different shade of blue. The differing lake depths account for the color variations. The trailhead is 5.6 miles (nine kilometers) south of town, off Highway 93.

Rafting
You can go white-water rafting on several rivers in the Jasper area. The gentlest rides are on the Athabasca River, while rafting tours on the Sunwapta (a First Nations word meaning "turbulent water") and Fraser Rivers are more wet and wild.

Jasper Raft Tours (780/852-2665 or 888/553-5628, www.jasperrafttours.com, May-Sept., adults $65, ages 6-17 $20, under age 6 $10) offers gentle 2.5-hour Athabasca River float tours, suitable for families and novice rafters.

Maligne Adventures (780/852-3370 or 866/625-4463, www.maligneadventures.com, May-Sept.) runs family-friendly **Atha B Expressway tours** (2 hours, adults $59, ages 5-14 $32) on the Athabasca, with mostly calm water and a few gentle class II rapids to add some excitement. For a little more adventure, the **Athabasca Falls Canyon Run** (2 hours, adults $79, ages 5-14 $42) starts at the base of Athabasca Falls south of town and mixes class II rapids with a gentle river float. The **Sunwapta River trip** (4 hours, $94 pp) has numerous class III rapids; the water is highest and fastest from mid-June through late July. For "big water," with class III+ rapids, take their **Mighty Fraser River tour** (5 hours, $109 pp).

Water Sports
You can go canoeing, kayaking, and even swimming (if you can brave the chilly

Jasper's Top-Secret Wartime Project

You might not think of Jasper as a place for a top-secret World War II mission or as a destination for scuba divers. But it was, and it is.

During the Second World War, the British government hatched a secret plan to build what they hoped would be an indestructible aircraft carrier out of a unique mixture of ice and wood pulp. The project team solicited Canada's participation, and after searching for a location that would be cold enough to build what essentially would be an ice boat, the designers began work at Jasper's Patricia Lake.

The clandestine project to construct this futuristic vessel took the code name "Habbakuk," based on the Old Testament's prophet Habakkuk, who wrote, "regard and wonder marvelously. For I will work a work in your days which ye will not believe."

In 1943, working in secret at Patricia Lake, the team constructed a scale model of the boat, measuring 60 by 30 by 19.5 feet (18 by 9 by 6 meters). At that point, however, the tide of the war turned, and despite the seemingly successful prototype, the project was quietly killed. The Canadian team members ordered that anything reusable be stripped off the boat and that the refrigeration units that kept the prototype afloat be turned off. As it began to melt, the Habbakuk project sunk to the bottom of Patricia Lake, where its remains remain today.

If you're a scuba diver, you can dive to the site of this abandoned wartime project. Based at the Patricia Lake Bungalows, **Jasper Dive Adventures** (780/852-3560, www.jasperdiveadventures.com) offer a **Guided Habbakuk Tour** ($75, rental equipment not included) for experienced divers (with Open Water Certification and 15 logged dives), where you can learn more about this wartime project and dive to the Habbakuk's final resting place.

---

waters) on scenic Jasper lakes close to town.

Named for the wife of Colonel Maynard Rogers, the first superintendent of Jasper National Park, **Lake Annette** (Lake Annette Rd.) has a sandy beach and turquoise water. The paved **Lake Annette Loop Trail** is a 1.5-mile (2.4-kilometer) lakeside walking path. From town, take Highway 16 east to Maligne Road, then take the first right onto Old Lodge Road (toward the Fairmont Jasper Park Lodge). Turn left onto Lake Annette Road and follow it to the shore.

Locals recommend swimming at **Lake Edith** (Lake Annette Rd.) in mid- to late summer when the lake level begins to drop and the water warms up slightly. The beach access is beyond Lake Annette on Lake Annette Road.

Ringed by mountains, **Pyramid Lake** (Pyramid Lake Rd.) is a scenic spot for canoeing or kayaking. Opposite the hotel of the same name, **Pyramid Lake Resort**

Boat Rentals (780/852-4900 or 888/852-7737) rents out canoes ($35 per hour), kayaks (single $35 per hour, double $40 per hour), rowboats ($35), and mountain bikes ($20 per hour). From town, follow Pyramid Lake Road (off Connaught Dr.) for four miles (6.5 kilometers) to the lake.

Horseback Riding

Jasper Riding Stables (1 Pyramid Lake Rd., 780/852-7433, www.jasperstables. com, daily mid-May-mid-Oct.) offers one-hour (over age 5, $42), two-hour (over age 7, $72), and three-hour (over age 8, $105) trail rides, which take you to viewpoints above the surrounding lakes and mountains.

Winter Sports

At 5,570 feet (1,698 meters), **Marmot Basin Ski Resort** (1 Marmot Rd., 780/852-3816 or 866/952-3816, www.skimarmot. com, 9am-4pm daily early Nov.-early May, lift ticket adults $89, seniors, students, and ages 13-17 $71, ages 6-12 $32.25) has the highest base elevation of all Canada's winter sports resorts. The mountain's seven lifts serve 1,675 acres (678 hectares) of terrain. The 86 runs are rated 30 percent novice, 30 percent intermediate, 20 percent advanced, and 20 percent expert.

Marmot Basin is 12.5 miles (20 kilometers) south of Jasper, off Highway 93. You need a Jasper park pass to visit the ski area, which is within the national park boundaries.

Entertainment and Events

On Sunday evenings in July and August, stop into the **Jasper Heritage Fire Hall** (411 Patricia St.) for the **Mountain Music Jam** (www.pc.gc.ca, 7pm Sun. July-Aug., free). Built in 1936, the Fire Hall also hosts other arts events; pick up a schedule at the **Jasper Information Centre** (500 Connaught Dr.). Note the tower atop the Fire Hall; it was once used as a drying rack for fire hoses.

Jasper is one of the world's largest **dark sky preserves,** where illuminated signs and other outdoor lighting are limited to keep the skies clear and the stars visible. The town celebrates its status as a go-to stargazing destination during the annual **Dark Sky Festival** (www.jasperdarksky. travel, Oct.), with several days of lectures, workshops, storytelling, and star-spotting events.

Accommodations
Under $150

As members of the **Jasper Home Accommodation Association** (www.stay-injasper.com, $60-190 d), many Jasper homeowners rent out a room or two to guests. Some offer breakfast, while others rent rooms only. Get a listing of available accommodations on their website or at the **Jasper Information Centre** (500 Connaught Dr.).

$150-250

Among the nicest features of the alpine-style **Whistler's Inn** (105 Miette Ave., 780/852-3361 or 800/282-9919, www.whistlersinn.com, $175-335 d) are the two rooftop hot tubs where you can soak as you take in the mountain views. The 64 guest rooms, with cherry-toned furniture, white bedding, and plaid accents, have mini fridges, coffeemakers, and Wi-Fi included. The location opposite the Jasper train station couldn't be more central. On the inn's lower level, stop into the **Wildlife Museum** (7am-10pm daily, $3, families $6, hotel guests free), which was set up in the 1950s and exhibits 100 taxidermy animals native to Alberta's parks, including cougars, elk, and bears. To experience a different type of wildlife, hang with the locals at the hotel's **Whistle Stop Pub.**

Centrally located but quiet, the **Park Place Inn** (623 Patricia St., 780/852-9770 or 866/852-9770, www.parkplaceinn. com, $159-269 d) has 12 upscale rooms and two suites, decorated in earth tones with mini fridges and coffeemakers; some have whirlpool tubs or fireplaces. No meals are provided, but there's a common microwave that guests can use, and you're surrounded by the town's cafés and eateries. Underground parking and Wi-Fi are included.

Want a no-frills place to sleep? Friendly **Mount Robson Inn** (902 Connaught Dr., 780/852-3327 or 855/552-7737, www. mountrobsoninn.com, $189-364 d), a two-story motel a few blocks from the center of town, fills the bill. The basic guest rooms have microwaves, fridges, and coffeemakers; the larger units can accommodate families. There's a laundry on-site and a hot tub facing the parking lot. Rates include continental breakfast, parking, and Wi-Fi. Staff are quick to help with tips on things to do, so you may not mind the painfully slow Internet connection.

Less than 15 minutes from town, the ★ **Patricia Lake Bungalows** (Pyramid Lake Rd., 780/852-3560 or 888/499-6848, www.patricialakebungalows.com,

Edmonton: Gateway to Jasper

If you're flying to Alberta, Edmonton has the closest international airport to Jasper National Park. And if you're planning an Edmonton stopover, here are some things to do.

Alberta's provincial capital has several worthwhile museums, starting with the **Art Gallery of Alberta** (2 Sir Winston Churchill Square, 780/422-6223, www.youraga.ca, 11am-5pm Tues. and Thurs.-Sun., 11am-9pm Wed., adults $12.50, seniors and students over age 6 $8.50, families $26.50), an exhibit center for contemporary art in a distinctive downtown building designed by the late American architect Randall Stout.

Housed in four glass pyramids, the **Muttart Conservatory** (626 96A St., 780/442-5311, www.edmonton.ca, 10am-5pm Fri.-Wed., 10am-9pm Thurs., adults $12.25, seniors and students $10.50, ages 2-12 $6.50, families $36) is Edmonton's botanical garden, with plants and flowers from around the world. The conservatory has an excellent contemporary café, **Culina at the Muttart** (780/466-1181, www.culinafamily.com, 10am-4pm daily, mains $13-18), serving salads, sandwiches, and inventive mains, like beef *mechado* (a Filipino beef stew) or cheddar-filled pierogi with beet-dill salsa and pickled onions.

To learn more about Edmonton's history, visit **Fort Edmonton Park** (Fort Edmonton Park Rd. NW, 780/442-5311, www.fortedmontonpark.ca, 10am-3pm Mon.-Fri., 10am-5pm Sat.-Sun. mid-May-June, 10am-5pm daily July-Aug., 11am-5pm Sat.-Sun. Sept., adults $26.20, seniors and ages 2-17 $20.90), where costumed interpreters take you back to the early fur-trading days, the pioneer era of the late 1800s, and the city's settlement at the beginning of the 20th century.

You can't visit Edmonton without stopping off at North America's largest shopping center, the **West Edmonton Mall** (8882 170 St., 780/444-5313, www.wem.ca, 10am-9pm Mon.-Sat., 11am-6pm Sun.), which has more than 800 stores, a waterpark, an aquarium, a casino, mini golf, a skating rink, and the world's biggest indoor amusement park.

Edmonton also has a great year-round showcase for local foods and crafts, the **Old Strathcona Farmers Market** (10310 83 Ave. NW, 780/439-1844, http://osfm.ca, 8am-3pm Sat.), with more than 130 vendors.

When you've worked up an appetite for a sit-down meal, squeeze into the tiny trattoria **Corso 32** (10345 Jasper Ave., 780/421-4622, http://corso32.com, 5pm-11pm daily, mains $21-38) for fine handmade pastas and other imaginative Italian fare. The buzzing **Three Boars Eatery** (8424 109 St., 780/757-2600, www.threeboars.ca, 5pm-10pm Sun.-Mon. and Wed.-Thurs., 5pm-midnight Fri.-Sat., small plates $4-22) has eclectic plates to share, like roasted potatoes with Sriracha mayo, Brussels sprouts with buckwheat honey, or smoked quail. Creative cocktails and more Canadian-inspired sharing plates, including crunchy salad with raw, pickled, and fried veggies, or garlic scape cavatelli with crab, are at **North 53** (10240 124 St., 587/524-5353, http://north53.com, 5pm-late Sun.-Thurs., 5pm-2am Fri.-Sat., small plates $4-28). For "untamed cuisine" using lots of Alberta ingredients, like bison with hazelnut spaetzle or clam-and-pastrami tart, try **RGE RD** ("Range Road," 10643 123 St., 780/447-4577, www.rgerd.ca, from 5pm Mon.-Sat., mains $24-32).

For more information about the Edmonton region, contact **Tourism Edmonton** (800/463-4667, http://exploreedmonton.com) or **Travel Alberta** (800/252-3782, http://travelalberta.com).

May-mid.-Oct., $109-355 d) feel like a world away. On a forested site by the lake, the 52 family-friendly units at this summer camp-style resort (the same family has run it for four generations) include everything from simple motel rooms to log cabins to deluxe suites. The newest units are in The Grove, where the modern one-bedroom cabins have barbecues and kitchens with cherry cabinets. Soak in the outdoor hot tub or rent kayaks, canoes, or row boats to go exploring; the intrepid can swim in the chilly lake. There's a playground and games for the kids as well as a guest laundry. Internet access is available in the office; as in many Jasper locations, the included Wi-Fi can be erratic.

Over $250

★ **The Crimson** (200 Connaught Dr., 780/852-3394 or 888/852-7737, www. mpljasper.com, $228-348 d) brought urban style to small-town Jasper, when the owners converted a 1950s lodge into a three-story boutique motel. In the 99 modern guest rooms, beige coverlets with red accents top the beds; all units have air-conditioning, microwaves, mini fridges, and Keurig coffeemakers, and many have kitchenettes. You can swim in the indoor pool (though it's in a window-less space) or soak in the hot tub. Rates include Wi-Fi and parking.

Across the road from a trout-filled lake 3.6 miles (5.8 kilometers) from town, **Pyramid Lake Resort** (Pyramid Lake Rd., 780/852-4900 or 888/852-7737, www.mpljasper.com, $239-409 d) has 62 rooms, cabins, and chalets that vary from rustic to lodge-modern. All have updated baths as well as gas fireplaces, mini fridges, coffeemakers, teakettles, and flat-screen satellite TVs. There's Wi-Fi, too, although staff caution that the signal can be intermittent. Other amenities include an outdoor hot tub, a sauna, and a guest laundry. You can rent canoes, kayaks, rowboats, and bikes at the lakeshore.

When the Jasper Park Lodge opened in the 1920s overlooking Lac Beauvert, it was reportedly the largest single-story log building in the world. Sadly, a fire destroyed that original structure in the 1950s, but the hotel now on the site is Jasper's most luxurious lodging. The ★ **Fairmont Jasper Park Lodge** (Old Lodge Rd., 780/852-3301 or 866/540-4454, www.fairmont.com, $435-929 d,

self-parking free, valet parking $20), a 10-minute drive from town, has a range of accommodations, the best with lake views, including upscale hotel rooms, deluxe cabins, a one-bedroom cottage, and an eight-bedroom manor. Join Fairmont's complimentary President Club for free Wi-Fi. To explore the lake and surroundings, rent canoes ($40 per hour), kayaks (single $35 per hour, double $40 per hour), or mountain bikes ($25 per hour) at **The Boathouse** (780/852-3301, May-Oct.). If you're not getting enough exercise in the mountains, you can work out in the fitness room or swim in the heated outdoor pool. The 18-hole golf course, opened in 1925, ranks among Canada's best. The lodge also has a lovely lake-view **Reflections Spa,** as well as several restaurants and lounges.

Food
Groceries and Markets
You can find local food at the summer **Jasper Farmers Market** (McCready Centre, 701 Turret St., 780/852-3599, noon-3pm Wed. late June-early Sept.).

For groceries, Jasper's largest market is **Robinsons Foods** (218 Connaught Dr., 780/852-3195, www.robinsonfoods.com, 8am-10pm daily summer, 8am-8pm daily winter).

Cafés, Bakeries, and Light Bites
Start your day with a scone or sticky bun and coffee from Jasper's favorite baked goods purveyor, ★ **Bear's Paw Bakery** (4 Pyramid Rd., 780/852-3233, www. bearspawbakery.com, 6am-6pm daily). A second location is called **The Other Paw** (610 Connaught Dr., 780/852-2253, www. bearspawbakery.com, 7am-6pm daily).

If you want a sandwich to take out on the trails, find your way to the ★ **Patricia Street Deli** (606 Patricia St., 780/852-4814, 10am-5pm daily, sandwiches $6-8), a take-out spot hidden behind the escalator in a mini mall. Choose your meat (roast turkey, black forest ham, smoked beef, roast beef), cheese, and loads of veggies—lettuce, peppers, carrots, beets, pickles, and sprouts—and your sandwich will be made to order. They've usually got homemade cookies, too.

Contemporary

There's nothing sinister about **Evil Dave's Grill** (622 Patricia St., 780/852-3323, www. evildavesgrill.com, dinner from 5pm daily, mains $23-35), an upscale but laid-back downtown eatery, except for the entertaining names of its dishes. Popular plates include Diabolical Tenderloin (Alberta beef in a red wine demi-glace) and Malevolent Meatloaf, made with bison and wild boar bacon. To finish, there's Wicked Cheesecake and a Sinful Sundae.

Italian and Pizza

Famoso Pizzeria (607 Patricia St., 780/852-5577, www.famoso.ca, 11am-midnight daily, mains $11-17), a Canadian chain, makes decent Neapolitan-style pizzas in their wood-burning oven, from standards like the Margherita (mozzarella and basil) and the Abruzzo (sausage, red onions, and mushrooms) to funkier pies like the Cavoletti (gorgonzola, dates, walnuts, and honey) and the Don Andreas (chicken, avocado, and corn-chipotle salsa). The lunchtime deal gets you a personal-size pizza with soup or salad for $11.50.

Starting with simple homemade pastas and moving on to grilled Alberta rib eye served with polenta or a boar chop with arugula pesto, ★ **Orso Trattoria** (Old Lodge Rd., 780/852-3301, www.fairmont. com, breakfast 6am-11:30am daily, dinner 6pm-10pm daily summer, 6pm-10pm Fri.-Sat. winter, mains breakfast $20-27, dinner $23-55), the classy main dining room at the Fairmont Jasper Park Lodge, channels Italy via the Rockies, using local produce and meats in its modern Italian meals. The restaurant, which has spectacular vistas across Lac Beauvert, also serves traditional **afternoon tea** (2pm-4:30pm daily summer, call for off-season hours, $32).

Pub Fare

For a casual meal and a pint, head for the local brewpub, **Jasper Brewing Company** (624 Connaught Dr., 780/852-4111, www. jasperbrewingco.ca, 11am-1am daily, mains $15-44), known for being the first brewery to open in a Canadian national park. They make several beers, including Sutter-Hill Pil (a pilsner), Rockhopper IPA (a hoppy India pale ale), and Jasper the Bear Ale, which is brewed with honey from B.C.'s Okanagan Valley. To pair with your brews, the food menu begins with basic burgers but quickly progresses to more inventive salads and sandwiches, like the beet and quinoa patty, plus heartier plates like Alberta beef or roast chicken.

The Downstream (620 Connaught Dr., 780/852-9449, www.downstreamjasper. ca, 5pm-2am daily, mains $17-28) takes good-value pub fare and amps it up with global flavors. You can nibble on miso-glazed steak bites or house-made falafel, travel the world with tandoori chicken or sweet potato and goat cheese lasagna, or come back to Canada for cabernet-glazed bison ribs or a bacon-topped burger. Vegetarians and other tofu-lovers should try the Legendary Samba, a substantial sandwich piled with grilled tofu, peppers, onions, melted mozzarella, and hot sauce overflowing out of its pretzel bun. The Downstream is on the lower level below the Fiddle River Restaurant.

Information and Services
Visitor Information

Tourism Jasper (780/852-6236, www. jasper.travel) produces an annual Jasper visitor guide, available in print and online, and also provides information about things to do, places to stay, and area events on its website.

In town, get your questions answered at the Parks Canada **Jasper Information Centre** (500 Connaught Dr., 780/852-6176, www.pc.gc.ca, 9am-5pm daily mid-Mar.-mid-May, 9am-7pm daily mid-May-mid-Sept., 9am-5pm daily mid-Sept.-Oct., 10am-5pm Wed.-Sun. Nov.-mid-Mar.).

Medical Services

The **Seton-Jasper Healthcare Centre** (518 Robson St., 780/852-3344, www.albertahealthservices.ca) provides 24-hour emergency medical services.

Local pharmacies include **Pharmasave** (610 Patricia St., 780/852-5903, www.pharmasavejasper.com, 9am-9pm daily) and **Rexall** (602 Patricia St., 780/852-4441, www.rexall.ca, 9am-9pm Mon.-Fri., 9am-7pm Sat., 9am-6pm Sun.).

Getting Around

The town of Jasper itself is small, and most accommodations, restaurants, shops, and in-town sights are within walking distance. However, many of the national park's attractions are spread out across a wide area. You either need to have your own vehicle, or book a tour with a local outfitter.

Parking

Jasper has three large **free public parking lots** on Connaught Drive; one is on the south side of the Jasper train station, while the other two are north of the station. You can park in these lots for up to 72 hours.

Street parking in Jasper is also free. Many parking spots in the center of town have a two-hour limit.

Car Rentals

Avis (414 Connaught Dr., 780/852-3970, www.avis.ca), **Budget** (414 Connaught Dr., 780/852-3222, www.budget.ca), and **National** (607 Connaught Dr., at the Jasper train station, 780/852-1117, www.nationalcar.ca) have car rental offices in Jasper.

Sightseeing Tours

Maligne Adventures (780/852-3370 or 866/625-4463, www.maligneadventures.com) runs several Jasper sightseeing tours, including the **Maligne Valley Wildlife & Waterfalls Tour** (5-6 hours), with stops at Maligne Canyon, Medicine Lake, and Maligne Lake, where you can choose a lake cruise (adults $109, ages 5-14 $60) or a guided hike (adults $65, ages 5-14 $40); an **Evening Wildlife Search** (3 hours, adults $65, ages 8-14 $40) that takes you to various Jasper locations where you might spot elk, bears, moose, sheep, or deer; and an **Edith Cavell Walk** (3-3.5 hours, adults $65, ages 8-14 $40), where you drive the 8.7-mile (14-kilometer) Cavell Road that snakes up the mountain and take a guided hike on the Path of the Glacier trail.

Maligne Tours (780/852-3370 or 866/625-4463, www.malignelake.com) operates the similar **Maligne Valley Wildlife and Waterfalls Tour** (5-6 hours), which includes stops at Maligne Canyon, Medicine Lake, and Maligne Lake for a lake cruise (adults $109, ages 5-14 $60) or guided hike (adults $65, ages 5-14 $40). If you just need transportation between town and Maligne Lake, take their **Maligne Lake Shuttle** (late May-early Oct., one-way adults $30, ages 5-14 $15).

SunDog Tours (780/852-4056 or 888/786-3641, www.sundogtours.com) offers several tours in the Jasper region. The **Maligne Valley Sightseeing Tour** (June-mid-Oct., 5-6 hours) takes you to Maligne Canyon, Medicine Lake, and Maligne Lake, with options for a lake cruise (adults $109, under age 12 $60) or a guided hike on the Mary Schaffer Loop (adults $65, under age 12 $35). The **Mount Edith Cavell Tour** (late June-mid.-Oct., 3-3.5 hours, adults $65, ages 6-12 $40) includes transportation up the winding Cavell Road and a guided hike on the Path of the Glacier trail. They can also take you to and from the **Jasper Sky Tram** (adults $42, ages 5-12 $28, including tram tickets).

Hiking Tours

Walks and Talks Jasper (780/852-4994 or

888/242-3343, www.walksntalks.com) offers several guided interpretive hikes in the Jasper area, including a hike to **Mount Edith Cavell Meadows** (adults $90, kids $50) and a **Maligne Canyon Guided 5 Bridges Adventure** (adults $90, kids $50).

Motorcycle Tours

Is riding a motorcycle on your bucket list? Then book a guided ride with **Jasper Motorcycle Tours** (610 Patricia St., 780/931-6100, www.jaspermotorcycletours.com, Apr.-Oct.), for a unique way to explore highlights of the Jasper region. You'll ride either on the bike behind your guide or in a sidecar attached to your guide's bike.

On a **one-hour tour** (adults $99), you can choose to follow winding Marmot Basin Road to a viewpoint over the Athabasca Valley or explore the lakes and lookouts on the outskirts of town. On a **two-hour tour** (adults $159), your options include riding south to Athabasca Falls, touring Maligne Canyon and Medicine Lake, or switch-backing up to Mount Edith Cavell near the base of the Angel Glacier.

The options on the **three-hour tour** (adults $209) are a ride to Maligne Lake or to Miette Hot Springs, with time to go for a dip in the pools. If you have five to six hours, you can take the **Icefields Parkway Tour** (adults $299), a 62-mile (100 kilometer) drive to the Columbia Icefield.

Before you set out, staff will outfit you in a leather jacket, leather pants, gloves, goggles, and a helmet. Yes, you're encouraged to take photos.

The Kootenays

Rambling through the Kootenays in southeastern British Columbia, you can soak in natural hot springs, hang out in funky mountain towns, and explore the region's multicultural past.

BANFF AND LAKE LOUISE

KOOTENAY NATIONAL PARK

85 MI/140 KM
2 HOURS

505 MI/260 KM
9.5 HOURS

BRITISH COLUMBIA

235 MI/375 KM
4.5 HOURS

THE OKANAGAN

NELSON

VANCOUVER

160 MI/260 KM
3.75 HOURS

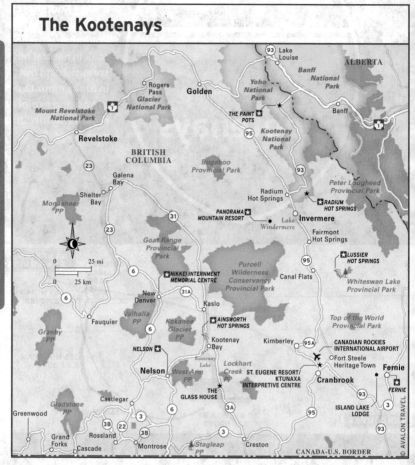

The Kootenays

The Kootenays' roads are made for meandering.

Covering a wide swath across British Columbia's southeastern quadrant, this region extends from the Rocky Mountain peaks along the Alberta border over several mountain ranges west toward the Okanagan Valley.

Two main highways cross the Kootenays region. The main east-west route across southern British Columbia, Highway 3, also known as the Crowsnest Highway, twists and climbs for 520 miles (840 kilometers) between Alberta and the town of Hope, near Vancouver and the B.C. coast. Heading north-south through the Kootenay region, Highway 93/95 runs between Golden, Radium Hot Springs, Cranbrook, and the U.S. border; dubbed the "Hot Springs Highway," this road passes numerous mountain mineral springs where you can stop for a soak.

Bordering Yoho and Banff National Parks, Kootenay National Park draws outdoor explorers to its varied landscape, encompassing mountain peaks, deep canyons, and arid grasslands. Throughout the Kootenays, down-to-earth mountain towns, like Fernie to the

Highlights

★ **The Paint Pots:** Among the distinctive geological features in Kootenay National Park are these mineral pools surrounded by orange ocher beds (page 312).

★ **Radium Hot Springs:** With a lap pool and a warm soaking pool, these natural springs in Kootenay National Park please everyone from kids to seniors (page 313).

★ **Panorama Mountain Resort:** Hikers and cyclists in summer and skiers and snowboarders in winter all come to get outdoors at this mountain playground near Invermere (page 320).

★ **Lussier Hot Springs:** Soak in a true natural hot spring, in an otherwise chilly river in remote Whiteswan Lake Provincial Park (page 321).

★ **Fernie:** With mountain peaks surrounding a historic downtown district, this charming East Kootenay community has lots to do, indoors and out (page 322).

★ **Nelson:** This funky town in the West Kootenays has everything you need for a road-trip stopover: excellent restaurants, independent shops, moderately priced accommodations, and

plenty of outdoor activities (page 333).

★ **Ainsworth Hot Springs:** At these hot pools near Nelson, you can soak and steam in a natural horseshoe-shaped cave (page 339).

★ **Nikkei Internment Memorial Centre:** Learn the dark heritage of Japanese Canadian wartime internment at this informative museum on the site of a World War II-era camp (page 342).

Best Hotels

★ **Cross River Wilderness Centre:** At this unique log-cabin getaway, you can choose outdoor adventures, wilderness trips, or aboriginal experiences (page 315).

★ **Fernie 901:** A former Fernie school has been transformed into striking modern condos, many available as short-term vacation rentals (page 326).

★ **St. Eugene Resort:** Once a residential school for aboriginal children, this Cranbrook hotel mixes its historic past with a casino, a golf course, and other modern amenities (page 331).

★ **Cloudside Inn:** You can walk to the town's cafés, restaurants, and shops from this well-run eight-room B&B in a Nelson Victorian home (page 338).

east and Nelson farther west, make interesting stopovers, with heritage buildings housing restaurants and shops, and plenty to do outdoors.

Another reason to travel through the Kootenays is to delve into its multicultural past. Sights throughout the region illustrate the history of First Nations people, settlers drawn by the gold rush, and Russian pacifists known as the Doukhobors. You can also learn about a darker past as well, visiting an internment camp that housed Japanese Canadians during World War II.

But wherever you travel in the Kootenays, take your time. These roads are made for a leisurely road trip.

Getting to the Kootenays

Driving from Banff and Lake Louise
To Kootenay National Park
Kootenay National Park is an easy day trip from either Banff or Lake Louise. Take **Highway 1** west from Banff or east from Lake Louise to **Highway 93** south, which runs through the park. The town of **Radium Hot Springs** is at the park's southern boundary.

The trip from **Banff** to Radium Hot Springs is **85 miles (140 kilometers).**

From **Lake Louise** to Radium Hot Springs, it's **80 miles (130 kilometers).** Each of these routes takes **1.75 to 2 hours.**

To Fernie
After passing through Kootenay National Park, continue south on **Highway 93**, and at **Highway 3**, turn east. Highway 3 runs directly into Fernie. It's **215 miles (350 kilometers)** to Fernie from either Banff or Lake Louise; the drive takes **four hours.**

To Nelson
If you're driving from Banff or Lake Louise to Nelson, you can choose several different routes.

One option is to take **Highway 93** south to **Highway 3** west. Then, to follow the **most scenic route**, turn north at **Creston** onto **Highway 3A**, which follows the east shore of Kootenay Lake. At **Kootenay Bay**, take the free 35-minute **Kootenay Lake Ferry** (250/229-4215, www.th.gov.bc.ca, 7:10am-10:20pm daily) across the lake to **Balfour.** Continue on **Highway 3A** to Nelson.

Alternatively, stay on **Highway 3** west beyond Creston to **Highway 6**, where you turn north to Nelson.

Both the Highway 3 and Highway 3A routes are **310 miles (500 kilometers)** from Banff or Lake Louise. The **Highway 3** route takes **six hours.** The **Highway 3A** route adds about an hour of travel time, for a total of about **seven hours;**

Best Restaurants

★ **Safta's:** Middle Eastern fare in the Kootenays? Yes, this Invermere eatery serves excellent falafel, tabbouleh, shawarma, and more (page 319).

★ **The Blue Toque Diner:** For the best breakfasts in Fernie, head to this inventive restaurant in the town's former rail station (page 327).

★ **Oso Negro Café:** Nelson's own coffee roastery runs this bustling café, where you can pair pastries or panini with your espresso or latté (page 338).

★ **Bibo:** In a cozy brick house with an outdoor terrace, this Nelson bistro uses local ingredients in its globally inspired comfort food (page 339).

on this winding road, you'll need to take it slow—the better to scan the beautiful lake views—and allow time for the ferry crossing.

There's another option from Banff or Lake Louise that takes you through several of **B.C.'s national parks** (Yoho, Glacier, Mount Revelstoke). Take **Highway 1** west into British Columbia. When you reach **Revelstoke,** turn south on **Highway 23.** Thirty miles (47 kilometers) south of Revelstoke, take the free 20-minute **Upper Arrow Lake Ferry** (250/265-2105, www.th.gov.bc.ca, 5am-midnight daily) from **Shelter Bay** to **Galena Bay.** Continue south on **Highway 23,** then take **Highway 6** south into Nelson. At **295 miles (475 kilometers),** this route is slightly shorter than the Highway 3 route from Lake Louise, but it takes an average of 30 minutes longer because of the ferry crossing.

Driving from the Okanagan
To Kootenay National Park

From **Kelowna,** the **most direct route** to Kootenay National Park is **Highway 1.** Follow **Highway 97** north to **Vernon,** where you continue north on **Highway 97A** to **Highway 1** east. Follow Highway 1 to **Golden,** then turn south on **Highway 95,** which will take you to **Radium Hot Springs** and the park's south entrance. It's **280 miles (450 kilometers)** from Kelowna to Radium; the drive takes **5.5 hours.**

From **Osoyoos** or the South Okanagan,

you can either go north through the Okanagan Valley on **Highway 97** and north to **Vernon,** where you continue north on **Highway 97A** to **Highway 1** east, or take **Highway 3,** which runs east from Osoyoos into the Kootenays. To Kootenay National Park, stay on Highway 3 east to **Highway 93/95** north toward **Cranbrook, Invermere,** and **Radium Hot Springs.** From Osoyoos to Radium via **Highway 1,** it's **360 miles (575 kilometers)** and the drive takes **7 to 7.5 hours;** via **Highway 3,** it's **365 miles (590 kilometers)** and the drive takes **7.5 to 8 hours.**

To Fernie

From **Kelowna** to Fernie, one option is to take **Highway 33** south to **Highway 3,** and then continue east on Highway 3. This route is **390 miles (625 kilometers)** and takes **eight hours.** A second option is to take **Highway 97 and 97A** north to **Highway 1,** follow Highway 1 to **Golden,** turn south on **Highway 95,** and then take **Highway 3** east. At **415 miles (670 kilometers),** this alternative is slightly longer, but it takes about the same amount of travel time; the route takes you through **B.C.'s national parks.**

From **Osoyoos** to Fernie, simply follow **Highway 3** east; it's **335 miles (540 kilometers),** a **seven-hour** drive.

To Nelson

From **Kelowna** to Nelson, the **shortest route** is to follow **Highway 33** south to **Highway 3** east. At **Castlegar,** turn northeast on **Highway 3A,** which will take you into Nelson. This route is **215 miles (350 kilometers)** and takes **4.5 to 5 hours.**

Alternatively, go north from Kelowna on **Highway 97,** then at **Vernon,** follow **Highway 6** east. This **scenic** two-lane road takes you to **Needles,** where you board the five-minute **Needles Cable Ferry** (250/265-2105, www.th.gov.bc.ca, 5:15am-9:45pm daily), a free shuttle across Lower Arrow Lake. Continue on **Highway 6** through Nakusp and New Denver to Nelson. The route is **240 miles (390 kilometers)** and takes **5.5 to 6 hours.**

From **Osoyoos** to Nelson, take **Highway 3** to **Castlegar,** then follow **Highway 3A** northeast to Nelson. It's **160 miles (260 kilometers),** a **3.75-hour** drive.

Driving from Vancouver
To Kootenay National Park

From Vancouver, follow **Highway 1** east to **Hope,** where you pick up **Highway 3** east, but exit immediately onto **Highway 5 (Coquihalla Hwy.)** north. Follow the Coquihalla over the mountains to **Kamloops,** where you rejoin **Highway 1** east and follow it to **Golden.** At Golden, turn south on **Highway 95,** which takes you to **Radium Hot Springs** and the park's south entrance. This trip is **505 miles (815 kilometers),** a **9.5-hour** drive.

To Fernie

You have two options to reach Fernie from Vancouver: **Highway 1** or **Highway 3.** Although the Highway 1 alternative is longer, both take **11.5 to 12 hours.** For either route, leave Vancouver on Highway 1 and continue east to Hope.

For the **Highway 1** option, which goes through **B.C.'s national parks,** continue east at **Hope** onto **Highway 3,** then exit onto **Highway 5 (Coquihalla Hwy.)** north. Follow the Coquihalla to **Kamloops,** where you rejoin **Highway 1** east and continue to **Golden.** At Golden, turn south on **Highway 95** and then take **Highway**

3 east to Fernie. This route is **645 miles (1,035 kilometers)** from Vancouver.

The second option is to pick up **Highway 3** east at **Hope** and follow it all the way to Fernie. This route is **585 miles (940 kilometers).**

To Nelson

From Vancouver to Nelson, go east on **Highway 1** to **Hope,** then continue east on **Highway 3** through **Osoyoos** and on to **Castlegar.** From there, follow **Highway 3A** northeast into Nelson. This trip is **410 miles (660 kilometers)** and takes **8.5 hours.**

Getting There by Air or Bus
By Air

The city of Cranbrook has a regional airport that serves eastern British Columbia. From **Canadian Rockies International Airport** (YXC, 9370 Airport Access Rd., Cranbrook, 250/426-7913, www.flycanadianrockies.com), **Air Canada** (888/247-2262, www.aircanada.com) flies to Vancouver and Calgary. **Pacific Coastal Airlines** (800/663-2872, www.pacificcoastal.com) flies from Cranbrook to Vancouver, Victoria, or Kelowna. **Budget** (250/426-5425 or 800/268-8900, www.budget.ca) and **Enterprise** (250/489-3689 or 800/261-7331, www.enterprise.com) have car rental offices in Cranbrook.

Otherwise, the main international airport closest to the Kootenay region is **Calgary International Airport** (YYC, 2000 Airport Rd. NE, 403/735-1200, www.yyc.com).

Spokane International Airport (GEG, 9000 W. Airport Dr., Spokane, 509/455-6455, www.spokaneairports.net), across the U.S. border in Washington State, is another option, particularly if you're going to Nelson or other parts of the West Kootenays. It's 155 miles (250 kilometers) from Nelson. Remember to add time for the international border crossing to what would otherwise be a three-hour drive.

By Bus

Greyhound (800/661-8747, www.grey-hound.ca) can take you from Vancouver to **Nelson** (1128 Lakeside Dr., 250/352-3939, 11.75 hours, adults $85-172) and **Fernie** (1561 9th Ave., 250/423-5577, 16.75 hours, adults $122-195), but it's a long, slow ride to either destination. Greyhound also runs an overnight bus from Calgary to Fernie (6.5 hours, adults $35-85) and Nelson (11.5 hours, adults $55-130).

From Golden, B.C., you can catch a Greyhound bus to the town of **Radium Hot Springs** (7507 Main St. W., 250/347-9726, 1.25 hours, adults $12.65), at the south entrance to Kootenay National Park. The bus depot is 1.9 miles (3 kilometers) from the park's hot springs pool.

Kootenay National Park

The 543-square-mile (1,406-square-kilometer) **Kootenay National Park** (250/347-9505, www.pc.gc.ca) covers a diverse landscape, extending from the mountain peaks of Banff and Yoho National Parks to the north, through several deep canyons, and to arid grass-lands regions at the park's southern end. Park staff describe its terrain as "from cactus to glacier."

Kootenay National Park owes its existence in part to a highway. In 1920, an agreement between the federal and provincial governments to build the first automobile route through the Canadian Rockies led to the creation of the park and the construction of the Banff-Windermere Highway. Now called Highway 93 or the Kootenay Parkway, this road runs 60 miles (100 kilometers) through the park.

As you drive through the park, you can't help but notice rows and rows of burned trees. In 2003, a lightning strike set off a massive fire, which burned for 40 days and scorched more than 42,000 acres (17,000 hectares) of forest in the northern half of the park, from the Stanley Glacier to Vermillion Crossing. While fires such as this one can be dangerous and appear devastating, the flames are an important element in the region's ecological restoration. New lodgepole pines, which actually need fire for their seeds to open, are sprouting, although it will take decades for the forest to regenerate. Wildflowers are growing throughout the burned area as well.

Kootenay National Park, particularly its northern side at the Alberta-British Columbia provincial border, is close enough to Lake Louise or Banff that you can visit on a day trip. If you're exploring the southern end of the park, where the hot springs are located, it's more convenient to stay in the gateway towns of Radium Hot Springs or Invermere. Golden, B.C., is also within day-trip distance; it's 65 miles (105 kilometers) northwest of Radium Hot Springs via Highway 95.

Visiting the Park
Entrances

The northern entrance to Kootenay National Park is 22 miles (35 kilometers) south of Lake Louise and 25 miles (40 kilometers) from Banff, on Highway 93. The park's southern entrance, where you can purchase a park pass, is on Highway 93, just north of Radium Hot Springs.

Park Passes and Fees

A **day pass** (adults $9.80, seniors $8.30, ages 6-16 $4.90, families $19.60) for Kootenay National Park is valid until 4pm on the day after you purchase it. Kootenay passes can be used at Mount Revelstoke, Glacier, and Yoho National Parks in B.C. and at Banff, Jasper, Waterton Lakes, and Elk Island National Parks in Alberta.

If you're driving through the park along Highway 93 without stopping, a park pass isn't required. However, you need a pass if you get out of your car anywhere within the park boundaries.

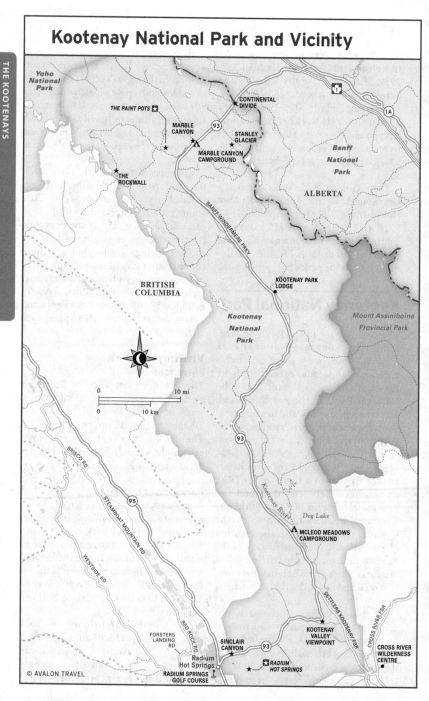

Kootenay National Park and Vicinity

Yoho National Park

THE PAINT POTS ★

MARBLE CANYON

CONTINENTAL DIVIDE

93

STANLEY GLACIER

MARBLE CANYON CAMPGROUND

THE ROCKWALL

Banff National Park

ALBERTA

1

1A

BANFF-WINDERMERE PKWY

BRITISH COLUMBIA

KOOTENAY PARK LODGE

Kootenay National Park

Mount Assiniboine Provincial Park

0   10 mi
0   10 km

BRISCO RD

STEAMBOAT MOUNTAIN RD

95

93

Kootenay River

WESTSIDE RD

Dog Lake

MCLEOD MEADOWS CAMPGROUND

SETTLERS KOOTENAY FSR

FORSTERS LANDING RD

RED ROCK RD

SINCLAIR CANYON

93

KOOTENAY VALLEY VIEWPOINT

CROSS RIVER FSR

CROSS RIVER WILDERNESS CENTRE

Radium Hot Springs

RADIUM SPRINGS GOLF COURSE

★ RADIUM HOT SPRINGS

© AVALON TRAVEL

Purchasing a Parks Canada **annual discovery pass** (adults $67.70, seniors $57.90, ages 6-16 $33.30, families $136.40), valid for a year, is a good deal if you're spending at least a week in one or more parks. It's valid at more than 100 national parks and national historic sites across Canada. You can buy an annual pass online from Parks Canada (www.pc.gc.ca) or at any of the parks' visitors centers.

For both day and annual passes, family passes cover up to seven people in a single vehicle, whether or not they're actually related.

Visitors Centers

In the village of Radium Hot Springs, just outside the national park, the **Radium Hot Springs Visitor Centre** (7556 Main St. E., 250/347-9331 or 888/347-9331, www.radiumhotsprings.com, 9am-7pm daily mid-June-early Sept., 9am-5pm daily early Sept.-mid-June) has information about the region. Parks Canada staff are on hand mid-May to mid-October to provide details about Kootenay National Park and about the Rocky Mountain national parks in general. The visitors center also has a small exhibit area about local wildlife.

If you're coming from Alberta, the **Lake Louise Visitor Information Centre** (Samson Mall, 403/522-3833, www.pc.gc.ca or www.banfflakelouise.com, 9am-7pm daily mid-June-early Sept., 9am-5pm daily May-mid-June and early Sept.-mid-Oct., 9am-4:30pm Thurs.-Sun. mid-Oct.-Apr.) or the **Banff Visitor Information Centre** (224 Banff Ave., 403/762-8421, www.pc.gc.ca or www.banfflakelouise.com, 9am-7pm daily late June-early Sept., 9am-5pm daily early Sept.-late June) can assist with information about Kootenay National Park. You can purchase a Kootenay park pass at either of these locations.

Reservations

Reservations are accepted at the park's Redstreak Campground, and they're recommended for stays in July and August. You can reserve campsites as well as oTENTiks, the park's canvas-walled platform tents. To book, contact **Parks Canada reservations** (877/737-3783, www.reservation.parkscanada.gc.ca).

Marble Canyon and McLeod Meadows Campgrounds are first-come, first-served; reservations aren't accepted for these areas.

Information and Services

Kootenay National Park has no fuel or other services within the park boundaries, so get gas in Banff or Lake Louise if you're coming from the north or in Radium Hot Springs, just south of the park. Radium has a grocery, a liquor store, and other basic services; you'll have more options for food and shopping in the larger town of Invermere, 10 miles (16 kilometers) south of the park's southern entrance.

There is cell phone service in Radium Hot Springs and in the park's Redstreak Campground, but no cell coverage or Wi-Fi elsewhere within Kootenay National Park.

Getting Around

Highway 93 runs north-south through Kootenay National Park, and the park's attractions are all located off this highway. The park has no shuttle service or public transportation, so you need a car to get around.

Sights and Activities

These things to see and do in Kootenay National Park are listed from north to south, along Highway 93.

The Continental Divide

Stop for a photo at the **Continental Divide**, which denotes the dividing line between the Pacific and Atlantic watersheds. It's also the provincial border between Alberta and British Columbia, as well as the boundary between Kootenay

One Day in Kootenay National Park

Have just one day? Pack a picnic lunch and you can see the highlights of Kootenay National Park. This itinerary starts at the park's north end, coming from Lake Louise or Banff; alternatively, you can follow this route from south to north if you begin in the town of Radium Hot Springs.

As you enter the park from the north on Highway 93, stop for a photo at the **Continental Divide,** which marks the divide between the Pacific and Atlantic watersheds, the B.C.-Alberta provincial border, and the boundary between Kootenay and Banff National Parks.

Continue 4.5 miles (7 kilometers) south to **Marble Canyon,** where you can follow the trail over several bridges that cross the deep, narrow gorge. You can hike from the canyon to the **Paint Pots,** or drive to the start of the short Paint Pots Trail; either way, don't miss the unusual orange ocher beds that surround these small mineral pools.

Back on Highway 93, drive south to the **McLeod Meadows picnic area,** where you can enjoy the lunch you packed. If you're up for another hike, follow the **Dog Lake Trail** from here, or keep driving south, stopping at the **Kootenay Valley Viewpoint,** and then hike the **Juniper/Sinclair Canyon Trail,** near the park's south gate.

Grab a bite to eat in the **town of Radium Hot Springs,** or head south to **Invermere** for the excellent falafel and other Middle Eastern dishes at **Safta's.** End your Kootenay National Park day with a relaxing soak in the **Radium Hot Springs.**

and Banff National Parks. It's along Highway 93, marked with a sign 22 miles (35 kilometers) south Lake Louise and 60 miles (100 kilometers) east of the town of Radium Hot Springs.

Marble Canyon

The turquoise waters of Tokumm Creek have carved a deep, narrow gorge into the limestone and dolomite rock at **Marble Canyon.** Follow the one-mile (1.6-kilometer) round-trip **Marble Canyon Trail,** which crosses the water on seven bridges above the canyon.

Marble Canyon is 4.5 miles (7 kilometers) south of the Alberta-B.C. border and 54 miles (87 kilometers) east of Radium Hot Springs, off Highway 93.

★ The Paint Pots

Among the most unusual geological features in Kootenay National Park are the **Paint Pots,** three small mineral pools surrounded by orange ocher beds. The Ktunaxa, Stoney, and Blackfoot First Nations used these natural pigments in ceremonies and later in trade, and aboriginal people still consider the ocher beds to be sacred. On the **Paint Pots Trail** (1.2 miles/2 kilometers round-trip), a short path through the woods and along the ocher beds, you may find the unique colors of the land more noteworthy than the small pools themselves.

If you'd like to hike between Marble Canyon and the Paint Pots, take the gentle 4.2-mile (6.8-kilometer) round-trip **Marble Canyon to Paint Pots Trail.** Part of the trail follows the Vermillion River.

The Paint Pots are off Highway 93, just south of Marble Canyon and 52 miles (84 kilometers) east of Radium Hot Springs.

Kootenay Valley Viewpoint

As you're driving through the park along Highway 93, pull off at the **Kootenay Valley Viewpoint** for vistas of the surrounding Mitchell and Vermilion Mountains and down to the Kootenay River. The viewpoint is at the southern end of the park, 10 miles (16 kilometers) east of Radium Hot Springs.

★ Radium Hot Springs

A highlight of a Kootenay National Park visit is a soak in the **Radium Hot Springs** (5420 Hwy. 93, 250/347-9485 or 800/767-1611, www.pc.gc.ca, 9am-11pm daily mid-May-mid-Oct., noon-9pm Sun.-Thurs., noon-10pm Fri.-Sat. mid-Oct.-mid-May, adults $6.30, seniors and ages 6-16 $5.40, families $19.10), natural outdoor hot springs pools surrounded by the reddish rock walls of Sinclair Canyon.

The minerals in the hot pool, where the water temperature is kept at 102°F (39°C), include sulfate, calcium, bicarbonate, silica, and magnesium. A large "cool" pool, designed for swimming rather than soaking, is 84°F (27°C).

You can rent both towels ($1.90) and swimsuits ($1.90) at the springs. Lockers are available for $1. Also on-site is the **Pleiades Spa Radium** (250/347-2288, www.pleiadesradiumspa.com, call for hours and rates), where you can add a massage, mud wrap, or other spa services to your soaking time.

Radium Hot Springs are located 1.9 miles (3 kilometers) east of the town of Radium Hot Springs.

Sinclair Canyon

Near the park's south gate, less than one mile (1.5 kilometers) east of the town of Radium Hot Springs, Highway 93 winds between **Sinclair Canyon** and the Redwall Fault Cliffs. You don't even have to get out of your car to take in the dramatic rock walls, but you can hike into the canyon on several different trails.

Hiking

Kootenay National Park has 143 miles (230 kilometers) of hiking trails, including many short hikes. The best months for hiking are July through mid-September. Some passes and trails at higher elevations can remain covered with snow until late June, and snow can begin to fall again in October. In addition to the trails

at Marble Canyon and the Paint Pots (above), the following are other popular park hikes.

Stanley Glacier and the Burgess Shale

In 1909, American geologist Charles Walcott unearthed surprisingly well-preserved fossils in the **Burgess Shale,** an area of what is now Yoho National Park. The fossils were the remains of soft-bodied marine organisms that lived in the Cambrian Sea. Estimated to be among the world's oldest fossils, they date back 505 million years.

In Kootenay National Park, visitors can tour a section of the Burgess Shale beds on a **full-day guided hike,** for which you must **book reservations in advance.** Make reservations with **Parks Canada** (877/737-3783, www.reservations.parkscanada.gc.ca, reservation fee online $11, phone $13.50), beginning in early January for the coming season. Check the website to confirm when reservations become available; you'll want to book them as early as possible.

On this guided hike to the **Stanley Glacier** (Sat.-Mon. mid-June-mid-Sept., adults $55, seniors $46.75, ages 8-16 $27.50, under age 8 free), guides will explain the Burgess Shale fossil beds and allow you to make fossil rubbings. You'll also get an up-close look at the glacier. Families are welcome, but make sure everyone is up to the challenge of this moderately difficult hike, a 7.5-hour, 6.3-mile (10-kilometer) round-trip, with an elevation gain of 1,500 feet (450 meters).

The Stanley Glacier hike departs at 8am from the Stanley Glacier parking lot on Highway 93, which is 9.3 miles (15 kilometers) south of Castle Junction and 59 miles (95 kilometers) north of Radium Hot Springs.

In addition to this Stanley Glacier hike, two other challenging guided Burgess Shale hikes are offered in Yoho National Park.

Juniper/Sinclair Canyon

The **Juniper/Sinclair Canyon Trail,** which starts near the hot springs, takes you high above the highway and deep into the canyon. It's a 3.7-mile (6-kilometer) loop, with an elevation change of 850 feet (260 meters). You can also hike a short section of the trail that switchbacks down into the canyon.

Redstreak Restoration

Starting near the Redstreak Campground, the 0.6-mile (1-kilometer) **Redstreak Restoration Trail** loops through a sunny meadow where a prescribed fire destroyed many of the trees but where vegetation is now growing back. Interpretive panels explain the role fire plays in the local ecosystem. You may spot grazing bighorn sheep as you walk.

Dog Lake

The moderate **Dog Lake Trail,** 3.2 miles (5.2 kilometers) round-trip, takes you through the forest and across two suspension bridges over the Kootenay River before reaching the lake. The trailhead is at the **McLeod Meadows picnic area,** 17 miles (28 kilometers) north of Radium Hot Springs, off Highway 93.

Floe Lake

For a challenging all-day or overnight hike, the **Floe Lake Trail** leads through open meadows and sections of burned forest, with 25 switchbacks en route to a large lake, with glaciers and mountain peaks all around. The trail is 13 miles (21 kilometers) round-trip, with an elevation gain of 2,345 feet (715 meters).

The trailhead is at the Floe Lake parking lot in the northern half of the park, 45 miles (72 kilometers) from Radium Hot Springs. If you don't want to go out and back in one day, you can camp at the Floe Lake backcountry campground.

Rockwall

Backpackers can tackle the 34-mile (55-kilometer) **Rockwall Trail,** a three- to

the Continental Divide

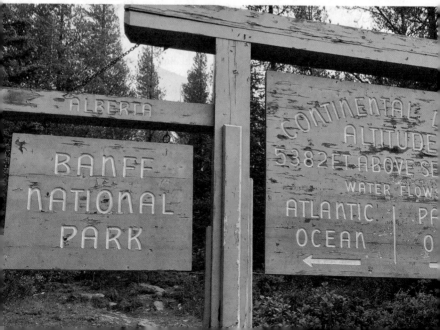

four-day adventure that takes you along a massive limestone cliff. At some points, this rock wall towers more than 2,950 feet (900 meters) above the trail.

For this multiday hike, you need to purchase a **wilderness pass** ($9.80 per day) from any Parks Canada visitors center. You also need to **reserve campsites** in advance (reservation fee $11.70) by calling Parks Canada at the **Radium Hot Springs Visitor Centre** (7556 Main St. E., 250/347-9505, www.pc.gc.ca, mid-May-mid-Oct.) or the **Lake Louise Visitor Information Centre** (Samson Mall, 403/522-3833 or 403/522-1264, Apr.-mid-May). You can reserve backcountry sites up to three months in advance.

Accommodations and Camping

If you don't want to camp, the only accommodations within the park itself are at the **Kootenay Park Lodge** (Hwy. 93, Vermillion Crossing, 250/434-9648 or 844/566-8362, www.kootenaypark-lodge.com, late May-mid-Oct.). As this

book went to press, new owners were updating the lodge and its restaurant; check with them for details.

Outside the park to the south, you can find convenient accommodations in the towns of Radium Hot Springs and Invermere. Another alternative is to stay in Lake Louise, Banff, or Golden and make a day trip to Kootenay National Park.

$150-250

The most uniquely Canadian place to stay in the Kootenay National Park area is just outside the park boundary, nine miles (14 kilometers) down a gravel road. Owners Robert and Marilyn Patenaude have been running the ★ **Cross River Wilderness Centre** (403/271-3296 or 877/659-7665, www.crossriver.ca, late May-early Oct., $225-250 d, meals $90 pp per day), their remote off-the-grid lodging, since 1996. Eight cozy log cabins, which originally came from the Cathedral Mountain Lodge near Field, have been rebuilt and modernized, with country-style furnishings, solar-powered lighting, and wood-burning fireplaces, as well as private baths with propane-heated showers.

Three hearty meals a day are served family-style in the main lodge, which has a comfortable lounge and an outdoor hot tub heated with a wood stove. Staff will pack you a picnic lunch if you're going hiking or exploring. Robert is of Métis heritage and has three tepees ($124-138) where guests can also stay; each sleeps up to six. With advance reservations, you can arrange a sweat lodge ceremony or cultural workshop with an aboriginal elder. The center hosts yoga retreats and offers a variety of wilderness workshops, guided hiking excursions, and backpacking trips as well. There's no Internet or cell service here, so plan to unplug. The owners provide detailed directions for getting to the lodge when you make your reservation.

Camping

Kootenay National Park has three campgrounds. The largest, **Redstreak Campground** (Redstreak Rd., 250/347-9505, www.pc.gc.ca, early May-mid-Oct., tents $27.40, electrical sites $32.30-38.20), is 1.6 miles (2.5 kilometers) uphill from the town of Radium Hot Springs. On foot, you can follow the steep 0.75-mile (1.2-kilometer) **Valleyview Trail** between the campground and the town; the 1.4-mile (2.3-kilometer) **Redstreak Campground Trail** leads to the Radium Hot Springs pools.

This 242-site campground, which accommodates everything from tents to large RVs, has restrooms with flush toilets and showers.

Another sleeping option in the Redstreak Campground is to stay in one of the **oTENTiks** (early May-mid-Oct., $120), canvas-walled platform tents that sleep up to six. You need to bring your own sleeping bags or bedding, as well as food, dishes, and cooking supplies. Flush toilets and showers are nearby.

The 61-site **Marble Canyon Campground** (mid-July-early Sept., $21.50), located near Marble Canyon in the north half of the park, and the 80-site **McLeod Meadows Campground** (late June-early Sept., $21.50), 17 miles (27 kilometers) north of Radium Hot Springs, both have restrooms with flush toilets but no shower facilities.

You can make reservations for campsites and oTENTiks in the Redstreak Campground by contacting **Parks Canada reservations** (877/737-3783, www.reservation.parkscanada.gc.ca). Reservations are recommended between late June and early September, and on any holiday weekend. The Marble Canyon and McLeod Meadows Campgrounds are first-come, first-served.

The Town of Radium Hot Springs

Just outside the southwestern boundary of Kootenay National Park, at the intersection of Highways 93 and 95, the small

soaking in the Radium Hot Springs

town of **Radium Hot Springs** (www.radiumhotsprings.com) has lodgings, a few restaurants, a grocery store, gas stations, and other provisions, as well as the national park visitors center. Basic motels, from mom-and-pop places to the **Best Western Plus Prestige Inn** (7493 Main St. W., Radium Hot Springs, 250/347-2300 or 800/780-7234, www.bestwestern.com), line Radium's streets.

You may see **bighorn sheep,** with their distinctive curved horns, as you wander through town or around the Redstreak Campground, particularly in May and June and again from September into the winter. In midsummer, the Radium herd of well over 100 bighorns tends to graze at higher elevations, returning to town in the colder months. A popular sheep-spotting site is the **Radium Springs Golf Course** (4714 Springs Dr., www.radiumgolf.ca). In late autumn, during the rutting season, when male sheep butt heads to establish their dominance before mating, the town hosts the **Headbanger**

Festival (www.radiumhotsprings.com, Nov.), with opportunities to see the bighorns, guided walks, and other interpretive programs.

Sports and Recreation

Another reason to stop in Radium Hot Springs is to go **white-water rafting,** and **Kootenay River Runners** (4987 Hwy. 93, 250/347-9210, www.raftingtherockies. com) offers rafting trips on several area rivers. On the **Kootenay River** (June-mid-Sept.) with Class I-III rapids, you can choose half-day (adults $82, ages 5-14 $63) and full-day (adults $118, ages 5-14 $93) rafting trips that depart from their Radium office.

The two-hour **Toby Creek** trip (June-Aug., adults $62, ages 8-14 $52), good for first-timers, includes Class I-III rapids and starts at Panorama Mountain Resort near Invermere.

The full-day **Kicking Horse River** trips (June-early Sept.) run Class I-IV rapids. You can choose the "classic" trip (over age 11 $115), which includes the river's Upper and Middle Canyons, or their "ultimate" trip (over age 15 $155) that adds the Lower Canyon. Both depart from their Kicking Horse River base, which is 15 miles (24 kilometers) east of Golden on Highway 1; from Radium Hot Springs, it's 83 miles (134 kilometers), about a 90-minute drive, on Highway 95 north to Highway 1 east.

Information and Services

The **Radium Hot Springs Visitor Centre** (7556 Main St. E., 250/347-9331or 888/347-9331, www.radiumhotsprings. com, 9am-7pm daily mid-June-early Sept., 9am-5pm daily early Sept.-mid-June) has information about the area and about Kootenay National Park.

Next to the visitors center, **Radium Mountainside Market** (7546 Main St. E., 250/347-9600, www.mountainside-market.com, 8am-10pm daily) sells basic groceries, along with sandwiches, salads, and barbecue chicken to go.

The East Kootenays

The **East Kootenays** region hugs the Alberta border and extends south to Canada's border with the United States. The city of Cranbrook, with 20,000 people, is the region's commercial center.

Highway 3 meanders through the East Kootenays from east to west and can take you toward the B.C. coast. Highway 93/95 is the East Kootenays' main north-south artery. Known as the **Hot Springs Highway,** Highway 93/95 runs south from Kootenay National Park and Radium Hot Springs through a region highly regarded for, yes, its mineral springs. Beyond these opportunities to soak, several scenic East Kootenays towns are worth a stop for outdoor activities, local history, and good food.

Invermere

Ten miles (16 kilometers) south of Radium Hot Springs, **Invermere** (www.invermerepanorama.com) is another potential base for visiting Kootenay National Park. It's an attractive town, where art galleries and cute shops line its main street and an in-town lake has a family-friendly sand beach.

Sights and Recreation

On Lake Windermere, **Kinsmen Park** (5th Ave. at 7A Ave.) draws families to its sandy beach, with a playground and splash pad for the kids, restrooms, picnic tables, and a snack bar. In winter, when the lake freezes, a local Nordic ski club creates and maintains the **Lake Windermere Whiteway** (www.tobycreeknordic.ca), a 21-mile (34-kilometer) groomed track for ice skaters and cross-country skiers; it's the longest skating path in the world.

The **Pynelogs Cultural Centre & Art Gallery** (1720 4th Ave., 250/342-4423, www.columbiavalleyarts.com), in a 1914 log building near Kinsmen Park and Lake Windermere, hosts art shows, concerts, films, and other cultural events. The **Pynelogs Café** (250/342-1445, www.scottyburger.com, 11am-4pm Tues.-Sat. late Apr.-late Sept., mains $10-19) serves soups, salads, sandwiches, and burgers in the gallery or on its terrace overlooking the lake.

Festivals and Events

Birders and others interested in the outdoors flock to the annual **Wings over the Rockies Festival** (www.wingsovertherockies.org, May) for bird-watching, guided hikes, environmental lectures, and other ecologically focused events held in Invermere, Kootenay National Park, and Golden.

Accommodations

The most upscale place to stay in the Invermere area is **Copper Point Resort** (760 Cooper Rd., 250/341-4000 or 855/926-7737, www.copperpointresort.com, $175-369 d, two-bedroom suite $399-469), with 173 contemporary lodgings that range from standard rooms with a queen bed, a mini fridge, and a microwave to one- and two-bedroom suites with full kitchens with stainless-steel appliances and granite countertops. If you haven't soaked enough in the region's hot springs, you can swim in the indoor or outdoor pools or lounge in several hot tubs. A fitness facility, kids playground, and golf course keep you busy on the property; for skiers and snowboarders, Panorama Mountain is only 14 miles (23 kilometers) from the hotel.

Food

Groceries and Markets

Invermere's several grocery stores include **Valley Foods** (906 7th Ave., 250/342-3330, www.agvalleyfoods.com, 7am-10pm daily), which carries some locally made and locally grown products.

Cafés, Bakeries, and Light Bites

Canada's number-one organic fair-trade coffee comes from the little town of

Invermere, where **Kicking Horse Coffee** sources, imports, and roasts their beans. Adjacent to their factory, you can taste their brews at the **Kicking Horse Café** (491 Arrow Rd., 250/342-4489, www.kicking-horsecoffee.com, 7am-5pm Mon.-Fri., 8am-5pm Sat., 9am-4pm Sun.), which sells pastries and serves all manner of coffee drinks.

Look for the giant pretzel on the roof to find the **Invermere Bakery** (1305 7th Ave., 250/342-9913, www.invermer-ebakery.com, 7:30am-6pm Mon.-Sat., 9am-4pm Sun. late June-early Sept., 7:30am-6pm Mon.-Sat. early Sept.-late June), which bakes flavorful pretzels, pastries, and other treats. They also make tasty sandwiches served on their chewy homemade pretzels.

Middle Eastern

This excellent Middle Eastern eatery started life as a falafel truck, and the Israeli chickpea dish is still a star at ★ **Safta's** (1321 7th Ave., 778/526-2424, www.saftas.ca, 4pm-midnight Mon.-Thurs., 11am-midnight Fri.-Sat., noon-10pm Sun., mains $12-23), a laid-back pub with a street-side patio in Invermere's downtown. Along with tabbouleh, chicken *shawarma,* and lamb *kefta,* plus burgers and steak for the less adventurous, Safta's serves local craft beer and B.C. wines.

Information and Services

Pick up information about the area or get your questions answered at the **Invermere Visitor Centre** (651 Hwy. 93/95, 250/342-2844, www.cvchamber.ca, 9am-5pm daily July-Aug., 9am-5pm Mon.-Fri. Sept.-June). **Tourism Invermere Panorama** (www.invermerepanorama.com) has a helpful area website.

Top to bottom: cabin at the Cross River Wilderness Centre, just outside Kootenay National Park; Invermere Bakery; falafel at Safta's in Invermere.

★ Panorama Mountain Resort

Summer or winter, **Panorama Mountain Resort** (2000 Panorama Dr., Panorama, 250/342-6941 or 800/663-2929, www. panoramaresort.com), 12.5 miles (20 kilometers) west of Invermere, has plenty of things to do, particularly for families who enjoy outdoor activities. It's located in the Purcell Mountains, with views to the Rockies. Contact the resort's **Adventure Centre** (250/341-3044) to find out what's happening.

Summer Activities

Hiking

In summer, you can ride the **Mile 1 Express Chairlift** (daily late June-early Sept., adults $14, seniors and ages 13-18 $12, ages 6-12 $10, families $44) to enjoy the mountain views or access several **hiking trails.** The family-friendly **Fort Hide 'n' Seek Trail** leads down from the top of the lift to a log playhouse with a slide. Just make sure the kids save some energy for the hike back up to the chair.

The short but steep **Lynx Loop** climbs through the woods above the lift for vistas across the mountains and down to the village. A challenging day hike, the **Panorama Summit Trail** takes you up to the mountaintop; riding the chair lift gives you a 1,246-foot (380-meter) vertical head start on this 4,000-foot (1,220-meter) climb.

Without riding the lift, you can walk the **Valley Trail,** a paved 2.1-mile (3.5-kilometer) loop from the village to the golf course and the Cliffhanger Restaurant.

Mountain Biking

Mountain bikers can ride the chair lift (daily late June-early Sept., adults half-day $36, full-day $45, seniors and ages 13-18 half-day $31, full-day $39, ages 6-12 half-day $20, full-day $25) up to 19 miles (30 kilometers) of mountain trails. Only 10 percent of the downhill routes are rated "beginner"; 40 percent are intermediate, and half are expert trails.

Yoga

Ride the Mile 1 Express for an outdoor **yoga class** (10:30am daily late June-early Sept.) with mountain views. The one-hour class is designed for all levels. Reservations are required; book at the resort's **Adventure Centre** (250/341-3044).

Water Sports

In summer, the large **Panorama Springs Pool** (daily late June-early Sept.) entices families to swim and whoosh down the water slide. Several outdoor **hot tubs** are open year-round. You must be staying at one of the resort's accommodations to use the pools.

Winter Sports

For **skiing and snowboarding** (www.panoramaresort.com, daily mid-Dec.-mid-Apr., full-day adults $88, seniors and ages 13-18 $75, ages 6-12 $41), Panorama has 120 trails across 2,847 acres (1,152 hectares) of mountain terrain. Trails are rated 20 percent beginner, 55 percent intermediate-advanced, and 25 percent expert. If you're staying on the mountain, you can purchase **discounted lift tickets** (full-day adults $66, seniors and ages 13-18 $56, ages 6-12 $31).

If you've wanted to try **heli-skiing** but haven't wanted to commit to a multiday trip, you can do a one-day adventure with **RK Heliski** (250/342-6941 or 800/663-2929, www.panoramaresort.com, adults $847-998 per day). Rates include a buffet breakfast, a helicopter flight up to untracked trails, lunch, and your choice of three or five runs through the powder.

The **Panorama Nordic Centre** (250/341-4106, www.panoramaresort. com) has more than 12.5 miles (20 kilometers) of trails for **cross-country skiing** (full-day adults $13, seniors and ages 13-18 $10, ages 7-12 $10), as well as 2.5 miles (4 kilometers) of **snowshoeing** (full-day adults $10, seniors and ages 13-18 $7, ages 7-12 $5) trails.

Another winter sport option is **fat-tire biking** (adults 2 hours $25, full-day

$40), where you ride specially equipped bicycles through the snow. Get details or reserve your bike from the Panorama Nordic Centre (250/341-4106, www.panoramaresort.com).

Accommodations

At the base of the mountain, **Panorama Mountain Resort** (800/663-2929, www.panoramaresort.com) has accommodations in a number of modern condominium buildings, with units ranging from studios to three-bedroom units. All have kitchen facilities and are short walk from the lifts.

Food

The resort has the usual fuel-up cafés, pubs, and restaurants; hours vary seasonally. At the base of the Upper Village, get pastries and sandwiches at casual **Picnic Café** (250/341-3354) or coffee at skier-friendly **Lusti's Cappuchino Bar** (250/341-3084). On the Valley Trail overlooking the golf course, **Cliffhanger Restaurant** (1860 Greywolf Dr., 250/341-4102, www.cliffhangerrestaurant.ca, mains $13-38) serves salads, sandwiches, and burgers all day, adding steaks and other grilled items in the evening; the terrace is a beautiful spot on a sunny day.

Getting Here

From Invermere, follow Panorama Drive, which becomes Toby Creek Road, to the mountain; it's a 25- to 30-minute drive.

During the winter season, the free **Mountain and Valley Shuttle** (www.panoramaresort.com, 9am-10pm daily) runs throughout the day between Invermere and Panorama Mountain. Service continues into the evening, so if you're staying on the mountain, you can take the shuttle into town for dinner and then back to your mountain accommodations.

If you're flying to Calgary in winter, you can take the **Panorama Mountain Resort Shuttle** (800/663-2929, www.panoramaresort.com, daily mid-Dec.-mid.-Apr., one-way adults $104, under age 13 $84) between the mountain and Calgary International Airport. The shuttle departs twice a day in each direction. Reservations are recommended, and guests staying on the mountain have priority for shuttle seats. The shuttle also provides daily service to Banff (one-way adults $94, under age 13 $74), by reservation only.

Fairmont Hot Springs

It may be the largest mineral pool in Canada, but that just means that more people of all ages can pack into the family-friendly **Fairmont Hot Springs** (5225 Fairmont Resort Rd., Fairmont Hot Springs, 250/345-6070 or 800/663-4979, www.fairmonthotsprings.com, 8am-9pm daily, adults $12, seniors $10, ages 13-17 $11, ages 4-12 $10, families $39), located at the Fairmont Hot Springs Resort. There are actually three pools where you can swim and soak: the 102°F (39°C) hot pool, a large 89°F (32°C) swimming pool, and a diving pool, which is kept at 86°F (30°C).

The springs offer a discounted late-night swim ($6 pp) at the end of every day, although the exact time varies with the season; call for details.

In addition to the pools, Fairmont Hot Springs has accommodations in lodge buildings, cabins, cottages, and two campgrounds.

If you're staying in the Kootenay National Park area, you can easily stop for a soak at Fairmont Hot Springs. It's 24 miles (38 kilometers) south of Radium Hot Springs and 17 miles (28 kilometers) south of Invermere, along Highway 95. The city of Cranbrook is 67 miles (108 kilometers) to the south.

★ Lussier Hot Springs

While the mineral pools run by Parks Canada and other commercial hot pools throughout the Kootenays-Rockies region are lovely, if you want a true natural hot springs experience, make your way to **Whiteswan Lake Provincial Park**

(250/422-3003, www.env.gov.bc.ca), off Highway 93/95 between Invermere and Cranbrook.

At the remote park's **Lussier Hot Springs** (dawn-dusk daily, free), you can soak in several natural rock-lined hot pools in an otherwise chilly river.

Two outhouses in the parking lot above the springs serve as changing rooms, but there are no other facilities. Wear study sports sandals or hiking shoes to walk up and down the short path to the springs. You'll also be more comfortable wearing sports sandals or water shoes into the spring, since you have to clamber over some slippery rocks.

The park has several campgrounds down the road beyond the hot springs, and Whiteswan Lake begins at kilometer 25. The provincial park has no cell service or public phones.

Getting There

It takes some effort to get to Lussier Hot Springs. From Highway 93/95, turn east three miles (4.5 kilometers) south of the town of Canal Flats onto the Whiteswan Forest Service Road. You don't need a 4WD or other special vehicle to follow this rutted gravel logging road; just watch your speed.

After you pass kilometer 14, Whiteswan Forest Service Road gets narrower as it winds along a ridge and through a canyon. Put your headlights on, take it slow, and use the pullouts if you meet a vehicle coming the other way. The hot springs are at kilometer 17.5.

★ Fernie

If you're traveling between the Canadian Rockies and the Okanagan Valley, it's a short detour along Highway 3 to the town of Fernie. It's a detour worth taking, particularly if you're interested in regional history or in outdoor adventures, or if you'd just like to chill in this down-to-earth mountain community. Victorian-era buildings line the downtown streets, home to cafés, restaurants, and eclectic

Lussier Hot Springs in Whiteswan Lake Provincial Park

shops, and the forested slopes and craggy peaks of the Rocky Mountains surround the town.

In 1919, Fernie's local newspaper wrote, "The scenery of Switzerland is no grander than our own." While it took some time before this southeastern B.C. district began drawing scenery-seeking visitors in any significant numbers, the area's first ski resort, which opened in the 1960s, became a major draw. Fernie now has a year-round population of just under 5,000, which almost doubles during the winter ski season.

Sights and Recreation

Fernie suffered two devastating fires in the early 20th century, in 1904 and again in 1908. After the second blaze, the town passed an ordinance decreeing that all downtown buildings must be made of brick. The result is that Fernie's downtown core is full of historic brick and stone buildings, most constructed between 1908 and 1912, including City Hall

(1905), Fernie Heritage Library (1908), and Fernie Court House (1908). Many of the town's cafés, shops, restaurants, and pubs are in heritage structures as well.

Get the scoop on Fernie's history at the compact but well-designed **Fernie Museum** (491 2nd Ave., 250/423-7016, www.ferniemuseum.com, 10am-5:30pm daily, donation), which has a mix of permanent and changing exhibits. In summer, the museum offers entertaining guided 90-minute **walking tours** (11am Sat. July-Aug., adults $10, families $25) that highlight the town's past, from its coal-mining heritage to a legendary First Nations curse. Also in the museum is a **visitor information desk,** where staff can provide details about local attractions.

In the town's former train station, built in 1908, **The Arts Station** (601 1st Ave., 250/423-4842, www.theartsstation.com, 9am-3pm Mon.-Fri. and during events) is a community cultural hub, with two art galleries, a theater, a craft and painting studio, and the **Blue Toque Diner** (250/423-4637, 9am-3pm Thurs.-Mon., mains $10-16).

Local craft beer maker **Fernie Brewing Company** (26 Manitou Rd., 250/423-7797 or 855/777-2739, www.ferniebrewing. com, call for hours) has a tasting room and shop at their brewery, off Highway 3 on the town's east side. Most restaurants and pubs in the area stock their beers, too.

In winter, Fernie is a center for **catskiing,** where, instead of taking lifts up to groomed runs, you ride into the backcountry in a heated snowcat, which resembles a cross between a bulldozer and a limousine. On these excursions, your guide will direct you to the day's best terrain before you head off into the powder. **Island Lake Catskiing** (250/423-3700 or 888/422-8754, www.islandlake-catskiing.com) operates catskiing tours from their deluxe wilderness lodge. **Fernie Wilderness Adventures** (250/423-6704 or 877/423-6704, www.fwapowder.

Fernie

To
Fernie Visitor Centre,
Fernie Brewing Company,
Sparwood, and Crowsnest Pass

Great Northern Trail

SCALE NOT AVAILABLE

Elk River

BURMA RD

Annex Park Trail

West Fernie Dyke Trail

17TH AVE

19TH ST

12TH ST

11TH ST

10TH ST

9TH ST

8TH ST

7TH ST

5TH ST

GREYHOUND
BUS STATION

ELK VALLEY
HOSPITAL

FAIRWAY DR

McDougall

Creek

8TH AVE

7TH AVE

6TH AVE

5TH AVE

YAMAGOYA

CLAWHAMMER
LETTERPRESS & GALLERY/
GHOSTRIDER TRADING CO

FERNIE
MOUNTAIN
MARKET

OLD NURSES
RESIDENCE B&B

2ND AVE

FERNIE 901

Kootenay Elk Trail

BEANPOD
CHOCOLATE

LOAF
BAKERY &
RESTAURANT

SAVE-ON-FOODS

4TH ST

5TH ST

LE GRAND FROMAGE

RIDGEMONT AVE

MUGSHOTS
CAFÉ

THE ARTS STATION/
THE BLUE TOQUE DINER

4TH ST

FERNIE
MUSEUM

LUNCH BOX

MCLEOD AVE

MCDONALD AVE

HISTORIC
PRECINCT

To
Fernie Alpine Resort,
Mt Fernie PP, and Cranbrook

© AVALON TRAVEL

com) offers one-day and multiday catskiing trips.

Fernie Alpine Resort

It's just three miles (5 kilometers) from the town of Fernie to **Fernie Alpine Resort** (5339 Ski Area Rd., 250/423-4655 or 800/258-7669, www.skifernie.com), where you can play outdoors in both summer and winter. The mountain is off Highway 3 on the west side of town.

Summer Activities

Fernie Alpine Resort is open for summer activities from late June to early September. For more information or to book summer experiences, call or visit the **Resort Adventure Centre** (250/423-4655, www.skifernie.com) at the mountain's base.

Ride the **chairlifts** (10:30am-4:30pm daily, adults $22.95, seniors and ages 13-17 $18.95, ages 6-12 $11.95, families $54.95) up the mountain to take in the views or reach several **lift-accessed hiking trails** that start from the top of the Elk or Timber chairs. If you prefer to go with a guide, choose from several **guided hikes** (adults half-day $36.95, full-day $49.95, seniors and ages 13-17 half-day $28.95, full-day $42.95, ages 6-12 halfday $22.95, full-day $35.95), ranging from easy to challenging.

Fernie is known for **mountain biking** (10:30am-4:30pm daily, adults single ride $22.95, full-day $47.95, seniors and ages

13-17 single $18.95, full-day $38.95, ages 6-12 single $11.95, full-day $24.95, families single $54.95, full-day $109.95), with 37 lift-accessed trails, from wide beginner routes to expert single track through the trees and down steep slopes.

For more thrills, test your balance in the **Aerial Park** (10:30am, 11am, 2pm, and 2:30pm daily, adults $64.95, seniors and ages 13-17 $44.95, ages 7-12 $24.95, families $149.95), a high ropes course, or whiz across the **Zip Lines** (10:30am-4pm daily, $13.95 pp, $9.95 per additional ride, families $49.95).

Winter Sports

With an average annual snowfall of 30 feet (nine meters) and a skiable area of more than 2,500 acres (1,000 hectares), Fernie Alpine Resort claims the most runs for **skiing and snowboarding** (9am-4pm daily early Dec.-mid-Apr., full-day adults $89.95, seniors $71.95, ages 13-17 $67.95, ages 6-12 $35.95) in the Canadian Rockies.

The resort has introduced winter **fat-tire biking,** where you ride specially designed bicycles with low gears and fat tires on snow-covered trails. Contact the resort activity desk (250/423-4655) for details.

Festivals and Events

The **Griz Days Winter Festival** (www. tourismfernie.com, Mar.) makes midwinter merriment with scavenger hunts, a craft fair, pancake-eating contest, lumberjack show, parade, dance parties, and fireworks.

Fernival (www.skifernie.com, Apr.), at Fernie Alpine Resort, wraps up the ski season with free concerts and other festivities.

Celebrating Canadian indie music, the **Wapiti Music Festival** (www.wapitimusicfestival.com, Aug.) brings established

Top to bottom: Fernie Brewing Company; ski lift in Fernie Alpine Resort; Fernie 901, a former school building turned into a condo complex.

and up-and-coming bands to town for a weekend of summer concerts.

Shopping

Sit on the purple and red couches and watch the chocolate makers at work at **Beanpod Chocolate** (691 2nd Ave., 778/519-5008, www.beanpod.ca, 10am-5pm daily) a family-run chocolate and gelato shop. Among their goodies are handmade chocolates, ice cream, and coffee.

Le Grand Fromage (672E 2nd Ave., 250/531-0030, www.legrandfromage.ca, 10am-6pm Mon.-Sat., 11am-5pm Sun.) sells cheese made locally and elsewhere, along with salami, jams, crackers, and other gourmet food items. Stop in for lunch, when they make several varieties of grilled cheese sandwiches ($8).

Check out the cool posters, cards, T-shirts, and artwork at **Clawhammer Letterpress & Gallery** (661 2nd Ave., 778/519-5010, www.clawhammer.ca, 10am-6pm Tues.-Sat., noon-4pm Sun.), which is a working letterpress studio, art gallery, and eclectic gift shop. The shop is inside the Fernie General Store building.

Also in the Fernie General Store building, **Ghostrider Trading Co.** (661 2nd Ave., 250/423-5541, 10am-6pm Mon.-Sat., 11am-5pm Sun.) carries stylish casual clothing and shoes, as well as funky Fernie T-shirts.

Accommodations and Camping

For accommodations on the mountain at **Fernie Alpine Resort,** contact **Resorts of the Canadian Rockies** (403/254-7669 or 800/258-7669, www.skircr.com or www.skifernie.com).

A former 1908 brick school building, a short stroll from downtown Fernie's restaurants and shops, has been converted into ★ **Fernie 901** (901 2nd Ave., 1-bedroom $185-225, 2- and 3-bedroom $205-380), a condominium complex with upscale one- to five-bedroom suites available for short-term rentals. The units' spacious modern kitchens have granite countertops, stainless steel appliances, and everything you'd need to make meals for a crowd; the high ceilings, wood floors, and fireplaces give the apartments a mix of mountain and urban style. Views of the surrounding peaks are a bonus. Units have washer-dryers, parking, and Wi-Fi. To book, contact **Fernie Central Reservations** (250/423-2077 or 800/622-5007, www.ferniecentralreservations.com), which manages short-term accommodations in several local buildings. Rates are higher during the winter ski season than from spring through fall.

Beginning in 1908, the Victorian manor that's now the **Old Nurses Residence B&B** (802 4th Ave., 250/423-3091, www.oldnurse.com, $139 s, $149-259 d), a few blocks off Fernie's main downtown street, was a lodging house for unmarried local nurses. Its four guest rooms and comfortable guest lounge channel that Victorian era with antique furnishings, polished wood floors, and original stained glass. Rates include Wi-Fi and a full breakfast, although the owners will discount your price by $10 pp if you choose to forgo your morning meal.

As you snake your way up the washboard track toward **Island Lake Lodge** (250/423-3700 or 888/422-8754, www.islandlakecatskiing.com, mid-June-Sept., $159-299 d), the road gets narrower and the trees get bigger; much of this area off Highway 3 south of Fernie is an old-growth cedar forest. A get-away-from-it-all place on 7,000 acres (2,830 hectares) of private land, the property has 26 guest rooms in three timber lodges. A fourth lodge houses the restaurants: the **Bear Lodge Patio** (11am-5pm daily mid-June-Sept., mains $13-19) and **Ancient Timbers Dining Room** (5pm-9pm daily mid-June-Sept., mains $27-35). The guest rooms have no TVs or phones, although there is cell service; rates include breakfast and Wi-Fi. Even if you're not staying at the lodge, you might explore its **hiking trails,** which are open to nonguests. From

Highway 3, turn onto Mount Fernie Park Road, travel past Mount Fernie Provincial Park, and continue to the lodge. In winter, the lodge is open only to guests booked for **catskiing.**

Camping
Off Highway 3, south of Fernie 1.9 miles (3 kilometers), **Mount Fernie Provincial Park** (Mount Fernie Park Rd., 250/422-3003, www.env.gov.bc.ca, May-Sept., $28) has 43 forested campsites and restrooms with showers.

Food
Groceries and Markets
The town's popular summer farmers market, **Fernie Mountain Market** (Rotary Park, 250/423-6674, www.mountainmarket.ca, 10am-2pm Sun. July-early Sept.) sells fresh produce, crafts, baked goods, and some prepared foods. The park is off Highway 3 at 5th Street.

Cafés, Bakeries, and Light Bites
Pop into laid-back **Mugshots Café** (592 3rd Ave., 250/423-8018, 7am-5pm Mon.-Fri., 8am-5pm Sat., mains $7-15) for your morning coffee and pastry, omelet, or breakfast skillet or for a *panini* and a cookie later in the day. The café has free Wi-Fi.

Colorful walls and equally colorful fruit- and veggie-filled plates make the **Lunch Box** (561A 2nd Ave., 250/423-4500, 10am-5pm Mon.-Sat., 11am-4pm Sun., mains $6-13), a smoothie and sandwich bar, a cheerful destination for freshly made soups, wraps, and blended drinks.

Located in the Arts Station, a cultural center in the town's former rail station, ★ **The Blue Toque Diner** (601 1st Ave., 250/423-4637, www.theartsstation.com, 9am-3pm Thurs.-Mon., mains $10-16) is *the* place for breakfast and brunch in Fernie. Try the Florentine Strata, bubbling ramekins of eggs, Swiss cheese, spinach, and bacon in creamy white wine sauce, or the Huevos del Karmalita, crispy corn tortillas piled with eggs, pulled turkey, and refried beans.

Contemporary
"Things you eat with bread" is the theme at the **Loaf Bakery & Restaurant** (641 2nd Ave., 250/423-7702, www.loafbakery.ca, 8am-9pm Wed.-Sat., 8am-4pm Tues. and Sun., mains brunch $7-13, dinner $12-34). It's a bakery by day, selling croissants, pastries, and fresh breads. It's a brunch spot and Italian restaurant, too, serving homemade pizzas, pastas, salads, and grilled dishes.

Asian
To satisfy your sushi cravings, visit the long-popular **Yamagoya** (741 7th Ave., 250/430-0090, www.yamagoya.ca, 5pm-10pm daily, sushi and sashimi $2-20) for traditional and funkier Japanese fare. The Fernie roll is made of tuna, kimchi, tempura, and green onion, while their fusion rolls include a curry version with prawns, mango, red pepper, and curry sauce. In addition to sushi, they serve tempura, salads, and teriyaki stir-fries. They also run a food truck, **Yama2Go,** that's frequently parked downtown around lunchtime or at the Sunday farmers market; to find it, check Yamagoya's twitter feed @Yama2GoSushi.

Information and Services
Visitor Information
The **Fernie Visitor Centre** (102 Hwy. 3, 250/423-6868, www.ferniechamber.com or www.tourismfernie.com, 9am-5pm daily July-Aug., 9am-5pm Mon.-Fri. Sept.-June) is on the east side of town. Out front is the last remaining **wooden oil derrick** (www.ferniederrick.com) still standing in B.C.

In downtown Fernie, there's a **visitor information desk** at the Fernie Museum (491 2nd Ave., 10am-5:30pm daily). Another excellent source of area information is the **Tourism Fernie** website (www.tourismfernie.com).

Medical Services

For emergency medical care in Fernie, **Elk Valley Hospital** (1501 5th Ave., 250/423-4453, www.interiorhealth.ca) is open 24 hours daily.

Save-On-Foods (792 2nd Ave., 250/423-7704, www.saveonfoods.com, grocery 8am-9pm daily, pharmacy 9am-7pm Mon.-Fri., 9am-6pm Sat., 11am-5pm Sun.), the large grocery store downtown, has a pharmacy.

Getting There and Around

Fernie is located on Highway 3 in the southeastern corner of British Columbia, 43 miles (70 kilometers) west of the Alberta border. It's 180 miles (290 kilometers), a three-hour drive, southwest of Calgary, which has the closest major airport. From Calgary, the shortest route is to follow Highway 2 south to Nanton, where you pick up Highway 533 west, then turn south on Highway 22 and west on Highway 3 to Fernie. You can also reach Fernie from Alberta by taking Highway 93 south through Kootenay National Park and continuing south to Highway 3, where you turn east to Fernie.

Fernie is 42 miles (68 kilometers) north of the U.S. border. Highway 93 leads north from Montana to Highway 3, which takes you east to Fernie. The closest U.S. airport, 115 miles (185 kilometers) from Fernie, is **Glacier Park International Airport** (FCA, 4170 Hwy. 2 E., Kalispell, MT, 406/257-5994, www.iflyglacier.com).

From late December through March or early April, several shuttle companies provide transportation between Calgary International Airport and Fernie, including the **Fernie Shuttle** (250/423-4023, www.thefernieshuttle.com, one-way adults $125, under age 6 $103), **Mountain High Shuttle** (877/423-4555, www.mountainhighshuttle.com, one-way adults $125, under age 15 $79), and **Ride Booker** (866/943-0416, www.ridebooker.com, one-way adults $150, under age 15 $95). The trip averages four hours.

Fernie Shuttle also runs a winter-season shuttle to and from the Canadian Rockies International Airport (one-way adults $95, ages 5 and under $70) in Cranbrook; they operate a summer weekend shuttle between Fernie and the Calgary's airport as well.

During the winter ski season, you don't need a car to get between town and the ski hill. **Mountain High Shuttle** (877/423-4555, www.mountainhighshuttle.com) runs the **Powder Chaser Shuttle** (8am to 11pm daily early Dec.-mid-Apr., one-way $3.50) throughout the day between downtown and Fernie Alpine Resort.

Cranbrook and Kimberley

The largest town in the East Kootenays, Cranbrook sits at the crossroads of two main travel routes: Highways 3 and 95. Primarily a commercial hub, it's worth a stop for several historic sights.

Nearby, the small community of Kimberley highlights its European heritage on its Bavarian-themed pedestrian promenade, **The Platzl,** which has Canada's largest freestanding cuckoo clock. Unless you're into this sort of kitschy attraction, it's not worth a special trip, although you may want to take a break for a beer or some sausages. Kimberley draws outdoor enthusiasts for white-water rafting in summer and skiing or snowboarding in winter.

Sights and Activities
Ktunaxa Interpretive Centre

The people of the Ktunaxa First Nation, known in English as the Kootenay, have lived in western North America for more than 10,000 years. Their traditional territory extends through B.C.'s Kootenay region east to Alberta and south into Washington, Idaho, and Montana. A complicated chapter in the Ktunaxas' history unfolded at the former St. Eugene Mission, a red-roofed Spanish-style stone church outside of Cranbrook that served as a residential school for aboriginal children from 1912 until 1970.

Once an Aboriginal Residential School, Now a Resort

Beginning in the 1880s, the Canadian government began establishing residential schools for aboriginal children. Aboriginal students were required to attend these church-run boarding schools, where children were removed from their families. The schools' objective was to assimilate aboriginal youth into mainstream Canadian culture.

While some students' experiences at the schools were positive, the vast majority suffered through poor education, inadequate food, isolation from their families and culture, and in some cases, physical or sexual abuse. The last residential schools closed, or were turned over to aboriginal communities to operate, in the 1980s.

Outside the city of Cranbrook, the **St. Eugene Mission** housed a residential school for most of the 1900s, opening to students in 1912 and remaining in operation until 1970. At its peak in the late 1950s and early 1960s, more than 200 students, both from local First Nations communities and from as far away as Port Hardy on Vancouver Island and Alberta, lived at the school.

The Roman Catholic Church had built the mission on aboriginal land, and in 1978, after the school was closed, the government stripped the building. In the process, workers found letters stuffed into the wall that students had written and hidden, attempting to send them home to their families.

The government returned the mission property to local First Nations bands, but it sat abandoned for many years. Eventually, several of the bands began redeveloping the former school and its surroundings, opening a golf course in 2000, a casino in 2002, and a hotel in 2003.

Today, the **St. Eugene Resort** (7777 Mission Rd., Cranbrook, 250/420-2000 or 866/290-2020, www.steugene.ca) is a resort hotel operated by the Ktunaxa First Nation, Chippewas of Rama First Nation, and Samson Cree Nation in the former mission building and adjacent new wings. Historic photos of the school, former students, and local First Nations residents line the hallways, where students' dormitories have been converted into guest rooms, and the former chapel is now a banquet hall.

Exhibits and artifacts tell the Ktunaxas' past and present-day story at the **Ktunaxa Interpretive Centre** (7777 Mission Rd., Cranbrook, 250/417-4001, www.steugene.ca, call for hours), which is on the lower level of the former mission, now **St. Eugene Resort**, a hotel and casino that several local First Nations bands operate. Take time to watch a documentary film with interviews of former Ktunaxa students who were removed from their families and forced to attend the church-run school.

Fort Steele Heritage Town

In the 1860s, when gold was discovered near Fort Steele on Wild Horse Creek east of Cranbrook, more than 5,000 prospectors inundated the region, hoping to strike it rich. A living history village, **Fort Steele Heritage Town** (9851 Hwy. 93/95, Fort Steele, 250/417-6000, www.fortsteele.ca, 10am-4pm daily May-mid-June and early Sept.-mid-Oct., 10am-5pm daily mid-June-early Sept., adults spring and summer $12, fall $7, seniors spring and summer $10, fall $5, ages 6-17 $5, families $27) takes you back to the gold rush days, with more than 60 restored heritage buildings. Wander into the barbershop (which advertises hot and cold baths), the jail, or the dry goods store, and chat with costumed interpreters as they ply their trades, from blacksmithing to dressmaking to panning for gold.

On the 30-minute **Gossip Tour** (included with admission), a costumed guide leads you through the village while sharing the local scuttlebutt about brothel owners, mail thieves, and other less-than-savory citizens. You can take a ride on the **Fort Steele Steam Railway** (adults $10, ages 6-17 $5) or see a musical production at the **Wildhorse Theatre** (adults $10, ages 6-17 $5). The village itself and the museum building remain open through the winter (10am-4pm daily mid-Oct.-Apr., donation), but the heritage buildings are closed.

Canadian Museum of Rail Travel

Train buffs may want to stop in Cranbrook to visit the **Canadian Museum of Rail Travel** (57 Van Horne St. S./Hwy. 3/95, Cranbrook, 250/489-3918, www. trainsdeluxe.com, 10am-5pm daily July-Aug., 10am-5pm Tues.-Sat. Sept.-June, adults $5-22, seniors $4-18, students $2.50-11, ages 5 and under $1.25-5.50), which has more than 15 historic rail cars that you can explore on a guided tour. Tours are priced based on the number of cars you want to see; the complete tour takes about two hours.

Sports and Recreation

Kootenay Raft Co. (250/427-3266 or 877/777-7238, www.kootenayrafting. ca) offers several water adventures from their Kimberley base, including the family-friendly half-day **St. Mary's Express Trip** (adults $75, ages 13-17 $62, under age 13 $52), a rafting excursion with Class I-III rapids; **Kayak Rafting** (adults $79, ages 13-17 $65), where you follow the St. Mary's route in an inflatable two-person kayak; a full-day **Wilderness Whitewater Rafting Trip** (adults $129, ages 13-17 $99) with Class II-IV rapids on either the White, Bull, or Elk Rivers (depending on river conditions); and the challenging full-day **Skookumchuck Creek Rafting Trip** (adults $159), with Class III-IV rapids, for experienced paddlers only. They also run half-day **stand-up paddleboard tours** (adults $75, under age 16 $65) on local lakes.

horse-drawn wagon at Fort Steele Heritage Town

Kimberley Alpine Resort (301 North Star Blvd., Kimberley, 250/427-4881, www.skikimberley.com, early Dec.-mid-Apr., adults half-day $57.95, full-day $72.95, seniors half-day $45.95, full-day $57.95, ages 13-17 half-day $43.95, full-day $54.95, ages 6-12 half-day $22.95, full-day $28.95) draws skiers and snowboarders to its 80 runs spread across 1,800 acres (729 hectares).

Accommodations

The former St. Eugene Mission, a residential school for aboriginal children from 1912 until 1970, is now the ★ **St. Eugene Resort** (7777 Mission Rd., Cranbrook, 250/420-2000 or 866/290-2020, www.steugene.ca, $139-235 d), which three First Nations communities operate in partnership. Twenty-five of the 125 guest rooms are in the original ivy-colored, red-roofed Mission building, where historic photos line the hallways; the remainder are in a newer lodge. All the units include Wi-Fi, flat-screen TVs,

mini fridges, and coffee- and tea-making equipment.

Also in the Mission building are a spacious fitness facility; the **Ktunaxa Interpretive Centre,** which showcases local First Nations history; and two restaurants, the casual **Fisher Peak Lounge** (11am-11pm Sun.-Thurs., 11am-midnight Fri.-Sat., mains $12-20) and the more formal **Purcell Grill** (7am-11am and 5pm-9pm daily, mains breakfast $6-16, dinner $24-50). Off Highway 95A, four miles (7 kilometers) north of downtown Cranbrook and 15 miles (25 kilometers) south of Kimberley, St. Eugene Resort has a large outdoor swimming pool, an 18-hole golf course, and a casino.

Food

The Heid Out (821 Baker St., Cranbrook, 250/426-7922, www.theheidout.ca, 11:30am-10pm Mon.-Wed., 11:30am-11pm Thurs., 11:30am-midnight Fri.-Sat., 3pm-9pm Sun., mains $13-31), a brewpub downtown, not far from the rail museum, serves burgers, sandwiches, ribs, and other pub fare.

A casual restaurant and lounge just off the Platzl, **Pedal and Tap** (215 Spokane St., Kimberley, 250/427-3325, www.pedalandtap.com, 4pm-9pm Sun.-Thurs., 4pm-10pm Fri.-Sat., call for off-season hours, mains $11-29) cooks up fun twists on pub grub, like Meat & Spaghettiballs (fried balls of spaghetti and cheese on a tomato-meat sauce) and the Tuk-Tuk, a Vietnamese-style sandwich of pulled pork, carrots, and sweet curry mayonnaise. They've got substantial salads, craft beer, and a sunny patio, too.

Information and Services

The **Cranbrook Chamber of Commerce Visitor Centre** (2279 Cranbrook St. N., 250/426-5914 or 800/222-6174, www.cranbrookchamber.com, 8:30am-5pm Mon.-Fri., 9am-5pm Sat.-Sun. late May-early Sept., 8:30am-4:30pm Mon.-Fri. early Sept.-late May) provides information about the area. For more local tips, see the **Cranbrook Tourism** (www.cranbrooktourism.ca) website.

Tourism Kimberley Visitor Information Centre (270 Kimberley Ave., Kimberley, 778/481-1891, www.tourismkimberley.com, 10am-5pm daily July-early Sept., 10am-5pm Mon.-Sat. early Sept.-June) can assist with area details.

Based in Kimberley, **Kootenay-Rockies Tourism** (1905 Warren Ave., Kimberley, 250/427-4838, www.kootenayrockies.com) has a detailed website with lots of itinerary suggestions and ideas for planning a trip through B.C.'s Kootenay-Rockies region.

The West Kootenays

Hot springs, quirky mountain towns, and the history of several different ethnic communities give you plenty to explore in the West Kootenays, from the agricultural town of Creston in the east to funky Nelson between the Purcell and Selkirk Mountains, and along Highway 3 toward the Okanagan Valley. Another popular driving route through the West Kootenays is the **International Selkirk Loop** (www.selkirkloop.org), which takes you from Creston north along the shore of Kootenay Lake, around to Nelson, and south to the U.S. border, continuing through eastern Washington State and northern Idaho.

Creston

Stop in this agricultural town along Highway 3 to stretch your legs, take a short hike, or explore the area's emerging wine industry.

Sights and Recreation

Follow the boardwalk trails through the marsh and along the river at the **Creston Valley Wildlife Management Centre** (1760 West Creston Rd., West Creston, 250/402-6908, www.crestonwildlife.ca, interpretive center 9am-4pm Mon.-Sat. mid-May-late June, 9am-4pm daily late June-Aug., 9am-4pm Tues.-Sat. Sept.-mid-Oct., trails dawn-dusk daily, adults $4, under age 12 $3, families $12), a 17,000-acre (7,000-hectare) nature preserve along the Kootenay River. For bird watching, climb the three-story wildlife-viewing tower on the March Trail loop. Check the website for guided canoe and walking tours. The center is seven miles (11 kilometers) west of Creston, off Highway 3.

Creston has several wineries where you can stop and sip. **Baillie-Grohman Estate Winery** (1140 27 Ave. S., 250/428-8767, www.bailliegrohman.com, 11am-5pm Sat.-Sun. Apr.-mid-May, 11am-5pm daily mid-May-mid-Sept.) and **Skimmerhorn Winery & Vineyard** (1218 27 Ave. S., 250/428-4911, www.skimmerhorn.ca, 11am-5pm Wed.-Sun. Apr.-late June and early Sept.-late Dec., 11am-5pm daily late June-early Sept., tours 2:30pm Sat.-Sun. late June-early Sept., $5 pp) are next door to each other on the south side of town. **Wynnwood Cellars** (5566 Hwy. 3A, 250/866-5155, www.wynnwoodcellars.com, 11am-6pm daily mid-May-mid-Oct.) is just north of town.

Food

Real Food Café (223 10th Ave., 250/428-8882, www.realfoodcafe.ca, 11am-2pm and 4:30pm-8pm Mon.-Fri., mains lunch $10-12, dinner $10-19), a homey downstairs eatery, lives up to its name, serving straightforward meals using lots of local ingredients. Try their excellent peppery wild salmon chowder or the Grown-Up Grilled Cheese, with a locally produced organic cheese, apple chutney, and fresh greens. They're also known for fish-and-chips and for homemade desserts, like carrot cake or sticky toffee pudding.

Information and Services

The **Creston Valley Visitor Centre** (121 Northwest Blvd., 250/428-4342, www.crestonvalleybc.com, 9am-5pm daily July-Aug., 9am-5pm Mon.-Fri.

Sept.-June) can assist with area information and with travel details for elsewhere in B.C. and Alberta. The visitors center also has free Wi-Fi.

★ Nelson

You may find yourself staying longer than you'd planned in this funky West Kootenays town, located between the Canadian Rockies and the B.C. coast. Mountains surround Nelson, on the west arm of Kootenay Lake, with the Purcells to the east and the Selkirk range to the west.

In the late 1800s and early 1900s, most Nelson-area residents were miners, farmers, or loggers. The town has more than 350 heritage buildings, many dating to the Victorian era.

In the 1960s and 1970s, a new wave of migrants settled in Nelson and helped shape the town's present-day culture. During the Vietnam War, between 50,000 and 125,000 Americans who opposed the war or who wanted to avoid the draft came to Canada, and many settled in Nelson or the surrounding small towns of the West Kootenays.

Nelson still has that countercultural vibe, with alternative health providers, yoga studios, and vegetarian restaurants sharing the downtown streets with art galleries, book shops, and outdoor gear stores. Although the town had its moment in the Hollywood spotlight in the 1980s, when the movie *Roxanne,* starring Steve Martin, was filmed here, those 15 minutes of fame didn't go to its head. Slow down and stay awhile; Nelson is a friendly, laid-back place.

Sights and Activities

Take time to explore **Touchstones Nelson: Museum of Art and History** (502 Vernon St., 250/352-9813, www.touchstonesnelson.ca, 10am-5pm Mon.-Wed. and Fri.-Sat., 10am-8pm Thurs., 10am-4pm Sun. mid-May-mid-Sept., 10am-5pm Mon.-Wed. and Fri.-Sat., 10am-8pm Thurs., 11am-4pm Tues. and Sun. mid-Sept.-mid-May, adults $8, seniors and students $6, ages 7-18 $4, families $22, 5pm-8pm Thurs. by donation), a well-designed museum in a 1902 former courthouse. Touchstones traces the region's history, beginning with its First Nations heritage, and follows the explorers, miners, steamship captains, fisherfolk, skiers, and draft dodgers who've influenced the town's development. The museum also hosts changing art exhibitions. Listen to the recorded stories of past and current Nelson residents, and check out the gift shop, which sells locally made crafts, jewelry, and gifts as well as books with local themes.

Kokanee Creek, which flows into Kootenay Lake east of Nelson, was once an important spawning ground for salmon. In an attempt to rebuild the salmon's breeding habitat, the Kokanee Creek Spawning Channel Salmon was built in **Kokanee Creek Provincial Park** (Hwy. 3A, 250/825-4212, www.kootenayswparks.com, May-mid-Oct.), where, from mid-August through mid-September, the waters of the channel are red with spawning fish. A walkway along the channel lets visitors see the salmon in action, and exhibits in the **visitors center** (www.kokaneevisitorscentre.org, 9am-9pm daily late June-early Sept.) tell you more about the fish and the region's ecosystem in general. The park, which is 12 miles (19 kilometers) east of Nelson on Highway 3A, also has a campground and beach along the lake.

Entertainment and Events

Local music, dance, and other performing arts students show off their stuff at the annual **Kootenay Festival of the Arts** (www.kootenayfestivalofthearts.ca, Apr.), a spring tradition in Nelson since 1930.

At the **Elephant Mountain Literary Festival** (www.emlfestival.com, July), a lineup of Canadian authors gives lectures, readings, and workshops on literary topics.

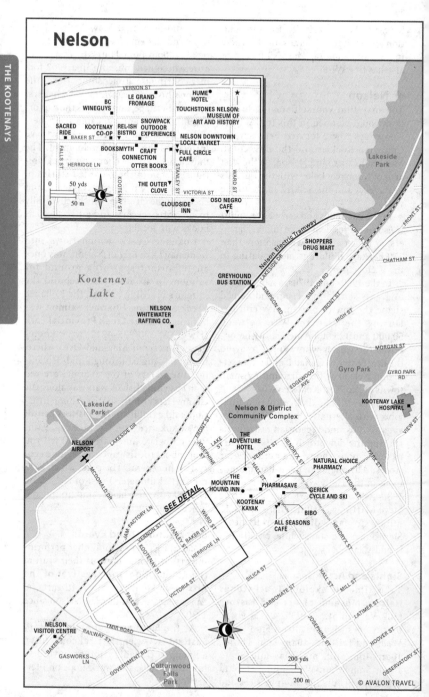

Nelson

VERNON ST

HUME HOTEL

LE GRAND FROMAGE

BC WINEGUYS

TOUCHSTONES NELSON: MUSEUM OF ART AND HISTORY

SACRED RIDE

KOOTENAY CO-OP

REL-ISH BISTRO

SNOWPACK OUTDOOR EXPERIENCES

BAKER ST

NELSON DOWNTOWN LOCAL MARKET

BOOKSMYTH

CRAFT CONNECTION

FULL CIRCLE CAFÉ

FALLS ST

HERRIDGE LN

OTTER BOOKS

KOOTENAY ST

STANLEY ST

THE OUTER CLOVE

VICTORIA ST

WARD ST

0   50 yds
0   50 m

CLOUDSIDE INN

OSO NEGRO CAFÉ

Lakeside Park

Kootenay Lake

Nelson Electric Tramway

SHOPPERS DRUG MART

POPLAR ST

FRONT ST

CHATHAM ST

LAKESIDE DR

GREYHOUND BUS STATION

SIMPSON RD

SIMPSON RD

FRONT ST

HIGH ST

NELSON WHITEWATER RAFTING CO.

MORGAN ST

Gyro Park

GYRO PARK RD

EDGEWOOD AVE

KOOTENAY LAKE HOSPITAL

Lakeside Park

LAKESIDE DR

Nelson & District Community Complex

VIEW ST

PARK ST

NELSON AIRPORT

FRONT ST

LAKE ST

THE ADVENTURE HOTEL

VERNON ST

HENDRYX ST

MCDONALD DR

JOSEPHINE ST

HALL ST

NATURAL CHOICE PHARMACY

THE MOUNTAIN HOUND INN

PHARMASAVE

GERICK CYCLE AND SKI

CEDAR ST

JAM FACTORY LN

SEE DETAIL

KOOTENAY KAYAK

BIBO

ALL SEASONS CAFÉ

HENDRYX ST

VERNON ST

STANLEY ST

BAKER ST

WARD ST

HERRIDGE LN

KOOTENAY ST

VICTORIA ST

SILICA ST

FALLS ST

NELSON VISITOR CENTRE

RAILWAY ST

YMIR ROAD

CARBONATE ST

HALL ST

MILL ST

LATIMER ST

JOSEPHINE ST

HOOVER ST

BAKER ST

GASWORKS LN

GOVERNMENT RD

Cottonwood Falls Park

0   200 yds
0   200 m

OBSERVATORY ST

© AVALON TRAVEL

Scenic Drive: Highway 3A Along Kootenay Lake

To travel between the East Kootenays and Nelson, you have two options. One is to follow Highway 3 east from Creston to the town of Salmo, where you pick up Highway 6 north. A scenic alternative, **Highway 3A,** takes you north from Creston along the eastern shore of Kootenay Lake.

Allow plenty of time to meander along this winding road to enjoy the views across the lake to the mountains beyond. One of the largest lakes in B.C., Kootenay Lake is 67 miles (108 kilometers) long, and at its widest point, it's three miles (4 kilometers) across. From Creston north to Kootenay Bay, it's just 50 miles (80 kilometers), but even without stopping, the drive will take at least 90 minutes.

The most unusual sight along Highway 3A is a former funeral director's home. David H. Brown built **The Glass House** (11341 Hwy. 3A, Boswell, 250/223-8372, 9am-4pm daily May-June and Sept.-Oct., 8am-7pm daily July-Aug., by appointment Nov.-Apr., adults $10, ages 13-17 $8, ages 6-12 $5) in the 1950s, constructing its walls from more than 500,000 empty embalming fluid bottles. Brown apparently felt there should be a practical use for this funeral industry byproduct; he collected discarded bottles from colleagues in the funeral business across western Canada. Guided tours of Brown's 1,200-square-foot (111-square-meter) home and the surrounding gardens overlooking Kootenay Lake 25 miles (40 kilometers) north of Creston tell you about its construction and its unique story.

The Glass House, made from 500,000 empty embalming fluid bottles

Another stop to make along Highway 3A is in the village of **Crawford Bay,** where you can visit studios and galleries of several artists and artisans, including a blacksmith, a broom maker, and a glassblower. Crawford Bay is 47 miles (76 kilometers) north of Creston.

To cross Kootenay Lake and turn west toward Nelson, take the free **Kootenay Lake Ferry** (250/229-4215, www.th.gov. bc.ca, 7:10am-10:20pm daily) from Kootenay Bay on the lake's eastern shore across to Balfour on the west. The 35-minute ferry bills itself as "the longest free ferry ride in the world"—who knew? Note, especially if you're coming from the east, that the ferry operates on Pacific time, one hour earlier than Alberta and the East Kootenays.

From Nelson to Fernie to Invermere, and in many towns in between, artists, galleries, and other cultural institutions open their doors to visitors during the weekend-long **Columbia Basin Culture Tour** (www.cbculturetour.com, Aug.).

The **Shambhala Music Festival** (www. shambhalamusicfestival.com, Aug.), an annual electronic music fest, draws music fans and partiers to the Salmo River Ranch, south of Nelson.

Sports and Recreation

Cyclists, hikers, and cross-country skiers all use the 30-mile (50-kilometer) **Slocan Valley Rail Trail** (888/683-7878, www. slocanvalleyrailtrail.ca) that follows the Slocan River west of Nelson, from Slocan Lake south toward the Kootenay River. In Nelson, **Gerick Cycle and Ski** (702 Baker St., 250/354-4622 or 877/437-4251, www. gericks.com, 9am-5:30pm Mon.-Thurs. and Sat., 9am-7pm Fri., 11am-5pm Sun.)

and **Sacred Ride** (213B Baker St., 250/354-3831, www.sacredride.ca, 9am-5:30pm Mon.-Thurs. and Sat., 9am-6pm Fri.) rent bikes and cross-country skis.

Water Sports

Go white-water rafting, or take a gentler river float trip, with **Nelson Whitewater Rafting Co.** (Prestige Marina, 701 Lakeside Dr., 877/808-7238, www.nelsonwhitewaterrafting.com). Among the trips offered are a leisurely all-ages 3.5- to 4-hour **Slocan River Scenic Float Tour** (June-Sept., adults $69, under age 16 $49); the family-friendly **Slocan River Facchina Rapids White-Water Trip** (June-Sept., adults $79, ages 5-15 $49), a 3.5- to 4-hour tour through Class II-III rapids; and the five-hour **Salmo River Shenango Canyon White-Water Trip** (late May-mid-July, over age 13 $95) that takes you down Class III-IV rapids. They also rent **stand-up paddleboards** (1 hour $20, full-day $60), **single kayaks** (1 hour $20, full-day $60), and **double kayaks** (1 hour $30, full-day $90) from their in-town marina.

Kootenay Kayak (250/505-4549, www.kootenaykayak.com) rents **single and double kayaks** ($40-50) and organizes **guided kayak tours** ranging from two hours to several days. They're based at the Rivers, Oceans, and Mountains shop (ROAM, 639 Baker St., 250/354-2056, www.roamshop.com) downtown, but they can deliver boats and gear to the lakeshore.

Zip-Lining

At **Kokanee Mountain Zipline** (Kokanee Glacier Park Rd., 866/358-8688, www.zipkokanee.com, 9am-5pm daily May-mid-Oct., adults $89, under age 15 $79), the six-line course takes you from a 90-foot (27-meter) warm-up line to a 2,400-foot (730-meter) zip across a canyon. It is located off Highway 3A, north of Nelson.

Kootenay Lake, Nelson

Winter Sports

Downhill skiers and snowboarders head for the 81 runs at **Whitewater Ski Resort** (250/354-4944 or 800/666-9420, www.skiwhitewater.com, early Dec.-early Apr.), which gets an average annual snowfall of 40 feet (12 meters). Although there are no accommodations on the slopes, Whitewater is just 14 miles (22 kilometers) south of town, so it's easy to stay in Nelson and spend the day at the resort. The mountain operates a daily ski-season shuttle (one-way $7.50, round-trip $11) with pickups and drop-offs at area hotels.

Shopping

Baker Street is downtown Nelson's main shopping district, with more shops on the surrounding streets.

Among the many outdoor clothing and gear shops in Nelson, **Snowpack Outdoor Experiences** (333 Baker St., 250/352-6411 or 877/669-7225, www.snowpack.ca) is Canada's only Patagonia outlet store.

Craft Connection (378 Baker St., 250/352-3006, www.craftconnection.org, 9:30am-5:30pm Mon.-Sat.), a local artists' cooperative, sells high quality jewelry, crafts, and gifts.

Nelson's independent bookstores include **Otter Books** (398 Baker St., 250/352-3434, 9:30am-5:30pm Mon.-Sat., 11am-4pm Sun.) and **Booksmyth** (338 Baker St., 250/352-1225, www.booksmyth.ca), which carries used books.

Selling only B.C.-made wines, **BC Wineguys** (410 Kootenay St., 250/352-1130, www.bcwineguysnelson.ca, 10am-7pm Mon.-Sat., noon-6pm Sun.) stocks 500 different varieties from British Columbia producers.

Le Grand Fromage (320 Vernon St., 778/463-3200, www.legrandfromage.ca, 10am-5:30pm Mon.-Sat., 11am-4:30pm Sun.) carries cheeses from local producers and from those farther afield.

Accommodations

Nelson has several moderately priced inns and B&Bs around downtown. Even if your lodging doesn't provide parking, you can park on most downtown streets for free between 5pm and 9am.

Under $150

In an older building on downtown's main street, **The Mountain Hound Inn** (621 Baker St., 250/352-6490, www.mountainhound.com, $79-99 d) has 19 no-frills but comfortable rooms, with private baths, air-conditioning, and flat-screen TVs. The vibe is friendly and hostel-like, although the only common space is the small lobby where a self-serve continental breakfast (muffins, fruit, and coffee or tea) is set up. If cinder block walls give you the creeps, though, look elsewhere, and note that many rooms have windows that face an adjacent building. Wi-Fi and local calls are included.

You choose what to pay for at **The Adventure Hotel** (616 Vernon St., 250/352-7211 or 888/722-2258, www.adventurehotel.ca), a vibrantly colored restoration of a historic building, where the three room categories offer different amenities. The least expensive of the 44 simple modern units, all with air-conditioning and Wi-Fi included, are the snug **budget rooms** ($69 d), with steel bunk beds (a double below and a twin above); the baths have a toilet and a sink, but you use the key-accessed shower down the hall. Want your own shower? Pick the **mid-priced rooms** ($99 d), with a queen bed or bunks and a full bath; you can lounge on the private rooftop deck. If you need more space and services, the larger **deluxe rooms** ($129 d) have iPod docks and private baths with blow-dryers; in addition to the rooftop terrace, you get access to the small gym and sauna. All guests can relax in the second-floor lounge and use the common kitchen and guest laundry. **Louie's Steakhouse** (11am-midnight daily, mains $16-61), the **Uptown Sports Bar,** and **Empire Coffee** (www.empire-coffee. ca) are all on-site.

In a heritage building on a quiet street in the town center, the ★ **Cloudside Inn** (408 Victoria St., 250/352-3226 or 800/596-2337, www.cloudside.ca, $109-185 d) is both personal and stylish. The eight rooms are individually furnished with a well-designed mix of modern and traditional pieces, with photos and other art pieces from around the globe. The two least expensive rooms share a bath; the more expensive rooms are larger suites. Guests can hang out on the front porch, the rear sundeck, or in the comfortable living room. In the morning, choose from two breakfast seatings, where a full meal, including homemade granola and muesli, fresh fruit, yogurt, and a hot dish, is served family-style.

$150-250

The most upscale of Nelson's downtown lodgings is the 45-room **Hume Hotel** (422 Vernon St., 250/352-5331 or 877/568-0888, www.humehotel.com,

$129-249 d), an updated heritage property with a parlor-like lounge, a busy pub, and a small spa. Historic photos decorate the walls, and the classically furnished rooms, while all somewhat different in layout, have white linens, brown upholstery, and dark wood furniture, as well as Keurig coffeemakers and mini fridges. Rates include Wi-Fi, parking, and a hot breakfast in the **General Store Restaurant.**

Food
Groceries and Markets
For fresh produce, local cheeses, and other groceries, and to pick up that Nelson vibe, wander the aisles at the **Kootenay Co-op** (295 Baker St., 250/354-4077, www.kootenay.coop, 7:30am-9pm daily), the town's local grocery store. As this book went to press, the co-op was preparing to move to a new location in the Nelson Commons development (700 block of Baker St.) in 2016.

Vendors at the **Nelson Downtown Local Market** (400 block of Baker St., 250/354-1909, www.ecosociety.ca, mid-June-late Sept. 9:30am-3pm Wed.) bring fresh produce, crafts, and prepared foods to the downtown streets. To be sold at the market, at least 80 percent of each vendor's wares must be made locally.

Cafés, Bakeries, and Light Bites
Nelson's own coffee roaster runs a bustling coffee-centric café, ★ **Oso Negro Café** (604 Ward St., 250/352-7661, www. osonegrocoffee.com, 7am-6pm Mon.-Sat., 8am-4pm Sun., mains $4-7), serving pastries, *paninis*, and, of course, coffee.

With a checkerboard linoleum floor and mauve tables, cheery **Full Circle Café** (101-402 Baker St., 250/354-4458, 6:30am-2:30pm Mon.-Sat., 7am-2pm Sun., mains $6-15) serves breakfast till early afternoon. It's known for the hash, which comes in Veggie (topped with beet pesto and miso-almond gravy) and Kick Hash versions, the latter mixing buffalo sausage with eggs, potatoes, peppers, and chipotle hollandaise. The grilled cinnamon buns and the burgers, from beef to buffalo to bean, have fans, too.

Contemporary

In a cozy brick house with an outdoor terrace, ★ **Bibo** (518 Hall St., 250/352-2744, www.bibonelson.ca, from 5pm daily, mains $16-32) serves what it calls "locally sourced, globally inspired comfort food." That means sharing plates like roasted beet and arugula salad with pepper-crusted chèvre and root chips or a platter of B.C. charcuterie, cheeses, and pickled vegetables, and hearty mains like sustainably caught fish, an Asian-style vegetable noodle bowl, or roast lamb paired with potato-parsnip mash.

If you don't like garlic (or a menu full of corny outer space puns), you might want to pass by **The Outer Clove** (536 Stanley St., 250/354-1667, www.outerclove.com, 11am-9pm Mon.-Sat., mains $12-23), an easygoing garlic-themed café. But if you do enjoy the stinking rose, try garlic-spiked burgers, quesadillas, salads, pastas, or dishes like Chicken Cordon Clove (stuffed with brie and roasted garlic) or lamb shank tempura with garlicky teriyaki sauce. Vegetarians have lots of options here. The signature dessert? Giant garlic chocolate chip cookies ($2) made with candied garlic. Yes, they provide breath mints.

One of Nelson's more upscale dining options, **All Seasons Café** (620 Herridge Lane, 250/352-0101, www.allseasonscafe.com, from 5pm daily, mains $18-34) sits on a narrow lane half a block south of Baker Street. On the menu, which changes with the seasons, you might find mushroom risotto made with locally foraged varieties, duck sauced with a cherry-port reduction, or venison chops served with butternut squash puree. The wine list is strong on B.C. labels.

Known for their burgers, which come in beef, chicken, salmon, and veggie varieties, **Rel-ish Bistro** (301 Baker St., 250/352-5232, www.rel-ish.com,

11am-10pm daily, mains lunch $9-12, dinner $12-32) also prepares updated home-style entrées that might include roast chicken with scalloped sweet potatoes, wild salmon with a caper-lemon beurre blanc, or grilled steaks. From lemon pie to blackberry cornbread pudding, desserts are homey, too.

Information and Services
Visitor Information

Tourism Nelson Kootenay Lake (250/352-7879, www.nelsonkootenaylake.com) produces an area visitors guide, with lots of information on its website.

For in-person assistance, stop into the **Nelson Visitor Centre** (91 Baker St., 250/352-3433 or 877/663-5706, www.discovernelson.com, 8:30am-5pm daily mid-May-early Sept., 8:30am-5pm Mon.-Fri. early Sept.-mid-May) downtown.

Medical Services

Serving the Nelson region, **Kootenay Lake Hospital** (3 View St., 250/352-3111, www.interiorhealth.ca) has 24-hour emergency services.

Nelson pharmacies include **Pharmasave** (685 Baker St., 250/352-2316, www.nelsonpharmasave.com, 9am-6pm Mon.-Fri., 9am-5:30pm Sat., 11am-3pm Sun.), **Shoppers Drug Mart** (Chahko Mika Mall, 1116 Lakeside Dr., 250/352-7268, www.shoppersdrugmart.ca, 8am-10pm daily), and **Natural Choice Pharmacy** (737 Baker St., 250/352-6928, www.naturalchoicerx.com, 9am-5:30pm Mon.-Fri., 10am-4pm Sat.).

Vicinity of Nelson
★ Ainsworth Hot Springs

One of the best places to relax in the Nelson area is **Ainsworth Hot Springs** (3609 Hwy. 31, Balfour, 250/229-4212 or 800/668-1171, www.hotnaturally.com, 10am-9pm daily, adults $12, seniors and students $11, ages 3-12 $9.50, families $38), a natural mineral pool, where its unique feature is a softly lit horseshoe-shaped cave where you can soak in

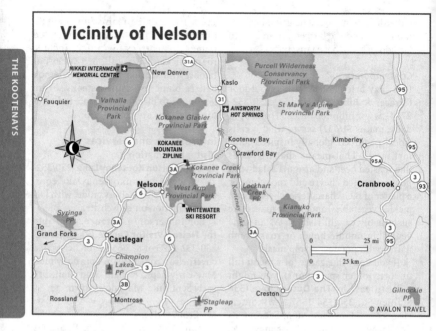

Vicinity of Nelson

secluded nooks. Immersing yourself in the steamy waters of the cave, which average 108°F (42°C), is especially romantic in the evenings. The springs have a large hot pool as well, kept at a soothing 96°F (35°C). The brave can cool off with a dunk in a bracing plunge pool.

The changing rooms at the springs don't have individual lockers, but staff give each guest a large plastic bag for their belongings, which they check at the front desk. A hotel and a restaurant are also on-site.

The hot springs are 30 miles (48 kilometers) northeast of Nelson and 14 miles (22 kilometers) south of Kaslo on Highway 31. If you're coming from eastern B.C., you can travel up the east shore of Kootenay Lake along Highway 3A and take the free ferry across the lake from Kootenay Bay to Balfour; from Creston, at the intersection of Highways 3 and 3A, to the hot springs is 65 miles (105 kilometers).

Kaslo

The pretty village of Kaslo, on the shores of Kootenay Lake, was incorporated in 1893, and many of its buildings date to the Victorian era.

Sights and Recreation

Docked on Kootenay Lake, the **SS Moyie National Historic Site** (324 Front St., 250/353-2525, www.klhs.bc.ca, mid-May-mid-Oct. 10am-5pm daily, adults $8.50, seniors and students $6, ages 6-12 $4, families $20) is the world's oldest intact passenger sternwheeler. Built in Nelson in 1898, the ship ferried passengers along Kootenay Lake until 1957. Watch a 10-minute video about the ship and then climb aboard to wander through the dining room, captain's quarters, and wheelhouse. The **Kaslo Visitor Centre** (10am-6pm daily mid-May-mid-Oct.) is near the ship's entrance.

To explore Kootenay Lake from the water, rent a stand-up paddleboard or kayak from **Kaslo Kayaking** (315 A Ave., 250/353-1925 or 855/505-2925, www.kaslokayaking.com). They also offer guided kayak tours, including a

Who Are the Doukhobors?

Traveling along Highway 3 through southern British Columbia, you might not expect to find communities that trace their ancestry back to Russia's Caucasus Mountains. Pull over to learn more about the Doukhobors.

In the 1700s, a Christian sect split from the Russian Orthodox Church, seeking a simpler form of worship and a more personal connection to God. A Russian Orthodox archbishop dubbed these dissidents *doukhoborsti,* meaning "spirit wrestlers," which he intended as a derogatory term. However, the community adopted the Doukhobor name (pronounced "DUKE-oh-bor"), saying that they were wrestling both "with and for the spirit of God."

The Doukhobors became pacifists, and in a dramatic 1895 act, 7,000 Doukhobor soldiers burned all their weapons. Doukhobor men refused to join the army, and most of the community adopted a vegetarian diet, with bread and borscht (a vegetable soup) as their staple foods. Doukhobor borscht differs from its Russian counterpart, which is a meat-based beet soup; the Doukhobors make their version from cabbage, potatoes, onions, and tomatoes, with one beet to provide color.

Both the czarist government and the Russian Orthodox Church opposed the Doukhobors' beliefs, and many Doukhobors were persecuted, exiled from their communities, and tortured.

the Doukhobor cemetery in Grand Forks

Their plight attracted attention from the Quakers and from author Leo Tolstoy, who became a patron of the community, raising funds that enabled 7,500 Doukhobors to leave Russia and immigrate to Canada in 1899, where most settled in Saskatchewan and established communal villages.

Still seeking to live their motto of "toil and peaceful life," many Doukhobors began migrating again in 1908-1910, leaving Saskatchewan for British Columbia's Kootenay region, where most took up residence in and around the communities of Castlegar and Grand Forks. Descendants of these early settlers still live in southern B.C.

two-hour **sunset paddle** ($65 pp), a half-day **Kootenay Explorer tour** ($135 pp), and the full-day **Adventure Exploration tour** ($185 pp).

Accommodations

A comfortable lodging with an interesting history, the **Kaslo Hotel** (430 Front St., 250/353-7714 or 866/823-1433, www.kaslohotel.com, $150-250 d) was originally built in 1896 when Kaslo was an active mining and logging community. As those industries declined, so, too, did the

hotel, which closed in the 1920s. During World War II, the run-down structure housed Japanese-Canadian internees who were relocated from the B.C. coast. After the war, the hotel was torn down.

Rebuilt in 1958 and later extensively renovated, the Kaslo Hotel is now a modern lodging with historic roots. The 11 rooms are traditionally furnished, with free Wi-Fi, mini fridges, coffeemakers, and updated baths. Rooms on the building's back side have views over Kootenay Lake. Guests can use a microwave in the hallway, or pick up something to read in the take-one, leave-one book box. Catering to active travelers, the hotel supplies rags for cleaning bikes, boots, and other outdoor gear. On the main level, a casual restaurant and pub overlook the lake.

Food

With rose-colored walls and wooden tables, homey **BlueBelle Bistro & Beanery** (347 Front St., 250/353-7361, 8am-8:30pm Mon.-Fri., 9am-8:30pm Sat.-Sun., mains breakfast $6-12, lunch and dinner $8-15) dishes up simple wholesome meals, from coffee, baked goods, and eggs in the morning to soups, salads, sandwiches, and pizzas later in the day. Try the Bistro Bowl, brown rice mounded with chicken, greens, shredded beets, and other veggies, and save room for a homemade dessert. BlueBelle has live music some evenings.

Kaslo's breakfast destination is **The Treehouse** (419 Front St., 250/353-2955, 6:30am-7pm daily summer, call for winter hours, mains $5-15), a local diner serving morning meals all day. Eggs benedict is a specialty, but they also cook up pancakes, sandwiches, and other home-style dishes.

Getting There

Kaslo is on the west shore of Kootenay Lake, off Highway 31. It's 44 miles (70 kilometers) northeast of Nelson and 14 miles (22 kilometers) north of Ainsworth Hot Springs. Between Kaslo and New Denver, it's a scenic 29-mile (46-kilometer) drive through the mountains on Highway 31A.

New Denver

★ Nikkei Internment Memorial Centre

During World War II, the Canadian government designated anyone of Japanese descent, whether they were Canadian citizens or not, an "enemy alien." The government created a 100-mile (160-kilometer) exclusion zone on Canada's west coast between the Pacific Ocean and the

the Heiwa Teien Peace Garden at the Nikkei Internment Memorial Centre in New Denver

Coast Mountains, extending south to the U.S. border and north to the Yukon. Anyone of Japanese heritage was prohibited from remaining in this area.

In 1942, the government sent more than 22,000 Japanese Canadians, many of whom had lived in Vancouver or surrounding coastal communities, to internment camps in British Columbia's Kootenay and eastern mountain regions. One such camp, known as The Orchard, was set up in the tiny town of New Denver, north of Nelson along Slocan Lake.

When you walk through the gates of what is now the **Nikkei Internment Memorial Centre** (306 Josephine St., 250/358-7288, www.newdenver.ca/nikkei, 10am-5pm daily May-Sept., adults $9, seniors and students $7, families $20), a National Historic Site of Canada, you're entering that former camp, which retains several original buildings. Walk into a 1940s-era 14- by 28-foot (4.25- by 8.5-meter) shack that would have housed

two families with up to six children each; The Orchard had roughly 200 of these rudimentary dwellings. Check out the outdoor latrine that would have served up to 50 people. Kyowakai Hall, built in 1943 as a bathhouse but used as a community hall for camp residents, is now a museum about Japanese Canadian history before, during, and after the internment period.

Also at the site is the **Heiwa Teien Peace Garden,** which Japanese Canadian master gardener Roy Tomomichi Sumi designed. Sumi, who was interned at the Rosebery camp north of New Denver, worked at Vancouver's Nitobe Japanese Garden at the University of British Columbia.

After the war, most of the interned Japanese Canadians were given the choice of moving east of the Rockies or returning to Japan; they were forbidden to return to the coast until 1949. Nearly all the internment camps were razed, but New Denver was an exception. Retained as a treatment facility for residents with tuberculosis, a number of the camp's buildings were preserved. In 1957, the B.C. government deeded the remaining shacks at The Orchard to their Japanese Canadian residents. One of these shacks, still on the property, was occupied until the 1980s.

Other Sights
On Slocan Lake, wander the peaceful paths of the **Kohan Reflection Garden** (1st Ave., www.kohangarden.com, dawn-dusk year-round, donation), a small Japanese-style garden that local community members created in 1989 to honor Japanese Canadians who were forcibly relocated to New Denver during World War II.

You could spend hours reading interviews with local residents compiled in books at the **Silvery Slocan Museum** (202 6th Ave., 250/358-2201, www.newdenver. ca, 9am-4pm daily late May-early Sept., adults and over age 11 $4, families $8), New Denver's community history museum, which is packed with artifacts and

Rest Stop: Canada's Smallest City

Blink and you'll miss it: Highway 3 runs directly through **Greenwood, B.C.,** Canada's smallest incorporated municipality.

Established in 1897, this hamlet of fewer than 700 people has some of the region's best-preserved heritage buildings. Stop into the **Greenwood Museum and Visitor Centre** (214 S. Copper Ave./Hwy. 3, 250/445-6355, www.greenwood-museum.com, 10am-4pm daily May, 9am-5pm daily June-Aug., 10am-4pm daily Sept.-Oct., by appointment Nov.-Apr., adults $4), with exhibits about local history, and ask for the free pamphlet outlining a short walking tour of the town's historic structures, including the 1903 city hall, 1915 post office, and 1899 saloon.

For a coffee break, **Copper Eagle Cappuccino & Bakery** (325 S. Copper Ave./Hwy. 3, 250/445-6121, 6am-4pm daily), in an 1899 brick building along Greenwood's main street, makes a variety of java drinks, along with soups, sandwiches, and cinnamon buns and other sweets. The butter tarts have legions of fans.

---

details from the area's past. Old musical instruments, stained glass from a local church, even an iron lung that had belonged to the local hospital are on view, as are belongings from the local Japanese community. The museum is inside the 1887 former Bank of Montreal building, used as a bank until 1969; you can peek into the vault or peruse the old ledgers. The museum also houses the **New Denver Visitor Centre** (250/358-2719, www.slocanlake.com), which is open during museum hours.

Getting There

You can visit New Denver on a day trip from Nelson or as part of a Nelson-Kaslo-New Denver loop through the Kootenay Lakes region.

New Denver is 60 miles (100 kilometers) north of Nelson via Highway 6. From Kaslo, follow Highway 31A west for 29 miles (46 kilometers). From Revelstoke, which is 95 miles (150 kilometers) north of New Denver, take Highway 23 south to Highway 6.

Castlegar

In the early 1900s, members of a pacifist religious community who had emigrated from Russia settled in B.C.'s West Kootenays. Known as the Doukhobors, from a Russian word meaning "spirit wrestlers," many made their home in the town of Castlegar, where you can learn more about the Doukhobors' legacy.

Located 28 miles (45 kilometers) southwest of Nelson and 80 miles (130 kilometers) west of Creston, at the intersection of Highways 3 and 6, Castlegar is an easy stop while traveling Highway 3 across southern B.C. It's 135 miles (220 kilometers) east of Osoyoos.

Sights and Activities

Built in 1969 to preserve the Doukhobors' heritage in the Castlegar area, **Doukhobor Discovery Centre** (112 Heritage Way, 250/365-5327, www.doukhobor-museum.org, 10am-5pm daily May-Sept., adults $10, seniors $8, students $5) illustrates how the community lived in the early 1900s. While most of the solid brick buildings aren't original, they represent the types of structures that the Doukhobors would have built. You can wander into the worship room stocked with bread, salt, and water (the three elements that the Doukhobors felt were necessary for survival), the communal kitchen, the *banya* (sauna and bathhouse), and the blacksmith shop, where craftsmen would have made spike-bottomed winter boots as well as rakes and other tools. Take time to chat with the guides who can explain more about Doukhobor history, life, and culture.

Another legacy of Castlegar's

Doukhobor community is the **Brilliant Suspension Bridge** (Brilliant Rd.) that a group of roughly 100 Doukhobor men constructed over the Kootenay River in 1913, using traditional hand tools and construction methods. A wooden bridge supported by concrete towers, it's 331 feet (100 meters) long. Designed by Vancouver engineer J. R. Grant, who later designed that city's Burrard Bridge (1932), the bridge, now a National Historic Site, is still standing, off Highway 3A at Robinson Road, and you can walk across it to take in the river views. It's no longer used as a transportation route, however; a new highway bridge replaced it in 1966.

Grand Forks

Like Castlegar, the town of Grand Forks drew Doukhobor settlers, with most arriving between 1909 and 1913.

Grand Forks is just north of the Washington border, 60 miles (100 kilometers) west of Castlegar and 80 miles (130 kilometers) east of Osoyoos on Highway 3.

Sights and Activities

In a historic brick schoolhouse on the west side of Grand Forks, the **Boundary Museum and Interpretive Centre** (6145 Reservoir Rd., 250/442-3737, www.boundarymuseum.com, 10am-4pm Tues.-Sat. early May-early Sept., 10am-4pm Tues.-Fri. early Sept.-early May, donation) has exhibits and artifacts about local history, including its mining and forestry heritage, and about the Doukhobor community. The Doukhobors constructed the building,

now called the Fructova Heritage Site, in 1929, and it served as a community school until the 1940s. From June to early September, you can watch bread-baking demonstrations (11am Thurs.), where volunteers use locally milled Pride of the Valley Flour and traditional outdoor ovens.

That local flour comes from the **Grand Forks Doukhobor Heritage Mill** (3620 Mill Rd., 250/442-8252, www.usccdoukhobors.org, 10am-4pm Tues.-Sat. early May-Aug.), originally a steam-powered stone-grinding mill that operated between 1915 and 1945. Reconstructed in the 1960s by a cooperative milling society, the mill continues to produce unbleached white, whole wheat, rye, and other flours. You can tour the historic mill; the flour is sold throughout the West Kootenay region.

Near the mill is a **Doukhobor cemetery** (Cemetery Frontage Rd.), where graves date back to the early 1900s. The cemetery is still in use today.

Food

If you've been learning about Doukhobor culture, you may want to tuck into a hearty Doukhobor lunch. **The Borscht Bowl** (214 Market Ave., 250/442-5977, 10am-4pm Mon.-Sat., mains $4-14), in downtown Grand Forks, serves traditional Doukhobor dishes, including *pyrahi* (a savory baked turnover stuffed with potatoes, spinach, or cheese), *voreniki* (filled dumplings similar to pierogi), and *nalesniki* (crepes). The tasty borscht is Doukhobor-style, with cabbage, tomato, and a little beet for color.

The Okanagan

Stop off for a wine tour or sunny lakeside detour in one of Canada's most popular wine-producing districts, often called the "Napa of the North."

KAMLOOPS

300 MI/480 KM
6 HOURS

BANFF

130 MI/210 KM
2.5 HOURS

245 MI/390 KM
4.5 HOURS

★ **KELOWNA**

75 MI/125 KM
1.5 HOURS

450 MI/725 KM
9 HOURS

VANCOUVER

OSOYOOS ★

250 MI/400 KM
4.5 HOURS

CANADA
UNITED STATES

The Okanagan

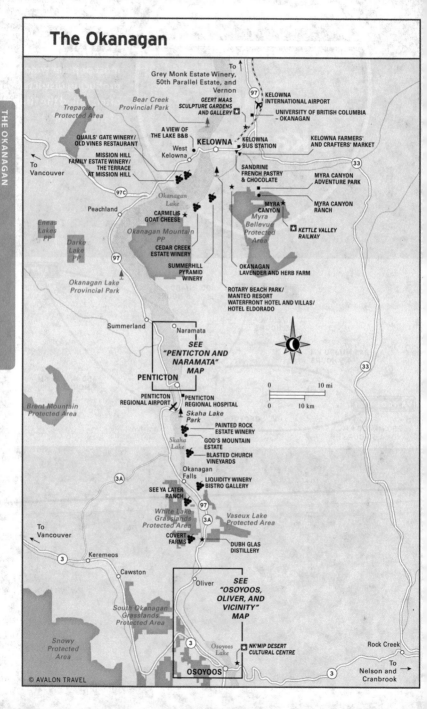

To Grey Monk Estate Winery, 50th Parallel Estate, and Vernon

To Vernon

KELOWNA INTERNATIONAL AIRPORT

GEERT MAAS SCULPTURE GARDENS AND GALLERY

UNIVERSITY OF BRITISH COLUMBIA – OKANAGAN

Bear Creek Provincial Park

Trepanier Protected Area

A VIEW OF THE LAKE B&B

QUAILS' GATE WINERY/ OLD VINES RESTAURANT

MISSION HILL FAMILY ESTATE WINERY/ THE TERRACE AT MISSION HILL

West Kelowna

KELOWNA

KELOWNA BUS STATION

KELOWNA FARMERS' AND CRAFTERS' MARKET

To Vancouver

SANDRINE FRENCH PASTRY & CHOCOLATE

MYRA CANYON ADVENTURE PARK

Okanagan Lake

Peachland

CARMELIS GOAT CHEESE

MYRA CANYON

MYRA CANYON RANCH

Eneas Lakes PP

Darke Lake PP

Okanagan Mountain PP

CEDAR CREEK ESTATE WINERY

SUMMERHILL PYRAMID WINERY

Myra Bellevue Protected Area

KETTLE VALLEY RAILWAY

OKANAGAN LAVENDER AND HERB FARM

Okanagan Lake Provincial Park

ROTARY BEACH PARK/ MANTEO RESORT WATERFRONT HOTEL AND VILLAS/ HOTEL ELDORADO

Summerland

Naramata

SEE "PENTICTON AND NARAMATA" MAP

PENTICTON

Brent Mountain Protected Area

PENTICTON REGIONAL AIRPORT

PENTICTON REGIONAL HOSPITAL

Skaha Lake Park

PAINTED ROCK ESTATE WINERY

GOD'S MOUNTAIN ESTATE

Skaha Lake

BLASTED CHURCH VINEYARDS

Okanagan Falls

LIQUIDITY WINERY BISTRO GALLERY

SEE YA LATER RANCH

White Lake Grasslands Protected Area

Vaseux Lake Protected Area

To Vancouver

COVERT FARMS

DUBH GLAS DISTILLERY

Keremeos

Cawston

Oliver

SEE "OSOYOOS, OLIVER, AND VICINITY" MAP

South Okanagan Grasslands Protected Area

Snowy Protected Area

Osoyoos Lake

NK'MIP DESERT CULTURAL CENTRE

Rock Creek

To Nelson and Cranbrook

OSOYOOS

0   10 mi
0   10 km

© AVALON TRAVEL

Highlights

★ **Wineries:** You've got more than 200 wineries to sample in British Columbia's "Napa of the North," making wine-touring and tasting the centerpiece of an Okanagan stay (pages 353, 369, and 375).

★ **Geert Maas Sculpture Gardens and Gallery:** One of Kelowna's most unexpected attractions is this gallery and sculpture garden that

the artist Geert Maas and his wife created at their rural home (page 358).

★ **Kettle Valley Railway:** This former rail line is now a cycling and walking path that stretches across the Okanagan and beyond. An especially scenic section near Kelowna crosses 18 historic trestle bridges high above Myra Canyon (page 358).

★ **Okanagan Wine Festivals:** Several times a year, the region celebrates its wine industry, with wine-tastings, wine dinners, and other special events (page 361).

★ **Nk'Mip Desert Cultural Centre:** The Okanagan includes Canada's only desert, which you can explore at this First Nations cultural center in Osoyoos (page 379).

Located in central B.C. along a chain of lakes, the Okanagan has become one of Canada's largest wine producing districts.

The weather changes dramatically when you approach the Okanagan, whether you're climbing over the Coast Mountains from Vancouver or crossing the Columbia Range from eastern British Columbia. Either way, you leave behind the rainforests and mountain passes as you descend into this sunny agricultural valley.

As wine regions go, the Okanagan is a youngster. It's been a fertile fruit-growing area for decades, producing peaches, apples, cherries, and more, but it wasn't until the 1980s that the modern wine industry took hold in earnest.

Now, more than 200 wineries hug the lakeshores and rocky hills between Osoyoos, in the desertlike lands near the U.S. border, and Kelowna, around the slightly cooler-climate growing areas to the north. The Okanagan makes a relaxing long-weekend getaway from Vancouver or road-trip stopover between the Rockies and the coast.

Getting to the Okanagan

Driving from Vancouver

From Vancouver to the Okanagan, the route you take will depend on which part of the wine region you're visiting. For all areas, leave the city via **Highway 1** and head east to **Hope.**

To Kelowna

To Kelowna, continue east at Hope onto **Highway 3,** then exit onto **Highway 5 (Coquihalla Hwy.)** north. Follow the Coquihalla over the mountains to **Merritt.** Exit onto **Highway 97C**, which becomes the Okanagan Connector. Stay on **Highway 97** north into Kelowna. Allow **4 to 4.5 hours** for this **245-mile (390-kilometer)** drive.

To Penticton and Naramata

To the Penticton and Naramata area, the shortest route is to follow the **Coquihalla Highway** toward **Kelowna,** but when **Highway 97C** meets **Highway 97,** turn south and continue past Peachland and Summerland to Penticton. Because Naramata is on Okanagan Lake's eastern shore, you have to go into Penticton, skirt the lakeshore, and turn north on Naramata Road to reach Naramata. It's about **4.5 hours** from Vancouver to **Penticton (260 miles/415 kilometers)** and another **20 minutes** to **Naramata.**

To Osoyoos

If you're traveling to Osoyoos, Oliver, and the South Okanagan, follow **Highway 3** east from Hope, which meanders over the mountains, through the Similkameen Valley, and to Osoyoos. This **250-mile (400-kilometer)** drive from Vancouver takes **4.5 to 5 hours.** Oliver is 12.5 miles (20 kilometers) north of Osoyoos along Highway 97.

Driving from Kamloops

To Kelowna

Driving from Kamloops to Kelowna, you have two options: Follow **Highway 5** south to **Merritt** and pick up **Highway 97C;** this route is **130 miles (210 kilometers)** and takes you through some beautifully remote ranchlands. Or take **Highway 97** south; it's a **105-mile (165-kilometer)** drive that follows some scenic stretches of lakeshore. The Merritt route is longer, but the roads are faster. Either option will take about **2.5 hours.**

To Osoyoos

To get from Kamloops to Osoyoos, follow

Best Hotels

★ **A View of the Lake B&B:** This West Kelowna bed-and-breakfast lives up to its name, with great views over Okanagan Lake. The welcoming hosts (including a professional chef) are known for their morning meals (page 362).

★ **Delta Grand Okanagan Resort and Conference Centre:** Combining urban and holiday pleasures, this large lakefront property has an indoor-outdoor pool, lots of activities, and a range of accommodations, all just a short stroll from downtown Kelowna (page 363).

★ **Watermark Beach Resort:** On Lake Osoyoos, this condo-style resort has everything you need for a lakeside getaway, from comfortable condos to complimentary wine-tastings (page 381).

★ **The Guest House at Burrowing Owl Estate Winery:** This upscale winery inn with a solar-heated pool and excellent restaurant makes a romantic escape (page 382).

the directions to **Kelowna** and continue south to Penticton, Oliver, and Osoyoos on **Highway 97.** The drive from Kamloops to Osoyoos is **180 miles (290 kilometers)** and takes **3.75 to 4 hours.**

If you're driving between Kamloops and Osoyoos and you don't want to meander through the Okanagan Valley, take **Highway 5** south to **Merritt,** then **Highway 5A** south to Princeton. At **Princeton,** follow **Highway 3** east to Osoyoos. This route is **180 miles (290 kilometers)** and takes **3.5 hours.**

Driving from Banff

From Banff and the Canadian Rockies to the Okanagan, the best route depends on where in the Okanagan you're heading and what you'd like to see en route.

To Kelowna

The most direct route between Banff and Kelowna is **Highway 1,** which travels west from Banff through the B.C. Rockies to **Sicamous.** There, head south on **Highway 97A** and continue south on **Highway 97** into Kelowna. It's **300 miles (480 kilometers),** a **5.5- to 6-hour** drive.

To Osoyoos

To get from Banff to Osoyoos, follow the directions to **Kelowna** and stay on **Highway 97** south to Penticton, Oliver, and Osoyoos. This Banff-Osoyoos route via Highway 1 and Highway 97 is a **375-mile (605-kilometer)** drive that takes **7.5 hours.**

An alternate route between Banff and Osoyoos takes you **through the Kootenays** region. Leaving Banff on **Highway 1** west, turn south onto **Highway 93** toward **Radium Hot Springs.** Continue following **Highway 93/95** south from Radium Hot Springs beyond Cranbrook to **Highway 3.** Take Highway 3 west to Osoyoos. This Banff-Osoyoos route is a **450-mile (725-kilometer)** trip; it takes **nine hours.**

Getting There by Air or Bus
By Air

The Okanagan's main commercial airport is **Kelowna International Airport** (YLW, 5533 Airport Way, Kelowna, 250/765-5125, http://ylw. kelowna.ca), which has regular flights from Vancouver, Victoria, Calgary, Edmonton, Toronto, Seattle, Las Vegas, and Phoenix. **Air Canada** (www.aircanada.com) and **WestJet** (www.westjet. com) are the airport's main carriers; **Alaska Airlines** (www.alaskaair.com) operates the Kelowna-Seattle route. The airport is nine miles (14 kilometers) north of the city center along Highway 97.

Best Restaurants

★ **The Terrace at Mission Hill:** At one of the Okanagan's grandest wineries, this contemporary West Kelowna restaurant on an outdoor patio is among the region's most scenic dining spots (page 366).

★ **Waterfront Wines Restaurant:** Long considered one of Kelowna's top dining destinations, this lively contemporary restaurant works its magic, whether you park at the bar for wine and small plates, or settle in for an inventive multicourse meal (page 366).

★ **RauDZ Regional Table:** This downtown Kelowna bistro sets a relaxed vibe with a long list of Okanagan wines and plates piled high with ingredients from around the region (page 367).

★ **The Bench Artisan Food Market:** You can get breakfast all day, espresso and pastries, or picnic fixings at this Penticton foodie destination that's part café and part gourmet grocery (page 373).

★ **The Sonora Room at Burrowing Owl:** Excellent food, polished service, and a panoramic vista over the Black Sage Bench make this South Okanagan winery restaurant a must-visit (page 384).

★ **Miradoro Restaurant at Tinhorn Creek:** Perched on an Oliver hillside, this winery dining room serves simple wood-fired pizzas and more adventurous dishes, paired with the vineyard's wines (page 384).

Car rental companies operating at the Kelowna Airport include **Avis** (250/491-9500, www.avis.com), **Budget** (250/491-7368, www.bcbudget.com), **Enterprise** (250/491-9611, www.enterprise.com), and **National** (250/765-2800, www.national-car.com).

Once you've arrived at Kelowna airport, it's possible to get to the city center by public transit. **B.C. Transit bus 23** (250/860-8121, www.bctransit.com/kelowna, adults $2.50, seniors and ages 5-18 $2) stops at the Kelowna Airport 6am-6:30pm Monday through Friday; however, it doesn't go directly downtown. To travel between the airport and downtown Kelowna, take bus 23 south to the UBCO Transit Exchange (at the University of British Columbia-Okanagan) and transfer to **bus 97.**

Another option for getting to the Okanagan by air is to fly to the small **Penticton Regional Airport** (YYF, 3000 Airport Rd., Penticton, 250/770-4422, www.cyyf.ca). **Air Canada** (www.aircanada.com) has daily flights to Penticton

from Vancouver. **WestJet** (www.westjet.com) flies between Penticton and Calgary.

By Bus

Greyhound (800/661-8747, www.greyhound.ca) runs regular buses to Kelowna from Vancouver (5.25-7.5 hours, adults $52-93) and from Calgary (9.75-13.5 hours, adults $69-110), via Canmore, Banff, Lake Louise, Golden, Revelstoke, and several intermediate points.

The **Kelowna Bus Station** (2366 Leckie Rd., 250/860-3036) is 3.5 miles (5.5 kilometers) east of downtown and the lakeshore. Several **B.C. Transit** (250/860-8121, www.bctransit.com/kelowna, adults $2.50, seniors and ages 5-18 $2) buses can take you between the bus station and the downtown area.

Greyhound also travels to the **Penticton Bus Station** (307 Ellis St., 250/493-4101) from Vancouver (6-7.25 hours, adults $43-79) and from Calgary (12-15 hours, adults $63-107), although the latter trip requires at least

Rest Stop: Hope

Most people end up in the small town of Hope when they're traveling between Vancouver and the Okanagan, since it's located near the junction of three major routes: Highway 1, Highway 3, and Highway 5. Take a break for gas and food here if you're heading east over the mountains or west toward the coast. For more area information, stop into the **Hope Visitor Centre** (919 Water Ave., 604/869-2021, http://hopebc.ca, 10am-4pm Mon.-Fri., 9am-5pm Sat.-Sun.).

Accommodations and Food

Hope has 20 motels where you can rest for the night. Most are basic chains or local lodgings on Highway 1 (Water Ave.), the Old Hope-Princeton Highway, or Wallace Street.

Need a coffee break? Look for the **Blue Moose Coffeehouse** (322 Wallace St., 604/869-0729, www.bluemoose.coffee, 7am-9pm daily, mains $5-9), where coffee is ground to order and you can choose from a wide selection of teas. Pastries and sandwiches can assuage most hunger pangs.

A time-honored stop for road-trippers, **Home Restaurant** (665 Old Hope-Princeton Hwy., 604/869-5558, www.homerestaurants.ca, mains breakfast $8-16, lunch and dinner $9-18) dishes up filling diner fare, including bacon and eggs, burgers, and roast turkey dinners. And yes, there's pie.

For something more interesting than ordinary roadside grub, try **293 Wallace** (293 Wallace St., 604/860-0822, www.293wallace.com, noon-9pm Wed.-Mon., mains $13-34), a contemporary dining room with dark wood tables and parquet floors. The menu includes homemade soups, fresh salads, and sandwiches, like a veggie wrap stuffed with feta, eggplant, peppers, or the well-loved beef dip.

one transfer. From Penticton, buses continue south to **Oliver** (5852 Main St., 250/498-2626) and **Osoyoos** (9912 Hwy. 3, 250/495-7252).

Kelowna and Vicinity

The largest city in the Okanagan, Kelowna has an enviable location directly on Okanagan Lake. The city's revitalized downtown district borders its beautiful park-lined waterfront, while orchards, wineries, and forests fill its surrounding rural districts. Alas, like many growing communities, Kelowna has plenty of not-so-bucolic suburban sprawl in between.

Because it's centrally located, Kelowna (population 117,000) makes a convenient stopover between Vancouver and the Canadian Rockies. You can tour numerous wineries, breweries, and distilleries, explore local cheesemakers, farms, and gardens, or go cycling along the lake or through the desert hills, before returning to the city for a first-rate meal. While some parts of Kelowna may not be as "resort pretty" as other areas of the Okanagan, you won't lack for things to do.

★ Wineries

Kelowna's wineries are concentrated in several different areas: south of the city's downtown on the east side of Okanagan Lake, on the lake's west shore, and north of Kelowna in the district known as Lake Country.

You don't even have to leave Kelowna's city center for wine-tasting, though. **Sandhill Wines** (1125 Richter St., 250/762-9144 or 888/246-4472, www.sandhillwines.ca, 9am-6pm daily June-Oct., 10am-5pm Mon.-Sat., 10am-4pm Sun. Nov.-May) has a downtown tasting room at the Calona Vineyards Winery Boutique.

Eastside Wineries

After releasing its first wines in 1987,

The Othello Tunnels

Just east of Hope, stop to stretch your legs with a short walk into history at the **Othello Tunnels** in **Coquihalla Canyon Provincial Park** (www.env.gov.bc.ca).

The Othello Tunnels were built in the early 1900s as part of the Kettle Valley Railway, which once provided the main rail link between B.C.'s interior and the coast. The five Othello tunnels enabled the railroad to pass through the Coquihalla Gorge, where the Coquihalla River had carved a 300-foot-deep (91-meter) channel of solid granite. And yes, the tunnels were named after Shakespeare's character.

The Kettle Valley Railway was dismantled in the 1980s, and along the Othello Tunnels section, you can follow a flat walking path that leads through these impressive granite passages. The trail from the parking area to the fifth tunnel and back is 2.1 miles (3.5 kilometers) round-trip. Bring a flashlight; the tunnels are very dark inside, and the path can be uneven and often wet.

To reach the Othello Tunnels coming from the west, take Exit 170 from Highway 1 at Hope and turn left at the end of the exit ramp. Turn right onto Old Hope-Princeton Highway junction, left at 6th

Othello Tunnels

Avenue, then right onto Kawkawa Lake Road. Take the second right onto Othello Road, and then stay right to continue on Othello Road to the parking area. It's five miles (8 kilometers) east of Hope.

If you're traveling south on Highway 5 from Kamloops or Kelowna, take Exit 183 and follow Othello Road to the tunnels. Heading west on Highway 3, turn north onto Highway 5. Follow Exit 183 off of Highway 5 and take Othello Road to the tunnels.

long-established **CedarCreek Estate Winery** (5445 Lakeshore Rd., 778/738-1027, www.cedarcreek.bc.ca, tasting room 11am-7pm daily May-June, 10am-7pm daily July-Sept., 11am-5pm daily Oct.-Apr., tours 11am, 1pm, and 3pm daily May-mid.-Oct., $8) now produces a lengthy catalogue of wine, including riesling, gewürztraminer, ehrenfelser, chardonnay, pinot gris, merlot, meritage, syrah, and pinot noir, which you can sample year-round in the tasting room. The **Vineyard Terrace Restaurant** (from 11am daily May-Sept., mains lunch $21-24, dinner $28-36) serves farm-to-table fare outdoors above the lake.

Summerhill Pyramid Winery (4870 Chute Lake Rd., 250/764-8000 or 800/667-3538, www.summerhill.bc.ca, wine shop 9am-7pm daily, tours noon, 2pm, and 4pm daily, adults $10) produces organic wines that it ages in, yes, its own pyramid. Tour guides tell you about organic wine production, about the process of making sparkling wines, and about the history and significance of the unusual pyramid; tours also include tastings of four wines. The winery's **Sunset Organic Bistro** (lunch 11am-3pm Mon.-Sat., "grazing" 3pm-5pm Mon.-Sat., dinner 5pm-9pm Mon.-Sat., brunch 11am-3pm Sun., mains lunch $15-24, dinner $22-36) uses ingredients from their biodynamic gardens and local organic farms in their contemporary dishes.

Two Days in the Okanagan

You can follow this route from south to north, as it's described here, or begin at the northern end and head to the south.

Start your day in Osoyoos at the southern tip of the Okanagan Valley with an early morning stroll along the Lake Osoyoos shore, ideally with a hot drink and a sourdough cinnamon bun from the **Lake Village Bakery.** Before it gets too hot, visit the **Nk'Mip Desert Cultural Centre** to learn about the region's ecology and First Nations culture. Stop into nearby **Nk'Mip Cellars** to sample the wares at Canada's first aboriginal-owned winery.

Then it's time to begin **wine touring** in earnest. You can make several stops along the Black Sage Bench; **Burrowing Owl, Black Hills Estate Winery, Church and State Wines,** and **Platinum Bench** (where you can do bread- and wine-tasting) are all here, and you can enjoy lunch on the patio at the **Vineyard Kitchen at Black Hills.** Another option is to follow Highway 97 north toward Oliver, visiting **Hester Creek, Tinhorn Creek,** and **Maverick Wines** along the way.

In the late afternoon, check into your accommodations—the **Watermark Beach Resort Hotel** in Osoyoos or **The Guest House at Burrowing Owl Estate Winery** are both excellent choices—to relax before dinner, maybe with a swim in the pool. Then have a leisurely evening meal at one of the winery restaurants, such as **The Sonora Room at Burrowing Owl** or **Miradoro at Tinhorn Creek.** Plan to arrive before the sun sets, so you can take in the views across the valley from their terraces.

The next morning, check out of your hotel and drive north on Highway 97 toward Penticton, where you can explore the wineries in **Naramata,** including

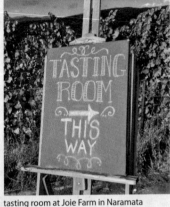

tasting room at Joie Farm in Naramata

Joie Farm, Therapy Vineyards, and **Upper Bench Winery & Creamery.** Pick up a picnic lunch at **The Bench Artisan Food Market** or sit down at one of the winery restaurants, like the **Patio at Lake Breeze.**

When you're done exploring Naramata, get back on Highway 97, continuing north around Okanagan Lake to Kelowna. If you'd like to check out more wineries along the way, stop at **Mission Hill Family Estate** or **Quails' Gate** on Kelowna's Westside. Then head for Myra Canyon for a late afternoon bike ride along the **Kettle Valley Railway,** where you can cross a series of reconstructed trestle bridges high above the canyon floor.

After settling into your Kelowna hotel, stop for a pre-dinner libation at one of the city's brewpubs, like the **Tree Brewing Beer Institute** or **BNA Brewing.** Then have dinner at **Waterfront Wines** or **RauDZ Regional Table,** where you can compare notes on the best wines that you've tasted during your two days in the Okanagan.

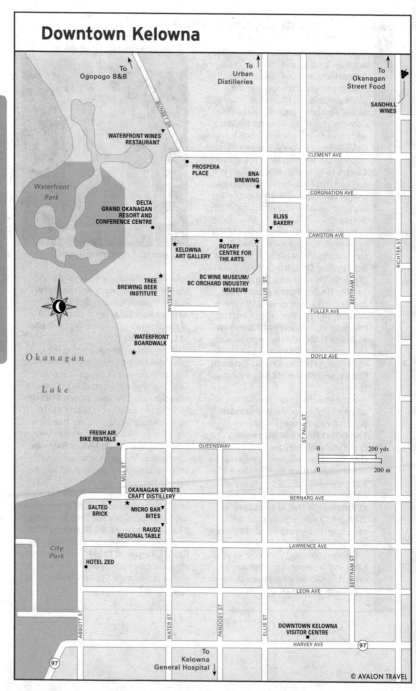

Downtown Kelowna

To Ogopogo B&B

To Urban Distilleries

To Okanagan Street Food

SANDHILL WINES

WATERFRONT WINES RESTAURANT

CLEMENT AVE

PROSPERA PLACE

BNA BREWING

CORONATION AVE

Waterfront Park

DELTA GRAND OKANAGAN RESORT AND CONFERENCE CENTRE

BLISS BAKERY

CAWSTON AVE

KELOWNA ART GALLERY

ROTARY CENTRE FOR THE ARTS

BC WINE MUSEUM/ BC ORCHARD INDUSTRY MUSEUM

FULLER AVE

TREE BREWING BEER INSTITUTE

WATER ST

ELLIS ST

BERTRAM ST

RICHTER ST

DOYLE AVE

WATERFRONT BOARDWALK

Okanagan

Lake

ST PAUL ST

0   200 yds

0   200 m

FRESH AIR BIKE RENTALS

QUEENSWAY

MILL ST

BERNARD AVE

OKANAGAN SPIRITS CRAFT DISTILLERY

SALTED BRICK

MICRO BAR BITES

RAUDZ REGIONAL TABLE

LAWRENCE AVE

BERTRAM ST

City Park

HOTEL ZED

LEON AVE

ABBOTT ST

WATER ST

PANDOSY ST

ELLIS ST

DOWNTOWN KELOWNA VISITOR CENTRE

HARVEY AVE

97

To Kelowna General Hospital

97

© AVALON TRAVEL

Westside Wineries

Among the grandest of the Okanagan wineries, **Mission Hill Family Estate** (1730 Mission Hill Rd., West Kelowna, 250/768-6483 or 800/957-9911, www.missionhillwinery.com, call for hours) welcomes guests through an imposing archway into a courtyard where a 12-story bell tower stands. From here, make your way to the wine shop where tastings are offered daily, or meet in the Wine Education Centre for one of several **tours** (60 to 90 minutes, $12-55). The winery hosts summer concerts in their outdoor amphitheater and offers culinary workshops and wine dinners throughout the year. **The Terrace** (noon-7pm Sun.-Wed., noon-8pm Thurs.-Sat. mid-May-mid-June and mid-Sept.-mid-Oct., 11:30am-3:30pm and 5pm-8:30pm Tues.-Thurs., 11:30am-3:30pm and 5pm-9pm Fri.-Mon. mid-June-mid-Sept., mains lunch $19-29, dinner $27-47), with vistas across the vineyards, is among the region's most scenic dining destinations.

Most winery tours aren't geared for kids, but at **Quails' Gate Winery** (3303 Boucherie Rd., West Kelowna, 250/769-4451 or 800/420-9463, www.quailsgate.com, 9:30am-8pm daily late June-early Sept., 10am-7pm daily May-late June and early Sept.-mid-Oct., 10am-6pm daily mid-Oct.-Apr.), all ages are welcome on the one-hour **family winery tour** (daily May-Oct., call for tour times, adults $10, under age 19 free), which covers a brief history of the Okanagan Valley, a short visit to the vineyards and production facilities, and a tasting. Their flagship Quails' Gate label includes pinot noir, merlot, marechal foch, gewürztraminer, riesling, chenin blanc, chasselas, chardonnay, and rosé, and they also produce ice wine, port, and other specialty wines. At **Old Vines Restaurant** (lunch 11am-2:30pm, wine bar 2:30pm-5pm, dinner from 5pm daily, mains lunch $17-24, dinner $29-40), you can enjoy lunch

or dinner overlooking the vineyards year-round.

Lake Country Wineries

Lake Country is north of Kelowna and south of Vernon. For more wineries in this emerging wine district, check out the **Scenic Sip Trail** (www.scenicsip.ca).

Named for its geographic location on a 61-acre (25-hectare) property above the lake, **50th Parallel Estate** (17101 Terrace View Rd., Lake Country, 250/766-3408, www.50thparallel.com, 10:30am-6pm daily Apr.-Oct., noon-5pm Thurs.-Sun. Nov.-Mar.) offers samples of their chardonnay, pinot gris, pinot noir, or other wines at a tasting bar inside in their modern production facility.

Grey Monk Estate Winery (1055 Camp Rd., Okanagan Centre, 250/766-3168 or 800/663-4205, www.graymonk.com, summer 10am-7pm daily summer, 10am-5pm daily spring and fall, call for winter hours) got its start in 1972, in the Okanagan's early wine-producing days. While it makes a range of varietals, it is especially known for its pinot gris. Free 45-minute winery tours (on the hour 11am-4pm daily) are offered. The winery's dining room, **Grapevine Restaurant and Patio** (250/766-3168, www.grapevinerestaurant.ca, lunch 11:30am-3pm daily Apr.-Oct., mains $18-23), serves upscale lunches that include duck confit with spaetzle, B.C. steelhead filets, and meatball sliders. From spring through fall, Grapevine is also open for afternoon wine, cheese, and charcuterie (3pm-5pm daily May-mid-Oct.) and for dinner (5pm-8:30pm daily May-mid-Oct., mains $22-36).

Breweries and Distilleries

While the Okanagan's beer and spirit brewing operations are younger industries than its wine-making, you can visit craft breweries and distilleries in and around Kelowna.

Tree Brewing Beer Institute (1346 Water St., 778/484-0306 or 800/663-4847, www.treebeer.com, 11am-9pm Sun.-Tues., 11am-10pm Wed.-Sat.) has a tasting room and lounge where you can taste pilsners, IPAs, and seasonal brews, and amuse yourself with tabletop Trivial Pursuit game cards. They also make excellent **pizza** using spent grain from the brewing process in the crust; try the bratwurst, sauerkraut, and arugula pie.

Stop in for a tasting flight or a snack at **BNA Brewing** (1250 Ellis St., 236/420-0025, www.bnabrewing.com, tasting room 1pm-6pm daily, food 4pm-late daily), a microbrewery that opened in 2015.

Okanagan Spirits Craft Distillery (888/292-5270, www.okanaganspirits.com) brews gin, vodka, fruit liqueurs, and Canada's first genuine absinthe. They offer tours and tastings at their main location north of Kelowna (5204 24th St., Vernon, 250/549-3120, 9am-6pm Mon.-Sat.) and have a tasting bar at their downtown Kelowna satellite (267 Bernard Ave., 778/484-5174, 10am-6pm daily).

Urban Distilleries (6-325 Bay Ave., 778/478-0939, www.urbandistilleries.ca, 11am-6pm daily Apr.-Oct., 11am-5pm Sun.-Fri., 10am-6pm Sat. Nov.-Mar.), in an industrial building in downtown's north end, offers tours and tastings of gin and vodka.

Sights and Activities

In downtown Kelowna, follow the 1.5-mile (2.5-kilometer) paved **Waterfront Boardwalk** along the Okanagan Lake shore. Along the way, besides enjoying the lake views, look for the 2010 sculpture called *Bear* by Brower Hatcher; it's illuminated at night.

★ Geert Maas Sculpture Gardens and Gallery

One of Kelowna's most unexpected attractions might be the **Geert Maas Sculpture Gardens and Gallery** (250 Reynolds Rd., 250/860-7012, www.geert-maas.org, 10am-5pm daily, donation)

that the artist Geert Maas and his wife created in their home northeast of the city. Inside the gallery are several rooms of the prolific Maas's bronze sculptures, stonework, and paintings, with many more pieces on the grounds outside. Born in the Netherlands in 1944, Maas immigrated to Canada in 1979. His works are included in public, private, and corporate art collections in more than 30 countries.

Other Museums and Galleries

In a modern downtown building, the **Kelowna Art Gallery** (1315 Water St., 250/762-2226, www.kelownaartgallery.com, 1pm-4pm Sun.-Mon., 10am-5pm Tues.-Wed. and Fri.-Sat., 10am-9pm Thurs. July-Aug., 10am-5pm Tues.-Wed. and Fri.-Sat., 10am-9pm Thurs., 1pm-4pm Sun. Sept.-June, adults $5, seniors and students $4, families $10, free Thurs.) shows works by Canadian contemporary artists in changing exhibitions throughout the year.

The **B.C. Wine Museum** (Laurel Packinghouse, 1304 Ellis St., 250/868-0441, www.kelownamuseums.ca, 10am-6pm Mon.-Fri., 10am-5pm Sat., 11am-5pm Sun., free) has a small exhibit area that traces the history of the region's wine industry. Housed in B.C.'s oldest remaining agricultural packinghouse, which operated from 1918 until the 1970s, it's primarily a wine store, selling wines from around the Okanagan. Staff can answer your wine questions and give you touring tips; the museum hosts a **wine-tasting** (3pm-5pm Fri.) featuring local products.

Also in the Laurel Packinghouse, the tiny **B.C. Orchard Industry Museum** (1304 Ellis St., 778/478-0347, www.kelowna-museums.ca, 10am-5pm Tues.-Sat., donation) has exhibits about another major Okanagan industry: fruit growing.

★ Kettle Valley Railway

Opened in 1915, the **Kettle Valley Railway** provided the main rail link

Planning an Okanagan Wine Tour

Making plans to go wine-tasting in the Okanagan Valley? Here are some tips to help you organize your wine tour.

Do Some Research (or Just Explore)

If you want to research local wines before you set out, the **British Columbia Wine Institute** (www.winebc.com) has an excellent, detailed website with all the information you might want about wineries in the Okanagan and elsewhere in the province. If you're stopping in Penticton, the staff at the **B.C. VQA Wine Information Centre** (553 Vees Dr., Penticton, 250/490-2006, www.pentictonwineinfo.com), which is both a wine shop and an information office, can tell you all about local wineries. But there's no harm in stopping wherever a winery catches your fancy.

Focus Your Travels

Because the Okanagan covers a large region, 75 meandering miles (125 kilometers) between Osoyoos and Kelowna, consider picking one or two areas to explore if you have just a day or two. You'll spend less time traveling around and get to know an area in depth.

Taste Large and Small

When planning your wine tour, visit a mix of larger producers and smaller family-run wineries. The larger facilities typically offer tours of their production facilities, while the smaller spots give you a more individualized experience, where you can often learn what led the owners to plant their Okanagan vineyards or why they chose particular grape varieties.

Include Beer or Spirits

While wine is the Okanagan Valley's major liquid asset, you'll find a growing number of craft distilleries and microbreweries as well. Consider balancing your wine-tasting with a beer sampling or distillery tour.

Break It Up

Take time out of your wine-tasting for other activities. Go cycling, hiking, or swimming. Explore the desert, or stop at a fruit stand. Tour an art gallery, or visit a cheesemaker. Or simply enjoy the views across the lakes.

Have a Designated Driver

You don't want to be driving if you're sampling a lot of wine. Limit your tasting, "sip and spit," or make sure one member of your party is the designated driver.

Alternatively, book a wine tour that includes transportation from winery to winery and back to your hotel. That way, you can leave the driving to your guide while you enjoy your wine.

Local wine tour companies include **Discover Okanagan Wine Tours** (250/763-1161, www.discoverokanagantours.com), **Distinctly Kelowna Tours** (250/979-1211 or 866/979-1211, www.distinctlykelownatours.ca), **Roots & Vines Tour Co.** (250/868-0611 or 844/868-0611, www.rootsandvinestours.com), and **Uncorked Okanagan Wine Tours** (250/769-3123, www.uncorkedokanagan.com).

Another enjoyable way to tour area wineries is by bicycle. Kelowna's **Monashee Adventure Tours** (250/762-9253 or 888/762-9253, www.monasheeadventuretours.com) offers a number of different sip-and-cycle tours. In the South Okanagan, **Heatstroke Cycle and Sport** (778/437-2453, www.heatstrokecycle.com) runs cycling tours to the wineries along the Black Sage Bench and the Golden Mile.

For more recommended wine tour companies, see the **Tourism Kelowna** (www.tourismkelowna.com) website or talk to the staff at area visitor centers.

between the mines, mills, and farms of B.C.'s Kootenay region and the port of Vancouver. Following a meandering path between Midway, near the Canada-U.S. border east of Osoyoos, through the Okanagan Valley and over the mountains to the town of Hope, the railroad was the main transportation and communications connection between B.C.'s interior districts and the coast until 1949.

Passenger train service continued along the line until the 1960s, but by the 1980s, the entire line had been abandoned. Fortunately, after the railroad ceased operation and the tracks were removed, the former rail line was eventually converted into a 370-mile (600-kilometer) cycling and hiking path across southern B.C.

The Myra Canyon Trestles

One of the most popular sections of the Kettle Valley Railway route is in the Kelowna area. The 7.5-mile (12-kilometer) trail through **Myra Canyon** crosses 18 historic wooden trestle bridges high above the deep canyon. It also passes through two tunnels in the rock cliffs. In 2003, a massive wildfire destroyed 16 of the 18 bridges; however, they've since been rebuilt and reopened.

Unless you're afraid of heights, cycling the Myra Canyon, high above the city of Kelowna, offers great views and a look back into the region's history. Interpretive panels along the way tell you more about the railroad and the trestle bridges.

Getting There

To reach Myra Canyon from downtown Kelowna, make your way south and turn left onto K.L.O. Road. At McCulloch Road, turn right and continue until you reach Myra Forest Service Road, where you turn right again. Follow Myra Forest

Top to bottom: Kelowna Art Gallery; trestle bridge over Myra Canyon; view from Myra Canyon Ranch.

Service Road five miles (8 kilometers) to the parking lot. Allow 25 to 30 minutes for the drive.

Monashee Adventure Tours (250/762-9253 or 888/762-9253, www.monashee-adventuretours.com) leads **guided rides** ($120 pp) of the Myra Canyon Trestles that include commentary and background about the bridges, the railroad, and the region in general, plus pickup and drop-off at Kelowna-area hotels. You can also do a **self-guided ride** ($100 pp) at Myra Canyon, where they'll provide transportation, a rental bike, maps, and directions, then send you on your way. They also **rent bikes** ($40-70 per day) for your own adventures.

Myra Canyon Rentals (Myra Station parking area, 250/878-8763, www.myra-canyonrental.com, 9am-5:30pm daily mid-May-early Oct., half-day rentals adults $39, kids $30, full-day adults $69, kids $50, bike trailers $25) rents bikes from a stand at the entrance to the Myra Canyon parking lot.

Agritourism

At **Carmelis Goat Cheese** (170 Timberline Rd., 250/764-9033, www.carmelis-goatcheese.com, 10am-6pm daily May-Sept., 11am-5pm daily Mar.-Apr. and Oct.), you can sample and purchase handcrafted goat cheeses, including soft chèvre, a firm gruyère-style cheese, and "goatgonzola," their distinctive blue. The goat's milk gelato is a perfect afternoon refresher. Carmelis is located 7.5 miles (12 kilometers) south of downtown Kelowna on the east side of Okanagan Lake.

Breathe deeply at **Okanagan Lavender and Herb Farm** (4380 Takla Rd., 250/764-7795, www.okanaganlavender. com, 11am-5pm daily mid-May-mid-Oct., mid-May-mid-June and Sept.-mid-Oct. adults $7.50, seniors and ages 13-17 $6.50, ages 7-12 $5, mid-June-Aug. adults $9, seniors $8, ages 13-17 $6.50, ages 7-12 $5), where you can tour the fields that bloom with aromatic purple plants. July is the best time to visit, when the lavender is at its purplest. Refresh with lavender treats, from lemonade to gelato, in the **Small Bites Café.** The farm is six miles (10 kilometers) south of downtown Kelowna.

Entertainment and Events
The Arts

The modern **Rotary Centre for the Arts** (421 Cawston Ave., 250/717-5304, www.rotarycentreforthearts.com) downtown presents theater, music, and visual arts events.

Prospera Place (1223 Water St., 250/979-0888, www.prosperaplace.com) is the city's sports arena and concert venue.

B.C.'s third-largest orchestra, the **Okanagan Symphony** (250/763-7544, www.okanagansymphony.com) performs in Kelowna, Penticton, and Vernon.

★ Okanagan Wine Festivals

The **Okanagan Wine Festivals** (www.thewinefestivals.com) are the largest celebrations of the region's wine industry, taking place several times a year, with wine-tastings, wine dinners, and other special events, from Kelowna to Osoyoos. The Spring Festival is held in late April and early May, the Fall Festival is for 10 days in early October, and the Winter Festival is in January.

Other Festivals and Events

At their 1,000-seat outdoor amphitheater, **Mission Hill Family Estate** (1730 Mission Hill Rd., West Kelowna, 250/768-6483 or 800/957-9911, www.missionhillwinery.com) hosts a summer concert series, where Tony Bennett, the Gipsy Kings, Lyle Lovett, jazz trumpeter Chris Botti, and country singer Martina McBride have been among the past performers.

Parks Alive! (www.festivalskelowna.com, July-Aug.) is a summertime series of more than 50 concerts and other arts events in Kelowna's parks and outdoor spaces.

Sports and Recreation
Beaches
Beaches line Okanagan Lake throughout the Kelowna area. Downtown, **City Park** (1600 Abbott St.) has a sandy beach, kids waterpark and playground, basketball courts, volleyball nets, and restrooms.

South of the city center, **Rotary Beach Park** (3726 Lakeshore Rd.) has a swimming beach, playground, and restrooms. Windsurfers and kite-boarders flock here for the winds.

Ropes Course
The Von Andrian family, who operate the Myra Canyon Ranch B&B, also run the **Myra Canyon Adventure Park** (4429 June Springs Rd., 250/869-8494, www.myracanyon.com, 2pm-7pm Fri., 10am-7pm Sat.-Sun. mid-May-June and Sept.-mid-Oct., 10am-8pm daily July-Aug., adults $39, under age 18 $34), where you can challenge yourself on several ropes courses. The adventure park is nine miles (15 kilometers) southeast of downtown Kelowna.

Winter Sports
Big White Ski Resort (5315 Big White Rd., 250/765-3101 or 800/663-2772, www.bigwhite.com, adults $87, seniors and ages 13-18 $74, ages 6-12 $49) is Kelowna's local mountain, and it's also Canada's largest fully ski-in, ski-out resort. With 2,765 acres (1,147 hectares) of patrolled terrain, Big White has 15 lifts serving 118 runs. Terrain is rated 18 percent beginner, 54 percent intermediate, 22 percent expert, and 6 percent extreme. The mountain typically opens in late November and closes in mid-April.

Big White is 35 miles (57 kilometers) southeast of Kelowna. From Highway 97, take Highway 33 southeast to Big White Road.

On weekends during the ski season, the resort operates an **Express Bus** (Fri.-Sun., one-way $19, round-trip $24) that can take you to the mountain from a number of locations in Kelowna; check the Big White website for schedules.

The **Big White Airport Shuttle** (daily late Nov.-mid-Apr., 800/663-2772, one-way adults $48.89, ages 6-12 $34.21, ages 5 and under $21.08, round-trip adults $79.47, ages 6-12 $56.22, ages 5 and under $27.11) picks up passengers at the Kelowna Airport and at Kelowna's Greyhound Bus Station and brings them to the mountain. Reserve your shuttle at least 72 hours in advance.

Accommodations and Camping
Under $150
From May through late August, the **University of British Columbia Okanagan Campus** (1290 International Mews, 250/807-8050 or 888/318-8666, www.okanagan.ubcconferences.com) rents out on-campus rooms to travelers. Options include single rooms ($48) that share a bath with one other room and have hardwired Internet access but no Wi-Fi, or studio suites ($69-129 d) and one-bedroom units ($119-189 d), both with private baths, kitchens, and included Wi-Fi. Parking is $3.15 per day. These aren't plush accommodations (think basic dormitory decor), but they're a reasonable value if you don't need frills. The campus is nine miles (14 kilometers) northeast of downtown Kelowna.

As this book went to press, **Hotel Zed** (1627 Abbott St., www.hotelzed.com), which operates a fun and funky boutique motel in Victoria, was planning to open a location in Kelowna; check their website for details.

$150-250
★ **A View of the Lake B&B** (1877 Horizon Dr., West Kelowna, 250/769-7854, www.aviewofthelake.com, $135-185 d) lives up to its name, particularly from the expansive deck, where the panoramic views extend across Okanagan Lake to downtown Kelowna. Guests can have their three-course breakfast on this sunny east-facing terrace, or inside in

the window-lined living room with a fireplace. Three of the four guest rooms, with modern furnishings, contemporary art, and Wi-Fi, look out to the lake; the Grand View suite has a whirlpool tub with lake vistas. Gregarious owner Steve Marston, a former professional chef who runs the B&B with his wife, Chrissy, offers cooking workshops and dinners fall through spring in his huge demonstration kitchen. The B&B is in a residential neighborhood, a 15-minute drive to downtown Kelowna.

Named for a mythical creature said to inhabit Okanagan Lake, **Ogopogo B&B** (845 Manhattan Dr., 250/762-7624, www.ogopogobedandbreakfast.ca, May-mid-Oct., $195-295 d) is an upscale inn, hidden in a residential neighborhood across the street from the lakeshore and a short walk from downtown. In the main house, the spacious Manhattan suite upstairs has a king bed, a fireplace, and a view of the lake; the smaller Sunset suite, on the main floor, also has a king bed. The third room, in the adjacent carriage house, is decorated in black and white, with a queen bed. All units have mini fridges, coffeemakers, teakettles, and complimentary Wi-Fi. Take the kayak and beach chairs to the lake, or borrow a bike to go for a ride. A full breakfast, alternating sweet and savory dishes like blintzes or frittatas, is served family-style in the modern open kitchen.

From the expansive deck at **Myra Canyon Ranch** (4675 June Springs Rd., 250/764-9731, www.myracanyonranch.com, $150-219 d), a six-room family-friendly B&B high in the hills above town, you have panoramic views across the valley to the city, the lake, and beyond. Owners Rolf and Kathrin von Andrian and their family relocated from Germany to open this modern wood-frame inn, where, inside, the clean-lined European-style furnishings and duvet-topped beds make the guest rooms simple but comfortable. They prepare hearty morning meals that often feature waffles (from a Berlin café's secret recipe), German whole-wheat bread, platters of cheeses and meats, and fresh fruits and vegetables. It's a working ranch, too, with **stables** where you can arrange **trail rides** (2 hours, $109 pp) and introductory **kids rides** (ages 3-7, 30-60 minutes, $55-75). Myra Canyon Ranch is nine miles (15 kilometers) southeast of downtown Kelowna.

Over $250

The family-friendly **Manteo Resort Waterfront Hotel and Villas** (3762 Lakeshore Rd., 250/860-1031 or 800/445-5255, www.manteo.com, $219-385 d) has plenty for everyone to do, with a small private lakeside beach where you can rent canoes, kayaks, and stand-up paddleboards; three pools (two outdoors, one inside); several hot tubs; a gym; a games room, with Ping-Pong and pool tables; tennis and basketball courts; a kids playground; and even a movie theater, where the gang can watch films or sporting events. When it's time to sleep, choose one of the 24 villas, comfortable two- or three-bedroom townhouses with full kitchens and beds for 6 to 10, or the 78 hotel rooms and suites, with dark wood furniture and puffy duvets; the best rooms have lake views, but all are just steps from the waterfront. Parking, local calls, and Wi-Fi are included in the room rates. **Smack DAB restaurant** (250/860-4488, www.smackdabmanteo.com, 7am-10:30am and 11am-10pm daily, mains $13-28), smack-dab on the lake, serves a good-value breakfast buffet (resort guests adults $9, under age 11 $4) and later in the day casual sandwiches, pizzas, and pub fare with local craft beer.

Right on Okanagan Lake a short walk from downtown, ★ **Delta Grand Okanagan Resort and Conference Centre** (1310 Water St., 250/763-4500 or 888/890-3222, www.deltahotels.com, $249-399 d, parking $19-23) combines urban and holiday pleasures. When you pull up a seat on the sunny patio overlooking the lakefront lagoon, lounge in the indoor-outdoor pool, or book a treatment in the on-site spa, you definitely feel like you're on vacation. During the summer, the resort hosts movie nights and other activities to entertain families; for the grown-ups, there's a fitness facility and a casino. In the two guest towers, the 265 modern rooms have smart desks with lots of outlets, included Wi-Fi, flat-screen TVs, mini fridges, and coffeemakers; the 60 traditionally appointed one-, two-, and three-bedroom suites feel more like vacation homes with full kitchens. A separate condo building, the Royal Private Residence Club, has large one- to four-bedroom apartments ($700-2,000), a private gym, and a gorgeous rooftop infinity pool above the lake.

An Austrian countess constructed the original **Hotel Eldorado** (500 Cook Rd., 250/763-7500 or 866/608-7500, www.eldoradokelowna.com, $259-489 d) in 1926, and the current lakeside property, decorated with old photos, has been rebuilt in a classic lake-villa style. Of the 49 guest rooms, those in the heritage wing are all different but have traditional furnishings and balconies overlooking the lake. In the newer four-story Arms wing, the cottage-style rooms are outfitted with white painted furniture and plaid comforters; eight one-bedroom suites have a small kitchenette and a living room with a pullout sofa and an electric fireplace. Popular for Sunday brunch, the window-lined Lakeside dining room resembles a cottage summer porch. You can swim in the indoor lap pool, or rent kayaks or stand-up paddleboards; there's a small gym, sauna, and hot tub. Free parking.

Camping

Several provincial parks in the vicinity of Kelowna have lakeside campgrounds. To make reservations at any of these parks, contact **Discover Camping** (519/826-6850 or 800/689-9025, www.discovercamping.ca), the park reservation service.

Delta Grand Okanagan Resort and Conference Centre

Bear Creek Provincial Park (Westside Rd., 250/548-0076, www.env.gov.bc.ca, Apr.-mid-Oct., $35), located on the west shore of Okanagan Lake, northwest of Kelowna, has 122 campsites, flush toilets, and showers. Reservations are required between mid-May and early September. From Kelowna, take Highway 97 west to Westside Road; follow Westside Road north for 4.5 miles (7 kilometers) to the park entrance.

Kekuli Bay Provincial Park (off Hwy. 97, 250/548-0076, www.env.gov.bc.ca, Apr.-late-Oct., $32) is on the west side of Kalamalka Lake, between Kelowna and Vernon. The 69-site campground, with showers and flush toilets, is a short distance from the water, although with a rocky beach, the area is more popular for boating than swimming. You can reserve sites between mid-May and early September. From Kelowna, take Highway 97 north toward Vernon, and watch for the park signs; it's about a 45-minute drive.

At **Ellison Provincial Park** (off 25th Ave., Vernon, 250/548-0076, www.env.gov.bc.ca, Apr.-mid-Oct., $32), located on the northeastern shore of Okanagan Lake, reservations are accepted for 51 of the 71 sites between mid-May and early September. Otherwise, you can arrive and take any available site. The campground has showers and flush toilets, and several beaches are nearby. There's no direct road access to the park from the south, so if you're coming from Kelowna, follow Highway 97 north toward Vernon. At 25th Avenue (the main intersection in downtown Vernon), turn left (west), and continue for 10 miles (16 kilometers) to the park. It's about an hour's drive to Ellison from Kelowna.

South of Kelowna, **Okanagan Lake Provincial Park** (off Hwy. 97, 250/548-0076, www.env.gov.bc.ca, $35) has two different camping areas, both with showers and flush toilets. The North Campground (Apr.-late Sept.) has 80 sites spaced out on three terraces overlooking the lake, while in the South Campground (mid-May-mid-Oct.), the 88 sites are closer together but closer to the lakeshore. You can make reservations for both campgrounds for stays between mid-May and early September; otherwise, sites are first-come, first-served. The park is on Okanagan Lake, 33 miles (53 kilometers) south of Kelowna and seven miles (11 kilometers) north of Summerland.

Food
Groceries and Markets
More than 150 vendors hawk their wares at the **Kelowna Farmers and Crafters Market** (Dilworth Dr. and Springfield Rd., www.kelownafarmersandcrafters-smarket.com, 8am-1pm Wed. and Sat. Apr.-mid-Nov.), featuring fresh fruits and vegetables, baked goods, jewelry, pottery, and other foods and crafts. In the colder months, the market moves into the Parkinson Recreation Center

(1800 Parkinson Way, 9am-1pm Sat. mid-Nov.-Mar.).

Cafés, Bakeries, and Light Bites

Convenient for breakfast or a light lunch downtown, sunny **Bliss Bakery** (109-1289 Ellis St., 778/484-5355, www.blissbakery.ca, 7:30am-6pm daily, mains $3-11) bakes excellent muffins (try the Kitchen Sink, with carrots, pineapple, and walnuts), scones, and other pastries, and also prepares several daily varieties of sandwiches. Wi-Fi is free. They have another location (4200 Beach Ave., Peachland, 250/767-2711, 7:30am-6pm daily) near the lakeshore south of Kelowna.

Despite its name, the **Okanagan Grocery** (Guisachan Village, 2355 Gordon Dr., 250/862-2811, www.okanagangrocery.com, 9:30am-5:30pm Tues.-Sat.) is primarily a bakery, selling their own delicious homemade breads and pastries, along with a small selection of locally made cheeses and other regional products. At the second bakeshop-only location (115-1979 Windsor Rd., 250/868-4929, 7am-6pm Tues.-Fri., 8am-5pm Sat.), you can pick up pastries and coffee.

Sandrine French Pastry & Chocolate (1865 Dilworth Dr., 250/860-1202, www.sandrinepastry.com, 8:30am-6pm Mon.-Sat.) would look more at home on a Parisian boulevard than it does in a strip mall opposite Kelowna's Orchard Park shopping center, so perhaps it's no surprise that this jewel-box patisserie specializes in traditional French pastries and chocolates. Pick up a croissant (the chocolate almond are particularly decadent), a *pain raisin*, or tart made with local fruits. They offer half-day **cooking classes**, focusing on French pastry-making or chocolate techniques; check their website for schedules and prices.

Winery Restaurants

One of the Okanagan's most scenic dining spots is ★ **The Terrace at Mission Hill** (1730 Mission Hill Rd., West Kelowna, 250/768-6467, www.missionhillwinery.

com, noon-7pm Sun.-Wed., noon-8pm Thurs.-Sat. mid-May-mid-June and mid-Sept.-mid-Oct., 11:30am-3:30pm and 5pm-8:30pm Tues.-Thurs., 11:30am-3:30pm and 5pm-9pm Fri.-Mon. mid-June-mid-Sept., mains lunch $19-29, dinner $27-47), a patio restaurant with vistas across the vines all the way to Okanagan Lake. Catering to the changing seasons, the contemporary menu varies but always includes fresh salads, seafood, and other preparations using ingredients from around the region. The gracious staff can assist you in pairing wines with your food selections. Plan your visit for a sunny day; this outdoor restaurant closes when the weather turns inclement.

At Quails' Gate Winery, you can dine overlooking the vineyards year-round at **Old Vines Restaurant** (3303 Boucherie Rd., West Kelowna, 250/769-2500 or 800/420-9463, ext. 252, www.quailsgate.com, lunch 11am-2:30pm, wine bar 2:30pm-5pm, dinner from 5pm daily, mains lunch $17-24, dinner $29-40). As at many Okanagan dining spots, Old Vines' seasonal menus incorporate regional products, from duck ravioli with pickled beets or a west coast bouillabaisse at lunch, to Cornish game hen with herb gnocchi or locally raised beef served with Brussels sprouts and celeriac puree in the evening. Reservations are strongly recommended in summer.

Contemporary

★ **Waterfront Wines Restaurant** (104-1180 Sunset Dr., 250/979-1222, www.waterfrontrestaurant.ca, 5pm-10pm daily, mains $26-32) has long been one of Kelowna's top dining destinations, in a compact space with honey wood tables that feels both lively and cozy. You can park at the bar for a glass of Okanagan wine and small plates (perhaps the simple but excellent wild mushrooms on toast or an organic vegetable salad with local blue cheese), or let executive chef Mark Filatow and his crew in the open kitchen work their magic on more elaborate dishes, like quail with a savory concord grape sauce, Indian-spiced brisket with coconut rice cake and cilantro-mint chutney, or house-made ricotta *cavatelli* with beluga lentils and a carrot-fennel sauce. Finish with a cheese plate or a sweet like the chocolate pear tart with bitter chocolate ice cream.

The kitchen cures its own charcuterie at **Salted Brick** (243 Bernard Ave., 778/484-3234, www.saltedbrick.com, 11am-6pm Mon.-Tues., 11am-10pm Wed.-Fri., 10am-10pm Sat.-Sun., small plates $8-14), housed in a narrow downtown storefront. Order a platter with local cheeses, pickled vegetables, and dried fruit for a light lunch or an evening snack, paired with local wines or craft beers. The small menu also offers several sandwiches, salads, and snacks, including meaty medjool dates stuffed with blue cheese and drizzled with olive oil; served warm, they're rather addictive.

The motto of this warm downtown bistro with exposed brick walls is "fresh, local, comfortable," and even though chef and co-owner Rod Butters is something of a local food celebrity, ★ **RauDZ Regional Table** (1560 Water St., 250/868-8805, www.raudz.com, from 5pm daily, mains $19-32)—pronounced "Rod's"—keeps the vibe relaxed and fun. Sip a glass of Okanagan wine along with the crab cappuccino, a rich bisque swimming with Dungeness crab, topped with milk froth and served in a coffee cup, or try the *poutine,* heaped with chicken confit. The oat-crusted arctic char comes with a big pile of local vegetables, while the signature dish, the RJB, is a decadent sandwich of beef tenderloin, butter-poached crab, bacon, and onion jam piled on a brioche bun. Fortunately, desserts like apple cinnamon-filled beignets or chocolate

Top to bottom: Indian-spiced brisket at Waterfront Wines Restaurant; crab "cappuccino" at RauDZ Regional Table; on Okanagan Lake in Naramata.

caramel crunch (rich mousse topped with salted caramel ice cream and crispy caramel) are served in slightly less huge "taster" sizes.

The same owners run tiny **micro bar bites** (1500 Water St., 778/484-3500, www.microkelowna.com, 3pm-late daily, small plates $6-20), down the street. Yes, it's petite (as the chef says, the space is so small, they don't even capitalize the *m*), but they find room to serve charcuterie, cheeses, oysters, salads, and other creative small plates.

Diners

On an industrial street north of downtown, **Okanagan Street Food** (812 Crowley Ave., 778/478-0807, www.okanaganstreetfood.com, 8am-3pm Tues.-Sat., mains $9-13) is a locals joint for breakfast and lunch, run by a former winery chef. With an organic fair-trade coffee, you can dig into breakfast wraps, huevos rancheros, or choose-your-filling omelets. Midday, the not-your-average-diner menu includes fish tacos, pulled pork sandwiches, pasta specials, and candied salmon risotto fritters.

Information and Services
Visitor Information

Tourism Kelowna (250/861-1515 or 800/663-4345, www.tourismkelowna.com) provides information about the city and the surrounding region. They assist visitors at the **Downtown Kelowna Visitor Centre** (544 Harvey Ave., 9am-5pm Mon.-Fri., 10am-3pm Sat.-Sun.) and at the **Kelowna International Airport Kiosk** in the airport arrivals lounge. You can also tweet a travel question to @KelownaVisitor, using the hashtag #AskKelowna.

Media and Communications

Glossy *Okanagan Life* (www.okanaganlife.com) magazine reports on the region's restaurants, producing an annual restaurant guide, and on community, business, and real estate news.

Kelowna's *Daily Courier* (www.kelownadailycourier.ca) and *Capital News* (www.kelownacapnews.com) both cover local news.

Medical Services

The Okanagan's main hospital facility, **Kelowna General Hospital** (2268 Pandosy St., 250/862-4000 or 888/877-4442, www.interiorhealth.ca), provides emergency services around the clock.

The pharmacy at **Shoppers Drug Mart** (2271 Harvey Ave., Unit 1360, 250/860-3764, www.shoppersdrugmart.ca) is open 24 hours daily.

Getting Around
By Car

Kelowna is located off Highway 97 on the west side of Okanagan Lake. Highway 97 runs east-west through the city, where it's called Harvey Avenue. The main downtown shopping and restaurant street is Bernard Avenue, which is parallel to Harvey Avenue, three blocks to the north.

In the downtown area, **street parking** is metered (9am-5pm Mon.-Sat., $1.25 per hour); purchase a parking ticket from the automated machines nearby. Metered spaces have a two-hour maximum. For longer stays, pull into one of the city-run parking structures: **Library Plaza Parkade** (1360 Ellis St., $1 per hour, $5 per day) or **Chapman Parkade** (345 Lawrence Ave., $1 per hour, $5 per day). Street parking is free in the evenings and on Sunday. The city parkades are free 6pm-6am Monday-Friday and all day Saturday-Sunday.

Most of the wineries are located outside the city center, either in West Kelowna, on the lake's west shore, via Highway 97 south, or south of downtown, off Lakeshore Road.

By Bus

B.C. Transit (250/860-8121, www.bctransit.com/kelowna, adults $2.50, seniors and ages 5-18 $2) runs bus service around Kelowna.

By Bike

Kelowna has more than 185 miles (300 kilometers) of on-street bicycle lanes and 25 miles (40 kilometers) of paved multi-use cycling and walking paths. Download a **bike map** from the City of Kelowna website (www.kelowna.ca), or pick up a copy at the **Downtown Kelowna Visitor Centre** (544 Harvey Ave.).

In summer, you can rent bikes on the downtown waterfront at **Fresh Air Bike Rentals** (238 Queensway, 250/317-0784, 11am-5pm daily June, 9am-7pm daily late June-early Sept., $15-20 per hour). **Monashee Adventure Tours** (1591 Highland Dr. N., 250/762-9253 or 888/762-9253, $40 per day) can deliver rental bikes to your hotel.

Penticton and Naramata

On the southern shore of Okanagan Lake, Penticton is the largest community in the Central Okanagan. The main reason to visit this city of 43,000 is to explore the wineries just east of town, in the bucolic area above the lake known as the **Naramata Bench.**

★ Wineries

The wineries along the south end of the Naramata Bench have Penticton addresses, while those to the north are in Naramata.

Producing both wine and cheese, **Upper Bench Winery & Creamery** (170 Upper Bench Rd. S., Penticton, 250/770-1733, www.upperbench.ca, 10am-6pm daily Apr.-Oct., 10am-5pm daily Nov.-Mar.) offers samples of both in their homey shop and tasting room. The U&Brie is especially flavorful. Under the arbor on the patio, you can sit down to a cheese platter and wine flight.

Another cheesemaker, **Poplar Grove Cheese** (1060 Poplar Grove Rd., Penticton, 250/492-4575, www.poplar-grovecheese.ca, 11am-5pm Sat.-Sun.

Apr.-May, 11am-5pm daily June-Oct.), makes several varieties, including a mild double-cream camembert and the full-flavored Tiger Blue. Sample them at the tasting bar, along with wines from **Lock and Worth** (www.lockandworth.com).

A small farm and winery, **Joie Farm** (2825 Naramata Rd., Naramata, 250/496-0092, www.joiefarm.com, 10am-5pm Wed.-Mon. May-Oct.) makes an excellent rosé as well as the Alsace-style Noble Blend, unoaked chardonnay, riesling, gewürztraminer, pinot blanc, gamay, and pinot noir, many of which sell out before they even reach the stores. In addition to sampling wine in their hospitable tasting room, you can tuck into a wood-fired pizza at **Picnique,** their patio eatery. The winery entrance is actually along Aikins Loop; turn off Naramata Road onto Old Main Road, then go left onto Aikins Loop to the winery.

Producing labels like Freudian Sip (a blend of pinot gris, riesling, sauvignon blanc, gewürztraminer, muscat, and viognier), Pink Freud (a pinot noir-merlot rosé), or Bruised Ego (made from sauvignon blanc, pinot gris, and viognier), cheeky **Therapy Vineyards** (940 Debeck Rd., Naramata, 250/496-5217, www.therapyvineyards.com, 10am-6pm daily May-Oct., 10am-5pm daily Nov.-Apr.) does make serious wine, too. Analyze it yourself in their tasting room.

In the modern **Painted Rock Estate Winery** (400 Smythe Dr., Penticton, 250/493-6809, www.paintedrock.ca, 11am-5:30pm daily May-Oct., by appointment Nov.-Apr.), you can sample chardonnay, merlot, cabernet sauvignon, and Painted Rock's signature red blend, Red Icon, which is made predominantly from merlot, cabernet franc, and petit verdot. The winery is six miles (10 kilometers) south of Penticton along the east shore of Skaha Lake.

Breweries and Distilleries

Doug and Dawn Lennie converted Naramata's former doctors' office into

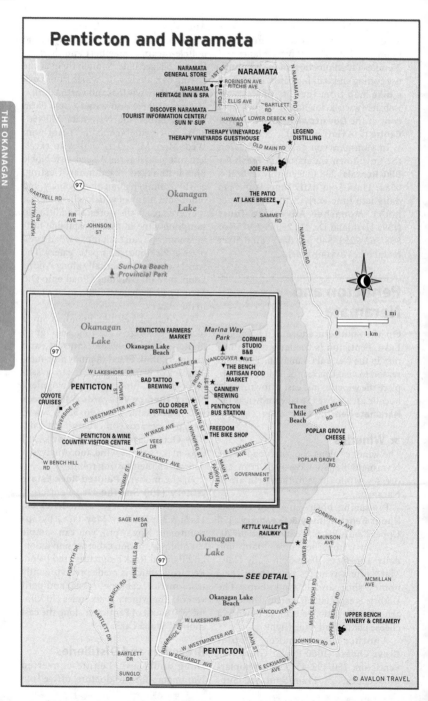

Penticton and Naramata

NARAMATA

NARAMATA GENERAL STORE

NARAMATA HERITAGE INN & SPA

DISCOVER NARAMATA TOURIST INFORMATION CENTER/ SUN N' SUP

ROBINSON AVE
RITCHIE AVE

ELLIS AVE

BARTLETT RD

HAYMAN RD

LOWER DEBECK RD

THERAPY VINEYARDS/ THERAPY VINEYARDS GUESTHOUSE

OLD MAIN RD

LEGEND DISTILLING

JOIE FARM

Okanagan Lake

THE PATIO AT LAKE BREEZE

SAMMET RD

N NARAMATA RD

NARAMATA RD

GARTRELL RD

HAPPY VALLEY RD

FIR AVE

JOHNSON ST

Sun-Oka Beach Provincial Park

Okanagan Lake

PENTICTON FARMERS' MARKET

Okanagan Lake Beach

W LAKESHORE DR

PENTICTON

COYOTE CRUISES

RIVERSIDE DR

POWER ST

BAD TATTOO BREWING

OLD ORDER DISTILLING CO.

W WESTMINSTER AVE

PENTICTON & WINE COUNTRY VISITOR CENTRE

W WADE AVE

VEES DR

W ECKHARDT AVE

W BENCH HILL RD

RAILWAY ST

E LAKESHORE DR

FRONT ST

ELLIS ST

MARTIN ST

WINNIPEG ST

MAIN ST

FAIRVIEW RD

Marina Way Park

VANCOUVER AVE

CORMIER STUDIO B&B

THE BENCH ARTISAN FOOD MARKET

CANNERY BREWING

PENTICTON BUS STATION

FREEDOM THE BIKE SHOP

E ECKHARDT AVE

GOVERNMENT ST

Three Mile Beach

THREE MILE RD

POPLAR GROVE CHEESE

POPLAR GROVE RD

SAGE MESA DR

FORSYTH DR

W BENCH RD

PINE HILLS DR

Okanagan Lake

KETTLE VALLEY RAILWAY

LOWER BENCH RD

CORBISHLEY AVE

MUNSON AVE

MCMILLAN AVE

SEE DETAIL

Okanagan Lake Beach

BARTLETT DR

BARTLETT DR

SUNGLO DR

RIVERSIDE DR

W LAKESHORE AVE

W WESTMINSTER AVE

PENTICTON

W ECKHARDT AVE

VANCOUVER AVE

MAIN ST

MIDDLE BENCH RD

S UPPER BENCH RD

JOHNSON RD

UPPER BENCH WINERY & CREAMERY

E ECKHARDT AVE

0   1 mi
0   1 km

© AVALON TRAVEL

Legend Distilling (3005 Naramata Rd., Naramata, 778/514-1010, www.legend-distilling.com, 11am-6pm daily), where they're producing gin, vodka, and a vodka-spiked cold-brew coffee they call Blasted Brew. They offer 30-minute tours of their facility (3pm Fri., noon Sat., $8 pp) that include a tasting of their spirits.

Small-batch producer **Old Order Distilling Co.** (270 Martin St., Penticton, 778/476-2210, www.oldorderdistilling.ca, noon-6pm Tues.-Wed., noon-8pm Thurs.-Sat.) is distilling vodka, gin, and whiskey from 100 percent B.C.-grown fruits and grains. They offer free tours at 1pm and 3pm most Saturdays, or by appointment.

In downtown Penticton, microbrewer **Cannery Brewing** (198 Ellis St., Penticton, 250/493-2723, www.cannerybrewing.com, 11am-7pm Sun.-Thurs., 11am-9pm Fri.-Sat., tours 1pm Fri.) produces an amber ale, an IPA, and a pale ale, among others, along with a number of seasonal brews. Sample them in their tasting room.

Festivals and Events

While grapes may be getting the glory these days, the Okanagan's agricultural heritage, and a significant part of its present-day economy, is in other fruits. The **Penticton Peach Festival** (www.peachfest.com, Aug.) celebrates one of its bumper crops with a sand castle competition, peach-bin races (where teams compete in peach crates), a grand parade, and, of course, fruit.

Sports and Recreation
Beaches

Right in town, **Okanagan Lake Beach** (Lakeshore Dr., Penticton) and small **Marina Way Park** (Marina Way, Penticton) both have popular sandy stretches.

In Naramata, you can swim at **Three Mile Beach** (Three Mile Rd., off Naramata Rd., Naramata).

On Okanagan Lake between Penticton and Summerland, **Sun-Oka Beach Provincial Park** (off Hwy. 97, 250/548-0076, www.env.gov.bc.ca, mid-Apr.-mid-Oct.) has a large sandy beach on a bay that's good for swimming.

Another excellent swimming beach is in **Skaha Lake Park** (Skaha Lake Rd. at Parkview St., Penticton), on Skaha Lake south of downtown Penticton.

Water Sports

Want to combine time on the water with wine-tasting? **Hoodoo Adventures** (250/490-6084, www.hoodooadventures.ca) offers four-hour **wine tours by kayak** (mid-Apr.-Oct., adults $115). From the starting point at Penticton's Marina Way Beach, you paddle along Okanagan Lake; then a shuttle brings you to a number of Naramata wineries. They offer other kayak tours as well, including **Paddle to the Pub** (adults $105), which combines kayaking and a pub stop; a two-hour **sunset paddle** (adults $75); and a **kayak brunch tour** (adults $85).

Grab your inner tube for a gentle **river float** along the Okanagan River Channel that runs between Okanagan and Skaha Lakes. **Coyote Cruises** (215 Riverside Dr., 250/492-2115, www.coyotecruises.ca, 10am-5pm daily mid-June-Sept., inner tube rental $6, bus $6) rents inner tubes from their office near the starting point, and they'll pick you up when you get to the other end of the channel. Bring sunscreen, water, and snacks.

Go paddling with **Sun n' Sup** (176 Robinson Ave., Naramata, 778/514-5594, www.sunnsup.com, 11am-5pm Wed.-Fri., 10am-5:30pm Sat., 11am-4pm Sun. Apr.-mid-June, 9:30am-6pm Mon. and Wed.-Sat., 9:30am-8pm Tues., 10am-5pm Sun. mid-June-Aug., 10am-5:30pm Wed.-Sat., 11am-4pm Sun. Sept.), which rents **stand-up paddleboards** (1.5 hours $25, 4 hours $45), **single kayaks** (1 hour $20, 4 hours $30), and **double kayaks** (1 hour $25, 4 hours $40) in Naramata Village.

Cycling

To cycle between the wineries, follow a section of the **Kettle Valley Railway** trail that runs along the Naramata Bench, parallel to and above Naramata Road. It's 10 miles (16 kilometers) along the trail between Penticton and Naramata Village, and you'll pass many of the Naramata wineries en route.

Freedom the Bike Shop (533 Main St., Penticton, 250/493-0686, www.freedombikeshop.com, 9am-5:30pm Mon.-Sat. full-day $40-70) rents road and mountain bikes.

In Naramata Village, you can rent **beach cruiser bikes** (one hour $10, full day $25) and **mountain bikes** (full day $45) from **Sun n' Sup** (176 Robinson Ave., Naramata, 778/514-5594, www.sunnsup.com, 11am-5pm Wed.-Fri., 10am-5:30pm Sat., 11am-4pm Sun. Apr.-mid-June, 9:30am-6pm Mon. and Wed.-Sat., 9:30am-8pm Tues., 10am-5pm Sun. mid-June-Aug., 10am-5:30pm Wed.-Sat., 11am-4pm Sun. Sept.).

Kelowna-based **Monashee Adventure Tours** (250/762-9253 or 888/762-9253, www.monasheeadventuretours.com) runs **Naramata Bench Winery Tours** (self-guided $80, guided $120-150) with approximately 12 miles (20 kilometers) of cycling between several Naramata wineries.

Accommodations

Several wineries in Penticton and Naramata run guest houses or rent rooms to visitors, and the area has a few lovely inns and B&Bs.

Owned by two artists who cater to independent art-loving travelers, **Cormier Studio B&B** (495 Vancouver Ave., Penticton, 250/493-3273, www.cormierstudio.com, $135-195 d, breakfast $15) has three comfortable adult-oriented guest rooms on the lower level of a contemporary home set back from the street. All units have kitchenettes with fridges, microwaves, and toasters. Breakfast, served upstairs in the living room that's also the owners' art gallery, is optional, but might include open-face bacon sandwiches with fresh tomatoes, arugula, and a fried egg, or homemade granola with locally grown blueberries or peaches. More than a dozen wineries are within three miles (5 kilometers) of the B&B.

Pack your sense of adventure for a stay at **God's Mountain Estate** (4898 Lakeside Rd., Penticton, 250/490-4800, www.godsmountain.ca, $215-299 d), an eclectic Mediterranean-style villa set on 115 secluded acres (47 hectares) above Skaha Lake. The most unusual accommodations are in the Roofless Room, a romantic rooftop unit that's open to the sky. The other 14 guest rooms, as you might envision in the home of an eccentric aunt, are an idiosyncratic mix of antiques and miscellanea. This adult-oriented property has no TV, radio, or phones, although Wi-Fi is included and is accessible in the main part of the house. Rates include a full breakfast. The inn is located on the east side of Skaha Lake between Penticton and Okanagan Falls.

A stay at **Therapy Vineyards Guesthouse** (940 Debeck Rd., Naramata, 250/496-5217, www.therapyvineyards.com, $170-290 d), adjacent to the winery that produces wines like Pink Freud and Bruised Ego, may feel therapeutic, or at least supremely relaxing. Settle into one of the eight comfortable rooms overlooking the vines, outfitted with sturdy wood furniture, a large-screen TV, a DVD player, a coffeemaker, and a wine fridge; the suites have separate sitting areas. Rates include a complimentary wine-tasting as well as breakfast pastries, fruit, and tea or coffee delivered each morning to your patio.

There's a lot of history at the **Naramata Heritage Inn & Spa** (3625 1 St., Naramata, 778/514-5444, www.naramatainn.com, May-Oct. $168-268 d), built in 1908 in Naramata Village, on the shores of Okanagan Lake. Fruit baron John Moore Robinson constructed the property, which over the years has been a hotel, a private girls' school, and the Robinson family home. It still has its original woodwork and Mission-style furnishings; some of the 12 guest rooms, most of which are on the small side, have claw-foot tubs. Rates include continental breakfast and use of the inn's mountain bikes. The on-site **Heirloom Spa** offers massages, facials, and other esthetics services.

Food
Groceries and Markets

Shop for local produce and picnic fixings at the **Penticton Farmers Market** (100 block of Main St., Penticton, 250/770-3276, http://pentictonfarmersmarket.org, 8:30am-1pm Sat. May-Oct.).

In the village of Naramata, you can find food and snacks at the **Naramata General Store** (225 Robinson Ave., Naramata, 250/496-5450, 7am-8pm Mon.-Thurs., 7am-10pm Fri., 8am-10pm Sat., 9am-8pm Sun.).

Cafés, Bakeries, and Light Bites

Part café and part gourmet grocery, ★ **The Bench Artisan Food Market** (368 Vancouver Ave., Penticton, 250/492-2222, www.thebenchmarket.com, 7am-5pm Mon.-Fri., 8am-5pm Sat.-Sun., mains $5-15) serves breakfast all day, including a yummy salmon "eggwich" with smoked salmon, egg, and organic gouda grilled in an English muffin. They pour espresso and tea drinks to go with the muffins, cookies, and other sweets, and lunches include *paninis* and salads. If you're planning a picnic, you can pick up locally made cheeses, gourmet crackers, and other treats.

Winery Restaurants

A peaceful place for lunch is **The Patio at Lake Breeze** (930 Sammet Rd., Naramata, 250/496-5659, www.lakebreeze.ca, 11:30am-3:30pm daily May-mid-Oct., mains $15-26), on the terrace at Lake Breeze Wine Farm. Simple sandwiches, like the Croque Monsieur (smoked

ham and gruyère) or roast chicken with smoked gouda and apple, get dressed up with homemade breads and creative condiments. You can also get more daring with dishes like peach- and chipotle-braised pork with corn fritters or lingcod in a mushroom-mint broth with wild rice risotto cake, cod sausage, and ginger confit. The restaurant doesn't take reservations (except for groups of 8 or more), so come early or late to nab a patio table.

Pizza

Pizza and beer—what's not to love? Especially at **Bad Tattoo Brewing** (169 Estabrook Ave., Penticton, 250/493-8686, www.badtattoobrewing.com, 11am-10pm Sun.-Thurs., 11am-11pm Fri.-Sat., mains $17-23), a lively microbrewery and pizzeria where you can pair the craft beers with pizzas that range from basic to (in their own words) "weird." The offbeat pies change, but among their recent creations are Carolina BBQ, topped with slow-roasted brisket, and the Grilled Cheese Sandwich, which actually has bread with cheese and tomatoes piled on the crust. To drink, try the medium-dark Los Muertos Cerveza Negra or the West Coast IPA.

Information and Services

The **Penticton & Wine Country Visitor Centre,** also known as the **B.C. VQA Wine Information Centre** (553 Vees Dr., Penticton, 250/490-2006, www.pentictonwineinfo.com, 9am-6pm daily spring and fall, 9am-7pm daily summer, 9am-6pm Mon.-Sat., 10am-5pm Sun. winter) is both a wine shop and an information office where staff can help you plan a wine tour, tell you about local wineries, and offer guidance on buying wines from their stock of more than 700 B.C. varieties. Staff from **Tourism Penticton** (250/276-2170 or 800/663-5052, www.visitpenticton.com) run the information desk.

For information about Naramata, stop into the **Discover Naramata Tourist**

Dinner on God's Mountain

A popular wine-country dinner takes place every week on God's Mountain. While some might consider the meals to be a religious experience, it has nothing to do with religion.

Joy Road Catering (250/493-8657, www.joyroadcatering.com), an Okanagan-based catering company, partnered with **God's Mountain Estate** (4898 Lakeside Rd., Penticton, 250/490-4800, www.godsmountain.ca), an inn outside Penticton, to present **Sunday Alfresco Vineyard Dining** (6:30pm Sun. mid-May-early Oct., $105 pp), a farm-to-table supper served outdoors at a long communal table on the inn's grounds. This four-course Sunday feast is paired with local wines and emphasizes seasonal ingredients.

At the same location, they also host the **Winery Series Dinners** (6:30pm selected Thurs. late June-early Sept., $120 pp), in partnership with local wineries. These multicourse meals, matched with wines from a specific Okanagan producer, are held on some Thursdays throughout the summer; check the Joy Road website for the schedule.

Advance reservations are required for both dinners. Book online at the Joy Road website or call them for details—and pray that there's space for you at these God's Mountain feasts.

Information Center (176 Robinson Ave., Naramata, 250/496-5450, www.discovernaramata.com, 10am-5pm Tues.-Sat., 11am-4pm Sun. May-June and Sept., 10am-5pm daily July-Aug.).

Penticton Regional Hospital (550 Carmi Ave., Penticton, 250/492-4000, www.interiorhealth.ca) provides 24-hour emergency services.

Getting Around

Penticton is on the south end of Okanagan Lake, off Highway 97. Naramata borders Penticton to the east. Wineries line Naramata Road between Penticton and Naramata Village, which is on Okanagan Lake at the north end of Naramata Road.

OK Wine Shuttle (250/495-3278, www.okwineshuttle.ca) operates a **hop-on, hop-off shuttle** (10am-5pm daily late May-Oct., $65 pp), which picks up passengers at the Penticton & Wine Country Visitor Centre and at a few local hotels. The van then circles past the Naramata Bench wineries throughout the day; the driver normally returns to each stop every 30 minutes.

Osoyoos, Oliver, and Vicinity

When you think about Canada, does "desert" come to mind? Probably not—but the South Okanagan region along the U.S. border is a desert area. Situated at the northern end of the Sonora Desert that extends south to Mexico, it's one of Canada's only deserts.

The warm, dry weather has long made the South Okanagan an agricultural area, growing fruits and vegetables years before the current grape boom took over. Orchards and farms are still abundant, but there are also plenty of wineries, from long-established producers to rising newcomers.

In addition to wine touring, the South Okanagan communities of Osoyoos, Oliver, and Okanagan Falls have other attractions, including several related to the desert environment and to the area's First Nations heritage. And when the warm, dry weather gets a little too warm, you can jump in the lake—Lake Osoyoos.

★ Wineries

For a directory of wineries in the South Okanagan, check the website for the **Oliver Osoyoos Winery Association** (www.oliverosoyoos.com) or pick up their brochure at area visitors centers. The following list includes some notable wineries to help start planning your wine itinerary.

Osoyoos East Side

Canada's first aboriginal-owned winery, **Nk'Mip Cellars** (1400 Rancher Creek Rd., Osoyoos, 250/495-2985, www.nkmip-cellars.com, 9am-6pm daily Apr.-late June and Sept.-Oct., 9am-8pm daily late June-Aug., 10am-5pm daily Nov.-Mar.) is owned by the Osoyoos Indian Band, which also manages the Spirit Ridge Resort and the Nk'Mip Desert Cultural Centre on the same property. You can take a one-hour winery tour (1pm daily Apr. and early-late Oct., 11am, 1pm, and 3pm daily May-June and Sept.-early Oct., 11am, 1pm, 3pm, and 5pm daily July-Aug., $10), where you can learn how the band got into the wine business, tour their production facilities, and taste several wines. The winery currently produces chardonnay, pinot blanc, riesling, pinot noir, merlot, cabernet sauvignon, syrah, an ice wine, and several red blends. **TIP:** The name is pronounced "in-ka-meep."

Years ago, Osoyoos had a gold mine, and according to legend, American miners trying to smuggle gold across the border would curse at the bright moon that threatened to expose them. These tales gave rise to **Moon Curser Vineyards** (3628 Hwy. 3 E., Osoyoos, 250/495-5161, www.mooncurser.com, 10am-5pm daily Apr.-Oct., 10am-5pm Mon.-Fri. Nov.-Mar.), where the winemakers may not swear at the night sky but instead produce wines from less common varietals. In their tasting room, you might sample their smooth Dead of Night (a blend of tannat and syrah), arneis (an Italian grape similar to sauvignon blanc), or an unusual carménère. Their grapes are all grown within two miles (3.2 kilometers) of Osoyoos.

Black Sage Road

One of the South Okanagan's most established wineries, **Burrowing Owl Estate Winery** (500 Burrowing Owl Pl., Oliver, 250/498-0620 or 877/498-0620, www.burrowingowlwine.ca, 10am-6pm daily May-mid.-Oct., 10am-5pm daily mid-Oct.-mid-Dec., 10am-4pm Mon.-Fri. mid-Dec.-Feb., 10am-5pm daily Mar.-Apr.) donates proceeds from **wine tastings** ($3) in its Tuscan-style shop to the Burrowing Owl conservation society, which is working to repopulate this endangered species; you can do your part for the local ecology as you sample chardonnay, pinot gris, pinot noir, merlot, and other varieties. Go into the cellar on a 30-minute **guided tour** (10:30am Sat.-Sun. late May-early Sept., $5) or take a free **self-guided tour** by walking up the observation tower to scan their fermentation tanks, blending room, crush pad, and, at the top of the 103 steps, across the vineyards; informational panels tell you about the winery as you climb. Want to stay longer? Burrowing Owl has an excellent dining room and an upscale guest house.

Black Hills Estate Winery (4190 Black Sage Rd., Oliver, 250/498-6606, www.blackhillswinery.com, 10am-6pm daily Apr.-Nov.) is something of a cult favorite among wine aficionados, particularly for their flagship Nota Bene, a Bordeaux-style blend of cabernet sauvignon, merlot, and cabernet franc. It's a "wow" wine, but if its $60 price tag is beyond your budget, try their white Alibi (a sémillon-sauvignon blanc blend), viognier, or lush and peppery syrah. They also make affordable everyday wines under the Cellar Hand label, including Free Run White and Punch Down Red. You can do your wine-tasting, led by a "wine evangelist," out on the patio in the **Vineyard Kitchen Restaurant** (11:30am-5pm Thurs.-Sun.,

THE OKANAGAN

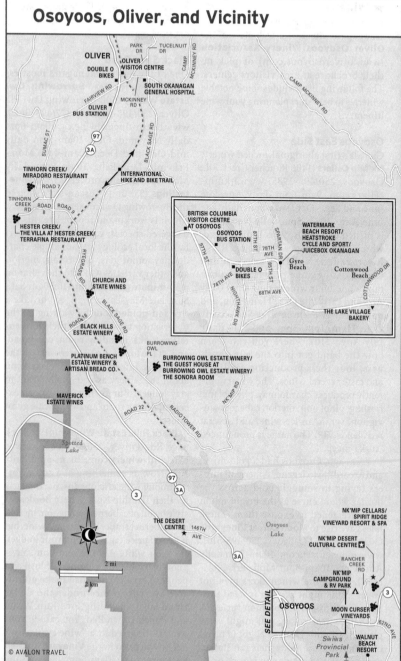

Osoyoos, Oliver, and Vicinity

OLIVER

PARK DR

TUCELNUIT DR

CAMP McKINNEY RD

DOUBLE O BIKES

OLIVER VISITOR CENTRE

SOUTH OKANAGAN GENERAL HOSPITAL

CAMP McKINNEY RD

FAIRVIEW RD

McKINNEY RD

OLIVER BUS STATION

SUMAC ST

97

3A

BLACK SAGE RD

TINHORN CREEK/ MIRADORO RESTAURANT

ROAD 7

INTERNATIONAL HIKE AND BIKE TRAIL

TINHORN CREEK RD

ROAD 8

ROAD 9

HESTER CREEK/ THE VILLA AT HESTER CREEK/ TERRAFINA RESTAURANT

RYEGRASS RD

CHURCH AND STATE WINES

BLACK SAGE RD

ROAD 18

BLACK HILLS ESTATE WINERY

BURROWING OWL PL

PLATINUM BENCH ESTATE WINERY & ARTISAN BREAD CO.

BURROWING OWL ESTATE WINERY/ THE GUEST HOUSE AT BURROWING OWL ESTATE WINERY/ THE SONORA ROOM

MAVERICK ESTATE WINES

ROAD 22

RADIO TOWER RD

NK'MIP RD

Spotted Lake

BRITISH COLUMBIA VISITOR CENTRE AT OSOYOOS

87TH ST

SPARTAN DR

78TH AVE

WATERMARK BEACH RESORT/ HEATSTROKE CYCLE AND SPORT/ JUICEBOX OKANAGAN

OSOYOOS BUS STATION

97TH ST

88TH ST

Gyro Beach

Cottonwood Beach

DOUBLE O BIKES

74TH AVE

NIGHTHAWK DR

68TH AVE

COTTONWOOD DR

THE LAKE VILLAGE BAKERY

3

97

3A

THE DESERT CENTRE

146TH AVE

Osoyoos Lake

NK'MIP CELLARS/ SPIRIT RIDGE VINEYARD RESORT & SPA

3A

NK'MIP DESERT CULTURAL CENTRE

RANCHER CREEK RD

NK'MIP CAMPGROUND & RV PARK

3

SEE DETAIL

OSOYOOS

MOON CURSER VINEYARDS

82ND AVE

Swiws Provincial Park

WALNUT BEACH RESORT

0   2 mi

0   2 km

© AVALON TRAVEL

mains $15-18), overlooking the 40-acre (16-hectare) property on the Black Sage Bench, while nibbling a meal-size salad, perhaps seared tuna with pea shoots and cherry tomatoes, or a creative pizza.

How do you pair wine with bread? Find out with a wine and bread tasting at **Platinum Bench Estate Winery & Artisan Bread Co.** (4120 Black Sage Rd., Oliver, 250/535-1165, http://platinumbench. com, 10am-5pm daily Apr.-Oct., 11am-5pm Sat.-Sun. Nov.-Dec., by appointment Jan.-Mar.), a winery with a bakeshop on its screened porch. Try Mur-Fi's White, a blend of chardonnay and viognier, named for husband-and-wife owners Murray Jones and Fiona Duncan, with their asiago cheese bread.

With cheeky labels suggesting "We Should Do This More Often" and "Tonight Is the Night," the Lost Inhibitions line at **Church and State Wines** (4516 Ryegrass Rd., Oliver, 250/498-2700, http://churchandstatewines.com, 11am-6pm Fri.-Sun. mid-Apr.-late Apr., 11am-6pm daily May-Oct., by appointment Nov.-mid-Apr.) makes great gifts for a special someone—or someone not so special, since others bear less printable slogans. Either way, they're good-value blends, designed for drinkers with a sense of fun. For something more serious, sample the Trebella (a white blend of marsanne, rousanne, and viognier), or the flagship Quintessential (blending cabernet sauvignon, merlot, cabernet franc, malbec, and petit verdot) in the über-modern tasting room.

Along Highway 97

At the small family-owned **Maverick Estate Wines** (3974 Hwy. 97, Oliver, 778/437-3133, www.maverickwine. ca, 10am-5pm daily), where the South African-born winemaker previously

Top to bottom: the wine shop at Burrowing Owl Estate Winery; wine tasting at Black Hills Estate Winery; wines from Platinum Bench Estate Winery & Artisan Bread Co.

worked for Burrowing Owl, try the Origin white (a full-flavored blend of gewürztraminer and sauvignon blanc), the spicy pinot gris, or the bold Rubeus, made from syrah, cabernet sauvignon, cabernet franc, and merlot.

A 95-acre (38-hectare) property along the Golden Mile Bench, where its first vines were planted in 1968, **Hester Creek** (877 Rd. 8, Oliver, 250/498-4435 or 866/498-4435, www.hestercreek.com, 10am-6pm daily May-Oct., 10am-4pm daily Nov.-Apr.) has a modern Mediterranean-style tasting room, where you can sample from their long list of wines. The winery hosts concerts, cooking classes, winemaker dinners, and other special events throughout the year. An Italian dining room and six-suite inn are also part of the business.

Tinhorn Creek (537 Tinhorn Creek Rd., Oliver, 250/498-3743 or 888/484-6467, www.tinhorn.com, 10am-6pm daily Mar.-Oct., 10am-5pm daily Nov.-Dec., 10am-4pm daily Jan.-Feb.)

produces whites (gewürztraminer, pinot gris, chardonnay, and the 2Bench White blend), rosé, and reds (cabernet franc, merlot, syrah, pinot noir, and the 2Bench Red blend). The hillside wine shop is open for tastings year-round, and in summer, the winery presents the **Canadian Concert Series** (May-Aug.) of music events in an outdoor amphitheater.

You can start with a sampling in the rustic tasting room at **Covert Farms** (Seacrest Rd., Oliver, 250/498-9463, www.covertfarms.ca, 11am-5pm daily mid-Apr.-Oct.), an organic winery and farm atop a steep hill north of Oliver that produces sauvignon blanc, sémillon, pinot blanc, rosé, and several proprietary red blends. Covert Farms also offer a unique experience: a one-hour **tour** (adults $40, ages 6-18 $20) of their farm and vineyards in a vintage 1952 truck. You can purchase organic produce from the farm stand (June-Oct.) or pick your own berries or other

Liquidity Winery Bistro Gallery, Okanagan Falls

seasonal crops. The farm is also the starting point for a hike to **McIntyre Bluff,** a rocky cliff with views across the valley.

Okanagan Falls

North of Oliver, there's a cluster of wineries in the community of Okanagan Falls. Places to visit include **Blasted Church Vineyards** (378 Parsons Rd., Okanagan Falls, 250/497-1125 or 877/355-2686, www.blastedchurch.com, daily May-Oct.) and **See Ya Later Ranch** (2575 Green Lake Rd., Okanagan Falls, 250/497-8267, www.sylranch.com, 10am-5pm daily Mar.-late June and early-Sept.-Oct., 10am-6pm daily late June-early Sept., 11am-5pm Wed.-Sun. Nov.-Feb.).

Another distinctive property is **Liquidity Winery Bistro Gallery** (4720 Allendale Rd., Okanagan Falls, 778/515-5500, www.liquiditywines.com, tasting room 11am-6pm daily May-mid-Oct., noon-5pm Thurs.-Sun. mid-Oct.-mid-Dec.), which, as the name suggests,

makes wine, shows art, and serves food in their **Bistro** (11am-9pm daily late Apr.-mid-Oct., noon-8pm Thurs.-Sun. Mar.-late Apr. and mid-Oct.-mid-Dec., mains lunch $16-21, dinner $26-32) in a sleek, art-filled setting high above the valley.

Distilleries

Dubh Glas Distillery (8486 Gallagher Lake Frontage Rd., Oliver, 778/439-3580, http://thedubhglasdistillery.com, 11am-6pm Fri.-Sun.) brews Noteworthy Gin from B.C.-grown barley. Try it at the distillery tasting room.

Sights and Activities
★ Nk'Mip Desert Cultural Centre

Have you ever touched a rattlesnake? Listened to the legend of the coyote? Wandered through the sagebrush on a desert trail? Explore the creatures and plants that live in the Okanagan desert and learn more about the region's First Nations culture at the **Nk'Mip Desert Cultural Centre** (1000 Rancher Creek Rd., Osoyoos, 250/495-7901 or 888/495-8555, www.nkmipdesert.com, 9:30am-6pm daily July-Aug., 9:30am-4:30pm daily May-June and Sept.-mid-Oct., adults $14, seniors and students $13, ages 3-17 $11, families $38), a facility for natural and cultural education run by the Osoyoos Indian Band. Interpreters introduce you to snakes and other desert inhabitants and lead daily guided trail walks.

The Desert Centre

In the hills between Osoyoos and Oliver, **The Desert Centre** (14580 146th Ave., Osoyoos, 250/495-2470 or 877/899-0897, www.desert.org, 9:30am-4:30pm mid-May-mid-Sept., 10am-2pm daily late Apr.-mid-May and mid-Sept.-early Oct., adults $7, seniors and ages 6-17 $6, families $16) lets you explore the Okanagan's desert plants and animals. On this 67-acre (27-hectare) protected site, a small exhibit area shows animal skulls, snakeskins, and displays about local wildlife. Outside, you can follow a one-mile (1.6-kilometer) boardwalk trail through the desert. Optional guided tours (10am, noon, and 2pm daily mid-May-mid-Sept.) are included with your admission, or you can explore on your own. The grounds are particularly vibrant in the spring, when the yellow antelope brush blooms.

Spotted Lake

The local Okanagan First Nation considers it a sacred site, known for its healing properties. **Spotted Lake** (Hwy. 3), called *Kliluk* in the Okanagan language, is certainly an unusual geological feature. It's a mineral-rich lake whose waters evaporate over the summer months, leaving behind mineral deposits in circular spots, giving the lake its name and its distinctive appearance. The lake is located on private property, six miles (9.5 kilometers) northwest of Osoyoos, but you can pull over and have a look from the side of the highway.

Festivals and Events

What do running and wine-tasting have in common? You can do both at the annual **Half-Corked Marathon** (www.oliverosoyoos.com, May), an 11-mile (18-kilometer) fun run with nearly a dozen stops for wine-tasting and food along the way. As the organizers advise, "If you're planning on setting a record, this might not be the race for you." A vehicle will pick up any runners who poop out en route.

Oliver's annual **Festival of the Grape** (www.oliverfestivalofthegrape.ca, Oct.) includes music, wine-tastings, and a grape stomping competition.

Sports and Recreation
Beaches

Osoyoos has an average summer temperature of 87°F (31°C), so a splash in the lake helps you beat the heat. On Osoyoos Lake, **Gyro Beach** (off Main St.) is the area's largest, with sand, shade trees, and restrooms, right in town behind

The Desert Centre

Watermark Beach Resort. **Cottonwood Beach** (Cottonwood Dr., off Main St.), on the town's east side, is another popular place to swim and sun.

On a skinny peninsula jutting into Osoyoos Lake, **S̓ w̓ iw̓ s Provincial Park** (off Hwy. 97, Osoyoos, 778/437-2295, www.env.gov.bc.ca), formerly known as Haynes Point before adopting its traditional Okanagan First Nations name, has a narrow swimming beach and a walking trail through the marsh. The park is 1.25 miles (two kilometers) south of downtown Osoyoos, off Highway 97; its name is pronounced "swee-yous."

Hiking and Cycling

The flat, 11.7-mile (19 kilometer) **International Hike and Bike Trail** follows the Okanagan River in the Oliver area. More than half of the route is paved; the rest is gravel. A convenient access point for the trail is behind the **Oliver Visitor Centre** (6431 Station St., Oliver).

Cycling from winery to winery on the region's back roads is also a great way to explore, as long as you don't mind some hills and can moderate your wine consumption.

Double O Bikes (www.doubleobikes. com, 4 hours $15-30, 24 hours $24-48) rents bikes from their shops in Oliver (6246 Main St., 250/535-0577, 9:30am-5pm Thurs.-Sat., 9:30am-3pm Sun.) and Osoyoos (8905 Main St., 250/495-3312, 9:30am-5pm Tues.-Sat.).

Heatstroke Cycle and Sport (225-15 Park Pl., Osoyoos, 778/437-2453, www. heatstrokecycle.com), based at the Watermark Beach Resort, rents road (1 hour $10, full-day $60), mountain (1 hour $10, full-day $40), hybrid (1 hour $8, full-day $30), and electric bikes (1 hour $25, full-day $99). They also offer a variety of **cycling tours**, including two where you travel by **electric bike:** the four- to five-hour **Golden Mile Wine Country Tour** ($160), a guided ride to seven South Okanagan wineries; or the **Black Sage Road Cycle Wine & Dine Tour** ($225), with wine and food samplings along the Black Sage Bench.

Accommodations and Camping

Osoyoos has several upscale resort hotels overlooking Lake Osoyoos, as well as a strip of aging motels. In Oliver, you can stay amid the vineyards in posh winery guesthouses.

You'd never know that stylish ★ **Watermark Beach Resort** (15 Park Pl., Osoyoos, 250/495-5500 or 888/755-3480, www.watermarkbeachresort.com, $229-359 d) was built on the site of a former fruit packinghouse. Today, this 153-suite resort has everything you'd need for a lakeside holiday. In the main building, the one-, two-, and three-bedroom suites, decorated in beachy terra-cotta or sage green, have full kitchens, washer-dryers, and balconies, many facing the sandy lakeshore or the large outdoor pool and patio. Families might also like the 30 townhouse-style beachfront villas. Rent a bike to go exploring

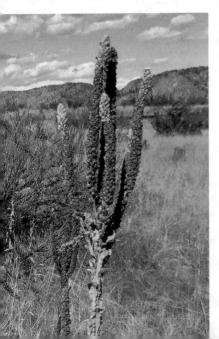

or take a yoga class in the on-site studio; in summer, you can stop into the lobby for a complimentary wine-tasting. The resort offers cycling tours, foraging excursions, cooking classes, and other activities. The **Watermark Restaurant** uses lots of local products in dishes like quinoa, cauliflower, and goat cheese salad or organic chicken pie. Try the potted salmon spread with pickled fennel and garlic crostini with a glass of Okanagan wine.

Part of a complex of businesses owned by the Osoyoos Indian Band, **Spirit Ridge Vineyard Resort & Spa** (1200 Rancher Creek Rd., Osoyoos, 250/495-5445 or 877/313-9463, www.spiritridge.ca, $199-419 d, 2-bedroom suite $249-469, 3-bedroom suite $349-559) is an upscale condo resort above the lake on Osoyoos's east side. Backed by rolling hills, with the vineyards of the Nk'mip Cellars winery all around, the Tuscan-style buildings house one-, two-, and three-bedroom suites, with full kitchens and balconies or patios. You've got all the expected amenities, with several restaurants, an outdoor pool, hot tubs, a fitness center, and a spa; the Nk'mip Desert Cultural Centre is also on the property. Although the resort has a private beach, the accommodations aren't lakeside; a shuttle takes guests down to the lakeshore. Rates include Wi-Fi and parking.

On the east side of Osoyoos Lake, condo-style **Walnut Beach Resort** (4200 Lakeshore Dr., Osoyoos, 250/495-5400 or 877/936-5400, www.walnutbeachresort.com, $159-329 d) has 112 straightforward earth-toned studio, one-, and two-bedroom suites, all with decks facing either the lake or the desert hills. The larger units have kitchens. The property has a small exercise room, a sauna, and a steam room, but the real action is outdoors, with a sandy lakeside beach, a year-round heated pool, two hot tubs, and a patio wine bar. You can rent kayaks, canoes, and Jet-Skis on the beach.

An intimate wine-country escape, ★ **The Guest House at Burrowing Owl Estate Winery** (500 Burrowing Owl Pl., Oliver, 250/498-0620 or 877/498-0620, www.burrowingowlwine.ca, mid-Feb.-mid.-Dec., $199-349 d) has 10 contemporary guest rooms, with fireplaces and decks that look over the winery's vineyards and across the valley. Decorated with light woods, slate floors, and cream-and-beige soft goods, the upscale suites are air-conditioned with mini fridges, flat-screen TVs, and Wi-Fi. A full "wine country" breakfast is served daily. If you need more space, the inn has a grand two-bedroom penthouse with a gourmet kitchen. With walls decorated with local art, this deluxe inn's best features are the 25-meter seasonal solar-heated pool with vineyard views, the excellent **Sonora Room** restaurant, and the proximity to the wineries on the Black Sage Bench.

You may spend all your time out on your patio at **The Villa at Hester Creek** (877 Road 8, Oliver, 250/498-4435 or 866/498-4435, www.hestercreek.com, Mar.-Nov., $229-379 d), sipping wine overlooking the vineyards or enjoying your breakfast, but the six Mediterranean-style suites are pretty special inside, too. Five of the units have a duvet-topped king bed, a fireplace, a bar fridge, a microwave, and a large bath with granite countertops and both a soaker tub and a walk-in shower. In the larger La Sirena Executive Suite, the bed is a queen, but there's a separate living room. Wi-Fi is included in the rates.

Camping

Run by the Osoyoos Indian Band, who also operate the nearby Spirit Ridge Vineyard Resort, the busy **Nk'mip Campground & RV Park** (8000 45th St., Osoyoos, 250/495-7279, www.campingosoyoos.com, tent sites $31-38, electrical sites $31-60, yurts $80-90 d) is located directly on Lake Osoyoos. The 400 sites

◈ Side Trip: Fruit and Wine in the Similkameen Valley

As the Okanagan's wine industry continues to mature, more wineries are opening in the agricultural **Similkameen Valley** (www.similkameenvalley.com), along Highway 3 west of Osoyoos. If you haven't had your fill of wines in the Okanagan, or you'd like to explore this up-and-coming destination, stop off when you're traveling between Osoyoos and Vancouver, or make a detour during your South Okanagan stay.

The Similkameen Valley has more than 15 wineries, most in and around the communities of Keremos and Cawston, where fruit stands selling peaches, apples, and other seasonal produce also line the roads. Many of the families who farm this area are of East Indian heritage, so at some markets, you might find samosas, *pakoras*, and curries as well.

To start your Similkameen winery tour, consider stops at the following destinations:

* **Clos du Soleil Winery** (2568 Upper Bench Rd., Keremeos, 250/499-2831, www.closdusoleil.ca, 10am-5pm daily May-Oct.)

* **Crowsnest Vineyards** (2035 Surprise Dr., Cawston, 250/499-5129, www.crowsnestvineyards.com, 10am-5pm daily May-Oct.)

* **Forbidden Fruit Winery** (620 Sumac Rd., Cawston, 250/499-2649, www.forbiddenfruitwines.com, 10am-6pm daily Apr.-Oct.)

* **Orofino Winery** (2152 Barcelo Rd., Cawston, 250/499-0068, www.orofinovineyards.com, 10am-5pm Thurs.-Mon. May-June, 10am-5pm daily July-mid-Oct.)

* **Seven Stones Winery** (1143 Hwy. 3, Cawston, 250/499-2144, www.sevenstones.ca, 10:30am-5:30pm daily May-Oct.)

And to keep up with what's new in the Similkameen region, check with the **Similkameen Wineries Association** (250/488-0878, www.similkameenwine.com).

---

accommodate everything from tents to big RVs, or you can stay in one of several **yurts.** The yurts sleep up to six and even have air-conditioning. Campground amenities include washrooms with showers, laundry facilities, and an indoor pool and hot tub (Oct. to May).

At **Sẁiẁs Provincial Park** (off Hwy. 97, Osoyoos, 778/437-2295, www.env.gov.bc.ca, Apr.-mid-Oct., $31), on a narrow peninsula jutting into the lake, the 41 campsites are close together, although most are right on the lake. The park, which has flush toilets and cold water taps, is 1.25 miles (2 kilometers) south of downtown Osoyoos. You can reserve sites in advance from mid-May through mid-September; **reservations** (519/826-6850 or 800/689-9025, www.discovercamping.ca) are recommended for all weekends

during that period and anytime in July and August.

Food
Cafés, Bakeries, and Light Bites

It's worth waking up early for the sourdough cinnamon buns at **The Lake Village Bakery** (6511 Main St., Osoyoos, 250/495-3366, www.thelakevillagebakery.ca, generally 9am-4:30pm Tues.-Sat., call for hours), a family-owned strip-mall bakeshop that turns out all sorts of baked treats. It's also known for sourdough croissants, fresh-baked breads, and various cookies. It closes when it sells out, so phone before making a special trip.

Beat the heat with a fresh juice or smoothie from **JuiceBox Okanagan** (223-15 Park Pl., Osoyoos, 250/689-0174, 10am-4pm daily spring-fall, call for off-season hours), located in the same building as the Watermark Beach Resort.

Winery Restaurants

Top-notch food, polished service, and panoramic vistas over the Black Sage Bench make ★ **The Sonora Room** (500 Burrowing Owl Pl., Oliver, 250/498-0620 or 877/498-0620, www.burrowing-owlwine.ca, lunch noon-4:30pm, dinner 5pm-8pm Thurs.-Mon. Apr., lunch 11:30am-3pm, tapas 3pm-4:30pm, dinner 5pm-9pm daily May-mid-Oct., lunch noon-4:30pm Fri.-Sun., dinner 5pm-8pm Thurs.-Sun. mid-Oct.-mid-Dec., mains lunch $18-32, dinner $26-39), at Burrowing Owl Winery, a must-visit dining destination. You might kick off your meal with tuna carpaccio atop apple slaw or an heirloom squash salad with candied prosciutto, and continue with local fish paired with watercress *arancini,* lamb sirloin served with goat cheese *gnudi,* or a grilled bison steak. The menu suggests a wine pairing for each dish, and staff can provide further assistance. A glass of the port-style Coruja and the sun setting over the vineyards wrap up an ideal evening.

The name is Italian, meaning "from the earth," so fittingly, **Terrafina Restaurant** (887 Rd. 8, Oliver, 250/498-2229, www.terrafinarestaurant.com, 11:30am-9pm daily Mar.-Dec., mains lunch $17-21, dinner $20-32), at Hester Creek Winery, serves Italian-influenced fare made from local Okanagan ingredients. At lunch, pizzas come out of the wood-fired oven layered with potatoes and arugula or butternut squash and brie, and the pastas might be topped with prawns and smoked bacon or chorizo with roasted garlic. In the evenings, the menu adds dishes like arctic char with fennel relish and basil gnocchi, or Cornish game hen with cannellini cassoulet and wilted greens. You can eat on the patio when the weather is fine.

Perched on a hill at Tinhorn Creek Winery, ★ **Miradoro Restaurant** (537 Tinhorn Creek Rd., Oliver, 250/498-3742, www.tinhorn.com, lunch 11:30am-3pm, tapas 3pm-5:30pm, dinner 5:30pm-9pm daily Mar.-Dec., mains $19-46) has a rustic elegance, whether you dine indoors in the window-lined dining room or out on the covered heated terrace. You can go simple with a Neapolitan-style pizza from the wood-fired oven, perhaps paired with a salad or a plate of house-cured charcuterie. The kitchen gets adventurous, though, with starters like bison carpaccio with beet fudge or cauliflower panna cotta with squash *mostarda,* and mains like duck with sage spaetzle or Moroccan-spiced lamb shoulder served with stewed chickpeas, apricots, and olives. The gracious service and thoughtful wine pairings help make your meal more special.

Information and Services
Visitor Information

The **British Columbia Visitor Centre at Osoyoos** (9912 Hwy. 3, at Hwy. 97, 250/495-5410, www.hellobc.com, 9am-5pm daily early May-mid-June, 9am-6pm daily mid-June-mid-Sept., 9am-5pm daily mid-Sept.-mid-Oct., 9am-4pm daily mid-Oct.-early May) can assist with travel questions and information about the Okanagan region. The center has free public Wi-Fi.

Located in a former train station built in 1923, the **Oliver Visitor Centre** (6431 Station St., Oliver, 778/439-2363 or 844/896-3300, www.winecapitalof-canada.com, 9am-5pm Mon.-Fri., longer hours July-Aug.) has details about local wineries and attractions.

Medical Services

South Okanagan General Hospital (911 McKinney Rd., Oliver, 250/498-5000, www.interiorhealth.ca) provides medical services for Osoyoos, Oliver, and the surrounding communities. The hospital has a 24-hour emergency room.

Getting Around

Osoyoos is at the intersection of Highways 3 and 97. Highway 3 runs east-west through town. Highway 97 will take you north from Osoyoos to Oliver and on to Penticton; heading south on Highway 97, you'll cross the U.S. border into Washington State.

OK Wine Shuttle (250/495-3278, www.okwineshuttle.ca) operates a **dinner shuttle** (round-trip $25 pp) providing evening transportation between the hotels and resorts in Oliver and Osoyoos and the area's restaurants and winery dining rooms. They also run a **hop-on, hop-off shuttle** (10am-5pm daily late May-Oct., $65 pp), which picks up at local hotels and then circles past the Oliver-Osoyoos wineries throughout the day; the driver normally returns to each stop every 30 minutes.

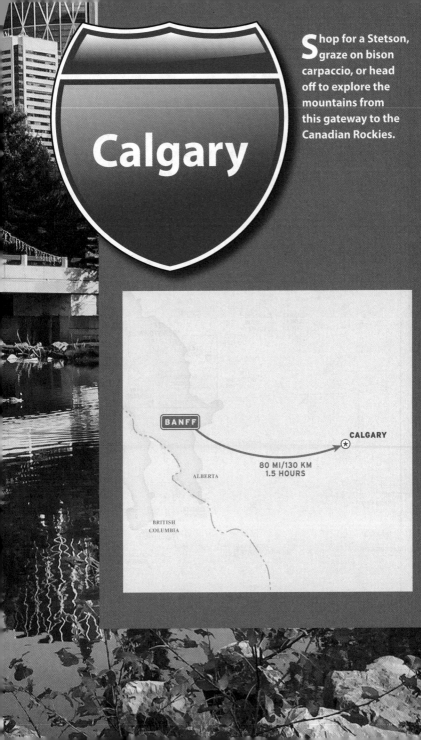

Calgary

Shop for a Stetson, graze on bison carpaccio, or head off to explore the mountains from this gateway to the Canadian Rockies.

BANFF

CALGARY

80 MI/130 KM
1.5 HOURS

ALBERTA

BRITISH
COLUMBIA

Calgary

To Cochrane

To Drumheller and Edmonton

Calgary International Airport

To Shoppers Drug Mart

Nose Hill Park

To Cochrane

To CANADA OLYMPIC PARK and Banff

CENTRO MOTEL

University Of Calgary

OLYMPIC OVAL

HOTEL ALMA

MCMAHON STADIUM

FOOTHILLS MEDICAL CENTER

PETER LOUGHEED GENERAL HOSPITAL

SHOPPERS DRUG MARKET

ALBERTA BALLET

RIVER SURFING

SEE "DOWNTOWN CALGARY" MAP

TELUS SPARK

CALGARY ZOO

GLENBOW MUSEUM

GREYHOUND BUS DEPOT

CALGARY STAMPEDE

SMITHBILT HATS

Inglewood Bird Sanctuary

WILD ROSE BREWING

ALBERTA BOOT CO.

HOTEL BLACKFOOT

SHOPPERS DRUG MART

ROCKYVIEW GENERAL HOSPITAL

CALGARY FARMERS' MARKET

To Bragg Creek

Glenmore Park

Glenmore Reservoir

Sarcee Reserve

HERITAGE PARK HISTORICAL VILLAGE

0 2 mi

0 2 km

© AVALON TRAVEL

Highlights

★ **Glenbow Museum:** Part history museum, part art gallery, and part cultural curator, this excellent museum tells Calgary's stories from its earliest days to the present (page 394).

★ **Heritage Park Historical Village:** From rum running to fur trading to a "Little Synagogue on the Prairie," you can explore western Canada from the 1860s to 1950s at the country's largest living history village (page 395).

★ **Canada Olympic Park:** Whiz down the bobsled track, try out the luge, or go zip-lining, mountain biking, and more at Calgary's 1988 Winter Olympics venue, which also houses Canada's Sports Hall of Fame (page 398).

★ **Calgary Stampede:** One of western Canada's biggest festivals, this rodeo, county fair, and crazy party rolled into one takes over Calgary for 10 days every July (page 401).

★ **River Surfing:** Surf in downtown Calgary? Yes, you can, where the Bow River has formed a permanent wave under the 10th Street Bridge (page 404).

With its trademark cowboy swagger, Calgary hosts one of Canada's biggest parties. The annual Calgary Stampede takes over the city every July, proclaiming itself "The Greatest Outdoor Show on Earth."

The rest of the year, this city of 1.2 million wears its western heritage a little more quietly. Canada's fourth-largest metropolis is often compared to U.S. cities like Houston, as a headquarters for the energy business, or Denver, a gateway to the Rocky Mountains. And there's truth to these comparisons. Oil, gas, and related energy industries are major drivers of Calgary's economy, and with its location just 90 minutes from Banff, Calgary is the closest major city to Canada's Rocky Mountain national parks.

Yet beyond its cowboy roots, its company-town ethos, and its proximity to western Canada's best outdoor experiences, there's a lot more to Alberta's most populous city.

Calgary has an excellent museum of western Canadian history, art, and culture, as well as the country's largest living history village, where you can wander back to the 19th and early 20th centuries. A new National Music Centre is the focus of a redeveloping downtown district that will also include a landmark New Central Library, along with urban condos, restaurants, and cafés. The city's food scene has taken off, with Calgary's restaurants regularly ranked among the country's top dining destinations.

Before you head for the mountains, you can get outdoors within the city limits. Try the unusual sport of river surfing right downtown, cycle the scenic pathways along Calgary's riverfront, or follow in the footsteps (and bobsled tracks) of the Olympians at Canada Olympic Park, where the city hosted the 1988 Winter Olympic Games.

Then, when you're ready to road-trip, set off from Calgary to Banff, Lake Louise, and Jasper, or travel across British Columbia to the Pacific coast. Just take time to shop for your Stetson and cowboy boots before you hit the road.

Getting to Calgary

Driving from Vancouver
Via Highway 1
The **most direct route** from Vancouver to Calgary is via the **Trans-Canada Highway (Hwy. 1).**

From Vancouver, take **Highway 1** east to **Hope.** Continue east at Hope onto **Highway 3,** then exit onto **Highway 5 (Coquihalla Hwy.)** north. Follow the Coquihalla over the mountains to **Kamloops,** where you rejoin **Highway 1.** Stay on Highway 1 east into Alberta, where you'll reach Lake Louise, Banff, and then Calgary. This route from Vancouver to Calgary is **605 miles (975 kilometers)** and takes **11 hours.**

Via Highway 3
You can also travel between Vancouver and Calgary via **scenic Highway 3.**

Through the Okanagan and Kootenays
Take the **Trans-Canada Highway (Hwy. 1)** from Vancouver east to **Hope,** where you pick up **Highway 3.** Highway 3 winds its way across southern British Columbia through the Okanagan and Kootenays regions. From here, the shortest route is to stay on Highway 3 into Alberta, then turn north on **Highway 22** and east on **Highway 533.** At **Nanton,** pick up **Highway 2** north that will take you into Calgary. This Vancouver-Calgary trip is **745 miles (1,200 kilometers)** and takes **14.5 hours.**

Best Hotels

★ **Hotel Alma:** If you don't need to be right downtown, this up-to-date hotel on the University of Calgary campus is a good value (page 405).

★ **Hotel Arts:** Featuring works by Canadian artists throughout, this contemporary hotel lives up to its name. It has good restaurants, too (page 406).

★ **Hotel Le Germain Calgary:** From the illuminated marble check-in desk to the purple lounge chairs in the 143 modern guest rooms, this downtown boutique hotel is one stylish lodging (page 406).

Through Radium Hot Springs and Kootenay National Park

Another alternative is to follow **Highway 3** east to **Cranbrook,** where you turn north on **Highway 95** through Invermere and Radium Hot Springs. From there, continue north on **Highway 93** through Kootenay National Park. North of the park, Highway 93 meets **Highway 1,** which will take you east through Banff and into Calgary. This scenic route from Vancouver to Calgary is **775 miles (1,250 kilometers)** and takes **15 hours.**

Via Highway 5 and the Icefields Parkway

Yet another option is to go northeast from Vancouver to Jasper, then turn south along the scenic Icefields Parkway to Lake Louise, before continuing south through Banff and on to Calgary.

To follow this route, leave Vancouver on the **Trans-Canada Highway (Hwy. 1)** east to **Hope.** Continue east at Hope onto **Highway 3,** then exit onto **Highway 5** north toward Kamloops. At **Kamloops,** continue north on Highway 5 until it intersects with **Highway 16** north of Valemount. Follow Highway 16 east to Jasper.

From Jasper, follow the spectacular **Icefields Parkway (Hwy. 93)** south to Lake Louise, where you rejoin **Highway 1** and continue east to Calgary. Vancouver to Calgary via this Jasper route is **750 miles (1,200 kilometers)** and takes **13.5 to 14.5 hours.**

Driving from Banff

The **Trans-Canada Highway (Hwy. 1)** runs east from Banff to Calgary, an **80-mile (130-kilometer)** drive that normally takes about **90 minutes.**

Driving from the Okanagan
From Kelowna

To travel from Kelowna in the Okanagan Valley to Calgary, take **Highway 97** north, then continue north on **Highway 97A.** At **Sicamous,** turn east onto the **Trans-Canada Highway (Hwy. 1)** that will take you into Alberta and on to Calgary. It's **375 miles (605 kilometers)** from Kelowna to Calgary; the drive takes **seven hours.**

From Osoyoos

From Osoyoos or other points in the South Okanagan, one option is to take **Highway 97** north to **Kelowna** and follow the directions from Kelowna. This route is **455 miles (730 kilometers)** from Osoyoos to Calgary; the drive takes **8.5 to 9 hours.**

Alternatively, follow **Highway 3** east from Osoyoos. Continue on Highway 3 east past Cranbrook and Fernie and into Alberta, where you turn north on **Highway 22.** Stay on Highway 22 until you reach **Highway 533** east. Follow Highway 533 toward **Nanton,** where you'll pick up **Highway 2** north, which will take you into Calgary. This latter route is **515 miles (830 kilometers)** from Osoyoos to Calgary; the drive takes **10 hours.**

Best Restaurants

★ **Sidewalk Citizen Bakery:** Calgary's most delectable breads, pastries, and other baked goods come out of the ovens at this East Village bake shop, where you can also get Middle Eastern-influenced sandwiches, salads, and toasts (page 408).

★ **Pigeonhole:** Difficult to pigeonhole, the ever-inventive small plates at this 17th Avenue hot spot are among Calgary's most exciting tastes (page 409).

★ **River Café:** Long considered one of Calgary's best restaurants, this eatery serving seasonal Canadian cuisine is still at the top of its game (page 409).

Getting There by Air, Train, and Bus
By Air

You can fly to **Calgary International Airport** (YYC, 2000 Airport Rd. NE, 403/735-1200, www.yyc.com) from across Canada and the United States and from Amsterdam, Frankfurt, London, Paris, and Tokyo, among other cities. The airport is located on the city's northeast side, about 20 minutes' drive from downtown.

Ground Transportation

Calgary Transit's **bus 300** (403/262-1000, www.calgarytransit.com, 5am-midnight daily, one-way $9.50) runs between the airport and downtown Calgary, every 20 to 30 minutes. The trip takes 40 to 50 minutes. Purchase a Calgary Transit Boarding Pass from an automated machine at the airport bus stop or pay cash (exact change) on the bus.

Allied Airport Shuttle (403/299-9555 or 877/299-9555, www.airportshuttle-calgary.ca, 3:30am-midnight daily, one-way adults $15, ages 4-12 $10) is a scheduled van service that can take you between the airport and downtown Calgary hotels. Vans leave every 30 minutes. From the airport, reservations are not required; buy your ticket at the Allied desk on the arrivals level or on the shuttle. When you're going to the airport, however, you must make a reservation to be picked at your hotel downtown. Depending on your downtown destination, the trip takes between 30 and 60 minutes.

Taxis wait for passengers on the airport's arrivals level around the clock. Cabs are metered, and average fares between the airport and downtown are $40-45.

To go directly to **Banff** or **Lake Louise** from the Calgary airport, without a car, you can take one of several shuttle services. **Brewster Banff Airport Express** (403/762-6700 or 866/606-7000, www.brewster.ca) provides bus service between the Calgary airport and both Banff (2.5 hours, one-way adults $57, ages 6-15 $28.50) and Lake Louise (2.5 hours, one-way adults $57, ages 6-15 $28.50). The **Banff Airporter** (403/762-3330 or 888/449-2901, www.banffairporter.com, one-way adults $58.95, seniors $50.11, ages 2-12 $29.48) can take you from Banff to the Calgary airport as well.

Numerous car rental companies can rent you a car from the Calgary airport, including **Alamo** (403/543-3985 or 888/826-6893, www.alamo.ca), **Avis** (403/221-1700 or 800/230-4898, www.avis.ca), **Budget** (403/226-1550 or 800/268-8900, www.budget.ca), **Discount** (403/299-1203 or 800/263-2355, www.discountcar.com), **Dollar** (403/221-1806 or 800/800-6000, www.dollar.com), **Enterprise** (403/233-8021 or 800/261-7331, www.enterprise.com), **Hertz** (403/221-1676 or 800/654-3001, www.hertz.ca), **National** (403/221-1690

One Day in Calgary

Get your Calgary day off to a delicious start in the East Village near downtown. In the restored Simmons Building, you can get excellent coffee at **Phil & Sebastian Coffee Roasters** to pair with the city's most delectable pastries at **Sidewalk Citizen Bakery.**

Make your first sightseeing stop at the **Calgary Tower** to get an overview of the city and what's where. Around the corner, the **Glenbow Museum** illustrates Calgary's history and culture and mounts changing art exhibitions.

Wander along the **Stephen Avenue Walk** to check out the downtown shops. Then cross the river for lunch at the fun **Container Bar** outdoors in a Kensington alley, or head south instead for an Italian lunch at **Mercato.**

In the afternoon, go back to Calgary's early days at the **Heritage Park Historical Village,** or if you'd prefer an active adventure, head west to **Canada Olympic Park** to test your mettle on the bobsled, luge, or zip line.

Back downtown, rent a bike to go **cycling** along Calgary's riverfront for an hour or so or try a unique water sport: **river surfing.** Have a quick rest at your hotel, then kick off your evening with a cocktail and Asian small plates at **Raw Bar** in the Hotel Arts.

For dinner, book a river-view table at the **River Café,** long considered one of Calgary's best restaurants, or head for 17th Avenue to try out one of the newer eateries, like **Pigeonhole, Model Milk,** or **Anju.**

Later, if you're not ready to wrap up your Calgary day, see what's happening at one of the **theaters,** then have a nightcap at a **brewpub** or at the stylish **Lounge Central 899** in Hotel Le Germain Calgary.

---

or 888/826-6890, www.nationalcar.ca), **Routes** (403/398-3930, www.routes.ca), and **Thrifty** (403/221-1961 or 800/847-4389, www.thrifty.com).

By Train

The **Rocky Mountaineer** (Calgary Tower, 115 9th Ave. SE, 877/460-3200, www.rockymountaineer.com, mid-Apr.-mid-Oct.), a privately operated luxury train, travels among Vancouver, Banff, Lake Louise, Jasper, and Calgary. The Rocky Mountaineer also has a route that starts in Seattle, stops in Vancouver, and continues on to the Rockies and Calgary. You can travel either route from west to east or east to west.

Neither **VIA Rail** nor **Amtrak** provide passenger service to Calgary.

By Bus

Greyhound (800/661-8747, www.greyhound.ca) runs buses to Calgary (850 16th St. SW, 403/263-1234) from many Canadian and U.S. destinations, including several buses a day between Calgary and **Banff** (1.75 hours, one-way adults $16.50-36.50) or **Lake Louise** (2.5 hours, one-way adults $18.70-48.10).

Brewster Banff Airport Express (403/762-6700 or 866/606-6700, www.brewster.ca) runs buses from Banff to downtown Calgary hotels (2.5 hours, one-way adults $57, ages 6-15 $28.50) and to the Calgary international airport (2 hours, one-way adults $57, ages 6-15 $28.50).

Red Arrow (403/531-0350 or 800/232-1958, www.redarrow.ca) runs buses to Calgary from Edmonton (3.5-4 hours, one-way adults $71) and other cities in Alberta.

Sights

Downtown Calgary has several sights to explore, including a first-rate museum of history and culture and the landmark Calgary Tower. Other attractions, notably Canada's largest living history village and Canada Olympic Park, are outside the city center.

A new neighborhood is developing east of the downtown core. Calgary's East Village will house a new music center, library, condos, and restaurants, and it's already worth checking out.

★ Glenbow Museum

Part history museum, part art gallery, and part cultural curator, the well-designed **Glenbow Museum** (130 9th Ave. SE, 403/268-4100, www.glenbow.org, 9am-5pm Mon.-Sat., noon-5pm Sun. July-Aug., 9am-5pm Tues.-Sat., noon-5pm Sun. Sept.-June, adults $16, seniors and students $11, ages 7-17 $10, families $40) tells Calgary's stories. The museum is downtown, one block from the Calgary Tower.

In the permanent exhibits, you can explore the early days in Calgary, southern Alberta, and western Canada, from the indigenous communities to the entrepreneurs, adventurers, and even scoundrels who helped shape the region. Changing exhibitions have focused on everything from Canadian art to aboriginal residential schools to gun sculpture.

Calgary Tower

Standing 4,023 feet (1,228 meters) above sea level, and 627 feet (191 meters) above the downtown streets, the **Calgary Tower** (101 9th Ave. SW, 403/266-7171, www.calgarytower.com, 9am-10pm daily July-Aug., 9am-9pm daily Sept.-June, adults $18, seniors $16, ages 4-12 $9) has the highest 360-degree observation deck in the world. When it opened in 1968, it was originally called the Husky Tower, not because it was portly, but because Husky Oil and Marathon Realty constructed this downtown landmark as a joint venture. It was renamed in 1971.

As you walk around the observation deck, listen to the free **audio tour,** which gives you historical background about the city and points out highlights of what you're seeing, from City Hall to the Saddledome (where the Calgary Flames ice hockey team plays) to Stampede

Park, which hosts the annual Calgary Stampede. On a clear day, you can see the Rocky Mountains.

A section of the observation area has a glass floor, so you can look down—way down—on the streets below.

Contemporary Calgary

Three of the city's contemporary art galleries, the Art Gallery of Calgary, the Institute of Modern and Contemporary Art, and the Museum of Modern and Contemporary Art, joined forces to become **Contemporary Calgary** (www.contemporarycalgary.com, free), a modern art showcase with two locations.

Both the Stephen Avenue gallery, called **C** (117 8th Ave. SW, 403/770-1351, noon-6pm Thurs.-Sun.) and the City Hall location, known as **C2** (104-800 Macleod Trail SE, 403/262-1737, noon-6pm Thurs.-Sun.) are open only during exhibitions, so check the website to see what's showing or phone before visiting.

National Music Centre

Featuring Canadian music, performers, and composers past and present, the **National Music Centre** (www.nmc.ca) is moving to **Studio Bell,** a new facility in Calgary's East Village.

As this book went to press, the new museum building, which will house the music center's more than 2,000-piece collection of instruments, artifacts, and music technology, as well as performance spaces and recording studios, is slated to open in 2016. The center will also be the home of the Canadian Music Hall of Fame and the Canadian Country Music Hall of Fame. Check the website for more details.

Fort Calgary

Where the Bow and Elbow Rivers meet, the Northwest Mounted Police built an outpost in 1875 that eventually grew to become the city of Calgary.

At **Fort Calgary** (750 9th Ave. SE, 403/290-1875, www.fortcalgary.com,

9am-5pm daily, adults $12, seniors and students $11, ages 7-17 $7, ages 3-6 $5), start by watching a short film about life in the late 19th-century when the fort was first established. Then explore the exhibits that illustrate life at the fort, and in the fledgling city, in the late 1800s and early 1900s. The fort operated until 1914 when it was sold to the Grand Trunk Railroad.

Fort Calgary is 0.9 miles (1.5 kilometers) directly east of the Calgary Tower, and a short walk from the East Village neighborhood. The C-Train's **City Hall station,** part of the free downtown light rail network, is a 10- to 15-minute walk from the fort. Several buses that run along 9th Avenue from downtown, including **buses 1, 302,** and **411,** stop near the fort.

★ Heritage Park Historical Village

Go back in time at the **Heritage Park Historical Village** (1900 Heritage Dr. SW, at 14th St. SW, 403/268-8500, www.heritagepark.ca, 10am-5pm daily mid-May-early Sept., 10am-5pm Sat.-Sun. early Sept.-mid-Oct., adults $26.25, seniors $20.50, ages 7-14 $18.75, ages 3-6 $13.50), Canada's largest living history experience.

As you walk through the history of western Canada from the 1860s to 1950s, you can explore a 19th-century fur-trading fort and First Nations camp, wander the streets of a 1910 prairie railroad town, checking out the mounted police barracks, the snooker parlor, and the old-time bakery (which sells gooey butter tarts), and talk with the costumed interpreters who reenact life in these past eras. There's even a "Little Synagogue on the Prairie," an original 1916 house of worship from a Jewish farming community in eastern Alberta.

You can ride a passenger train, pulled by an antique steam locomotive, through the 127-acre (51-hectare) park, and take part in activities throughout the day, including butter-making, wagon rides, First Nations games, and street theater.

Near the park entrance is the **Gasoline Alley Museum** (10am-5pm daily mid-May-early Sept., 10am-5pm Sat.-Sun. early Sept.-mid-Oct., 9:30am-4pm daily mid-Oct.-mid-May, winter admission adults $10.75, seniors $8.50, ages 7-14 $6.75, ages 3-6 $5.50), a car buff's fantasy of antique cars and trucks, along with North America's largest collection of restored gas pumps. The museum is open year-round, even when the rest of the park is closed. There's a separate museum-only admission fee in winter, while in summer, you can visit the museum as part of your standard park admission.

Getting There

Heritage Park is six miles (10 kilometers) south of downtown Calgary, a 20-minute drive.

By public transit from downtown, take the C-Train **Red Line 201** (Somerset/Bridlewood) to Heritage Station. From there, catch **bus 502** (Heritage Park Shuttle), which takes you to the park. The shuttle runs only when the park is open, daily from mid-May to early September and on weekends from early September to mid-October, and for special events at other times of year.

Telus Spark Science Centre

At the **Telus Spark Science Centre** (220 St. George's Dr. NE, 403/817-6800, www.sparkscience.ca, 10am-5pm daily June-Aug., 10am-4pm Sun.-Fri., 10am-5pm Sat. Sept.-May, last entry 90 minutes before closing, adults $19.95, seniors $17.95, ages 13-17 $15.95, ages 3-12 $12.95), Calgary's modern science museum, you and the kids can explore the earth and the human body, build things in the open studio workshop, watch live science demonstrations, and generally immerse yourself in the world of science.

Take in the planetarium show or a movie at the **HD Digital Dome Theatre** (adults $26.45, seniors $22.45-24.45,

Downtown Calgary

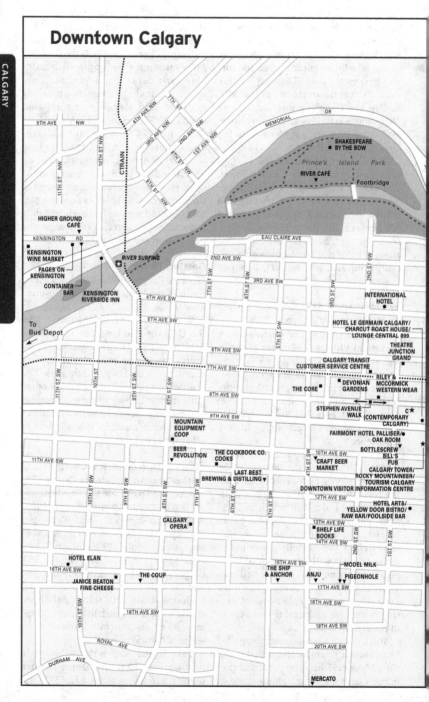

5TH AVE NW

4TH AVE NW

7TH ST

3RD AVE NW

2ND AVE NW

1ST ST NW

8TH ST NW

MEMORIAL DR

SHAKESPEARE BY THE BOW

Prince's Island Park

11TH ST NW

10TH ST NW

CTRAIN

9TH ST NW

RIVER CAFÉ

Footbridge

HIGHER GROUND CAFÉ

KENSINGTON RD

EAU CLAIRE AVE

KENSINGTON WINE MARKET

PAGES ON KENSINGTON

RIVER SURFING

2ND AVE SW

3RD AVE SW

2ND ST SW

INTERNATIONAL HOTEL

CONTAINER BAR

KENSINGTON RIVERSIDE INN

4TH AVE SW

7TH ST SW

8TH ST SW

3RD ST SW

5TH AVE SW

HOTEL LE GERMAIN CALGARY/ CHARCUT ROAST HOUSE/ LOUNGE CENTRAL 899

To Bus Depot

5TH AVE SW

5TH ST SW

6TH AVE SW

THEATRE JUNCTION GRAND

CALGARY TRANSIT CUSTOMER SERVICE CENTRE

7TH AVE SW

RILEY & McCORMICK WESTERN WEAR

11TH ST SW

10TH ST

9TH ST SW

8TH ST SW

THE CORE

DEVONIAN GARDENS

8TH AVE SW

STEPHEN AVENUE WALK

C ★ (CONTEMPORARY CALGARY)

9TH AVE SW

MOUNTAIN EQUIPMENT COOP

FAIRMONT HOTEL PALLISER/ OAK ROOM

BEER REVOLUTION

THE COOKBOOK CO. COOKS

10TH AVE SW

4TH ST SW

CRAFT BEER MARKET

BOTTLESCREW BILL'S PUB

11TH AVE SW

10TH ST

9TH ST SW

8TH ST SW

7TH ST SW

6TH ST SW

LAST BEST BREWING & DISTILLING

CALGARY TOWER/ ROCKY MOUNTAINEER/ TOURISM CALGARY

DOWNTOWN VISITOR INFORMATION CENTRE

12TH AVE SW

HOTEL ARTS/ YELLOW DOOR BISTRO/ RAW BAR/POOLSIDE BAR

CALGARY OPERA

13TH AVE SW

SHELF LIFE BOOKS

2ND ST SW

1ST ST SW

14TH AVE SW

HOTEL ELAN

16TH AVE SW

15TH AVE SW

THE SHIP & ANCHOR

MODEL MILK

JANICE BEATON FINE CHEESE

THE COUP

ANJU

PIGEONHOLE

17TH AVE SW

10TH ST

18TH AVE SW

18TH AVE SW

19TH AVE SW

ROYAL AVE

20TH AVE SW

DURHAM AVE

MERCATO

6TH AVE NE
5TH AVE NE
4TH AVE NE
3RD AVE NE
2ND AVE NE
1ST AVE NE
CENTRE ST
1ST ST NE
2ND ST NE
3RD ST NE
4TH ST NE

DRURY AVE
5TH AVE NE
4TH AVE NE
2ND AVE NE
6TH ST NE
7TH ST NE
7A ST NE
8TH ST NE
9TH ST NE
10TH ST NE
11TH ST NE
1ST AVE NE
MURDOCK RD

CENTRE STREET BRIDGE
Bow River
RIVERFRONT AVE
EDMONTON TR.
MEMORIA DR
MCDOUGALL RD

To
Telus Spark and
Calgary Zoo

CENTRE ST
4TH AVE SE
5TH AVE SE
6TH AVE SE

PHIL & SEBASTIAN COFFEE ROASTERS/
SIDEWALK CITIZEN BAKERY/
CHARBAR

St Patrick's
Island

CALGARY TRANSIT
CUSTOMER SERVICE CENTRE

C2
(CONTEMPORARY CALGARY)
GLENBOW MUSEUM

4TH ST SE
5TH ST SE
3RD ST SE
3 ST SE

THEATRE CALGARY
3RD ST SE

NATIONAL MUSIC CENTRE

FORT CALGARY

ALBERTA THEATRE PROJECTS
CALGARY PHILHARMONIC ORCHESTRA
9TH AVE SE

LUNCHBOX THEATRE

VERTIGO THEATRE

11TH AVE SE
12TH AVE SE
13TH AVE SE
14TH AVE SE
1ST ST SE
MACLEOD TRAIL
OLYMPIC WAY
5TH ST SE
6TH ST SE
MACDONALD AVE
8TH ST SE
9TH ST SE
17TH AVE SE

C-TRAIN

Stampede Park

CALGARY STAMPEDE

SCOTIABANK SADDLEDOME

Elbow River
SALISBURY AVE
RAMSAY ST
MAGGIE ST
BURNS AVE
19TH AVE SE

0   400 yds
0   400 m

© AVALON TRAVEL

ages 13-17 $20.45-22.45, ages 3-12 $17.45-19.45) or let the youngsters explore the Brainasium, an outdoor playground.

The museum isn't just for children. The second Thursday of every month is **Adults Only Night** (6pm-10pm) at the science center, where people over age 18 can explore the exhibits and check out the demonstrations and other programs.

Telus Spark Science Centre is east of downtown, off Memorial Drive Northeast. By public transit, take the C-Train **Blue Line 202** (Saddletowne) to Zoo Station. From the station, it's a 0.6-mile (1-kilometer) walk north to the science center.

Calgary Zoo

From bears to penguins to tigers, from the Canadian wilds to Africa, the **Calgary Zoo** (1300 Zoo Rd. NE, 403/232-9300 or 800/588-9993, www.calgaryzoo.com, 9am-5pm daily, mid-Mar.-mid-Oct. adults $24.95, seniors $22.95, ages 3-15 $16.95, mid.-Oct.-mid-Mar. adults $23,

seniors $21, ages 3-15 $15, parking $8) shows off animals and their habitats.

The zoo is east of downtown, off Memorial Drive Northeast, near the Telus Spark Science Centre. By public transit, take the C-Train **Blue Line 202** (Saddletowne) to Zoo Station.

★ Canada Olympic Park

Calgary hosted the Winter Olympics in 1988, the year that an unlikely team from Jamaica captured the world's attention when they competed in the bobsled event. Immortalized, at least in movie fiction, in the 1993 film *Cool Runnings,* the Jamaican team sledded on the track at what is now WinSport's **Canada Olympic Park** (88 Canada Olympic Rd. SW, 403/247-5452, www.winsport.ca), where many events were held during the XV Olympic Winter Games, and where activities now draw both sports fans and the athletically inclined in winter and summer.

Year-round, you can visit **Canada's**

wagon ride at the Heritage Park Historical Village

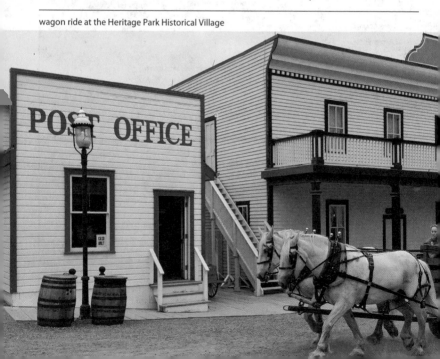

Sports Hall of Fame (169 Canada Olympic Rd. SW, 403/776-1040, www.sportshall.ca, 10am-5pm daily July-Aug., 10am-5pm Tues.-Sun. Sept.-June, adults $12, seniors $10, ages 4-18 $8, families $35), with a dozen galleries featuring more than 60 sports, from swimming and wheelchair racing to curling, snowboarding, and, of course, ice hockey, with plenty of hands-on things to do and exhibits about Canada's athletic legends.

For other activities, hours vary throughout the year, so call or check the park website to see what's open when. In general, the summer activities are open from May to early October.

Summer Activities

Have Olympic dreams? In a wheeled sled driven by a professional pilot, you can reach speeds up to 50 mph (80 km/h) on the **summer bobsled** (over age 13, $59.99).

Whiz down the world's longest luge track at the park's **Skyline Luge Calgary** (403/776-0617, www.skylineluge.com, single ride $13). If one ride on the wheeled sled isn't enough, you can buy packages of tickets for multiple rides, as well as family tickets.

Another way down the mountain is on the park's **zip-line course,** which comprises three lines: the Trainer; the Plaza Zip Line, where you might reach speeds of 50 mph (80 km/h); and the Monster Zip Line, where you start at the sky jump tower and zip 1,640 feet (500 meters), with a vertical drop of more than 325 feet (100 meters), and speeds up to 75 mph (120 km/h). You can choose just the Trainer ($10.99), the Trainer plus the Plaza ($39.90), or all three lines ($59.99).

The park has a network of lift-accessed trails for **mountain biking** (full-day adults $24.99, seniors and ages 4-17 $19.99, families $69.99), as well as a skills park with dirt jumps and other obstacles. For something tamer, play the family-friendly 18-hole **mini golf** course (over age 5 $9.99, under age 6 $4.99, families $18.99).

Winter Activities

In winter, you can whip down the Olympic **bobsled track** (over age 15, $149.99) at speeds up to 60 mph (100 km/h) in a four-person sled with a professional driver, or slide feet-first down the **luge** run (over age 7, $35).

You can **ski** or **snowboard** (full day adults $44.99, seniors $24.99, ages 13-24 $39.99, ages 6-12 $24.99, ages 3-5 $15.99, families $94.99) on the small ski hill, although serious powder hounds will want to go to Banff or Lake Louise. In addition to full-day passes, you can buy lift tickets for two hours (adults $29.99, seniors $18.99, ages 13-24 $24.99, ages 6-12 $18.99, ages 3-5 $11.99, families $60.99) or four hours (adults $37.99, seniors $22.99, ages 13-24 $33.99, ages 6-12 $22.99, ages 3-5 $14.99, families $74.99).

The park has an **ice-skating rink** (adults $5.99, ages 13-17 $4.99, seniors and under age 13 $2.99, families $14.99)

SIGHTS

and 1.25 miles (2 kilometers) of groomed **cross-country ski trails** (adults $21.99, seniors $14.99, ages 13-24 $19.99, ages 6-12 $17.99, ages 3-5 $10.99) as well.

Getting There

Canada Olympic Park is on Calgary's west side, off Highway 1 (16th Ave. SW), nine miles (15 kilometers) from downtown, about a 25-minute drive. It's an easy stop on the way to or from Banff.

It's possible to reach Canada Olympic Park by public transit from downtown, but the trip will take about an hour. The most direct route is to take the C-Train **Red Line 201** (Tuscany) to Brentwood Station. Change to **bus 408** (Valleyridge), and get off at Canada Olympic Road.

Entertainment and Events

Nightlife

Fans of craft beer should head for **Last Best Brewing and Distilling** (607 11th Ave. SW, 587/353-7387, www.lastbest-brewing.com, 11:30am-midnight Sun.-Thurs., 11:30am-2am Fri.-Sat.), which brews their own, as does **Wild Rose Brewing** (Currie Barracks, 2-4580 Quesnay Wood Dr. SW, 403/727-5451, www.wildrosebrewery.com, 11am-11pm Mon.-Sat., 11am-9pm Sun.) in a former Air Force barracks.

Craft Beer Market (345 10th Ave. SW, 403/514-2337, www.craftbeermarket.ca, 11am-1am Mon.-Wed., 11am-2am Thurs.-Fri., 10am-2am Sat., 10am-1am Sun.) keeps more than 100 varieties on tap, **Beer Revolution** (1080 8th St. SW, 403/264-2739, www.beerrevolution.ca, 11am-midnight Sun.-Mon., 11am-1am Tues.-Thurs., 11am-2am Fri.-Sat.) rotates 24 taps that they pair with pizza and rock and roll, while long-standing **Bottlescrew Bill's** (140 10th Ave. SW, 403/263-7900, www.bottlescrewbill.com, 11am-2am

Mon.-Sat., 4pm-midnight Sun.) serves 300-plus varieties, from local to international brewers.

To watch soccer or listen to local bands, join the diverse crowd at **The Ship & Anchor** (534 17th Ave. SW, 403/245-3333, www.shipandanchor.com, 11am-2am Mon.-Fri., 10am-2am Sat.-Sun.), a Calgary dive-bar landmark.

For cocktails, consider the sedate **Oak Room** (133 9th Ave. SW, 403/262-1234, www.fairmont.com, 11am-midnight daily), at the Fairmont Hotel Palliser, which has weekly live jazz, or the more contemporary **Lounge Central 899** (899 Centre St. SW, 403/264-8990, www.leger-mainhotels.com, 11:30am-11pm Mon.-Fri., 4pm-10pm Sat.-Sun.) at Hotel Le Germain Calgary.

You might imagine you're in Miami on a sunny afternoon at the **Hotel Arts' Poolside Bar** (119 12th Ave. SW, 403/266-4611, www.hotelarts.ca, May-Oct.), where you can have a drink and go for a swim in the courtyard pool. A DJ keeps things hopping on weekends.

The Arts
Theater

Launched in the 1960s, the professional **Theatre Calgary** (Arts Commons, 220 9th Ave SE, 403/294-7447, www.theatrecalgary.com) produces an annual season of contemporary and classical drama. They also present the summertime **Shakespeare by the Bow,** a pay-what-you-can production performed outdoors at Prince's Island Park.

Focusing on contemporary Canadian and international works, the **Alberta Theatre Projects** (403/294-7402, www.atplive.com), a professional nonprofit company, presents six plays a year. They perform in the **Martha Cohen Theatre** (215 8 Ave. SE) in the Arts Commons complex.

Canada's only professional mystery theater, **Vertigo Theatre** (115 9th Ave. SE, 403/221-3708, www.vertigotheatre.com) produces a season of thrillers and

Bloody Caesar

Spend any time in a Canadian bar, and you'll likely spot someone drinking a "Caesar." Canada's version of a Bloody Mary, this spicy cocktail blends vodka, Worcestershire sauce, and hot sauce, with the uniquely Canadian addition of Clamato juice—tomato-clam juice substituting for standard tomato.

Though you'll find Caesars, often called bloody Caesars, at pubs and lounges across the country, credit for the first of these tomato-clam cocktails goes to a bartender in Calgary. In 1969, Walter Chell, a hotel bar manager, was asked to create a signature drink to celebrate the opening of the Calgary hotel's new Italian restaurant.

The flavors of spaghetti vongole (pasta with clams) reportedly inspired Chell's version of a Bloody Mary, which he concocted by mashing clams into tomato juice, before adding vodka and spices. He garnished his creation with a stick of celery.

Around the same time, the California-based Mott's company began working on a clam tomato juice and hired Chell as a consultant. Clamato juice was born. And with a premixed tomato-clam juice available, far easier than mashing clams by hand, Calgary, and Canada, had a new favorite drink.

who-done-its. Their performance space is located at the base of the Calgary Tower.

Have an hour for lunch? Then you can see a play at the **Lunchbox Theatre** (115 9 Ave. SE 403/265-4292, www.lunchboxtheatre.com), which presents a season of one-act noon-hour productions in the Calgary Tower complex. Bring your lunch to eat during the show.

In western Canada's oldest theater building, **Theatre Junction GRAND** (608 1st St. SW, 403/205-2922, www.theatrejunction.com) presents "contemporary live art," including theater, music, and dance.

Music

The city's symphony orchestra, the **Calgary Philharmonic Orchestra** (403/571-0849, www.calgaryphil.com), performs at the Arts Commons downtown in the 1,700-seat **Jack Singer Concert Hall** (205 8th St. SE). They also play at various venues around town, so check the details of any performance you plan to see.

The **Calgary Opera** (1315 7th St. SW, 403/262-7286, www.calgaryopera.com) converted a former church in the Beltline district south of downtown into the Arrata Opera Centre, where the company produces its mainstage season. In August, the 10-day **Opera in the Village** festival features performances in a 900-seat open-air tent in the East Village.

Dance

With both classical and contemporary productions in its repertory, the **Alberta Ballet** (box office 341 17th Ave. SW, 403/245-4549, www.albertaballet.com), Canada's second-largest professional ballet company, splits its time between Edmonton and Calgary, where they take the stage at the **Southern Jubilee Auditorium** (1415 14th Ave. NW).

Festivals and Events
★ Calgary Stampede

Alberta's biggest festival is the annual **Calgary Stampede** (www.calgarystampede.com, July), which has its roots in the region's cowboy culture. Taking over the city for 10 days every summer, the Stampede, which is a rodeo, county fair, and crazy party rolled into one, bills itself as "The Greatest Outdoor Show on Earth."

The Stampede opens with a huge parade through downtown. Other attractions include chuck wagon races, calf roping, bull riding, horse shows, a carnival midway, concerts by big-name entertainers, and plenty of partying by cowboy hat-sporting locals and visitors. The Stampede draws more than a million people every year, so pull on your boots and come on down.

Other Festivals

The **Calgary International Children's Festival** (www.calgarykidsfest.ca, May) presents three days of theater, magicians, jugglers, musicians, and acrobats, all performing for kids.

Performers from more than a dozen countries take to the eight stages in Prince's Island Park for the annual **Calgary Folk Music Fest** (www.calgaryfolkfest.com, July).

Pride Calgary (www.pridecalgary.ca, Aug.-Sept.) hosts a week of events, including a big parade, celebrating the city's LGBTQ community.

What do you get when you mix art, science, and engineering into a weirdly fun five-day festival? That's quirky **Beakerhead** (www.beakerhead.com, Sept.), where the technical meets the creative in street performances, competitions, food labs, and other unexpected events.

Shopping

Shopping Districts

The main downtown shopping district, known as the **Stephen Avenue Walk,** is along Stephen Avenue, which is 8th Avenue Southwest, between 1st Street Southeast and 4th Street Southwest. From 6am to 6pm daily, it's a pedestrian only street.

At **The Core** (8th Ave. SW, between 2nd St. and 4th St., 403/441-4940, www.coreshopping.ca, 9:30am-6pm Mon.-Wed. and Sat., 9:30am-8pm Thurs.-Fri., noon-5pm Sun.), a shopping mall on Stephen Avenue, Holt Renfrew and Brooks Brothers share space with other

Stampede Park hosts the annual Calgary Stampede.

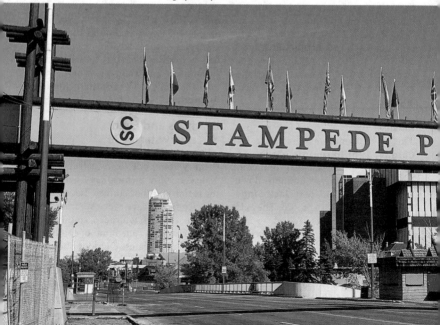

Canadian and international chains. Make your way to the top floor for the secret-feeling **Devonian Gardens** (free), a sky-lit indoor park with benches, café tables, and lots of greenery, including more than 10,000 shrubs, 500 palm trees, and a living wall.

Wander the **17th Avenue District** (www.17thave.ca), along 17th Avenue Southwest between 1st and 14th Streets, for funky independent clothing and specialty shops, but even more for its cool cafés and hip restaurants.

Across the Louise Bridge from downtown, the brick storefronts in **Kensington Village** (www.visitkensington.com) house an eclectic mix of bookstores, food businesses, and independent boutiques. The neighborhood's hub is near the intersection of Kensington Road and 10th Street Northwest.

Western Wear
Founded in 1901, **Riley & McCormick Western Wear** (220 8th Ave. SW,

403/228-4024 or 800/661-1585, www.realcowboys.com, 9am-6pm Mon.-Wed. and Sat., 9am-8pm Thurs.-Fri., noon-5pm Sun.) stocks shirts, jeans, hats, boots, and other "real cowboy" stuff. In addition to their downtown location, they have a branch at the Calgary Airport (departures level, Main Terminal, 403/250-8830, 7am-9pm daily).

If you're in town for the Stampede, of course you need cowboy boots. Calgary's longstanding supplier of proper western footwear is the **Alberta Boot Co.** (50 50th Ave. SE, 403/263-4623, www.albertaboot.com, 9am-9pm Mon.-Fri., 9am-6pm Sat., 11am-4pm Sun.). They stock thousands of pairs, and they also make custom boots to order. Prices start at around $350 a pair.

Another essential Stampede accessory is a cowboy hat. Known for creating the white hat that's become a symbol of the Calgary Stampede, **Smithbilt Hats** (1103 12th St. SE, 403/244-9131 or 800/661-1354, www.smithbilthats.com, 9am-5pm Mon.-Fri.) is a long-established vendor who can outfit your head in proper Calgary style.

Books
In a building that once housed a branch of Calgary's library, **Pages on Kensington** (1135 Kensington Rd. NW, 403/283-6655, www.pageskensington.com, 11am-6pm Mon.-Wed. and Sat., 11am-7pm Thurs.-Fri., noon-5pm Sun.), a classic independent bookstore, sells thousands of titles and hosts readings and other literary events.

Another independent bookseller, **Shelf Life Books** (1302 4th St. SW, 403/265-1033, www.shelflifebooks.ca, 10am-8pm Mon.-Fri., 10am-6pm Sat., noon-6pm Sun.) is in the Beltline neighborhood just south of downtown.

For food-related titles, visit **The Cookbook Co. Cooks** (722 11 Ave. SW, 403/265-6066, www.cookbookcooks.com, 10am-8pm Mon.-Fri., 10am-5:30pm

Sat., noon-5pm Sun.), a bookstore that also offers **cooking classes.**

Gourmet Goodies

Janice Beaton Fine Cheese (1017 16th Ave. SW, 403/229-0900, www.janicebeaton.com, 10am-6pm Sun.-Mon., 9am-6pm Tues.-Wed., 9am-7pm Thurs.-Fri., 9am-6pm Sat.) sells cheeses from near and far, along with pâtés, salads, and other prepared foods. They'll pack fancy picnic baskets for, well, fancy picnics.

Besides selling wine, beer, and spirits from near and far, **Kensington Wine Market** (1257 Kensington Rd. NW, 403/283-8000 or 888/283-9004, www.kensingtonwinemarket.com, 10am-8pm Mon.-Wed. and Sat., 10am-9pm Thurs.-Fri., noon-6pm Sun.) holds regular evening **tasting events.** Check their website or call for schedule and prices.

Outdoor Gear

Calgary's branch of **MEC** (Mountain Equipment Co-op, 830 10th Ave. SW, 403/269-2420, 10am-9pm Mon.-Fri., 9am-6pm Sat., 11am-5pm Sun. mid-May-early Sept., 10am-7pm Mon.-Wed., 10am-9pm Thurs.-Fri., 9am-6pm Sat., 11am-5pm Sun. early Sept.-mid-May), the nationwide outdoor gear chain, can supply clothing and equipment for hiking, cycling, camping, and other active pursuits.

Out There Adventure Centre (151 8th Ave. SW, 403/263-9651, www.outtherestore.com, 10am-6pm Mon.-Wed., 10am-8pm Thurs.-Fri., 10am-6pm Sat., 11am-5pm Sun.) sells clothing, packs and travel bags, and shoes for outdoor adventures from its downtown shop.

Sports and Recreation

Cycling

Calgary has 500 miles (800 kilometers) of pedestrian and cycling paths that you can follow throughout the city, one of the longest urban pathway networks in North America. A good introduction to cycling in the city is to ride along the **Bow River Pathway** that follows the river through downtown Calgary.

Rent bikes from **Eau Claire Rapid Rent** (200 Barclay Parade SW, 403/444-5845, May-Sept., one hour $10-15, full-day $40-60) at the Eau Claire Market, near the Bow River Pathway, or from **Bike Bike** (1501A 17 Ave. SW, 403/457-2453, www.bikebike.ca, mid-Apr.-Sept., one hour $8, full-day $35) south of downtown.

★ River Surfing

Here's a unique sport: In landlocked downtown Calgary, you can try **river surfing** where the Bow River has formed a permanent wave underneath the 10th Street Bridge. In summer, **Rocky Mountain River Surfing** (www.rockymountainriversurfing.com, lesson $80, board rental $20, wetsuit rental $20) offers two-hour lessons that get you started on the river; call or check the website for more details and schedules.

Winter Sports

Skate where the Olympians skated at the **Olympic Oval** (2500 University Dr. NW, 403/220-7954, www.oval.ucalgary.ca, adults $7, seniors and ages 6-17 $4.75, families $18.50), which was one of the venues for the 1988 Winter Olympic Games. It's on the University of Calgary campus northwest of downtown; you can take the C-Train **Red Line 201** (Tuscany) to University station.

At WinSport's **Canada Olympic Park** (88 Canada Olympic Rd. SW, 403/247-5452, www.winsport.ca), you can try out an Olympic bobsled, slide down the luge track, or go downhill or cross-country skiing or ice-skating.

Spectator Sports

Calgary's National Hockey League team is the **Calgary Flames** (403/777-4646 or 888/535-2637, www.flames.nhl.com), who play from October through April at the **Scotiabank Saddledome** (555

Saddledome Rise SE). When they score a goal, watch for actual flames to shoot up toward the ceiling.

If you'd like to see what the professional Canadian Football League is about, go see the city's CFL team, the **Calgary Stampeders** (403/289-0258, www.stampeders.com) at McMahon Stadium (1817 Crowchild Trail NW), near the University of Calgary campus.

Accommodations

Many Calgary accommodations cater to business travelers during the week, so except during holidays or the annual Calgary Stampede, lodging rates often drop on weekends when road warriors go home. Shop for deals on the hotels' websites directly, particularly if you can be flexible with your dates.

$150-250
Calling itself a "boutique motel," the **Centro Motel** (4540 16th Ave. NW, 403/288-6658, www.centromotel.com, $159-169 d) was built in the 1960s, but its 30 renovated rooms are much cooler than its roadside surroundings on the city's northwest side suggest. They all have white bedding, dark wood furnishings, and updated baths, along with flat-screen TVs, mini fridges, and Keurig coffeemakers. Rooms aren't large, so they're better suited to couples than families. Rates include Wi-Fi, North American phone calls, parking, and a light continental breakfast. The motel is about 20-minutes' drive from downtown.

On the University of Calgary campus northwest of downtown, the stylish ★ **Hotel Alma** (169 University Gate NW, 403/220-3203 or 877/498-3203, www.hotelalma.ca, $175-215 d, parking $10 per day) is a modern seven-story hotel. The best rooms are the one-bedroom suites on the top floor, with king beds and separate living rooms with a pullout sofa. Most of the guest rooms are more compact, with one queen bed, a lounge chair, and a work desk. All units have mini fridges, microwaves, and coffeemakers. There's no air-conditioning, but the windows open. Wi-Fi and North American phone calls are included, as is the continental breakfast served in the lobby-level Bistro Alma, which offers light meals (grilled *paninis,* soups, pastries) and drinks later in the day. Guests can use the nearby university fitness facility, with an Olympic-size pool; the Olympic Oval, also a short walk away, has public ice-skating. The hotel is a 10- to 15-minute walk from the C-Train's University station that can take you downtown in 15 minutes.

Much nicer than most of the chain motels that cluster in the Motel Village near the University of Calgary, **Aloft Calgary University** (2359 Banff Trail NW, 403/289-1973, www.aloftcalgaryuniversity.com, $165-219 d, parking $10) is a sociable spot, with a pool table and iPads in the lobby, weekly live music in the WXYZ Bar, and a once-a-week "mix and mingle" event with complimentary beer and appetizers. A trendy pool in an indoor courtyard is outfitted with lounge chairs and private cabanas. Other facilities include a 24-hour fitness room, a spa, and guest laundry. The 143 guest rooms across three floors are decorated with colorful Calgary-themed artwork and white linens accented with multicolored pillows. Rooms feature work desks, flat-screen TVs, coffeemakers, safes, and fridges. Rates include a hot buffet breakfast. The hotel is one block from the Banff Trail C-Train station.

A good-value downtown lodging, the 35-story all-suite **International Hotel** (220 4th Ave. SW, 403/265-9600 or 800/661-8627, www.internationalhotel.ca, $199-449 d, parking $29) opened in 1970, though it's since been updated with cherry-hued furnishings, white bedding, an indoor pool, and free Wi-Fi. The studio suites are comfortable, with separate sitting and sleeping areas, plus a wet bar with a fridge; the spacious two-bedroom units could easily accommodate a family or group of friends. Rates include a hot breakfast buffet. Popular with tour groups, the International can feel chaotic at times, but the central location makes up for it.

Though it's somewhat out-of-the-way southeast of downtown, **Hotel Blackfoot** (5940 Blackfoot Trail SE, 403/252-2253 or 800/661-1151, www.hotelblackfoot. com, $159-239 d) offers 193 comfortable, modern rooms at reasonable rates that include Wi-Fi, local calls, and parking. The standard units on the first through fifth floors have safes tucked into the night table drawers, mini fridges, teakettles, coffeemakers, and modern baths with rain showers. The sixth-floor Element rooms (typically $30 more than the standard units) have Keurig coffeemakers, robes, nightly turndown service, and a grab-and-go breakfast of yogurt, pastries, and fruit. The seventh-floor "Club" rooms add a private lounge with continental breakfast and evening appetizers. The heated pool is outdoors in a private courtyard; the fitness center, with several cardio machines and free weights, overlooks the pool. Dining and drinking outlets include Green's Restaurant, which serves a morning buffet, a sports bar, and a comedy club.

Over $250

Three blocks south of the Calgary Tower, in the Beltline neighborhood, ★ **Hotel Arts** (119 12th Ave. SW, 403/266-4611, www.hotelarts.ca, $229-429 d, parking weekday $24-30, weekend $10) lives up to its name. The 12-story property features works by Canadian artists throughout, and it's a popular place for musicians and other performers to stay. You can lounge around the courtyard pool, where a DJ spins tunes on weekends, or drop in for a poolside yoga class ($15). The contemporary guest rooms have all the expected amenities, including triple-sheeted duvets and work desks with ergonomic chairs, Wi-Fi included in the room rates, Keurig coffeemakers, and safes. Breakfast, lunch, and dinner are served in the **Yellow Door Bistro** (6:30am-10pm Mon.-Thurs., 6:30am-11pm Fri., 7am-11pm Sat.-Sun., mains breakfast $10-24, lunch $14-25, dinner $16-35), which also offers an excellent weekend brunch; the **Raw Bar** lounge whips up handcrafted cocktails and Vietnamese-influenced sharing plates.

From the illuminated marble check-in desk to the purple lounge chairs in the 143 modern guest rooms, ★ **Hotel Le Germain Calgary** (899 Centre St. SW, 403/264-8990 or 877/362-8990, www.legermainhotels.com, $279-359 d, parking weekday $40, weekend $10) is one stylish lodging. In a centrally located downtown tower, even the standard rooms are spacious, measuring 450 square feet (42 square meters), with honey-hued furniture, down comforters, rain showers, and Nespresso machines. There's no pool, but you can work out in the huge top-floor fitness center with windows overlooking downtown or relax in the **Santé Spa.** Rates include a generous breakfast buffet and Wi-Fi. The on-site restaurant is the well-regarded **CHARCUT Roast House** (11am-11pm Mon.-Wed., 11am-1am Wed.-Fri., 5pm-1am Sat., 5pm-10pm Sun., mains lunch $15-29, dinner $28-26), which also manages the sleek lobby lounge.

Staff deliver a coffee and tea tray with a morning newspaper to your room at the intimate boutique **Kensington Riverside Inn** (1126 Memorial Dr. NW, 403/228-4442 or 877/313-3733, www.kensington-riversideinn.com, $219-449 d, parking $15 per day), a 19-room lodging where you might feel like a guest at a stately manor house. The modern rooms (some with fireplaces) feel understated, with dark-gray upholstery and rich woods; the granite baths are luxurious, with robes and slippers waiting when you come out of the soaker tub or rain shower. Rates include Wi-Fi, local phone calls, and a $20 pp food and beverage credit that you can use toward breakfast, drinks, or dinner (handy if you can't face a big morning meal), served at **Chef's Table** (7am-10am and 5:30pm-9:30pm Mon.-Fri., 8am-1pm and 5:30pm-9:30pm Sat., 8am-1pm Sun., mains breakfast $11-21, dinner $26-38), the petite French-inspired dining room. You can stroll across the bridge to downtown or cruise off on one of the complimentary bikes.

In a former 1980s apartment building that was completely gutted, soundproofed, and updated, the **Hotel Elan** (1122 16th Ave. SW, 403/229-2040 or 855/666-6612, www.hotelelan.ca, $249 d, $309-399 suites, parking $18 per day) is one block from the 17th Avenue shopping and dining district. The standard rooms, at 250 square feet, are small but smart, with fun features like heated toilet seats and heated bath floors, as well as mini fridges and Keurig coffeemakers. Larger one-bedroom units add a living room with a sleep sofa; the two-bedroom units are nearly 1,000 square feet (93 square meters), and some have their own workout space with a recumbent bike and yoga mat. Rates include deluxe continental breakfast, Wi-Fi, and international phone calls; several nights a week there's a free evening social hour with local craft beer, wine, and appetizers.

A traditional downtown luxury hotel, the **Fairmont Hotel Palliser** (133 9th Ave. SW, 403/262-1234 or 866/540-4477, www. fairmont.com, $299-549 d, parking weekdays $42, weekends $30) opened in 1914, and in the lobby, the sparkling chandeliers, red velvet lounge chairs, and stone archways recall that bygone era. The indoor pool still has its traditional black and white tiles, though the health club is modern and there's an on-site spa. The 407 guest rooms on 12 stories feel classic; the baths are generally small, although

---

Top to bottom: Hotel Alma, on the University of Calgary campus; the stylish lobby at the Kensington Riverside Inn; sweet and savory pastries at Sidewalk Citizen Bakery.

most have natural light. Wi-Fi is included for Fairmont President's Club members, the frequent stay program that's free to join, so there's no reason to pay the $14.95 per day connection charge. The **Rimrock,** the hotel's formal dining room, serves breakfast, dinner, and a popular weekend brunch; more casual meals are available in the **Oak Room lounge.**

Food

Groceries and Markets

With more than 80 vendors, the year-round **Calgary Farmers Market** (510 77th Ave. SE, 403/240-9113, www.calgaryfarmersmarket.ca, 9am-5pm Thurs.-Sun.) sells Alberta products like bison jerky, gouda cheese, and locally grown produce, alongside prepared food and crafts.

Cafés, Bakeries, and Light Bites

Calgary's most delectable breads, pastries, and other baked goods come out of the ovens at ★ **Sidewalk Citizen Bakery** (Simmons Bldg., 618 Confluence Way SE, 403/457-2245, www.sidewalkcitizenbakery.com, 8am-6pm Mon.-Fri., 8:30am-6pm Sat.-Sun., mains $7-13) in the East Village. Try a *bureka,* an Israeli puff pastry baked with cheese, stuffed with egg, and served with *harissa.* They make sandwiches on house-made sourdough, including tuna confit with preserved lemon or shaved ham with arugula and kale. Naturally, there are sweets, too, including croissants, brownies, and single-serving cakes. They have another location in the Kensington neighborhood inside the Sunnyside Natural Food market (338 10th St. NW, 403/460-9065, 9am-8pm Mon.-Fri., 9am-7pm Sat., 9am-6pm Sun.).

If you're serious about your coffee, you should meet Phil & Sebastian: **Phil & Sebastian Coffee Roasters** (Simmons Bldg., 618 Confluence Way SE, 587/353-2268, www.philsebastian.com, 6:30am-9pm Mon.-Wed., 6:30am-11pm

brunch at the Yellow Door Bistro

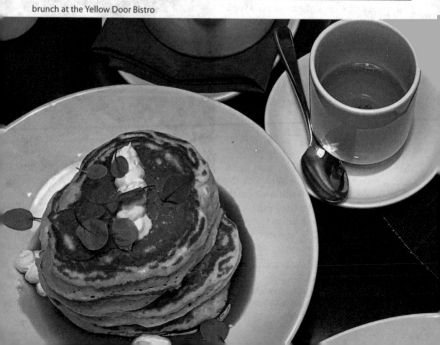

Thurs.-Fri., 7:30am-11pm Sat., 7:30am-9pm Sun.), that is. They roast their own beans and offer coffee tasting flights at their East Village location. They have additional branches in the Mission neighborhood (2207 4th St. SW, 403/245-1111, 6:30am-9pm Mon.-Fri., 7am-9pm Sat., 7am-6pm Sun.) and the Marda Loop (2043 33rd Ave. SW, 403/686-1221, 6:30am-9pm Mon.-Fri., 7:30am-9pm Sat., 7:30am-6pm Sun.), among others.

Since 1982, **Higher Ground Café** (1126 Kensington Rd., 403/270-3780, www.highergroundcafe.ca, 7am-11pm Mon.-Thurs., 7am-midnight Fri., 8am-midnight Sat., 8am-11pm Sun.) has been giving the Kensington neighborhood its caffeine fix from early morning to late at night. The brews are all fair trade and organic, and the atmosphere is laid-back.

Contemporary

Model Milk (308 17th Ave. SW, 403/265-7343, www.modelmilk.ca, 5pm-1am daily, small plates $15-20, larger plates

$24-36, 4-course family-style supper $40) occupies a former dairy, providing the exposed brick walls and heritage pedigree to back up the imaginative modern fare. The old dairymen would never have supped on barbecue quail with beer granola, sweetbreads with anchovy cream, halibut with Chinese broccoli and Manila clams, or any of the other imaginative dishes, though they might have appreciated the multicourse Sunday supper served family-style.

Under the same ownership as Model Milk, ★ **Pigeonhole** (306 17th Ave. SW, 403/452-4694, www.pigeonholeyyc.ca, 4pm-late Mon.-Sat., sharing plates $11-45), this newer sibling next door, is rather hard to pigeonhole, but the ever-inventive small plates, served on green marble tables in this buzzing room, are among Calgary's most exciting tastes. Prime your palate for chewy beets with goat cheese meringue, salted cod crepes with pickled onion, charred cabbage mounded with shredded mimolette cheese, or a particularly rich and creamy chicken-liver mousse. Fun cocktails and wines from around the world keep things even livelier.

Long considered one of Calgary's best restaurants, ★ **River Café** (25 Prince's Island Park, 403/261-7670, www.river-cafe.com, 11am-10pm Mon.-Fri., 10am-10pm Sat.-Sun., mains lunch $15-26, dinner $32-52, brunch $16-26), overlooking the river on a downtown island, is still at the top of its game. The room is warm, almost rustic, and the gracious staff makes you feel at home. The kitchen lives and breathes seasonal Canadian cuisine, so if you haven't sampled Alberta beef, try it here, where it might come with grilled new potatoes and Okanagan peaches, or with caramelized parsley root and wild ramps. The prairie pickerel with lobster mushrooms, or a terrine of winter squash, glazed carrots, and wild rice, might also tempt. To finish? Maple wild rice pudding, plum pavlova with almond cream, or a perfect dark chocolate truffle.

The wine list is strong on Canadian labels, along with selections from across the globe.

Take an alley, add a shipping container and a few picnic tables, then serve indulgent bar snacks like salted chicken skin and duck fat potato chips paired with fun cocktails and weird beers, and you have the recipe for the hip **Container Bar** (1131 Kensington Rd. NW, 403/457-4148, www.container-baryyc.com, 4pm-10pm Mon., 11:30am-10pm Tues.-Thurs., 11:30am-midnight Fri., 10am-midnight Sat., 10am-10pm Sun., mains $15-26), in a lane next to Brasserie Kensington (a French bistro, which has the same owners). It's not just a crazy-munchies idea, though; excellent sandwiches like a chicken club, updated with juicy thigh meat, bacon, and gruyère, creative salads, and several variations on the *poutine* theme give it serious dining credentials, too. Outside of summer or in uncertain weather, call or check their Twitter feed @Container_Bar to confirm that they're open.

For a hotel brunch that goes beyond the same-old thing, go behind the yellow door. The **Yellow Door Bistro** (119 12th Ave. SW, 403/206-9585, www.yellowdoorbistro.ca, 6:30am-10pm Mon.-Thurs., 6:30am-11pm Fri., 7am-11pm Sat.-Sun., mains breakfast $10-24, lunch $14-25, dinner $16-35), the comfortably trendy restaurant at the Hotel Arts, serves a weekend brunch that will kickstart your day with a duck confit omelet, a changing choice of pancakes, and salads like hibiscus-cured steelhead layered with butter lettuce, endive, and charred grapefruit. The rest of the day, the bistro fare is interesting enough for foodies but versatile enough for a business meal. The restaurant's enomatic wine system (that preserves open bottles) lets you sample wines in one-, three-, and five-ounce pours.

While a restaurant that butchers its own meats, cures charcuterie, and makes pickles and preserves could remind you of Grandmother's kitchen, **CHARCUT Roast House** (101-899 Centre St. SW, 403/984-2180, www.charcut.com, 11am-11pm Mon.-Tues., 11am-1am Wed.-Fri., 5pm-1am Sat., 5pm-10pm Sun., mains lunch $15-29, dinner $28-26) is anything but old-fashioned. Located in the same building as the Hotel Le Germain Calgary, this chic downtown dining spot does handle its local ingredients with care but shakes off the apron strings with steak served with chimichurri and wild arugula, bison brisket with beech mushrooms and boar bacon, or the lunchtime rotisserie chicken sandwich with *piri piri* aioli. Homey desserts like preserved fruit in a jar with whipped cheesecake or french toast pie with bourbon ice cream would make Grandma proud.

A spin-off of CHARCUT Roast House, **Charbar** (Simmons Bldg., 618 Confluence Way SE, 403/452-3115, www.charbar.ca, lunch 11:30am-5pm Mon.-Fri., dinner from 5pm daily, brunch 10:30am-3pm Sat.-Sun., mains lunch $15-22, dinner $15-49, brunch $11-36), in the East Village, is built around an Argentine wood-fired grill that turns out deep-dish pizza and grilled meats to pair with ceviches, salads, and small plates to share. In mild weather, have your cocktails up on the rooftop bar.

Asian

Crispy tofu with pork belly and maple-sesame kimchi, gochujang-glazed fried chicken with cheddar grits, and Brussels sprouts seasoned with lemongrass and Chinese sausage are just a few of the imaginative Korean tapas you can sample at hip **Anju** (344 17th Ave. SW, 403/460-3341, www.anju.ca, lunch 11am-5pm Mon.-Fri., dinner 5pm-1am daily, brunch 11am-5pm Sat.-Sun., small plates lunch $3-16, dinner $3-30), which serves what it describes as "Korean drinking food." Speaking of drinking, there's *soju,* beers from near and far, and unusual cocktails, like the Doctor's Orders, made with rye, ginger liqueur, Korean herbal tea, and

🔷 Side Trip: A Day with the Dinosaurs

Drive east from Calgary and you're in the prairies, with farmland undulating along the gentle hills. Then as you turn slightly north and approach the small town of Drumheller, the terrain changes again. Suddenly, you're in the **Canadian Badlands.**

Known for its unusual hoodoo rock formations and rocky canyons, Canada's Badlands region also has some of the world's most extensive deposits of dinosaur fossils.

Survey the Badlands landscapes and discover their dinosaur legacy on a day trip from Calgary. Take Highway 2 north to Highway 567 east to Highway 9 east to Drumheller, which is 87 miles (140 kilometers) northeast of Calgary. It's less than two hours' drive from the city to the dinosaurs.

Royal Tyrrell Museum

In 1884, Canadian geologist Joseph Burr Tyrrell put Alberta on the dinosaur map when he unearthed the 70-million-year-old skull of a carnivorous dinosaur near Drumheller. Tyrrell's discovery was christened *Albertosaurus sarcophagus*, the "flesh-eating lizard from Alberta."

Named for this geologist, the **Royal Tyrrell Museum** (Midland Provincial Park, Hwy. 838, Drumheller, 403/823-7707 or 888/440-4240, www.tyrrellmuseum. com, 9am-9pm daily mid-May-Aug., 10am-5pm daily Sept., 10am-5pm Tues.-Sun. Oct.-mid-May, adults $15, seniors $12, ages 7-17 $7.50, families $40) is Canada's only museum devoted to paleontology. Highlights include a gigantic *Tyrannosaurus rex* skeleton and the partial skull of an *Atrociraptor,* discovered nearby.

Outside the museum, follow the trails through the hoodoo-filled landscape in **Midland Provincial Park** (www. albertaparks.ca), or take a guided one-mile (1.6-kilometer) **Seven Wonders of the Badlands** walk (11am and 2:30pm Sat.-Sun. mid-May-late June, 11am, 1:30pm, and 4:30pm daily late June-Aug., 2:30pm daily Sept., $5) that museum staff lead through the desert-like terrain. The museum also offers fossil-collecting workshops and other kid-friendly programs.

The museum is four miles (6 kilometers) northwest of Drumheller on Highway 838. As you come into town, follow the museum signs, and turn left (west) onto Highway 838 (N. Dinosaur Trail).

The World's Largest T. Rex?

It's hard to pass through Drumheller without stopping for a photo with this kitschy attraction: the **World's Largest Dinosaur** (60 1 Ave. W., Drumheller, 403/823-8100 or 866/823-8100, www. worldslargestdinosaur.com, 10am-5:30pm daily, over age 5 $3, families $10).

This steel and fiberglass *Tyrannosaurus rex* stands 86 feet (26 meters) high, more than four times bigger than an actual T. Rex would have been. You can climb up inside the dinosaur to its mouth; there are 106 stairs to the top.

The dino is located off Highway 56, next to the **Drumheller Visitor Information Centre** (60 1 Ave. W., Drumheller, 403/823-1331 or 866/823-8100, www.traveldrumheller.com).

Other Badlands Attractions

Continue along Highway 838 past the Royal Tyrrell Museum to **Horsethief Canyon,** with its multihued rock layers. On Highway 9, about 10 minutes' drive west of Drumheller, receding glaciers carved rock formations into a "U" shape, or horseshoe, in striking **Horseshoe Canyon.**

You can hike into both of these dramatic canyons or simply enjoy the views from above. Hikers should wear sturdy shoes, bring sunscreen, and carry water. Summer temperatures in the canyons can approach 104°F (40°C).

ginseng bitters. It's a fun spot for sipping and grazing.

The ever-so-stylish **Raw Bar at Hotel Arts** (119 12th Ave. SW, 403/206-9565, www.rawbaryyc.ca, 4pm-11pm Mon.-Thurs., 4pm-midnight Fri.-Sat., small plates $7-19, larger plates $18-31) riffs on Vietnamese flavors to create Asian-inspired sharing plates to match with classic and more unusual cocktails. Once you've settled in with a drink, like the Derelict, which blends vodka, lychee liqueur, lemon and pineapple juices, and a spiced plum-clove jelly, or their version of bubble tea, where popping lychee pearls enliven prosecco, it's time to eat. Order tastes for the table, like crispy taro and mango slaw, steamed buns filled with beef short ribs, or squid *a la plancha* served with preserved lime aioli.

Italian

Half gourmet market and half bustling Italian dining room, **Mercato** (2224 4th Ave. SW, 403/263-5535, www.mercatogourmet.com, market 9:30am-7pm daily, restaurant 11:30am-2pm and 5:30pm-10pm daily, mains $15-49), in the Mission district south of downtown, sells deli sandwiches, cheeses, and salads to go and serves updated Italian classics at long bars lining the upscale dining space. Specialties consist of traditional pastas, like *bucatini alla carbonara* or handmade gnocchi with spicy sausage and rapini, and grilled dishes, including swordfish with Sicilian tomatoes and caper berries or balsamic-glazed lamb. Dishes are sized and served family-style, designed to share.

Vegetarian

Alberta beef is ubiquitous on local menus, which may be why Calgary vegetarians considered it a coup when **The Coup** (924 17th Ave. SW, 403/541-1041, www.the-coup.ca, 11am-3pm and 5pm-10:30pm Mon.-Thurs., 11am-3pm and 5pm-11pm Fri., 9am-3pm and 5pm-11pm Sat.,

Calgary Transit's C-Train

9am-3pm and 5pm-9pm Sun.) opened in the 17th Avenue district. Fresh juices, *kombucha,* and cocktails pair well with the world-roaming vegetarian menu of small plates, salads, and heartier dishes, including Vietnamese-style subs piled with cheese, eggplant, carrots, and kimchi, or falafel quesadillas, with falafel, hummus, tahini, feta cheese, pickles, and veggies grilled into a tortilla.

Information and Services

Visitor Information

Tourism Calgary's Airport Visitor Information Centre (2000 Airport Rd. NE, 403/735-1234, www.visitcalgary.com, 6am-11pm daily), located on the arrivals level (opposite baggage carousels 7 and 8) at the Calgary International Airport has travel information and maps, as well as free Wi-Fi. If you're heading for the

national parks, you can purchase a Parks Canada Annual Discovery Pass here.

The **Tourism Calgary Downtown Visitor Information Centre** (120-101 9 Ave. SW, 403/750-2362, www.visitcalgary.com, 9am-7pm Mon.-Fri., 9am-5pm Sat.-Sun. June-Sept., 9am-5pm daily Oct.-May) provides travel information and has free Wi-Fi.

The provincial tourism agency, **Travel Alberta** (800/252-3782, www.travelalberta.com) has detailed information on its website about planning a trip to Calgary, the Canadian Rockies, and elsewhere in the region. They also publish provincial visitor guides, available online or at visitors centers throughout the area.

Media and Communications

Calgary's local daily newspapers include the *Calgary Sun* (www.calgarysun.com) and *Calgary Herald* (www.calgaryherald.com). The daily Toronto-based *Globe and Mail* (www.theglobeandmail.com) covers news across Canada, including Calgary, as does the **CBC** (www.cbc.ca), Canada's public television and radio outlet.

Avenue Calgary (www.avenuecalgary.com) is a monthly lifestyle magazine with extensive restaurant coverage and features about city neighborhoods, people, and activities.

Medical Services

The Calgary area has several hospitals that can provide emergency medical care to visitors, including **Peter Lougheed General Hospital** (3500 26th Ave. NE, 403/291-8555, 24-hour emergency 403/291-8999, www.albertahealthservices.ca), **Foothills Medical Centre** (1403 29th St. NW, 403/670-1110, 24-hour emergency 403/670-1315, www.albertahealthservices.ca) on the University of Calgary campus, and **Rockyview General Hospital** (7007 14th St. SW, 403/541-3000, 24-hour emergency 403/541-3449, www.albertahealthservices.ca).

For emergency services or other medical issues for children ages 18 and younger, contact the **Alberta Children's Hospital** (2888 Shaganappi Trail NW, 403/955-7211, 24-hour emergency 403/229-7070, www.albertahealthservices.ca), near the University of Calgary.

Several of Calgary's **Shoppers Drug Mart** (www.shoppersdrugmart.ca) locations have 24-hour pharmacies, including the **North Hill Shopping Centre** (1632 14th Ave. NW, 403/289-6761), the **Chinook Centre** (6455 Macleod Trail S., 403/253-2424), and **McKnight Village** (5500 Falsbridge Dr. NE, 403/293-2560).

Getting Around

Calgary is divided into four quadrants: northwest, northeast, southwest, and southeast. Numbered avenues run east-west, while numbered streets go north-south. Both begin downtown.

Two rivers also define Calgary's geography. The Bow River runs through the center of the city; downtown is on the Bow's south bank. The Elbow River meanders into the city center from the southwest and joins the Bow east of downtown.

In the downtown area, you can get around easily on foot or using the city's light rail system. Thanks in part to its extremely changeable weather, Calgary has built the world's largest indoor pedestrian pathway network. Calgary's **+15 Skywalk** (www.calgary.ca) runs 11 miles (18 kilometers) through the downtown area, with weather-proof walkways between buildings 15 feet (5 meters) above the street (hence, the +15 name). Signs on the sidewalk can direct you to a +15 entrance. The City of Calgary publishes a +15 map that's available on its website and from the **Tourism Calgary Downtown Visitor Information Centre** (120-101 9 Ave. SW).

By Light Rail and Bus

Calgary Transit (403/262-1000, www.calgarytransit.com) runs the city's public transportation network, with two Light Rail Transit lines, known as the C-Train, and more than 160 bus routes. Use the **trip planner** function on the Calgary Transit website to plot your transit trip.

C-Train and bus schedules vary by route, but regular service on major routes begins between 5am and 5:30am and runs until 12:30am or 1am.

Transit Fares and Passes

Fares (adults $3.15, ages 6-17 $2.10) for the C-Train and buses are valid for 90 minutes.

Buy your C-Train ticket from the vending machines in the station before you board the train; machines accept coins, credit cards, and debit cards. If you're transferring from the C-Train to the bus, show the driver your validated ticket from the light rail. You don't have to purchase an additional bus ticket.

When you board a bus, you can pay cash for your ticket, but you need to have exact change.

You can buy transit tickets in advance at the **Calgary Transit Customer Service Centres** (Centre Street Platform, 125 7 Ave. SE, and Bow Parkade, 234 7 Ave. SW, 10am-5:30pm Mon.-Fri.), and at many convenience stores and other shops around the city. Tickets are sold individually or in books of 10. Insert your ticket into the fare box when you board the bus, or validate it using the machines in the C-Train station before boarding the light rail.

If you're going to use transit extensively during a single day, purchase a **day pass** (adults $9.50, ages 6-17 $6.75).

By Light Rail

Calgary's **C-Train Light Rail System** (www.calgarytransit.com) has two lines: the **Red Line/Route 201** (Tuscany/Somerset-Bridlewood), which goes to the city's northwest and southeast neighborhoods, and the **Blue Line/Route 202** (69th Street/Saddletowne), which crosses the city between west and northeast.

Both C-Train lines run through the city center along 7th Avenue, where you can ride **free downtown.** The free zone is between the Downtown West/Kerby (10th St. SW) and City Hall (Macleod Trail SE) stations.

By Bus

Calgary Transit's **bus 300** (403/262-1000, www.calgarytransit.com, 5am-midnight daily, one-way $9.50) can take you between the airport and downtown Calgary. These express buses, which have a different fare structure than the standard buses, run every 20 to 30 minutes; the trip takes 40 to 50 minutes.

For other routes, the **trip planner** on the Calgary Transit website (www.calgarytransit.com) can help you figure out how to get to your destination.

At any bus stop, text the posted stop number to 74000, and you'll receive a reply listing the next buses scheduled to arrive at that stop.

By Car

Highway 1, the Trans-Canada Highway, runs east-west across Calgary's north side, where it becomes 16th Avenue. Highway 2, also known as the Queen Elizabeth II Highway, is the main north-south route to the city, extending north to Edmonton and beyond, and south to the Montana border.

Other major roadways include the Crowchild Trail (Hwy. 1A), which crosses northwest Calgary and then turns south; Macleod Trail, which runs south from downtown; and Glenmore Trail (Hwy. 8), which can take you east-west through Calgary's southern suburbs.

Downtown Calgary is south of the Bow River, between 1st and 9th Avenues Southwest. A rail line crosses the city south of 9th Avenue Southwest, so some downtown streets stop at 9th Avenue, rather than continuing southbound.

Parking

Calgary's on-street **parking meters** ($1-5 per hour) operate 9am-6pm Monday-Saturday. Parking is free after 6pm and all day Sunday. Rates vary by location. You can park at most metered spaces for up to two hours.

You can look up meter rates and typical parking availability in different areas using the **Calgary Parking** website (www.calgaryparking.com). This site also shows the location and prices for parking garages and parking lots around the city.

By Taxi

Calgary taxis are metered, with a $3.80 base fare and 20 cents for each additional 120 meters. Most trips within the downtown area will cost less than $10. A cab between the Calgary International Airport and downtown averages $40-45.

Local taxi companies include **Associated Cab** (403/299-1111, www.associatedcab.ca) and **Checker Yellow Cabs** (403/299-9999, www.thecheckergroup.com).

Essentials

Getting There

For a trip to Vancouver and the Canadian Rockies, the main gateway cities, particularly for international travelers, are Vancouver, British Columbia, and Calgary, Alberta.

Getting to Vancouver
By Car
Coming from the United States, **I-5** takes you north from Seattle to the U.S.-Canada border. When you pass through border control, you'll be on **Highway 99** in British Columbia, which leads to metropolitan Vancouver.

The main east-west route across Canada is **Highway 1**, the Trans-Canada Highway. It's possible to follow Highway 1 from eastern Canada, Calgary, and the Canadian Rockies all the way to Vancouver; however, it's not the fastest route.

If you're coming from Calgary or Banff to Vancouver, follow Highway 1 west into British Columbia and continue west to the city of Kamloops. From Kamloops, take **Highway 5**, the Coquihalla Highway, southbound, toward Merritt and Hope. Highway 5 meets **Highway 3**, which you take westbound to rejoin **Highway 1** at the town of Hope and continue west to Vancouver.

From Jasper to Vancouver, the shortest route is to follow **Highway 16** west to **Highway 5**, where you turn south toward Kamloops. At Kamloops, continue south on **Highway 5**, to **Highway 3** west, to **Highway 1** west.

By Air
Vancouver International Airport (YVR, 3211 Grant McConachie Way, Richmond, 604/207-7077, www.yvr.ca) is a

major international gateway with flights from across Canada, the United States, Mexico, Europe, Asia, and the Pacific. The airport is located south of the city center in the suburb of Richmond; it's 25 minutes from the airport to downtown by public transit, taxi, or by car. All the major car rental companies have offices at the Vancouver airport.

By Train
Pacific Central Station (1150 Station St., Vancouver), near the intersection of Main and Terminal Streets on the edge of Chinatown, is Vancouver's main rail depot. It's also the city's long-distance bus station.

Amtrak
Amtrak (800/872-7245, www.amtrak. com), the U.S. passenger rail carrier, runs trains to Vancouver from Seattle, Washington, and Portland, Oregon. You can make connections in either Seattle or Portland to U.S. points farther south or east. Trains from Seattle (5.5 hours) operate twice a day; the direct Portland-Vancouver train (8 hours) runs once a day in each direction. These trains have electrical outlets and free Wi-Fi in both standard economy and business classes; the latter seats give you additional legroom.

Tip for cyclists: You can walk your bike onto the Seattle or Portland trains for a fee of just US$5.

VIA Rail
Canada's national passenger rail carrier, **VIA Rail** (514/989-2626 or 888/842-7245, www.viarail.ca), runs cross-country trains to Vancouver from Toronto. The major stops along the Toronto-Vancouver route of *The Canadian*, VIA Rail's flagship train, are Winnipeg (Manitoba), Saskatoon (Saskatchewan), Edmonton and Jasper (Alberta), and Kamloops (British Columbia).

If you do the 2,775-mile (4,466-kilometer) Toronto-to-Vancouver rail trip nonstop, it's a four-night, three-day

VIA Rail is Canada's national rail carrier.

journey. *The Canadian* operates three times a week in each direction from May through mid-October, and twice a week from mid-October through April. It's possible to get off en route and continue your journey on a subsequent train. For example, you could take the train from Toronto to Jasper in the Canadian Rockies, get off the train for two or three days (depending on the schedule), and catch the next train onward to Vancouver.

VIA Rail offers several classes of service on *The Canadian*. In **Economy class,** the cheapest option, you have a seat that reclines and access to a washroom (but no shower). Meals aren't included, although you can buy meals and snacks on the train or outside the train during a few brief stopovers.

A more comfortable alternative is **Sleeper Plus** class, where you have several choices of accommodations. The least expensive is a **berth,** which is a seat by day that converts into a bunk, shielded by a heavy curtain, at night; the bunks can be either a lower or upper unit. Berth passengers have access to men's and women's restrooms and private shower rooms in the corridor.

Another Sleeper Plus option is a **cabin,** which can sleep one, two, three, or four people. Cabins have their own toilets and sinks, and passengers can use the shower rooms in the corridor. Note that in the one-person cabin, the bed folds down over the toilet, so if you need to use the facilities during the night, you have to fold up your bed or use the restroom in the hallway.

The top-end sleeper accommodations are in **Prestige Sleeper** class, which gives you a more modern cabin with a private bathroom and shower. These units have an L-shaped leather couch by day with a Murphy bed for two that folds down at night.

All the Sleeper class fares include three meals a day in the dining car, nonalcoholic drinks, and access to a window-lined viewing car. You can also sit in the bar-snack car, with complimentary coffee, tea, fruit, and cookies.

Outside of the busy summer travel season, VIA Rail frequently offers discounts of up to 50 percent off their standard fares. Check their website or sign up for their newsletter to find out about seat sales. They also offer occasional last-minute travel deals, which are posted on the VIA Rail website (www.viarail.ca).

The Rocky Mountaineer

The **Rocky Mountaineer** (1755 Cottrell St., at Terminal Ave., Vancouver, 604/606-7245 or 877/460-3200, www.rockymountaineer.com, mid-Apr.-mid-Oct.) is a privately run luxury train that offers rail trips between Vancouver, Banff, Lake Louise, Jasper, and Calgary. You can travel round-trip from Vancouver to the Canadian Rockies and back, or you can book a one-way journey through the Rockies from Vancouver to Calgary (or vice versa). Another route starts in Seattle and stops in Vancouver before continuing to the Rockies. Rocky Mountaineer trains travel during the day and stop overnight in Kamloops, where you stay in a hotel, en route to or from the Rockies.

Unlike a standard train trip, many Rocky Mountaineer packages include activities that range from gondola rides to helicopter tours, as well as accommodations along the way. It's also possible to book a Rocky Mountaineer holiday that covers rail fare and accommodations only; for example, they offer two-day train trips between Vancouver and Lake Louise, Banff, or Jasper. Rail packages start at $1,699 pp and depend on the destinations, number of travel days, and the level of service and accommodations.

Rocky Mountaineer trains do not use Vancouver's Pacific Central Station, where VIA Rail and Amtrak trains depart; they have a separate depot nearby.

By Bus
Greyhound (800/661-8747, www.greyhound.ca) runs buses to Vancouver's **Pacific Central Station** (1150 Station St., Vancouver) from across Canada and from many U.S. cities, including direct service from Seattle.

Between Seattle and Vancouver, other bus services include **Bolt Bus** (877/265-8287, www.boltbus.com) and **Quick Shuttle** (604/940-4428 or 800/665-2122, www.quickcoach.com). Bolt Bus arrives and departs from Pacific Central Station, but Quick Shuttle stops at Canada Place and will also pick up or drop off passengers at a number of downtown hotels, with advance reservations.

Getting to Calgary
By Car
Highway 1, the Trans-Canada Highway, brings you to Calgary from Banff, Lake Louise, and points west in British Columbia. From the east, Highway 1 leads to Calgary from Medicine Hat (Alberta), Regina (Saskatchewan), Winnipeg (Manitoba), and eastern Canada.

Highway 2, also known as the Queen Elizabeth II Highway, is the main north-south route to Calgary. It extends north to Edmonton and beyond, and south to the United States border and the state of Montana.

By Air
You can fly to **Calgary International Airport** (YYC, 2000 Airport Rd. NE, 403/735-1200, http://yyc.com) from across Canada, from many U.S. cities, and from Amsterdam, Frankfurt, London, Paris, and Tokyo, among other cities. The airport is located on the city's northeast side, about a 20-minute drive from downtown.

By Train
Neither VIA Rail nor Amtrak have passenger service to Calgary. The closet VIA Rail passenger station is in Edmonton, 185 miles (300 kilometers) to the north.

The privately run **Rocky Mountaineer** (877/460-3200, www.rockymountaineer.com, mid-Apr.-mid-Oct.) offers luxury train trips that can start or end in Calgary and travel to Banff, Lake Louise, Jasper, and Vancouver. The Rocky Mountaineer also has a route that starts in Seattle, stops in Vancouver, and continues on to the Rockies and Calgary; you can do this trip from east to west as well.

By Bus
Greyhound (800/661-8747, www.greyhound.ca) runs buses to Calgary from many Canadian and U.S. destinations, including several buses daily between Calgary and **Banff** or **Lake Louise.**

Brewster Banff Airport Express (403/762-6700 or 866/606-6700, www.brewster.ca) runs buses from Banff to downtown Calgary hotels and to the Calgary international airport. The **Banff Airporter** (403/762-3330 or 888/449-2901, www.banffairporter.com) can take you from Banff to the Calgary airport as well.

Red Arrow (403/531-0350 or 800/232-1958, www.redarrow.ca) runs buses to Calgary from Edmonton and other cities in Alberta.

Road Rules

Car Rental

The major North American car rental companies have outlets at Vancouver International Airport and Calgary International Airport. They also have offices in downtown Vancouver, downtown Calgary, and in many smaller cities across British Columbia and Alberta.

Many agencies provide discounts for weekly rentals and additional discounts for rentals of a month or more. Some also offer discounts for members of the Canadian Automobile Association (CAA) or American Automobile Association (AAA).

If you're considering renting a car in the United States and driving it across the Canadian border, confirm with your car rental company in advance that you're allowed to drive out of the country. Make sure you have a copy of the rental contract handy at the border crossing.

RV Rental

Renting an RV is a popular way to travel across western Canada. Whether you rent a small van or a mega motor home, you're combining your transportation and lodging. The national and provincial parks, as well as privately run facilities across the west, have campgrounds where you can park for a night or more.

Some companies allow you to book one-way rentals. For example, you can pick up your RV in Vancouver, drive to the Canadian Rockies, and drop off the vehicle in Calgary, where you can depart from the international airport.

The following companies rent RVs in western Canada: **CanaDream RV Rentals** (888/480-9726, www.canadream.com), **Cruise Canada** (800/671-8042, www.cruisecanada.com), **Discount RV Rental** (866/669-9758, www.discountrv.biz), **Fraserway RV Rentals** (877/747-7947, www.fraserway.com), **Traveland RV** (800/922-6326, www.travelandrvcanada.com), and **Westcoast Mountain Campers** (888/608-8766, www.wcmcampers.com).

Driving Rules

In Canada, each province determines its rules of the road, so for a trip to the Canadian Rockies, you need to be aware of the laws in both British Columbia and Alberta. Differences between the provincial laws are typically minor but still worth knowing.

Driver's Licenses

If you have a valid driver's license from your home country, that license will be valid in British Columbia for up to six months and in Alberta for a year.

If your license is not in English, you should either obtain an International Driving Permit (IDP) in your home country, which will be valid for six months in B.C. or one year in Alberta, or have your license translated into English. Always carry both your driver's license and the IDP (or translation of your license) when you're driving.

Even if your license is in English, Alberta recommends that you obtain an International Driving Permit and carry it along with your driver's license.

Insurance

If you're driving a rented car in B.C. or Alberta, make sure you always carry a copy of the rental contract and proof of insurance.

If you're driving over the border from the United States, bring the car's registration forms and proof of insurance. Either carry the insurance policy itself or get a free **Canadian Non-Resident Insurance Card** from your insurance agent.

In both B.C. and Alberta, you must have a minimum of $200,000 in third-party liability coverage. Check with your insurance provider in your home country to ensure that you have sufficient insurance.

Speed Limits

Canada uses the metric system, so speed limits are posted in kilometers per hour.

In British Columbia, speed limits in urban areas are 50 km/h and those outside the metropolitan areas are 80 km/h, unless otherwise posted. On many B.C. highways, speed limits range from 90 to 120 km/h.

In Alberta, speed limits on all roads in urban areas are 50 km/h, on roadways outside the metropolitan areas are 80 km/h, and on provincial highways are 100 km/h, unless otherwise posted. On Alberta highways, the maximum speed limit is 110 km/h.

Traffic Signals

You can make a **right turn at a red light** in British Columbia and in Alberta (as long as you stop and make sure it's clear), unless it's otherwise posted.

A **flashing red traffic signal** is equivalent to a stop sign. It means you must stop, allow any cross traffic to proceed, and then you can proceed when it's safe to do so. A **flashing yellow traffic signal** is a warning light, advising drivers to use caution in the area.

A **flashing green traffic signal** indicates that the traffic light is pedestrian-activated. That is, the signal remains flashing green and cars can proceed as you would on a standard green signal, until a pedestrian who wants to cross the street presses the "walk" button. The signal will turn yellow and then red, indicating that traffic must stop to allow the pedestrian to cross.

Even when there is no traffic signal, drivers must stop for pedestrians **in a crosswalk.**

Electronic Devices

In both B.C. and Alberta, it's against the law to drive while using a **handheld cell phone** or other electronic device. No texting or emailing while you're driving!

Drivers may use a hands-free cell phone if it is voice activated; the device must be attached to the vehicle or the driver's body (using an earpiece in one ear only). Similarly, you can't program a Global Positioning System (GPS) while you're driving; you can issue voice commands, but you can't touch it.

Seat Belts

By law, **you must wear a seat belt** when you're driving in B.C. or Alberta.

In both provinces, infants must ride in rear-facing car seats until they are at least one year old and weigh 20 pounds (9 kilograms). When children outgrow these infant seats, they're required to sit in forward-facing car seats until they weigh at least 40 pounds (18 kilograms).

In B.C., children who weigh more than 40 pounds must sit in a booster seat with a seat belt until they are nine years old or at least 4 foot 9 (145 centimeters) tall. Alberta law does not require booster seats, but they're still recommended.

Road Conditions

To check current road conditions in British Columbia, visit **www.driveBC.ca** online or phone 800/550-4997.

In Alberta, visit **www.511Alberta.ca** or call 511, which is a toll-free call within the province.

Many of western Canada's highways pass through high mountain elevations, where it can snow at any time of year, even in the summer. Although heavy snow is uncommon outside the winter months, it's smart to check the weather forecast regularly.

When you're traveling through the mountains between October and March, your vehicle must be equipped with **winter tires.** Among the roads on which winter tires are required are the Sea-to-Sky Highway between Vancouver and Whistler, and many sections of Highways 1, 3, and 5 throughout B.C., as well as

Highway 1 and the Icefields Parkway in Alberta.

Maps and Tourist Information
Destination Canada (www.canada.travel) is the government of Canada's official guide to travel across the country.

British Columbia Visitors Centers
Destination B.C. (www.hellobc.com), British Columbia's provincial tourism agency, runs visitors centers across the province that provide maps and other travel information. The offices have public restrooms, and many offer free Wi-Fi.

If you're driving from the U.S. on I-5, you can get information from the visitors center at the **Peace Arch** (298 Hwy. 99, Surrey), as soon as you cross into Canada.

The **Vancouver Visitor Centre** (Plaza Level, 200 Burrard St.) is downtown, opposite Canada Place and the cruise ship terminal.

On Vancouver Island, look for visitors centers in **Victoria** (812 Wharf St.), **Nanaimo** (2450 Northfield Rd.), **Tofino** (1426 Pacific Rim Hwy.), and **Ucluelet** (2791 Pacific Rim Hwy.).

On the Sea-to-Sky Highway (Hwy. 99), get information at the visitors centers in **Squamish** (Squamish Adventure Centre, 38551 Loggers Lane) and **Whistler** (4230 Gateway Dr.).

En route between Vancouver and Kamloops or the Okanagan, there are B.C. visitors centers in **Hope** (919 Water Ave.) and **Merritt** (Hwy. 5 at Hwy. 97C).

Along Highway 1, heading toward the B.C. Rockies, there are visitors centers in **Kamloops** (1290 W. Trans-Canada Hwy.), **Revelstoke** (301 Victoria Rd. W.), and **Golden** (111 Golden Donald Upper Rd.).

In the Kootenays, you'll find visitors centers in **Radium Hot Springs** (7556 Main St. E.), **Invermere** (651 Hwy. 93/95 Cross Roads), **Fernie** (102 Hwy. 3), **Kaslo** (324 Front St.), and **Nelson** (91 Baker St.).

In the Okanagan, get your questions answered at visitors centers in **Kelowna** (544 Harvey Ave./Hwy. 97), **Penticton** (553 Vees Dr.), and **Osoyoos** (9912 Hwy. 3, at Hwy. 97).

Alberta Visitors Centers
In Alberta, you can pick up travel information at visitors centers operated by the provincial tourism agency, **Travel Alberta** (800/252-3782, www.travelalberta.com) and at local visitors centers around the province.

Alberta Visitor Centres are located at the **Calgary International Airport** (arrivals level, May-Sept.), and in the Rocky Mountain region, in **Canmore** (2801 Bow Valley Trail), **Field, B.C.** (Hwy. 1, May-Oct.) in Yoho National Park, and in **Hinton** (309 Gregg Ave., May-Oct.), on Highway 16 northeast of Jasper National Park.

There's also an Alberta Visitor Centre at **Crowsnest Pass** (Hwy. 3, Blairmore, May-Sept.) 3.7 miles (6 kilometers) east of the B.C.-Alberta border, and another near the Canada-U.S. border near **West Glacier, Montana** (Hwy. 2 at Going-to-the-Sun Rd., May-mid-Sept.).

Canadian Automobile Association
The **Canadian Automobile Association** (CAA, www.caa.ca) provides road maps for its members through its provincial chapters. It has reciprocal agreements with the **American Automobile Association** (AAA, www.aaa.com), so that AAA members can get maps and assistance in Canada. Members can order maps by mail or pick them up at local CAA offices.

The CAA's British Columbia chapter, the **B.C. Automobile Association** (BCAA, www.bcaa.com), has several offices in **Vancouver,** including their Cambie Village location (2301 Cambie St., at W. 7th Ave., Vancouver, 604/268-5600, 9am-6pm Mon.-Fri., 9am-5pm Sat.), **Victoria** (115-1644 Hillside Ave., Victoria, 250/414-8320, 9:30am-5:30pm Mon.-Sat., 11am-5:30pm Sun.), **Kamloops** (400-500 Notre Dame Dr., Kamloops, 250/852-4600, 9am-6pm Mon.-Fri., 9am-5pm

Sat.), **Kelowna** (18-1470 Harvey Ave., Kelowna, 250/870-4900, 9am-6pm Mon.-Fri., 9am-5pm Sat.), **Penticton** (100-2100 Main St., Penticton, 250/487-2450, 9am-6pm Mon.-Fri., 9am-5pm Sat.), and **Nelson** (596 Baker St., Nelson, 250/505-1720, 9am-5pm Mon.-Sat.)

The **Alberta Motor Association** (AMA, http://ama.ab.ca), the CAA's Alberta chapter, has several offices in Calgary. The **Calgary Main Office** (4700 17th Ave. SW, Calgary, 403/240-5300, 9am-6pm Mon.-Fri., 9am-5pm Sat.) is west of the city center, and they also have a **Calgary Downtown** location (Watermark Tower, 100-530 8th Ave. SW, 403/262-2345, 9am-5pm Mon.-Fri.).

Roadside Assistance

In an emergency, call **911** to reach police, fire, ambulance, or other emergency services. Never leave the scene of an accident without contacting the police.

The **Canadian Automobile Association** (CAA, www.caa.ca) provides roadside assistance for its members and for members of the **American Automobile Association** (AAA, www.aaa.com).

Visas and Officialdom

For the most up-to-date requirements for visitors coming to Canada, visit **Citizenship and Immigration Canada** (www.cic.gc.ca).

Important note: If you have a criminal record, including misdemeanors or driving while impaired (DWI), no matter how long ago, **you can be prohibited** from entering Canada, unless you obtain a special waiver well in advance of your trip. Refer to the Citizenship and Immigration Canada website (www.cic.gc.ca) for additional information.

Passports and Visas
U.S. Citizens

The simple answer to the question of what documents U.S. citizens need to visit Canada is "a valid **passport.**" It's always a good idea to travel with your passport, if you have one.

If you are driving over the border, you can use a **NEXUS** card, issued as part of the U.S. government's Trusted Travel Program, as your entry document. See the U.S. Customs and Border Protection website (www.cbp.gov) for NEXUS details.

If you're driving, a valid **U.S. Passport Card** can also be used instead of a passport. Get more information about U.S. Passport Cards, which cannot be used for air travel, from the U.S. State Department (www.travel.state.gov).

Several U.S. states and Canadian provinces issue **Enhanced Drivers Licenses** that can be used as an alternative to a passport or passport card when you're crossing a land border; they're not valid for air travel. The U.S. Customs and Border Protection website (www.cbp. gov) has details about Enhanced Drivers Licenses.

Citizens of the United States do not need a visa to visit Canada for stays of less than six months.

Citizens of Other Countries

All other foreign visitors to Canada must have a valid passport, and depending on your nationality, you may also need either a visitor visa or an Electronic Travel Authorization (eTA). Check with Citizenship and Immigration Canada (www.cic.gc.ca) to confirm what documents you require.

British, Australian, and New Zealand citizens don't require a visa, nor do citizens of many European nations. However, in 2016, Canada introduced the **Electronic Travel Authorization (eTA)**, which is required for visa-exempt visitors who are traveling to Canada **by air.** For example, a British citizen who is driving into Canada from the U.S. would not require a visa or an eTA but would need the eTA to fly into Canada. If you need an eTA, apply for this document online on the **Citizenship and Immigration Canada** website (www.cic.gc.ca).

Embassies and Consulates

American citizens in western Canada can get assistance from the **U.S. Consulate General-Vancouver** (1075 W. Pender St., 604/685-4311, www.vancouver.usconsulate.gov) or **U.S. Consulate General-Calgary** (615 Macleod Trail SE, 10th Fl., 403/266-8962, www.calgary.usconsulate.gov).

British nationals needing consular assistance can contact the **British Consulate General-Vancouver** (1111 Melville St., Suite 800, 604/683-4421, www.gov.uk) or **British Consulate-General-Calgary** (5100-150 6th Ave. SW, main office 403/705-1755, emergencies 403/538-2181, www.gov.uk).

The **Australian Consulate and Trade Commission, Vancouver** (1075 W. Georgia St., Suite 2050, 604/694-6160, www.canada.embassy.gov.au) provides consular assistance to Australian citizens in western Canada.

The **New Zealand Consulate General, Vancouver** (1050 W. Pender St., Suite 2250, 604/684-7388, www.nzembassy.com/canada) can assist citizens of New Zealand in western Canada.

Customs

Visitors to Canada can bring a reasonable amount of personal baggage, including clothing, camping and sports equipment, cameras, and computers for personal use.

Travelers must declare all **food,** plants, or animals they bring into Canada. In general, you're allowed to bring food for personal use, although there are restrictions on fresh fruits, vegetables, meats, and dairy products. Get the latest information from the **Canadian Food Inspection Agency** (www.inspection.gc.ca).

As long as you're of legal drinking age (at least age 19 in B.C., age 18 in Alberta), you can bring a small amount of **alcoholic beverages** into Canada

duty- and tax-free. You're allowed to bring one of the following: two bottles of wine (up to 53 fluid ounces or 1.5 liters), one standard bottle of other alcohol (40 ounces or 1.14 liters), or 24 cans or bottles of beer or ale (up to a total of 287 ounces or 8.5 liters). Visitors are also allowed to bring in up to 200 cigarettes or 50 cigars.

In general, visitors cannot bring weapons into Canada. You're specifically prohibited from bringing automatic weapons, sawed-off rifles or shotguns, most handguns, and semiautomatic weapons into Canada. There are some exceptions for hunters, and all visitors must declare any firearms in writing. Check the detailed requirements with the **Canada Border Services Agency** (www.cbsa.gc.ca).

Note that when you're flying to Canada from the United States or other international destinations, you clear immigration and customs at the Canadian airport after you land in Canada. However, if you're **flying to the United States** from Vancouver, Calgary, or other major Canadian cities, you clear U.S. immigration and customs at the Canadian airport *before* you board your flight. For example, if you were traveling from Vancouver to Los Angeles, you would clear U.S. immigration and customs at the Vancouver airport. **Allow extra time** for these immigration and customs procedures, in addition to the time it takes for standard airport passenger screening.

Travel Tips

In Canada, each province sets its own laws regulating activities such as drinking, smoking, and drug use. The **drinking age** in British Columbia is 19; in Alberta, it's 18.

Each province has its own laws about when and where you can **smoke,** too, and some cities have laws that are more restrictive than those at the provincial level. You must be 19 to smoke in B.C., 18 in

Winter Travel in the Canadian Rockies

When you're road-tripping in western Canada's mountain regions between October and March, your vehicle needs to be equipped with winter tires, since it can snow—a lot—at any time. Listen to the weather forecast regularly, and prepare to get off the road if you need to wait out a storm.

In January, the average daytime high temperature in Banff is 19°F (-7°C). In Jasper, it's 21°F (-6°C). For outdoor activities, make sure you have a warm water-repellent jacket, ideally with long underwear, fleece, and a vest that you can layer underneath, as well as gloves, a hat that covers your ears, and warm waterproof boots. Don't forget your sunscreen and sunglasses; even in winter, the sun can be strong, particularly when it's reflecting off the snow.

If you're not comfortable with winter driving conditions, or don't want the hassle of winter driving, you can make your winter trip without a car. Shuttles pick up passengers at Calgary International Airport, bringing you to Banff or Lake Louise, and you can take a shuttle from town to the ski areas.

Alberta. In both B.C. and Alberta, you can't smoke in any indoor public place, including restaurants, bars, shopping centers, and public transit, or in a car where anyone under age 16 is a passenger. Vancouver also prohibits smoking at any city parks or beaches and on restaurant patios. Similarly, in Calgary, you can't smoke in the +15 walkways or within 16 feet (5 meters) of outdoor pools, skating rinks, playgrounds, or sports fields.

Access for Travelers with Disabilities

Many of western Canada's attractions, hotels, restaurants, entertainment venues, and transportation options are accessible to travelers with disabilities. A useful general resource about accessible travel to and around Canada is the government's **Access to Travel** website (www.accesstotravel.gc.ca). It includes details about transportation between and around B.C. and Alberta cities and towns, as well as general tips and travel advice.

Most national and provincial parks offer accessible facilities. Many picnic areas, campsites, and park washrooms, as well as some trails, can accommodate wheelchairs and other mobility aids. Get details on facilities in specific parks from **Parks Canada** (www.pc.gc.ca), **B.C. Parks** (www.env.gov.bc.ca), and **Alberta Parks** (www.albertaparks.ca).

Traveling with Children

Western Canada is an extremely family-friendly destination. Not only are there tons of fun things for families to do, but plenty of resources also help support traveling families or make travel more affordable.

Many museums, attractions, and recreational facilities offer free admission for kids under a certain age (often 5 or 6, but sometimes 11 or 12). Many offer discounted family admission rates, which generally include two adults and at least two children. Ask about family discounts when you're buying tickets.

Kids stay free at many major hotels. Other good lodging options for traveling families, besides the typical chain motels, include suite hotels (in cities) and cabins or cottages (in more rural areas), which often provide more space for the money, as well as kitchen facilities where you can prepare your own food. Some bed-and-breakfasts don't accept kids, so always ask.

Many restaurants in Canada offer children's menus with a few kid-approved food selections. Encourage your kids to try new things, though, since they may surprise you with their newfound love for bison burgers, handmade noodles, or sushi.

When you're visiting a national park or national historic site with kids, ask for a free **Parks Canada Xplorer** booklet, which has child-friendly activities to help them explore that destination. At most parks, Parks Canada staff offer interpretive programs, from wildlife talks to guided hikes, that are designed for kids or suitable for families; ask at the park visitors center or check the Parks Canada website (www.pc.gc.ca) for details and schedules.

Note that if only one parent is traveling with his or her children, the Canadian government recommends that the parent carry a written letter of permission from the other parent. Divorced parents who share custody should also travel with a copy of their legal custody documents. If you are traveling with a child who isn't your own (or for whom you're not the legal guardian), you should carry written permission from the parents or guardians indicating that you're allowed to travel with the child. You may be asked to present these letters at the border when you enter Canada. For a sample letter of consent, see the **Travel and Tourism** section of the Government of Canada's website (www.travel.gc.ca).

Women Traveling Alone
Overall, western Canada is a relatively safe destination compared to many spots around the world, and women shouldn't hesitate to travel alone. However, exercise caution wherever you go, and particularly in urban areas, avoid venturing out alone late at night or in the wee hours of the morning. If you are out late on your own, don't walk; take a cab. Take your cues from local women, too. If you don't see other women walking or waiting for the bus, that's a clue that maybe you shouldn't either.

Carry a cell phone with you, so you can phone for assistance if you need it.

However, be aware that many parks and remote regions have limited or no cell phone coverage.

When hiking, many women suggest finding other groups of travelers that you might join, or hiking on busier trails where you won't be alone for long periods of time.

An excellent resource for women travelers is **Journeywoman** (www.journeywoman.com), a Toronto-based website where women travelers can share tips and ask for advice from local women around the world.

Senior Travelers
The good thing about getting older is that you can often get discounts. Many B.C. and Alberta attractions, lodgings, and transportation providers offer discounts for seniors. Normally, you need to be 65 to qualify for a senior discount, although occasionally these discounts are extended to travelers at age 60 or 62.

Parks Canada offers discounts at the country's national parks and national historic sites, with reduced rates for single-day admissions and annual passes.

Gay and Lesbian Travelers
Canada is far more welcoming to gay and lesbian travelers than many other destinations. Marriage equality is the law in Canada.

Western Canada's largest LGBTQ community is in Vancouver. The hub of the community is along Davie Street in the city's West End, with another popular area along Commercial Drive in East Vancouver, although accommodations, restaurants, and other facilities across the city (and indeed across B.C.) welcome gay travelers. **Tourism Vancouver** (www.tourismvancouver.com) publishes a quarterly LGBT newsletter, *Out in Vancouver.* **Gayvan Travel Marketing** (www.gayvan.com) can tell you more about the local community, events, and resources. *Gay Calgary Magazine* (www.gaycalgary.com) can tell you what's happening in that city.

Other resources for gay and lesbian travel to Canada include **Travel Gay Canada** (www.travelgaycanada.com), the country's gay and lesbian tourism association, and **TAG Approved** (www.tagapproved.com), which highlights gay-friendly hotels and attractions.

Traveling Without Reservations

You can travel without advance reservations across western Canada, leaving your itinerary flexible to explore intriguing areas that you discover en route or to alter your plans to accommodate the weather.

However, July and August are peak travel months across the region, and in the major cities and national parks, you may have trouble finding last-minute accommodations. Holiday weekends, particularly **Victoria Day** (3rd Mon. in May), **Canada Day** (July 1), **August Civic Holiday** (1st Mon. in Aug.), **Labour Day** (1st Mon. in Sept.), and **Thanksgiving** (2nd Mon. in Oct.), are also especially busy travel times, as is the week of **Christmas** and **New Year's.** Note that Canada celebrates Thanksgiving in October, while the U.S. Thanksgiving holiday is in late November.

If you are looking for last-minute lodgings, begin your search early in the day. You're far more likely to find a room before noon than you are at 5pm. Some area visitors centers keep lists of available accommodations or can provide suggestions for same-day places to stay. Similarly, if you're camping, claim your site early in the day.

When you're taking a car on the ferries between the mainland and Vancouver Island, you don't need to reserve a spot in advance. However, on weekends and holidays, you may have a long wait if you don't. Making a reservation will ensure that you get your car on the boat you want.

Hotel and Motel Chains

Western Canada has many of the same roadside motels and urban chains that you find across the United States.

Best Western (www.bestwestern.com), **Choice Hotels** (www.choicehotels.ca, including Comfort Inn, Econo Lodge, Quality Inn, Rodeway Inn), **Hilton Hotels** (www.hilton.com, including Hampton Inn), **Holiday Inn** and **Holiday Inn Express** (www.ihg.com), **Hyatt Hotels** (www.hyatt.com), **Marriott Hotels** (www.marriott.com, including Courtyard, Fairfield Inn, Residence Inn), **Starwood Hotels** (www.starwoodhotels.com, including Sheraton, Westin, Aloft, Four Points), and **Wyndam Hotels** (www.wyndham.com, including Days Inn, Howard Johnson, Ramada, Super 8, Travelodge) all have properties in British Columbia and Alberta.

Other Canadian hotel chains include **Delta Hotels and Resorts** (www.delta-hotels.com) and the upscale **Fairmont Hotels and Resorts** (www.fairmont.com).

Time Zones

Most of British Columbia is in the Pacific time zone, the same as the U.S. West Coast. Alberta is one hour later, in the mountain time zone.

However, some B.C. national parks and communities close to the Alberta border follow their neighbors to the east and use mountain time. Revelstoke, Mount Revelstoke National Park, and Glacier National Park are on Pacific time, but Golden, Yoho National Park, Kootenay National Park, Fernie, and Cranbrook are on mountain time.

Both B.C. and Alberta observe daylight saving time. Clocks move ahead one hour on the second Sunday in March and move back one hour on the first Sunday in November.

Health and Safety

Travelers should always carry a basic first-aid kit, including bandages, aspirin or other pain reliever, sunscreen, insect repellent, and an antiseptic or antibiotic ointment. You might want to include an ointment or other product to relieve the itching of mosquito bites; if you're prone to allergic reactions, consider packing an antihistamine, too. If you wear glasses, bring an extra pair. If you take prescription medication, carry a copy of your prescription.

Emergencies
In an emergency, call **911** to reach police, fire, ambulance, or other emergency services.

Nonemergency Medical Information
In **British Columbia,** to speak with a nurse for medical information 24 hours a day, call **811** to reach the **HealthLink BC** service (www.healthlinkbc.ca). You can also reach HealthLink BC at 604/215-8110.

In **Alberta,** call **811** to reach that province's **Health Link** (www.albertahealth-services.ca) 24-hour medical information line.

Health Care and Insurance
If you become ill or injured while traveling in B.C. or Alberta, go to the nearest hospital emergency room or walk-in health clinic.

If you're a resident of another Canadian province, your provincial health plan may not provide health coverage while you're out of your home province. If the plan does provide coverage, it may pay only the amount it would pay for the service in your home province, not what you might be billed in B.C. or Alberta. Either way, before your trip, it's a good idea to purchase supplemental travel health insurance to cover any unexpected medical costs while you're on the road.

If you live outside Canada, make sure that you have health insurance that will cover you and your family in Canada. You normally have to pay for any medical services provided in Canada and then file a claim with your health insurance provider after you return home.

Wilderness Safety
Poison Ivy
Touching the sap of the poison ivy plant can give you an intensely itchy skin rash. Found throughout Western Canada, poison ivy often grows in wooded areas, beside hiking trails, and along the roadside. Its identifying characteristics are its leaves, which grow along a woody vine in clusters of three. The leaves can have a reddish cast, particularly in the spring and fall, although they may appear deep green during the summer.

A poison ivy rash usually appears within 24 to 48 hours after contact. The sap can also get on an animal's fur, and while your dogs won't get a rash, they can transfer the rash-inducing sap to you.

The best way to avoid getting a poison ivy rash is to avoid touching the plant. Wear closed-toe shoes, socks, and long pants when hiking or walking in the woods, and check for poison ivy before you sit down in a meadow or spread out your picnic blanket. If you think you may have come in contact with poison ivy, wash your skin with soap and cool water right away. Wash your clothing as soon as possible, too.

If you develop a poison ivy rash, applying calamine lotion or a hydrocortisone cream to the skin may help alleviate the itching. Go to a hospital emergency room right away if you have any trouble breathing or swallowing or if the rash causes swelling, particularly around your eyes. Seek medical attention as well if the rash appears on your face or if you develop a fever or any other signs of infection.

Ticks
Ticks are tiny bugs—a type of arachnid—that feed on the blood of animals or people. Most are harmless, although some varieties of ticks, primarily black-legged or deer ticks, can carry Lyme disease. Lyme disease is a bacterial infection

Stay Safe in Bear Country

It's important to know how to stay safe in wildlife country and how to protect bears and other animals from human encounters.

Wildlife on the Roads

If you spot animals by the roadside or along the trails, keep your distance. Parks Canada staff recommend staying at least 100 feet (30 meters), or the equivalent of three bus lengths, from deer, sheep, goats, elk, and moose, and more than 300 feet (100 meters), or 10 bus lengths, from bears, cougars, or wolves.

If you're in your car or RV and want to stop for wildlife along the road, pull over to avoid creating "wildlife jams," where traffic can't pass because cars are blocking the road. Use your warning lights to alert other vehicles. If you've stopped close to an animal, don't get out of your car! Snap a photo and move on.

Be extra careful when driving at dawn or dusk, when animals are most active. Scan the roadway and shoulders frequently for wildlife. And if you see one animal, others may be nearby.

Bear Safety on the Trails

If you're hiking or cycling, Parks Canada suggests three general steps to stay safe in bear country:

* **Prepare:** Carry bear spray and learn what to do if you encounter a bear.

* **Be aware:** Scan your surroundings and look for tracks, droppings, or diggings.

* **Let bears know you're there:** Make noise (consider singing), and ideally travel in a group of at least four.

During certain times of year, Parks Canada posts "bear warnings" on certain trails. Trails can be closed due to bear activity, or in some cases, park staff require that you hike in close groups of 4 to 6. These warnings are posted on the Parks Canada website (www.pc.gc.ca), in park visitors centers, and at trailheads. Always check for bear restrictions before you set out on a hike.

Be Careful with Garbage

Take care with food and garbage, too. Throughout western Canada, even in towns, you'll notice bear-proof garbage containers, where you have to reach under a covered metal handle to open the container; use them.

If you're camping, never leave food outside or in your tent. That includes food scraps, dirty dishes, empty bottles or cans, and toothpaste, soap, or other toiletries. These items need to be secured in your vehicle or in a bear-proof container. Coolers are not bear-proof.

Want to Learn More?

To learn more about Rocky Mountain wildlife and bear safety, talk to staff at any of the national park visitors centers. Interpretive programs held regularly in national park campgrounds often focus on bear safety.

---

that can cause flu-like symptoms, and if left untreated, more severe illnesses of the nervous system, joints, and heart. To date, Lyme-carrying ticks have infrequently been found in British Columbia or Alberta, except in certain parts of the Lower Mainland, parts of Vancouver Island, and some areas along the B.C. coast, where they are found more often.

It's still a good idea to reduce your exposure to ticks when you're hiking, camping, or exploring forested areas, by wearing closed-toe shoes, socks, and long pants. Do a "tick check" whenever you finish any of these outdoor activities, examining your skin, and that of your kids or pets, to spot any ticks. You can generally avoid infection by removing a tick within 24 to 36 hours.

If you do find a tick attached to your skin, remove it by using clean tweezers to grab the head and pull it straight out. Then wash the skin with soap and water or disinfect it with alcohol or hand sanitizer.

Giardia

Crystal clear lakes and rushing rivers flow across Western Canada, but that doesn't mean that the water is safe to drink. While tap water in most parts of B.C. and Alberta is of excellent quality, Health Canada, the nation's public health agency, advises that you shouldn't drink any water in the great outdoors without treating it.

The main risk to backcountry travelers who drink untreated water is giardiasis, an intestinal illness caused by the *giardia* parasite that lives in streams, rivers, and lakes. Giardiasis symptoms, which include severe diarrhea, abdominal cramps, nausea, and sometimes vomiting or fever, typically begin between six and 16 days after you ingest the parasite.

If you must drink water from a backcountry source, boil it for 3-10 minutes or treat it with iodine. You can also use a water filter as long as it's small enough to block the *giardia*. Get more information about water treatment methods from **Health Canada** (www.hc-sc.gc.ca) or from staff at an outdoor equipment store like **MEC** (Mountain Equipment Coop, www.mec.ca).

Heat Illnesses

When you're outdoors on especially hot days, wear loose-fitting, breathable clothing, sunglasses, and a hat with a brim to protect your face and head from the sun. Make sure to drink plenty of water, particularly when you're active. The higher elevations in the Canadian Rockies can make you more susceptible to **dehydration** or **heat exhaustion** than you might be at sea level.

Symptoms of heat-induced illness include dizziness or fainting, headache, decreased urination and/or unusually dark yellow urine, nausea or vomiting, and rapid breathing and heartbeat. Try to move to a cool place and drink water right away.

If someone has a high body temperature, becomes confused, stops sweating, or becomes unconscious, they may be suffering from **heat stroke.** Call 911 or seek medical attention immediately.

Winter Travel

Winter in the Canadian Rockies and in the mountainous regions of B.C. is cold, and it can snow at any time, particularly between October and March. For outdoor activities, dress in layers: a warm, water-repellent jacket, a fleece sweater, and long underwear, along with gloves or mittens and well-lined waterproof boots. Wearing a hat, ideally one that covers your ears, is especially important, since you lose a significant amount of heat through your head.

One risk of cold-weather travel is **frostbite,** which occurs primarily in the extremities: hands, feet, ears, and nose. To protect its core temperature, your body restricts blood flow to these outlying body parts when the temperature dips below freezing (0°C or 32°F). In the early stages of frostbite, your skin can turn white or yellow. Once you get warm, the skin should regain its normal color; if it doesn't, or if the area remains numb, seek medical attention.

If your overall body temperature begins to drop due to extreme cold, you're at risk of **hypothermia,** a condition where your body is losing heat faster than it can retain it. You begin to shiver, and your hands or feet may turn numb.

To treat mild hypothermia, try to get to a warm place and keep your muscles moving. Remove wet clothing, wrap up in a blanket or sleeping bag, and drink warm sweet liquids. While drinking alcohol may make you think that you're warmer, it can actually prevent you from recognizing the degree to which your body is losing heat, increasing your risk of hypothermia.

Fatigue, nausea, or rapid shallow

breathing can indicate that the hypothermia is becoming more severe. As it worsens, you may feel confused or uncoordinated. Call 911 or go to a hospital emergency room if these symptoms occur.

Internet Resources

Canada
Destination Canada
www.canada.travel
The government of Canada's official guide to travel across the country.

Parks Canada
www.pc.gc.ca
The federal government agency that manages national parks and national historic sites across Canada. The Parks Canada website has details about things to do, camping, hiking, and other activities in the parks in the West and throughout the country.

Parks Canada Reservation Service
www.reservation.pc.gc.ca
Reservations booking service for Canada's national park campgrounds.

Citizenship and Immigration Canada
www.cic.gc.ca
The federal government agency responsible for overseeing visitors and immigrants to Canada, including information about visitor visas, work permits, study permits, and applications for permanent residence.

Canada Border Services Agency
www.cbsa-asfc.gc.ca
The federal government agency that manages Canada's borders, including what items visitors can bring into Canada. Their website also shows wait times at highway border crossings.

Environment Canada
www.weather.gc.ca
Provides weather forecasts and historical weather data for locations across Canada.

British Columbia
Destination British Columbia
www.hellobc.com
British Columbia's provincial tourism agency, which provides travel tips and information for the region and operates a network of visitors centers.

British Columbia Wine Institute
www.winebc.com
Has a detailed website with information about wineries and wine-touring tips in the Okanagan, Vancouver Island, and elsewhere in British Columbia.

Tourism Vancouver
www.tourismvancouver.com
Vancouver's tourism agency provides event schedules, tips for getting around, neighborhood profiles, and other information about the city's sights, hotels, restaurants, shops, and experiences.

Tourism Vancouver Island
www.vancouverisland.travel
Their free guide to things to do across Vancouver Island is available online and in print from area visitors centers.

Tourism Victoria
www.tourismvictoria.com
Promoting tourism in the city of Victoria, this organization runs a year-round information center on Victoria's Inner Harbour and provides information about attractions and activities, events, accommodations, and restaurants.

Tourism Whistler
www.whistler.com
Representing the Whistler region, this tourism agency has information to help you plan a mountain trip in any season.

Tourism Kamloops
www.tourismkamloops.com
Operates the Kamloops Visitor Centre and provides detailed information about the Kamloops region, including things to do and local events.

Tourism Kelowna
www.tourismkelowna.com
Provides information about the city of Kelowna and the surrounding Okanagan region, including wineries, wine tours, outdoor activities, and events.

Tourism Revelstoke
www.seerevelstoke.com
This tourism organization publishes a free guide to the Revelstoke area that's available online and in print at the local visitors center.

Tourism Golden
www.tourismgolden.com
Golden's tourism agency provides information about the B.C. Rockies region, including the area national parks, on its website, which also has an online trip-planning tool.

Kootenay Rockies Tourism
www.kootenayrockies.com
This regional tourism organization in eastern British Columbia has a detailed website with lots of itinerary suggestions and other ideas for planning a trip through the Kootenay-Rockies region.

Tourism Fernie
www.tourismfernie.com
Provides information about things to see and do, festivals, events, and other travel details for the town of Fernie and vicinity in southeastern B.C.

Nelson Kootenay Lake Tourism
www.nelsonkootenaylake.com
Provides travel information for Nelson, Kaslo, and the surrounding Kootenay Lake area in B.C.'s West Kootenays region.

Alberta
Travel Alberta
www.travelalberta.com
Tourism agency for the province of Alberta, providing travel tips and information about the region and operating a network of visitors centers.

Banff-Lake Louise Tourism
www.banfflakelouise.com
This area tourism organization has a detailed website with information about the towns of Banff and Lake Louise and about Banff National Park in the Canadian Rockies.

Tourism Jasper
www.jasper.travel
Produces an annual Jasper visitors guide, available in print and online, and also provides information on their website about things to do, places to stay, and events in and around Jasper National Park.

Tourism Calgary
www.visitcalgary.com
Calgary's tourism agency provides event schedules, tips for getting around, neighborhood profiles, and other information about the sights, hotels, restaurants, shops, and experiences in this city that's a gateway to the Canadian Rockies.

INDEX

INDEX

LIST OF MAPS

PHOTO CREDITS

ACKNOWLEDGMENTS

It's impossible to thank all the people who provided information, suggestions, and support while I was researching and writing *Moon Vancouver & Canadian Rockies Road Trip*, but I'd like to give a special shout-out to the following individuals and organizations.

I'm grateful for the assistance and advice I received from Destination BC and Tourism Vancouver. On Vancouver Island, many thanks to Heather McEachen, Tourism Vancouver Island; Holly Lenk and Katie Dabbs, Tourism Victoria; Chelsea Barr, Tourism Nanaimo; Samantha Fyleris, Tourism Tofino; and Ronette Nyhan, Magnolia Hotel and Spa.

Many thanks to Steve Ogden and the Tourism Whistler team; Monica Dickinson, Tourism Kamloops; Kyle Taylor, Tourism Sun Peaks; Alexa Creelman, Tourism Kelowna; Oliver Osoyoos Winery Association; and Ingrid Jarrett, Watermark Beach Resort.

Heidi Korven at Kootenay Rockies Tourism provided a wealth of information and contacts across eastern British Columbia. Andy Brown at Tourism Golden; Jikke Gyorki and Rebecca Hall at Tourism Fernie; Dianna Ducs at Nelson Kootenay Lake Tourism; Momoko Ito, Paula Cravens, and Bruce Woodbury in New Denver; and Dean Thornton and Daphne Hunter at Kaslo Kayaking were all generous with their time, as were Donald Sam and the staff at Ktunaxa Interpretive Centre and Gordie Sebastian at St. Eugene Resort.

Thanks, too, to Thom Tischik and Meghan Tabor in Revelstoke; Max Cretin, Kicking Horse Mountain Resort; Marilyn and Robert Patenaude and the staff at the Cross River Wilderness Centre; Ken Wilder, Tourism Invermere Panorama; and Jamie Hurschler, Panorama Mountain Resort.

I especially appreciate the support I received from Rose Chase and her colleagues at Travel Alberta; Kymberley Hill and Jonny Bierman, Banff Lake Louise Tourism; Alison McPhail, Tourism Canmore; Nancy Gordy and April Henry, Tourism Jasper; Andrea Visscher, Tourism Calgary; Katie Mayer, Hotel Arts; and Lonna Hoggan, Canadian Badlands Tourism.

I'd like to thank the countless helpful Parks Canada staffers, who offered advice and information, particularly Jennifer Burnell, Guy Thériault, Rick Reynolds, and Karin Smith, and to fellow members of the Travel Media Association of Canada for always being ready with ideas and contacts.

More thank-yous to Paula Amos at the Aboriginal Tourism Association of BC; Kate Rogers and Brian Cant at the Tartan Group; Marisa Cuglietta, Brianna Prasloski, and the staff at Hawksworth Communications; Samantha Geer, Tiffany Soper, Gemma Brown, and the Avenue PR crew; Wendy Underwood and Kristine George, Fever Pitch Communications; Nancie Hall, Fairmont Hotels; and Noelle Aune, NA Communications.

Many thanks to the excellent team at Avalon Travel, including acquisitions editor Elizabeth Hansen, senior editor Kathryn Ettinger, senior cartography editor Albert Angulo, and publishing technologies manager Darren Alessi.

Travel buddy extraordinaire Lynn Bryant deserves special mention for being game for yet another crazy adventure, good-naturedly putting up with last-minute plan changes, huff-and-puff hikes, and picnics of contraband peanut butter.

Finally, a million thanks to my team at home: to Michaela for snorkeling with the seals, testing deep-fried Nanaimo bars, and coaxing me onto the Via Ferrata; to Talia for reminding me to take breaks for swimming and supper; and to Alan, for always understanding when I need to hit the road.

ALSO AVAILABLE

MAP SYMBOLS

▦ Expressway	○ City/Town	✈ Airport	⛳ Golf Course
▦ Primary Road	◉ State Capital	✈ Airfield	🅿 Parking Area
Secondary Road	◉ National Capital	▲ Mountain	⬟ Archaeological Site
▫▫▫ Unpaved Road	★ Point of Interest	✚ Unique Natural Feature	⛪ Church
Feature Trail	• Accommodation		⛽ Gas Station
- - - - Other Trail	▾ Restaurant/Bar	🦅 Waterfall	Glacier
⋯⋯ Ferry	■ Other Location	▲ Park	Mangrove
▦ Pedestrian Walkway	Λ Campground	Trailhead	Reef
⊞⊞⊞ Stairs		Skiing Area	Swamp

CONVERSION TABLES

°C = (°F - 32) / 1.8
°F = (°C x 1.8) + 32
1 inch = 2.54 centimeters (cm)
1 foot = 0.304 meters (m)
1 yard = 0.914 meters
1 mile = 1.6093 kilometers (km)
1 km = 0.6214 miles
1 fathom = 1.8288 m
1 chain = 20.1168 m
1 furlong = 201.168 m
1 acre = 0.4047 hectares
1 sq km = 100 hectares
1 sq mile = 2.59 square km
1 ounce = 28.35 grams
1 pound = 0.4536 kilograms
1 short ton = 0.90718 metric ton
1 short ton = 2,000 pounds
1 long ton = 1.016 metric tons
1 long ton = 2,240 pounds
1 metric ton = 1,000 kilograms
1 quart = 0.94635 liters
1 US gallon = 3.7854 liters
1 Imperial gallon = 4.5459 liters
1 nautical mile = 1.852 km

MOON VANCOUVER & CANADIAN ROCKIES ROAD TRIP

Avalon Travel
An imprint of Perseus Books
A division of Hachette Book Group
1700 Fourth Street
Berkeley, CA 94710, USA
www.moon.com

Editor: Kathryn Ettinger
Series Manager: Leah Gordon
Copy Editor: Christopher Church
Graphics Coordinator: Darren Alessi
Production Coordinator: Darren Alessi
Cover Design: Erin Seaward-Hiatt
Interior Design: Darren Alessi
Moon Logo: Tim McGrath
Map Editor: Albert Angulo
Cartographers: Albert Angulo, Brian Shotwell
Indexer: Greg Jewett

ISBN: 978-1-63121-335-9
ISSN: 2471-6065

Printing History
1st Edition — July 2016
5 4 3 2 1